Plate section The copyright notices
Blocks' is to Robert Eisler, *The Messi*
Monastery' is © Trip/I Mitchell. Cred

Text pages

xii,   l.5 'to of'; l18 'or a second'
xxvii, l.2 'Several had writing ...'
xxix, n.6 DSSU; "the Star Prophecy"
13,   n.7 'See below, p.48'
54,   n.105 l.28 'See above, p.40'
80,   l.8 'was dated'
116, n.1 '29–30, 32–34, 109–110 above'
191, l.9 "Violence done *to the land*..."
      l.18 'the blood of Man' not 'Men'
194, l.3 "with a worthless work ..."
203, n.22 'Lex Cornelia de Sicarius'
216, l.36 'Iehinnazer/Iehazzir'
238, l.32 "Jews *dwelling at* Damascus"
241, l.30 Josephus' (apostrophe)
246, l.19 delete repetition 'we mentioned ...'
253, l.15 'is at' not 'at of'
263, l.19 delete quote after 'statement';
      l.33 'emerges'
265, l.36 'God's Divine "Wrath" is ...'
267, l.38 'However *surprising* this ...'

3
33
34,
347
348,
369
402, [
432, l.

THE
DEAD SEA SCROLLS
AND THE
FIRST CHRISTIANS

Robert Eisenman is Professor of Middle East Religions and Director of the Institute for the Study of Judeo-Christian Origins at California State University, Long Beach, USA. The author of several books on the Dead Sea Scrolls and consultant to the Huntington Library in San Marino in California on its decision to open its archives, he was a leading figure in the worldwide campaign to gain access to the Scrolls. A United States Endowment for the Humanities Fellow at the Albright Institute of Archaeological Research in Jerusalem (where the Scrolls were first inspected) and a Visiting Senior Member at Linacre College, Oxford and the Oxford Centre for Postgraduate Studies, he was the first to publish all the photographs of the unpublished Scrolls in *A Facsimile Edition of the Dead Sea Scrolls*, Washington DC, 1991.

THE
DEAD SEA SCROLLS
AND THE
FIRST CHRISTIANS

Essays and Translations

ROBERT EISENMAN

ELEMENT
Shaftesbury, Dorset • Rockport, Massachusetts • Brisbane, Queensland

Text © Robert Eisenman 1996

First published in Great Britain in 1996 by
Element Books Limited
Shaftesbury, Dorset SP7 8BP

Published in the USA in 1996 by
Element Books, Inc.
PO Box 830, Rockport, MA 01966

Published in Australia in 1996 by
Element Books Limited
for Jacaranda Wiley Limited
33 Park Road, Milton, Brisbane 4064

Cover design by Bridgewater Book Company
Page design by Roger Lightfoot
Typeset by Wyvern Typesetting Ltd, Bristol
Printed and bound in the USA by Edwards Brothers, Michigan.

British Library Cataloguing in Publication
data available

Library of Congress Cataloging in Publication
data available

ISBN 1-85230-785-4

Contents

PART THREE

Introduction

The books published in this volume were originally published separately when the debate over the Dead Sea Scrolls was just gathering momentum. Ground-breaking works, they presented an entirely new viewpoint from which to consider the Scrolls—one which combined "Jewish-Christian" and "Zealot" approaches to produce a new synthesis which has become the driving force behind the Qumran debate today.

To be sure, there have been spin-offs of these works, but they were the first to identify Qumran as "Sadducean"—albeit relating to a new kind of Sadduceeism not attested heretofore. They also coined a new phrase to refer to this: "Messianic Sadducees", a variation on such parallel phraseologies as "Essene", "Zealot", and/or "Jewish-Christian" or "Nazoraean".

The ideas contained in the books were used extensively by Michael Baigent and Richard Leigh in their publication *The Dead Sea Scrolls Deception* (Jonathan Cape, 1991), constituting the foundation of the more popular historical and literary approach they adopted. The same ideas featured likewise in the more recent *The Hidden Scrolls: Judaism, Christianity and the War for the Dead Sea Scrolls* by Neil Asher Silberman (Putnam, 1994).

But from the start *Maccabees . . .* and *James . . .* were never widely available to the general public. Moreover, although the original editions were sold out by the early 1990s and new editions were definitely planned, these were held up because of the scholarly animosities and controversies inherent in breaking the monopoly and the final publication of the Scrolls. This volume seeks to remedy that situation, reprinting them as they originally appeared, but in a single volume, as the publisher believes it is time these books were available to a much wider audience.

Together with these published books, this volume contains more recent papers published or delivered during the late 1980s and the 1990s to the Society of biblical Literature, to the Mogilany Conferences in Poland, at the University of Chicago, and to the Groningen Conference in Holland, relating to points raised in the two books, but developing them further.

It was patently the appearance in 1983 of the first of these monographs, *Maccabees, Zadokites, Christians and Qumran: A New Hypothesis of Qumran Origins* (hereafter abbreviated to MZCQ), that touched off the lively debate that has been going on ever since over the origin, date, and identification of the Movement responsible for the writings at Qumran. Not only did this book act as a catalyst for this debate (if not inspiration) but without it the debate might never have arisen. We use the term "Movement" advisedly: the documents found at Qumran are styled in the character of "a Movement", that is they are all of a piece, constructed with the same concepts and emphases, the same vocabulary and, from document to document, containing the same allusions and *dramatis personae*.

The more that is published, the more this impression is reinforced. For instance, across the whole corpus of material published to date there is not one single document that suggests accommodation, nor recommends compromise with the powers-that-be or the ruling Establishment. There is not one that is conciliatory or proposes "turning the other cheek" (as the New Testament so graphically puts it), nor "loving one's enemies" rather than "hating the sons of the Pit", as the Scrolls colorfully express it, not one that wishes anything other than "Eternal hatred and damnation to all the Sons of Darkness" and to "all the Hosts of Belial".

It is this impression of an unremittingly xenophobic, nationalistic and apocalyptic attitude on the part of the Qumran Community that the author has been particularly identified with having brought to light. Minor stylistic differences and shifts in emphasis in line with ostensibly different writers may be observable between documents, but the main doctrines, principles, characters, and elements of vocabulary occur and recur. The *dramatis personae* include:

the Righteous Teacher
the Wicked Priest
the Liar, Spouter of Lying, or Scoffer/Comedian
the Traitors
the Violent Ones or the Violent Ones of the Gentiles
the Simple Ones of Judah doing *Torah*.

Recurrent vocabulary, the Hebrew originals of which are always important, includes (and I have capitalized fundamental concepts throughout for emphasis):

Zedek—Righteousness
Hesed—Piety

Tom and *Tamim*—the Perfect, Perfection
Ebion/Ebionim—the Poor
ma'asim—works
Derech—the Way
Shomrei ha-Brit—Keepers of the Covenant
Emet—Truth
Hon—Riches
Mishpat—Judgement
zanut—fornication
Tom-Derech or *Tamim ha-Kodesh*—Perfection of the Way or Perfect Holiness

More are listed in the introduction to MZCQ. Imagery centering on "Light" and "Dark" also features prominently, as does constant stress on words formed from the basic consonantal Hebrew roots *Z-D-K* "Righteousness"/"Justification", *B-L-'*/"Swallowing", *R-SH-'*/"Evil", and others.

In attempting a new ideological and historiographic reconstruction, MZCQ looked at these matters from the internal perspective of the writings themselves and followed the progress of the Movement—which it ultimately termed "the Messianic Movement"—from the Maccabean Period, through the Herodian and the Roman, to the destruction of the Temple and the rise of early Christianity, and beyond.

In developing the notion of an Opposition and non-compromising group, which it called "Purist Sadducees", it also posited a new definition of Pharisees different from the normal understanding and more in line with the terminology found at Qumran, "the Seekers after Smooth Things". This emphasized political rather than religious distinctions—the "Smooth Things" (*Halakot*) in question clearly being a play on the normative Pharisaic/Rabbinic activity of seeking after *Halachot* or Legal Traditions. Wordplay of this kind was a favorite activity of the writers of the Qumran Scrolls, but straightforward enough for even the non-specialist to recognize it.

Following these notions, MZCQ coined a more accurate definition of the term in line with the Qumran vocabulary for Pharisees and their fellow-travelers, "seeking accommodation with foreigners". This is totally different from the more common view of Pharisees as mainstream Jews or as legalistic hair-splitters. Rather, it emphasizes their role in *opposing* the Maccabean Priesthood and cooperating with foreign rulers—first Seleucids and finally Herodian kings and Roman governors. Continuing this approach, MZCQ demonstrated how the Herodians were apprehended basically as foreigners at least by "Opposition" Zealot-style groups like the one represented by the literature at Qumran.

We are not speaking here about wrangling over minor legal issues, which certainly happened, but "seeking accommodation with foreigners" along the broad lines of *foreign kingship* and *foreign rule* generally—which the Pharisees not only tolerated but willingly cooperated with, and derivative complaints over the foreign appointment of high priests, the acceptance of foreign gifts and sacrifices in the Temple, polygamy, divorce and niece marriage—all things the Pharisees and Establishment Sadducees, whom Josephus says were dominated by the Pharisees during the Herodian period, seem to have approved of, but which groups like the one represented by the literature at Qumran definitively condemned.

This definition of Pharisees is new and revolutionary—but accurate if we consider the period before us carefully. To regard the Pharisees and their allies as quasi-quislings or collaborators would probably not sit very well among many Jews today, for whom the Pharisees have always been portrayed as the religiously orthodox and rather heroic party, but it meshes well with the point of view expressed in the documents at Qumran. It also has repercussions when considering the Historical Jesus and the New Testament presentation of him as basically another accommodator—after all, he is pictured as speaking positively about Roman centurions, Roman governors, and seemingly even Herodians, and adopting an accommodating position on some burning issues of the time, notably the tax question.

MZCQ thus did not hold to the view that the group responsible for the writings at Qumran was anti-Maccabean—as did most "consensus" scholars, despite the fact that this makes it impossible to come to grips with the internal thrust of the documents themselves. Nor did it try to find in one or another of the Maccabean rulers of the time—for example Judas Maccabee (*c.* 167 BC), his brother Jonathan (*c.* 150 BC), their grand-nephew Alexander Jannaeus (*c.* 100-75 BC), or even Mattathias the father of the Hasmonaeans himself—"the Wicked Priest", a central figure among the *dramatis personae* of the Scrolls. MZCQ instead took the position that the Movement represented by these writings was *pro*-Maccabean or, at least, certainly *not* anti-Maccabean.

The illogicality of considering any of these Maccabeans, except perhaps Hyrcanus II (*c.* 70–40 BC—the only Pharisee-leaning one among them, and the one who gave the country over to Herod and the Romans), to be the ones against whom the principal Qumran documents were directed was further concretized with the publication of the remaining Dead Sea Scrolls, in which there is even a Paean of Praise, written seemingly to extol the Maccabean Alexander Jannaeus, and a Testament of

Kohath opposing the foreign appointment of high priests and recommending non-cooperation with foreigners generally.

The point, though, was already amply clear in the existing published corpus. Since the Maccabees were nothing, if not zealous, apocalyptic, nationalistic, and xenophobic—what we call in this book "Zadokite", understood in the more esoteric sense of the word—how is it possible to consider them the group the Qumran writings were condemning (as opposed to, let us say, the Pharisees), when the Scroll documents have precisely the same xenophobic, nationalist mindset one normally attributes to these Maccabees?

This question has never been adequately answered. It was arrived at on the basis of the internal data, that is, the vocabulary, allusions, and internal ethos of the texts themselves, as opposed to the external, archaeological, paleographic, and now even carbon-14 evidence—and it was the arguments presented in these books that went a long way towards undercutting external evidence of this kind or at least rendering it insufficiently secure to stand in the face of counter-indicative internal data. Despite the fact that new carbon testing has now been done, so compelling is the internal data that it is impossible to accept the results of some of this, especially since it was done with the express purpose of attempting to discredit views such as the one presented in this book.

But one can go further than this. As noted, the conceptualities engendered by these kinds of external data contradict the clear thrust of the internal data, defeating any attempt to make sense of it. This has been the case from the beginning of Qumran research and still is. Therefore, since the earliest days of Qumran research, little or no clear understanding of the Qumran documents has emerged—and this is still the case today since the consensus has ever so subtly been reforming.

The results of the new carbon tests, while originally done at the urging of the present writer, were inconclusive and completely skewed. These tests suffered from a number of drawbacks including lack of objectivity and proper safeguards, lack of double or even triple "blinds", lack of proper external proficiency checks of laboratories, lack of objective conveyance of materials by persons not party to the debate, and the known predilection of laboratories to arrive at results those employing them desire.

Nor can the accuracy claimed for such tests be anywhere near the accuracy that can be said to properly apply, carbon testing notoriously tending to "archaize", that is, make documents seem older than they really are. This not only has to do with the callibration of the system in the first place and pollutants, ancient and modern, but also the fact that such tests only measure when a given animal or plant was supposed to have grown or died, not when a given manuscript was actually written on the finished product—an interval impossible to estimate.

This bears on the problem just alluded of to the tendency of a given laboratory to arrive at the results those using their services or sponsoring the tests desire. Whether evident upon first inspection or not, there is interpretation involved in reaching such results, and this is where the personal dimension comes into play. This problem is inherent even in the final reports written up following the two series of tests done, which go out of their way to support hitherto majority theories of archaeology and paleography, giving vivid evidence of such an original predisposition.

However this may be, the tests that were done on the Qumran documents were inconclusive and, as almost everyone acknowledges, produced skewed results: some far too early and some far too late. Where the results turned out to be at odds with what laboratories had previously been led to expect—as, for instance, a fourth-century BC dating for the Testament of Kohath (probably a first century BC—first century CE document) second/third-century CE dating for the Community Rule—they were simply dismissed. Moreover, even the dated documents supplied to the labs as controls were known in advance to be from the second century CE, as there are no extant written documents from any other *known* provenance. Even here, one papyrus document with an actual date of 135 CE produced a radio-carbon date of 231–332 CE and another with an actual date of 128 CE produced a radiocarbon dating of 86–314 CE[1].

But perhaps the best argument against the results of these tests, whatever they may be, is that they cannot stand together against the *clear thrust of the internal data* itself, and, in a sense, one must be grateful for these tests in that they re-focus one's reasons for disagreeing with such external indicators in general, and make one realize that one was correct in relying on internal data. In fact, because of the consistency of the "internal data"—the same usages, turns-of-phrase, and *dramatis personae* (most with a clearly discernible first-century milieu)—many of these "sectarian" documents, like the Community Rule, the Habakkuk *Pesher*, and the Damascus Document, had to have been written at more or less the same time—regardless of the results of such "external data". As stated as a conclusion in MZCQ, given the uncertain character of the external data and the kind of results obtained, these are insufficient and cannot be used to disqualify an argument which can otherwise make sense of the internal data.

These were the new positions entertained in MZCQ (Chapter 1 in this book). It and *James the Just in the Habakkuk Pesher* three years later (henceforth JJHP and Chapter 2 in this book), insisted that it was through an intelligent and insightful reading of the internal data rather than relying on the external data, such as it was, that one could get at the truth of the Qumran documents. The points made in the Introduction to MZCQ regarding psychological or subconscious predispositions by many Qumran scholars to distance the materials as far as possible from Christian origins in Palestine and the first century, and the concomitant animus displayed towards the Maccabean family, have never been controverted. These are still relevant today.

JJHP took a specific Qumran document and applied these positions on a point-by-point basis, thus arguing from the general theory of MZCQ to the specific case. Not only did it show how intimately these passages could be applied to known data within the early Church in Palestine from the 40s to the 60s CE before the fall of the Temple, but shed light in turn on hitherto only dimly perceived characters like James the Just, called "the brother of Jesus" and the leader of the early Church in Palestine during this period. Perhaps central of all, it showed how materials in the Habakkuk *Pesher*—specifically the interpretation of Hab 2:4, "the Righteous shall live by his Faith", one of the foundation pieces of Christian theology as we know it—could be linked up with the "Jamesian", as opposed to the Pauline, interpretation of this key scriptural passage.

Materials contained in this book were further concretized in a long paper delivered to the Groningen Conference in Holland in 1989, "Interpreting *Abeit-Galuto* in the Habakkuk *Pesher*", but never published in the *Revue de Qumran*, the official organ of consensus scholars, in contravention of the agreed terms for participants in that conference, because of unspecified objections concerning it, which raises questions about free debate in this field.

This article, which was subsequently published in Poland, is also included in this book (as Chapter 5), and the reader will be able to judge for him or herself as to its merits or defects. It carried the arguments of JJHP further in showing that it was material from the life of James—in particular, the fact of James' condemnation at a Sanhedrin trial for blasphemy in 62 CE—that could enable one to approach in an extremely convincing manner otherwise esoteric or defective usages in a principal Qumran document such as this and, in so doing elicit new information that could not even have been envisioned without it. This is extremely persuasive proof of the validity of a given theory.

It was problems of this kind that were at the heart of the struggle for freedom of access to the Scrolls. The point was that, given the previous editorial oversight system set up in the early 1950s by the Jordanian Government in conjunction with the Catholic-sponsored École Biblique in Jerusalem—and to some extent, thereafter, Harvard University—where the editing and interpretation of the Scrolls had been controlled by a tightknit and secretive network of scholars, all indebted to each other and all having the same basic perspective; it was impossible to have free and open debate in this field. I expressed this quite succinctly in other forums using the phrase, *"control over the unpublished manuscripts meant control over the field"*.

In fact, so effective was the dead hand of these scholarly cabals that the field of Dead Sea Scrolls Studies was virtually moribund from the late 1950s to the mid-1980s when MZCQ and JJHP appeared. In first employing the language of "consensus" to describe Establishment theorizing in Qumran Studies, MZCQ also called attention to the preconceptions as they expressed themselves in "the Essene Hypothesis", some psychological, some spiritual, and some emanating from clear religious predispositions, which either accidentally or otherwise tended to obscure the links of the tradition represented at Qumran to early Christianity in Palestine.

We use the latter term advisedly, because there was *no Christianity per se* in Palestine at this point, only Essenism, Zealotism, Messianic Sadduceeism, Nazoraeanism—or perhaps even "Naziritism" (the wordplay is probably deliberate)—and a kind of "Essene" Zealotism. As we shall show, these are all simply variations on a theme well developed at Qumran. "Christianity", even according to the New Testament, was first called Christianity in Antioch in the 40s or 50s CE (Acts 11:26)—whether Antioch on the Orontes in Syria or Antioch-by-Callirhoë further north, i.e., Antioch of the Osrhoaeans (Assyrians), also called Edessa (now "Urfa").

It was this consensus, followed blindly as it were by its proponents and their students—who seemed hardly to read the manuscripts for themselves or, if they did, missed their thrust—that insisted on pressing the dates of principal Qumran documents back into the second and in some cases, even the third century BC. MZCQ, in calling this whole elaborate, but basically obfuscating, structure into question, was the first to subject the archaeological and paleographical assumptions behind it to severe and thoroughgoing criticism.

The other side of the struggle was to publish all the Scrolls immediately without hesitation, to open them up to general research and in so doing, break the cartel. This was basically accomplished in 1991 by two decisions, in which the author was intimately involved: 1) the publication of *A Facsimile Edition of the Dead Sea Scrolls* (B.A.S., Washington DC), originally scheduled and ready for publication in April, 1991, but for reasons politic and otherwise, delayed until November, 1991, and even then not published without *deleterious legal wrangling*, and 2) the decision by the Huntington Library of San Marino, California, in September, 1991, to open its archives of Dead Sea Scrolls photographs.

Since the publication of all the remaining unpublished materials and attenuant works, and their translation in many languages, this consensus, aided and abetted now by persons within Israeli official circles, has in the aftermath of the initial blush of excitement over the new freedom engendered by open access, begun to reconstitute and reassert itself, now backed by all the new people brought into the continuing process of preparing "official editions". In fact, adherence to the consensus view or its variation was a *sine qua non* for being invited to participate in this process. This, in turn, once again highlighted the control exercised by those previously charged with editing the unpublished texts over the parameters and direction of debate in a field where there is still *no really free* exchange of ideas.

At the time MZCQ and JJHP were written, most people were unaware that there even were a substantial amount of Qumran documents awaiting publication, let alone the fact of this consensus and its bases. This extended to the present writer, who knew about the consensus, though not the extent of the unpublished corpus. In the event, the number of unpublished Qumran documents proved to be far larger than anyone imagined, but their existence did not change the basic approach enunciated in these two works and their addenda—on the contrary, they supported and gave it renewed vigor.

With the publication of *A Facsimile Edition of the Dead Sea Scrolls*, conceived of and midwifed by the writer, many works have begun to appear in Qumran studies which before were considered impossible, including the complete translations mentioned above of the entire corpus (however poor some of these new editions might be). Two years later, a competing, officially-sponsored Israeli Government *Facsimile Edition* appeared, following the lead and virtually overwriting the present author's own. But nothing has appeared in any of the remaining texts that would contradict anything developed in the works in this book. On the contrary, they simply complemented and extended what had already been pointed out in these works previously.

The Dead Sea Scrolls even seem to have been used as a kind of catalyst to thaw and cement hitherto cool relations between Israel and the Vatican, the Scrolls being perhaps one of the few items on which agreement could be fairly easily achieved. As things transpired, coinciden-tally or otherwise, not only did Vatican recognition of Israel follow soon after many of these problems were resolved and mutual interests disco-vered, but the official Israeli Government exhibit of the Scrolls that subsequently toured Western countries (even highlighting newly disco-vered fragments "opposition" scholars had published *over official disapproval*) also finally turned up at no less a final destination than the Vatican Library itself.

As we have repeatedly averred, many consensus scholars had not understood the implications of the already published texts, let alone the newly published ones. Even before the final opening of the Qumran archive in 1991, several new documents like the Temple Scroll and the Songs of the Sabbath Sacrifice had begun, however hestitantly, to appear. The latter, extant at both Qumran and Masada, strengthened the indi-cations of an intrinsic relationship to Kabbalistic tradition, in particular, *Hechalot* Mysticism or the Mysticism of Heavenly Ascents. Not only are these "Songs" replete with "Tongue" imagery, which we discuss in MZCQ and JJHP in relation to famous allusions to "the Tongue" in the Letter of James 3:5–6, but the theme of "Ascents" implicit in its imagery has additional reverberations connected to the person of James, in par-ticular to the title of a lost work called "The Ascents of James", so called after a series of lectures James is reputed to have given on the steps of the Temple.

In these Ascents, mentioned by Epiphanius at the end of the fourth century, James is pictured as "complaining against the Temple and the sacrifices". It does not take much lateral translation to transform this into one of the intrinsic Qumran themes, complaining against *gifts and sacrifices on behalf of foreigners in the Temple* and the manner in which *Temple service* was being performed by the basically compromised Establishment Priesthood.

The Temple Scroll, in addition to having more parallel material on the barring of Gentiles from the Temple, evokes the Deuteronomic King Law—"You shall not put a foreigner over you" (Deut 17:5)—already predicated by MZCQ, which, had it not been evoked, we would have had to postulate. Evoking the same basic themes we shall encounter in the Damascus Document of condemnation of "niece marriage" and "divorce", the Temple Scroll also emphasizes the Deuteronomic idea that the King *marry once and only once* (at least during the lifetime of his wife) and *not divorce*, and this, *only to a Jewish woman*. Its basic xenophobia could not be clearer. All these were points stressed previously in MZCQ and JJHP.

Other texts published since the opening of the rest of the Qumran archive, like the one I called the Paean to King Jonathan and the Testament of Kohath, mentioned above, and the Hymns of the Poor (*Ebionim*) simply reinforce the xenophobic, Zealot and/or Jewish Christian appearance of the literature. In the Testament of Kohath, ascribed to Moses' grandfather, for instance, one encounters many of the themes about *antagonism to foreign rule*, and the concomitant *foreign appointment of high priests*, stressed in MZCQ previously and, in effect, the same telltale "Zealot" approach, which certainly appears anti-Herodian not anti-Maccabean. Kohath's descendants are cautioned "not to give their inheritance to foreigners lest they become a laughing-stock and an object of contempt in their eyes". This is one of the texts dated to the fourth century BC by recent carbon testing. There is no way that this could be accurate.

Such antagonism to foreigners also forms the basis of another Cave IV prayer, the extant translations of which are so misleading and poor as to be virtually incomprehensible and miss its xenophobic thrust altogether. Written, seemingly, in the throes of some traumatic wartime scenario, it opens with the line, "Do not give our inheritance to strangers and our built-up areas to foreigners."[2] Like both 1 Macc 2:42, the War Scroll, and the *Paean to King Jonathan*, it appears to evoke the term "Volunteers for War", and paralleling the Habakkuk *Pesher* and Community Rule, "the Poor and the Meek" again, expressing the pious hope that God would not allow them to be overwhelmed by the foreign forces invading the country, but rather, as in the War Scroll, that it would be the Poor who would "execute vengeance by the Hosts of His Power".

As far as the question of the Historical Jesus is concerned, in the original Introduction to MZCQ I set it aside, considering it too contaminated by the retrospective imposition of later theological consenses and overwritten by material relating to other contemporary Messianic pretenders and the veneer of Pauline experience ever to be adequately clarified on the basis of the sources available to us. Even the historicity of Jesus, where New Testament accounts go, is a question fraught with uncertainty. I preferred rather to deal with the more accessible ones of the *Historical James* and the *Historical Paul*.

It was from this perspective that it was possible to arrive at a picture of the Historical Jesus *if he existed*. The reasoning was simple. Whatever James was—Jesus' reputed closest living heir and successor in Palestine—so was Jesus. In fact, the existence of James is perhaps the best proof of the existence of Jesus. Here the documents at Qumran do help us, because, in so far as they can be shown to relate to James, they also relate to Jesus. The New Testament—particularly Acts—has gone far towards obliterating this connection, but it also inadvertently preserves it, albeit while remaining extremely reticent about who this James was who comes so to dominate Acts. In fact, once we have found the Historical James, we have found the Historical Jesus. We have certainly *not* found him by treating the ideas of his ideological adversary and the man Ebionite tradition calls "the Enemy", Paul, who even admits he persecuted Christians in the early days in Palestine—according to Acts, even "unto death".

We can speak about how the Qumran documents saw the figure of the Righteous Teacher and his nemesis "the Lying Spouter" or "Comedian"; we can speak about the Wicked Priest, responsible in some way for the destruction or death of the Righteous Teacher—and MZCQ and JJHP were the first books to definitively distinguish between him and "the Liar", the one a troublesome internal ideological adversary within the Movement; the other, an external High Priest responsible for his death. But we do not know how Qumran saw the figure of the Messiah because we cannot yet say if they had developed a personalized idea of the general concept apart from the idea of "Righteousness".

Qumran does have a concept of *Yesha'/Yeshu'a* ("Salvation"), and this is evinced in quite a few documents, including the note of "seeing His Salvation"/*Yeshu'ato* at the end of important passages in the Damascus Document about "Justification". We shall treat this passage in another of the papers collected in this volume, "Interpreting some Esotericisms in columns V–VIII of the Damascus Documents from Qumran" (Chapter 7). Another new Qumran document we published, which we called "The Children of *Yesha'* and the Mystery of Existence", even speaks of "the Salvation of His works" and "the Children of *Yesha'*"/ "the Children of Salvation" in the same breath as "inheriting Glory".

This notion of "Salvation", coupled with that of being "saved from the House of Judgement" or "saved on the Day of Judgement", as the Habakkuk *Pesher* puts it on two separate occasions, is very new in the history of ideas, particularly when it is translated into a Hellenistic lifesetting. In fact, there was no god in the Greek Pantheon representing this concept until "Jesus"—which actually means "Salvation" or "Savior" in Hebrew.

This might be all that can be said about the Historical Jesus from the perspective of the Qumran documents: that Qumran had a very developed concept of "Salvation", which at some point may have become personified in the Gospels as they have come down to us—common in Greek literature. In respect of the widely circulated picture of *two*

Messiahs at Qumran, we suggested as early as in MZCQ, following R.H. Charles even earlier, that these might correspond to a singular Messiah descended from two genealogical roots of Aaron and Israel, which is what Jesus, in fact, was, at least according to the Gospel of Luke—or a series of these—and in the Damascus Document, too, where references to a "Messiah" or "Messiahs" occur, the pronominal and verb usages surrounding such allusions are *always singular*.

Throughout the Damascus Document there are references to a divine "Visitation" of some kind—in The Messiah of Heaven and Earth text we published expressed as God (or His Messiah) "visiting the Pious Ones and calling the Righteous Ones by name". This last is also a phrase applied to "the Sons of Zadok" in the Damascus Document, increasing the overlaps between *Righteous Ones* and *Sons of Zadok* we emphasize in this book. Not only does the Damascus Document refer several times to these "Visitations", but also the "*standing up* of the Messiah of Aaron and Israel" (possibly denoting either "to be resurrected" or "to return"— verb usage, as noted, singular), and with it, a nationalistic antagonism to both foreign kings and foreign ways expressed in terms of "the Kings of the Peoples"—an expression in Roman law used to designate lesser kings of the eastern provinces like Asia Minor, Syria, and Palestine— and "the Head of the Kings of Greece"—in this case, clearly the Roman Emperor—as the "head of the asps". This, too, will be treated in the paper about the esotericisms in the Damascus Document mentioned above.

This "Zealot"-style theme of antagonism to foreigners is also discernible in a work we called "Two Letters on Works Reckoned as Righteousness"—known to others by the somewhat more obscure "*MMT*". In these two "Letters" this theme is combined, as it is in the Temple Scroll, with an extreme attention to the details of purification, often relating to gifts and sacrifices in the Temple. Because it contained what could be identified—according to *Talmudic* parameters—as discernible Sadducean legal positions, a flurry of interest developed in the "Sadducean" character of the corpus, which had already been concretized in MZCQ in 1983 without benefit of this document.

As the existence of *MMT* was purposely leaked out, debates began about whether Qumran was "Essene" or "Sadducee". But this was not the main issue. The main issue was, what kind of "Sadducees" could the Sadducees responsible for the Qumran corpus be? MZCQ, using the then available documents, had already arrived at an idea of "Messianic" or "Purist Sadducees", postulating, as the reader will discover, *two groups* of Sadducees: one Establishment and the other Opposition. As it turned out, the orientation of *MMT* was right in line with the general theory enunciated in MZCQ concerning "Opposition Sadducees" with an esoteric, eschatological, or *Righteousness*-oriented understanding of the Zadokite Covenant as opposed to the strictly genealogical one of more familiar "Boethusian" or "Establishment Sadducees" of the Herodian Period and the New Testament.

This Zealot-like animus against foreign gifts and/or sacrifices in the Temple exhibited in *MMT* is one I concretize in this book as at once seminal to the understanding of Qumran and fundamental to the period leading up to the Uprising against Rome—the period in which James the Just, the brother of Jesus, according to early Church accounts, held sway in Jerusalem among the Messianic mass. As we shall see, it is in this period from the 40s to 60s CE that Josephus accuses the insurgents of introducing "innovations" into the religious practice of the people, with which, as he puts it, "our fathers were before unacquainted". By this he means their *banning gifts and sacrifices on behalf of foreigners in the Temple*, including the Roman Emperor, which triggered the War against Rome. But this is just the orientation of *MMT*.

In fact, central to this hostility to foreign gifts and sacrifices in the Temple *MMT* is an allusion to a kindred antagonism to "things sacrificed to idols", one of the key categories of James' prohibitions to overseas communities, bitterly attacked and countermanded by Paul in 1 Co 8:1–10:33, leading up to his proclamation of "Communion with the *blood of the Christ*" in 1 Co 10:16 and 11:25, the esoteric sense of which we shall attempt to delineate in *James the Brother of Jesus* (Faber and Faber/Penguin, 1996). In *James the Brother of Jesus*, we shall also outline the reasons for thinking *MMT*—considered either a "letter" or "letters"—a "Jamesian" letter to "the Great King of the Peoples beyond the Euphrates", either "Agbarus", or possibly even Helen of Adiabene's favorite son Izates. This would, therefore, give it strong link-ups to "the Letter to Agbarus", delivered either by Ananias, Thaddaeus, or Judas Thomas in Syriac sources. This is not to mention James' own "letter", sent down to "Antioch" with someone called "Judas Barsabus", in Acts 15:22–30, containing these prohibitions to overseas communities, including these same "things sacrificed to idols".

Earlier, however, Josephus denoted Herod as being the principal "innovator" introducing changes into the customary practices of the people, to the detriment of their religion. Sycophant that he is, Josephus calls the rejection of gifts and sacrifices on behalf of Romans and other foreigners by "the Revolutionaries" in the Temple "an innovation", but from the time of Ezekiel—a fundamental Prophet for the vocabulary of

Qumran—and the Covenant of Phineas evoked in 1 Macc 2:26 on behalf of the High Priestly claims of the Maccabees, this attitude is strong among "Zealot"-style groups, culminating in the final stopping of sacrifice in the Temple on behalf of foreigners by the lower priesthood in 66 CE, with which the Uprising began.

While groups like the Zealots and breakaway Sadducees as those at Qumran ("Essenes" if one prefers, as long as the term is used advisedly, meaning *militant* and *uncompromising "Essenes"*) supported this action, groups like the Pharisees, Phariseeizing Sadducees, and Herodians, of course, opposed it. I have expressed this in terms of looking at groups on the basis of common enemies and friends. Those that had common enemies probably basically had a common orientation on these issues as well.

This theme of *antagonism to foreigners*, particularly foreign kings, but also the pollution engendered by contact with them—seen as *including Herodians*—is part and parcel of the general xenophobia at Qumran. In Josephus' *Antiquities*, as we shall see, this even goes so far in the 40s CE as the presentation of one Simon—identified as the Head of his own *Ecclēsia* or "Church" in Jerusalem (paralleling the "Simon Peter" in the Bible)—as wishing to *bar Herodians from the Temple as foreigners*. The only difference here is that whereas the "Simon Peter" in the Bible learns he should not make distinctions between clean and unclean, "nor call any man profane", the Simon in Josephus does just the opposite. As we shall show in the Appendix to JJHP, this antagonism to foreigners is part and parcel of the *pollution of the Temple* charge which, in turn, is the third part of the Three Nets of Belial charges in the Damascus Document.

Aside from this kind of nationalist orientation, *MMT* also outlines the position of extreme Righteousness required of either the priesthood or the king it would support. It does so by evoking the idea of "works of the Torah" (*ma'asei ha-Torah*), from which it derives its popular name. This ends in an allusion straight out of the letters of Paul and echoed in Ja 2:21 having to do with how Abraham "was justified". This focus on *Abraham* will also be very important to people in a northern Syrian, Edessa, or Adiabene cultural framework. In Ja 2:23, just as in the Damascus Document, this is evoked in terms of Abraham being "the Friend of God"—and, by implication, not "the Enemy"—terminology familiar to the whole tradition of Jewish Christianity and, in particular, the Ebionites where the orientation of Paul is at issue. James 4:4 puts this in terms of "he who would make himself a Friend of the world turns himself into an Enemy of God".

For its part, *MMT* ends by setting forth in language drawn from Ge 15:6 and echoed to reverse effect in Paul, that these are the "works that would be reckoned for you as Righteousness", or, if one prefers, using the Pauline language of "Justification", "that would justify you". For Paul, in Romans and Galatians, it will be recalled, basing himself directly on Ge 15:6, it is Faith that supposedly "is reckoned for you as Righteousness". The conclusion is that the whole recitation that preceded these words was the sum total of minutiae that would be considered soteriological at "the End of Time", i.e., salvational. However, unlike Paul's evocation of Ge 15, the emphasis as per the Habakkuk *Pesher*'s interpretation of Hab 2:4, which we shall examine in this book, is on "works Righteousness" and the whole recitation is "works" oriented.

Probably more than any other allusions in the Qumran corpus, "the Three Nets of Belial" in the Damascus Document provide the best dating measure for the ambiance of many of these texts, in particular, the charge of "Riches" against the Establishment and prohibitions on "niece marriage", "polygamy", "divorce", and "sleeping with women during their periods". These are all part of the "fornication" charge, coupled with the "Riches" one above, and connected with the charge of improper "separation" in the Temple. This is the basis of the *pollution of the Temple* charge, the third Net of Belial in the Damascus Document above, against what has to be considered the Herodian/Roman Establishment—it could hardly be the Maccabean—calling down divine vengeance and damnation on those supporting it. It only remains to set these into their proper historical framework.

Originally found at the Cairo *Genizah* in 1897, the Damascus Document contained, in addition, numerous passages important for the chronology of Qumran, including those about the appearance of a Messianic "root of planting out of Aaron and Israel" and the pursuit of the Righteous Teacher and his colleagues—the other "Walkers in Perfection"—by the Liar and his confederates. It was important to see whether allusions like that to "Damascus" in the Damascus Document interpretation of the "Star Prophecy" above, "the Kings of the Peoples", "seeing *Yeshuʿa*", Jannes and Jambres, and Gehazi in its later columns—all constituting important *internal* dating parameters—were paralleled in the unpublished corpus. A selection of these allusions is treated in the "Esotericisms" paper mentioned above (now Chapter 7).

There was also thought to be a reference, which had never been published, in the Damascus Document to an annual convocation of the Community at Pentecost and a flight to the wilderness "camps", which paralleled to some degree the well-known flight to Pella by the early Jewish Christians in Jerusalem after the death of James. For these reasons in mid-March, 1989, Prof. Philip Davies of Sheffield University and I formally requested Prof. John Strugnell, then Head of the International Committee, for access to the Qumran parallels to the Damascus Document and other documents.

We copied this letter to Amir Drori, the then Head of the newly reconstituted Israel Antiquities Authority. In the event, our request was ignored, but the Damascus Document fragments from Qumran were mysteriously and quite abruptly immediately transferred to a Jewish scholar outside the International Team of Qumran editors. Still, it became the beginning salvo in the debate over scholarly access, so that in just two years everything was open.

Prof. Davies and myself also called, in a follow-up letter to Drori on May 2, 1989, for AMS carbon-14 dating. This time, our recommendations were not ignored—at least, not completely—and the Israelis publicly announced their decision to conduct such tests four months later, albeit neglecting to note that they were responding to our original proposal. Our caveat had been that "opposition" scholars be present during the process. In the event, those evincing the greatest need for such tests were excluded from them; instead, those conducting the tests represented them as *an answer to my work*, in the process seeming to purposefully misrepresent my ideas as implying the whole of the Qumran corpus to be "Christian". This is untrue. As the title of MZCQ makes clear, I argue for a development of ideas from the Maccabean Period, through the Herodian, into the "Christian", the "Jerusalem Community" of James the Just representing the last phase of the development of that Movement I designate as the "Messianic"—not the first—but this would have been clear to anyone who took the trouble to read my work.

In other work since the publication of MZCQ and JJHP I have been able to further concretize allusions linking the interpretation of the "Star Prophecy" in columns xi–xvi of the War Scroll both to the Messiah and the coming of the Heavenly Host. This is expressed in columns xi and xix in terms of a violent apocalypticism incorporating Dan 7's ideal of "one like a Son of Man coming on the clouds of Heaven" with the Heavenly Host "to rain down Judgement"/*Mishpat* on all the sons of men. That the famous prophecy from Daniel is actually at the root of the interpretation of the "Star Prophecy" in the War Scroll is no mean proposition.[3]

The imagery used is that of *eschatological rain* that falls like Judgement equally on the Righteous and the Wicked alike (compare with Mt 5:45). Not only does this reverberate with the eschatological "rain" and "rain-making" tradition which is delineated in MZCQ, but also with the evocation of "rain" and "rain-making" and "Judgement" in Chapter 5 of the Letter of James. This in turn cannot be separated from James' pronouncement, as portrayed in early Church sources, in the Temple on Passover, of the Messiah "standing at the right hand of the Great Power" and coming eschatological Judgement, which ends up in his trial and execution—allusions which have, in their turn, become almagamated into the portrait of the trial, vision, and stoning of Stephen in the book of Acts as we presently have it (Acts 7:56).

Josephus identifies the "Star Prophecy" (Num 24:17) as the moving force behind the Uprising against Rome in 66 CE, as it seems to have been the Second Uprising under Bar Kochba ("Son of the Star") in 132–36 CE. As we show at several points in these essays, it is evoked at key junctures in at least three Qumran documents: the War Scroll, the Damascus Document, and a collection of Messianic proof-texts known as 4QTestimonia. The conclusion is that the Movement before us was at once Messianic, Law-oriented, and nationalistic. One may choose to term this "Essene", but if so, one should redefine one's understanding of Essenes, for such militancy is not generally part of the normative understanding of the term. If one does, it is not clear how these would now differ from what otherwise go by the name of "Zealots", "*Sicarii*", or for that matter "Zadokites" or Messianic Sadducees of a Qumran frame of mind.

In the meantime, further new theories of Qumran origins appeared. Like the proponents of the Zealot Hypothesis, supposedly *vanquished* by de Vaux, Milik, Cross, and company in the 1960s, Norman Golb of the University of Chicago, for instance, used the Copper Scroll as the jumping-off point for his re-evaluation of Qumran origins. His arguments for a *Jerusalem* origin of the corpus at Qumran do not differ appreciably from the points made in MZCQ and JJHP, which see the Community Leadership as moving freely between Jerusalem and a number of "camps" in the wilderness, referred to under the codename "Damascus"—whether on the other side of the Jordan or at Qumran.

But his notion of the materials at Qumran as an eclectic collection of Jerusalem "libraries"—itself, little more than a refurbishment of earlier "*genizah*" theories of Qumran origins—does not sufficiently come to grips with the homogeneity of the literature, because, as already noted, the same basic concepts and allusions permeate the corpus. While the texts are certainly those of a major, not a minor, Movement in Judaism and can be looked upon as "popular Judaism" of the day, this Judaism must be seen as *opposed* to the Establishment. Nor, as explained, was the group or Movement responsible for this literature particularly forgiving, retiring, or non-violent. Neither was it passive, though it did counsel the kind of patience recommended, for instance, in Ja 5:7. Nor did it follow the more accommodationist Gospel dictums of "loving one's enemies" or "turning the other cheek", but rather, as we have seen, "eternal hatred towards the Sons of the Pit", inclusive of "Traitors", Jewish backsliders and collaborators, and, in fact, Gentile idolators generally.

It is the homogeneity of allusions of this kind that makes the approach of Golb, who seems to read the Qumran documents about as incisively as consensus scholars, unconvincing. Though this is not the Judaism of an Establishment like that of the Herodian/Pharisaic one, it most certainly represents that of an Opposition Movement of some kind, more in harmony with popular Maccabean-style nationalism than anything else. In MZCQ, as explained, I call this "the Messianic Movement", and this kind of intense Messianism was certainly displayed in The Messiah of Heaven and Earth text mentioned above that we published for the first time in *The Dead Sea Scrolls Uncovered*, not only making the singular nature of this Messianism clear, but even possibly a kind of quasi-supernatural aspect to it.[4]

Another text we demonstrated—one that had earlier been published in a somewhat fragmentary form—related to the interpretation at Qumran of the famous "*Shiloh* Prophecy" of Ge 49:10 about the *Mehok-kek*/"the Staff" that would not pass from Judah until "the *Shiloh*" came.[5] Both "the *Mehokkek*" and "Scepter", mentioned in this text and referred to in allusions in Deuteronomy—the latter also being an integral allusion in the "Star Prophecy", also subjected as well to exegesis in the War Scroll—are also developed further in column vi of the Damascus Document. In this fragment, which we identified as being part of a text we called "The Genesis Florilegium", "the Scepter" and "the *Mehokkek*" are related to a singular individual called "the Messiah of Righteousness". He, in turn, is said to be equivalent to "the Branch of David"—additional Messianic terminology found elsewhere in the Qumran Scrolls.[6] Together with "the Men of the Community", all are said to be "Keepers of the Torah", the terminological definition, as noted above, of "the Sons of Zadok" at Qumran.

Included in this work too will be several additional essays already signaled in the text and notes of both MZCQ and JJHP. These include a paper given to the Society of Biblical Literature in 1991, further developing the Qumran interpretation of Ezek 44:15 in the Damascus Document on "the Priests, the Levites, and the Sons of Zadok". This paper (Chapter 8) argues that the term developed out of the underlying reference to "Levites", "the *Nilvim*" or "Joiners", implies a cadre of Gentile adherents joined to the Community in the wilderness camps in associated status, just as to some extent (if Acts is any measure) Christians seem to have originally been drawn from a class of Gentile "God-Fearers" attaching themselves to Jewish synagogues around the Mediterranean—"*Nilvim*" in Hebrew implying just such a caste.

In addition, we shall present here for the first time a paper given to the Society of Biblical Literature in November, 1984, immediately following the publication of MZCQ. This was entitled "Paul as Herodian"—it is now Chapter 4 —and follows up some of the points made in the lengthy footnotes of that book. This article arose out of the suspicion that in some manner many Qumran positions arose out of opposition to the Herodian family and the consideration of them as foreigners. It became clear, too, that Paul's inordinate influence as such a young man and his easygoing relations with persons in the ruling circles of Jerusalem, the antinomian thrust of his "Gentile Mission"—in particular, its opposition to circumcision—and the fact of his Roman citizenship, were all comprehensible in the light of such an identification.

Furthermore, this suspicion of an actual family relationship to Herodians was evident not only in the tenor of his beliefs, but further strengthened by the actual reference Paul makes in Ro 16:11 to "my kinsman Herodion"—that is, "the Littlest Herod"—which to my knowledge had never been remarked by any commentator previously. Paul's putative "Herodian" connections also led to a closer consideration of an actual character in Josephus' works named "Saulus" or "Saul", a contemporary of Paul, whom Josephus specifically identifies as a "kinsman" of the Herodian family. This Saulus disappears from sight after a mission to Nero—then in Corinth overseeing the construction of the Canal—to brief him on the seriousness of the Uprising in Judea in 66 CE. As we shall see, this Saulus knew this first hand, having been a key player in the events following James' death in Jerusalem leading up to the Uprising.

It is apparently as a result of this intelligence that Nero sends for Vespasian (the future Emperor) from Britain and dispatches him to Palestine to put down the rebellion. The Saulus in Josephus drops from sight around 66 CE, the same time as Paul himself does in Christian history. The paper also suggests that it was possible Paul returned to Palestine after his first appeal to Nero in Rome in 60 CE, six years before the events being described here, since nothing is said of his fate after this trip and Acts portentously and inchoately simply trails off at this point (coincidentally with *James' death* in 62 CE), so it is impossible to say whether Paul did or did not. If Josephus' "Saulus" is Paul, he did, to return again to report to Nero six years later at the beginning of the Uprising.

Recently, three to four sherds were discovered by accident in rubbish heaps on the Qumran plateau near the graves.[7] These had writing on them and appear to have been receipts for supplies received from Jericho. Not only are these some of the only really secular documents found at the site of Qumran, they are extremely important in showing that the settlement was *not isolated*, but part of the general network of communities in that region. But what is even more important, they contain an allusion to "Year 2"—meaning "Year 2 of the Redemption of Zion" or of the Revolt against Rome. Again, not only does this conclusively demonstrate that the site was not an isolated one during this period, but that the inhabitants at Qumran were participating in the Revolt against Rome and *using its calendar*—along with many others in the region. This is precisely the position we have argued for in this book on both archaeological grounds, and also *internal* textual grounds.

Also appended are new translations of several previously published Qumran documents, forming the basis for the ideas presented in these works. The reader will be able to see what a difference a translation sensitive to the mindset of the authors and the precise vocabulary they use, makes. This is a crucial point because in the past the only publicly available translations have been consensus ones, on the whole totally ignoring this mindset and the consistency of the vocabulary employed by these wilderness-dwelling extremists. These include the Cairo *Genizah* version of the Damascus Document, at least the first eight or nine columns, mentioned so often above; the Habakkuk *Pesher*, forming the basis of JJHP; and the first nine columns, again, of the Community Rule.

These works have always been available only in vague, generally imprecise, translations by Establishment scholars, and the public has never had the benefit of an "Opposition" approach to these texts, translated in the style of *The Dead Sea Scrolls Uncovered* above. The difference is quite surprising, because key concepts are identified in a uniform and consistent manner throughout, and the reader will then be in no doubt concerning the aggressive and militant nature of this fundamental vocabulary ranging across the breadth of the Qumran corpus and the precise translations of key phrases in English which *never vary*.

Finally we append a paper given at the Society of Biblical Literature in 1994, "The Final Proof that James and the Righteous Teacher are the Same" (Chapter 9). This paper picks up where JJHP and the "*Abeit-Galuto*" paper left off, developing a proof of the identity of James and the Righteous Teacher from Qumran so astonishing that even the present writer could not believe it when first considering it. It centers on the fact that the same linguistic configurations were being used in the

Greek to apply to key episodes in James' life—and spun off in a sometimes comical and always very playful manner in the New Testament to relate to episodes in Jesus' life and his teaching—as were being used in the Hebrew regarding the life and teaching of the Righteous Teacher at Qumran, but the latter with altogether different signification.

It should be stated that it is allusions of the kind treated in this article and JJHP that go a long way towards proving the case. If a theory can elicit more from the internal data than we knew previously or could have been known without it, it is good reason for taking that theory seriously. This is the case with the theory about James or "the First Christians"—more is elicited from the material than was known hitherto. No other theory of Qumran origins does as much. On the contrary. Other theories of Qumran origins purposely skirt these issues and give no meaningful interpretation of them—in fact, they often abjure identifications altogether. This, of course, has always been a very safe vantage-point from which to attack the position of one's adversaries.

The James theory allows us to come to grips with allusions and puzzling usages in the Qumran corpus in a way no other prior or competing hypothesis does, allowing us to venture further into the texts than we could have before. This is very powerful proof indeed, and normal to the way most attempts at scientific verification are constructed. It is hoped that readers will be encouraged to continue to approach analyses and historical investigations of the kind included in these previously published books and articles in order to further deepen their understanding of the roots of the Community represented by the literature deposited at Qumran.

Robert Eisenman   Fountain Valley, California
                                                              June, 1996

[1] G. Bonani, M. Broshi, I. Carmi, S. Ivy, J. Strugnell, and W. Wolfi, "Radiocarbon Dating of the Dea Sea Scrolls", *Atiqot*, xx, July, 1991, 127–32, and more recently in July, 1995, in the same journal, T. Jull, D. Donahue, M. Broshi, and E. Tov, "Radiocarbon Dating of Scrolls and Linen Fragments from the Judean Desert".

[2] See R.H. Eisenman, "Dead Sea Scroll Update", *Biblical Archaeology Review*, Nov/Dec, 1991, p. 65 and Plate no. 924, PAM no. 42.601 in Eisenman and Robinson, *A Facsimile Edition of the Dead Sea Scrolls*, Washington DC, 1991. The translations of this text in Baillet, *DJD*, vii, and Vermes dependent on it, inexplicably omitting lines 8–9 calling down God's vengeance on the foreign armies invading the land, miss the militant xenophobia inherent in them. Vermes also mysteriously omits a very important phrase about the exposition of the Messiah's "Name" (singular!) in line ii.13 of the Damascus Document. The reader will judge for himself or herself whose translations are the more accurate.

[3] See "Eschatological 'Rain' Imagery in the War Scroll from Qumran and in the Letter of James", *Journal of Near Eastern Studies*, April, 1990, pp. 183–84 (Chapter 6 of this book).

[4] See *The Dead Sea Scrolls Uncovered*, Element Books, 1992, pp. 19–23.

[5] Ibid, pp. 83–85.

[6] See CD, vi, 14–20 also interpreting "The Star Prophecy" (Num 24:17), and the Messianic Leader fragment (4Q285) and my detailed discussion there; *DSSO*, pp. 24–29.

[7] See note in *Archaeology*, May/June, 1996, p. 21 and *Biblical Archaeology Review*, May/June, 1996, p. 14.

PART ONE

Judas, called Maccabaeus, with some nine others, withdrew into the wilderness, and lived like wild animals in the hills with his companions, eating nothing but wild plants to avoid contracting defilement (2 Macc 5:27).

The disciples said to Jesus: "We know that you will depart from us. Who is he who shall be our leader?" Jesus said to them: "In the place where you find yourselves, go to James the Righteous One, for whose sake Heaven and Earth came into existence" (Gos Th 12).

Noah was a Righteous One. Assuredly so after the supernal pattern. It is written, "The Righteous One is the Foundation of the World," and the Earth is established thereon, for this is the Pillar that upholds the world. So Noah was called "Righteous" below . . . and acted so as to be a true copy of the supernal ideal . . . an embodiment of the world's Covenant of Peace (Zohar 59b on "Noah").

When God desires to give healing to the Earth, He smites one Righteous One . . . with suffering . . . to make atonement . . . and sometimes all his days are passed in suffering to Protect the People (ibid., 218a–b on "Phineas").

CHAPTER 1

Maccabees, Zadokites, Christians and Qumran: A New Hypothesis of Qumran Origins

INTRODUCTION

Various preconceptions have dominated Qumran research. These, in turn, have blurred the significance of documents of the most incalculable historical value, so that only thirty-five years after their discovery, they have become objects of only passing interest to many scholars. Primarily, these preconceptions stem from an animus towards and derogation of the Maccabean family and the additional underlying motive—albeit at times unconscious—of trying to distance the materials in question as far as possible from Christianity's formative years in Palestine. These preconceptions subtly deform archaeological and paleographic studies as well, so that scholars end up with "results" that are psychologically and spiritually more in keeping with their original assumptions and beliefs. In turn, these are used to render stillborn solutions that are based on the clear thrust of internal data and the reality of the historical *sitz im leben*.

Though Josephus is properly recognized as the important source he is, his associations with both the "Essene" and "Zealot" Movements (and what we shall refer to as "the Messianic Movement"), and his canny evasions resulting from these, are in large measure ignored. It is forgotten, too, that apart from the period 55–75 CE, when he was a mature observer, he too was working from sources—sources he sometimes either treated too hastily or did not fully understand himself—and his confusions compound our own. For example, he repeats data (probably from different sources) about Herod's regard for both Pharisees and Essenes and sets them side by side without realizing his sources were themselves most likely talking about the same group. This confusion of "Pharisee" and "Essene" terminologies is also at the root of the contradictory notices about "Hassidaeans" in 2 Macc and 1 Macc as both the supporters of Judas *par excellence* and his betrayers. Elsewhere, Josephus contradicts himself in what he says about James' nemesis, the High Priest Ananus, heaping praise on him in the *War*, while abusing him in the *Antiquities* and the *Vita*. In fact, many startling omissions in the *War* are made good in this way in the *Antiquities* and the *Vita*. Compounding this particular confusion, early Church accounts insist that Josephus connected James' death with the fall of Jerusalem, which is precisely what he tells us about Ananus' death in the extant copy of the *War*.

The inability to come to grips with a whole new vocabulary in Hebrew also prevented many scholars from seeing through to the real implications of the materials before them. In particular, it proved difficult to recognize the Hebrew originals of familiar expressions known only through Greek, Latin, and more modern translations, e.g., *Derech* ("the Way"), *Tamim* or *Tom* ("Perfection"), *Da'at* ("Knowledge"—"*Gnosis*" in some traditions), *'amal/ma'asim* ("works"), *yazdik/yizadek* ("justify" or "be justified"), *Yom* or *Beit ha-Mishpat* ("the Last Judgement"), etc. Perhaps because of a dearth of really credible translations, specialists also found it difficult to come to grips with the use of interchangeable metaphor where the names of numerous familiar groups were concerned, e.g., "Essenes" (*Hassidim*), Zadokites (*Zaddikim*), Ebionites (*Ebionim*), Nazoraeans (*Nozrim*), "the Meek" (*'Anayyim*), "the Saints" (*Kedoshim*), "Zealots" (*Kanna'im*), etc. This is compounded by the basically secretive nature of the tradition, which itself was connected with an ongoing "hidden" tradition, and in turn, accounts for the seemingly dizzying multiplication of sects and groups, when in fact one has to do essentially with one "Essene" or "Zealot"-type orientation. Part of the problem, too, stems from the inability to recognize subversive groups in what on the surface, anyhow, appeared to be harmless "ascetics". Here, Josephus is more forthcoming, albeit still using his familiar circumlocutions, when he tells us that "the imposters and deceivers" (that is, those whom we shall call our "Zadokite" leaders) were scheming to bring about *both* "innovations" (i.e., religious reform) *and* "change in Government".

One must be prepared to put aside all preconceptions stemming from one's own terms of reference, usually either the viewpoints of Rabbinic Judaism or Christianity as it has devolved upon us, since the tradition under consideration is implacably hostile to both. For example, the authenticity of the Letter of James has been consistently undermined from Eusebius' time to Luther's; but aside from some polishing and minimal ideological tinting, it fits perfectly into the materials of concern to us in this study. Exhibiting that studied reticence in identifying its antagonists which is usually the result of fear of powerful, hostile forces, its "not one jot or tittle" approach to Torah, its constant stress on "keeping (not "breaking") the Law", and its antagonism to "fornication" (cf. Ja 2:8ff., the formulations of which appear to predate and underlie Mt 5:17ff.) all have their parallels in Qumran usage. Its application of "tongue" imagery, extant at Qumran, to describe a troublesome internal adversary, is also generically parallel to the "Lying", "Spouting", and insolent "Scoffing" allusions there. Elsewhere, the interpolation in Paul's presentation of the order of resurrection appearances in 1 Co 15.4ff. is widely assumed to involve the reference to "James and all the apostles". However, we prefer to turn this around, considering it rather to consist of the improbable "Cephas and the twelve" (there were only eleven at the time). Neither can the historical *sitz im leben* of the Qumran tradition be reconstructed solely on the basis of traditions to which Rabbinic Judaism is the heir. In fact, in this period both it and "Gentile Christianity" exhibit a telltale pattern of deference to Herodian religious requirements and political designs.

Some words should be said about our reference in passing to *Zohar* tradition, correspondences to which are pointed out in the footnotes. It should be noted that I confine myself to the *Noah* and *Phineas* sections only, where allusions relevant to James' person are found. Though I prefer to stand aside on the question of the Second Temple or medieval origins of *Zohar* tradition (cf. Paul on Mosaic "splendor" in 2 Co 3:8ff.), the appropriateness of these allusions to the materials under consideration should give those who dogmatically adhere to the latter position something to consider; certainly these references have nothing whatever to do with thirteenth-century Spain.

Correspondences are also pointed out in the footnotes to Karaite traditions and selected use is made of materials in the Slavonic Josephus. Anyone who would object to recourse to such parallels should realize that Gospel and Rabbinic traditions are not much better attested to and all such materials, anyhow, must be treated *equally* according to the *same* criteria. Here, attention to work done in traditions in the Islamic field of *a completely disinterested kind* might prove helpful. Its results illustrate that traditions of the most surprising content, considered poorly authenticated for some reason, or "divergent" by majority opinion, often turn out to carry the earliest strata of historical data. Where the documents at Qumran are concerned, of course, we are in possession fortunately of contemporary accounts in large measure unaffected by the distortions of tradition-manufacture and the retrospective imposition of a later historical consensus.

Another serious problem in Qumran textual studies is the inability to come to grips with literary genre and literary device; in particular, the Hebrew love of word-play. This is true, for instance, of the Qumran exegesis of the crucial "Zadokite Statement" of Ezek 44:15 (which is very definitely *eschatological*, as is that of Hab 2:4), the use of the term "the Many" in Qumran community organization and (together with both *'amal* and *Da'at*) in "Justification"-theorizing going back to Is 53:11 usage (the currency of which is attested to by Paul in 1 Co 15:4 above), and figurative allusion to the central priestly triad as "the Holy of Holies" in a general context of Is 40:3 "making a Way in the wilderness" and Ps 118:22 "Cornerstone" imagery.

Two basic Hebrew concepts, *Hesed* and *Zedek* ("Piety" and "Righteousness"), run through all descriptions of opposition groups in this period. Justin Martyr identifies these as the twin components of the "all Righteousness" doctrine. Putting them side by side with the elemental Noachic proscriptions on "idolatry, fornication, and manslaughter" (also at the root of James' "Jerusalem Council" directives), he shows how this duality was expressed in the two scriptural commandments of "loving God" (*Hesed*) and "loving one's neighbor" (*Zedek*; cf. Mt 22:34ff. and Mk 12:28ff.).

Starting with the description of the *Anshei-Hesed/Zaddikim* in Hebrew Ecclesiasticus and Josephus' parallel note about Simeon the *Zaddik* in the *Antiquities*, this dichotomy is the common thread running through all Josephus' descriptions of "Essenes", Josephus' description of John the Baptist's wilderness activities, and all early Church accounts of James; and comprises the essential basis of what we shall describe as the "Zadokite Hassidaean" Movement. Where James and "the Essenes" were concerned—and probably Jesus as well—the "Righteousness" Commandment (cf. Ja 2:8 on "the Supreme Law of Scripture") underwent the additional fundamental metamorphosis into a demand for economic equality, which is at the root of "the Poor" terminologies and the hostility towards "the Rich" so closely connected with all these Essene-like or "Jewish Christian" personalities.

Another important theme in this period is the "hidden" ideology we have alluded to above. This is linked in our literature to "hiding in *caves*" and taken all the way back via *Zohar* tradition to the first *Zaddik* Noah's paradigmatic experience of "being hidden" (by God) in the ark to escape the destruction that was being unleashed. It finds additional expression in a strong *redivivus* tradition adhering to these "Noachic" priest-*Zaddiks*, which, in turn, is closely associated with another element in the "Noachic" tradition: *rain-making*. An additional echo of all of these motifs is to be found in the *Talmud* in the *redivivus* and "hidden" traditions circulating about Honi, the circle-drawing *Zaddik*, not to mention in Josephus' "magician" and "imposter" accusations.

Not only does the *ARN* associate rain-making (not insignificantly under the heading of "Simeon the *Zaddik*") with proper (that is, "Zadokite") "Temple service", but in the War Scroll eschatological "rain" imagery is definitively connected to the exegesis of "the Star" Prophecy. This is expressed in terms of "the Messiah" coming to give "Judgement" (*Mishpat*) and the coming of "the Heavenly Host" to "rain judgement" from the clouds "on all the sons of men". The connection of both of these allusions with the well-known Messiah "coming on the clouds of Heaven" imagery should be clear (cf. also Paul in 1 Thess 3:13–4:17 and Jude 14f.). This is precisely the proclamation early Church tradition attributes to James, to whom the rain-making tradition also adhered, and it is repeated in the letter conserved under his name, which itself culminates in Messianic "rain" imagery and, in the process, specifically refers to one of the key rain-making forerunners in the *redivivus* tradition: Elijah.

Two titles, *Zaddik* and *Oblias* (or "Protection of the People"; the last paralleled in Qumran "Shield"/*Ma'oz* and "Fortress"/*Migdal* imagery), were applied as if integrally to James' being; and it is specifically acknowledged that Qumran-style scriptural exegesis was carried on with regard to his person (as at Qumran, the passage in question, Is 3:10, is a *Zaddik*-passage of the kind applied to the events of the life of the Righteous Teacher; cf. Hab 2:4, Ps 37, etc.). Also, two adversaries can be readily identified with regard to his life. These, in turn, precisely parallel the two nemeses of the Righteous Teacher: one an establishment High Priest outside the Movement called "Wicked" and the other a "treacherous" individual within the Movement who follows a more antinomian approach to the Law (including "denying the Law in the midst of the whole congregation"), "leads Many astray" (in contradistinction to the more proper "Justification" activity of "making Many Righteous"), and is variously dubbed "the Liar", "the Pourer out of Lying", "the Scoffer" or "Boaster". Tradition, too, actually places James with *all his community* in the Jericho area in the early 40s, corresponding to an impressive rise in Qumran coin distribution under Agrippa I (Ps *Rec* 1.71, a notice which can hardly be ascribed to historical interpolation).

It should be appreciated that according to the scheme of the Damascus Document, the Messianic "Root" has already been killed, and that, therefore, dwelling too much on the person of "the Messiah" (who even for Gospel artificers and their modern-day form-critical and redactionist inheritors is a figure shrouded in mystery) will not prove very productive.

This was the defect of J. Teicher's fantastic theorizing, which did more to discredit work on this subject than advance it, itself prefigured in the earlier and more solid work done on the Damascus Document by G. Margoliouth. However, the Damascus Document does conclude with the unmistakable evocation of a "Messianic" *return* (repeated three times). The language it uses precisely corresponds to James' several like-minded proclamations noted above and Paul in 1 Thess 3:13. A proper grasp of the Hebrew usage, *'amod*, which does not only mean "coming" as per most translations, but also "standing up", as per the original reference in Ezekiel, would clarify these matters.

Finally, it should be appreciated that Qumran exegetical interpretation raises the clear presumption of a first-century provenance for most Qumran sectarian materials. This is as true of the exegesis of Hab 2:4 (including the notice about "the delay of the *Parousia*" which precedes it), as it is for the citation of "the Star" prophecy (which Josephus definitively connects with the Uprising against Rome and which all available evidence attests was "in the air" from the 40s to the 60s CE and beyond) upwards of three times in the extant corpus—once in connection with the Messianic "rain" imagery described above; the reference to "the True Prophet" proof-text (Deut 18:15) well-known in Jewish Christian tradition; and the application of "Lebanon" imagery to the fall of the Temple, which *ARN* definitively ties to the fall of the Temple in 70 CE.

In addition, there is the implied presence of the terminology of Is 53:11 in the very structure of Qumran organization itself, as well as in Qumran eschatological exegesis of Ezek 44:15 and Hab 2:4, and the fairly large collection of Qumran allusions, including "the Way" (which Luke identifies as an alternative name for first-century "Christianity" in Palestine), "the Poor", "the Meek", *Yom ha-Mishpat* ("the Day of Judgement"; cf. Jude 6), "works", "the *Kez ha-Aharon*" ("the Last End"; cf. Heb 9:27), etc., all with a fairly well attested first-century provenance.

Then what principally holds researchers back from arriving at such conclusions? Aside from a strong psychological and spiritual predisposition not to arrive at such results, the answer is to be found in the supposedly secure "results" paleographers and archaeologists have claimed for themselves. Here, a small group of specialists, largely working together, developed a consensus which was used to press the provenance of the most important Qumran sectarian texts back into the first (and sometimes even the second) century BC.

In *lieu* of clear historical insight or a firm textual grasp, preconceptions and reconstructions, such as they were, were stated as facts, and these results, which were used to corroborate each other, in turn became *new* assumptions, that were used to draw away a whole generation of students unwilling (or simply unable) to question the work of their mentors. The archaeological evidence they used was mainly based on a questionable treatment of coin data; while the flaws in paleography (a subject notorious for its imprecision) were mainly connected with F. M. Cross' and S. Birnbaum's assumptions of a "rapid", *straight-line* development of scripts.

In fact, where paleographic sequences are concerned and the rather simplistic straight-line functions developed to describe these, the situation is probably far more uneven and complex than either scholar originally envisioned; and historical and textual studies will be able to do much to clarify these, not vice versa. Despite the fact that a majority of concerned persons do not appear to have seriously examined the various positions of those principally responsible for this consensus or their methodologies, this consensus has been allowed to stand. Therefore, I have felt obliged to treat and criticize their arguments and conclusions in detail in the latter part of this work, particularly in the footnotes.

In providing an alternative historical and textual framework in which to fit the most important Qumran sectarian documents, it is hoped that most of the preconceptions that have dominated Qumran research for so long will fade away, and that new ideas will be brought into play and previously unused sources given their proper scope. When this is done, individual beings, the facts of whose lives tradition has distorted beyond recognition, or who have been consigned to historical oblivion, spring immediately to life and a whole block of associated historical fabrications and accusations evaporate.

I wish to express my appreciation to Robert Morgan of Oxford University, Luigi Cirillo of the University of Calabria, William Farmer of Southern Methodist University, and Morton Smith of Columbia University, all of whom took the time to offer suggestions, or read through parts of the book. Also, I wish to thank the Office of Research of California State University Long Beach for encouraging the research that went into this study. Finally, I dedicate this work to my wife and to my children without whose patience and forbearance it could never have been accomplished.

Robert Eisenman   Fountain Valley, California
                                                            April, 1983

LIST OF ABBREVIATIONS

ANF	The Anti-Nicene Fathers
Ant.	Josephus, *Antiquities of the Jews (Antiquitates Iudaeorum)*
1 Apoc Ja	First Apocalypse of James
2 Apoc Ja	Second Apocalypse of James
Apost. Const.	*Apostolic Constitutions*
APOT	*Apocrypha and Pseudepigrapha of the Old Testament,* ed. R. H. Charles
ARN	*Abot de Rabbi Nathan*
BASOR	*Bulletin of the American Schools of Oriental Research*
CBQ	*Catholic Biblical Quarterly*
CD	Cairo *Genizah*: Damascus Document
Comm. in Matt.	Origen, *Commentarium in Evangelium Mattheum*
De Mens et Pond	Epiphanius, *De Mensuris et Ponderibus*
Dial.	Justin Martyr, *Dialogue with Trypho*
E.H.	Eusebius, *Ecclesiastical History*
Gos Th	Gospel of Thomas
Haeres.	Epiphanius, *Adversus Haereses*
Hist. Nat.	Pliny, *Natural History (Naturalis Historia)*
IEJ	*Israel Exploration Journal*
In Flacc.	Philo, *In Flaccum*
JBL	*Journal of biblical Literature*
JJS	*Journal of Jewish Studies*
JTS	*Journal of Theological Studies*
Mur	Wadi Murabbaʿat Cave I
NTS	*New Testament Studies*
PEQ	*Palestine Exploration Quarterly*
Ps *Rec*	Pseudoclementine *Recognitions*
Quod Omnis	Philo, *Quod Omnis Probus Liber Sit*
Qumran	*Revue Qumran*
RB	*Revue biblique*
REJ	*Revue des études juives*
SBL	Society of Biblical Literature
Test. L.	Testament of Levi
TZ	*Theologische Zeitschrift*
Vir. ill.	Jerome, *Lives of Illustrious Men (De Viris Illustribus)*
Vita	Josephus, *Life of Flavius Josephus*
V.T.	*Vetus Testamentum*
War	Josephus, *Jewish War (Bellum Iudaicum)*

I
QUMRAN RESEARCH

Over and over again in Qumran research one comes upon the assertion that one or another of the Maccabee family had some connection with "the Wicked Priest" and/or "the Spouter of Lies". Furthermore, it is claimed that the Maccabee family, including even Mattathias or Judas, "usurped" the high priesthood from an earlier, purer line known as the "Zadokite".[1] These ideas have on the whole dominated Dead Sea Scroll research, but they are at variance with the evidence found at Qumran itself including material in the Book of Enoch, Daniel, and the Testament of Levi. They display a curious insensitivity to the true meanings and origins of the Sadducee, Zealot, and "Christian" (or what in Palestine probably should be called the "Messianic") Movements.[2]

Josephus is usually taken at face value with little attempt to analyze the data he provides beyond a superficial comparison of it with other known facts. Where religious movements were concerned, however, he was a self-serving and inadequate observer. Like the final redactors of the Gospels—whose contemporary he was—he was at pains to avoid certain potentially incriminating facts: in his case, his own association with the "Zealot" and/or "Messianic" Movements.[3]

---

[1] See F. M. Cross, *The Ancient Library of Qumran*, New York, 1961, pp. 127–160 for perhaps the classic discussion of this problem; for his use of the word "usurpation", see pp. 135 and 140; G. Vermes, *The Dead Sea Scrolls in English*, London, 1962, pp. 62ff.; J. T. Milik, *Dix ans de découvertes dans le Désert de Juda*, Paris, 1957, Chapter 3 (Eng. tr., *Ten Years of Discovery in the Wilderness of Judaea*, London, 1959, pp. 44–98), etc. F. F. Bruce in *Second Thoughts on the Dead Sea Scrolls*, Exeter, 1956, p. 100, perhaps sums up the prevailing view admirably with the words ". . . in the eyes of the Qumran community every ruler of the Hasmonean dynasty, not being a member of the House of Zadok, held the high-priestly office illegitimately and was *ex officio* a Wicked Priest."

[2] For these purposes, it is often overlooked that the "Christians" were not and could not have been called "Christians" in Palestine if the testimony of Luke in Acts is to be credited: "It was at Antioch that the disciples were first called 'Christians'" (Acts 11:26). Epiphanius, for whatever his testimony is worth—and in this instance I see no reason to quarrel with him, since, however he garbles the traditions he presents, there is often a credible core to them—thinks that "before the Christians began to be called 'Christians' at Antioch", they were called at least in Palestine "Jessaeans", by which, apart from his facile derivation of this term, he clearly intends "Essenes"; *Haeres.* 29.1. He repeats this in 29.4 in no uncertain terms: "therefore either by that Jesse or from Jesus Christ our Lord we call them by the name of 'Jessaeans', because their teaching arises from Jesus and they became his disciples . . . "

[3] It should be remembered that Josephus advertises himself in the *Jewish War* as military commander of Galilee under the insurgent government in Jerusalem, though in the *Vita*

The curious lack of reference to the Christian movement in his works is passed over by a scholar as eminent in the field as M. L'Abbé J. T. Milik with the words: " . . . we should remember that Josephus hardly mentions John the Baptist and Jesus; *his interest lay in other things*" (italics mine).[4] The same writer, whose work is one of the foundation pieces of Qumran research, pokes fun at Dupont-Sommer's outrage over his suggestion to identify the "heroic and holy" Mattathias with "the Man of Belial", and defends his own position as follows: "Whatever may have been the attitude of the Asidaeans . . . to Mattathias", their successors "could easily include in their disapproval the ancestors of the ruling dynasty. *This Semitic custom needs no comment*" (italics again mine).[5]

Milik's response is biased and based on an inability to come to grips with the true nature of the documents under consideration, and by implication, that of the movement upon which Christianity is predicated. In this instance, Dupont-Sommer's righteous indignation is justified, though his passion is on firmer ground than his scholarship, as his identifications in the beginning at least were only little better than Milik's (and for that matter Cross', whom Milik includes with himself).[6] Not only are these

his role seems more that of a priestly commissar. Depending on his audience and purposes Josephus is always altering his facts in this way. Since the Uprising was actually begun by young priests who stopped sacrificing on behalf of the Romans, Josephus is compromised by this association as well. S. G. F. Brandon, *Jesus and the Zealots*, New York, 1967, pp. 114–41, covers the role of the lower priesthood in the War against Rome in some detail.

Several other curious matters must be explained with regard to Josephus. The first has to do with his trip to Rome in order to obtain the release of two priestly prisoners. Here he seems very quickly to gain access to the imperial family itself. As well, he makes the contacts on this trip that are to prove so useful to him in his later betrayal of the "Zealot" cause. His knowledge of the importance of "the Messianic Prophecy" in the atmosphere of the times is made clear in his use of it to flatter Vespasian, not to mention his inadvertent revelation of it as the basis of the Uprising against Rome; cf. *War* 6.6.4. A second interlude in Josephus' life which needs explanation is his novitiate period with the mysterious "*Banus*" in the wilderness, *Vita* 2. Who *Banus* was and what role he played in ensuing events remain a mystery. Note, however, the parallel themes of "bathing", wearing only "linen" (cf. "clothing that grew on trees" for *Banus*), and vegetarianism (*Banus*, Rechabite-like, ate "food growing of itself") in descriptions of *Banus*' contemporary James; cf. below, pp. 60 and 64.

[4] Milik, p. 74

[5] *Ibid.*, pp. 63f. His actual words are: "Dupont-Sommer practically accuses us of blasphemy in proposing this slander."

[6] His understanding that the sect would be violently opposed to the machinations of the Phariseeizing Hyrcanus II, who in effect invites the Romans into the country, and his grasp of the significance of a *Zaddik*-type like Honi the Circle-Drawer, whose life

kinds of assumptions derogatory to the Maccabees who with perhaps the single exception of Alexander Jannaeus were held in the highest esteem by the common people (including Christians), as we shall show;[7] they are self-serving and should never have so easily passed the tests of critical scholarship, so that now twenty years later one finds them dutifully recited by most students and textbooks in the field.

One should perhaps quote finally from the concluding sentence of Milik's book: " . . . although Essenism bore in itself more than one element that one way or other fertilized the soil from which Christianity was to spring, it is nevertheless evident that the latter religion represents something completely new which can *only be adequately explained by the person of Jesus himself*" (italics mine).[8] It is perhaps unfair to single out one author in this way, but his remarks are representative of a wide segment of Qumran scholarship. Granting even that these last might have been included to a certain extent to satisfy Church authorities, they are still illustrative of the crux of the problem.

It is difficult to acknowledge that there is a relationship between Judas Maccabee and the priesthood growing out of his activities, and Jesus

and death prefigure those of the above-mentioned *Zaddik*-type, James the Just, are very close to the mark; A. Dupont-Sommer, *Nouveaux aperçus sur les Manuscrits de la Mer Morte*, Paris, 1953, pp. 33–61. Actually, he adopts the suggestion of R. Goosens that Onias the Just was the founder of the Community and therefore Hyrcanus, the enemy, in "Onias le Juste, Le Messie de la Nouvelle Alliance, lapidé à Jerusalem en 65 av. JC", *Nouvelle Cleo*, vii, 1950, pp. 336–53. Cross, who rightly criticizes Dupont-Sommer on his misuse of the Testament of Levi, on the other hand, cannot in any way understand why Dupont-Sommer should prefer to include Aristobulus in his list of "saviors" while leaving off Hyrcanus II and makes what can only be considered an uninformed remark in saying the "Essene author" of the Testament presumably "was unaware that Judas never functioned as high priest"; cf. his comments, pp. 158ff.

[7] See below, pp. 40ff. W. R. Farmer in *Maccabees, Zealots, and Josephus*, New York, 1957, pp. 28f. has observed the proliferation of Maccabean names by the time of Jesus and these are particularly in evidence in the Gospels themselves among the ʿ*am* (probably equivalent to the ʿ*am ha-arez* in the *Talmud* and the ʿ*am* that James protects through his Righteousness); cf. Eusebius, *E.H.* 2.23.8).

[8] *Op. cit.*, p. 143. Note how this attitude is reflected in a preceding statement: "One has the impression that there is a perpetual increase in Essene influence on the early Church. In the generation of *our Lord and of his first disciples* there are *hardly any similarities*. In the earliest phase of the Church in Palestine, as we find it in Acts, institutional parallels become more frequent. Slightly later we find in one part of the Church Essene influence almost taking over and submerging the *authentically Christian* doctrinal element; indeed, it may be considered responsible for the break between the Judeo-Christians and the *Great Church*" (italics mine), pp. 142f. "Essene", as Milik uses the term here, is synonymous with "Jewish Christian".

and the priesthood growing out of his.[9] But on closer examination, why this should be is itself puzzling. The events surrounding the appearance of Judas form the background of every sectarian movement in the Second Temple period including that coalescing about Jesus and to a lesser extent John the Baptist. Both Judas and Jesus are referred to or treated in the extant texts as *Zaddik*s (as was Jesus' brother James, his successor and heir in the priesthood he represented);[10] both are priests "after the Most High God", as the Maccabees styled themselves, and if R. H. Charles is right, of "the order of Melchizedek";[11] both seem to be ascetics of some kind possibly abjuring marriage;[12] both are probably "zealous for the Law" (witnesses to the contrary in the New Testament notwithstanding);[13] both come from large families of five brothers and are succeeded by their brothers;[14] both seem to be acknowledged as

[9] Unlike Cross and most other observers I take Josephus literally when he tells us Judas Maccabee was *elected* to the High Priesthood, i.e., "The people bestowed the High Priesthood on Judas"; *Ant.* 12.10.6. He repeats his reference to "the High Priesthood" of Judas in two other places. Indeed, even in 1 Macc, Judas presides over the cleansing of the Temple in Ezra-like fashion. However, most observers cleave to the incomplete testimony of the *Jewish War* where Judas' Priesthood is concerned and often underrate native procedures such as election. I take all couplings of putative *Zaddikim* with their natural constituency, "the people", as significant and worth cataloguing.

[10] Judas' role as one of "the Ten *Zaddikim*" is evoked by 2 Macc 5:27. Jesus is specifically referred to as "*Zaddik*" in Acts 3:14, 7:52, and 22:15; Pilate and his wife both refer to him as such in Mt 27:19ff. without the theological implications of Luke. His father Joseph is so designated in Mt 1:19. In Herod's description of John in Mk 6:20 the term "Pious", that is, "*Hassid*", accompanies the usage; cf. *Ant.* 18.5.2. In transliterating *Hassid*/Hassidaean, I prefer the double "s" to conserve the parallel with *Zaddik*.

[11] Of the numerous references to this in Charles' works, see for instance *APOT*, ii, pp. 9, 32, 61, 309, and 418 with reference to Jub 13:25, 32:1, As. Mos. 6:1–2, Test. L. 8:14–15. He rightly points out the crucial position of John Hyrcanus in this and the reference to such in *Ant.* 16.6.2. Fitzmyer discusses the matter in " 'Now this Melchizedek . . .' (Heb 7:1)", *Essays on the Semitic Background of the New Testament*, Montana, 1974, p. 235, unfortunately without citing his source, Charles.

[12] Though Judas is referred to in 2 Macc 14:25 as having "married and settled down", there is never any mention of children, which would have been important genealogically speaking, and the reference has more the character of a narrative device. In any event, Judas soon resumes his warrior ways.

[13] The claim is specifically raised on behalf of Jesus in John 2:17 in reference to the Temple-cleansing incident; Judas' similar zeal is not in question.

[14] See Mt 13:55, Mk 6:3, Ga 1:19, 1 Co 9:5 etc. The problem of Jesus' brothers bedevils Apostle lists and resurrection appearances. We take the Emmaus road appearance in Lk 24:13–35 involving "Cleopas" as being the lost one regarding Jesus' family members and the analogue of Paul's "Damascus Road" experience. The reference to "Simon", preceded by allusion to "True Prophet" ideology and "Nazoraean" terminology, we take to refer to Simeon bar Cleophas. Cf. Origen in *Contra Celsum* 2.62 and Jerome's report

"messiahs" by their enthusiastic followers;[15] and both purify the Temple in some way.[16]

While the Maccabean movement emerged in response to the destruction and corruption of the previous priesthood represented by Simeon the Just and his son, Onias, and the forcible imposition of Hellenistic civilization; the events and sentiments culminating in the Messiahship of Jesus came to fruition as a response to the destruction of the Maccabean priesthood by the "Herodians" and their Roman overlords. So closely do the movements crystallizing about the two resemble each other that the only observably incontrovertible difference between them is that the Christianity born of Jesus' death developed a non-Jewish overseas wing because of the general oppression in the Roman Empire at the time. In addition, it is arguable that this latter gradually supplanted the native and indigenous one in perspective and via retrospective historical insight obscured it, so that its actual nature has become lost to us. The Scrolls have restored the balance in viewpoints by helping to rescue these native sectarian movements from the oblivion into which they were cast by both *Roman* Christianity and *Rabbinic* Judaism either intentionally or via benign neglect.

II
THE ZADOKITE PRIESTHOOD

The Scrolls have delineated what a Zadokite priesthood has to have been from the second century BC onwards. Though there might be a genealogical component to this conception, its main thrust is qualitative, namely,

---

in *Vir. ill.* 2 of a first appearance to James including the common theme of *breaking bread*. Unlike von Harnack, we consider the interpolation in Paul's 1 Co 15:5ff. resurrection-appearance sequence to comprise the orthodox "Cephas and the Twelve"—patently impossible—not "James then all the Apostles". Note tradition often confuses Simon Cephas with Simeon bar Cleophas, identified as "a Rechabite priest" in *E.H.* 2.23.17 (cf. *Haeres.* 78.14)—"cousin" and "uncle" often being euphemisms for brother and father. For a fuller treatment, see below, pp. 62 and 78.

[15] Judas' Messiahship is reflected in the Messianic sword episode of 2 Macc 15:12–16 where Onias and Jeremiah (a kind of "Ancient of Days") play the role of priestly forerunners.

[16] Jesus' Temple-cleansing activities are well known, as are Judas', though they are rarely linked. In the wake of the latter *Hanukkah* is ratified by a vote of "the people"; 2 Macc 10:5ff. much as Judas' Priesthood was; cf. Ezra's similar activities below, p. 36.

"those who keep the Covenant" or "follow the Law".[17] Primarily, the Zadokite priesthood must relate, as the Damascus Document explicitly denotes, to the Book of Ezekiel where it was first introduced.[18] In Ezekiel "the Priests", who are "the *Bnei-Zadok* Levites, . . . *kept charge of My sanctuary*", i.e., "kept the Covenant", while "the sons of Israel *went astray from Me*" (translation and italics mine).[19]

[17] Cf. "Keepers of the Covenant" for "Sons of Zadok" in 1QS, v, 2–9. In CD, ii–iv's exegesis of Ezek 44:15 the definition turns more eschatological, that is, it is linked to the role of the *Zaddikim* ("First" and "Last"—*Rishonim* and *Aharonim*) in "the Last Days" and probably the Resurrection. Here, too, the stress is on "doing the exact sense of the Law" (4.8 and 6.15). "Doing" and its variations, *ma'asim* and *ma'aseihem*, are constant themes at Qumran linking up with the stress on "works" and "keeping the whole Law" in Ja 2:7ff. In the Letter of James, "keeping the Law" is repeatedly stressed as opposed to its ideological opposite "breaking the Law".

"Doing" or "Doers of the *Torah*" is, also, important in 1QpHab, viii, 1–3, and xii, 4–5 regarding "the Delay of the *Parousia*", the exegesis of "the Righteous shall live by his Faith" (also eschatological), and "the Last Judgement". This is also true in 4QTest, including both "True Prophet" and "Star" proof-texts ("the Star" is the *Doresh ha-Torah* in CD, vii, 18). The reference there to Deut 33:8ff.'s "teaching the Law" and "keeping (*yinzor*) your Covenant" is the clue to "Nazoraean" terminology; cf. *Nozrei-Brito* (paralleling *Shomrei-Brit*) in Ps 25 and Ps 119 addressing "the Perfect of the Way walking in *Torah*" and saturated with Qumran imagery. Cf. too the use of Ezek 44:7's "Covenant-Breakers" in 1QpHab, ii, 6 for "the Liar" and his confederates "the Traitors" (*Bogdim*) and "Violent Ones" ('*Arizim*).

[18] See Ezek 40:46, 43:19, 44:15, and 48:11. The best discussion of "the Zadokite Statement" is by J. Bowman, "Ezekiel and the Zadokite Priesthood", *Transactions of the Glasgow University Oriental Society*, xvi, 1957, pp. 1–14. Albright, too, understands the problem noting that the Greek Septuagint conserves a reading of "Sons of Saddok", not Zadok; and he understands that "Sons of Zadok" can just as easily be understood as "sons of the Righteous One"; cf. the reading "Sons of the Zadok" in 1QS, ix, 14 and W. F. Albright and C. S. Mann, "Qumran and the Essenes: Geography, Chronology, and Identification of the Sect", *BASOR*, Suppl. Studies, 10–12, 1951, pp. 17ff. Le Moyne in *Les Sadducéans*, Paris, 1972 shows little insight into these problems. His preconceptions resemble Milik's; cf. his comments about the "righteousness" of the Sadducees, p. 160.

[19] In Ezekiel's wording "priests" and "*Bnei-Zadok* levites" are appositives. "*Bnei-Zadok*" is used adjectivally to describe which "levites" will serve as "priests", not vice versa. Any genealogical sense this might have had is broken open in CD, iii, 21ff. by the deliberate addition of *waw*-constructs. There, "Sons of Zadok" are defined as "the *Elect of Israel* called by *name* (note the predetermination) who will *stand* in the *Last Days*" (italics mine—the usage is from Ezek 37:10 and also carries with it the implication of "be resurrected". Note too the Ebionite "Standing One" ideology here). The usage "wandered astray" is common at Qumran and is usually used in contradistinction to "the Sons of Righteousness" who "do the *Torah*", often in connection with allusion to the treacherous activities of "the Man of Lying", who "pours out the waters of Lying" and teaches "straying from the Law" and "stubbornness of heart"; cf. CD, i, 15; ii, 13, 16f.; iii, 1, 4, 14; iv, 1; 1QS, iii, 21f.; iv, 11f.; 1QpHab, x, 9; 1QH, i, 23f.; ii, 14; iii, 21f. etc. The use of "Sons of

That there may be a genealogical connotation to this description is self-evident. However, it is also clear from studying Ezekiel's account (whether authentic or pseudepigraphic is beside the point) that there are other priestly Levites, members of families as respectable as Shaphan's (who was involved in "the reform of Josiah"). These, comprising the former reigning priestly aristocracy, doubtless could have made equally legitimate "Zadokite" claims—though it is not clear such claims counted for anything before the Restoration—and are now being disqualified on the basis of their idolatry, etc. from service in the Temple.[20]

The Dead Sea Scrolls further emphasize the ethical aspect of Ezekiel's usage. As they employ this terminology, it definitely has a component in "Righteousness", which is of course the root of the personal noun, "Zadok", or in observation of "the Law" (what in other language might be characterized as "*zeal* for the Law"—phraseology current at Qumran).[21] It cannot be stressed too strongly that this moral component

Zedek" twice in 1QS, iii, 20ff. in this context is deliberate; cf. also 4QpPs 37, iv, 15.

The context here, important for all subsequent Second Temple problems from the "Zealot" opposition to the Herodian family to the Pauline Gentile Mission's problems with the Jerusalem Community, is keeping "the uncircumcised in heart and uncircumcized in flesh" out of the Temple (Ezek 44:7–10). It belies Josephus' contention that the 66 CE rejection "by those in charge of Temple service" of gifts and sacrifices from *any* foreigner (including the Emperor and presumably *Herodians*) was an "innovation". The "heart" and "flesh" imagery forms the backbone of the allusion to "Holy Spirit" baptism from 1QS, ii, 1–iv, 26 and is the basis of Josephus' description of John's baptism. The "idolatry", "fornication", and "Riches" charges (all themes associated in extant data with James) comprise "the Three Nets of Belial" accusation against the priestly hierarchy in CD, iv, 18ff. For the confrontation between "Simon" and Agrippa I—probably the original behind Acts 10:1–11:18—and the related "Temple wall" incident directed against his son Agrippa II (which leads inexorably to James' death), see below pp. 30 and 53 and *Ant.* 19.7.4 and 20.9.11. In *War* 2.17.1 Agrippa II *is* ultimately barred from the Temple and all Jerusalem by "the Innovators".

[20] See Ezek 44:10: "those levites who abandoned me when Israel strayed from me . . . They are to become servants in my sanctuary . . . "; these are contrasted to those levites who are "*Bnei-Zadok*" in 44:15. It becomes clear that "Sons of Zadok" is being used as an antonym of "going astray" and "broke my Covenant". Cf. 4QFlor, i, 17, where "the Sons of Zadok and the men of their community" are identified with those who "shall not defile themselves with idols" (the reading here is disputed, but the context is clear). For Ezek 8:11 those levites who abandoned their duties "to follow idols" include the former priestly establishment including the family of Shaphan. Cross does not treat these matters in "Reconstruction of Judean Restoration", *JBL*, v, 1975, pp. 4–18.

[21] See, for instance, the introduction of the Damascus Document addressed to "all Knowers of Righteousness" amid the language of "the heart", "the Way", "works" (*ma'asei/ma'aseihem*), and "Walkers in Perfection". 1QS, ii, 15 and iv, 4 refer to "zeal for his Judgements" and its variant "zeal for the Judgements of Righteousness" as opposed to "stubbornness of heart", "zeal for fornication", "slackness in the service of Righteous-

is the absolute determinant of a proper "Zadokite" priest at least as far as the Damascus Document is concerned, and probably Ezekiel as well.

The play on words implicit in this esoteric analysis of the term constitutes a favorite device at Qumran. The artful craftsmanship practiced there is missed by many Qumran scholars who do not adequately come to grips with literary devices in such an environment. This play on words is reinforced in the conjunction of the *Moreh ha-Zedek* with the "Son of Zadok", or more precisely the "Zadok" *par excellence*. It is extended even further in the *pesharim*, where the identification is always consciously and explicitly drawn between "the *Zaddik*" in the text and "the *Moreh ha-Zedek*" in the exegesis.[22]

What would Jesus' relationship be to the kind of ideology we are developing here? According to perhaps the oldest and probably most "Jewish" stratum of New Testament Christology, Jesus was the suffering "Just One"; i.e., "the suffering *Zaddik*" and is specifically so designated in Acts. The origin of this phraseology is "the suffering servant" simile of Is 53. Here, it should be noted, not only is "the servant" identified with "the *Zaddik*", but his "justifying" action is to be accomplished by his "Knowledge" (probably through teaching; cf. that *Da'at* widespread at Qumran) and his *'amal-nephesh*, that is, works with soteriological force. This *yazdik-Zaddik* theology of Is 53 is not only recognizable in the

ness", and "a tongue full of insults" (cf. "the Tongue" imagery in Ja 3:5ff. itself generically parallel to "Lying"/"Spouting"/"Scoffing" imagery at Qumran). See also 1QH, ii, 15 "a spirit of zeal" against "the Seekers after Smooth Things". In 1QS, ix, 23 the usage "zealous for the Law" actually occurs relating to two citations of the famous Is 40:3 "making a Way in the wilderness" and reference to the three central "priests" as a spiritualized "Holy of Holies" who *atone for the land* by "suffering the sorrows of affliction" and practicing Righteousness and "Perfection of the Way". They are "the offering", their Righteousness "the fragrance", and through them "the Holy Spirit is established on Truth" (viii, 1–ix, 25); cf. also the "Cornerstone", "Wall", "Rock", and "Fortress" symbolism in this passage and in 1QH, vi, 25f., vii, 7f., etc.

[22] I have treated this correspondence in two SBL papers, "James as Righteous Teacher" (1977) and "The *Zaddik*-Idea and the Zadokite Priesthood" (1979), but its verification is readily made by even a cursory inspection of Habakkuk and Ps 37 *Peshers*. 1QpHab, i, 12 actually draws it in the exegesis. The context of "the Wicked devouring" or "seeking to slay the Righteous" (4QpPs 37, iv, 7) also closely parallels Is 3:10, another *Zaddik*-passage expressly applied to the death of James (about whom "the Prophets declared") in *E.H.* 2.23.15. Cf. also CD, i, 20 specifically referring to "the *Zaddik*" and alluding to the *nephesh-Zaddik* vocabulary of the Is 53:11f. *Zaddik*-passage. If one catalogues all references to *zaddik* in Prophets and Psalms—the usual exegetical texts employed at Qumran—further collating them with words like Lebanon, *Ebionim*, *'Anayyim* ("the Meek"—also *Dallim*), *Bogdim* (Traitors), etc., one achieves an approximation of the method used for choosing exegetical texts at Qumran; cf. Is 2–5, 10f., 14, 25, 29–33 (Zech 10–11), Hab 2–3, Nah 1, etc.

Pauline corpus, it is also present in the Damascus Document and the Qumran Hymns.[23] By extension, it is also present working off the word *'amal*—in recognizably parallel fashion in the Habakkuk *Pesher* and the Letter of James; however, Paul parts company with these on whether this "Justification" is to be achieved by "Faith" or through works of Righteousness and "the Law".[24]

According to the esoteric interpretation of "the Zadokite Priesthood", as we have expounded it, since Jesus was "*Zaddik*", to his heirs belong the High Priesthood. The word-play we have already signalled is further extended in the Letter of the Hebrews with the allusion to "the priesthood after the order of Melchizedek". The reference here is not only to the concept of "Righteousness" as being the primary basis of legitimacy in the succession, but also to the personality of the Righteous priest/king Jesus, in whose name the new order is established.[25]

---

[23] See CD, iv, 6f. in the Ezek 44:15 exegesis. Here "the Sons of Zadok", now identified with "the *Kodesh Shonim*", i.e., "the *Rishonim*" or "the *Anshei-Kodesh Tamim*"—usage widespread in CD and 1QS—"through whom God grants atonement", "justify the Righteous", i.e. *yazdiku Zaddik*. Cf. the purposeful reversal "justify the Wicked" in CD, i, 19 in relation to "the Lying Scoffer" who abolishes "the Ways of Righteousness" and his attack on "the soul of the Righteous One" and the parallel reversal of *yizadek* ("to be justified") in 1QS, iii, 2f.; cf. also Ps *Rec* 1.70. For *yizadek* in Hymns see 1QH, vii, 28; ix, 14f.; xiii, 16f. etc. See also "you justified" used in relation to Righteous "works" in 1QH, i, 7 and "to justify" in 1QM, xi, 14 in relation to eschatological reference to "the Poor", "the Star Prophecy", and Messianic "rain" imagery. That Is 53:11f. was very early applied (presumably in the Jerusalem Church) to Jesus' death is confirmed by Paul in 1 Co 15:3ff. in his preface to resurrection-appearance sequences. It is never remarked that the whole structure of Qumran organization of *Moreh-Zedek/Zaddik* and *Rabbim* is based on Is 53, that is, "My servant the Righteous One will justify"/"bear the sins of the Many" (*Rabbim*). Cf. as well Ja 5:6 below, pp. 30 and 54.

[24] The preservation of something resembling the "Jerusalem Church" or "Jamesian" interpretation of Hab 2:4 in 1QpHab, viii, 1ff. is often missed. Not only does the exegesis parallel Paul's, but in contradistinction to the more antinomian Gentilizing approach of the latter, its effect is twice restricted to "all *'Osei ha-Torah* in the House of Judah", meaning only to *Jews*, and of these, only to those "who do the Law", with an accent on "doing". These "will be saved from the House of Judgement by their works (*'amalam*) and their Faith in the Righteous Teacher". Note the telltale reversal of the sense of the underlying text as per Pauline exegesis. Its eschatological nature is confirmed in xii.3ff. where it is now "the Simple of Judah doing *Torah*" who will be "saved at the Last Judgement", "Lebanon" is referred to, and the usage "*Ebionim*" is deliberately introduced into the *Pesher* (though *'Ani* does not appear till Hab 3:15). Cf. how in x, 9ff. "the *Mattif ha-Chazav* . . . leads Many astray . . . with works of Lying so that their *'amal* will count for nothing".

[25] Heb 3:1ff., 4:14ff., and 7:1ff. Note Heb 7:26 already knows the doctrine that only "an absolutely pure and Holy High Priest beyond the influence of Sinners" (in the peculiar code of this period "Herodians" and "foreigners") , that is, a Priest-*Zaddik*, can pro-

Here it should not be forgotten that the title "the *Zaddik*" was also accorded to Jesus' brother James, who was on this basis in addition to being Jesus' genealogical successor, his spiritual heir. Early Church literature, whether through over-enthusiasm or otherwise, depicted James as having worn the breastplate of the High Priest and actually entering the Holy of Holies.[26] Whether this priesthood of Jesus and James was also "the Zadokite" one is debatable. In terms of the analysis we have presented of Righteousness or "the Righteous One" being the basis for the esoteric understanding of Ezekiel's prognoses, it was.

Through this analysis, also, sense can be made of the testimony, referred to above, of James actually functioning as High Priest. Whether the Maccabean priesthood "of the Most High God" is, also, to be identified with the Melchizedek one of Christianity and the Letter to the Hebrews remains open to question. Whether this latter usage of the term can be extended to the Qumran (or Zadokite) use of the term as well has been debated. The writer would take a position in the affirmative, considering all such juxtapositions of the letters *Z-D-K* to be interrelated. In this regard, it should be remembered that the formula "men of the lot of Melchizedek" of 11QMelchizedek corresponds almost precisely to the terminology "Sons of Zadok" in the Damascus Document; and therefore, by simple reduction, "Zadok" and "Melchizedek" are equivalent usages.[27]

---

vide an efficacious atonement for sin. Cf. too its evident Qumranisms: the doctrine of "Righteousness" (5:14), the doctrine of "Perfection" (2:10 and 7:28), adoptionist sonship (5:5f), and in connection with "bearing the sins of the Many", "*the End* of the Last Age" (9:27f.) actually echoing CD, iv, 10f., "the completion of *the end* of those years", and "*ha-keẓ ha-aharon*" of 1QS, iv, 16f. and 1QpHab, vii, 12 (italics mine).

[26] *E.H.* 2.23.6 and Epiphanius, *Haeres.* 29.3. and 78.13. Jerome, *Vir. ill.* 2, supports Epiphanius' claim that James went into the Holy of Holies, which suggests his atoning activities in his role as Righteous "Priest" and appears to relate to at least one *Yom Kippur* atonement he made. These testimonies are contemptuously dismissed by most scholars. T. Zahn's reference to James as "the pope of Ebionite phantasy" (quoted in H.-J. Schoeps, *Paul: The Theology of the Apostle in the Light of Jewish Religious History*, Philadelphia, 1961, p. 67) is representative. Since it has become possible within the framework of the opposition "Priest"/*Zaddik*/*Moreh-Zedek* at Qumran to make sense out of such testimonies, I submit they should be treated more seriously. Note *Talmudic* tradition preserves material that the sons of Rechab married the daughters of the high priests (*Siphre Num* 78 on 10:29 reverses this) and their sons did service in the Temple; *Yalqut Shim'oni* on Jer 35:12—"Sons of Rechab" being in our view a euphemism for "Essenes"/"Zadokites", evoking—like "life-long Nazirite" allusions—the similarity in life-styles.

[27] 11QMelchizedek has been translated and commented upon variously by A. S. van der Woude, "Melchisedek als Himmlische Erlösergestalt in den Neugefundenen Escatologischen Midraschim aus Qumran Höhole XI", *Oudtestamentische Studien*, iv, 1965,

Finally, if there is substance to any of these extensions and identifications, "the Priesthood after the order of Melchizedek" must be related to what we have called "the Zealot", based on "the zeal of Phineas" and invoked on behalf of Simeon the Righteous, Mattathias, and Onias in the Hebrew version of Ecclesiasticus, 1 Macc, and 2 Macc respectively.[28] Correspondingly, J. Bowman has argued in a much overlooked article on this subject that the Zadokite one bases its claims for legitimacy on this selfsame "Covenant of Phineas".[29]

By now it should be clear that these are not all separate reckonings, but rather esoteric or poetic variations around the same theme, "Righteousness" and/or "zeal"—just as the various appellations the community at Qumran used to refer to itself, e.g.,"Sons of Light", "Sons of Truth", "Sons of Zadok", "Sons of *Zedek*", "the Sons of *Hesed*", "*Ebionim*", "the Elect of Righteousness", "the Meek", "*Ebionei-Hesed*" (the Poor Ones of Piety), "*Nimharei-Zedek*" (the Zealous for

pp. 354–73; J. T. Milik, "Milkīṣedq et Milkī-reša' dans les anciens écrits juifs et chrétiens", *JJS*, 23, 1972, pp. 95–144; J. Carmignac, "Le document de Qumran sur Melkisédeq", *Qumran*, vii, pp. 343–78; M. de Jonge and A. S. van der Woude, "11Q Melchizedek and the New Testament", *NTS*, xii, pp. 301–26; J. A. Fitzmyer, "Further Light on Melchizedek from Qumran Cave 11", *JBL*, 86, pp. 25–41, etc.; but it is incontrovertible that "Men of the Lot of Melchizedek" of line 8 is used synonymously with "the Sons of Light" in line 7 and with the general way "Sons of Zadok" is used throughout the Qumran corpus; cf. 1QS, iii, 18ff. equating "Sons of *Zedek*" with "Sons of Light". Once the basic parallelism of all these usages, i.e., "Sons of Zadok", "Truth", "Light", "Heaven", etc., is comprehended, and with it, adoptionist *sonship*-notions centering around the "Perfection" ideal, the question whether or not the Melchizedek Priesthood is found at Qumran becomes academic.

[28] See Sira 50:24, 1 Macc 2:26f., and 2 Macc 3:1 and 4:2. Note Onias III plays the same literary role in 2 Macc as Mattathias does in 1 Macc.

[29] *Op. cit.*, pp. 4f.; J. Trinquet, "Les liens 'Sadocites' de l'écrit de Damas des Manuscrits de la Mer Morte et de l'Ecclésiastique", *V.T.*, i, 1951, pp. 290ff., is also aware of the same point, but is able to develop it less. For confusion of "Zadokites" and "Sadducees", see Justin Martyr, *Dialogue with Trypho* 80, where "Sadducees" are listed with other Jewish heretical groups; Filaster in *Diversarum Haereseon Liber* 5; and Jerome in Migne, *Patrolog. Lat.*, xxvi, pp. 163ff. For problematic *Talmudic* references (which abound), see *b. Erub* 68b–69a, *Sanh* 38a and 100b, *Hullin* 87a, *Niddah* 33b–34a, *M. Yadaim*, iv, 6–8, etc. In the Pseudoclementine Rec 1.53–54 it is specifically asserted that the Sadducees are a group considering themselves "more Righteous" than the others who came into existence about the time of John the Baptist; cf. Josephus' characterization of them as "harsher in Judgement", *Ant.* 20.9.1, and his play on John Hyrcanus' desire "to be righteous", *Ant.* 13.11.5f. Cf. also Mt 11:12 and Lk 16:16 associating the beginning of "the Men of Violence" with John's coming and the material in *ARN* 5.2 associating sectarian strife with "Zadok and Boethus" (i.e., "Saddok" and Joezer b. Boethus). Strikingly, Josephus' discussion of Jewish sects in *War* and *Ant.* is also triggered by mention of Judas and/or "Saddok"; see below pp. 50 and 97.

Righteousness), "*Tamimei-Derech*" (the Perfect of the Way), "*Anshei-Tamim ha-Kodesh*" (the Men of the Perfection of Holiness), etc., do not all designate different groups but function as interchangeable metaphors.[30] In this view, the Covenant of Phineas operated over and above the general Aaronite one (Bowman considered the Covenant of Phineas to be the prior one), setting forth which among the various Aaronite heirs could be considered suitable candidates for the High Priesthood, that is, the "zealous" or "Righteous" ones.

It is significant that one of the original demands at the time of the first uprising in 4 BC, inspired according to Josephus by "the Zealots", was to appoint "according to the law" a High Priest of "more perfect purity".[31] For their part it was the "messianically"-inspired zealous young priests who by stopping sacrifice on behalf of the Romans gave the signal for the start of the uprising in 66 CE.[32] Commentators who cannot make a determination as to whether the Dead Sea Scroll sect was anti-Herodian or pro-Herodian, pro-Hyrcanus or pro-Aristobulus, and consequently are unable, for instance, to make any sense out of the destruction of the community in the 40s or 30s BC by fire, are equally unable to understand any of the considerations delineated above, or rather simply do not wish to, preferring to take a position on the relatively safer and less controversial questions of paleography and archaeology.[33]

---

[30] See 1QH, ii, 10, 12, 33f.; iii, 22; v, 8, 31–32; vi, 20, 29; ix, 35f.; 1QS, iv, 28; v, 13; viii, 17ff.; ix, 8; CD, viii, 24ff. etc. Unfortunately for the premises of most modern scholarship terms like "*Ebionim*", "*Nozrim*", "*Hassidim*", "*Zaddikim*" (that is, Ebionites, Palestinian Christians, Essenes, and Zadokites), turn out to be variations on the same theme. The inability to relate to changeable metaphor, particularly where subversive or estericizing groups are concerned, has been a distinct failure in criticism ancient as well as modern.

[31] *Ant.* 17.9.1. One should follow the variations of this "Perfection" terminology, i.e., *Tom*, *Tamim/Tamimim*, *hatem*, etc., at Qumran and in the New Testament. At Qumran it is often used in connection with the "Way" terminology. Since it is based on the description of the first *Zaddik*, Noah, as "*Tamim*" in Ge 6:9, it should perhaps be called "Noachic".

[32] *War* 2.17.2. That these priests who halted the sacrifice on behalf of or payed for by foreigners in the Temples were moved by the "Messianic" prophecy is made clear in *War* 6.6.4. The application of it to Vespasian by Josephus and Rabbi Yohanan ben Zacchai not only testifies to its currency in 68 CE, it is also in keeping with general "Pharisaic" policy. It further illustrates Josephus' description of the followers of "Judas and Saddok" in *Ant.* 18.1.6 as being "in all matters like the Pharisees except they have an inviolable attachment to liberty and . . . could not bear to call any man Lord".

[33] See below, pp. 43ff. and 80–97ff.

III
ECCLESIASTICUS AND PRIESTLY LEGITIMACY

The all-important Hebrew text of Ecclesiasticus ("Ben Sira" as it is often denoted), found at three locations over the last century: the Cairo *Genizah*, Qumran, and Masada (each of which is important in itself), is crucial to the matter of Zadokite/Sadducean priestly claims and one of the keys to unraveling the Second Temple sectarian puzzle. The "Sadducean" or scribal character of the text has generally been recognized. What was not so plain was its sectarian character, nor how the key material in chapters 50–51, missing from the Septuagint/Vulgate version, was used to legitimize priestly claims by all the sects heir to the legacy, spiritual or otherwise, of the saintly Simeon the *Zaddik*.

These include, as we shall see, the Maccabees, Zealots, Zadokites, and probably even the Christians, namely, all the groups outside of the Pharisaic/Herodian establishment of 40 BC onwards. The Pharisees also used Simeon, but not to establish priestly legitimacy; rather as a link in the transmission of right-guided tradition.[34]

I have left both Essenes and Sadducees off the list. It is, strictly speaking, imprecise to refer to the "Zadokites" at Qumran as "Essenes", which the majority of scholars in the field tend to do for polemical reasons of their own. The sectaries at Qumran might be "Essenes", but the case is by no means proven. Nor is it clear how "the Essenes" saw the problem of priestly succession, nor how they would then differ from Hassidaeans, Zealots, partisans of Judas Maccabee, or even his enemies. One is on safer ground to use the sectaries' own terminology, whether "Sons of Zadok", "*Ebionim*", "*Zaddikim*", "*Hassidim*", or some other, all terms found generously sprinkled throughout their literature and meaningful in the light of sectarian history in Palestine.

For their part, the so-called "Sadducees" are dominated by the Pharisees in their post-Herodian embodiment, as Josephus tells us in no uncertain terms.[35] They are in no way "Zadokite" if Qumran is typical

---

[34] The association in both *Pirke Abot* 1.2 and *ARN* 4.1 (the section delineating R. Yohanan's relations with the Romans and applying "Lebanon" imagery to the 70 CE Temple fall) of "Torah", "Temple-service"—the basis of Ezekiel's Zadokite Statement— and "*Hesed*" or "the practice of the *Hassidim*" with the person of Simeon the *Zaddik* needs no further elucidation. Note that this section of *ARN* (4.4) associates *rain-making* with proper *Temple-service*; drought with its cessation.

[35] *Ant.* 18.1.4. It is noteworthy that what Josephus describes as "Sadducees" and "Pharisees" in *War* 2.8.14 sound very close to what Rabbinic literature is referring to as *Beit-*

of what we mean by Zadokite. We have already noted that their legal and spiritual legitimacy was called into question by those Josephus calls "desirous of innovation" as early as 4 BC (*War* 2.1.2); quite properly, as it were, since these new-model "Sadducees" are thoroughly compromised by their Roman/Herodian connections.

Let us attempt a reconstruction following priestly lines of legitimacy, but without adhering to the interpretation of "Zadokite" as implying only or even primarily genealogical descent.[36] It is generally accepted that Simeon the *Zaddik* (whether the earlier one of Josephus and imprecise Rabbinic speculation or the later one of Ecclesiasticus) is a true son of Zadok, meaning a lineal descendant of the Davidic/Solomonic High Priest, but there is nowhere any proof of this.[37] This is one of the implicit assumptions of Qumran scholarship, and should it be found wanting, most of the edifice so artfully constructed upon it becomes extremely fragile.

There is no proof that Ezra is "a Zadokite" Priest, or Ezekiel who first employs the term in a significant way, or even Elijah for that matter. It is true that someone wants us to think that Ezra is a Zadokite Priest, and he is supplied with a good "Zadokite" genealogy, but on closer

Shammai and *Beit*-Hillel. In this period one has to be careful with one's terminologies which tend to become unglued. Terms like "Zealots", "Essenes", even "Pharisees", which we take to be "parties", Josephus and his sources often use generically. Josephus himself confuses Essenes and Pharisees saying the same things about Pollio and Sameas as he does about "Essenes". "Menachem the Essene" repeats a prophecy earlier ascribed to Sameas, and Pollio and Sameas are even confused with each other; cf. *Ant.* 14.9.3f., 15.1.1, and 15.10.4f. Elsewhere, Josephus cuts a part from his description of "the Essenes" in *War* 2.8.10 and adds it to his description of "the Fourth Philosophy" of Judas and Saddok in *Ant.* 18.1.6. See below, pp. 47 and 69.

[36] See Albright, *loc cit.* The idea that "*Zaddik*" is as good a basis for the derivation of the term Sadducee as "Zadok" is also understood by P. Wernberg-Moeller, "*Zedek, Zaddik*, and Zadok in the Zadokite Fragments (CDC), the Manual of Discipline (DSD) and the Habakkuk Commentary (SSH)", *V.T.*, iii, 1953, pp. 309–315, and R. North, "The Qumran 'Sadducees'", *CBQ*, 17, 1955, pp. 164–188. Wernberg-Moeller incisively states in his conclusion, p. 315, "Probably *Zadok* is not meant as a name at all, requiring the reading *Zaddik*; and we may translate: 'it was (not) revealed until *a righteous one* arose' (of CD, iii)". Le Moyne, p. 160, is unable to understand North's presentation, no less rebut it. See also A. Michel, *Le Maître de Justice*, Avignon, 1954. That *waw* and *yod* are indistinguishable at least in 1QpHab was developed by Y. Ratzaby in *JQR*, 41, 1950, pp. 155ff. See also Ps *Rec* 1.54 and John Hyrcanus' "Righteousness" associated with Sadducees above, p. 21.

[37] The problem of the dating of Simeon the *Zaddik* has been discussed in detail by G. F. Moore in "Simeon the Righteous", *Jewish Studies in Memory of Israel Abrahams*, New York, 1927, pp. 348–64, including all the relevant references from the *Talmud*, Josephus, and Ben Sira.

inspection one finds he is given the exact same genealogy as Jesus ben Yehozedek 100 years earlier, the First High Priest after the return from captivity.[38] Even this genealogy has gaps in it and contradicts what is known about priestly succession in other parts of the Bible.[39] For Bowman, all such genealogies are artificial since very little survived the Babylonian destruction. biblical ploys (old or new) on matters of genealogy are, in any event, something to be handled with circumspection.

More importantly, what has never been remarked is that the claim being put forward on behalf of Ezra is not the normal "Zadokite" one at all, but rather what we have been calling "the Zealot" (as Bowman has argued, this is prior to and functions as the Zadokite). Indeed, Ezra is the "zealous" priest *par excellence*, showing incontrovertible *zeal for the Law* even to the extent of demanding the divorce of alien, including Samaritan, wives—a typical Phineas-style procedure.[40] No doubt Ezra would have preferred a harsher penalty than excommunication had the "Yehud" of his day not simply been autonomous and had he had the powers to impose the death penalty. In any case, his powers seem to

---

[38] Cf. Ezra 7:1f. with 1 Chron 5:34ff.

[39] For instance, Josephus tells us in his famous statement about the priesthood in *Ant.* 20.10.1 that there were eighteen in number "one in succession to the other from the days of King Solomon until Nebuchadnezzar . . . took Josadek the High Priest captive", but this contradicts the numbers on the list of *Ant.* 10.9.6—only fifteen names, which in turn contradicts the genealogy given Ezra and Yehozedek in 1 Chron 5:34ff.—only six names—or 1 Chron 5:5–14, which gives thirteen names. With so many repetitions, the last-named has the air of concoction about it; for instance, a second Azariah far down the list is said to have officiated in Solomon's Temple. Even a cursory examination of Josephus' list will reveal several significant omissions as well as conflicts with known facts he himself provides: for instance, the Amariah who served in Jehosephat's time and the Azariah of Hezekiah and Hilkiah's time. One garbled genealogy of 1 Chron 9:10 gives the ancestors of Yehozedek's grandfather, Azariah, but lists only three generations between him and the Zadok of Solomon's time. In addition, it groups him in a genealogical milieu that seems to reflect a pre-Davidic time—*pace* genealogical knowledge at the time of the composition of Chronicles. In Neh 11:10, one Jedaiah (the name Chronicles gives to the second priestly course and evidently meant to be a high priest) is listed as the son of Joiarib (the first priestly course) and given the genealogy of Ezra and Jesus ben Yehozedek. Cf. too Eusebius' statement following Julius Africanus in *E.H.* 1.7.12 about Herod's purported destruction of all priestly genealogical records.

[40] For this grisly episode, see Num 25:6–15: "Phineas the Priest . . . has turned *my wrath* away from the sons of Israel . . . In reward for his *zeal* for his God he shall have *the right to perform the ritual atonement* over the sons of Israel" (italics mine). It is precisely the problem of "Gentiles" in the Temple that forms the background to the Zadokite Statement in Ezek 44:7 as we have seen, and later surfaces in the Herodian period with the posting of "Zealot" warning markers. Cf. too *Ant.* 19.7.4 on "Simon"'s opposition to Agrippa I entering the Temple noted above, p. 17.

have reached right into the "Zadokite" High Priestly household itself. Not only does he occupy its Temple chambers, but he banishes one of its heirs, Sanballat's son-in-law, which seems to be the birth-moment of Samaritan "Zadokite" claims.[41]

If we are unable to prove the legitimate "Zadokite" descent of any priestly hero of the Bible after the Solomonic period, imagine the embarrassment of the priests of Judas' day, who certainly could not do so either. Of the twenty-four courses of the Temple, only sixteen could even be "Zadokite", and which ones these might be is impossible to determine. Though Chronicles attempts a retrospective portrait of these, the names it includes are identifiably Second Temple.[42] One of these is accused in Ezra's time of not even being of priestly descent.[43]

In any event, the Maccabees put forth in the safest manner possible their "Zadokite" claim in 1 Macc by signaling their membership in the first and largest priestly course, that of Jehoiarib. It is as good a claim as any, especially when reinforced by the portrait of Mattathias' Phineas-like behavior. Where did the assumption come from that the Maccabees could not be considered "Zadokite", or even that they were not "priestly", appertaining rather to some lower "levitical" order?[44] This is nothing but a confused distortion of historical data to suit desired theoretical aims. We do not even know to what course Simeon's family belonged (unless it be that of Jedaiah), and it is not at all outside the

---

[41] Ezra 10:6ff. and Neh 13:4ff. Strictly speaking, the banishment recorded in Nehemiah is claimed by Nehemiah, which raises questions as to who is actually behaving in this zealous way, Ezra or Nehemiah. Ezra 10:18f. only mentions the members of the high priestly family whose marriages Ezra dissolved. Curiously enough, one of these last is named "Jarib", which must be identical with the first priestly course in Chronicles, the one the Maccabees later claim affiliation with. For Ezra with his Phineas-like behavior as a priestly gloss (possibly Maccabean), see below, p. 36.

[42] The sixteen orders are given in 1 Chron 24:3ff. and dated to David's time. The genealogy of Azariah of 1 Chron 9:10 above presents three of the course names as brothers and dates them in Saul's time. The names figure prominently in the list of returnees in Ezra 8 (repeated in Neh 7–8). Many are repeated among the signatures of the agreement of Neh 10, in the population list of Neh 11, and the list of returnees of Neh 12. One course, "the sons of Delaiah", Ezra 2:34ff. considers not even to be able to prove "that their families and ancestry *were of Israelite origin*" (italics mine).

[43] Ezek 2:34ff.

[44] 1 Macc 2:1, 24–28, 50, 54, 58, etc. Note how in what can only be called Mattathias' *Zealot* farewell, Elijah is said to be consumed by "zeal for the Law". For good examples of this kind of assumption, see Milik, pp. 82–3, and Cross, pp. 129–41. Josephus in *Ant.* 20.10.1 never doubts the legitimacy of Maccabean family claims to the priesthood, contrasting them with the meaner ones of the Herodian priesthood, and as *Vita* 1 confirms, never considered his own Hasmonaean priestly ancestry an embarrassment.

realm of possibility that the Maccabees constituted a lesser branch of his family as the Tobiads had in a previous generation.[45]

To claim Zadokite descent in Jesus' time (not to mention Davidic) would be like being able to claim descent from Dante in our own. Ecclesiasticus, especially Chapter 51, was so important because it delineated an instrumentality for claiming priestly legitimacy in the days when all priestly genealogies had difficulty in going back to Ezra's time. First, Simeon is the High Priest, but he is so on "Zadokite" lines; i.e., he is a *Zaddik*, a pious man. *Hassid* and *Zaddik* are in some sense parallel usages probably going back to Isaiah and have continued as such in Scroll literature, Karaism, and Jewish mysticism up to the present day.

In this manner, the crucial list of "*Anshei-Hesed*" (the familiar "famous men" of Greek translation) in the Hebrew Ecclesiasticus begins and ends with the *Zaddikim*, Noah and Simeon.[46] I think we must grant that Simeon the Just (Mattathias too) is "Aaronite" according to the normal usage of that term. In Second Temple period times the priests (or "sons of Aaron") seem more of a caste, as they were in Zoroastrianism or as the Brahmins in India, than a specific genealogy. But is he a "Zadokite" to whom in Ezekiel's language "the charge of God's Sanctuary" must go until the end of time? He is, says Ecclesiasticus, on the basis of his perfect Piety (*Hesed*) and Righteousness (*Zedek*).

In this we have the stirrings of both the "Hassidaean" and "Zadokite" movements, which are related (cf. *War* 2.1.2 where the demand of "the innovators" is for greater priestly "Piety"—*Hesed*). The Hebrew version of Ecclesiasticus adds that as such he also accedes to "the Covenant of Phineas". This Covenant is a bridge over any supposed genealogical

---

[45] For the relation of the Tobiads to the high priestly family, see *Ant.* 12.4.2. The garbled high priestly genealogy of Neh 11:10 also points to a relationship between the first and second courses, Jehoiarib and Jedaiah, one or the other of which presumably being the reigning high priestly line.

[46] Is 57:1 is perhaps the best example of this coupling of "*ha-Zaddik*" with the "*Anshei-Hesed*", the exact language of Ecclesiasticus. For "Noah the Righteous", see Hebrew Ben Sira 44:17 (actually found intact at Masada and in the *Genizah*). For "Enoch the Righteous" see Enoch 1:1–2, beginning with the revealing words "he [Enoch the Righteous] blessed the Elect and the Righteous who will be living in the Day of Tribulation when all the wicked and godless are to be removed". In 12:4 Enoch is "the scribe of Righteousness", and both titles are coupled again in 15:1. Cf. Test. L. 10:5 and Wis 10:4 in the context of Genesis history told in "*Zaddik*" symbolism. The coupling of *Hesed* and *Zedek* also forms the backbone of Josephus' description of John the Baptist's baptism, *Ant.* 18.5.2. Justin Martyr in *Dial.* 23, 47, and 93 uses them to describe early Christianity and they form the basis of Josephus' description of Essene doctrine in *War* 2.8.2ff. and *Ant.* 15.10.5 on Menachem above. See also how Josephus applies these two categories to the person of Simeon the *Zaddik* himself in *Ant.* 12.2.5.

deficiencies, in that being based on "zeal for the Law", it is qualitative, extending to all descendants of Aaron through Eleazar. It is also to a certain extent "Zadokite" in a genealogical sense, since theoretically it should not extend to the descendants of Ithamar. It is not clear, however, if it ever should be construed in this sense, though originally this might have been part of its thrust. It is also "Zadokite" in the esoteric sense explaining just how "a son of Zadok" or "a *Zaddik*" distinguished him-self, i.e., through "zeal for the Law".

Ecclesiasticus is patently a priestly book as the amount of space spent praising Aaron and Phineas, to say nothing of Simeon—more than for Jacob, Moses, David, and others put together—attests. That it should have been prized at Qumran among the Zadokites, at Masada among the *Sicarii*—the terminology is Josephus'—and in a probable Karaite synagogue in Old Cairo, is not surprising.[47] What is often overlooked

---

[47] Josephus relates how 600 surviving *Sicarii* fled to Egypt to escape Roman repression, as a consequence of which the Temple at Heliopolis was very likely suppressed. The terminology *"Sicarii"* is pejorative, since this group obviously did not refer to itself in this fashion. The first use of concealed weapons in this manner in Palestine was actually employed by a Roman Governor, Pontius Pilate: *War* 2.9.4; *Ant.* 18.3.1. Seen in this light, "the *Sicarii*" were simply adopting already existing Roman stratagems. Their hostage tactics (*War* 2.13.2; *Ant.* 20.8.5) resemble those of modern Islamic revolutionaries.

The connection with Shi'ism is not fanciful, "the *Sicarii*" being Apocalyptic Judaism's *Assassins*. The *Imam*-idea at the heart of Shi'ism closely parallels the pre-existent *Zaddik*-idea at Qumran; cf. 1QH, i, 20ff.; ix, 28ff. (in the context of adoptionist sonship); xv, 5 (echoing Nazirite-from-womb themes in Ga 1:15 and *E.H.* 2.23.4); and CD, ii, 7ff. Ps *Rec* 1.52 conserves a perfect facsimile of "the Hidden Imam" doctrine (cf. "hidden" themes below, p. 34): "Know then that Christ, who was *from the beginning and always*, was *ever present with the Pious, though secretly*, through all their generations" tying it to "the Righteousness doctrine" (italics mine; cf. also Paul in 1 Co 2:8 and Col 1:16. Note that he hints here at the "Hidden" ideology and in 1 Co 15:44f. at that of "the Primal Adam". For the *Zohar* on Noah the Righteous as the progenitor of the "Hidden" notation, see below p. 41–2; on the Primal Adam, p. 109).

R. de Vaux's criticism of the "Zealot" Hypothesis of Roth and Driver again displays the peculiar inability to come to grips with the true nature of such groups: "According to its literature the community of Qumran was pre-eminently a religious group and was opposed pre-eminently to the official Judaism. The Party of Zealots, on the other hand, was, according to all that Josephus tells us of it, first and foremost a nationalist party and was opposed, first and foremost, to the Romans"; R. de Vaux, *Archaeology and the Dead Sea Scrolls*, Oxford, 1973, p. 120. De Vaux misunderstands that Josephus describes events to the Roman public in terms that they can understand; cf. the language he uses in describing revolutionary events relating to the downfall of Caligula and the elevation of Claudius, *Ant.* 19.1.2. The rise of militant Islam, particularly Shi'ite Islam, in modern times should help place such movements in a more realistic light.

by those considering Josephus' data is the link of what he ultimately chooses to label as "the Zealot" Movement to the priestly class despite the fact of his own affiliations as a young priest with this Movement.[48] The *Talmud* in its own manner alludes to the priestly connections of the orientation.[49] Though Josephus describes it to his Roman readers in the primarily political terms they could understand (the same could be said for how they could understand "Christianity"—a deficiency the New Testament goes a long way towards making up); "the Zealot Movement" is first of all a Movement making certain claims about priestly legitimacy, and not the primarily revolutionary one Josephus and the New Testament have caused us to think of it as. Chief among these claims is the requirement of "zeal for the Law" as a prerequisite for service at the Temple altar.

In an age where the high priesthood was to a certain extent up for barter, that this should have political ramifications is not surprising. Jesus himself displays some of these attitudes in the Gospel portrayal of the Temple-cleansing affair where "Zealot" language is explicitly attributed to him.[50] Similar "zeal" for the Temple is attributed to his brother James in the portraits of his "Piety" (*Hesed*) and Righteousness (*Zedek*) in early Church literature. Not only does Ja 2:10 stress his "zeal for the Law", but all accounts dwell on how the flesh on his knees resembled "camel's hide" from all the importuning of God he did in the context of what

---

[48] S. G. F. Brandon, *Jesus and the Zealots*, New York, 1967, pp. 114–141, has dealt at length with this issue of priestly connections. Not only did Josephus as a young priest occupy an official position in Galilee under what should probably be termed the "Directorate" period of the Revolt, 66–68 CE, but his earlier trip to Rome (where he probably made the connections that he later used to betray the "Zealot" cause) is also interesting in this regard; cf. *Vita* 3. Technically, Josephus never actually calls "the Fourth Philosophy" or Judas' "Galilean" Movement "Zealot" until after the "election" of Phannias/Phineas in *War* 4.3.8f.; even here he applies it only to those, seemingly, who take vengeance for James and later only Eleazar's group *in the Temple* (5.1.1), but the usage has attained a wide currency.

[49] The famous passage in *M. Sanh*, ix, 6 implies at least some connection of the *Kanna'im* with priestly matters. B. Salomonsen in "Some Remarks on the Zealots with Special Regard to the term '*Qannaim*' in Rabbinic Literature", *NTS*, 12, 1966, pp. 164–76, has supplied a list of others; but his general orientation reflects the same general preconceptions as Milik, de Vaux, Le Moyne, *et al.*

[50] Noted above, p. 15. The whole problem of Jesus and the Zealots has been debated at length in well-known works by Brandon, Cullmann, Hengel, etc. The lack of issue relates very much to the inability to grasp that Zealotism as such was an orientation and not a religio-political movement with a distinct ideology as, for instance, Messianism was.

appears to have been a *Yom Kippur* atonement.[51] Similar "zeal" (as well as "Rock", "Fortress", "Shield", and "Protection" imagery) is also referred to in the Qumran Hymns usually attributed to the personal composition of the Righteous Teacher himself.[52]

Here, it is significant to remark that Ecclesiasticus has also been conserved by what perhaps should be called non-Palestinian Christianity, i.e., Roman, Greek Orthodox, Ethiopic, etc., albeit in a somewhat sanitized form, though not by Rabbinic Judaism true as always to its Pharisaic/Herodian roots. Many readers will be shocked at my linking of the latter two and yet the *Talmud* proudly proclaims the links of Pharisaic Judaism with the Herodian family,[53] as it does Rabbi Yohanan ben

---

[51] Epiphanius and Jerome, *loc. cit.*, mention entering the Holy of Holies, and in general all accounts agree that James' praying involved an "atonement" on behalf of "the people"; cf. sectarian difficulties over the issue of *Yom Kippur* in 1QpHab, xi, 4ff. between the Righteous Teacher and the Wicked Priest. Note James' nemesis Ananus was "called by the name of truth" (*War* 4.5.2; cf. the parallel *E.H.* 2.23.20 about James), twice "ruled over Israel", and "his corpse" was violated—in 1QpHab, ix, 2 the word *is* "corpse"! That James' surpassing "Righteousness", revealingly testified to by his sobriquet, and "Piety" would have entitled him in Zadokite circles to make such an atonement should be clear.

In connection with these priestly claims, *Haeres.* 78.14 evokes his *rain-making*, performed too by his *Zaddik*-precursor, Honi (whose death anticipates James'), which Rabbinic tradition also ascribes to Phineas/Elijah and Habakkuk, cf. *Ant.* 14.2.1f., *b. Ta'an* 22b–23b, and *ARN* 4.4. M. Sanh. 9:6 specifically notes: "If a priest served in a state of uncleanness . . . the young men among the Priests took him outside the Temple and split open his brain with clubs", which appears to have been absorbed into accounts of James' death in *E.H.* 2.23.17 and *Haeres.* 78.14, as opposed to *Ant.* 20.9.1. Whatever James' ritual purity, he was subjected to "Sanhedrin" trial by the Herodian Priestly Establishment. In his regard, one should take seriously the violent attitude towards "the Rich" in Ja 2:6 and 5:1–10, following which Elijah's rain-making miracle is evoked (5:17). Note that the first political act when "the Zealots" took over the Uprising in 68 CE in its "Jacobin" phase, apart from the wholesale slaughter of the high priests (including Ananus), was to destroy the debt records "to enable *the Poor* to rise against *the Rich*" (italics mine); *War* 2.17.8. Cf. in this context Ja 5:6 blaming "the Rich" for the death of "the Righteous One" (and Paul in 1 Thess 2:15 blaming *the Jews*).

[52] 1QH, i, 11; ii, 15; iii, 37; iv, 3; vi, 17ff.; vii, 8ff.; viii, 22ff., ix, 28f., etc.; cf. James as "*Oblias*", "Protection of the People", and "Bulwark" in *E.H.* 2.23.7, 3.7.8, and *Haeres.* 29.4 and note the Cleophas/Alphaeus/*Oblias*/Lebbaeus tangle.

[53] See particularly *M. Sota* 7:8 and the cry there, when Agrippa (whom "the sages praised") reads the Law on *Succot* and comes to the passage, "You may not put a foreigner over you which is not your brother"; cf. also *Bikk* 3:4 and *Siphre Deut* 157 on 17:15. The mirror image of this episode for Zadokite history must once again be that Simon with "a very accurate knowledge of the Law" who convenes "an assembly" (this is literally "Ecclēsia" or "Church") in Jerusalem in *Ant.* 19.7.4 and wants to exclude Agrippa from the Temple *as a foreigner* ("since it belongs only to native Jews"); see above, p. 17 and below, p. 79.

Zacchai's Romanizing self-humiliation before Vespasian by way of disassociating himself from the Zealot (and in this case "Messianic") Movement.[54] Josephus, another self-professed "Pharisee", not uncharacteristically flaunts his own similar behavior.[55] If the extant literature is any yardstick, Vespasian must have become very impatient at all these Jewish turncoats vying with each other to proclaim him Messiah.

The anti-nationalist, Romanizing policy of the Pharisees will be dealt with at length below. It can be traced back to the earliest stages of the Party in 2 Macc and the time of Alexander Jannaeus and his son Hyrcanus II. At this point it is sufficient to assert that if the patriarch Hillel was ever head of the Sanhedrin, as Pharisaic tradition proclaims, then the Sanhedrin in which he exercised such influence was the Herodian one.[56] Of all the parties so far mentioned, the Pharisees alone make no perceivable insistence on the high-priestly qualification of Righteousness, being satisfied to accept appointment from foreign or non-Jewish rulers. In this orientation is probably to be found the original basis for their split with the "Zadokites".[57]

---

[54] For this clear misuse and cruel mockery of the Messianic Prophecy in the episode usually taken as being the birth moment of Rabbinic Judaism, see *ARN* 4.5. Those who doubt that the fall of the Temple discussed in the Qumran Habakkuk and Isaiah *Peshers* applies to the one in Vespasian's time should note that the same passage, Is 10:33–4 applied to the 70 CE fall in *ARN* above, is also to be found subjected to exegesis. Since there is no evidence of exegesis of this kind relating to an earlier fall, the burden of proof in the face of such decisive evidence must rest on its detractors.

[55] *War* 3.8.8f. For his discussion of the "Messianic Prophecy" see 6.5.4.

[56] For the relationship of the Hassidaeans in 1 Macc to the Pharisees, see below, pp. 37ff. For Alexander's crucifixion of the 800 Pharisees, see *War* 1.4.6 and *Ant.* 13.14.2. That these are Pharisees is clear from the revenge they take against Alexander's associates when they come to power after his death, under his wife Alexandra, as it is from their support of the Priestly claims of her eldest son Hyrcanus II against the "Sadducee"/"Zealot" supporters of his younger brother Aristobulus. We have already noted Herod's affection for "Pollio the Pharisee". Equally illuminating is the famous *Prozbul* associated with Hillel, which is at the root of the problem of debt records above. For its relationship to James' attitude towards "the Rich", see below, p. 54.

[57] This "split" is vividly illustrated in 1 Macc 7:9–18, where the "Hassidaeans" are said to be "the first among the Israelites to ask them for peace terms". This is in line with their policy under Alexander and Hyrcanus. It accords vividly with the words of "Pollio the Pharisee and Sameas, *a disciple of his*" (italics mine), who, "when Jerusalem was besieged . . . advised the citizens to open their gates to Herod, for which advice they were well requited"; *Ant.* 15.1.1 (*Ant.* 14.9.3 attributes this advice to Sameas alone). The same policy is followed by Yohanan ben Zacchai, who before having himself smuggled out of Jerusalem in a coffin, had his friends shoot an arrow "over the wall saying that Rabban Yohanan ben Zacchai was one of the Emperor's friends". It also epitomizes the foreign policy of two other self-professed Pharisees, Josephus and Paul (cf. Ro 13:1ff.

IV

THE MACCABEES AS ZEALOTS AND ZADOKITES

The "Zealot" and "Zadokite" claims of the Maccabees are put forward in the "official" history of these claims, 1 Macc. Made in the name of the eponymous family head the Hasmonaean Mattathias, these are meant to be blanket claims covering not just Judas and his descendants,[58] but all of Mattathias' descendants, including most notably Jonathan, Simon, and the latter's progeny.

2 Macc puts forth the same "Zealot" claim for the person of the saintly Onias III, presumably the son of Simeon the Just.[59] In this account Judas is the "Messianic" savior/Priest and Onias plays the role of Mattathias. For it, there is no interruption between the family of Simeon the Righteous and Judas. Judas and the nine others who go out into the wilderness to live in caves and subsist on vegetarian fare are nothing but Noachic *Zaddikim*.[60]

---

for Paul's views). Our use of the term "Pharisees" here parallels what Qumran calls "Seekers after Smooth Things" and their fellow-travelers, "the Liar", "Traitors", and "Men of Violence"; cf. CD, i, 12ff.; 1QpHab, ii, 1ff.; 4QpNah, ii, 1ff., etc.

[58] Here one might wish to quote from Mattathias' testament to his sons (itself a paraphrase of Ben Sira's famous "Praise of the *Anshei-Hesed*"). 1 Macc 2:49–64: "This is the time my children . . . to have a *burning zeal for the Law* and to give your lives for the Covenant of your ancestors. Remember the deeds performed by our ancestors, each in his generation, and you shall win great honor and everlasting renown. Was not Abraham tested and found Faithful, was that not counted *as making him Righteous*? . . . Phineas, our father, in return for his *burning zeal* received a Covenant of everlasting Priesthood . . . Elijah for his *consuming zeal for the Law* was caught up to Heaven itself. . . . My children, play the man and be courageous for the Law, for it will bring you Glory." Note the reference to the zeal of Phineas/Elijah, combined with the favorite Pauline allusion, "Justification by Faith". The question of Judas' descendants we cover elsewhere. Unlike Ezra, who confines himself to excommunication, Mattathias' "zeal" is expressed in killing the backsliding Jew about to offer illegal sacrifice on the altar at Modein. His cry in 1 Macc 2:21–28 to his followers, "Let everyone who has *zeal for the Law* and takes his stand *on the Covenant* follow me" (italics mine) resembles nothing so much as the behavior of Levites in Ex 32:25–30, who slaughter their backsliding countrymen, and to whom Moses says, "You have won yourself investiture as Priests of Yahweh today."

[59] 2 Macc 4:2 calls him "this Zealot for the Laws" and "Protector of his fellow countrymen" after already applying the *Hesed*/"Perfection" imagery in 3:1f. Note the "Protection" (in Hebrew probably *Ma'oz*) imagery once again, prefiguring its later application to James. See below, p. 37.

[60] 2 Macc 5:27. The significance of this concept of "the Ten *Zaddikim*" for the events surrounding the birth of the Hassidaean Movement should not be underestimated. Judas' behavior, including his vegetarianism, is the prototype of John the Baptist's. The problem

Here, of course, is the archetypical episode for the founding of a community such as Qumran, but so thick is the obscurity surrounding Maccabean claims in Qumran research, it is never remarked. Judas is a *Zaddik* in the sense that Noah the Righteous was considered a *Zaddik* (so surnamed in various Second Temple books). In some sense the continued existence of mankind is predicated on his righteous behavior,[61] and his "Nazirite" (or "Rechabite")-style vegetarianism is tied to this.

This episode regarding Judas also relates to the second episode in Genesis regarding Righteous Men, the Lot episode, and takes place in a locality very near that of the events recorded of Lot. Lot, too, is a *"Zaddik"*. The Lot story goes further even than that of Noah and specifies the minimum number of *Zaddikim* required for the world to continue in existence—ten.[62] It is important to note that Abraham, too, is usually referred to in these sources as "Righteous", an appellation which has

relates to Noah's vegetarianism before the institution of sacrifice (Ge 9:1ff.; note the additional theme of *abstention from blood*) and has to do, as 1 Macc 1:62–7 suggests, with "standing firm and having the courage to refuse unclean food". Cf. the second escape and salvation episode involving *Zaddikim* in Ge 18, also including the theme of "cave-dwelling" (in a Qumran locale).

[61] In the words of Prov 10:25, "the *Zaddik* is the Foundation of the World". This passage is subjected to exegesis in *Zohar* 59b with the conclusion that the existence of the world is predicated on the Righteous (note the *Zohar* 218a–b on "Phineas" knows the doctrine of "the suffering *Zaddik*", whose death is expiatory and who "suffers to protect the people"). 59b and 222a use the "Pillar" imagery, which relates to its application to "James, Cephas, and John" (the Central Triad) in Ga 2:9. *Zohar* 59b on Noah explains the mysterious saying about James in the Gospel of Thomas, to wit: "In the place where you are to go, go to James the Just for whose sake Heaven and Earth came into existence." The "Heaven and Earth" theme is reiterated in relation to Jesus' words in Mt 24:34ff. (somewhat condensed in Mk 13:30f. and Lk 21:32f.) amid eschatological allusion to "the days of Noah".

Of course, according to this ideology, when James, "the Protection of the People" and "Righteous One", is killed, Jerusalem could no longer remain in existence. This is reflected in the attribution in Origen's Josephus of the fall of Jerusalem to his death and in the appearance directly thereafter of a man Jesus ben Ananias, whom Josephus described as having suddenly appeared on the streets at that time crying "Jerusalem is doomed", *War* 6.5.3. Josephus relates this episode in the context of discussing the relationship of the "Star Prophecy" to the events culminating in the fall of Jerusalem. It is perhaps helpful to point out that the treatment of Jesus ben Ananias by the Jewish and Roman authorities is exactly parallel to that described in the New Testament for Jesus, except Jesus ben Ananias is freed; in the Slavonic Josephus so is Jesus.

[62] Noah and Lot are specifically so designated in Ge 6:9ff., 7:1, and 18:22ff. Later Rabbinic tradition is fond of augmenting this to 36.

clung to him in Islam and by which he is referred to several times in the *Koran*, i.e., Ibrahīm *as-Sadīq*.[63]

Here, one should be aware that the *Koran*, preserving as it does lost traditions from sectarian and Apocalyptic Judaism, provides us with the reference to Ezra as "the Son of God", in what is perhaps a more interesting testimony to his Zadokite heredity than the genealogy provided him in the book of his name.[64] John the Baptist is portrayed as another of these *Zaddiks*, who goes out in the wilderness in imitation of Judas Maccabee and his nine *Zaddikim*, and whose followers will be saved in good Noachic fashion from the universal flood of fire and water soon to descend on mankind.[65] He is distinctly referred to as "*zaddik*" in the New Testament and possibly in Josephus as well. The latter reference is followed by a capsule description of John's philosophy of *Righteousness* more perfect as a reflection of its time and place than anything comparable in the New Testament and containing

[63] See for instance *Koran* 2:35 and 3:67; the second reflects the "Justification" material in Ge 15:6, which in turn is reflected in 1 Macc 2:52 and of course Paul. Note the *Koran* in 3:39–59 and 6:86 knows that both John and Jesus were *Zaddikim*, and knows Jesus as "Primal Adam".

[64] *Koran* 9:30. Ezra's sonship is here grouped beside Jesus'. Such a peculiar notion can be understood if one consults Ben Sira 5:11 on almsgiving, *Zedakah* (*Zakat* in Islam): "you will be like a Son to the Most High" and the parallel passage in Wis 2:16: "The Righteous Man (*Zaddik*) is God's son." Cf. *Zohar* 222a above and 1QH, ix, 28–36: "You have known me before ever my father was and from the womb of my mother, You have dealt kindly with me . . . for my father knew me not and my mother abandoned me to You, for You are a Father to all the Sons of Your Truth. . . . " and xv, 14f.: "You alone created the *Zaddik* and established him from the womb." These allusions to "the pre-existent *Zaddik*" and adoptionist sonship at Qumran are often presented in association with baptismal imagery and the language of the descent of the Holy Spirit and "being joined to the Community of the Sons of Heaven"; cf. 1QS, iii–iv; xi, 2ff.; 1QH, iii, 20ff., etc.; cf. also adoptionist sonship and baptism in Justin, *Dial.* 88 and 103; also Heb 1:15 and 5:6. In particular, the pre-existent *Zaddik* links up with the "*Logos*" doctrine in the Gospel of John and the notion of the "*Imam*" in Shiʿism ("the Hidden *Imam*"— like the Hidden Messiah—to return at the end of time in the person of the *Mahdi*). That all the *Zaddikim* are the Sons of God and, as such, will be resurrected at the End of Time—an event of which Jesus is but the special case—is widespread in the literature; cf. Mt 5:9ff., 45ff.; Lk 20:36 etc. A parallel idea is expressed in CD, iv, 5 on Ezek 44:15 above, p. 16.

[65] For the coming fire and "burning"—which the Righteous will of course escape— see Mt 3:10f. and Lk 3:16f. At Qumran its counterpart is to be found in 1QM, xi, 10 where the "fire in the chaff" allusion is actually employed following an allusion to "the Star"/"Messiah" and Judgement executed by "the Poor" leading up to the evocation of eschatological "rain" imagery. Mt 24:37, cited above, also compares the saving activity of the Messiah with that of Noah at the time of the Flood, i.e. "as were the days of Noah, so shall be the coming of the Son of Man." We consider all these escape and Salvation episodes involving *Zaddikim* to be "Noachic".

within it the explicit mention of the two key words, *"Hesed"* ("Piety") and *"Zedek"* ("Righteousness") so characteristic of these tendencies as we have described them.[66]

We are now in a position to reconstruct some of the history of the so-called "Sadducean" or Zadokite Movement. I propose this to stand as an alternative to some of the "History of the Essenes" we see so often in Qumran research and which have stood so unchallenged for the last twenty years.[67] Perhaps the first truly *Zadokite* Priest, leaving aside the originator of the terminology Ezekiel himself, was Ezra. Here, too, we leave aside possible plays on the name of the last high priest before the Captivity, Yehozedek, and the possibility that the author of the Zadokite Statement was preparing the way for the return of Yehozedek's family in the person of his son Jesus.

A century later Ezra, with the same genealogy as Jesus, is superficially

[66] Mk 6:20. Curiously enough, but in line with the New Testament's working method, it is always foreigners or their satraps who first recognize and/or identify *Zaddik*s like Jesus and John. John, according to the ideology of 1 Macc, even in his role of Elijah/Phineas *redivivus*, would be a Priest/*Zaddik* as well as being a "Zealot". The last he confirms by hounding Herod over a minor legal point. The New Testament also refers to Joseph the Righteous (in this case Jesus' father, but classically, too, the biblical Joshua was "ben Joseph") and Abel the Righteous, Mt 1:19 and 23:5, characterizations perhaps derived from the *Zaddik*-style history in Wis 10.

In *Ant.* 18.5.2 Josephus characterizes John as "a good man who commanded the Jews to exercise virtue, both as concerning Righteousness (*Zedek*) towards one another and Piety (*Hesed*) towards God and so to come to baptism ... for purification of the body, supposing still that the soul was thoroughly cleansed beforehand by Righteousness". The Slavonic adds, "God sent me to show you the Way of the Law." Cf. 1QS, viii–ix, where the words attributed to John in the New Testament are expounded in terms of "the Way" terminology and "studying the Law", and 1QS, iii–iv's description of Qumran baptismal procedures against a background of "heart"/"body" imagery evocative of Ezek 44:9 (see above, p. 16–17) and varying Josephus' "soul"/"body" notation above.

This *Zedek* and *Hesed* dichotomy constitutes the surest basis for confirming the identity of these various Second Temple groups. Justin Martyr, as noted (*Dial.* 93), pinpoints it as the basis of Jesus' teaching (cf. Mt 22:34–40): "He summed up all Righteousness and Piety in two Commandments, namely, 'You shall love the Lord Your God with all your heart' (i.e., "Piety towards God") and 'your neighbor as yourself' " (i.e., "Righteousness towards one another"); and we have already shown it to constitute the totality of Josephus' description of "the Essenes", whom he calls "despisers of Riches"—an extension of "the Righteousness towards men" theme into the sphere of economic equality; cf. "the Poor"—who "exercise Piety towards God and Righteousness towards all men", *War* 2.8.2–7.

[67] See, for instance, Milik, Chapter 3, pp. 44–98; J. Murphy O'Connor, "The Essenes and their History", *RB*, 81, 1974, pp. 215–44; A. Dupont-Sommer, *The Essene Writings from Qumran*, Oxford, 1961; and Cross, Chapter 2, "The Essenes, the People of the Scrolls", and Chapter 3, "The Righteous Teacher and Essene Origins".

at least more substantial, though much overlapping exists between his actions and those of Nehemiah's. For this reason, the possibility that the character of Ezra himself might simply be a priestly fiction superimposed on more secular material should not be ruled out, but this does not affect the "Zealot/Zadokite" character of the presentation. Given the portrait we have, however, Ezra certainly can lay claim to the priestly "zeal" of the Covenant of Phineas, for no more zealous priest is on record unless it be the Lawgiver himself. Whether he actually did service at the altar is impossible to determine since our sources are so imperfect. He presides over festivities in the Temple like some powerful vice-gerent.[68] The rededication of the Temple implicit in his reading of the Law is echoed in Judas Maccabee's presiding over a similar rededication 250 years later accompanied by the institution of a similar festival.[69] Whether Ezra's piety and zeal are sufficient to entitle him to the sobriquet "the *Zaddik*" as the *Koran* would imply, is open to question. If the Zadokite priesthood does not go back to pre-Exilic times (and there is little evidence that it does), then our renascent "Zadokite" or "Righteous" Priesthood must date from this period.

From Ezra's time to the time of Simeon the Just in the third to second centuries BC we go into something of a "tunnel", and very little is clear until we emerge with what appears to be a "Zadokite" Priesthood in the person of Simeon the *Zaddik* himself. Whatever else this priesthood

---

[68] See above, p. 25–26. That Ezra might be a priestly fiction was proposed some time ago in a book by C. C. Torrey, *Ezra Studies*, Chicago, 1910. When viewed from a Maccabean/Zealot point of view, the suggestion has considerable merit. Whether true or not, the fundamentally Zadokite/Zealot/*Zaddik*ite character of the presentation of Ezra remains unaffected.

[69] That Judas' Temple rededication was also accompanied by an Ezra-like reading of the Law is implied by the institution of a *Succot*-like Festival commemorating another wilderness sojourn, *Hanukkah*. This in turn is actually ratified by popular vote (a democratic feature of the new "Zealot" mentality that has escaped most modern criticism anxious as it is to distance Christianity from movements like the Zealots, Maccabees, and Zadokites); 1 Macc 4:59 and 2 Macc 10:1–8. 2 Macc actually recommends that the "Feast of Tabernacles now be kept in the month of Chislev" (1:9), and the more one reads it the more one sees it as a kind of *Hanukkah Haggadah*. The implication of moving the Feast of Booths to *Hanukkah* is of course that just as Moses went into the wilderness for the First Law, so Judas and his nine *Zaddikim* went into the wilderness for its reconsecration—the second. 2 Macc 2:13–15 even compares the collecting activities of Nehemiah concerning Kings, Prophets, and Psalms with how "Judas made a complete collection of the books dispersed in the late war, and these we still have. If you need any of them, send someone to fetch copies for you." It is striking too that this correspondence knows no Ezra (1:18–36); neither does Ben Sira (49:13f.). Both refer only to Nehemiah.

adhering to Simeon's family might have been, it was obviously considered a "Righteous" one with the title of "the *Zaddik*" prominent among its accoutrements.

The confusion of dates for this first definitive *Zaddik* may simply be the confusion of two Simeon the *Zaddik*s, since the family names seem to alternate back and forth between use of the names Onias and Simeon. Onias III—possibly also surnamed "the Just", martyred at the time of the Maccabean uprising and probably the son of the Simeon in Ecclesiasticus—is very definitely presented as a *"Zaddik"* and probably "a Suffering Servant" as well. In an extremely important section of 2 Macc—the book which presents Judas' claims to be a *"Zaddik"* and, as "Messianic" battle-Priest, the leader of the "Hassidaean" Movement—Onias is not only called a *"Hassid"* (Pious One) and "this zealot for the Laws", but also "Protector" or "Shield of his fellow countrymen".[70] Despite its equal importance to the notice about Judas and his nine *Zaddikim*, this passage has also been totally ignored by modern scholarship, though it is quite possibly the basis for similar statements about the person of James the Just the brother of Jesus, another *Zaddik* and putative priestly heir according to early Church testimony.[71]

---

[70] 2 Macc 3:1, 4:2, and 15:12. We have already mentioned the titles *"Zaddik"* and *"Oblias"* ("Protection" or "Strength of the People") above, p. 30, as being repeatedly (or intrinsically as it were) applied to James in *E.H.* 2.1.2ff., 2.23.4ff., 3.7.8 and *Haeres.* 29.4–7 and 78.7–14; cf. too Josephus in Origen, *Contra Celsum* 1.47, 2.13, and *Comm. in Matt.* 10.17.

[71] J. Brashler suggested re-interpreting the difficult *"Oblias"* to read *"Obdias"*, or what he would translate as "Servant of Yahweh". It is at least as plausible to consider *"Oblias"* a garbled version of *Onias*. That Onias is distinctly surnamed "Protection of his fellow countrymen" in the passage above seems the clear prototype of the statement about James. The implication, of course, in both instances was when this "Shield", "Strength", "Pillar", or *"Zaddik"* was removed from the city, the city could no longer remain in existence. *E.H.* 3.7.8 puts this proposition as follows: "By their dwelling in Jerusalem (i.e. James and his companions), they afforded, as it were, a strong Bulwark to the place." Origen, *loc. cit.* (echoed in *E.H.*), insists that Josephus affirmed that "so great was James' reputation for *Righteousness* among the *People*" (italics mine), that the more discerning attributed the siege of Jerusalem and its subsequent destruction to his death. Origen's own impatience with this notice is probably not a little connected with its disappearance in extant texts.

In *War* 4.5.2, Josephus makes a precisely parallel statement about James' nemesis, Ananus. He calls Ananus "venerable and very Righteous", "egalitarian", "concerned for the proletariat", etc., even though later in *Ant.* 20.9.1, he calls him "overbearing", "insolent", and in *Vita* 39 "corrupted by bribes". That there is some confusion of Onias III with Honi the Circle-Drawer ("circle-drawing" is the mechanism for rain-making—in Josephus, "Onias the Just"), the events of whose life are mirrored in James', further

It is perhaps because of this extremely pious presentation of Onias (who cures/resurrects an enemy of God through his righteous sacrifice and is resurrected himself along with the prophet Jeremiah as a kind of "Ancient of Days" to offer Judas the Messianic battle sword in the concluding episode) and the miraculous appearances of heavenly horsemen, that 2 Macc is held in such low esteem.[72] Yet, aside from these shortcomings attributable to lapses of pious enthusiasm, it describes itself as being based on an earlier and much longer work by Jason of Cyrene. It contains much that is authentic, including official correspondence, a portrait of Onias patently more reliable than the confusion of 1 Macc, and first-rate material on Judas' relation to the Hassidaeans.

As should be obvious by now to the reader, unlike majority scholarly opinion I consider it more reliable on the whole than 1 Macc. The latter suffers from certain apologetic aims regarding the whole of the Maccabean family—in particular the progeny of Simon through John Hyrcanus, the real hero of its narrative.[73] Pro-Hassidaean in a manner that 1 Macc

strengthens the Onias/James connection and raises the additional possibility of an Onias *redivivus* tradition alongside the Phineas/Elijah one, if all three are not in fact variations on the same theme; cf. also Goosens, *op. cit.*

[72] For it, there is no break between the priesthood of Onias and the activities of Judas. The Zadokite (or the equivalent *Zaddik*ite) and the Hassidaean Movements are the same. Its stress is on resurrection of the dead and "making a pious end", providing the *sitz im leben* out of which Christianity was to emerge. Following its terminology, Jesus very definitely "makes a pious end" and in so doing must be resurrected. That 2 Macc has not been found at Qumran requires explanation, because of its patently similar orientation to Qumran literature. However, that Josephus does not seem to know it argues very strongly either that it was not yet written or was not known in Palestine. Indeed, it has the form simply of a letter to the Jews of Egypt as Hebrews does to the Jews of Rome. 1 Macc would have been rejected out of hand by the Qumran sectaries—as Esther probably was—because of its slanderous portrayal of the Hassidaean Movement.

[73] It may even have been written to combat certain slanderous material regarding John Hyrcanus' origins, perhaps originally set forth in Jason of Cyrene's earlier work championing the cause of Judas Maccabee: see *Ant.* 13.10.6. Here a mysterious Eleazar—an Essene-type—castigates him with the words, "if you would really be *Righteous*, lay down the Priesthood and content yourself with the civil government of the people" (italics mine). Note the play on the *Zaddik*ite aspect of the Zadokite Priesthood. The thrust of the episode concerns priestly purity or a priesthood without blemish, not genealogy. It does not dispute John's right to serve, nor his family's. It only complains that his mother was a captive and carries with it the imputation of bastard birth. Here, too, the text first introduces Pharisees and Sadducees and we hear of John's being priest, prophet, and king, as well as his desire "to be Righteous". The attempt by 1 Macc to acquit Simon, John's father, of the treachery of handing over his brother Jonathan's two sons to be slaughtered is patent and also bears on the problem of John's dubious origins; cf. 1 Macc 13:17–20.

is not, 2 Macc exhibits many of the characteristics of what must be called "Hassidaean-type" literature—to cite two: "thorough-going" apocalyptic and a stress on resurrection of the dead. Besides having something of the appearance of a *Hanukkah Haggadah*, it seems to have been written to correct the inaccurate portrayal of Judas Maccabee and the slanderous presentation of the Hassidaean movement he headed in 1 Macc. That Judas and Onias are found so closely linked in its account argues very forcibly that its author(s) felt no break from the "Zadokite Priesthood" of the one to the "Zadokite Priesthood" of the other. That both were also "Zealots" needs no further elucidation.

The testimony of books like Daniel, Enoch, the Testament of Levi, etc., can be employed at this point to clinch the case for the similarity in aims between the Maccabees (perfectly good Zadokites in the several senses of that word as I have argued), the previous priesthood of Simeon and Onias, and the Hassidaeans.[74] One must, to be sure, concede the point that the saintly "*Kedoshim*" of Daniel are equivalent to what is called "Hassidaeans" in the Maccabee books and Josephus, a correspondence not difficult to acknowledge.[75]

I take Daniel in any event, if not Enoch as well, to be products of this "Hassidaean-type" literature. Here, among other things it will be objected that 1 Macc portrays the Hassidaeans as having deserted Judas Maccabee for a Quisling high priest loyal to the Seleucids.[76] For 2 Macc, Judas is the leader *par excellence* "of those Jews called Hassidaeans ... who are warmongers and revolutionaries".[77] As at Qumran and in Ecclesiasticus, no distinction is made between "*Zaddik*" and "*Hassid*",

[74] See Dan 9:26 and 11:22 and the subsequent rising of the *Kedoshim*, "the learned" and "the elect" who will be "made white", implied thereafter in 11:33 and described in 7:15–23. As most scholars have realized there can be little doubt of the provenance of these events. The reference to Jeremiah and "the Ancient of Days" is picked up in the Messianic sword scene with Judas Maccabee at the climax of 2 Macc. Enoch 90:8 refers to the martyrdom of Onias in portions extant at Qumran, followed immediately in 90:9 with the description of Judas, probably "the Great Horn", and his activities which follow in 13–19; cf. the "Horn" imagery applied to the teacher in 1QH, vii, 22f.

[75] I think there can be little doubt that those who are called "Saints" in Daniel must relate to those who are called "Hassidaeans" in the Maccabee books. In any event, the terminology is used interchangeably at Qumran with a host of other epithets including "*Zaddikim*", "*Ebionim*", "Sons of Light", etc.

[76] 1 Macc 7:8–18. Note the interesting use of Qumran-style exegesis in applying *Hassid-eicha* in Ps 79 to this breakaway party who sue for peace and are prepared to recognize foreign appointment of high priests. It is not yet a case of confusion of terminologies since the terminologies are fluid and still developing. It is this Josephus fails to appreciate when taking his sources too literally and later speaking about "Pharisees" and "Essenes".

[77] 2 Macc 14:6.

and Judas' *Zaddikim* double as Hassidaeans. In one account the Hassidaeans are the loyalist partisans of Judas Maccabee; in the other they are treacherous backsliders who go over to his Seleucid-backed opponents.

How can the two be reconciled? Actually it is not so difficult if one remarks that the behavior of the so-called "Hassidaeans" in 1 Macc resembles very much the behavior of the Pharisees during the reign of Alexander Jannaeus at the time of the incursion by Demetrius.[78] The way out of the impasse is to assume both accounts are true and that there are *two groups* of Hassidaeans: one loyalist or purist which must be identical with those whom we have been calling "the Zadokites"; the other a breakaway which has rightly been termed "Pharisees". It even might be assumed that both saw themselves as authentic "Hassidaeans" until gradually the new terminology supplanted the old.

What was the "split" about? When viewed in this light it is about instrumentalities—in particular, who should appoint the high priest: whether it should be by a native and purist procedure, meaning "an election" or "by lot", or whether appointment by foreign rulers or their agents was to be considered legitimate. Josephus mentions the "high priesthood of Judas" three times and that it was "bestowed on him by the people".[79] He also tells us that the "Zealots" not only demanded selection by lot in 4 BC, but actually proceeded to carry it out in the extremist phase of the Uprising against Rome in 68 CE. For their part, the Pharisees consistently supported and upheld the legitimacy of Priests appointed by foreigners.[80]

[78] That these men are Pharisees is clear from the vengeance they take in retribution later under Alexandra; cf. *War* 1.4–5.

[79] *Ant.* 12.10.6 and 11.2. That he did not mention this in the *Jewish War* is perhaps best understood in terms of his fuller and freer elucidation of events in the *Antiquities* when his position in Rome had become more secure. Note the parallel "election" of James as "Bishop of Jerusalem" in early Church tradition and its likely reflection in the story of "the election" of the Twelfth Apostle "Matthias" who defeats "Barsabas *Justus*" in Acts 1:23f. Note, also, the *bloody* Jamesian-like *fall* Judas Iscariot purportedly takes in 1:18, not to mention the actual use of the term "Episcopate" for the "Office" that was filled.

[80] Cf. *Ant.* 17.9.1, where the main demand of the followers of the two rabbis slain in the "Temple Eagle" incident was that "the People" should choose the High Priest. For the election of Phannias (i.e. Phineas) ben Samuel, see *War* 4.3.8 and *Tos. Yoma* i, 6.180. Josephus' words of indignation over his elevation are worth quoting: "He was a man not only unworthy of the High Priesthood, but that did not even know what the High Priesthood was; such a mere commoner was he! Yet did they haul this man without his own consent from the countryside, ... put upon him the sacred garments, and upon every occasion instructed him what he was to do." It is hard to imagine a "Poorer" priesthood than this. That he was a "Stone-cutter" as well is not without its symbolism;

How can the presentation of 1 Macc be explained according to this picture? What it has preserved is probably the *birth moment* of the Pharisee Party, but according to Josephus the later Simon and the early John supported the Pharisee Party.[81] Later John went over to the Sadducees and was followed in this by his son, Alexander Jannaeus. The latter, together with his son, Aristobulus, are the epitome of what we must mean by *Sadducees* in this period. Aristobulus very definitely exhibits the "nationalist" tendencies of this movement, as we have described it, and the telltale inability to fawn on foreign potentates (in Josephus' words, "he turned sick of servility and could not bear to abase himself in order to secure his aims at the expense of his dignity"). In this he is supported by a "zealous" lower priesthood in the Temple who go about their chores and sacrifices even while the Romans are slaughtering them.[82] As against

cf. "Rock" and "Cornerstone" symbolism in the early Church and at Qumran. Note that *War* 6.8.3 mentions a Temple Treasurer named Phineas, who gives over to Titus what is left of the Temple treasure.

[81] *Ant.* 13.10.5.

[82] *War* 1.7.1: "Pompey was amazed at the unshakable endurance of the Jews ... Not even when the Temple was being captured and they were being butchered around the altar did they abandon the ceremonies ordained for the day ... the Priests quietly went on with the sacred rites and were cut down as they poured libations and offered incense putting *service to God before* their own preservation" (italics mine). Josephus adds the important political note: "Most of those who fell were killed by their own countrymen of the rival faction" (i.e., the Pharisees and proto-Herodians). Nothing could be more "Zealot" (and "Zadokite") than the dedication to "Temple service" exhibited by Aristobulus' priestly supporters.

Even the typically Zealot resort to suicide finds expression here. Cf. the "Zealot" suicide of the old man (whom Josephus identifies with cave-dwelling "robbers" of *Galilean* origin) and his seven sons in a Jordan valley location 100 years before Masada, below p. 68–69 and *Ant.* 14.15.4f. Not only is this event reflected in "the Seven Brothers" episode in 2 and 4 Macc, which definitively link the doctrine of resurrection to the martyrdom ideal; it coincides with the period of the end of phase 1B of Qumran habitation, i.e., 37 BC when Herod is on his way like Pompey before him and Vespasian after him to assault Jerusalem. Note the purposeful trivialization of this "Seven Brothers" episode in the Mt 22:23, Mk 12:18, and Lk 20:27 responses to "Sadducee" beliefs on *resurrection*. These parodies, following references to Jesus' "right-teaching" on the question of paying taxes to Caesar, conclude with citation of Justin Martyr's "all Righteousness" dichotomy of *Hesed* and *Zedek*, namely, the *Piety* Commandment of "loving God" and the *Righteousness* Commandment of "loving one's neighbor as oneself". Jesus quotes these in order "to silence the Sadducees". Note the general context of the allusion to "the Way of Righteousness", and "God in Truth", "the Prophet", "Stone" and "Cornerstone" imagery, plural sonship, and spiritualized sacrifice; cf. Ja 2:8ff. on the "all Righteousness" Commandment.

For Honi ("Onias the Righteous")'s attitude towards these Pharisee and Romanizing supporters of Hyrcanus, see *Ant.* 14.2.1. Honi's refusal to condemn Aristobulus is the

this, his brother Hyrcanus II returns, following his mother's lead and her connections with Simeon ben Shetach, to the Pharisee fold. Hyrcanus is definitely Pharisaic, which his connections with Herod's family and cooperation with the Romans to secure his priesthood conspicuously confirm.[83]

But Jonathan and Simon Maccabee have already at an earlier time betrayed the purist program of their brother Judas and in effect assimilated themselves to the policies of "the Pharisees" who split with Judas and supported the Seleucid appointee Alcimus on the grounds of his supposed greater purity.[84] This break can explain the negative portrayal

direct cause of his murder. Here, Josephus alludes to the "Hidden" tradition, which appears to have attached itself to Honi's family, seems to involve cave-dwelling, and comes all the way down through Simeon bar Yohai, the *Zohar*'s eponymous source (see below, pp. 76. Note that the *Zohar*, 63a and 67b on "Noah", knows the "hidden" tradition. For it, Noah, who "sought *Righteousness*", "*withdrew*", "*hid himself in the ark*" or "*was hidden* in the ark on *the Day of the Lord's Anger*, and was placed beyond the reach of *the Adversary*"—italics mine. Note also the connection of these notions with "rain" and eschatological "Flood"). Josephus tells us that Honi "hid himself" because of the war; but his grandson "Hanan", possibly identifiable with John the Baptist, is also called "Hidden" in the *Talmud*, and the thrust probably relates more to what goes by the name of "the Hidden *Imam*" ideology in Shi'ite Islam than it does Josephus' rather charming misunderstanding of it. The *Talmud*, too, misunderstands the true implications of the ideology when it recounts a "Rip van Winkle" story about Honi and tells of another, otherwise unidentifiable, grandson Abba Hilkiah, who repeats his grandfather's rain-making feat: *b. Ta'an* 23a–b. Not only must "Abba Hilkiah" have been a contemporary of James, but if the Lukan account of a kinship between Elizabeth and Mary has any substance, then James, too, was very likely a descendant of Honi. Epiphanius' (*loc. cit.*) ascription to James of a parallel rain-making miracle increases the points of contact (note the common elements of "working in the fields" and antagonism to the Pharisaic Herodian establishment in both traditions).

[83] See *War* 1.6.2; *Ant.* 13.16.1. For Hyrcanus' general connections with the Herodian family, see his relations with Antipater, *Ant.* 13.16–14.6. That Aristobulus is anti-Pharisaic is confirmed in *Ant.* 14.5.4. For Hyrcanus' behavior towards Pompey, see *Ant.* 14.4.2, i.e., "Hyrcanus zealously assisted him [Pompey] in everything." As we have suggested, such behavior also epitomizes Pollio and Sameas', Josephus' "Essenes", Yohanan ben Zacchai's, and Josephus' own attitudes towards Emperors or their agents, as it does Paul's. It has also been retrospectively assimilated into the portrait of Jesus in the New Testament. Here the charge in Acts 15:5—echoed in modern scholarship—that Christianity was infiltrated by "Pharisees" at an early stage is true; but its import is rather the opposite of what the New Testament implies. The "Pharisee the son of a Pharisee" is Paul, and his approach in Ro 13:1–7 typifies "Pharisaic" policy, as no Pharisee rabbi other than Akiba is on record as having been crucified or beheaded. Akiba, in any event, is ridiculed by his colleagues for his behavior; see below, p. 61–62.

[84] Which is why 2 Macc chooses to end on the triumphal note of Judas' Messianic appointment. For it, Jonathan and Simon have already betrayed the "Zadokite Hassidaean" ideal of their brother. Given the almost obligatory martyrdom of those who espoused it, their defection is not surprising.

of the Hassidaean Movement in the official family history of 1 Macc, an attitude of antagonism, which by the time of its composition, had permeated the Hasmonaean family. But 1 Macc, while conserving the anti-*Hassidaean* spirit of Jonathan and Simon, "forgets" that the original Hassidaeans were Zadokites and followers of Judas conserving only their current embodiment in the Pharisee movement. John Hyrcanus very soon attains the status of an independent monarch—Josephus tells us that he alone embodied in his person the three attributes of prophet, priest, and ruler, and that his son, Aristobulus, actually assumed the crown—and, therefore, has no further need of the temporizing policies of the Pharisees.[85] He returns to the policies of the "Zadokite" wing, which he assimilates to his own, no longer treating it as an independent entity, nor remembering its original differences with his two ancestors. For him, the Hassidaeans are the group who betrayed his uncle Judas and follow a temporizing foreign policy inimical to the new interests of his "Kingdom".

On this basis 1 Macc, though "Phariseeizing" of necessity in its portrait of Jonathan and Simon, is a product of the later part of John Hyrcanus' reign (or even early Alexander Jannaeus). It purposely obscures the connections of the original "Zadokite" Hassidaeans led by Judas with the priesthood of Onias and Simeon, and at the same time uses the terminology "Hassidaean" to heap abuse upon the breakaway temporizing Pharisee Movement.[86]

V

ARCHAEOLOGICAL RECONSTRUCTION

Here, some archaeological evidence based on the coins so dear to Qumran archaeologists should perhaps be employed.[87] If one observes

---

[85] *Ant.* 13.10.6 and 11.1. His father, Simon, had assumed the High Priesthood "until a trustworthy prophet should arise": 1 Macc 14:41 (prefiguring the later "True Prophet" ideology); Simon no doubt must have considered this to mean permanently. We have already seen above, p. 38, how the Pharisees, who contest John's right to the High Priesthood, do so on the grounds of his questionable purity and prod him on the basis of his own presumable interpretation of the Zadokite Covenant, that is, on the basis of *Righteousness*.

[86] 1 Macc's rather clumsy handling of the priestly infighting in which Onias is replaced by Mattathias gives further evidence of its unreliability. By comparison, 2 Macc clarifies the political ramifications of the squabbles over priestly succession.

[87] See R. de Vaux, "Fouille au Khirbet Qumrân", *Revue Biblique*, 60, 61, and 63, 1953, 1954, and 1956, pp. 93, 229–231, and 565–569, and *Archaeology and the Dead Sea Scrolls*, pp. 18–23, 33–41, 44–45, 64–67, 70–71. De Vaux, and almost all specialists who base

in a general way the distribution of coins found at Qumran, it will be remarked that it increases and decreases in a consistent pattern. The first rise in distribution begins at the time of John Hyrcanus (the later period) and reaches a peak under Alexander Jannaeus. It then falls away almost to zero in Herod's reign. It starts increasing again around the time of Herod's death and the revolts of 4 BC–7 CE, rising steadily until it hits a peak during the crucial years 50–60 CE before the War against Rome.

To judge by the numerical distribution of coins, the monastery is destroyed at the height of its power.[88] Numerous scholars have been

their work on his, employ this coin data to arrive at a final determination for the abandonment of the site by the sectaries. De Vaux himself, however, states, p. 138, "It is quite certain that in the study of the Qumran documents archaeology plays only a secondary role". Elsewhere, though, he states in response to Driver's contention, *The Judaean Scrolls*, Oxford, 1965, p. 394, that "internal evidence afforded by a document must take precedence over external evidence": "No—other things being equal, there is no precedence between the two kinds of evidence; a correct solution must make use of both, must prove the worth of both", *NTS*, 13, 1966–7, p. 97.

[88] De Vaux, *loc. cit.* There are some ninety-four coins which are all from the second and third years, 67–8 and 68–9 of the Revolt (six too oxidized to read). By contrast there are only about eleven coins from the period of Archelaus, one for Herod—though there are seventy-eight coins from the period of Agrippa I, another period of high revolutionary activity ending with the execution of Judas' two sons. By contrast there are 143 coins from Alexander Jannaeus, five coins from Hyrcanus II and four for Antigonus b. Aristobulus. One cannot resist remarking here that if one coin had been found from 69–70, de Vaux's theory of abandonment, and that of those basing their theories on his, would be in grave jeopardy. See also E. M. Laperrousaz, *Qoumrân L'Établissement Essénien des bords de La Mer Morte*, Paris, 1976, p. 30.

No coins have been found for instance from the first year of the revolt. Should we therefore conclude the sectaries only arrived during the second? No coins have so far been found from the second year of the Revolt in Jerusalem. Should we likewise conclude the Temple fell before then? Y. Meshorer confided in a personal comment to me that he has not even seen de Vaux's coins, which are safely locked up in the École Biblique, and doubt must persist as long as six are too oxidized to read. Very few coins would have escaped from the city when it was under siege from 68 CE onwards in any event; and at least in the Jericho area, under Roman occupation as it was, they would have been of no use even if they had. De Vaux points to one hoard of coins found near Jericho from the fourth year, but this is just that: a hoard.

Note the precipitous rise in coin distribution during the periods of Alexander Jannaeus and Agrippa I. These correspond chronologically to two known flights in these periods: Alexander's flight with "6,000 of his followers" to a mountainous area outside Jerusalem (*War* 1.4.7 and *Ant.* 13.14.2) and James' flight with "5,000" of his followers to an unspecified location "outside Jericho" after the attack by Paul on the Temple Mount, Ps *Rec* 1.70ff. Significantly, this last actually places James and his community in the region of Qumran, from where he sends out Peter on his first missionary journey to Caesarea. It also contains the highly original notice that James broke his leg in a fall down the Temple steps and was still "limping" some weeks later when Peter arrived in Caesarea. For an

particularly puzzled over the clear destruction of the settlement some-where on or before 31 BC.[89] The usual conclusion drawn is that the monastery was destroyed by fire during the earthquake of 31 BC. De Vaux, whose hypothesis this was, admitted its weakness when criticized, but this admission never made the same impression as his original pro-posal.[90] Or, for those who realize the absurdity of thinking that the sectaries could not have rebuilt the monastery in 30 or 29 BC if they did so in 4 BC, comments such as, "Perhaps the Persians destroyed the mon-astery in the war between Antigonus and Herod/Hyrcanus", are common.[91]

To these I should like to add a third possibility. Cross was very close to the mark when he observed that control of the Jericho road was all-important, and the sectaries could not maintain themselves at Qumran in the face of Roman control over it. But he missed the self-evident corollary of this, of which the settlement's several destructions give unmistakable proof. Only some twenty-odd walking miles from Jerusa-lem, the monastery could not maintain itself in the face of a strong determined central authority in Jerusalem.[92]

additional numerical parallel to this flight of the "5,000", see Philo's remarks in *Quod Omnis* 12, numbering "those people called Essenes ("who derive their name from their Piety") at something more than 4,000". For Mt 15:38 and Mk 8:9 this is the same number of men Jesus feeds in the wilderness!

[89] See Milik, pp. 51ff., Bruce, pp. 49–52, Cross, p. 60, etc.

[90] Though originally extremely dogmatic on the question of the earthquake, in his final work de Vaux took a much more conciliatory stance: "The question remains open, therefore, and my real reason for believing that the fire coincided with the earthquake of 31 BC is that this solution is the simplest and that there are no positive arguments to contradict it." The criticism came from de Vaux's own colleague, Milik, pp. 51ff., and a despised enemy, S. Steckoll, "Marginal Notes on the Qumran Excavations", *Revue de Qumran*, 7, 1968, pp. 34ff. But *there are positive* arguments to contradict it, namely, besides the question of evidence of some habitation in the Herodian period, why a group that returned in 4 BC could not return in 30 BC, or even left in the first place instead of quite simply repairing the damage. To think an earthquake could have caused, in addition to masonry damage, the kind of total conflagration the evidence suggests, is far-fetched. (Those who contend that superstition could have kept the sectaries away—Morton Smith in a personal comment to me—still must explain why they subsequently returned and the evidence for a less than total abandonment.) But de Vaux's methods were already being criticized by R. North as early as 1954 in "Qumran and its Archaeology", *CBQ*, 16, pp. 426–37 and more recently by Laperrousaz.

[91] See Milik, p. 94, Laperrousaz, pp. 41–45, and B. Mazar, T. Dothan, and I. Dunayev-sky, *En-Gedi, The First and Second Seasons of Excavations: 1961–62*, Jerusalem, 1966, p. 5.

[92] Cross, pp. 75ff. His sharp critique of Driver, Rabin, and Roth in these pages is intemperate. It is true that the theories of Driver and Roth could not account for the whole expanse of Qumran literature, but they at least had the virtue of pointing out the

Alexander Jannaeus was one such ruler; Herod the Great another. The Romans under Vespasian and subsequently under Titus plainly constitute a third such determined force, as they do under Hadrian and Severus when Bar Kochba's guerrillas first occupied the site and then abandoned it and made a more determined stand further into the Wadi Murabba'at or Nahal Hever.[93] I do not consider the period of the Tetrarchies and Procurators by definition to at any time have exhibited this characteristic of "strong central government". The power of the procurators probably

"Zealot" nature—that is to say, non-pacifist and apocalyptic—of the sectaries. Even de Vaux finds himself in difficulty on this account, stating in *NTS*, p. 93, that "the Essenes, who were pacifists, offered resistance to attack . . . " and in *Archaeology*, p. 122, "We were already aware that the Essenes took part in the Revolt." Milik was forced by the theories of Roth and Driver to admit that in the last phase, "Essenism had taken on something of the character of the Zealots . . .", *NTS*, p. 93. Oblivious to the contradiction he had involved himself in, de Vaux held to his pacifist preconceptions, while at the same time terming the Essenes "eschatological". One early Church historian, Hippolytus, whose works may be pseudographic, actually seems to retain a variant and more detailed version of Josephus, in which "Zealots" and even "*Sicarii*" are simply "Essene" groups with a more nationalist, extreme, more uncompromising ideology. For him there are *four* groups of "Essenes", one that even kills backsliders who refuse to circumcize, just as Josephus' "Zealots" do in the *Jewish War*.

Here it is worth quoting Cross, "Military control of Qumran from Masada in the face of Roman power immediately north (i.e., Jericho) is quite incredible." Additionally, Cross assumes the Masada group participated in the final stages of the war, although like the Christians before them they had already withdrawn from Jerusalem in 68 after the assassination of Menachem. As long as they refrained from harassing commerce on the Jericho road, which most evidence suggests they did, the Romans would have had no interest in bothering any final holdouts, who might have remained in or slipped back to the caves and ruins. Control of the Jericho road by a hostile and determined authority would make life difficult at the monastery, but *in wartime conditions* not impossible, and the site was a good forward observation post for Masada. It is just as likely the Romans did not immediately garrison it (coin data notwithstanding—otherwise why burn it?), but rather moved on to the siege of Jerusalem—actual garrisoning would have come later in the course of operations against Masada. Life could certainly have continued at Qumran, its isolated location and natural caves being the *raison d'être* for its settlement in the first place.

[93] For description of Nahal Hever finds, see Y. Aharoni, "Expedition B—The Cave of Horror", Y. Yadin, "Expedition D", and "Expedition D—The Cave of Letters", *IEJ*, 12, 1962, pp. 186–99; 11, 1961, pp. 36–52, and 12, 1962, pp. 227–257. Here, too, the evidence shows that Bar Kochba's followers returned to site at Qumran at a time of weakened central authority and abandoned it in the face of superior, more determined, forces. Actually, as Driver has noted, the presence of Bar Kochba's forces at the site must be explained, particularly in relation to Cave IV, which they could not have remained unaware of. 68 CE, far from being a *terminus ad quem* for the deposit of the scrolls, is only a *terminus a quo*, meaning, not the last, but rather *only the first possible moment* for their deposit.

rarely extended very far outside Jerusalem except in occasional bursts of energy as under Tiberius Alexander and Felix.[94]

That the monastery seems to have flourished under Alexander while it lay buried in ashes under Herod (the same monarch who built a winter palace near by and had the last of the Maccabean claimants to the High Priesthood strangled while frolicking in its swimming pool) *must say something*. Yet majority opinion tends to identify Alexander Jannaeus as *the Wicked Priest* while at the same time identifying the sect with "the Essenes", about whom both Herod and Josephus speak with such evident cordiality.[95]

---

[94] The robbery of the crown messenger, Stephen, not far outside the walls of Jerusalem (see below, p. 77, for the relationship of this Stephen to the "Stephen" in Acts) shows the impunity with which guerrilla forces operated in these years. The bandit chief, Eleazar bar Dinaeus, operated for almost a generation until Felix was able to curtail his activities. The inability of procurators to protect Galilean pilgrims on their way through Samaria, and even the activities of John the Baptist and Jesus, give further proof of this proposition; cf. *Ant.* 20.5.4; *War* 2.12.2; *Ant.* 20.6.1 and 8.5; *War* 2.13.1–3.

As for Felix' activities in the years 52–60, Josephus states "as to the number of the robbers whom he caused to be crucified and of whom were caught among them, and those he brought to punishment, they were a multitude not to be enumerated." Still the next procurator, Festus, was forced to tackle "the chief curse of the country", killing "a considerable number of the bandits" and capturing "many more"; *Ant.* 2.14.1. Elsewhere, Joseph calls the "cheats and deceivers claiming inspiration" and scheming to bring about revolutionary changes by leading the people "*out into the wilderness* on the pretenses that there God would show them *signs of approaching freedom*" an even greater scourge (italics mine), *Ant.* 2.13.4, and claims "the religious frauds and bandit chiefs joined forces and drove numbers to revolt, *inciting them to strike a blow for freedom*" (language reminiscent at once of the two Rabbis in the 4 BC Temple Eagle incident and the Slavonic descriptions of John the Baptist and Jesus): *Ant.* 2.13.6.

[95] Milik understands this proposition very well, pp. 93–5, citing the relevant data from Josephus (*Ant.* 15.10.4–5: "He always treated all the Essenes with honor and thought higher of them than their mortal nature required"); yet he resists its self-evident corollary, preferring to hold out for token habitation of the monastery in the Herodian period. For Josephus' own pro-Essene sentiments, one has only to cite his description of the sects in *War* 2.8.2ff. This is not really a description of the sects at all, but a description of the Essenes, the customs of whom he labors over in loving detail; see above, p. 24, for Josephus' incorporation of elements from this description in his expanded treatment of the Movement of Judas and Saddok, in *Ant.* 18.1.1ff. He first mentions "Essenes" in the period between John Hyrcanus and Alexander Jannaeus; cf. *War* 1.3.4 and *Ant.* 13.11.2 on "Judas the Essene" portrayed as a Temple fortune-teller on the fringes of the establishment (see similarly "Simon the Essene" in *Ant.* 17.13.3).

We have already called attention to the overlap in the portraits of "Menachem the Essene" and the Pharisees Pollio and Sameas. The obsequious behavior of all three resembles nothing so much as Yohanan ben Zacchai's (and Josephus' own) treatment of Vespasian. The technique is always the same, predicting for the patron either his

Very few specialists doubt that the sect was vociferously—even vindic-tively, as John the Baptist was—anti-Pharisaic. Yet the scholarly consen-sus insists that Alexander Jannaeus, who in his person exhibited the same characteristic, persecuted the sect, while Herod, whose open alliance with the Pharisee-sponsored Hyrcanus and special treatment of Pollio and Sameas (who advised the Jerusalem polity to open its gates to him) pat-ently show to have been pro-Pharisaic (as his descendants, Agrippa I and Agrippa II, indisputably were, confirming the Gospel picture of the "Herodian"-Pharisaic alliance), treated it with solicitude.[96]

One text at Qumran actually deals with these events—the Nahum *Pesher*. While it does not condone crucifixion *per se* for reasons that in the first century CE should be obvious (and even paleographers agree that this is what they call a "Herodian" text, i.e., first century CE), it does not condemn the "Furious Young Lion"'s action in taking vengeance on the members of the party who invited "Demetrius" into the country. The stance, rather, is very similar to that of Honi the Circle-Drawing

imminent coming to power or long life on the throne. Once again, I feel our explanation of the origins of the "Hassidaean" split goes a long way towards resolving these discrep-ancies. This is also true for Hippolytus' picture above of "Zealot Essenes". Whoever these early "Essenes" are they are not our Qumran sectaries, who are never obsequious and whose eschatology never panders to anyone; on the contrary, it is violently apocalyp-tic. Nor are they the "Essenes" whose martyrdoms Josephus describes in such detail in the *War*, a description probably embodying elements of his own eye-witness account of the fall of Qumran. In the *Antiquities* these same martyrs are now "zealot" followers of Judas' and Saddok's "Fourth Philosophy". Milik's description of a change in the character of the Essenes is not sufficient to explain these discrepancies.

[96] See n. 95 and above, p. 42. The grouping of "the Pharisees and the Herodians" together on the questions of loyalty to Caesar and paying taxes in the section of the New Testament preceding the discussion of "the Sadducees" and "the Seven Brothers" is for once very incisive: Mt 22:15ff., Mk 12:13ff., and Lk 20:20—parodying the "Righteousness" notation (cf. also Mk 3:6). Once the *two* groups of Hassidaeans/Essenes are understood, as we have described them, namely, as "Pharisee" Essenes and "Zadoki-te" Essenes, then most of these problems that so bedevil Josephus' narratives, evaporate. When "Essene" is used, we must often substitute "Pharisee", as for instance, in all the examples of Herod's regard for "Essene" teachers. When "Pharisee" is employed, we must *sometimes* substitute "Essene"—or better yet, "Zadokite"—as for instance, in Jose-phus' reference to "Saddok a Pharisee".

In the Slavonic (in what is perhaps as good a proof as any of its authenticity), we hear how Simon, a toadying "scribe of Essene origin", runs at "the wild Man" and attacks him, which is patently preposterous since John is the "Essene"-type (cf. "Simon the Essene" in *Ant.* 17.13.7, possibly identifiable with the legendary "Shammai"). If we read here "Pharisee", the situation is clarified considerably; for more on the relationship of Saddok and John, see below, pp. 107–8.

Zaddik, who when called upon to condemn the priestly supportors of Aristobulus in the next generation who had opened the Temple gates to Aristobulus and given him refuge, refuses in good *Zadokite* style. In return, these Herodian-aligned and Romanizing Pharisees stone him.[97]

VI
A *ZADOKITE* RECONSTRUCTION

Our hypothesis is that the "Zadokite" monastery at Qumran is "Sadducean", but not Sadducean according to the portraits in Josephus and the New Testament, which relate to a later period.[98] In like manner the so-called "Karaites" of the Middle Ages refer to themselves and are referred to by others as "Sadducees"—strikingly enough they also seem

---

[97] This event has been rightly signaled in the work of Goosens and Dupont-Sommer as very important. We have noted it above, p. 13. In it, we must see the basis for the charge, repeated so often in the New Testament and early Church history—and then echoed in the *Koran*—that Israel stoned all the Prophets and Righteous Ones: Mt 23:29ff. and Lk 13:34ff., 11:47 etc. There can be little question that Honi is one of "the Righteous Ones" referred to, the "tombs" of whom are also mentioned in Mt 23:29 (cf. "the whitened sepulchres" in the Ps *Rec* 1.71 reference to James' flight to Jericho probably related to the "making white until the time of the End" allusion in Dan 11:35. See also how this imagery is picked up in the *Koran* 73:13 in the description of "the Day on which the hair of the children will be turned white"). Other than Zechariah, and excluding the apocryphal Martyrdom of Isaiah, no other prophets are on record as having been killed by Jews unless we include Honi's namesake Onias and John the Baptist, the latter linked in New Testament tradition with Zechariah.

The connection of both Oniases to James has already been signaled. In addition to the *rain-making*, the bringing of James—again by "Sadducees and Pharisees"—into the Temple at Passover to quiet the Jewish masses, the "Messianic" proclamation he makes, and his subsequent stoning are extremely close to the circumstances of this Honi episode; cf. Eusebius, Epiphanius, and Jerome, *loc. cit.* The reference to James' fall from "the Pinnacle of the Temple" in these accounts is a garbled version of his earlier "fall" from the steps in Ps *Rec* 1.70 which has been assimilated by Church tradition into a single attack.

[98] The hypothesis is not new; see for instance the articles of North, Goosens, Wernberg-Moeller, Trinquet, and the remarks of Albright above, p. 24. However, none of these ever developed the proposition in any detail; neither did they couple it with "Christian" and "Zealot" hypotheses as we are doing. Up until now it has been something of a three-cornered hat—the partisans of the "Zealot" theory and the Sadducees knowing nothing about Jewish Christianity; the partisans of Jewish Christianity—Teicher is its only well-known representative, but actually G. Margoliouth preceded him—knowing little or nothing about Sadduceeism and Zealotism.

to have used this terminology interchangeably with *"Zaddikim"*—but have more in common with the Qumran sectaries than they do with what I shall call "Herodian" or normative Sadduceeism.[99]

Far from being at odds with the Jerusalem authorities during the

[99] See Maimonides on *Abot* 1.3 and Abraham ibn Ezra on Dan 11:31 in Gallé, *Daniel avec Commentaires*, p. 141 for the view from outside. From inside, see Embden and Fili-powski, *Liber Juchassin . . . R. Abraham Zacuti*, 13a; Trigland, *Diatribe de Secta Karaeorum*, pp. 16f., and Hassan b. Massiah, quoted in Poznanski, *REJ*, xliv, pp. 76ff. That the Karaites actually referred to themselves as *Zaddikim* is confirmed in S. Luzki, *Orah Zaddi-kim*, Vienna, 1830, pp. 19ff. Indeed, no one has yet satisfactorily explained the double "d" in the Greek transliteration of Sadducee, nor the fact that the Zadok in the Zadokite statement in the Septuagint Ezekiel is rather transliterated *Saddok*, just as the teacher who arose with Judas the Galilean, as the shift to "Messianism" occurred, is called "Saddok" in the *Antiquities*.

Here it would be worth quoting from the Karaite author al-Kirkisani, who not only knows—as Rabbanites did not, or had forgotten—that Jesus was "a *Zaddik*", but "that his Way was the same as that of Zadok and Anan . . . Jesus forbade divorce just as the Sadducees did [but the Sadducees did not forbid divorce; rather the sectaries at Qumran and the early Christians did]. As for the religion of the Christians which they profess today, it was Paul who introduced and established it. He was the one who invested Jesus with divinity and he claimed to be a prophet ordained by his Lord Jesus . . . As for the religion of the Christians which they profess today, it is outright heresy"; *al-Qirqisani's Account of the Jewish Sects of Christianity*, tr. by L. Nemoy, *Hebrew Union College Annual*, v, 7, 1930, pp. 364–5. A more "Ebionite" account of "Christian" history could not be imagined. Even today one has to be amazed by al-Kirkisani's perspicuity in an age of otherwise utter confusion.

Al-Kirkisani also preserves the tradition from *ARN* 5.2 that there were *two* groups of Sadducees (i.e., "the Sadducees and the Boethusians") taking their origins from the "split" between two leaders, "Zadok and Boethus", pp. 326 and 364. Though al-Kirkisani's generation count places this in the second generation after Simeon the *Zaddik* (that is, the time of our Zadokite "Hassidaean"/Pharisee "Hassidaean" split) close attention to generation counts in *ARN* 5.2 ("they taught them to their disciples and their disciples to their disciples") places it *three* generations beyond that or in the period of the confron-tation (the *second split*) between "Saddok" and the *Herodian* "Sadducee", Joezer b. Boethus, over the issues of *taxation*, priestly *Hesed*, etc. (note that for *ARN*, Zadok's "Sadducees" *espouse* the doctrine of Resurrection, not reject it and heap abuse on the "Pharisees" on this basis). Not only is this the *sitz im leben* of Josephus' discussions of sectarian strife, it links up with traditions in the New Testament and Pseudoclementines dating "Messian-ic" and sectarian strife to the time of the coming of John the Baptist; see above, p. 21. Note also that for the *Ant.* and the Slavonic, "Saddok" and "the Wild Man" play parallel roles; see also below, p. 108. For al-Kirkisani, *Zadok* broke with the "Rabbanites" (and presumably their "Boethusian" confederates) on *the issue of marriage with a niece*. The prac-tice was widespread in the first-century establishment, particularly among "Herodians" themselves, and constitutes the basis of the "fornication" charge at Qumran, a matter that also exercises James; cf. CD, iv, 15–v, 11 specifically delineating these matters in connection with "the standing up of Zadok", and Acts 15:20ff., 21:25, and 1 Co 5–7 on James' directives to overseas communities, in particular, "fornication".

Maccabean period, Qumran Sadduceeism was in large measure sponsored by them. Therefore, its high point according to coin data comes in the John Hyrcanus/Jannaeus period, also the high point of the Maccabean family priesthood. Its rise is coincident with the split in the later part of John Hyrcanus' reign between the Maccabean family and the Pharisee Party which is carried to an extreme of brutality in the conflict of the Jannaeus period.[100] How then could John Hyrcanus have "returned" to the Sadducee Party? He did so because this was the original party of Judas Maccabee, deserted by his family during the somewhat dubious machinations of his uncle Jonathan and father Simon to curry Seleucid favor for their claims to the high priesthood.

The monastery at Qumran was probably the extreme expression of Sadduceeism. In the manner of both Daniel and 2 Maccabees this extreme and pietistic expression of Sadduceeism, embraced by the Hassidaean partisans of Judas Maccabee, differed from normative Sadduceeism of the Herodian period (which seemed to have more in common with Samaritanism or the Shammai wing of the Pharisee Party) in its radical espousal of the relatively "new" doctrine of resurrection of the dead—or rather resurrection of "the Pious Ones" or "the Righteous Ones", for these were the only ones to whom the privilege applied, all others in the language of the time going straight to *Sheol*.[101]

That the Sadducees of the Herodian Period did not embrace the

---

[100] Both Laperrousaz, p. 31 and Cross, p. 122, realize that the evidence of coin data invariably points to an origin about the time of John Hyrcanus. We should add the corollary that its establishment was not inimical either to the aims of John or his children (it is in relationship to the demise of the first two of these that John derives his reputation as a "prophet" in *Ant.* 13.10.7; cf. the parallel "prophesying" of "Judas the Essene").

[101] This idea is so widespread in Second Temple literature, including the Scrolls and the Gospels, that one hardly knows where to begin; cf. Wis 1:1, 1:15, 2:16ff., 3:1, 4:7ff.; Enoch 38–62, where the doctrine is developed in its entirety and "the Righteous" and "Elect" are identified, 92:3, 93:10, 94:1, repeating the "love Righteousness" admonition of Wis 102:4–5, the basis of a similar *Koranic* expectation, and 103:1–4; Test. L. 5:7 and 13:5; A. Bar 14.12 and 15.7f.; A. Ezra 7.17–8, 35ff., 99 (encouraging martyrdom), 102 (adding the additional notion of intercession on the Day of Judgement), 8:33, 55, and 9:13ff.; cf. CD, i–iv; 1QS, xi; 1QH, vi, 29 and xi, 10–14. That the doctrine, announced first in 2 Macc 12:38–45, was meant (as implied in A. Ezra 7.99) to encourage martyrdom is clear from the "Seven Brothers" episode, the martyrdom of Eleazar, and the words, "If he had in view the splendid recompense reserved for those who make a pious end, the thought was holy and devout"; cf. 6:28, 7, and 14:46. What better inducement could there be for sacrifice in Holy War? This is the thrust which is picked up in Islam. Paul, while stressing the doctrine, rather emphasized its Greek mystery parallels, i.e., "entering the tomb with Jesus", in the interests of appealing to a wider (less "Zealot"-minded) clientele.

doctrine is difficult to understand, except that Herod after destroying the Maccabean family (those who doubt the popularity of the Maccabean family should note the reaction of the crowd to Herod's murder of Mariamme and her brother, Aristobulus, and its support of Antigonus in opposition to the advice of Pollio and Sameas) brought in a priest from Egypt, Simon ben Boethus, whose daughter he married as he had the Maccabean heiress previously.[102] Because of this, the "new" priesthood he instituted should more properly be called the "Boethusian", as it is often referred to in *Talmudic* literature.[103]

[102] For the crowd's reaction to Aristobulus/Jonathan, see *War* 1.22.2: "When he put on the sacred vestments . . . the whole crowd burst into tears." Josephus is even more effusive in *Ant.* 15.3.3f.: " . . . a warm zeal and affection towards him appeared among the people, and the memory of the actions of his grandfather Aristobulus evidently came to their minds . . . The city . . . was in very great grief, every family looking on this calamity (his death) . . . as if one of themselves had died." That Mariamme's memory was also cherished by the progenitors of Christianity is clear from the proliferation of Marys in the Gospels. In Antigonus' case, it is because of his equally wide *popularity* that Herod bribes Mark Anthony to *behead* him—the first recording of such in Palestine.

Like stonings, these beheadings are worth cataloguing; they are all applied to *popular* leaders for the same reason. Josephus (*Ant.* 15.1.2) quotes Strabo of Cappadocia to explain: "Anthony supposed he could in no other way bend the minds of the Jews to receive Herod . . . for by no torments could they be forced to call him king [cf. Josephus on 'the Essenes' in *War* 2.8.10: "though they were tortured and tormented . . . they could not be forced to flatter their tormentors"], so he thought that this dishonorable death would diminish the value they had for Antigonus' memory"—this directly following his description of how Herod paid such honor to "Pollio the Pharisee and Sameas". Note the progression: Antigonus, John the Baptist, and *Theudas* (a contemporary of the New Testament's "James the son of Zebedee"; see also below, pp. 78f).

[103] *Ant.* 15.9.3. This Simon ben Boethus is a citizen of Jerusalem but comes from an Alexandrian priestly family "of great note". In typical fashion Josephus seems to confuse him with Simon Kanthera "the son of Boethus" under Agrippa I more than fifty years later (*Ant.* 19.6.2), while at the same time comparing the Boethusian family with that of Simeon the *Zaddik* in the number of sons doing the high priestly service and in the process providing the interesting aside that the latter had three sons. J. Jeremias, *Jerusalem in the Time of Jesus*, Fortress Press, 1975, pp. 194f. and 229f., gives credence to this suggestion. For *Talmudic* references, see *Tos Sukk* iii.1.195; *Tos Yoma* i.8.81; *Yal R. Sh.* i.15.210; *b. Sukk* 43b; *b. Shabb* 108a; *b. Men* 65a; *b. Yoma* 18a, etc.

The ancestral tomb of the Boethusian family is probably to be found in the Kedron Valley beneath the "Pinnacle of the Temple" at the foot of the Mount of Olives. There the memorial plaque identifies a family of the course of "Hezir" and contains the names of some four of the Boethusians who actually served as High Priests. Curiously enough, this is the Tomb which is usually ascribed in Christian tradition to St James, i.e., James the Just. Allegro romantically queries, though perhaps not without substance, whether this could be the "Tomb of Zadok" mentioned in the Copper Scroll, line 52, *The Treasure of the Copper Scroll*, New York, pp. 103–112.

Herod also "leased" out the Priesthood to a variety of other pro-Pharisaic claimants as the Procurators did after him. This importation of foreign claimants is a typical totalitarian or colonial device for controlling local party unrest, and probably is very much evidenced by the pliant Hillel's arrival from Babylon at about this time coincident with Herod's destruction of the previous classically Sadducean Sanhedrin that had opposed him.[104] Anyone who doubts the flexibility—even the

The Christian tradition linking this tomb with James is extremely old and one should be chary of lightly setting such folk memories aside. If indeed James was buried here—and most Church fathers make pointed mention of the location of James' burial place just outside the Temple wall—the question of an actual link with the Boethusian family is not completely far-fetched. Indeed, this is precisely what is implied in the Rabbinic nickname for Jesus, "ben Panthera", i.e., probably a slight distortion of "ben Kanthera". If there is any truth to this suggestion, then the takeover of the Boethusian Tomb—whose in-laws the sons of Kanthera were—by Christian tradition becomes more comprehensible; cf. Epiphanius' constant assertion that "Joseph the brother of Cleophas" (*sic*) was called "Panther"; *Haeres* 78.7. Since Joseph Cabi—and possibly Joseph Kami, as well, if the two can be separated—the High Priest preceding the execution of James, was one of the sons of Simon ben Kanthera—i.e., a Boethusian called "Joseph", we have the additional possibility of material relating to the burial of James being assimilated into the "Joseph of Arimathaea" legend in Jesus burial traditions; cf. *Ant.* 20.8.11f. In fact, it is Agrippa II's removal of Joseph Cabi that sets the stage for the judicial murder of James. One should remember that Agrippa II, like his father before him in the confrontation with "Simon", was already smarting from his defeat by the Temple "Zealots" in the Temple wall incident; see below, p. 78. It was shortly after these events that Josephus undertook his mission to Rome to see Poppea on behalf of certain "Essene"-type priests who, because of their "Piety towards God", ate only "figs and nuts": *Vita* 3.

[104] Josephus records in *Ant.* 15.2.4 that he had first set up "an obscure Priest from Babylon" named Ananel, though the *Talmud, M. Para*, iii, 5 considers him to have been an Egyptian; see Jeremias, pp. 66–69. Herod seems to have elevated four principal families, the Boethusians, that of Ananus, Phiabi, and Kamith; see Jeremias, pp. 193ff. Their popularity may be judged by the well-known lament preserved in *Tos Men* xiii.21.533 and *b. Pes* 57a: "Woe to me for the Boethusians; woe unto me for their curses. Woe to me from the sons of Ananus; woe unto me for their slanders. Woe to me for the sons of Kantheras; woe unto me because of their reed pens. Woe to me for the house of Ishmael ben Phiabi; woe unto me because of their fists. For they are the high priests, their sons are Treasurers, their sons-in-law are Temple Captains, and their servants smite the people with sticks."

Josephus' opinion of these families, even though severely compromised by his relationship with them, is as follows: "And Herod, who was made king by the Romans, did no longer appoint high priests out of the descendants of the Hasmonaean's house, but appointed to that office men of no note and barely priests, with the single exception of Aristobulus" (Mariamme's brother); *Ant.* 20.10. The key to this process, of course, was possession of the high priestly garments, which Herod took over immediately on coming to power and which the Roman governors inherited in succession to him. The

exploitability—of the Pharisaic *Nasi* and Davidic descendant from Baby-lon should examine his celebrated innovation of "the *Prozbul*" and com-pare the attitude it evinces towards "the Rich" or upper middle classes (by this time all with Roman, Herodian, and "Pharisaic" connections) with the attitude in the Letter of James—a true *Zaddik* in the parlance of this period—towards these same classes.[105]

machinations concerning this are well described in *Ant.* 20.10. Of course, what had in effect been instituted from 37 BC onwards was the Greek custom of selling the High Priesthood to principal families of wealth on a temporary basis; cf. *Ant.* 15.11.4.

[105] "Isn't it always the Rich who are against you? Isn't it always their doing when you are dragged before the court [cf. Paul's "only criminals have anything to fear from magistrates"]? Aren't they the ones who insult the honorable name to which you have been dedicated? ... Now an answer to the Rich. Start crying, weep for the miseries that are coming to you. It was a burning fire that you stored up as treasure for the last days [cf. John's attack on "the Pharisees and Sadducees" in Mt 3:7ff. and CD, vi–viii—also referring to "vipers"—on "Riches" and "fornication"]. Laborers mowed your fields and you cheated them ... realize that the cries of the reapers have reached the ears of the Lord of Hosts. In the time of slaughter you went on eating to your heart's content. It was you who condemned the Righteous One and killed him; he offered you no resist-ance. Now be patient brothers until the Lord's coming" (Ja 2:6f. and 5:1ff.). Echoing this passage's climax in the allusion to "Messianic" rain, James actually proclaims "the Lord's coming" or the Messianic return in the Temple on Passover in terms of "coming on the clouds of Heaven" (*E.H.* 2.23.13; cf. CD, vi, 10), thereby linking, as already suggested above, the Dan 7:13 "clouds" allusion with this "rain" imagery as per "the Star Prophecy" and "rising up of the Poor" material in 1QM, xi, 5–xii, 7.

Though early Church accounts have conflated two separate attacks on James (one in the 40s by "the Enemy" Paul in the Temple with one in the 60s by the High Priest Ananus; cf. the two adversaries of "the Righteous Teacher"/"Priest" whose presence dominate the Habakkuk and Ps 37 *Peshers*—"the Pourer out of Lies"/"Scoffer" with "a Tongue full of insults" within the Community and the Wicked Priest outside it), such a proclamation in these circumstances was incendiary. James' attitude, of course, cannot be separated from that of the priestly "Zealots", who having regard for "the Messianic Prophecy" start the final uprising by stopping sacrifice "on behalf of foreigners". We have already signaled their concern "to persuade the Poor to join the Insurrection" by burning all the debtors' records—a demand initially voiced *seventy years* before in the 4 BC events—and their election of the lowly Stone-Cutter Phannias as high priest; see above, p. 80 and *War* 2.1.2 and 2.18.6.

We have also already noted above, p. 17, the common theme of "admission of Gen-tiles" whether into Church or Temple. Hostility towards "Herodians" is but a variation of this theme, as is the Pharisaic/Pauline involvement with them. Note that among the founders of the Church at Antioch, where "the disciples were first called 'Christians'" (Acts 13.1f.), were *Herodians*; and Paul's "Gentile Mission", overriding the demands of the Law and addressed equally "to Jews and Gentiles alike" (cf. Ro 3:22, 1 Co 12:13, etc.), is perfectly in line with the exigencies of *Herodian* family policy.

Timothy, for instance, "whose mother was a Jewess" and who carried Roman citizen-ship, is typical of this "Herodian" mix, as is Paul himself; cf. Ro 16:11, where Paul hints

That this Boethusian Priesthood abjured the doctrine of Resurrection of the Dead is probably attributable to its overseas and earlier roots. These are discernible in both Ecclesiasticus, despite its preservation in all the localities so far described, and the Samaritan "Zadokites" going back to a time before its introduction by the Maccabean/Hassidaean practitioners of "Holy War".[106] The Pharisees true also to their "Hassidaean" roots embraced the new doctrine.

As we have discussed, Simon probably broke with this original

at his own Herodian ties, and Acts 10:15ff., 11:20ff., 16:1ff., and Ga 2:4ff. See also, that "Saulus", a "kinsman of Agrippa who used violence with the People", in *Ant.* 20.9.4, who is the go-between between "the Men of Power" (the Herodians), "the High Priests" and "the principal Pharisees" and Agrippa II in *War* 2.17.3f. and 2.20.1. The constant linking of Saulus in these episodes with the Idumaean convert "Costobarus" and a namesake of Herodias' husband "Antipas" probably reflects his genealogy back through Bernice I to Agrippa I's maternal grandfather Costobarus—note the repetition of the telltale themes of *marriage with nieces* and blatant *fornication* here). "Saulus" is also closely associated in these descriptions with "Philip b. Jacimus", the intimate of Agrippa II *in Caesarea* and Commander of his guard. For Josephus' pointed reference to "Philip's" two daughters, see *War* 4.1.10 and *Vita* 36. For Acts 21:9, Paul's associate, "the Evangelist" Philip has "four virgin daughters who were prophetesses" (*sic*)!

Among other Herodians at Antioch are very likely "Niger" and "Silas" and "the foster brother of" or the individual "brought up with Herod the Tetrarch" is most likely *Paul himself*. This *Herod the Tetrarch* is Herod Antipas, the individual responsible—along with Herodias and Salome—for the death of John the Baptist. Niger and Silas are very likely deserters from Agrippa II's army and are grouped with Queen Helen of Adiabene's two sons or "kinsmen", Monobazus and Kenedaeos, and "John the Essene" as some of *the bravest commanders of the Revolt*; cf. *War* 2.19.2, 2.20.4, 3.2.1ff., and 4.6.1. These Herodian *Men-of-War* present valuable parallels to "the Men of War"/"Men of Violence" allusions at Qumran themselves linked to the mysterious "Idumaeans" of Josephus' allusion—responsible for the death of Ananus and participants, as well, to a certain extent in the War.

Brandon, *op. cit.*, pp. 124ff., has already discussed in detail James' relationship with the Messianic/Zealot lower priesthood, and Josephus describes how the High Priests "ventured to send their slaves to the threshing floors to take the tithes . . . so that *the Poor* among the priests died for want" (italics mine): *Ant.* 20.8.8—developed with greater emphasis on "the Riches" of the High Priests in the context of the stoning of James and the description of Saulus' violent rioting in Jerusalem in *Ant.* 20.9.1ff. Compare this with the parallel sequencing in Acts 6–8, including problems in collection distribution and the reference to the conversion of "a large number of Priests"—also our further remarks below, p. 77.

[106] Ecclesiasticus is still following the Stoic/Cynic/Epicurean philosophy of Ecclesiastes, though in "the Zadokite Statement" at the end, there is a distinct shift; cf. 10:11f, and 15:20 with 49:12, 50:24f., 51:1–22 (extant as a separate psalm at Qumran), and 51:30. The doctrine was probably abjured as much at Leontopolis—the probable venue of "the Boethusians"—as at Samaria both because of its revolutionary tendencies and the innate conservatism of each.

Hassidaean Movement. 2 Macc is anxious to counter the charge that Judas was not a Hassidaean and pointedly ignores the subsequent priest-hoods of Jonathan and Simon—with their "Pharisaic" tendencies—as being unworthy of note. Associated with this Pietistic Sadduceeism that believed in Resurrection of the Dead and was more *zealous for the Law* even than the Pharisees (note Jesus' stance in this regard in the Sermon on the Mount: "Unless your *Righteousness exceed* that of the Scribes and Pharisees . . ." [107]) was the production of apocalyptic literature which in turn gave rise to both the "Messianic" and "Zealot" Movements of the first century CE.[108]

This Pietistic Sadducee Movement did not follow Pharisee *Halachah*, nor its style of expressing this in "traditions" culled from the practice and teachings of "the Fathers"—much like Sunni Islam. Rather, in the style of the Temple Scroll and much other similar literature

---

[107] Mt 5:20. For other statements in Matthew on "Righteousness" and "Righteous Man", see 3:15 on the commands of "all Righteousness" (compare this with Justin Mar-tyr's use of the "all Righteousness" terminology in *Dial.* 93 in summing up the *Hesed* and *Zedek* Commandments and the reference to the "all Righteousness" Commandment in CD, vi, 20 above); 5:6, "blessed are those thirsting for Righteousness"; 5:10, "those persecuted for Righteousness"; 10:41, "He that receives a Righteous Man in the name of a Righteous Man shall receive a Righteous Man's reward (cf. Wisdom); 21:32, "John came in *The Way of Righteousness*" (italics mine—terminology current at Qumran and remi-niscent of statements in Josephus and al-Kirkisani); 25:37, Jesus' followers as "the Righte-ous"; 25:46, "the Righteous (shall go) into eternal life"; 13:43, "then shall the Righteous shine forth as the sun in the Kingdom of their Father" (note the *sonship* motif); and 13:49f., "so shall it be at the end of the world: the angels shall come forward and sever the Wicked from among the Righteous." The reference to Abel as "a Righteous One" in 23:35 comes in the context of comparing his fate with that of Zechariah ben Barach-iah, obviously another *Zaddik*—note the traditional ascription of the Kedron Valley tomb next to James' to his name.

See also Paul in an unguarded moment in 2 Co 11:5ff. amid "Light" imagery referring to the *Hebrew* "Archapostles" as "dishonest workmen disguised as *Servants of Righteousness*" (italics mine). For other Qumranisms, see "Sons of Light" and Light imagery in 1 Thess 5:4ff., Eph 5:9, Col 1:12, and 2 Co 6:11ff. (including reference to "*Beliar*"); the reference to Noah as "preacher of Righteousness" in 2 Pe 2:5; "the service of Righteousness" in Ro 6:17ff.; "weapons of Righteousness" in 2 Co 6:7; adoptionist sonship in Ga 3:24ff., Ro 8:14, Eph 1:5, 1 John 3:1ff.; and 3 John 11's "he that does what is right is a Son of God"; the "heart" imagery in Ro 10:10; the "fragrance and offering" metaphor of 1QS, viii.9 and ix, 4, in 2 Co 2:14ff. (including reference to Qumran-style *Da'at*), Eph 5:2f., and Phil 4:18, and the allusion to "Perfection of Holiness" in 2 Co 7:1. For a combination of "Perfection", "Sons of Light", and "Truth" motifs, see Ja 1:17f.; for "Truth" motifs in Paul, see 2 Thess 2:11, Eph 5:9, Ro 2:20, 9:1, etc.

[108] See below, pp. 105ff, for our contention that the "Zealot" Movement was not new in 4 BC to 7 CE, only what we are delineating as its "Messianic" variation.

at Qumran—including Jubilees—the Movement expressed itself in pseudepigraphic pronouncements of an exoteric kind, whether *halachic* or apocalyptic.

This is the literature found at Qumran. It is massive as it is widely disseminated through the Oriental world via Jewish Christianity, other "Zealot" or "Messianic" Movements—in fact, all groups outside the orbit of Phariseeism and official Judaism—and apocryphal literature. As the disappointment of its Messianic hopes became permanent, its covert tendencies increased, and its ideas grew ever more esoteric. These, in turn, were transmitted to various groups outside the orbit of official Judaism and Christianity in the East, namely Ebionites, Elkasaites, Manichaeans, Gnosticizing groups like Sabaeans, Mandaeans, and at Nag Hammadi, and even Syriac Christians, Nestorians and Jacobites (note the telltale nomenclature).

Many of its fundamental ideas, while distorted by subsequent overlays, were preserved in *Kabbalah*; and traces of them are clearly discernible in Karaite and Islamic literature, most notably in its Shi'ite variation. Indeed, the latter is the Islamic counterpart to the "Zadokite Movement" as we have described it—as Sunnism is to Rabbinism.[109] Judas, following in the footsteps of Simeon and Onias before him, is the quintessential *Zaddik* or Righteous Teacher-type, who in Rechabite/"Essene"-style "withdrew into the wilderness"—usage current at Qumran—and lived "like a wild animal" (presumably in caves), eating "nothing but wild plants to avoid contracting defilement". He is the

---

[109] For the pre-existent *Zaddik*-notion at Qumran and its connections with the *Logos* doctrine of John's Gospel and the incarnate *Imam* doctrine of Shi'ism, as well as its relation to Proverbs' "The-*Zaddik*-the-Foundation-of-the-World", the Gospel of Thomas, and the *Zohar*, see above p. 33. The constant reiteration of the notion of *Da'at* ("Knowledge"), itself tied up with the "Justification" processes of Is 53:11, in all Qumran sectarian texts easily translates itself into what goes by the name of *Gnosis* in other milieus.

For the comparison of "the coming of the Son of Man" to "the days of Noah" amid imagery regarding the passing away of "Heaven and Earth", see Mt 24:34ff., already cited above. For Noah as the "Perfection" ideal or "the Perfect Man" who was, therefore, like Shem and Melchizedek "born circumcised", see *ARN* 2.5 and *Zohar* 59b. For the relationship of "the Poor" and "the Pious" to Phineas and David, see the section on "Balak and Balam" preceding "Phineas" in *Zohar* 193a–197a. Not surprisingly, this section knows "Yunus and Yamburus" (cf. the material in CD, vi–ix, including Ms. B). Though the *Zohar* may be the thirteenth-century forgery it is often considered to be, the whole "Phineas" section, which includes reference to the Book of Enoch and "the supernal Priest"—as well as "the future Jerusalem", "the celestial Temple", "the supernal Israel" and "the Primal Adam"—should be treated very carefully.

type of the warrior High Priest presented in the War Scroll.[110] This is not to say that any Qumran identifications should be attached to Judas, either in the *pesher*s, which are late, or the Damascus Document,

---

[110] For the role of this warrior High Priest and the priests generally (in their white "battle dress" in the War Scroll which de Vaux refers to as "apocalyptic"), see 1 QM, vii, 10–ix, 9. The war in question is not metaphorical, though it is idealized. Here, the same preconceptions which inhibit coming to grips with the metaphor embodied in the term "Zadok" now dictate an allegorical approach to the war. Attention to literary genre and care over literary devices would help. That these priests do not follow the Pharisaic policy of compromise with foreigners is plain: "they are not to defile the oil of their priestly annointment with the blood of vain heathen". One battle priest is separate and goes up and down the line encouraging the ranks. This is undoubtedly the same priest who "is chosen by the vote of his brothers" to officiate on "the Day of Vengeance" (xv, 4–7). This "Vengeance" is to be accomplished by "the Saints" or "Holy Ones of his People", as well as "the Poor" and "those downtrodden in the dust", with the help of the Heavenly Warrior Angels. Compare this with the employment of these Angels for just such a purpose in 2 Macc and the general discussion of the angel Michael in Milik's "*Milkî-sedq et Milkî-reša'* ... ", pp. 106ff. and 141ff., van der Woude, pp. 304ff., and Fitzmyer's "Further Light on Melchizedek", *JBL*, 86, 1967, pp. 32ff.

Compare, too, this Priest's "election" with both "Phannius" in the last phases of the uprising and that of Judas Maccabee discussed above. We have, also, noted the parallel theme of the election of James as successor and head of "the Jerusalem Church" in early Church literature, and its counterpart the election of "the Twelfth Apostle" in Acts. Though some accounts speak of a direct appointment of James by Jesus (Gos Th 12 and Ps *Rec* 1.43), others generally agree that an "election" of some kind occurred (*E.H.* 2.1.2–4, 2.23.4, 7.19.1 and Jerome, *loc. cit.*; cf. *E.H.* 4.22.3f. on Simeon bar Cleophas' succession after James' martyrdom, because "being a cousin of the Lord—namely, the son of his uncle—it was *the universal demand* that he should be *the second*" —italics mine. If Acts had at this point discussed *the succession to Jesus* and not *the succession to Judas Iscariot*, then, of course, the puzzling appearance of James in 12:17 would need no further explanation).

Whether this avenging battle priest is identical with the "High Priest" who rises to recite the War Prayer from the Rule and also all their Hymns, and generally "arranges all of the order of formation according to what is written in the War Scroll" (xv, 4f.) is difficult to determine from the context. Compare this with Eisler, pp. 262ff., interpreting Lk 3:14ff. in terms of "John's field sermon"; also Jesus' arranging of those who follow him "into the wilderness" in military formation (Mk 6:40). We have already called attention to such battle order, "warrior angels", and "the horsemen who come like clouds" over the earth to rain "Judgement on all that grows on it", which is mentioned in the context of reference to the "Messiah" who "justifies the true Judgement of God in the midst of mankind"—"the Mighty One" whose foot will be on the necks of his enemies, who will smite the Nations, and whose "sword will devour the flesh of the Sinners filling the land with glory"; 1QM, xi–xii. For Enoch 90:9ff., Judas was "a Great Horn" and probably even "a Great Sword" (cf. 2 Macc 16:16), an appellation probably echoed in Ps 148:14: "He lifted up the horn for His People; the praise for all his Pious Ones" (that is, *Hassidim*) quoted in the Hebrew version of Ben Sira (51:15). Note that Philo,

the date of which, for the moment must remain indeterminate.[111]

Judas, too, is probably observing the extreme purity regulations associated with lifelong Naziritism, reflected in both Philo's and Josephus' description of "Essene" practices—including sexual continency. As such, he is probably the model for John the Baptist, Jesus, and James, one could also add Simeon bar Cleophas, Jesus' probable second brother, called "a Rechabite Priest"—read "Essene"—in Eusebius.

Where sexual continency is at issue, though argument from silence is not a proof, in each of the above-mentioned cases it offers a strong presumption. As far as James is concerned, all early Church accounts make a point of calling him "Holy" or "a Nazirite from his mother's womb" (parodied to a certain extent by Paul's rival claims in Ga 1:15f.;

Quod Omnis 12.75 and 13.91, knows very well that the name "Essenes" derives from the word "Piety", that is, "Hassidaeans".

[111] Cf. below, p. 94–96. The dating of the Damascus Document is complex because of one exemplar considered "early" on paleographic grounds. Many point to the doctrinal shift that appears to occur between it and the Community Rule on the issue of "the Messiah of (from) Aaron and Israel" in the former (viii, 24; xii, 23f.; and xiv, 18) and "the Messiahs of Aaron and Israel" in the latter (ix, 11) as a dating aid. R. H. Charles, *APOT*, ii, Oxford, 1913, pp. 795ff., argued that the former related to an Israelite father and an Aaronite mother. G. Margoliouth, "The Sadducean Christians of Damascus", *The Expositor*, vols 37–38, 1911–12, pp. 499–517 and 213–235, made the initial identification of this with Jesus.

Curiously enough, and unremarked in subsequent commentary, the possibly plural usage in 1QS may imply a series of "Messiahs of Aaron and Israel", as much as it does *two separate* messiahs. When it is appreciated that the usages *'amod/'omdim*, used in the exegesis of Ezek 44:15, carry something of the sense of "be resurrected" with them (cf. "the Standing One" in Ps *Rec* 2.7ff. and the phrase, "stand up", used with just such a connotation in *Zohar* 63a on "Noah") and that the *Messianic* "shoot out of Israel and Aaron" (after whom the teacher comes) of CD.i.7 has already died, then it will be realized that these usages, accompanying all references to "the Messiah of Aaron and Israel" and also coupled with references to "Zadok" and "the *Yoreh ha-Zedek*" in CD, v, 4f. and vi, 10f., are eschatological. Since, as we have remarked, the usages surrounding them are always singular, never plural, it may be we have an idiomatic appellative here—which seems to be the case as per the suggestion of Milik, *op. cit.*, pp. 151f., pp. xv–xvi are inserted before p. ix; then, in fact, ms. A ends on p. xiv with fragments from 1QS, vii, 4ff. Since CD quite properly ends with the pious hope for the return (or "resurrection") of the Messiah of Aaron and Israel who *"will pardon their sins"* (xiv, 18—italics mine), the conclusion is that, whoever the Cairo redactors of the Damascus Document might have been, they also knew materials from the Community Rule and they, anyhow, did not see the two documents as particularly separate. Also the usage, regardless of epigraphy, seems *very definitely* to have been *singular*—i.e. a *single* Messiah from the two roots of Aaron and Israel—and this seems to have been borne out in the publication of more recent texts.

cf. the stress on Nazirite-oath procedures in Paul's confrontations with James). In Judas' case, any children would have changed the political picture for succeeding generations considerably; however, none are mentioned.[112] Contrariwise, Judas' uncle Simon took care to dispose of the children of his brother Jonathan, who were killed under very questionable circumstances, thereby insuring the succession of his own heirs.[113]

At this point one is probably witnessing the break between the Hassidaeans supporting Judas and holding his memory sacred and the faction increasingly influencing the actions of Simon (by this time already beginning to be called "Pharisees") in his machinations to gain endorsement for his priesthood from the several Syrian kings and pretenders. Judas is simply from the original and more Pietistic wing of the Zadokite Movement and proves it by the manner of his life—imitated to a certain extent by John the Baptist and Jesus—and in the "Zealot" manner of his

---

[112] We have discussed why the note in 2 Macc 14:25 about Judas' "marrying and settling down" should not be taken too seriously; above, p. 14. For the Essenes, see *War*. 2.8.2ff. The description, after the one indicating their contempt "for Riches", of their view of oil as a defilement precisely accords with James' habits. Together with the description of "bathing in cold water", it points the way towards the harmonization of James' and *Banus'* bathing habits noted above, p. 12. James only abjured *Roman*-style *hot* baths, where *oil was used, not ritual immersion*; compare this with Josephus' description in *War* 2.8.3 of how the "Essenes" prefer "being unwashed"). The original model for such an extension of the rules of priestly purity, ultimately going back, as Ecclesiasticus well knew, to "the zeal of Phineas", was Elijah, but the ideology underwent a formidable development in the person of Judas.

Of course 1QM, vii, 1–7 provides the best explanation for Judas' family condition, as it also does John's, Jesus', James' and the people of Qumran generally: "No toddling child or woman is to enter their camps *from the moment they leave Jerusalem* to go to war until they return . . . They shall all be freely enlisted [i.e. "volunteers"] for war, *Perfect in spirit and body* and prepared for and ready for *the Day of Vengeance*. Moreover, any man who is not cleansed from a bodily discharge on the day of battle is not to go down with them. *For Holy Angels march with their hosts*" (italics mine). The echo of this in the use of the word "camp" in the Damascus Document and "volunteer" in the Community Rule and 1 Macc 2:43 (used to describe "Hassidaeans") should not be overlooked. More recently published Qumran texts also refer to this idea of "Volunteers for War".

We have noted Eisler's presentation, above, p. 58, of John the Baptist as opposition High Priest of the Last Times, calling his followers to the pursuit of Holy War or, as CD, xii, 22–3 puts it, "This is the rule for camp-settlements and those who live accordingly at the End of the Era of Wickedness until the rising ["standing up"] of the Messiah of Aaron and Israel"; cf. also CD, xiv, 18 above. So strict was the sect in the pursuit of ritual cleanliness that some have taken the Temple Scroll as implying copulation was forbidden in Jerusalem—cf. Uriah the Hittite's query to David when advised to enjoy his wife: "Are not the ark and the men of Israel and Judah lodged in tents?" (2 Sam 11:11).

[113] 1 Macc 13:17f.

death—i.e., he makes "a pious end" as do John, Jesus, and James among numerous others after him. So "zealous for the Law", in fact, is John that he continually harangues the Herodian monarch, Herod Antipas, over a minor point of law—incomprehensible to anyone but the specialist—until the latter is forced to put him to death.[114] It is interesting to note that aside from the relatively late example of Rabbi Akiba, who in any event is ridiculed by his Rabbinic contemporaries, this is not the Pharisaic way;[115] nor is it Josephus' or Paul's, both of whom identify themselves as Pharisees and prefer the obsequious self-abasement before

---

[114] Cf. Mt 14:1–12 and Mk 6:14–29 with *Ant.* 18.5.2 and Slavonic Josephus. Note that Slavonic Josephus knows the precise point, violation of the levirite law of marriage. Where al-Kirkisani's "Zadok" and Qumran are concerned, there is the additional issue of *marriage with a niece*, Herodias being Agrippa I's sister (as *Ant.* 18.5.1 is quick to point out while missing the connection with John's execution; cf. the tangle regarding Costobarus and Antipas, who was supposed to be the son of the Temple Treasurer Helcias, with regard to Saulus' genealogy above, pp. 54–55. This would make Antipas, Saulus' cousin). This, in turn, links this confrontation to the general hostility to Agrippa I's family and the recurrent theme of "fornication" at Qumran and in the Jerusalem Church. *Antiquities* knows that John was put to death as a public agitator—therefore the "Jewish" punishment of beheading—because Herod "feared the great influence John had over the people might lead to some rebellion". Note its prototype and only recorded precedent in the Second Temple period, the beheading of the last Maccabean Priest/King Antigonus, above, p. 52. The New Testament portrait of Salome dancing at Herod's birthday party is childish fantasy, though in this instance consistent with its religio-political aims of acquitting the Romans or their appointees of complicity in the deaths of or malice towards "Christian" leaders.

Indeed, according to its polemic, non-Jews never have any difficulty in recognizing Jesus' messiahship, whereas his closest disciples like Peter sink into the Sea of Galilee for *lack of Faith* or *deny him three times* on his death-night. Caesarean legionnaires—whom Josephus identifies as the most brutal in Palestine (*Ant.* 19.9.2)—are complimented for their "devoutness" and "generosity to Jewish causes" (Acts 10:1ff. means, of course, Agrippa I; see below, p. 79. The provenance of this episode becomes clear from the reference to "Italica", the birthplace in Spain of both Trajan and Hadrian). That Herod, Pilate's wife, Pilate, and a Roman centurion recognize John or Jesus as *Zaddikim* in Mk 6:20, Mt 27:19, 24, and Lk 23:47 is consistent with the working method we are describing.

One particularly appropriate example of this kind, in the context of "receiving and keeping table fellowship with Sinners" (read "Gentiles"—cf. Paul in Ga 2:15), is the statement that "there is more joy in Heaven over the repentance of one Sinner than ninety-nine Righteous Ones" ("in the wilderness"); Lk 15:1ff. Often the motifs of "prostitutes" (read "fornicators"), "publicans" or "tax-collectors", including people who do not abstain from *table fellowship*, are added for emphasis. The "wine-bibbing" assertion (Mt 11:19; Lk 7:34) serves to distinguish Jesus from James—and other presumably "Rechabite" Nazirite-types—who, of course, *shunned wine*.

[115] *P. Ta'an* 68d. Yohanan b. Torta's retort to R. Akiba over the messiahship of Bar Kochba, "Grass will grow on your grave before the Messiah comes", is proverbial; cf. *b. Sanh* 97b. Akiba in the "Zealot"/"Messianic" tradition is operating within the

Romans and their Palestinian appointees of Rabbi Yohanan ben Zacchai to martyrdom.[116] Nor was it the way of Simon Maccabee.

It was, however, the way of the extreme wing of the Zealot Party, conserving Ecclesiasticus and Qumran material on Masada, namely "making a Pious end" in the manner recommended by 2 Macc. That they expected the imminent return of their bodies is implicit in the *purposeful* burial of the "standing-up-of-the-bones" passage from Ezekiel under the synagogue floor.[117] These "Saints" whom Josephus maligns, derogatorily referring to them as *"Sicarii"*—terminology which has stuck—were Hassidaean *Zaddikim par excellence*.[118]

The behavior of Aristobulus' supporters on the Temple Mount during the siege of Jerusalem and its fall in 63 BC is illustrative of the mentality of the whole "Zadokite"/"Zealot" Movement. As we have noted, Hyrcanus, following the policy of Alexandra and her presumed relative Simeon ben Shetach (a Pharisee "Father"), is certainly the Pharisaic

framework of "the Star Prophecy" and not cynically manipulating it, subjecting it to mockery as Yohanan b. Zacchai, Josephus, and others did.

[116] For Paul's claims to be a Pharisee, see Phil 3:5 (echoed in Acts 23:5 and 26:5); for Josephus', *Vita* 2.

[117] See Y. Yadin, *Masada*, London, 1966, pp. 187ff. In his usual manner, Yadin is impressed with finding Chapter 37 of Ezekiel buried underneath the synagogue floor, but at first sees no *special* significance in it. Finding also the last two chapters of Deuteronomy dealing with the *blessing and death of Moses*, he finally decides he has come upon a *genizah*! In like manner, finding a fragment of the Songs of the Sabbath Sacrifice from Qumran Cave IV at Masada, he sees this as proving only that "some Essenes" joined the refugees and took refuge on Masada with "the Zealots"; pp. 173–4 and "The Excavation of Masada", *IEJ*, 15, 1965, pp. 81–2, 105–8. Of course, this ignores the fact that, strictly speaking, the partisans of Masada were those Josephus calls *"Sicarii"*.

[118] The name *"Sicarii"* was derived from the Roman *sica*—a type of curved Arab-style dagger they carried under their cloaks; *Ant.* 20.8.10; *War* 2.13.3 and 2.17.6. Note, however, that Pilate was the first to use such enlightened methods of crowd control in Palestine. Driver, pp. 183ff., thinks he has found a reference to this weapon in 1QM, v, 12; and Brandon, pp. 39f. and 203f., thinks he sees it in the episode of Lk 22:38 when the disciples appear to be armed with two concealed weapons in the *Sicarii* manner. One should also note the reference in *Apost. Const.* 8.25 (v. mss.), identifying Thaddaeus with "Judas the Zealot" and the further variation of the latter name in "Judas Iscariot". Jn 6:71 speaks of "Judas of Simon Iscariot" (read "brother of") and Lk 6:16 speaks of "Judas of James" (read "brother of"). "Simon Iscariot" is, of course, equivalent to "Simon the Zealot" (cf. also "Cananaean") and his place in Gospel Apostle lists approximates that of Jesus' *second brother* "Simeon bar Cleophas", e.g., "James the son of Alphaeus (read Cleophas), Simon, who was called the Zealot, and Judas (the son) of James" (Acts 21:20, of course, testifies to the overwhelming number of "Zealots for the Law" the movement actually consisted of). For a complete discussion of these confusing matters, see below, pp. 78f.

Priestly contender and cleaves to a Pharisaic political line as we have expounded it. Who are Aristobulus' supporters? They are a combination of nationalists and Sadducees. That they are also "the popular party" is indisputable, belying the oft-quoted testimony of Josephus in this regard, just as the popularity of Aristobulus' son, Antigonus, puts the lie to any claim that Pollio's (Hillel's?) typically Pharisaic recommendation to open the gates to Herod could in any way be considered popular.

But what kind of "Sadducees"?[119] Their behavior refutes, as nothing else can, the idea that they could have anything in common with the

[119] The most extensive testimony of the popularity of the Pharisees (as opposed to "the Sadducees") comes in relation to John Hyrcanus, *Ant.* 13.10.5–6; however this cannot represent the state of affairs 200 years later at the time of the Uprising against Rome. In addition, it contradicts what the *Antiquities* says about the followers of "the Fourth Philosophy". Discussing the "Innovations" of Judas and Saddok and the calamities their movement brought upon the nation, Josephus states, *Ant.* 18.1.1: "So great did the alteration and change from the customs of our fathers tend to bring all to destruction who thus banded together, for Judas and Saddok who introduced a fourth philosophic sect among us and had a great many followers therein, filled our state with tumults at that time and laid the foundations of future miseries by their system of philosophy which we were before unacquainted with ... and that rather because the infection which spread thence among our younger men, who were zealous for it, brought our nation to destruction."

The word "infection" was also used to describe the itinerant messengers the Emperor Claudius cautioned the Jews against receiving in his famous letter to the Alexandrians; cf. H. Idris Bell, *Jews and Christians in Egypt*, London, 1934, pp. 25ff. Paul, too, is described in similar terms in Acts 17:7, a passage that makes it clear that the problem concerned "Messianic" messengers like the Apostles: "These are the people who have been turning the whole world upside down ... They have broken every one of Caesar's edicts by claiming there is another emperor, Jesus"; and in Acts 24:16: "The plain truth is that we find this man a perfect pest; he stirs up trouble among the Jews the world over and is a ringleader of the Nazoraean Heresy"; cf. 16:20–22. For a recital of these "calamities" with inverted polemical intent, see all versions of "the Little Apocalypse": Mt 24:1ff.; Mk 13:1ff.; and Lk 21:5ff.

But the Pharisees are not even the popular party in Alexander Jannaeus' time, since in spite of his cruelties the people rally to him; nor in Aristobulus' or Antigonus' time: cf. *Ant.* 15.3.3. Josephus in *Ant.* 17.2.4 puts their number at "6,000", the same figure he gave in 13.14.2 for the number of Alexander's supporters; cf. 2 Macc 8:2 putting Judas' supporters at "6,000" and Jeremias' comments, p. 252. We must remember, too, that Josephus himself was working, usually in an uncritical manner, from sources—in this instance, probably Nicolaus of Damascus, an intimate of Herod. Since we are dealing with a 200-year period, a party having a degree of popularity at one point might not even be the same 100 years later—and Josephus doesn't take the trouble to inform us to which period his sources relate. From 4 BC to 70 CE, and perhaps beyond, it is clearly "the Zealot Party" which is the popular one, as "nationalist" parties predictably are— not the Pharisees with their restrictive religious practices and contempt for the *'Am ha-Arez* (the "Zealot"/"Zadokite"/"Nazoraean" sectaries?).

corrupt Sadducee Priesthood introduced under Herod and the Procurators. They are of a different stripe altogether, of which the "Herodian
Sadducees" are barely a caricature. They are "zealous" priests doing service for God on the Temple Mount even as the carnage going on around
them ultimately overwhelms them, eliciting even the grudging admiration
of their Roman conquerors. They are what we have identified as "Zadokites", that is, the zealous Lower Priesthood, and very probably received
part of their training at Qumran, as Josephus himself relates he received
part of his training in a later period living three years among rock caves
with a person he chooses to identify in his usual cryptic style only as
"*Banus*" (probably meaning "Bather").[120] Josephus is canny, always careful to cover his footsteps and not reveal the overt role of the priesthood—the lower at first (which would have inevitably implicated him),
but eventually the higher—in the so-called "Zealot Movement" (and/or
"the Messianic") in the revolution against Rome.[121]

[120] *Vita* 2; cf. Ga 1:17–18, where Paul reports he went off immediately after his vision
"into Arabia", possibly for "three years". Luke's knowledge of Paul's activities is probably
defective, since he states in Acts 9:22, covering the same period that "Saul's power
steadily increased and he was able to throw the *Jews who dwelled at Damascus* into complete
confusion" (italics mine; cf. below, p. 66).

For the resemblance of "*Banus*" to James see above, p. 12. That the bathing practices of
both are highlighted by tradition is important in itself. We have already seen how Josephus'
description of the Essenes points the way towards resolving discrepancies between how
both are pictured. Both Eusebius and Jerome, *loc. cit.*, also link the question of James' bathing habits with anointing with oil, and Epiphanus in *Haeres.* 78.14 confirms: "he never
bathed in the (*public*) *baths*"; but, of course, if he went on the Temple Mount in the manner
described, he underwent *ritual purification.* Josephus' charming transposition into Greek of
"clothing that grew on trees" links up with the stress in all early Church sources of James'
wearing only "linen", as it does the right won by the Lower Priesthood to wear linen shortly
before the Uprising (directly following the account of James' death, the High Priests robbing "the Poor", and "Saulus'" violent behavior: *Ant.* 20.9.6).

[121] The *Autobiography* itself seems to have been written to combat damaging charges
made in this regard against Josephus by Justus of Tiberius and others: *Vita* 65 and 74.
For instance, it completely contradicts the claims made by Josephus in the *War* inflating
his role in Galilee, though the business activities he describes in the *Vita* are no less
shameful. He also as we have seen above, p. 37, completely contradicts himself on his
personal assessment of his erstwhile associate, the High Priest Ananus.

Now and then he lets down his guard enough to reveal "the Star" Prophecy as the
moving force behind the Uprising against Rome and the cessation of sacrifices in the
Temple on behalf of all foreigners—including the Emperor—by the Lower Priesthood
as the signal for its commencement. We have noted his mission to Rome to obtain the
release of "certain priests" of his acquaintance above, p. 12. He describes them in *Vita* 3
as "very excellent persons" (*Righteous?*), who "on a small and trifling charge were put into
bonds and sent to Rome to plead their cause before Caesar" (note the Pauline-like appeal
to Caesar, but the non-Pauline-like note of vegetarianism—Paul's pretensions in 1 Co

Qumran can almost be considered a training center for the Jerusalem Priesthood. As the "monastery" is probably very near the site where Judas Maccabee and his nine "*Zaddikim*" hid in "caves" (accepting the testimony of 2 Macc), one cannot resist the admittedly speculative suggestion that it might have been "founded" by John Hyrcanus to commemorate his return to the "Sadducee" Party of his uncle, much as his father had embellished the family's ancestral tombs at Modein before him. It is not sectarian until it is rendered sectarian after the assumption of power by Herod in alliance with the Roman-inclined Pharisees.

8:13f. notwithstanding—and abstention from "table fellowship"). He also reports the ritual shipwreck; cf. Acts 27:1ff. In Rome he makes the acquaintance of Nero's wife Poppea, whom in *Ant.* 20.8.11 he describes as "a religious woman", as well as the contacts he later employs so effectively to save himself and launch himself into Imperial favor. Poppea's obvious interest in "Jewish" causes (or "Christian"—in Claudian Rome there was no distinction; note she takes the side of the Temple Wall "Zealots" against Agrippa II) parallels Helen of Adiabene's; *Ant.* 20:2. The "Christian" character of the latter's conversion emerges from the person of the Pauline-like "Ananias" and Helen's own intractable opposition to circumcision. In contrast, her more "Zealot"-minded son—and those "kinsmen" who later distinguish themselves in the Uprising against Rome (cf. above, p. 55)—embraces it. The *Christian* character of her conversion is echoed in Syriac sources, the antiquity of which is given additional support in *E.H.* 1.13.1ff. and 2.1.6ff. That the matter of famine relief, whether involving Helen or Paul, the "Agbarus legend", and the issue of Thaddaeus/Theudas/Judas Thomas lie behind the distortion of these same in Acts 5:34, 11:19, etc., is hinted at in *E.H.* 2.12.1ff.'s remarks on Helen; cf. below, pp. 79f.

Who the priestly beneficiaries of Josephus' rescue mission were and what the "trifling" charge was are interesting questions. In addition to Helcias and Ishmael retained at the pleasure of Poppea in the wake of the Temple Wall Affair, Josephus reports that the High Priest Ananias and Ananus "the Temple Captain" were earlier sent to Rome in bonds "to give an account of what they had done to Caesar"; *Ant.* 20.6.2. This latter controversy apparently also involved both Jewish and Samaritan "Innovators" persuading "the multitude to revolt against the Romans" and a crucifixion at Lydda (also reflected in Jewish "Messianic" tradition).

It would appear, as well, to be the occasion of the consolidation of relations between Agrippa II and Ananus. It may be protested that Josephus was too young at this point for such a mission, which is true; however, his youth may have been just the reason for sending him to Poppea in the first place, as Roman sources make no secret of her apparent preference for young men; cf. Tacitus, *Annales* 13.44ff. She evidently found him quite pleasing as he returned, as he himself attests, a success, bearing "many presents" from her. Josephus tells us he was twenty-six at the time, which places the episode in 63–64, the year after the execution of James. Nero, who married Poppea in 62, proceeded to kick her to death not long before the Uprising. However these things may be, we might be dealing with more "Essene"-like priests, as Josephus' account implies. Given the fairly positive attitude evinced in Josephus' writing towards both *Banus* and James, the possibility cannot be ruled out of a connection between these priests and events centering around the death of the latter described above.

Josephus and priests like him (John the Baptist for instance) probably went out to it for a two- or three-year novitiate period as young men, where they were indoctrinated with "Zadokite" ideas.[122] As coin distribution testifies, it flourishes under the Maccabees; it is not inimical to them, though it is somewhat opposed to Phariseeism and any Pharisaic tendencies among them. It only begins to decline with the coming of the Romans under Pompey and the assumption of power by Herod the Great.

The Nahum *Pesher*, already referred to, though condemning crucifixion—as any good "Messianic" text would in this period—is not otherwise antagonistic to Alexander Jannaeus, but rather to the presumable Pharisees he crucifies. The sectaries at Qumran knew their history as well as anyone else, in any event as well as Josephus, who may even have received some of his training with them, and this is just the point. The example of Alexander Jannaeus is cited for polemical purposes only, to condemn those who are guilty of having invited the Romans into the country in the first place (namely, the Pharisees, as they had previously the Seleucids under Demetrius and probably at the time of Judas Maccabee) and to condemn the effects of this presence, that is, the crucifixion of the Just, which the Romans indulged in so promiscuously.

At this point, it is helpful to observe that the Damascus Document

---

[122] See 1QS, vi, 13–23. Cf. *Vita* 2 and *War* 2.8.7, where Josephus shows extensive knowledge of "Essene" customs; also Cross, p. 86, n. 61. It would have been impossible for anyone going "into the wilderness" in this region to have remained unaware of, or for that matter, unaffected by a settlement the size of Qumran.

Acts 9:3ff., after delineating Paul's commission to arrest "those of the Way" at "the synagogues in Damascus" and his vision on "the road to Damascus", speaks of how he "threw the Jewish settlement at Damascus into total confusion". Ga 1:17ff., following Paul's claims to being "specially chosen from his mother's womb", knows no *Damascus-road* vision. Rather it recounts how he went *directly* "into Arabia" (which is usually taken to refer to the area around Petra but may indeed mean further, even as far East as Edessa or Adiabene) and spent "three years" there and later in Damascus. CD, vi, 5; vii, 21, 35's references to "the Land of Damascus" and "the New Covenant" associated with it—from which the followers of "the Lying" Scoffer who "departed from the Way" by abandoning the Law, and "the Men of War" who deserted to them, are to be excluded—are well known.

Of particular interest is the exegesis in CD vii, 18ff. identifying "the Star" as "the Interpreter of the Law who came to Damascus". We have already noted above, pp. 14–15, the relationship of Paul's Damascus-road encounter to the Emmaus-road encounter associated with members of Jesus' family. Ga 1:15f., in parodying James' "being Holy from his mother's womb" and other Nazirite claims, also makes a claim for "the Son in" Paul. Seen in this light, the possible parody of both the Emmaus-road encounter and Qumran "Star" exegesis implicit in Acts' Damascus-road episode should not be discounted.

actually prescribes death as the punishment for those "whose sworn testimony has condemned another to be executed according to the laws of the Gentiles".[123] It is also striking to see that the sectaries do not hesitate to call by name foreign opponents whose regimes are now regarded as past history, i.e., "(Deme)trius King of the Greeks".

It is another thing with regard to the present when their peculiar and by now familiar code comes into play. As anyone familiar with the technique of literary criticism will immediately grasp, the thrust of this commentary actually relates to the first century CE, "the period when the Seekers after Smooth Things hold sway", as do most of the other *pesharim* at Qumran, its examples being provided by way of historical confirmation of the points it wishes to make.[124] "The *Kittim*" in the Nahum *Pesher*—as in Dan 11:30—regardless of how the terminology might be used in any other literary work, specifically denotes "the Romans", since these are portrayed not only as being distinct from the Greeks under Demetrius, but as having succeeded them.[125]

---

[123] CD, ix, 1–2; Gaster's translation of sworn as "a private vow" and Vermes' "vows another to destruction" make the extremely important thrust—clear from its placement at the head of what one should designate the civil law section—incomprehensible.

[124] Since the *pesharim* are found in single copies only, there is general agreement on paleographic grounds on their fairly "late" character. The subject of the Nahum *Pesher* is "the Seekers after Smooth Things", the period in which they hold sway (i.e., according to our interpretation, the Herodian Period), its effects, and the coming dispersal of "their community" (note the stress on "leading Many astray"—the inversion of our interpretation of Is 53:11f.; "Lying" and "the Lying Tongue"—cf. Ja 3:1ff.; and the grouping of "those who walk in Lying and Evil during the Last Days" with "the Seekers after Smooth Things"). Driver, p. 94, attributes the suggestion that "the Seekers after *Halakot*" is a parody of that favorite Pharisaic legal activity "seeking *Halachot*"—equivalent in its thrust to the play on "*Zaddik*" and "Zadok" we have identified—to Brownlee. But there is, also, its wider, more generic, sense, applying to all those who sought accommodation with the Romans, namely, Pharisees, Herodians, Pauline Christians, "the Congregation of Traitors", and "the Men of War".

[125] The same conclusion is unavoidable in relation to 1QpHab's use of the expression; cf. Driver's detailed discussion, pp. 197–216, which for command of difficult materials and its scope is unrivaled. Where the Habakkuk *Pesher* is concerned, this is also true because of the presence in it of at least three exegetical interpretations identifiably current in 70 CE, *viz*. the material on "the Delay of the *Parousia*" (vii, 10ff, applied only to "'*Osei ha-Torah*" or "the Doers of the Law"), the "Jamesian" exegesis of Hab 2:4 (viii, 1ff., applied only to "Doers of the Law in the House of Judah", meaning *only Torah-doing Jews* or *only Jews walking in the Way of Torah*), and the use of "Lebanon" imagery (xii, 2ff., which *ARN* 4.5 definitively ties to the fall of the Temple in 70 CE) amid eschatological allusion again to "the Simple of Judah doing *Torah*", "the Wicked Priest robbing the Poor", and "the Day of Judgement"; see above, p. 19. We have also provided the provenance for the alliance of "the Lying Scoffer," "the Men of War," and "the Congregation of

There is no doubt as to how and why the monastery was destroyed after the events depicted in the Nahum *Pesher*. It was destroyed in the struggle between Aristobulus/Antigonus and Hyrcanus/Herod, very probably by Herod himself. As governor of Galilee he hunted down insurgent leaders like Hezekiah, who had the support of the "Sadducee"-dominated Sanhedrin. When he was able, he then turned on this Sanhedrin killing all its members, except for the two Pharisees, Pollio and Sameas, the latter having already recognized Herod's "leadership potential" after the Hezekiah affair.[126]

On his way towards his final assault on Jerusalem, he even stopped to brutally and mercilessly dispose of the "Galileans" of Sepphoris who had fled to "caves" with all their families.[127] In effect, this is the end of

Traitors" (cf. CD, i, 14ff. and viii, 38) with "the Seekers after Smooth Things"; see above, p. 32. Our explanation of the generic use of expressions like "Seekers after Smooth Things"—in this instance applying to those who sought accommodation with the Romans—and our identification of "the Violent Ones" as Herodian "Men of War" (including Josephus' "Idumaeans"), who first support the Uprising and later desert it (cf. *War* 6.8.2), goes a long way towards clarifying many of these seemingly complex relationships.

[126] A more obsequious speech is hard to imagine. The identification of Pollio and Sameas awaits final clarification. G. F. Moore, *Judaism*, i, 1927, Cambridge, p. 313 and n. 89a, puts the case for an identification with Abtalion. There is little disagreement that Sameas is Shammai (though some would prefer Shemaiah, if the two can in fact really be distinguished). I would submit that Josephus thinks he is talking about *Hillel and Shammai*, as his whole presentation implies they are *well known*. In any event, the *Talmud* notes proudly that both Shemaiah and Abtalion were descendants of "Sennacherib" (i.e., foreign converts, or is the allusion metaphoric?); *b. Sanh* 96b and *Gittin* 57b.

See above, p. 24, for Josephus' confusion of Pollio and Sameas with each other, as well as his additional confusions of Pharisees and Essenes generally. Most scholars will agree that Hillel was patriarch at some point during Herod's reign, that is, *c.* 30 BC; J. Neusner, *First Century Judaism in Crisis*, Abingdon, 1975, gives a *terminus ad quem* of about 20 CE, pp. 49–55, but rightly refers to these years as "obscure". Since there seem to be two sets of events referred to in Josephus, one dealing with the Sanhedrin that attempted to put Herod on trial say between 55 and 50 BC, the other with his destruction of the followers of Antigonus after 37 BC, a way out of the impasse is to assume *both* presentations contain some truth and that Josephus was referring to both sets of pairs, the earlier around 60–55 BC and the later around 35–30 BC.

[127] *Ant.* 14.15.4f. Josephus labors over this episode in loving detail. It includes the "Zealot" suicide of the old man, his wife, and "seven sons" while Herod begs them to desist, which we have already treated above, p. 41, including its parody in Mk 12:20ff., Lk 20:29ff., and Mt 22:25ff. The episode, together with the martyrdom of Eleazar, has received its literary transformation in 2 and 4 Macc; and the Eleazar material has received an additional transformation via *Gematria*—including the allusion to cave-dwelling—in the "*Taxo*" material in As. Mos. 9:1ff. In 4 Macc "Eleazar" has seven sons. The cave-like

the first stage of our Zadokite Movement. Its pious priests have been slaughtered on the Temple Mount by the Romans and their Pharisaic collaborators. Others fall victim to Herod's destruction of the Sanhedrin and though the struggle is protracted, their fate is sealed with Herod's final assumption of power around 37 BC. In the course of these events, the monastery is burned (giving way to the construction of Herod's pleasure palace near by) and remains more or less uninhabited until the death of Herod when his sons are too weak to prevent its rehabilitation.[128] De Vaux and Albright notwithstanding, the earthquake of 31 BC was hardly

---

terrain is an important element in all traditions. The emphasis on "cave-dwelling" and martyrdom carries right through Bar Kochba times via Akiba's student Simeon bar Yohai, who functions as the keystone of *Zohar* tradition; cf., *b. Shabb* 33b. For Josephus the locale is south or east of Galilee, because Herod chases the refugees "as far as the River Jordan". That "the bandits" described are not bandits is made clear in the old man's impugning Herod's right to kingship (compare this with how the mass of Jews responded to Herod in connection with Antigonus' beheading; below, n. 130, i.e., "by no torments could they be forced to call him King", which further translates into the more general, "nor could any such fear make them call any man Lord", so characteristic of Josephus' descriptions of the followers of Judas and Saddok). As with Josephus' descriptions of the martyrdom of "the Essenes" coinciding with the end of period 2A of Qumran habitation, one can suppose that in this description one has a facsimile of the fall of Qumran ending period 1B.

[128] It was de Vaux who first proposed as a reason for the abandonment of the monastery the earthquake of 31 BC; cf. "Fouilles de Khirbet Qumran", 1956, pp. 544f. and *Archaeology* . . . , pp. 21–23, where he softens his stand under criticism. However, the conflagration that seems to have occurred on the site is not evidence of an earthquake; nor is an abandonment, as something else must explain the 30–40 year interruption in habitation. Laperrousaz in *Numen*, vii, 1960, pp. 26–76 would push the abandonment back to 67–63 BC. Milik, pp. 52–5, on the basis of some five Herodian coins questions the evidence for an abandonment at all, though he admits the evidence does suggest "a very violent conflagration . . . the traces of an *intentional* destruction of Qumran" (italics mine) and a "substantial interval before rebuilding". He also questions his colleague de Vaux's archaeology on the question of the broken dishes which the latter associates with the earthquake, but which he rather equates with the destruction in 68 CE. C. Roth, *The Dead Sea Scrolls: A New Historical Approach*, Oxford, 1958, pp. 22ff., took the interruption in habitation as demonstrating that a new group, "the Zealots", reinhabited the settlement after 4 BC (and Milik agrees that the "Essenes" do appear to have changed character between 4 BC and 70 CE). Roth's theory, while original, was poorly argued and hastily put together and he displays little or no knowledge of Jewish Christianity or the link of the "Zealot" movement to what we have been calling "Messianism". As it is, to him belongs the distinction of having pointed out the "Zealot" nature of the sect, even if he could not explain or account for it, and even if his identifications sometimes bordered on the absurd. Where identifications were concerned, Driver publishing seven years later, while giving a more solid presentation, was little better.

of any consequence except as a possible archaeological aid in helping to date the period of the monastery's destruction and relative dormancy.[129]

Herod, as would any clever monarch interested in undermining his opposition, brings in leaders from outside, most notably Hillel from Babylonia and Simon ben Boethus from Egypt. The Establishment which he sponsors and creates—partially by confiscating the wealth of the previous one, which had been destroyed much as its central figures, the members of the Maccabean family themselves, had been destroyed— is the Pharisaic/Sadducean one so familiar to us from portraits in the New Testament and Josephus.[130] With the appearance of "the Zealot Movement" in 4 BC, coincident with Herod's own demise, habitation at Qumran revives as the coin distribution verifies.

But this Movement is more than just "Zealot", as Josephus so pejoratively designates it to conceal its other tendencies after the election of "Phannius" and the killing of Ananus and the other high priests in the

---

[129] Steckoll, pp. 33–4, argues that no earthquake damage ever occurred at Qumran. The kind of acidity that can be generated by these disputes can be measured by de Vaux's caustic aside on his critic: "The authorities of the Israel occupation have forbidden this Sherlock Holmes of archaeology to continue his researches at Qumran", *op. cit.*, p. 48. This kind of comment compares with his final reaction to Driver. Having admitted on p. 133 that "The solution to the question [of the Essene character of the sect] is to be sought from the study of texts, and not from that of archaeology", de Vaux then goes on to state on p. 138 "that in all probability none of the manuscripts deposited in the caves is later than this date" (i.e. 68 CE). Finally, he puts it more unequivocally in his review in *NTS* of Driver's book: "No manuscript of the caves can be later than June 68 CE", ending with the intemperate: "Driver's theory is not 'as nearly valid as possible', as he says on the last page of his book, it is impossible": p. 104. Albright, who uncritically accepted de Vaux's archaeological explanation that Stratum 1B came "to an end with an earthquake and a fire, which can scarcely be separated from one another", dismissed Driver's work with the following words: " . . . the latest proposal for a different solution by a scholar of standing . . . has failed completely. This failure is not caused by any lack of philological learning or of combinatory talent, but to an obvious scepticism with regard to the methodology of archaeologist, numismatists, and palaeographer. Of course he had the bad luck to run into head-on collision with one of the most brilliant scholars of our day—Roland de Vaux . . . "; "Qumran and the Essenes", pp. 14f.

[130] The change is vividly evinced by Josephus' laconic comment after Pompey's troops stormed the Temple Mount: "So the Jews were now freed from kingly rule, and were governed by an aristocracy": *Ant.* 14.5.4. The character of this aristocracy we have dealt with variously above, but it is perhaps best summed up in the following description: "Since Herod had now the government of all Judea put into his hands, he promoted such of the private men in the city as had been of his party, but never left off punishing and revenging himself every day on those that had chosen the party of his enemies. But Pollio the Pharisee, and Sameas a disciple of Pollio, were honored by him above all the rest, because when Jerusalem was besieged, they had advised the citizens to receive Herod, for which advice they were well requited": *Ant.* 15.1.1.

last stages of the Uprising. The terminology is also picked up and applied in the New Testament, not to others, but to the followers of Jesus (cf. James in Acts 21:20 on the members of "the Jerusalem Church"). A better description of it would be "Messianic", as it is marked by a series of "Messianic" pretenders from the Shepherd Athronges and Judas in 4 BC to "the Egyptian" for whom Paul is mistaken, Menachem ben Judas (who, if he was really the latter's son, must have been about seventy years old), and Bar Kochba.[131] It is "Messianic" because it believes the time of the end or "the last days" is at hand and that the Messiah of Israel (or of Aaron and Israel) must arise.

It is often overlooked how "Messianic" the Qumran sect actually was, and one is not just speaking here about the well-known notion of "the two Messiahs", which has been widely commented on presumably because it is so perplexing. Rather, what is even more striking is the reference to and quotation of the all-important "Star Prophecy" from Num 24:17 upwards of three times in the extant corpus: once in the Damascus Document, once in the War Scroll, and at least once in what should be called the sect's "Messianic" proof-texts.[132] Josephus in a rare moment of candor describes this Prophecy as the moving force behind the whole of the Uprising against Rome, the signal for the actual start

---

[131] The phrase, "I have called my son out of Egypt", of Mt 2:15 is perhaps better applied to this *Egyptian*, who also attempts the *pro forma* wilderness exodus. As it is, Matthew goes to considerable effort to get the infant Jesus to Egypt (an effort Luke and the other Gospel writers spare themselves). The Movement, as we have stressed, is on the whole priestly, and is combined in interesting ways with the Messianic with the demise of the Maccabean Priest Kings. A good place to begin the study of the early Christian concept of Jesus as High Priest is Justin Martyr's *Dial.*, where it is laboriously laid out, as are the associated doctrines of Jesus as *Zaddik*; Enoch, Noah, Abel, etc. as the *Zaddikim* of old; adoptionist baptism and adoptionist sonship; "Stone" and "*Ma'oz*" imagery; and the "Righteousness" ideology (cf. Heb 7:26ff. on Jesus as the *Perfect* "Son" and supernal High Priest, above, p. 18 and note that Justin never mentions Paul). Justin also provides the basis for Epiphanius' Essenes as "Jessaeans", i.e., "Jesus" being a Greek pseudonym for Jesus' real name, "Oshea" or Hosea; cf. also *E.H.* 1.2.2ff. The priests, therefore, that should be coupled to this list of Israelite Messiahs in this period are "*Saddok*", i.e., "a Pharisee teacher" (read "Essene") *who was* "the *Zaddik*", John, Jesus, and James, just as the Priest "Eleazar" is added to Bar Kochba's coins in a later embodiment of this duality. Only in Jesus' case, and James'—and Simeon bar Cleophas' following him—are we justified in thinking that a change in the ideology has occurred as per the Damascus Document—and perhaps the series of "Messiahs of Aaron and Israel" in the Rule—becoming permanent in Christianity as it has been passed down to us.

[132] CD, vii, 18–21; 1 QM, xi, 5ff.; and 4 QTest 9–13, the last coming amid a flurry of references to "*ish-Hassideicha*", "*yinzor*", and "Yeshua" (not the biblical "Yehoshua" one would expect), as well as "the True Prophet" citation of Deut 18:18f. so dear to the Ebionites.

of which was the halting of sacrifice in the Temple by the zealous lower priests.[133]

Examples and reflections of the currency of this prophecy in the first century CE and beyond can be seen in Josephus' and R. Yohanan ben Zacchai's derisive misuse of it (that is, in improperly applying it to the Roman conqueror Vespasian,[134] behavior akin to the supposed jeering

---

[133] The young priests officiating at the Temple were persuaded "to receive no gift or sacrifice for any foreigner"; cf. the charge of "fornication, Riches, and profanation of the Temple" leveled in CD, iv, 12ff. against the Jerusalem Establishment; above, p. 17. The first is explained, not only in the Document itself, but also in al-Kirkisani's account of the similarity of Jesus' and Zadok's teaching on the subject. Like Mt 19:4 and Mk 10:6, CD, iv, 21f. cites Ge 1:27, "male and female he created them", to explain the ban on taking more than one wife—cf. al-Kirkisani, pp. 363ff., who insists "Jesus forbade divorce just as the Sadducees did"—something we know, of course, that Herod *did* to excess. Yet Josephus' report of cordial relations between Herod and "the Essenes" is still taken seriously in many quarters.

The second aspect to this "fornication" charge, "marriage with a niece", we have treated in detail above, p. 50. It also relates to "Herodians". The charge of "Riches" is self-explanatory; note that James' antagonism to *Riches* is developed out of his citation of Justin's "all Righteousness" commandment—according to which James calls "the Supreme Law of the Scripture", "love your neighbor as yourself"; cf. Ja 2:8f. (including his "keep the whole Law" directive) with CD, vi, 21f. The "large group of *Priests* who made their submission" in Acts 6:7 (cf. Ps *Rec* 1.44) certainly must be included among those "thousands" of believing Jewish "Zealots for the Law" James mentions to Paul in 21:20f.

To quote Josephus: "And this was the true beginning of our war with the Romans ... And when many of the High Priests and principal men [i.e., the Herodian Pharisaic/ Sadducean Establishment] besought them not to omit the sacrifice which it was customary for them to offer for their princes, they would not be prevailed upon, relying much upon their multitude": *War* 2.17.2f. When this is combined with the words: "But their chief inducement to go to war was an ambiguous oracle found in their sacred writings announcing that at that time a man from their country would become ruler of the world" (*War* 6.6.4), and this, in turn, with the quotation from *Ant.* 18.1.1: "the *infection* which spread thence [i.e., the alteration in customs preached by Judas and Saddok] among our younger men *who were zealous for it*, brought our nation to destruction" (italics mine), then I believe the true historical current of this period becomes clear. (This charge is only slightly deformed in the "Herodian" reformulation of it in the New Testament.)

[134] For the most detailed account of this see *ARN* 4.5; also b. *Gittin* 56a–b. Cf. *Mid. R. Lam* i.5.31 and *b. Yoma* 39b. That the interpretation of Is 10:34, the classical allusion to the fall of the Temple in 70 CE in *Talmudic* literature, is to be found at Qumran (4QpIsᵃ) interpreted in exactly the same way points as nothing else can to the chronological *sitz im leben* of this interpretation; and, indeed, much of this exegetical literature generally, especially in the absence of any indication whatsoever that this passage was ever applied in like manner to any earlier fall of the Temple.

This is also the case with Zech 11:1 (the fragmentary commentary of a related passage, Zech 11:11, also being found at Qumran spliced into 4QpIsᶜ). The "keys", which are

by the Jewish crowd at the Messiah Jesus crowned by thorns) and further afield in the peculiar twists given it in the infancy narrative of "the Star over Bethlehem" in Matthew's Gospel and in the name accorded Bar Kosiba by tradition, i.e., "Son of the Star".[135] One might add to this, the obvious game being played by Tiberius Alexander, Philo's nephew (presumably with Josephus' connivance), to convince Vespasian that he was indeed the Messiah called from Palestine to rule the world.[136] This is to say nothing of Agrippa I's seeming possession by it and his posturing in silver garments in all probability to evoke "the Star's" glitter before a theater crowd in Caesarea prior to his suspiciously sudden death.[137]

flung into the heavens at the fall of the Temple in the *Talmudic* exegesis of Zech 11:1, and which for the *Talmud* are in the possession of the Sadducees or Priests, are also a favorite topic in the New Testament. Cf. *War* 6.6.3 in the same section as that containing Josephus' explanation of "the Star Prophecy", the portents of the fall of the Temple, including heavenly hosts riding to and fro, the Temple gate opening of its own accord, and an overwhelming voice emanating from the Inner Sanctum crying, "Let us remove hence." The reference to "Lebanon", in some sense most often related to the Priesthood and the fall of the Temple, is discussed in detail in Driver, pp. 458–9, G. Vermes, "The Symbolic Interpretation of Lebanon in the Targums", *JTS*, 1958, pp. 1–12, and Neusner, p. 75; cf. also Tacitus, *Historiae* 5.13.

[135] This star is also alluded to in Josephus' portents for the fall of the Temple, but here it resembles a sword that stood over the city for a whole year. That the early Christian Community knew that "the star over Bethlehem" was connected to "the Star that would arise from Jacob" of Num 24:17 and linked to the person of Jesus is clear from Justin Martyr's discussion of the subject in *Dial.* 106; cf. the *Zohar*'s flawed, but striking presentation of these matters (212b introducing "Phineas"). That "the Star Prophecy" was "in the air" in Justin's time is clear from the application of it to Bar Kochba in *j. Ta'an* 68a–b, which does not deny that R. Akiba interpreted Num 24:17 to refer to Bar Kochba, but rather turns it around (probably retrospectively) to read: "A Liar has gone forth from Israel"; note the typical juxtaposition of "Liar" and "Star".

[136] The suggestion was first made by W. Weber in *Josephus and Vespasian*, Stuttgart, 1921, p. 43; Eisler, pp. 554–61, discusses the charade in detail. The point, of course, of all these messianic exercises, so lovingly detailed in the Gospels, is Isaiah's prophecy that "the lame would walk" and "the blind would see"; Is 35:5ff. and 42:16ff. Cf. Dio Cassius, *Roman History*, lxvi, 8 and lxxiv, 3.

[137] *Ant.* 19.8.1. Cf. his triumphal arrival in Alexandria after being appointed king by his friend Claudius (after similarly predicting Caligula's demise), where he is hailed by the Jewish crowds as "Lord" ("*Maran*"): *Ant.* 18.6.11 and Philo, *In Flacc.* 5ff. (2.521M). It is interesting that in the Slavonic Josephus' rendering of the World Ruler citation that most moved the Jews to revolt against Rome, it is stated in place of the usual *pro forma* ascription of it to Vespasian: "Some took this as a reference to Herod, others to the crucified miracle-worker Jesus, and others to Vespasian." For Herod's messianic claims, see the discussion of the priests around the time of the earthquake (i.e., 31 BC) in the Slavonic Josephus, secs. 373–79, though in fact the allusion is most likely to Agrippa I's

A succession of priestly *Zaddik*s had already been in existence for a century or two before the official appearance of this so-called "Zealot" Movement: to identify at least four so indicated in the extant literature: Simeon, Onias, Judas, and Honi.[138] This sequence is, strictly speaking,

pretensions. The whole question of Herodian family ambitions in the East, and the family's interest in "Messianic" matters tied to these, must be thoroughly investigated. Agrippa I is first suspected of plotting against Rome in *Ant.* 19.7.2ff., which appears to lead directly to his death. Antiochus of Commagene, one of his co-conspirators, did ultimately revolt in 71 CE: cf. *War* 5.11.3f. and 7.7.1ff. and also the pro-Roman role of Herod of Chalcis' son Aristobulus in "Lower Armenia" bordering on Commagene.

[138] As noted above, one should probably include John, Jesus, and James in the list. The all-important rain-making capacity adhering to the *Zaddik*-tradition seems to have been transmitted from Honi to his daughter's son, Hanin or Hanan *ha-Nehba* (i.e., Hanan the Hidden); *b. Ta'an* 23a–b. It was ascribed by tradition to Phineas and Elijah, and here also to *Habakkuk*. Note how the "rain-making" and the "Hidden" traditions come together in the *Zohar*'s description of the archetypical "rain-maker" Noah (63a and 67b). Note, too, Hanan the Hidden's outlook towards "the Rabbis" (equivalent to "the Pharisees and Sadducees" of Mt 3:7), who send schoolchildren to ask him to make rain, obviously because they are afraid to approach him themselves.

Not only does the "Hidden" tradition attach itself to the person of Honi, Hanin's grandfather (*Ant.* 14.2.1), but it persists in clinging in Christian tradition to John (cf. Onias=Honi=Hanin=John), whose mother in Lk 1:24 "hid herself" for five months (fearing the authorities?); see the *Protevangelium of James* 18.1, A. R. James, *Apocrypha of the New Testament*, Oxford, 1924, p. 46, where Elizabeth "hides" him *in a mountain cave* when Herod sought to destroy John (the basis of the similar tradition about Jesus?) and asks Zechariah: "Where have you *hidden* your son?" (italics mine), the typical note of cave-dwelling. See also al-Kirkisani's "*Magharians*", also associated with cave-dwelling and whom al-Kirkisani places between "Zadok and Boethus" and Jesus; pp. 326f. and 363f. The notice he gives in regard to their penalizing "guffawing" parallels 1QS, vii, 14—the section of the Community Rule we have already identified as having been attached to the Damascus Document in the Cairo *Genizah*.

Syriac tradition actually identifies Elizabeth's father as "*Anon*"; cf. Eisler, p. 244. *B. Ta'an* 23a–b tells of another grandson of Honi and the contemporary of James treated above, p. 42, "Abba Hilkiah". In the time of the drought, he was approached by "Rabbis", whom he treats quite gruffly, and asked to make rain. *J. Ta'an* 66b mentions yet another grandson of Honi (also named Honi), who drew circles and prayed for rain shortly before 70 CE (cf. our comments above about Honi/Onias and "*Oblias*" and the "Rip van Winkle" tradition adhering to Honi, above, pp. 37 and 42).

Jeremias, pp. 141ff., accepting Rabbinic tradition at face value, dates the first drought in Honi's time around 65 BC. Its end, despite Rabbinic hyperbole, appears to have been quite dramatic; *M. Ta'an* 3:8 and *b. Ta'an* 23a. The second was certainly around 48 CE and is referred to in the New Testament apocalypses mentioned above and in connection with Helen of Adiabene's famine-relief efforts; *Ant.* 20.5.2, itself sandwiched between references to the beheading of Theudas and the crucifixion of Judas the Galilean's two sons, James and Simon. It is also linked to a certain extent to Paul's activities: Acts 11:27ff. We have already noted James' rain-making activities in this period, and the very similar kinds of requests for aid by the Sadducees and Pharisees, reported in all traditions anterior to the "Messianic". It undergoes a Messianic transformation once the Maccabean family, the last properly "Zadokite" line, is finally destroyed. Then a new variation of it is invoked for priestly and secular legitimacy. This is what Josephus is at pains to conceal in his "Zealot"-theorizing.

What the Movement in its new guise now anticipates is the coming of the Messianic Kingdom, i.e., the Kingdom of the Messiah of Israel— "the Star".[139] The notion of a movement based on priestly "zeal" is not new, as 1 Macc corroborates in its portrayal of the Maccabean ancestor, Mattathias, and W. R. Farmer has shown in his much underrated book. The Zealot Movement has effectively been in existence at least as long as the first Maccabean purveyors of it in "the Covenant of Phineas".

What is new is the coupling of this Movement with Israelite Messiahs in the wake of the demise of the Maccabean Priest/Kings. This is reflected in the literature of Qumran as we have it. It is preached by a teacher named "Saddok"—as much a transliteration of "*Zaddik*" as "Zadok"—whom Josephus neglected to mention in his first account of this Movement in the *Jewish War*, and Judas, the son of a former Messianic pretender and guerrilla leader, Hezekiah.[140] Here is the first

relating to him, as those Rabbinic tradition reports regarding "Abba Hilkiah", Hanan *ha-Nehba*, and Honi.

Beyond this, and the very real spiritual links between all these individuals—that is, the *Zaddik*-tradition or "*Zaddik*ate" they represent—there is also the possibility, should one choose to regard it, of a genealogical relationship as well. I should note that the tradition of "the Zealot woes" against the reigning High Priesthood reproduced above, p. 53, is ascribed to one "*Abba Joseph b. Hanin*", identity otherwise unknown (as for that matter is Abba Hilkiah's, who appears to come from a village in Galilee). These "Abba" names in first century Rabbinic tradition should be carefully reviewed, as they often carry traditions related to our subject; cf., as well, New Testament confusion over names like "Barabbas", "Barsabas", and "Barnabas", all linked to names with known counterparts in the "Messianic" family itself, e.g., "Justus", "Joses", "Judas", etc. (and note the curious parallel represented by the transliterations "Joses"/"Jesus").

[139] Note the interesting seventy-year period that elapses from its first apperance in 4 BC to the final stopping of sacrifice on behalf of non-Jews in the Temple in 66 CE. That Bar Kochba's followers were understood to have persecuted "Christians" (*E.H.* 4.8.4) is not particularly relevant, because one must first inquire what sort of "Christians" these were. Rabbinic Judaism also preserves a tradition that he was anti-Rabbinic; cf. his trampling of R. Eleazar of Modein and the *Talmud*ic quotation from Zech 11:17 applied to him: "Woe to the worthless shepherd that leaves the flock . . .": *j. Ta'an* 68d.

[140] *Ant.* 18.1.1. Josephus' omissions from the *Jewish War*, which are corrected in *Antiquities* and the *Vita*, are extremely revealing; these include: Honi, Saddok, John, Jesus, *Banus*, and James, namely, all persons connected in some way with the inspirational or spiritual side of the "Zadokite"/"Messianic" Movement (as Josephus himself was at least until his trip to Rome). Even in the *Vita* and *Antiquities*, Josephus' references to these individuals are

palpable manifestation—aside from Jesus ben Yehozedek and Zerubabbel long ago—of our *Zadokite*/Israelite dual messiahship.[141]

It is also preached by a mysterious Baptist named John, succeeded by Jesus, James, and others.[142] In the latter two we have the type of "the Messiah of Aaron and Israel" of the Damascus Document, and there does appear to be a shift between the ideology of this document on this point and that of the Community Rule, though the Rule may imply *a series of*, not dual, Messiahs. The ideology on these points is not stationary. It is developing, as we have shown—the challenge is to be able to fit the appropriate ideology into its proper *sitz im leben* and not passively rely on the problematic results of archaeology and paleography. In fact, more recent Qumran documents reveal that the concept of a *single* Davidic-style Messiah of the normative kind was very strong at Qumran.

The settlement at Qumran is fed by waves of refugees from the corrupt Pharisaic/Sadducean regime of the procurators. The monastery is not suppressed in this period because the various governments are just not strong enough to do so. Besides, it employs an esoteric form of exegesis, the true meaning of which, to a certain extent, is difficult to pinpoint. For the moment, too, it seems to have adopted a quietist stance (cf. James counseling "patience" in the letter attributed to him "*until* the coming of the Lord", that is, "the second coming" or "return" of the

reticent and fragmentary. For the interesting links between *Banus* and James, see above, p. 64; for Saddok and John, below, p. 107.

[141] Cf. the interesting imposition of Eleazar on Joshua's activities in Josh 14:1, Jesus ben Yehozedek and Zerubbabel, John and Jesus, and Bar Kochba and Eleazar.

[142] R. Eisler, pp. 221–80, was the first to identify John as "Opposition" High Priest, and he did this without the Scrolls to assist him, though the Damascus Document was already known. Though he is generally held in contempt by modern scholars, his contentions about John—in contradistinction to those about the Slavonic Josephus—have never seriously been challenged. Anyone who doubts James' "revolutionary" sentiments, though they were discreetly covered in a veneer of counseling "patience", should examine his words to the assembled Passover crowd reported in early Church literature. Though these accounts conflate the *two* attacks on James—one by "the Enemy" Paul in the early 40s and one by Ananus in the early 60s—they are nevertheless informative. When asked to quiet the crowd's revolutionary fervor in the Temple, he rather fans the flames of Messianism: *E.H., loc cit.*

That Jesus was seen as a revolutionary, at least by the Romans, needs no further elucidation. The manner of his death gives vivid confirmation as nothing else can, despite mythologizing and retrospective attempts to transform it, of what party and movement he adhered to. For a true picture of "Christian" revolutionary propaganda in this period, the reader would do well to turn to Revelation and the Sibylline Oracles. These might be the propaganda exercises of militant Shi'ism in Iran in our own time, which indeed, owes a debt, however indirect, to the Messianic/*Zadokite* Movement.

Messiah).[143] Messianic disturbances are the rule from 4 BC to 62 CE, mostly coming at Passover, and as a consequence usually involving some sort of "exodus" to the desert ("the Land of Damascus") for a "New Covenant" (and revelation?) and presumable return.[144]

[143] Ja 5:7ff.: "Now be patient, brothers, until the Lord's coming. Think of a farmer, how patiently he waits for the precious fruit of the ground until it has the autumn rains and spring rains" (cf. above "until the coming of the Messiah of Aaron and Israel" of 1QS, xi, 11 and "until the rise" or "standing up of the Messiah of Aaron and Israel" of CD, viii, 24; xii, 23f.; xiv, 19). One cannot overemphasize, too, that the "rain" allusion, which continues in this section, and which we have already taken note of above, relates to James' proclamation of "the Son of Man coming on the clouds of Heaven" at Passover in n. 142 above. For the Karaites, the Messiah was even called "Anani" (that is, Anan ben David, and also "Cloudy One"), the last recorded scion of the family of David in 1 Chron 3:24. In Hebrew, the expression carries with it the additional connotation of "magician", which, of course, has interesting implications for this period.

[144] See, for instance, that of Theudas, *Ant.* 20.5.1 of 44–45 CE (mistakenly reported in Acts 5:36f. about 6–7 CE). What Luke has done, probably owing to an over-hasty reading of this passage in the *Antiquities*, to produce this anachronism in Acts is to conserve the reference to "Judas the Galilean" and "at the time of the Census"—which immediately follows along with reference to Helen's famine relief effort in *Ant.* 20.5.2—but inadvertently (or otherwise) dropped the reference to Judas' two sons "*James and Simon*". Pursuant to these notices, Josephus then tells the story (*Ant.* 20.5.4) of the "Stephen a servant of Caesar" who was beaten (and perhaps killed) just outside Jerusalem by "robbers" (that is to say "those who raised the tumult" in the Temple at Passover time over the legionnaire who scurrilously exposed himself to the assembled crowds). This is precisely the sequence of events followed in Acts 5–7. Schoeps in *Theologie und Geschichte des Judenchristentums*, Tübingen, 1949, pp. 441ff., has already suggested the basic interchangeability of Stephen and James, but he missed the error in the speech of "Stephen" which provides the clue to the speech's original provenance. Stephen claims (Acts 7:16) that *Abraham bought the ancestral tomb from the sons of Hamor in Shechem.* The whole speech is based upon Joshua's farewell address in Josh 24; and the error arises, once again, from an over-hasty reading, this time of the notice with which the latter concludes, about *the ancestral tomb that Jacob bought and paid for* "from the sons of Hamor the father of Shechem" (Josh 24:32). This attack on "Stephen", anyhow, though presented as a stoning, textually rather takes the place of the 44 CE attack on James by "the Enemy" Paul in Ps *Rec* 1.70f. and the riot the latter led there around 40 CE.

Theudas who wants to part the Jordan and "the Egyptian" who assembles his followers on the Mount of Olives—cf. *Ant.* 20.8.6 with Acts 21:38—function, in any event, as "Joshua" *redivivus*es. In this context, one must review the whole question of "lookalikes" or "twins". That Paul is mistaken for this so-called "Egyptian" shows that in Roman eyes, anyhow, such agitators were indistinguishable from one another. Note the consistent pattern of ruthlessness and violent repression in the Roman response to these "imposters and deceivers". Cf. above, p. 46, and *War* 2.13.4f., where Josephus characterizes them as being "in *intent* more wicked even than the murderers" and desirous of "procuring *innovations* and change of government" (italics mine). The Felix who butchers them is the same man with whom Paul converses so felicitously in Acts—"who knows more about the Way than most people". His alliance with the Herodian family through

There are innumerable crucifixions.[145] Aside from Jesus' (and the beheading of James—probably an overwrite for an individual referred to in both Josephus and Acts, called "Theudas" (Acts 5:36))—the most important are those of Jacob and Simon, the two sons of Judas the Galilean in anticipation of Passover in 48 CE at the hands of the Jewish collaborator, Tiberius Alexander, Philo's nephew, who along with Josephus was in a position to understand the significance of these individuals.[146] By the 50s the country is in chaos, fanned by the incompetent,

his illicit union with Drusilla should be carefully noted—a union connived at by a man who can be none other than *Simon Magus* (cf. Acts 8:9ff.). Simon convinces Drusilla to *divorce* her previous husband, a practice even Josephus admits "violated the laws of her forefathers"; *Ant.* 20.7.2.

[145] Where Felix was concerned, as we saw, Josephus informs us that "the number of robbers whom he caused to be crucified . . . were a multitude not to be enumerated"; *War* 2.13.2. In 5.11.1, Josephus describes how the "poor people" who "made no supplications for mercy . . . were first whipped, and then tormented with all sorts of tortures before they . . . were crucified", concluding, "so great was their multitude that room was wanting for the crosses and crosses wanting for the bodies". See also *War* 7.6.4 for an additional example of the terrible effect of crucifixion on the people and note the parallels with Gospel portraits.

[146] *Ant.* 20.5.1. In this episode one wonders if one does not have an echo of the *Boanerges*, "the two Sons of Thunder"; note the "rain" imagery again: Mk 3:17. "James" might well have been beheaded in the time of Agrippa, but neither he nor "his brother" drinks "the same cup" as Jesus (Mt 20:22 and Mk 10:38); however, James and Simon, the two sons of Judas the Galilean, did. At the beginning of this study, we noted how the problem of Jesus' brothers bedevils Apostle lists and post-resurrection appearances; above, p. 14. Josephus calls Theudas "a magician". Like "Judas Thomas", he is a Joshua *redivivus* or Jesus "lookalike". His relationship with "Addai" (cf. "Thaddaeus" above, p. 62) and with Jesus' family is signaled at Nag Hammadi (cf. "Theuda the father of the Just One"—read "brother of"—2 Apoc Ja 5.44; for "Addai", see 1 Apoc Ja 5.36). The additional phrase found there, "since he was a relative of his", shows the way towards sorting out all these confusing references to "brothers", "sons", and "fathers". What Acts has done is to substitute the beheading of "James *the brother of John*" for Theudas/ Thaddaeus/Judas (also Lebbaeus, "of James", and probably Judas *Thomas*) *the brother of Jesus*.

Note that it is "the brother" theme which is the constant, and the whole fictional exercise of "John and James *the sons of Zebedee*" is part and parcel of the process of downplaying and eliminating Jesus' brothers (and successors in Palestine) from scripture. The Central Triad of the early Church in Palestine can now be definitively identified as "James (*the brother of Jesus*), Cephas, and John" of Ga 2:9, not the misleading "Peter, James, and John *his brother*" of Gospel portraits, and the bewildering proliferation of "Mary's" also evaporates. "Mary (*the sister* of Jesus' mother Mary) the wife of Clophas" (John 19:25), "the mother of James and Joses and the mother of the sons of Zebedee" of Mt 27:56 (of "James the less, Joses, and Salome" in Mk 15:40; of "James" in Lk 24:10), now simply becomes identifiable with *Jesus' mother*. This is, in any event, the implication of the Papias fragment 10 in *ANF*, which identifies *Thaddaeus* as *the son of*

venal, and increasingly brutal administration of the procurators, and again as coin data attest, the monastery is in its most populous phase rising to a peak in the Second Year of the War against Rome.[147] Thereafter, it is downhill.

I will not at this point be drawn into the controversy over whether the monastery fell in 68 CE or thereafter, except to say that the destruction of its buildings would in no way make life untenable at the location in the conditions engendered by war. On the contrary—the site would have constituted an important forward outpost for the partisans at Masada even if its buildings had been burned, unless the Romans *actually garrisoned it*. This they would not necessarily have done in any serious manner as long as the partisans refrained from harassing the Jericho road before

Mary and Cleophas and *the brother of James, Simon, and Joses* and, in the process, *affirms* the identification of Alphaeus and Cleophas. Even the "Mary the mother of *John Mark*", to whose house Peter goes in Acts 12:12 to leave a message for "James and *the brothers*" (the "brother" theme again), simply reduces to "Mary *the mother of James*" (italics mine).

We have already shown above that "Thaddaeus" in Mt 10:3/Mk 3:8 corresponds to "Judas (the son) of James"—read "brother"—in Lk 6:16/Acts 1:13, and that two variant mss. of *Apost. Const.* 8.25 identify this same "Thaddaeus" as "Judas the Zealot who preached the truth to the Edessenes and the people of Mesopotamia when Agbarus ruled over Edessa." Once our comments about the relationship of Theudas to Judas Thomas and Addai are appreciated, we can make almost a one-for-one correspondence between all the executions referred to in Josephus and their *fictional* counterparts in the New Testament. Perhaps, even more importantly, that "Agabus who predicts the Famine" in Acts 11:28 is but a thinly disguised version of Helen's husband "Agbarus" or "Abgarus"—probably a title meaning something like "Great King", that is, "the Great King of the Peoples beyond the Euphrates". "Adiabene" becomes part of what goes under the title of "the Land of Edessenes" or "the Peoples beyond the Euphrates", a rival center to the expansionist aims of Agrippa's brother—and Paul's probable "kinsman" cf. Ro 16:11—Herod of Chalcis in "Asia".

The preventive execution of James and Simon in the time of the great drought (both drought and census are mentioned in the same sentence; cf. "the *Boanerges*" above) gives vivid indication of the existing unrest, as does the visit that preceded it of "Simon" to Agrippa I in Caesarea with complaints similar to those of John the Baptist (above, p. 17; note that Herod of Chalcis had married Agrippa I's daughter Bernice, later mistress of Titus, and it is Agrippa's sister Herodias whose marital practices are the issue in the death of John the Baptist). Agrippa, as one would expect, handles the incident patronizingly, but diplomatically. That Simon would ultimately have been arrested by Agrippa or by his brother Herod of Chalcis, who succeeds him (cf. Acts 12:1ff.) is a foregone conclusion; and that Luke, drawing also on the Agrippa II dining episode, would distort this into an episode where "Peter" learns to accept non-Jews (and in doing so, unwittingly reveals that Jesus never taught *table fellowship* with Gentiles, otherwise why would Peter need a "Pauline" vision to reveal it?) is typical of the working method of these documents, as we have already expounded it.

[147] See above, pp. 43ff. Also the new shards found with this date above, p. xxvii.

the commencement of actual operations against Masada *after the fall of the Temple* in 71/72 CE. Any token garrison left on the spot of the kind most commentators propose could easily have been dealt with by the refugees themselves, by this time having found temporary sanctuary at Masada their ranks swelled by new recruits.

Recently, as noted in the Introduction, three to four shards were found in the area of the Qumran plateau. Several turned out to be receipts for supplies from Jericho and one, anyhow, dated "Year 2", meaning "Year 2 of the Uprising against Rome". Not only do they confirm that Qumran was not an isolated Community, but part of the general Jericho nexus; they also confirm it was participating in the general Uprising against Rome and *using its calendar*—just the argument set forth in this book.

VIII
PALEOGRAPHIC PROBLEMS

The above reconstruction, I submit, is as good as any constructed around "Essenes" as such, or so-called "Zealots", and unlike any of these, has the virtue of being able to give a plausible explanation to the whole expanse of "Zadokite" literature from the third century BC to the second century CE. In addition, it does not resort to unknown or hypothetical individuals and/or teachers to do it. Everyone mentioned is known. As tempting as escapism might be, we have enough historical evidence from different sources in this period—even if some are patently folkloric or mythological—to demand that scholars toe the line on making *historical* identifications.[148]

It is also in keeping with paleographical finds, such as they are—as it is with archaeological, historical, and literary critical evidence. For instance, it very easily explains the archaizing Maccabean script so promi-nent among the scripts at Qumran, difficult to explain for those who

---

[148] Cross agrees, p. 72, n. 33: "The Qumran sect was not a small, ephemeral group. Its substantial community at Qumran persisted some two centuries or more ... Our task is to identify a major sect in Judaism. And to suppose that a major group in Judaism in this period went unnoticed in our sources is simply incredible." Having said this, he proceeds to make major identifications using unknown "Essene" teachers! De Vaux, p. 138, concurs: "This community, the life of which has been traced by archaeology over a period of two centuries and which has left behind a considerable literature is no small unknown sect"; he then proceeds to follow Cross in failing to grasp the import of his own statement.

see the group as being anti-Maccabean.[149] What is more, it does not resort to thinking that first-century CE *pesher*s of biblical material give intimate explanations of events that occurred in the second century BC.[150] This is as absurd as thinking that nowadays a preacher would interpret

[149] This archaizing "paleo-Hebrew" Maccabean script, a characteristic of some biblical manuscripts at Qumran and, for instance, writing the Tetragrammaton in the Habakkuk *Pesher*, was also used on the coinage, not only of the First, but also of the Second Jewish Revolt—another argument against the claim of anti-Maccabean feeling at Qumran and for the involvement of the sect at Qumran in what Brandon would call "Israel's national cause"; cf. R. S. Hanson, "Paleo-Hebrew Scripts in the Hasmonean Age", *BASOR*, 175, 1964, pp. 39 and 42, F. M. Cross, "The Oldest Manuscripts from Qumran", *SBL*, 74, 1955, pp. 147 and 159; "The Development of Jewish Scripts" in *The Bible and the Ancient Near East*, ed. G. E. Wright, 1961, p. 189, no. 4; and S. A. Birnbaum, *The Hebrew Scripts*, Leiden, 1971, pp. 78 and 94ff.

[150] Cross, *The Ancient Library*, pp. 113–5 agrees: ". . . virtually all commentaries and testimonia appear in manuscripts written in late hands . . . duplication (or multiplication) of copies among the various caves is significantly absent in a single category of literature: the commentaries . . . such works were rarely if ever copied, and hence are mostly original works . . . the date of the script of a commentary will indicate normally its date of written composition." However having admitted these probably represent the "regular sessions of the sect" mentioned in our sources, where scripture was read and expounded, he draws the rather lame conclusion "that a corpus of traditional exegesis was put into writing only toward the end of the sect's life", implying some oral transmission, but avoiding the question of why people would bother recording such intimate explanations of scripture (except in a fragmentary way as in the *Talmud*) 100–150 years after the fact, particularly when they did not judge them important enough to bother making more than single copies. As is so often the case in this research, Milik, p. 58, reproduces Cross' words almost precisely. For a description of the friendship of these three scholars, i.e., Milik, Cross, and de Vaux, see Cross' description in "Scripts", p. 190, n. 9 on how he wavered back and forth between the other two on the matter of the bowl graffiti— relating to the problem of the wall and broken dishes—which Milik on paleographic grounds dated to the second destruction and de Vaux true to his "earthquake" thesis claimed for period 1B. He was finally—against his original judgement—won over by de Vaux. That this would throw the chronology off perhaps 100 years is passed off with the comment: "the possibility should be borne in mind that the minimal dates in our absolute chronology on shifts of certain letter forms . . . *may be slightly low*" (italics mine).

The matter of de Vaux's obvious personal charm is commented on by R. North, *op. cit.*, pp. 433f.: "fortunately the trump-card [of direct exploration of the caves] eventually fell into the hands of de Vaux, whose loyal cooperation with the authorities has smoothed procedural details ever since." At the same time in n. 31, he notes "de Vaux's shrewdness in inducing the apprehensive Bedouin to cooperate with the Jordan govern-ment . . . " I am quoting these remarks at length throughout this work because I have the distinct impression that most scholars leave the details of these matters to a few specialists. They assume rather in the manner Tolstoy reports of most Christians, when coming into his new pacifist stage he inquired of the disquieting tendency of Christians

Biblical scripture in terms of the events surrounding the lives of George Washington, Napoleon, or the Duke of Wellington.[151] Indeed, this is the time span involved, since the homiletical/exegetical texts, known as *peshers*, are all from the first century CE. Found only in single copies, they are not the "classical" but rather represent the "current" literature of the sect, which is why the Habakkuk *Pesher* found so *neatly* deposited in Cave I is so important. To think they relate to events in the Maccabean period or those covered by Daniel, except where this is expressly so stated for internal historiographical demands of the text itself, as already noted, is unrealistic.

These texts were very likely the quickly written records of weekly sabbath scripture sessions held by "the Teacher" ("Righteous" or "of the *Yahad*", whoever the current office-holder might have been) in his role as unique interpreter of the Bible.[152] It is inconceivable that the

---

to serve in armies and Christian prelates to bless them, that "these matters were decided long ago". Upon further inquiry, Tolstoy never could find out by whom.

[151] See, for instance, Vermes' reconstructions, pp. 61ff., who remarks on p. 55 with the kind of discernment one has come to expect in Qumran research: "*No properly Judeo-Christian characteristic emerges from the scrolls, and unless we are much mistaken, the Zealots were scarcely a company of ascetics.* For the events reported in the Qumran literature *it therefore seems reasonable* to turn to the historical period prior to 66–70 CE, and *more precisely . . . to the epoch beginning with the accession of Antiochus Epiphanes* (175 BC) and ending with the fall of Hyrcanus II (40 BC)" (italics mine). Vermes' own preconceptions, of course, should be clear from these comments.

[152] If Cross is correct in seeing the establishment at Qumran as something of "a library", then, of course, caves with massive hoards like IV would represent something of its storehouse, and the literature in a cave like I what was actually circulating at the time. If the location was abandoned in haste, as the helter-skelter condition of the materials in Cave IV suggests—not the most ideal hiding place as even Cross admits—then the finding of an all-important commentary like Habakkuk neatly placed in a jar along with the other materials in Cave I probably implies it was actually in use or being studied at the time of the fall of the monastery and represents the latest literature; an assessment with which paleography, while offering uneven results, on the whole concurs.

As far as the textual content of Habakkuk is concerned, Driver's discussion is unrivaled for its development of war data. Since to any intelligent observer, Jerusalem's fall was a foregone conclusion once the main Roman army under Vespasian appeared, the allusions it and 4QpIs ᵃ appear to make to the fall of the city need not necessarily reflect a period of composition after 70 CE though they could. For the *Pesher*, the coming of and destruction inflicted by the *Kittim* are events in progress, not necessarily completed. The inexorable advance of the *Kittim*, as in other *Pesharim* at Qumran, only forms the literary backdrop to the commentary, whose main foci are actually on the Wicked Priest "who *polluted* the Temple of God" and "plundered *the Poor* of their belongings" (italics mine; xii, 2ff.), and on "the Last Priests of Jerusalem", who amassed wealth by plundering the people (ix, 4f.); as well as on the "Lying *Mattif*" ("Spouter"), who *attacked* the Righteous Teacher and "rejected the Law" in the midst of the whole Congregation (v, 7ff.).

In contrast to the *right*-guided exegesis of Is 53:11f. (see above, pp. 18 and 67), he "sets up a congregation of Lying", "leading *Many astray* . . . with *works of Lying*". His eschatological "*'amal* [and that of his followers] *will count for nothing*" at *the Last Judgement* (x, 9ff.; note in CD, i, 14ff. this "Scoffer" is described as "*pouring—hittif—over Israel the waters of Lying*", "*leading astray* without *a Way*", and abolishing the boundaries which the *Rishonim* had set up"—italics mine; cf. 4QpNah, ii, 8 on the Tongue "leading Many astray").

In such a context, the allusion to "building a worthless city with blood and erecting a Congregation on Lying" (x, 10) is easily explained. Having regard for CD, iii, 6's "Noachic" horror of the eating "of blood", to which it ascribes the *cutting off* of "the Children of Jacob" in the wilderness, and the comparable insistence in James' directives to overseas communities—so disingenuously discussed by Paul in 1 Co 6–10—to "abstain from blood"; the allusion can be seen as figurative, of the same genre as the allusion to "pouring over Israel the waters of lying" above, the figurative allusion to the Central Priestly Triad as a spiritualized "Holy of Holies" in 1QS, viii, 8 and ix, 6, and the general play on the word "Zadok" itself. (Cf. Paul's use of precisely this kind of imagery in 1 Co 3:9ff., 8:1, etc., where he describes his community as "the building" and himself as "the architect", and actually uses extant Qumran language when referring to his followers as "the Temple", i.e., "laying the Foundations" and the "Cornerstone", this in a letter that goes on to describe his idea of "the New Covenant in" and "communion with the blood of Christ"; 1 Co 10:16, 11:25, etc.).

Again, attention to the methods of literary criticism would help specialists here. The much-labored reference to the *Kittim* sacrificing to their standards (vi, 3f.) is *generic*, not specific. Though Josephus pictures the Romans as doing this in the midst of the carnage on the Temple Mount (*War* 6.6.1), the reference need not be to this particular sacrifice (though it might be), but rather to others which no doubt occurred after each successful siege as the Romans made their bloody way down from Galilee (e.g. Yotapata, *War* 3.7.3ff., and Gamala, 4.1.1ff.). For the Habakkuk *Pesher*, "the booty and Riches" of the High Priests would in the end be "delivered over to the Army of the *Kittim*" (cf. above, p. 41, on "Phineas the Temple Treasurer"—which was demonstrably not the case in 37 or 63 BC; in fact, Josephus makes a specific point of telling us that neither Herod nor Pompey torched *the Temple Treasure*, which indeed they would have had no interest in doing, wishing to conciliate the population), these last to be condemned with "Sinners" and "idolatrous men" generally on "the Day of Judgement" (xiii, 1ff.). This could have been written in 68 CE, or 69 CE, as well as in 70 or thereafter.

In this context, it should not be overlooked that both so-called "Christians" and the extreme "Zealot" (or rather *Sicarii*") occupiers of Masada left Jerusalem on or before the year 67/68 CE, the first in response to a mysterious oracle, the second because of the killing of Menachem. The first reportedly fled to a location Christian tradition identifies as "Pella"; the second, to Masada. Brandon, pp. 208ff., G. Strecker, *Das Judenchristentum in den Pseudoklementinen*, Berlin, 1958, pp. 229ff., and more recently, G. Lüdemann, "The Successors of pre-70 Jerusalem Christianity: A Critical Evaluation of the Pella-Tradition", *Jewish and Christian Self-Definition*, i, Philadelphia, 1978, pp. 161–73 (recapitulating Strecker), have questioned the historicity of the "Pella"-flight tradition. But their doubts do not alter the fact of the basic resemblance between the two traditions, nor do they rule out the possibility of a "flight" to an alternative location (cf. below, p. 94–95, and James' similar flight to the Jericho region in the 40s and the precipitous rise in Qumran coin distribution in both these periods). For Christians, anyhow, once the *Zaddik* James was killed, the city of Jerusalem could no longer remain in existence. Both disassociated themselves from the further progress of the Revolt; and indeed, "the *Sicarii*" on Masada do not seem to have undertaken any offensive action even up to its fall. Even their suicide was not an offensive action, though it robbed the Romans of the glory of triumph.

In paleography, S. Birnbaum—whose work Albright regarded as "expert" ("On the Date of the Scrolls from Ain Feshka and the Nash Papyrus", *BASOR*, 115, 1948, p. 15) and Cross regarded as "a major contribution" ("Scripts", p. 135), in "How Old Are the Cave Manuscripts? A Palaeographical Discussion", *V.T.*, 2, 1951, p. 105—originally put both Habakkuk and the War Scroll sometime before the "Herodian" period. However, Cross, *op. cit.*, p. 198, nn. 118 and 123, calls Habakkuk "early Herodian", having already informed us, p. 173, that a relative chronology of the Herodian period is "easily worked out" because of the rapid development in scripts; cf. also "The Oldest Manuscripts from Qumran", *JBL*, 74, 1955, p. 163. Birnbaum subsequently changed his mind and in *BASOR*, 115, 1949, he placed it "about the middle of the first century".

This he developed further in *The Hebrew Scripts*, Leiden, 1971, pp. 38–43, where using his peculiar form of mathematics, i.e., a (the number of early characteristics): b (the number of late characteristics) as c (his artificial time span based on supposition and unexamined archaeology): x (his answer, the number of years above his starting point: 300 BC), he ends up with a date (finally in agreement with Cross') of the last quarter of the first century BC. Here, it should be pointed out, for him c is always a constant equaling 368, i.e., 300 plus his presumed *terminus ad quem*, 68 CE. On p. 27, oblivious to hyperbole, Birnbaum states, echoing Cross above, it was "possible to build an unassailable basis for establishing order out of chaos" in this way and that he was "justified in applying the law of averages and *do not run much risk if, as a general rule*, we regard dated (*or datable*) *documents* as representative of their time" (italics mine). Presumably Birnbaum had never heard of differential equations—more applicable to a situation involving multiple variables and limits. His archaeological assumptions, along with his rather superficial historical ones, which are not insignificant to his conclusions, I shall deal with separately, below, pp. 88f.

N. Avigad, who should perhaps be considered the most moderate of all these individuals, in "Palaeography of the Dead Sea Scrolls and Related Documents" in *Aspects of the Dead Sea Scrolls, Scripta Hierosolymitana*, Jerusalem, 1958, pp. 72 and 82, calls Habakkuk late, noting the presence of some very late characteristics in both it and Hymns, which almost everyone acknowledges as contemporary. Here we are already speaking of a gap of some 120 years in these three assessments. The following is an example of Avigad's moderation. "We shall refrain here from suggesting absolute dates for each of them [i.e., the documents including Habakkuk under consideration] since the speed of development of the individual letters is a factor we cannot yet make out."

Scholars have taken advantage of all of these considerations, especially de Vaux's imperfect archaeology and Birnbaum's sophomoric calculus, to claim that the Kittaean advance referred to and the fall of the Temple implied in the Habakkuk *Pesher* must relate to earlier such events, i.e., that of Herod's assault in 37 BC or Pompey's of 63 BC, despite the fact that the cult of the military standards does not seem to have begun until the Imperial period; cf. Driver, pp. 211–216 and North, p. 433. For my part, I shall state categorically, on the basis of internal criteria alone, Habakkuk *is* late. Aside from the numerous allusions to 50–60s-type events and the "falling of the cedars of Lebanon"

Community as a whole had nothing new to say or no new reactions while 150 years of the most vital and controversial history in Palestine passed before its eyes; that on the contrary it sat passively and piously by studying or penning texts relating to the period leading up to 63 BC or before. It should be properly understood that this is what would be involved in following the generally accepted theories and yet acknowledging that the documents were deposited in the caves in 68 CE or thereafter (to which there are no serious objections). It should be also stated categorically that 68 CE is the *terminus a quo for the deposit of scrolls in the caves*, not the *terminus ad quem for the cessation of habitation* in the region of Qumran which it is generally taken to be.[153]

Only in the case of the Damascus Document are there any real difficulties, paleographically speaking, for the above theory. But for the moment we have made no claims concerning the date of this document. As to its "relative chronology", we would agree with the paleographers who see it as being somewhat "later" than the Community Rule.[154] It is only when putting in "the pegs", as they are referred to by those in the field, that real differences would emerge. But Milik himself says that

imagery of Is 10:34 already expounded above, which *Talmud*ic literature applies to the fall of the Temple in 70 CE, one should note the extremely important—and distinctly "Jamesian" as opposed to "Pauline"—exegesis of Hab 2:4 certified by the extant Pauline corpus as *current* in the 50–60s.

[153] This de Vaux and Driver properly realize. De Vaux to his credit states, p. 41: "It is perfectly true that strictly speaking the coins only provide a *terminus post quem*", and on p. 103 in *NTS*, "I concluded that this year 68 *has a good chance* of representing the end of Period II and the beginning of Period III" (italics mine); but hardens this in his conclusion, p. 138: " . . . in all probability none of the manuscripts deposited in the caves is later than this date"; cf. Avigad, p. 72, with more caution designates "the end of the Qumran settlement at 70 CE as the fairly certain *terminus ante quem*" (italics mine); and Birnbaum, p. 27, who with customary obliviousness states: "Archaeological evidence confirms the post-Christian era part, and even enables us to arrive at a precise *terminus ad quem*: the year 68 CE, when the Romans put an end to the Qumran settlement." Typically, he then proceeds to use this date as a principal "peg" in every one of his scores of calculations. Fitzmyer in "The Qumran Scrolls, the Ebionites, and their Literature" in *Essays*, p. 446, follows him in this mistake: "The latest possible date for the deposit of the manuscripts is the destruction of Qumran in AD 68." Fitzmyer has turned it completely around. His sentence should read (however unpopular it might sound): "the *earliest* possible date for the deposit of manuscripts is AD 68–69", the date of the last Jewish coins found before the Bar Kochba period. Cross' "Oldest Manuscripts", p. 163, realizes the "absolute *terminus ad quem* for Qumran script types" are the dated documents from the Wadi Murabba'at (though sometimes he behaves as if he doesn't).

[154] See Milik, pp. 58 and 91, and Cross, *Library*, pp. 81–82, n. 46. See below, too, for our discussion of why a single "early" exemplar on such a crucial text cannot be considered definitive.

paleographic evidence can be considered accurate only within two generations, and de Vaux admits that such evidence cannot be taken as absolute in and of itself, but must be ranged alongside textual, historical, and
other kinds of data.[155] The two-generation rule presupposes a correct

[155] Milik, p. 57: "Palaeography however enables us to establish, at least within two
generations, the time in which our earliest exemplar of a book was copied." Cross understands this but typically tries to narrow it, "Scripts", p. 136: "the palaeographer can fix
a characteristic book hand within fifty years in terms of absolute dates, or even a generation in terms of relative (typological) relationships" (a key escape word here is
"characteristic"). Avigad, as usual, is more circumspect, pp. 86–87: "Far more problematic is the question of absolute chronology. Ancient Hebrew manuscripts and inscriptions
are notorious for their lack of dating formulae. Comparative palaeography is doing its
best with the help of a few absolute data at hand", and notes that while "Hebrew
palaeography is rapidly advancing towards the status of a scientific discipline . . . many
lacunae still exist which need completion, and questions of overlapping and archaizing
are to be settled."

Vis-à-vis archaizing, Birnbaum, p. 138, admits that sometimes scripts "are frozen" for
hundreds of years, but when faced with persistence of paleo-Hebrew, calls it "an artificial
revival", p. 87 or an "isolated" rendering, p. 107, and when faced with its final revival
in the Bar Kochba coinage, explains it by saying the "grandfathers" used the old coins
and the "fathers" remembered them, p. 78, having already concluded elsewhere that
because of poor workmanship in the First Revolt, "die-cutters were not familiar" with
it. Actually, Birnbaum does not concern himself with such niceties as margins of error:
"By working out a comprehensive system of measurement, letter by letter and age by
age, it is possible to establish an unassailable palaeographical basis." Errors come from
not having "a good eye, patience, and training" and from lacking "the necessary palaeographic equipment" (whatever this means): *V.T.*, p. 92 (echoed verbatim in *Hebrew Scripts*,
p. 27). He sets out his method, such as it is, in detail, in *V.T.*, p. 105.

De Vaux, p. 97, in responding to Driver's contention that "internal evidence . . . must
take precedence over external", makes perhaps his clearest allusion to the worth of tools
like paleography. Although referring primarily to archaeology, he is at least willing to
admit: "other things being equal, there is no precedence between the two kinds of evidence; a correct solution must make use of both, must prove the worth of both." Cross,
Library, p. 74, n. 33, also, berates Driver's "peculiar refusal to accept the validity and
precision of these newer techniques" citing the existence of "a sufficient number of
specimens of Hebrew script of assured dating *however narrowly the phrase is defined*" (italics
mine). For him, in addition to materials dated by stratigraphic context (which afford
absolute termini—sic!), "there are documents of the first century AD which bear date formulae, and thus can be dated to the year, and in some instances to the day, month, and
year of their writing." He means, of course, the Wadi Murabba'at and Nahal Hever finds
and one unpublished date formula from Cave IV. However, aside from these, the only
absolutely secure "peg" he can come up with from 150 BC to 100 CE are the funerary
inscription of Queen Helen of Adiabene and the Bene Hezir inscription—hardly a precise tool (see below, p. 91).

In relation to the ossuaries he and Birnbaum so securely date in Herod's time,
Albright, his mentor, "Scrolls from Ain Feshka", p. 17, only says "all antedate the year
AD 70 and that the earliest of them are not later than the reign of Herod the Great."

identification of the general chronological provenance of a given script in the first place, and barring this, the deviation could be much wider. Even where a document as crucial as the Nash Papyrus is concerned, where most scholarly opinion has ranged itself behind the religiously conservative Albright—due in no small part to the successful efforts of

North, p. 435, at an early stage of Qumran research, lamented "the lack of an independent documented analysis with drawings and descriptions of pottery pieces from other sites giving ground for a chronological judgement." Citing the disquieting symptom on the part of other archaeologists "to leave everything to the decision of one judge, however skillful" and to accept de Vaux's numerous revisions with submissiveness, he also attacks Qumran stratigraphy and ceramic typology (in this he has since been backed up to a certain extent by Laperrousaz), which he contended were "not simple facts black and white", but had to be carefully evaluated on the basis of "many prudent judgements, aesthetic comparisons, and detached awareness of literary data".

As against this, Cross, whose wavering over the issue of the 100-year gap in stratigraphy between Milik and de Vaux has already been noted above, claims that "the rapid accumulation of discoveries . . . provide additional data for fixing absolute dates within relative dating systems provided by typological analysis." Yet he has the temerity to rely on de Vaux's controversial 31 BC date for the end of Period 1, while at the same time claiming this stratigraphy has made ostracon and ceramic dating more secure. Willing now to step out "boldly" in making use of the evidence of ossuary scripts, he claims that this "variety of archaeological and palaeographic advances" has made it possible to *peg* "a series of absolute datings at intervals throughout the Herodian Age and the subsequent era between the two Jewish Revolts against Rome". With considerable more modesty, however, he admitted that chronology for "proto-Jewish" scripts would be "less precise" and for Hasmonaean "more difficult to fix with precision than Herodian hands"; "Scripts", pp. 133–135.

The final insight, however, perhaps belongs to North. Despite Cross' attack on Driver and those dependent on him as "uninformed" (echoed later by de Vaux), he had some time before already cautioned in the manner of Avigad that "it must be admitted by a prudent observer that the materials at our disposal are simply not adequate" (i.e., to make absolute chronological sequences). Noting Vermes' pronouncement that "the palaeographers acquitted themselves remarkably well of their task" given the materials at their disposal, North cautions, "he can mean only that they came to a relative agreement which however is far from being a genuine or independent scientific *consensus*": pp. 430–1.

For his part, Cross finally admits also that scholars in the medieval field "have expressed skepticism concerning the precision of dating claimed by workers in the early Jewish field". However, he brushes it aside with his usual brusqueness, saying it "is based on a fallacious transfer of problems occasioned by experience with a surpassingly conservative script to scripts of a radically different tradition". Still he concludes, contradicting his original contention above: "the dating of a script of Qumran to a single generation on typological grounds, in the case of individual manuscripts, cannot, of course, be converted into absolute dating"; "Scripts", p. 192, n. 29. All of these comments and polemics are quoted at length because earlier criticism of paleographic methods have simply made no impression on the scholarly community.

his students—and upon which most subsequent data has been con-
structed, early voices, such as Idris Bell of the British Museum and F.
C. Burkitt, initially represented a three- or four-century deviation from
Albright.[156]

S. A. Birnbaum, who along with Cross has laid the foundations to
this paleographic structure, employs what in any other field would be
considered the most pseudo-scientific and infantile methods in determining these "pegs".[157] In this way he adds new "pegs" to aid in determining

---

[156] See Albright, "A Biblical Fragment from the Maccabean Age: the Nash Papyrus",
SBL, 56, 1937, pp. 149ff. and 171ff. Sukenik originally placed Nash in the first century,
Megilloth Genuzoth, i, Jerusalem, 1948, p. 14, but later in a letter to Albright, cited in "Ain
Feshka", p. 19, n. 10, revised it back to the first century BC; E. R. Lacheman put it in
the second century CE. Under these pressures Albright in "Ain Feshka", p. 19, who first
dated Nash at the start of the Maccabean age, now changed his estimate: "So far as the
evidence goes, it thus supports a date for the Nash papyrus not later than the first half
of the first century BC." See also, p. 15, n. 5a and J. C. Trever's article, "A Palaeographic
Study of the Jerusalem Scrolls", *BASOR*, 113, 1949, pp. 18–22, who preceded him in
this revision. Later, under Birnbaum's prodding, Albright was to revise it back again.
Cross, in "Oldest Manuscripts", p. 148, calls his mentor's original dating of the Nash
Papyrus (if one can remember what it was after all the shifts) "definitive"; elsewhere in
"Scripts", p. 135, he calls the analysis that produced it "exemplary" and notes, "his date
in the Maccabean Period remains undisturbed. Indeed, his original preference for a date
in the second half of the second century needs scant revision." His generosity to his
mentor is understandable, as probably also under Birnbaum's pressuring—who in
BASOR, 115, 1949, p. 22, had pressed for a date in the second quarter of the second
century "very near the maximum figure 165 BCE—suggested by Albright in his masterly
examination in . . . 1937"—he supports a date of 150 BC; "Scripts", p. 166.
Regardless of what the final truth is (which despite any claims to the contrary will
never be known), we see here an outside range of some 400 years and an inside one of
100–200 years for one of the most important "pegs" in the structure. Birnbaum's system
of reflecting this is particularly colorful; he uses square brackets when a document's
dating is *practically certain* from external evidence; "broken brackets" when *certain from his
own analysis* (italics mine), "Scripts", p. 28. Perhaps the most perceptive insight into this
sad spectacle of imprecision is once again North's, who obviously knew personally all
the *dramatis personae*: *CBQ*, p. 430: "The fact should be faced that it is extremely difficult
to divorce Albright's *arguments* from the considerable authority of his person; consequently his dating, ±50 BC, has attained a diffusion not strictly proportioned to the
proofs . . . . "
[157] Cross, "Scripts", p. 135, called Birnbaum's *The Hebrew Scripts* (*even before its publication*),
"a monumental attempt to deal with all periods of Hebrew writing . . . which will remain
for many years a standard handbook for student and scholar alike" (was this perhaps
intended for the book jacket?). He excuses the author's "polemical tone" (hardly
Birnbaum's principal flaw) in an earlier work with the comment that "it should be
remembered that it was written by *a professional palaeographer* tried to the limit by the
Lilliputian attacks of non-specialists" (italics mine): n. 20, p. 191.
The question of "pegs" is of course all-important. I have noted Birnbaum's

mathematical procedure, which he repeats with single-minded obliviousness on virtually every page leaving the intelligent reader in speechless amazement. See, for instance, nos. 80* (4QSam^b), 81 (1QIs.^{a}), 82 (1QS), 84 (1QpHab), 87^a (1QIs^b), 87^b (1QM), 87^d (1QH^2), 87^e (1QH^1), etc. His outside limits, based on general previous paleographic estimates of the Edfu scripts and archaeological acceptance of 68 as the *terminus ad quem* for the deposit of the scrolls at Qumran, are 300 BC and 68 CE. For comparison purposes he uses the Edfu scripts to determine "early" characteristics; and "the ossuaries"—by which he means 88 and 95–100*—"late". But these ossuaries (including Uzziah, Beit Schur, Ein Roghel, Wadi Saliʿa, and that of Queen Helen), which he himself dates anywhere from 50 BC to about 70 CE, averaging about early first century, are themselves, except for Queen Helen of Adiabene (his only secure peg), hardly secure.

In any case, his use of them as a measuring standard in one pole of his proportions, since they do not match the upper pole limit of his basic 368-year time span, vitiates his schoolboy mathematics even before he starts. Take 4QSam^b, which he says has forty-five features in common with the Egyptian scripts and eleven with the ossuaries. He, therefore, sets this up as: $\frac{45}{11} = \frac{368}{x}$ and subtracts x from 300 BC to get a result of 228 BC (*sic*—the computational error is Birnbaum's). "The result", he claims, "will be something like *the absolute date* . . . " (italics mine; p. 130), which is, of course, preposterous. Or on the other extreme, take 1QM, which he says has fifty-two features in common with the ossuaries and one with the Egyptian scripts, or $\frac{52}{1} = \frac{368}{x}$. He subtracts the result from 68 CE and gets 61 CE. He is even willing to use this methodology on notoriously conservative scripts like Samaritan ones, i.e., no. 70, the Abisha Scroll, choosing two *termini*, the eighth and thirteenth centuries, and finding that the characteristics point to the eleventh century as the "not unlikely date", p. 117.

This is not a proper working methodology, Cross and Albright notwithstanding. He may end up, if he is lucky, with a rough relative chronology, but it does not take into consideration the multiple variables of the age of scribe, his school of training, his personal expertise, his conservatism, and the speed of evolution of individual letters—which Avigad rightly abstains from attempting to estimate and which Cross invariably assumes to be "rapid"—none of which can even be conceived of as straight-line functions. To obtain a proper working method, he would have to define separate functions for each of these variables and then plug them into a differential equation, the solution to which would tax even the abilities of a space engineer. To think that his errors simply cancel themselves out, as Birnbaum does, is in itself a good illustration of the unscientific nature of his methodology.

What is worse he goes on to corroborate his "results" using results he previously obtained by the same method and with the same parameters, punctuating his discussion at various intervals with remarks like "results check", "tallies", "corroborated", which of course they cannot help but do. In reality, he might just as likely be compounding his errors and could be out 100 years, or even more, depending on the mistakes he has compounded in his "pegs". It is pretentious to call such a methodology "unassailable", and what is more to use it to rule out credible solutions which can at least make sense of internal data—which Birnbaum doesn't even understand, no less make intelligible—which is what is being done by dutiful students of this technique at the present time. You cannot deal with your opponent's charges by calling them "Lilliputian", contemptuously dismissing them as "uninformed", or what is even worse, ignoring them—the normal manner in Qumran studies of dealing with criticism—when you are using a methodology

the provenance and date of the next manuscript, and so on down the line.[158] Far from homing in on the true dates of a manuscript by such a methodology, what he does—as any good student of mathematics will realize—is to *compound* his errors increasing his margin of error

such as this. Certainly, you cannot claim you have cut your margin of error down to "one generation" even in relative chronology.

Before leaving this rather sad subject, let us set out a few of Birnbaum's "historical" assumptions. First, Birnbaum's answer to the lack of footnotes or bibliography in his work is simple: "The present study has not utilized any printed sources but ... the written documents themselves. For this reason no reference to previous work has been made in my book, and the compilation of a bibliography is not called for": p. 26. Where he does give references, they are usually either from the *Talmud* or to make additional comments. In discussing Ezra, whom he credits *with introducing the Aramaic script*, he is completely unaware of questions concerning Ezra's own chronology, or even his existence, and assumes without question he pre-dates Nehemiah. Claiming in a thinly disguised version of Wellhausen that such changes are invariably religiously motivated, he explains: "When a nation adopts a new religion, it discards also the script of its former creed and adopts that of the new religion", pp. 69–75. Pointing out that John Hyrcanus issued the first coins (recently a massive amount of new coins have been found from the Persian period), he categorically asserts John was "a Hellenistic ruler", not "a nationalist". For him, on the other hand, "the Pharisees" were the "religious nationalists". John's war, therefore—since John was a Sadducee—against the Samaritans could not be "nationalistic"; he rather terms it "expansionistic".

Pressing these historical insights further, he states that since John sided with the Sadducees, breaking with the Pharisees, the former "from what we know of their principles would have been the last people to dig out the old script" (i.e. the paleo-Hebrew)! He refers to this paleo-Hebrew with endless scorn, as if he were personally antagonized by it, as "not a living script", "an artificial revival", "an isolated rendering", concluding— for whatever it's worth—with the observation that even now the State of Israel declined to use it, since it was "consigned to oblivion by the Jewish people": pp. 77–79, 87, 94, and 103. Finally, he uncritically accepts de Vaux's archaeology. *Vis-à-vis* the 31 BC date, he has this to say: "We know that there was a break in the settlement at Qumran during the last third of the first pre-Christian century and a renewed settlement at the beginning of the next century" and he completely misunderstands the import of the 68 CE date. He uses both dates without reservation and unquestioningly, and like Cross, finds them an "important help" in turning a "relative date into an absolute one", pp. 149 and 127ff.

[158] Cf. how he uses 115 and 151 to corroborate his dating for 80*. Obviously, they must corroborate since they have been arrived at on the basis of the same parameters. He uses 115 again in 81, corroborates 82 by 81, corroborates 84 (Habakkuk) with 87a, and actually makes a slight shift back from 25 to 50 BC, saying he is more sure of 87a (1QIs^b—25 BC). Then finding the difference between it and 81 (1QIs^a—150 BC) "considerable", he says, results "check": p. 143. Milik, p. 64, would rather put Habakkuk in the mid-first century and even later, saying it "could not come from any part of the first century BC". Here we are out nearly 100 years on a key document. *Pace*, peace among paleographers. Birnbaum's approach to 87a (1QIs^b) is classic. He invokes de Vaux's archaeology to show that the date for the temporary abandonment of Qumran corresponds with his own projection, *turning it into an absolute date*, and corroborates his

exponentially. The methods of the other "paleographers" working in the Second Temple Period do not differ markedly from his (though they are not quite so forthcoming in their presentation of them). All involve a certain amount of subjective reckoning based on the assumptions and preconceptions I have been at pains to upset in this study.[159]

dating by comparison with 84. But he has just used 87a to corroborate his results with 84. Nothing loath, he concludes: "Thus each of the two dates corroborates the other", p. 150; his logic could hardly be more circular. He then confidently proceeds to corroborate 87b (1QM) and 87e (Hand A of Hymns) by 87a again, commenting it "goes well" (they should), p. 155. Cross, too, is quite prepared to use his tenuous relative dates as "pegs" in the absolute chronology. He is even willing to "project backward" ("not as complicated as it sounds") along separate typological lines to achieve these. For his classic discussion of this in relation to Jewish, Palmyrene, and Nabataean scripts, see "Scripts", pp. 160–1; cf. also 196–7, n. 105.

[159] I think we have covered these subjective preconceptions both in archaeology and other disciplines adequately for Birnbaum. Milik's were noted earlier above. Cross uses archaeology, as we have seen, for transforming relative to absolute chronologies; "Scripts", pp. 133ff. and "Oldest Manuscripts", pp. 147f. Here, while seeing relative chronology as secure, he admits that, "Absolute dating of the documents poses a more complicated problem . . . ", p. 163. He very definitely relies on de Vaux's "earthquake" hypothesis in dating "Herodian" script, i.e., 30 BC to 70 CE, but unlike Birnbaum, does not consider that the "abandonment" of Qumran produced any "equivalent *lacuna* in the typological sequence of manuscripts"; "Scripts", pp. 173 and 199, n. 127. Avigad, as we have noted, as always is more modest, but rarely stands against his peers. Cf. also Vermes, p. 55, quoted above. It is interesting, when one comes to investigate Cross' claims for "a series of absolute dating" pegs "at intervals throughout the Herodian Age", that, while protesting against Avigad's late dating of the Dominus Flevit ossuaries, he can only come up with the fact, citing Milik, that "the Herodian dating ['as Milik himself would insist'] of the great mass . . . is certain"—a range of some 125 years. Actually, as stated above, he has only the Queen Helen of Adiabene inscription as really certain.

Another "peg" is, of course, the Bene Hezir inscription, which is of special interest to us, which he (Cross), Avigad, p. 174, and Albright, "Nash", p. 159, all seem to agree on a date of about the turn of the Christian era; "Scripts", pp. 174, 198, n. 123, and 199, n. 133. In "Oldest Manuscripts" Cross is so secure in this date (in his usual manner) that he even terms it "a *terminus ad quem*" for first-century BC scripts. Avigad in *Ancient Monuments in the Kidron Valley* (Hebrew), Jerusalem, 1954, pp. 62–64, originally sought an even earlier dating. The key analysis here is Albright's. Attributing the thesis to de Vogüé (cf. Klein, *Jüdisch-Palästinisches Corpus Inscriptionum*, Vienna, 1920, pp. 14ff.), he says the latter "is clearly right" in claiming "that the tomb of the Bene Hezir (popularly ascribed to St James) belongs to the priestly family that contributed three high priests during the reigns of Herod and Archelaus . . . it would then date from the end of Herod's reign or a little later . . . ."

There are, however, at least four names mentioned on the plaque, and Jeremias has shown with considerably more precision than de Vogüé that the Boethusians contributed at least eight high priests, the last probably being Joseph Cabi, 62 CE, "the son of the high priest Simon"; cf. Jeremias, pp. 94 and 194ff. and *Ant.* 19.6.2–4 and 20.8.11–9.1.

This is to say nothing of the other variables: for instance, that in a given community there might have been an archaizing conservative tradition, as, for instance, the paleo-Hebrew script at Qumran: even today Samaritans use an archaizing script with roots going back perhaps some twenty centuries for biblical manuscripts.[160] Or that one might have been dealing with older scribes.

To posit for the purposes of argument the extreme case, let us suppose that an eighty-year-old scribe was sitting next to a twenty-five-year-old scribe trained in a more "up-to-date" scribal school (whatever this might mean in such circumstances).[161] Here, of course, is where Milik's margin

It is not without interest, nor significance, that Joseph Cabi loses the High Priesthood in the political machinations leading up to the judicial murder of James (see above, p. 53). There is, therefore, absolutely no proof (other than paleographic; cf. Cross and Albright on the use of ligatures) that this tomb was built, nor the inscription made, before about the middle of the first century CE; and the unfinished condition of adjoining tombs, and to a certain extent its own, would argue for the later, not earlier, dating. Certainly, it cannot be considered a *secure terminus ad quem* for the first century BC, as Cross would have it—at least not a precise one. This is to say nothing of the inherent imprecision of attempting to use lapidary work as a "*peg*" in dating manuscript sequences.

[160] Birnbaum, p. 138. Cf. his discussion of paleo-Hebrew, pp. 76ff.; of Samaritan, pp. 98ff.; and Cross, p. 189, n. 4.

[161] Cross is very much aware of this problem: "Despite the speed of evolution in this period, allowance must be made always for the extension of the professional life of a conservative scribe beyond his generation, or for the individualistic hand which holds out against the powerful current of scribal styles and fashions", p. 161. So is Avigad, who with typical caution, but considerably less élan, in the section where he asserts "the speed of development of individual letters is a factor we cannot yet make out," says, "It should, however, be kept in mind that various scribes are naturally inclined to conservatism in the case of formal styles", pp. 72–3. Cf. also Laperrousaz defending his own theories, p. 98.

Cross' charm and aesthetic sensibility—evident throughout his work—undoubtedly help to win him many supporters; cf. p. 160 on "archaic semiformal", p. 173 on "Herodian" (expressed even more sensitively on p. 192, n. 27 and p. 200, n. 141), and again on p. 105, n. 4 on "paleo-Hebrew"—though sometimes deteriorating into jargon or incomprehensibility as on p. 141 on the "Aramaic hand" or p. 153 on 4QEx[f]. Morton Smith has put the case well. In personal comments to me he notes that Cross originally considered the greater part of Qumran documents to be in "private hands". He claims that, only later, probably under Birnbaum's influence, did Cross begin to grasp the significance of and come to see them as being primarily in "book hands". Smith cites Mount Athos and similar communities, where documents are datable, as verification of the proposition that often several different book hands with widely differing dates of origin can be found simultaneously in the same community. He concludes that, even if accurate sequencing and dating of the original could be established—in themselves highly unlikely propositions—a given ms., written in a particularly durable hand, might in fact have been written years later than one written in a hand of more recent development.

of error comes into play, but this is hardly very comforting when we are using one manuscript to date another, as Birnbaum does, none of which with an actual dating formula. What date would two manuscripts copied by these two scribes at exactly the same time appear to be?

If the older scribe copied a manuscript using the script he learned when he was twenty, what date would we give a manuscript found in only one exemplar that was actually copied in 4 BC? 63 BC or before? Suppose the older scribe's teachers themselves were all old or very old-fashioned, what then would be the margin of error? Or suppose that a given student just had not learned his lessons very well and made errors which looked to paleographers either like scriptual developments or regressions (there are many such confusing mixtures of innovative and regressive scripts at Qumran, depending of course on what is meant by "innovative" and "regressive").[162]

It is not possible to say on paleographic grounds that a manuscript was written in 63 BC and not, for instance, in 45 CE. In particular, when one has only one exemplar of a given work (the case for instance of all the *Pesharim* at Qumran and many other texts) or when one has one "older" copy as opposed to several or a cluster of "newer" ones—the actual case of the Damascus Document—one must exercise extreme caution. The best one can hope for is a rough "relative chronology". Only when manuscripts begin to bunch up in a clearly discernible manner is one justified in thinking in terms of *possible* dates. In any event, it is certainly incautious to date it by its earliest exemplar, however

---

Our purpose in criticizing the paleographers is not to rule out a certain amount of value to such work *when taken within strict limits*, but to caution them to be more modest in their claims for precision: for instance, in the supposedly secure "Herodian" lapidary work and in the case of relative chronologies down to a single generation (Birnbaum claims even more precision); and to open their admitted fifty-year margin of error to 100 years (in some instances even more), particularly where sectarian works are concerned. Even their own disagreements on mss. such as Habakkuk and Hymns exceed this. Cross, for instance, knows that all of Birnbaum's estimates are too early, but so probably, too, are many of his own; cf. "Oldest Manuscripts", p. 148.

[162] See, for instance, Birnbaum's discussion of the earliest book hands at Qumran, in particular 1QLev and 1QEx, pp. 68–70 (nos. 28–32), where he says some features imply a later date for 1QLev, and some a later date for 1QEx. His conclusion is completely unscientific: "From this we cannot but conclude that both were written during the same period, each of the scribes using some 'earlier' and some 'later' forms." But, of course, this is Birnbaum's method of dating every manuscript at Qumran; cf. his discussion of 4QSam[b] and Cross' general discussion of 4QEx[f], 4QSam[b], and 4QJer[a], pp. 140–58. Birnbaum's estimate of the mid-fifth century for these hands is based on the purest supposition having to do, as we have noted above, p. 88–90, with his preconceptions about Ezra's importance.

tempting this may be, as all scholars in the field rush to do, but rather where the distribution peaks.[163] Yet Qumran scholars make these kinds of assumptions regularly, claiming a precision that comes down in some cases to a handful of years, while dismissing better theories than the one on which their own methodological assumptions are based.

---

[163] Cross, p. 61, has signaled his awareness of this problem following up his caution concerning the longevity of a conservative scribe: "However, in the case of a group of scripts belonging typologically to a certain generation, we can assume methodologically that the majority of the group were copied in the normal span of a generation." The contrapositive, however, which he misses, involves exceptions to the "majority": either the case of a scribe whose longevity extends beyond the group or that of a single manuscript that "appears" substantially earlier than a given group.

This is exactly the situation of the "early" fragments of the Damascus Document (4QD^b) found in Cave IV. Fragments from at least seven other mss. of the Damascus Document have been found in Cave IV, most of which appear to be "Herodian". Milik, pp. 38–9 and 57–8, gives 4QD^b a date of between 75 and 50 BC (cf. Cross, *Library*, p. 120), which paleographically probably presents the only serious stumbling-block to the historical reconstruction we set forth above. Fitzmyer, prescient as ever in grasping the cruciality of this fragment in the scheme of Qumran origins, tried to push it even further back in time by attacking Starcky's "Pompeian" dating in "Theory of Qumran Messianic Development" (cf. Starcky, "Les Quatres Étapes du Messianism", *RB*, 70, 1963, pp. 496ff.) and asserting that this copy was "scarcely the original monograph"; cf. his revision of "The Aramaic 'Elect of God' Text from Qumran Cave IV", *Essays*, pp. 138–9.

Milik, however, parts company with him on this issue, citing 4QD^b in a follow-up to his "two-generation" remark as an example of a Qumran text "more or less contemporary with the events to which they refer" (cf. Cross, p. 114, but also Cross' discussion, pp. 81–3, n. 46, where he rather agrees with Fitzmyer). In the same context, Milik also discusses the general class of mss. called *pesharim*, all of which he places in "the last phase of the Qumran settlement"; see also Additional n. 3, pp. 151–2 and "*Milkî-sedq et Milkî-reša'* ", pp. 135f. Surely Fitzmyer is asking more from paleography than it can scientifically sustain in attacking Starcky on the issue of such a paleographically insignificant time differential (the same might be said for Cross, who agrees with Fitzmyer on the matter of 4QD^b).

A few pages earlier, pp. 132ff., Fitzmyer had already pointed to how 4QD^b confirmed that the reference to a *singular* "Messiah of Aaron and Israel" in CD, xiv, 19 was not a medieval copyist's mistake, as has often been suggested, and, in addition, pointed out perhaps even more importantly that the same manuscript actually contained a reference to "the flight of the Essenes to their Damascus Camps". What could echo more the early Christian tradition of a flight by the Jerusalem Community to Pella (i.e., "in the Damascus region" or perhaps as Acts 9:22 would have it "the Jewish settlement at Damascus"), since as Brandon points out, an actual flight to Pella in this period was probably precluded by the political and military situation? For the whole controversy, including the positions of Strecker, Munck, Filson, Schoeps, etc., see Brandon, pp. 208–214. One should also keep in mind the use of the allusion "Damascus" as a codename (here Cross agrees with us, pp. 82f.; see also R. North, "The Damascus of Qumran Geography", *Palestine Exploration Quarterly*, 1955, pp. 34–48), and possibly too, even "Pella".

We have already noted above, p. 83, the similarity of the "Pella flight" tradition with the Masada flight of the *Sicarii*, both undertaken for similar reasons, namely, the stoning of their respective leaders. Both groups, too, appear to have withdrawn from further participation in the Uprising against Rome, which was moving quickly into its "Jacobin" phase. We have, however, not mentioned the possible confusion of "a flight to Pella" with a "flight to Sela' ", a name used both to refer to Petra—Paul's "Arabia" reference?— and an unidentified Dead Sea Valley location. Even Masada may have been known to the sectaries by such a codename (cf., for instance, the reference in Mur 45.6 to staying at the "*Meẓad-Hassidin*", i.e., "the Fortress of the *Hassidim*", which very likely refers to the area around Qumran, and which by implication identifies it as the original stronghold or location of "the Hassidaean" Movement).

Here, I think, it may be possible to identify the actual scriptural passage containing "the mysterious oracle" referred to in Church tradition (cf. Eusebius, *E.H.* 3.5.2f. and Epiphanius, *Haeres.* 29.7 and 30.2; also *De Mens et Pond* 15) as the basis for this flight. Significantly, it comes in direct proximity to the famous passage which tradition tells us was actually used to arrive at an exegetical understanding of James' death (Is 3:10). I refer to Is 2:10ff. In considering it, one should try to visualize what a Qumran-style *pesher* on the first four to five chapters of Isaiah would look like.

The whole passage is addressed pointedly and several times to "*the House of Jacob*" and as in Habakkuk, the context is the imminent destruction of Jerusalem ("Jerusalem is ruined and Judea fallen"). Amid the telltale imagery of the Righteousness of "works" (cf. the use of *ma'asim* at Qumran, above, p. 16), allusion to "plundering the Meek" (3:14; cf. CD, vi, 16 and "plundering the Poor" in 1QpHab, xii, 10), "justifying the Wicked" (cf. 5:24 with CD, i, 19 in the context of an allusion to "assaulting *the soul of the Zaddik* and pursuing the Walkers in Perfection with the sword"), the imminent coming of "the Day of *Yahweh*", and the equally telltale overthrow of "*the cedars of Lebanon*" (2:12f.); the people are urged to throw away their gold and idols to the moles and the bats (cf. Ja 5:2f. and 1QpHab, xi, 12ff.) and "enter into the Rock . . . for *the day of the Lord of Hosts* shall be upon every one that is proud and lofty [cf. Ja 4:6ff.] . . . and upon all *the cedars of Lebanon* that are high and lifted up [cf. 4QpIs[a] and 1QpHab, xii, 2] . . . go into the holes *of the Rocks* and *into the caves* of the earth for fear of the Lord [cf. once more the allusion to cave-dwelling] . . . go into *the clefts of the Rocks* and into the tops of the ragged *Rocks* [here "*Sela'im*" is actually used; anyone familiar with Qumran terrain will see the connection] for fear of the Lord and for the glory of his majesty when he arises to shake terribly the earth" (italics mine).

This is followed up at the beginning of Chapter 3, leading up to the passage we know was applied to James' death, with the words (Is 3:1): "For behold, the Lord, the Lord of Hosts is taking away from Jerusalem and from Judah the stay and the staff, the whole stay of bread, and the whole stay of water." Anyone familiar with the techniques of Qumran exegesis would know the kinds of exegesis that would have been developed from such passages. In close proximity to this passage is also the famous "Zion shall be redeemed through Judgement (*Mishpat*) and her converts through Righteousness" (*Zedakah*—in this context, more properly, "Justification") and the reference to the restored Jerusalem as "Faithful City" (*Kiryah-Ne'emanah*) and "City of Righteousness" ('*Ir ha-Zedek*), not to mention the well-known call to all peoples to come up "to the House of the God of Jacob", ending with: "O House of Jacob, come ye and let us walk in the Light of the Lord" (Is 1:26–2:5; cf. "Ways of Light", "eternal Light", and "walking in

I would like to state a rule of thumb that might be helpful. Paleo-graphic data cannot in and of itself be considered definitive. Scholars who use it to disqualify an otherwise convincing picture, which in most other ways fits the available evidence, do so at their own peril. At no time can it be used to dismiss a theory which within these general param-eters can make meaningful sense of internal textual evidence. Where "pegging" is so precarious and in the general absence of secure date formulae, "meaningful textual evidence" must be accorded precedence, as it is in any case by a majority of scholars—including even paleogra-phers as we have seen—albeit in a subconscious manner.

Ultimately, we shall probably have to admit that the situation regarding paleography is much more chaotic and difficult to describe than was originally envisioned by Cross' and Birnbaum's assumptions of "rapid" *straight-line* development of scripts in the Second Temple period, which lie at the heart of their reconstructions and *equations* such as they are. Such a circumstance, anyhow, would be more in keeping with the reality of the historical *sitz im leben* of the period. Here, textual and historical studies will be able to play a role in helping to clarify the true, probably highly complex, character of paleographic sequences, not vice versa as heretofore.

On the basis of internal textual data alone (namely, the use of Hab 2:4, Is 40:3, Is 10:29f., Num 24:17, Deut 18:15ff., and the evocation of the terminology of Is 53:11f. in Qumran communal organization and in eschatological interpretations like those of Ezek 44:15 and Hab 2:4, demonstrably all scriptural passages enjoying a vogue in first-century Palestine, but not before), one is entitled to conclude that almost all

the Ways of Light" imagery at Qumran generally, particularly in 1QS, iii, 7–25; iv, 2–7, etc.).

Here, therefore, one has considerable incentive to revive G. Margoliouth's original dating of the Damascus Document when it was first discovered in 1896, trusting that the cautions I have outlined above, *vis-à-vis* a conservative use of paleographic evidence and a healthy restraint on related preconceptions, will be taken seriously (note we are not making any claims that this reference in 4QD^b is to the actual "Pella flight", only that it echoes and is representative of the flight traditions of this period). See also Milik, p. 117, who admits 4QD^b places the "ceremony of the renewal of the Covenant" at Pentecost, a festival of the greatest significance to the early "Church"; cf. Paul's rush to get to Jerusalem in time for the community's convocation at Pentecost, Acts 20:16, and the transformation of "the descent of the Law" implicit in the celebration of this festival into "the descent of the Pauline Holy Spirit" and its Gentile Mission accoutrements of "speaking in Tongues", etc. (note the ready-made scope for the additional possible exten-sion of the "Tongue" and "Spouting" imagery at Qumran and in the Letter of James here).

Qumran sectarian texts are "late", namely first century CE. Paleography will have to accommodate itself to these results, not vice versa.

Such a conclusion where "sectarian" works are concerned, implying as it does the fact of *new* ideological departures, is completely in keeping with Josephus' repeated allusions to "innovations" and "innovators" since the appearance of Judas and Saddok at the beginning of the first century and the statements in the *ARN* and al-Kirkisani identifying the start of really destructive sectarian strife with the "split" between "Zadok and Boethus", as well as the parallel, albeit highly refracted, testimonies in the New Testament and Pseudoclementine *Recognitions* placing in conjunction "the division of the People into many parties", the birth of "the Sadducees" (who, "considering themselves more Righteous", "withdrew from the community"), and the *coming of John*.[164]

IX
ARCHAEOLOGICAL PROBLEMS

The above caution about the precedence "meaningful textual evidence" must take over the claims of paleography should be applied, as well, to claims in archaeology based on coin data, the use of which has gone so far as to convince the community at large that an absolute determination of the date of the destruction of the monastery can be made down to the year and the month.[165] The reason this destruction, in particular, is

[164] Of the *two* "splits" or "withdrawals" we have discussed in this study (i.e., that between "Zadokite Hassidaeans" and "Pharisee Hassidaeans" and that between "Messianic Sadducees" and "Boethusian Sadducees"), we are speaking about the later one which triggers Josephus' descriptions of the "sects" in *Ant.* and *War*. For the early first-century provenance of this and its connection with the split between Saddok and Joezer b. Boethus, see above, pp. 21 and 50. For the basic interchangeability of John and "Saddok", see below, p. 107. For the denouement of this split approximately seventy years later, see how "the Men of Power" (i.e., "the Herodians"), "the High Priests", "the principal of the Pharisees", and "all those desirous of peace"—principal among whom is one "Saulus . . . of the King's kindred"—the descendant of the *Idumaean convert* "Costobarus" probably either through Agrippa I's sister Herodias or the family of Herod of Chalcis in Cilicia—try to convince "the Innovators" that the rejection of gifts from foreigners and sacrifices from Romans or Caesar was "impious" or "seditious". Thereupon *they invite* the Roman army into the city "to cut off the sedition before it became too hard to subdue"; *War* 2.17.2–6. Note that it is these same Innovators who ban Agrippa II from the Temple and all Jerusalem; above, p. 17.

[165] De Vaux proposes a date of June, 68; pp. 37–41 and "Fouilles", 1954, p. 233, echoed in Cross, p. 63. Despite noting quite a few additional coins of 68/69 found at Ein Feshka, Laperrousaz, pp. 85 and 90, agrees.

so important is that the Habakkuk *Pesher* refers to the fall of Jerusalem including giving particulars that unmistakably point to the fall of 70 CE. Yet our commentators use the archaeological data they have developed to contend this fall could not be that of 70 CE but rather must be that of 40 BC or 63 BC (or even before), thereby pushing the provenance of all Qumran material back almost 150 years or more.[166]

Nor do they worry in this regard what the sect might have been doing in the meantime until the deposit of the scrolls in the caves, expecting us rather to believe that it sat passively studying archaic scriptural exegesis and ignored 125 years of the most eventful Palestinian history.[167] To be sure, I, too, make use of coin data in this study, but only *in the most general way* to make comments about *general trends* and, in the process, to show of what acceptable usage of such data might consist.

For instance, no coins have yet been found in Qumran—though they

---

[166] Cross, p. 126: "Just as we cannot date the foundation of the sect in the Roman era because of *reference to Pompey's conquest of Jerusalem in the Habakkuk Commentary* . . . " (italics mine). Cf. how he uses 4QD[b] in the same way, pp. 81–3, n. 46. De Vaux is not slow to follow him, p. 122. While willing to utilize Pliny's testimony in *Hist. Nat.* 5.17.4 about an "Essene" settlement near the shores of the Dead Sea between Jericho and Ein Gedi to further their own theories (de Vaux, pp. 134ff., and Cross, pp. 15 and 70ff.), they ignore the clear implication it contains of continued habitation in the region—regardless of the condition of the permanent structures at Qumran—a circumstance also hinted at by Mur 45.6 as we have seen, because it doesn't suit their preconceptions or archaeological conclusions. For an opposing view, see Farmer, "The Economic Basis of the Qumran Community", *TZ*, 1955, pp. 295ff.

Here, one is obliged to point out that Simeon bar Cleophas, the man Eusebius appears to identify as "a Rechabite Priest" and the successor to James and putative second brother of Jesus, martyred under Trajan sometime after 106 CE, while probably never going to "Pella", certainly subsisted with his followers somewhere in the environs of Jerusalem. Note the Qumran-style language *E.H.* 3.32, relying on Hegesippus, uses to describe his "end"—"like the Lord's" (i.e., "until then the church remained a virgin . . . then godless error began to take shape *through the Deceipt of False Teachers* . . . who preached against the *Truth* ["*Emet*" at Qumran] the counter-proclamation of *False Knowledge*" ["*Da'at Sheker*"]; italics mine). The passage, while obscure, seems to include data, also based on Hegesippus, about the simultaneous executions of those descendants of Jesus' *third brother Judas*, who he attests *still* "presided over every church" because they belonged to "the Lord's family".

[167] Cross and Milik explain—in the view of the writer rather lamely—that *the traditions were preserved orally to be set down at a time close to the fall of the monastery*, yet they do not deny that other mss. contain records of contemporary events: see Cross, pp. 94, 113–4, and 120, nn. 21, 24, 28, and Milik, pp. 57–9, 64, and 89 (with another slur on the Maccabees). That such intimate and intense commentaries could be thought to be the product of "oral transmission", the generally fragmented and disoriented nature of which is well illustrated in the *Talmud*, is typical of the unreal world these specialists are permitted to inhabit by their peers.

have at Ein Feshka—from the fourth year of the Revolt, 69/70. A substantial number, though, have already been found from the third year of the Revolt, 68/69, the year de Vaux and his supporters claim the monastery fell. They go so far as to claim this as a *terminus ad quem* for the deposit of the scrolls in the caves, meaning that habitation ceased at the location and its surroundings, though it has been observed that the sectaries living in the caves probably did not carry money on their persons. Since no coins of any kind have been found in the caves and their environs, no judgement whatever can be made on this basis about the extent or lack of Rechabite-style habitation in the caves.[168]

De Vaux claims that minting must have begun in the Spring of the year 68, which would have left enough time for this substantial number of coins to get to Qumran before its fall, which he places in June. But in the year 68 the siege of Jerusalem began, and it is surprising that as many coins got out to Qumran as did. In fact, it is not even clear if

---

[168] Sometimes de Vaux drops his diplomatic approach and categorically states, p. 112: "The community installed itself at Qumran in the second half of the second century BC. It abandoned the site for a period of some thirty years during the reign of Herod the Great, and *definitively left the area in* AD *68*" (italics mine). No wonder some commentators have taken this for a "*terminus ad quem*" and not the *terminus post quem* he admits it is on p. 41 (however de Vaux is notorious for shifts of this kind; cf. North, "Archaeology", p. 430, who lists four retractions by de Vaux in the first three years of his work).

See Laperrousaz, p. 91, on the pottery found in many of these caves. De Vaux admits the caves were inhabited, though he tries to reduce the number; even so, he cannot get it down below forty; cf. pp. 44ff., 50f., and 57. On p. 107 he admits that some pottery even appears to be of a later date than the outside limit he set for the life of the settlement and that some of the repositories were hardly more than mere "depressions" in the cliff walls (p. 57). In spite of this, though he acknowledges habitation took place in the Bar Kochba Period, he still feels utterly secure in insisting, "The manuscripts of Qumran . . . were certainly not deposited in the caves at the time of the Second Jewish War." The caves, of course, in the marl terrace (where Cross' "Library" is to be found, i.e., Cave IV), while not inhabited, could certainly not have escaped notice in the Bar Kochba Period; de Vaux, pp. 52ff. and 56f.

The fact that Cave I shows clear signs of habitation and no money was found in any of these cave locations is important for our contention above that regardless of whether the buildings were destroyed or not in 68 CE, to claim an absolute abandonment of the "total site" on the basis of coin data is wishful thinking. De Vaux thinks he has proved the absolute abandonment of the site in 68 CE in his retort to Roth on p. 123, n. 1, but once more he has proved nothing, only a *terminus post quem* for the abandonment of the site and that its buildings might have been burned. What no commentator has yet succeeded in explaining, if the site (and the caves) were clearly inhabited at various times up to 136 CE, is why the manuscripts survived at all in many of these locations, some of which were hardly more than "crevices", and in Cave IV itself which was hardly a hiding place at all.

Roman troops did invest the area until 69–70 CE. It would be equally surprising if many more got out after that year, and given the conditions in the city in 69 and 70, very few were likely to have been minted anyhow. In any event, Jewish coins would hardly have been very good tender in Jericho or similar outlying regions any longer.[169]

In this context de Vaux claims that Phoenician and other non-Jewish coins were found in the layer overlaying that of the presumed destruction in 68 CE. Finding such foreign coins is taken as proof positive that a Roman contingent occupied the location from 68 CE onwards despite the fact that the number of such coins are few and finding coins in a given place says nothing about who the given individual was who happened to drop them there, or for that matter, when, only that he could not have dropped them there before the said date on the coin.[170] In

---

[169] De Vaux, *NTS*, p. 102, cites five silver shekels from the year 4 found in a treasure near Jericho in 1874; but this is just the point. No one denies that with the fall of Jerusalem hoards of coins, big or small, would have made their way out of the city, but it is doubtful if these coins would have been very widespread in this area as popular tender, for they would have had no value. Take the counter example: no coins have yet been found either at Qumran or Ein Feshka from the Year 1 of the Revolt, when such coins would have freely circulated. Do we, therefore, conclude there was no habitation in that year at Qumran? It is, therefore, textual evidence, of which there is a substantial amount, as de Vaux himself admits, p. 133, which must finally decide these questions. De Vaux counters: "This would be true if it were not for the fact that some Roman coins, the earliest of which belong to 67/68, had not been found in the level of reconstruction, and if this date did not coincide with the arrival of the Roman troops in the vicinity of Qumran": *Archaeology*, p. 123, n. 1. But this proves absolutely nothing, as de Vaux well knows. For his explanation of how so many coins managed to appear at Qumran between April and June of the year 68 CE, see p. 41.

[170] See pages 44ff. and 66ff., recapitulated in Laperrousaz, pp. 61ff. As has already been noted, de Vaux's stratigraphy is also cause for some concern. That he considers 68 to be the year "at which the two numismatic sequences meet" is hardly a scientific assessment. In any event, it would seem to be dubious in the extreme that de Vaux's archaeology was precise enough to determine the difference between a year or two in stratification. Evidences of destructions and earthquakes aside, we are talking here of small coins supposedly suspended between stratification layers. If he and Milik can't even agree on a 100-year gap concerning a pile of broken dishes and the wall adjacent to them, what are we to conclude about such supposed coin data?

Finally, that coins do persist at Qumran, including some seventeen or more coins from the reign of Agrippa II (78–95) at Ein Feshka, is evidence that habitation did continue in the area in a not insignificant manner until the period of Bar Kochba and beyond. That de Vaux and his colleagues do not choose to analyze in any significant way the import of these coins has, of course, to do with their own peculiar preconceptions and somewhat lopsided interpretation of the texts; just as the fact that I do, has to do with my own.

This is where the battle must be joined, and I submit the presentation I have set forth

particular, it says nothing about the precise date of the fall of the monastery.

To counter some of the objections I raise, it has been pointed out that a hoard of coins from the Fifth Year of the Jewish Revolt was found in the Masada excavations.[171] This is true, but many refugees from Jerusalem undoubtedly fled in a straight line across the Bethlehem plain to Masada after the fall of Jerusalem. In these circumstances, they probably would not have fled to Qumran, which would have afforded little or no protection (particularly if de Vaux and his supporters are correct in believing that its *buildings* were destroyed in 68 CE by the Roman army on its way up from Jericho to the siege of Jerusalem).

I would like to offer a counter example: no coins have yet been found on the Temple Mount from the Fifth Year of the Revolt. Are we, therefore, to conclude using the kind of reasoning one finds in de Vaux's theorizing that Jerusalem fell in 69 CE—obviously an untenable thesis?[172] Suppose, for instance, that in his digging Father de Vaux happened to miss a single coin from the fourth year of the Revolt, or that he had gone on to dig a little further before propounding his thesis? As it is, we are well into the third year of the Revolt with the coin data he provides. Father de Vaux responds, "I think we can be pardoned for not having dug up the whole hillside outside the walls in search of others"; I for one am tempted to respond in the negative.[173]

in the above pages is as or more credible than theirs. When a coin appears, for instance, that does not suit de Vaux's preconceived parameters—e.g., the "very worn coin of Aelia Capitolina from the reign of Antonius Pius, 138–61CE"—he sets it aside with the remark: it "must have been lost by a passer-by", p. 67. Elsewhere, he calls it a "stray". For his comments on other ubiquitous passers-by, see p. 45: "The few surface finds of coins, the date of which extend from the third century CE to the Turkish period, indicate nothing more than the passing of chance travellers." On the basis of the evidence he presents he certainly is not entitled to say: "No manuscript of the caves can be later than June 68 CE", *NTS*, p. 104. For remarks on de Vaux's sensationalist discovery of a coin from the Tenth Roman Legion, see below, p. 103.

[171] See de Vaux, *NTS*, pp. 102f. and 126, and Yadin, *op. cit.*, pp. 108f. and 170f.

[172] B. Mazar, "The Archaeological Excavations near the Temple Mount" in *Jerusalem Revealed: Archaeology in the Holy City 1968–1974*, ed. Y. Yadin, Jerusalem, 1976, p. 32, where it is also noted only one coin from the first year has so far been found. Even if more subsequently do turn up, this makes the number of coins at Qumran and its environs from 68–69 appear quite substantial—even too substantial for simply the first three months of minting, another example of preconceptions pressing more from the data than the data legitimately allows.

[173] Strictly speaking, he makes this remark in regard to his search for Roman arrowheads, but the mentality is illustrative, and the problem analogous; *NTS*, p. 101. One should remember, here, the existence of a certain amount of unidentified coins which

The same father in his zeal for his dating theories let it be broadcast to the scholarly world that a coin from the Tenth Roman Legion had been found at Qumran, thereby sending colleagues like Cross into a frenzy of activity to trace the movements of this legion, since previously it had been assumed it was quartered somewhere else at the time.[174] When it was subsequently pointed out to de Vaux that the "X" on the coin in question was not the quartermaster's mark of the Tenth Roman Legion, he was forced to retract his claim, but his retraction was hardly

de Vaux, not uncharacteristically, usually neglects to mention. In questioning Ya'acov Meshorer on the matter of de Vaux's numismatic evidence, I was told that he himself had never seen or checked de Vaux's coins, nor did he know anyone else in Israel who had. No doubt the members of de Vaux's "team" have, but apparently the coins are now locked up at the École Biblique. Some, perhaps, might harbor doubts of the kind expressed by J. Allegro in his description (necessarily personal, but not on that basis as fanciful as some of his other well-advertised ideas) of the machinations surrounding the publication of the Copper Scroll; *op. cit.*, pp. 28–38.

Where the Copper Scroll itself is concerned, it is hardly worth while commenting on the contortions some scholars are willing to go through in order either to divorce it from "the Essenes" or render it harmlessly "allegorical" (Domitian and Trajan would have been pleased; cf. *E.H.* 3.19 and 3.33 where they learn *for the first time* that the Kingdom of God "is not of this world", and either "despised" their informants "as simpletons" or Pilate-like "could find no harm in them"). It is not that "the Essenes" were not interested in money; rather like James' "Jerusalem Community"—from which they are hardly to be distinguished—they were against "Riches" and class distinctions, an antagonism they derived, as we have seen above, from their extension of the "all Righteousness" commandment into the realm of economic equality. Like the early "Christians" in Palestine, they kept a common purse, and as in the case of the keen interest taken both by Paul and in Jerusalem in overseas fund-raising activities, they were no doubt mindful of the economic necessities of administering a fair-sized community.

As with the War Scroll, where specialists ignore the direct evocation of the coming of the Messiah and "the Heavenly Host" on the clouds of Heaven—as per Jamesian proclamation and Paul in 1 Thess 3.13ff.—and see only allegory, here once again one group of specialists see only "allegory"—yet when figurative allusion *is* intended, as with "Zadok" and the Community Council as a "Temple" or "sweet fragrance"—again as per Pauline allusion—it is very often ignored. The impetus behind such flights from reality should be gradually becoming clear.

[174] See (however futile) Cross' complete discussion of this matter, pp. 62ff., particularly n. 18. At this point he refers to Roth's and Driver's attempt "to lower the date of the fall of Khirbet Qumrân to AD 73", protesting that "archaeological data" cannot be manipulated so "cavalierly", though in the same breath, he himself refers to Josephus' description of the fanatic resistance of "the Essenes". See also de Vaux's own description of the movements of this legion—presumably now minus the coin—pp. 38f. For the opposing view, see C. Roth, "Did Vespasian Capture Qumran", *PEQ*, 1959, pp. 122–29. De Vaux is also tight-lipped on the existence at Qumran of what appears to be a good-sized forge presumably because it, too, does not fit his stereotype of the "peaceful" Essenes. Cross, p. 69, neatly skips over it.

ever heard and one still sees the original contention repeated in many quarters as fact.[175]

Milik, who in so many ways is closely identified with de Vaux, in addition to disagreeing with him on whether the fallen wall and "broken dishes" reflect the Herodian destruction or that of the Jewish Revolt, has on the basis of coin data queried the master's evidence for the absolute abandonment of the monastery in the Herodian period.[176] One is permitted on the basis of coin data to say certain kinds of general things, as Milik does, but one is not permitted to say that the monastery was destroyed in 31 BC, any more than one is permitted to say *anything more than the monastery was not deserted before 68/69 CE*. Certainly not the opposite. When making a case for the absolute abandonment of the site, one must take into account all information from other habitable locations around Qumran, since the sectaries probably lived in caves, "Rechabite" booths, or slept outside—not in "the monastery", which was reserved for communal activities of one kind or another.

On the basis of the available coin data, one is not even permitted to assert that it was abandoned until 136 CE (a distinct possibility, since little else can explain why such an obvious hiding place as Cave IV was not disturbed even more than it was between 70 and 136 CE when the site was inhabited by several unspecified groups).[177] As far as this continuing

---

[175] On the matter of the existence of this coin, de Vaux is quite insistent in *RB*, 61, 1954, pp. 232f. (followed, as always, faithfully by Cross; e.g., his comment concerning Milik's *wall* hypothesis: "De Vaux has reviewed the archaeological evidence with the writer, notably the pottery typology, and appears to have the stronger case"; p. 65). In *RB*, 63, 1956, p. 567, de Vaux, once again, treats this as a proven fact and speaks without reservation of the Roman conquest and occupation "by the soldiers of the Xᵉ Legion" (typical of his working method). As against this, let us review his humble retraction in *Archaeology*, p. 40 (given only in a footnote). "Recent discussions refer to the existence of a coin with the countersign of the Tenth legion, which, so it is held, was found at Khirbet Qumran and which I have in fact recorded. . . . The mention of this was unfortunate for this coin does not exist. Faced with a coin which was incomplete and much oxidized I believed that I could read the remains of an X, the countersign of the Tenth legion. But Fr Spijkerman has convinced me that it is the cruciform mark which appears on the stern of a galley in the designs of the coins of Ashkelon of AD 72/73." To such embarrassments will the injudicious use of evidence and the precipitous rush to judgement invariably lead.

[176] See Milik, pp. 51ff., particularly p. 55, n. 1, where the whole matter is discussed in detail, including de Vaux's non-existent "wall". See de Vaux's discussion of this pp. 24ff. (including his "wall", p. 25).

[177] Cross agrees, p. 64, n. 20. While at times referring to Cave IV as "the library" of the sect—elsewhere, p. 25, n. 29, as "the remnants of the great collection originally housed in the community center"—he attests, p. 27, n. 32, that the materials in the cave

habitation goes, there is to be sure a diminution of coins after about 75 CE, and these coins until the Bar Kochba period are all pagan. After the fall of Jerusalem, however, no one would be using anything but pagan coins until the time of Bar Kochba and, as I have noted, there is a substantial distribution of coins at other sites like Ein Feshka even after 75 CE.

What then can be said archaeologically speaking about the deposit of the scrolls in the caves and the final abandonment of the site? Almost nothing: only that we have a *terminus a quo* of 68 CE and a *terminus ad quem* probably of 134–136 CE.

X
SUMMING UP

To sum up: no member of the Maccabee family can be identified in any way with the "Wicked Priest" and/or "the Spouter of Lies", or for that matter any other pejorative title in Qumran literature, not even the infamous Alexander Jannaeus who is very probably referred to, albeit retrospectively, in the Nahum *Pesher* (an expression like "the Furious Young Lion" is not necessarily pejorative). On the contrary, the Qumran Community flourished during his reign and probably even under his tutelage as a training ground for young priests (and others) adept at pseudepigraphic and apocalyptic literature and opposed to the Pharisaic "gathering of traditions".

were probably in great disorder and had already begun to decompose even before their abandonment. He refers to the manuscripts in the upper caves as *individually owned*, without seeing the implication of this in regard to the calendar from Cave IV citing the names of Aemilius Scaurus (62 BC) and Shlomzion (Alexandra, 76–67 BC—which, of course, again he wishes to use as proof positive for an early dating for the identification of historical personages), i.e., that the cave was already being used as a repository (or according to some theories a *genizah*) even before the final abandonment of the site. This document has since been published. For my discussion of it, see *DSSU*, pp. 119–27.

For habitation in the caves, see de Vaux, pp. 51ff. and 107. There is, of course, even the possibility that the Romans simply burned the monastery and never bothered going after the people in the caves above, a difficult operation in the best of circumstances, for as high as a pursuer wished to go, one could always retreat back higher even to the Bethlehem plain (cf. the terrible modernday experiences of Mrs Pike who, after leaving her husband, was able to negotiate such a passage even in the dead of night; *Search*, London, 1970). Also, see my notes on pp. xxvii and 80 above, with reference to the three to four shards with writing on them, referring both to the "Year 2" and that they were receipts for supplies from *Jericho*.

Judas Maccabee himself is very likely one of these Righteous Teacher/ "*Zaddik*"-types closely akin to the *Hassidic* authors of Daniel and Enoch (and very probably Jubilees and the Testament of Levi). He is the proto-type of the warrior-Priestly Messiah of the War Scroll, as he is most probably of John the Baptist, who exhibits characteristics akin to such a warrior High Priest (despite the highly stylized and doctrinaire presen-tation of John in the Gospels). Some exceptions to these statements are necessary in the cases of the "Phariseeizing" Simon, early John, and Hyrcanus II, the attitudes of whom, for instance, vitiate the historical accuracy of 1 Macc (as do similar ones the historical accuracy of the Phariseeizing Josephus), but not to the extent of defamatory characteriza-tions of what was otherwise a priesthood extremely popular among "the people".

The monastery was destroyed during the struggles from 63 BC to 37 BC—prior to the earthquake of 31 BC—that ended up in the assumption of rule by Herod in Palestine, probably in 37 BC by Herod himself on his way, like Vespasian thereafter, to invest Jerusalem. It was destroyed, as it was, around 70 CE, because it took the part of the "Zadokite" Priest line, understood as much in its esoteric as its exoteric signification, that is to say, "the Righteous Priesthood" (the "Melchizedek Priesthood" being a further variation on this theme), and certainly not because it adopted anything even remotely smacking of Pharisaic-style collaboration with Herodians and Romans.

Qumran gives ample evidence of an attitude of Priestly "zeal for the Law", and with it a certain amount of xenophobia—an attitude also discernible in the relations of the Jamesian "Jerusalem Church" with the Pauline "Gentile Mission". This "zeal" was most notably expressed in the condemnation of "fornication", by which Qumran specifically denotes marriage with a niece and divorce—practices condoned by Phariseeism and widely indulged in by Herodians—as a result of which not a few of the Movement's leaders were executed. Such a monastery so close to the Herodian summer palaces near Jericho, in whose swimming pool the last Maccabean High Priestly claimant was drowned, *was intolerable*.

The outbreak of the "Zealot Movement" in the disturbances of 4 BC to 7 CE is a misnomer foisted on an uncomprehending public—including the modern—by Josephus, since there was always a "Zealot Move-ment"—or Orientation—as such ever since the events portrayed in 1 Macc, 2 Macc, and Ecclesiasticus, and even before. The orientation, including a predilection towards martyrdom and suicide, is also in evi-dence among the supporters of Aristobulus and Antigonus in their struggles with the Romans and the latter's Herodian protégés.

Here, it is important to realize that terminologies like "Zealots", "Essenes", and "Pharisees" are often being used generically, not specifically. For instance, both Paul and Josephus describe themselves as "Pharisees", which they are most certainly, but primarily in a *generic* sense, or part and parcel of what Qumran would group under the heading "Seekers after Smooth Things" (that is, *Those Seeking Accommodation with Foreigners*). Though Josephus only applies the "Zealot" terminology as a pejorative after the killing of the High Priest Ananus, he hints at it earlier in his original description of the followers of Judas and Saddok.

The Gospels use this terminology non-pejoratively as a cognomen for one of Jesus' closest collaborators "Simon the Zealot" (probably interchangeable with "Simeon bar Cleophas") and evoke it also in regard to Jesus' own attitude towards "Temple service". Even more significantly, Paul shows his awareness of the currency of the terminology, particularly where his opponents within the early "Christian" Movement itself were concerned, by repeatedly playing on it in Ga 1:14 (cf. Acts 22:3) and 4:17, Ro 10:2, 2 Co 7:11 and 9:2, Phil 3:6, etc.; and Acts 21:20 unerringly designates the vast majority of James' "Jerusalem Church" followers as "zealous for the Law". The attitude clearly expresses the approach of Qumran and parallels the well-known "not one jot or tittle" kinds of allusions in James 2:10, Matthew's Sermon on the Mount, and Lk 16:17.[178]

---

[178] Note how this proposition is reflected in 1QS, viii–ix in the same passage where the term "zealous for the Law" actually occurs. In the context of "Cornerstone" and "Foundation" imagery, allusion to the Central Council as a "sin offering" ("a sweet fragrance") or "Temple", and the Is 40:3 allusion tradition applies to the activities of John the Baptist, it is categorically stated that "anyone from the Holy Community ("the Walkers in perfection of the Way") . . . who transgresses one jot from the *Torah* of Moses either *overtly or covertly* is to be expelled from the community"—transgression through negligence is to be punished by denial of *"table fellowship"* (italics mine).

In the "not one jot or tittle" passage in Lk 16 many of these parallel, by now familiar, themes come together, namely, antagonism to *the Rich*—directed against "the Pharisees", who are called "lovers of money"—the "heart" and "Justification" allusions, the *Zaddik*-style allusion to "the passing away of Heaven and Earth", and the reference to violent strife coincident with John's preaching "the Kingdom of Heaven" ("the *Messianic* Kingdom"). The passage culminates with a reference to "fornication", in particular "divorce" and "marrying divorcees" so characteristic of Herodian family practices (substituting the word "nieces" here would bring about an absolutely perfect convergence of themes; cf. CD, iv, 15ff.).

These same themes also come together in Ja 2:1ff. on "the Royal Law according to the Scripture", culminating in allusion to "fornication" and "divorce", a passage which is clearly at the root of the parallel succession of themes—and their subtle deformation—in Mt 5:15–48. For Qumran parallels to the use of "Men of Violence", see 1QpHab, ii,

What is new in 4 BC is the appearance of the "Messianic" variation of this "Zealot Movement", which fits in very well with the promise made by Simon at the time of his "election" to the High Priesthood, that the Maccabees would only continue in that dignity until "a Prophet" arose who would make a new determination (1 Macc 14:41). That Prophet may very well have been John the Baptist, from the time of whose coming "the Men of Violence have not ceased attempting to take the Kingdom of Heaven by storm".[179] He plays a parallel role to, and is

6, 1QH, ii, 21, and the "*'Arizei-Go'im*" who take vengeance for the Righteous Teacher in 4QpPs 37, ii, 19; iv, 10. These last definitely parallel our "Niger" (one of Josephus' "Idumaean" leaders), "Silas", Helen's two "kinsmen" Monobazus and Kenedaeos, etc.

[179] The subject of John's dating is fraught with pitfalls. Certainly he appears to be a much more prestigious individual than Jesus at the time of the latter's appearance. This, of course, carries with it an implication of some seniority in age. Mt 11:12f./Lk 16:16f. leave little doubt that these evangelists, anyhow, considered John's appearance to have been simultaneous with that of the "Zealot Movement", i.e., with that of the mysterious "Saddok" of Josephus' portraits—Ps *Rec* 1.54 considers it simultaneous with "those called *Sadducees*" who "*separated themselves* from the community"—cf. 1QS, viii–ix and the theme of "separating" in *ARN*'s treatment of "Zadok and Boethus"—because they were "*more Righteous* than the others"—italics mine—and that a considerable amount of time elapsed between his coming and the coming of Jesus. This is reinforced by Mt 2:22–3:1, where there is the definite implication (obscured in translation) that John came in *the time of Archelaus*, a notion stated categorically in the long passage about the confrontation between "the *Man*"—who came "*in the Way of the Law*" and called upon "the Jews to reclaim their *Freedom*"—and "Simon *a scribe of Essene* origin" in the Slavonic, which makes no sense as an interpolation (italics mine).

While Luke's narrative contains an echo of valuable historical data—where it signals a genealogical link between John and Jesus, and the latter's priestly blood—it can hardly be considered very historical where the chronology of this relationship is concerned. We have already commented, above, pp. 41f, on the relationship of the Honi/Hanan the Hidden material of *Talmud*ic tradition and Josephus to the Lukan narrative. That Luke thinks John's father is named Zechariah may even reflect information relating to Honi's martyrdom; on the other hand, John's father, in fact, might have been called Zechariah, which leads to interesting questions regarding the Tomb by that name in the Kedron Valley next to the one usually ascribed to James. That the traditions relating to John in Matthew and Luke and the fragmented one concerning "Saddok" Josephus is ultimately willing to reproduce in the *Antiquities* imply that there is a relationship between the two individuals John and "Saddok"—without saying what that relationship is—is inescapable.

It will be objected at this point that to claim a connection between John and "Saddok" is absurd, since Josephus doesn't know of it. Strictly speaking this is true, but Josephus' knowledge of even Judas the Galilean (the Gaulonite/Sepphoraeus) is extremely shaky. He reproduces the circumstances relating to a rabbi, "Judas", together with another rabbi encouraging the tearing down of the "Temple Eagle" in about 4 BC and Judas and Saddok preaching the tax uprising in 6–7 CE as different events. But Judas Sepphoraeus of the earlier event is quite clearly equivalent to Judas the Galilean who broke into the armory at Sepphoris. The teaching ascribed to both is identical, though Josephus thinks

possibly identical with, the mysterious "Saddok" mentioned by Josephus in the *Antiquities*, from whose first appearance and/or appointment of Judas, the "Messianic" agitation begins in earnest.

It does not cease until the destruction of the Temple in 70 CE, only to break out sporadically again with the executions of Simeon bar Cleophas and Jesus' brother Judas' two sons and in the widespread 115/116 CE "Messianic" disturbances in the Roman Empire under Trajan until the last "Star" Simeon bar Kosiba (perhaps not just figuratively but physically related to earlier "Stars").[180]

The "Messianic Movement", called in Antioch in the late 40s or early 50s "Christian" according to Luke in Acts, appears at precisely the moment one would expect it to, following Herod's total destruction of the Maccabean family including Mariamme and her two sons, her brother Aristobulus, and her grand uncle Hyrcanus II. Henceforward, secular rule will be accorded, at least on a popular level, only to Israelite "messiahs" or "sons of David". Herod, always one step ahead of his

---

Judas Sepphoraeus was burned alive with his colleague by Herod while "Judas the Galilean" went on functioning.

Here, too, one should note that the Slavonic Josephus—which, if authentic, was written perhaps twenty or more years before the *Antiquities*—does not appear to know the name of "the Wild Man" it portrays as coming in the time of Archelaus, and at the same time, like the *War* and unlike the *Antiquities*, makes no mention of a "Saddok" contemporary with him. However, the doctrine it ascribes to him is once again *exactly* equivalent to that attributed to that of Judas and Saddok in the *Antiquities* and Judas Sepphoraeus in the *War*, cf. *War* 1.33.2 with *Ant.* 18.1.1.

[180] The whole question of the physical relationships of these "Messianic" families is something which remains to be investigated. The parallel developments of Judas' (also from Galilee) and Jesus' families, including even *preventive* (cf. John 11:50) and the almost contemporary crucifixions of "Jacob and Simon"—equivalent also to the names of two of Jesus' brothers—the second of whom, Eusebius insists, "won the prize of an end like that of the Lord"— and the *stoning* of Menachem, an event both parallel to and contemporary with the stoning of Jesus' brother James (not to mention the additional parallel crucifixions of the sons of Jesus' third brother Judas) must give historians some pause. That Bar Kochba, too, seems to come from the area of the Messianic villages "Nazara" and "Chochaba" either in the region of Jericho, Galilee or Gaulonitus, *E.H.* 1.17.14 (cf. the modern city in Southern Lebanon of Kaukabe) must also present food for thought. That the documents at our disposal, characterized as they are by individual polemical aims, do not tell us of such a relationship is no reason for dismissing it *a priori*. We have already seen that Karaite documents with differing polemical aims do testify, not only that Jesus followed "Zadok" and was a "Righteous Man", but that their doctrines, and those of Anan ben David's, were identical. Others, while late, tell us of the identity of the Sadducees with the *"Zaddikim"* (or "Righteous Ones"), a term, they claim, the Rabbis purposefully corrupted into *"Zaddukim"*.

adversaries, manages to equip himself with a relatively mild one from Babylon, the legendary Hillel.

It also expresses itself in a series of "Messianic" pretenders from 4 BC to 66 CE, from Judas the Galilean to "the magician" Theudas, "the Egyptian" mistaken for Paul, and Menachem son or grandson of Judas the Galilean, most of whom attempt to lead their followers out to the wilderness for a reaffirmation of the Deuteronomic Covenant of "Damascus", or purify the Temple in the manner of Judas Maccabee (and Ezra). The High-Priestly Messiah—for as in the days of Zerubbabel and Jesus ben Yehozedek and Joshuah and Eleazar, a dual Messiahship appears to have been envisioned—was to be elected by lot on the basis of "Perfect Righteousness" although this is not certain. At Qumran, where the allusion to "the Messiah of" or "from" Aaron and Israel are concerned, the verbal, pronomial, and adjectival usages associated with it are always *all* singular.

This process is probably to be seen reflected in the events centering about the lives of Jesus and his brother James—and Simeon bar Cleophas thereafter—as much as it is in those centering about Judas Maccabee and his predecessor Onias III two centuries earlier. This "election", which was demanded in 4 BC probably on the basis of Judas' earlier elections, was actually carried out in 68 CE with the selection, not insignificantly, of *Phineas the Stonecutter*.[181] Josephus rails against the meanness of the blood and social status of this man in a manner reminiscent of the way in which Eusebius rails against the "meanness" of the Christological conceptions of the Ebionites ("the *Ebionim*"/"the Poor").[182]

The reflection of such an election is probably, also, to be seen in "the Messianic acclamation" of Jesus upon his triumphal entry into Jerusalem, who in good Maccabean style proceeds directly to the business of

[181] We have developed this "Stone" and "Cornerstone" imagery above, pp. 41 and 83. It relates to the "Fortress", "Wall", "Protection", and "Pillar" imagery *vis-à-vis* the Righteous Teacher, the central priestly triad at Qumran, and James and the central three in early Church tradition. See also its development in the "Noah" and "Phineas" chapters of the *Zohar*—including reference to both "Primal Adam" and "Pillar" ideologies (59bff., 65a, 70aff., 76a, 213aff., 218a–b, 231a, and 241a). See too its further variation in both Paul's and Qumran's "laying the Foundations" and "building" imagery above, p. 83. For a corresponding Pauline reference to "the Primal Adam" ideology, see 1 Co 15:45. For Community as "City" imagery, see Mt 5:14 and Heb 11.

[182] Cf. *E.H.* 3.27.1. Observing that the Ebionites *"evince great zeal to observe every detail of the Law"*, he complains that "they cherish low and mean opinions concerning Christ", whom they regard "as *a Poor* and *common* man *justified through his advances in virtue, nothing more*" (italics mine).

purifying the Temple. It is also to be seen in the election of the Twelfth Apostle to replace "Judas Iscariot" in Acts 1:15ff., a probable Lukan counterfeit of James' Episcopal election as successor to his brother. The confession of the sins of the People by such a Priestly "Righteous One" in the Holy of Holies on *Yom Kippur*, a kind of "Noachic" atonement, could alone be considered soteriologically efficacious, particularly in eschatological anticipation of "the End of the Last Times" (*ha-Kez ha-Aharon*).

It is the esoteric approach to "the Zadokite Priesthood", developed at Qumran in the context of "Righteous Teacher"/"*Zaddik*"/"Zadok" theorizing that provides us with the conceptuality necessary for understanding this process. It is at least one such "Zadokite" atonement— paralleled as well in the *somewhat obscure* notice in the Habakkuk *Pesher* about difficulties between the Righteous Teacher and the Wicked Priest over events on *Yom Kippur*—which very likely ultimately leads to James' judicial murder on a charge of blasphemy, that is, pronouncing the ineffable Name of God, the only recorded incidence of an execution of this kind—aside from that of the largely imaginary Stephen—since that of his predecessor (and putative forebear) Honi 125 years before.[183]

---

[183] See for instance *Zohar* 195a on "the prayer of the Poor Man"—including how "King David" (the Messiah) "placed himself among the Poor"—considered co-extensive with "the Pious" and designated as "those willing to sacrifice themselves and their lives for sanctification of the Name"). Cf. also Heb 7:26ff. and the Righteous Teacher as "High Priest" in 1QpHab, ii, 8, 4QpPs 37, ii, 18, iii, 15, and iv, 7, and probably 4QpHos[b], i, 3. Once the inherent fallacies in supposedly secure archaeological and paleographic "results" are properly appreciated, it is a fairly straightforward matter to make a point-for-point link-up between the events of James' life and those of the Righteous Teacher's in CD, i and vii–viii, 1QpHab, and 4QpPs 37.

CHAPTER 2

James the Just in the Habakkuk Pesher

INTRODUCTION

This work is the second in a series of publications attempting to develop
a more secure foundation for studying Qumran origins and moving
Second Temple historiography into a new framework, i.e., seeing the
sectarian situation as Qumran would have seen it and not from the point
of view of the more familiar traditions that have come down to us.
*Maccabees, Zadokites, Christians and Qumran: A New Hypothesis of Qumran
Origins*, Leiden, 1983—the first chapter in the present book—treated the
relationship of James the Just to the Qumran Community at some length
and proposed new conceptual and historical parameters for viewing
some of the problems associated with Qumran research. It set forth the
connections of the "Righteousness" doctrine with the Zadokite Priesthood, in the process making the case for an esoteric or qualitative—
even an eschatological—exegesis of "the Zadokite Covenant" and the
twin concepts of *Hesed* ("Piety towards God") and *Zedek* ("Righteousness
towards men") as the fundamental orientation of all "opposition" groups
in this period.

In attempting to tie the term "Pharisees" closer to the group intended
by the Qumran circumlocution "Seekers after Smooth Things", a more
generic definition of the Pharisees was proposed and both groups were
viewed as coextensive with those "seeking accommodation with foreigners" (inclusive of Herodians and Romans—at Qumran "'*Amim*" and
"*Yeter ha-'Amim*" respectively). In doing so, some terminological and historical confusions between "Pharisees" and "Essenes" were pointed up,
and Qumran paleography and archaeology were subjected to thorough-
going criticism. Once the import of these re-evaluations was appreciated,
I suggested that it was a comparatively easy task to link the events and

teachings of the Righteous Teacher in the Habakkuk *Pesher* to those of James the Just in the early "Jerusalem Community".

James the Just in the Habakkuk Pesher is the application of the theory to the special case. An Appendix extends it to both the Damascus Document and the Temple Scroll. Providing the kind of detailed exposition, specific identifications, and substantive argument necessary to support the overall thesis, it analyzes the Habakkuk *Pesher* passage by passage, systematically signaling the connections between the life and teachings of James the Just and those of the Righteous Teacher of Qumran.

Not only was the "Righteousness" ideal integrally associated with James' being—that is, he was a Teacher of Righteousness and the sobriquet "the Just" or "Righteous One" was attached in an integral manner to his name—but early Church sources also confirm that scriptural exegesis of a Qumran kind was carried on with regard to his person ("and the Prophets declare concerning him": *E.H.* 2.23.8—the actual passage applied to James' death being Is 3:10–11, a *Zaddik*-passage paralleling the sense and signification of *Zaddik*-passages like Hab 1–2 and Ps 37 applied at Qumran to the death of the Righteous Teacher).

The Pseudoclementine *Recognitions* actually place James together with *all* his community in the Jericho area in the early 40s, from where he sends out Peter to confront Simon Magus in Caesarea—not "Samaria" as per the here weaker Acts tradition. Paralleling John the Baptist's earlier confrontation with Herodians, the confrontation bears on the themes of marriage, divorce, and "fornication" and links up with data in Josephus suggesting Simon to have been in the employ of "Herodians"/Romans and connived at Drusilla's legally reprehensible divorce and remarriage to Felix.

Two antagonists are also readily discernible with regard to James' life. One was an Establishment High Priest responsible for his death, Ananus. Ananus was killed in the early stages of the Uprising by "Violent Gentiles" and his body was violated and thrown outside the walls of Jerusalem without burial—events we think are reflected in the Habakkuk *Pesher*. The other, a self-willed, often rebellious and argumentative individual within the Movement, Paul. Following a more antinomian approach to the Law, he had a new version of "Salvation" which he proposed "teaching to the Gentiles".

These two antagonists of James can be linked to the *two antagonists* of the Righteous Teacher in the Habakkuk *Pesher*: one a "Man of Lying"/ "Pourer out of Lying" within the community itself, who "speaks derogatorily about the Law in the midst of the whole congregation", "leads Many astray"/"tires out Many with a worthless service"—the opposite of the Righteous Teacher's proper "justifying" activity of "making Many Righteous"—and "leads astray in a wilderness without a Way"—the opposite of 1QS, viii. 27's proper *teaching* activity of "making a Way in the wilderness" by showing "zeal for the Law" (*hok*). In the context of terminological allusions such as these and their doctrinal reversal or inversion in the New Testament, one should not forget Acts 21:20's description of the majority of James' "Jerusalem Church" supporters as "zealous for the Law".

The *Pesher*, in addition to accusing the Establishment High Priest it refers to as "Wicked" of being responsible for the death of the Righteous Teacher, also charges him with "polluting the Temple". This charge comprised one of the "Three Nets of Belial" following the exegesis of the "Zadokite Covenant" in CD, iv–v—the other two: "fornication" and "Riches" have *real* applications to Herodians, as opposed to artificial ones to Maccabeans and others; both are echoed in the *Pesher*. Two persistent themes relating to the personal status of Herodians also exercised Qumran legal theorists in the Damascus Document and the Temple Scroll: *divorce* and *marrying nieces*. Together with a third theme, incest, they bear on the "fornication" charge above.

Antagonism to "fornication" is a significant theme, too, in all extant traditions attaching themselves to James' name. In the Appendix we shall be able to delineate the provenance of these "fornication" and "pollution of the Temple" charges with some precision, together with their culmination and combination in the Damascus Document's curious charge of "sleeping with women in their periods".

In the Habakkuk *Pesher*, it will become clear that the "polluting the Temple" charge relates to accepting gifts (and sacrifices) from *Herodians* and other *violent* Gentiles, as well as incurring their "pollution" by associating with them. Priests like Ananus, it should be remembered, took their appointment from Herodians, who from the time of Herod the Great shared possession of the High Priest's vestments with the Procurators, and their guilt therefore was one of association. Another aspect of the "pollution" charge was the fact that Herodians were even allowed into the Temple, a theme which is at the center of the internecine squabbling from the 40s to the 60s CE, triggering the Uprising against Rome. The problem of Herodians in the Temple will ultimately have to be seen, Qumran paleography notwithstanding, as being at the root of the allusion to improper "separation" introducing the Damascus Document's "sleeping with women in their periods" and the Temple Scroll's "*balla'*"/"Bela'"/"things sacrificed to idols" interdiction materials.

Perhaps even more importantly, I suggest that what can only be understood as the "Jerusalem Church" or "Palestinian" version of the exegesis of Hab 2:4 is present in the *Pesher*. In our view, the presence in the *Pesher* of this much-overlooked exegesis is the real reason for its composition. Framed as if with the "empty" or "guilty" exposition of "the Liar" in mind, the Habakkuk *Pesher* restricts the efficacy of this exegesis in a twofold manner, firstly only to "the House of Judah" (i.e., *only to native Jews*) and secondly, only to "*Torah*-Doers" (in this context, one should pay attention to the parallel reiteration of the "Doers" theme in the first chapter of the Letter of James, a letter also alluding to Qumran "empty", "Lying", and "Jewish Christian" "Enemy" terminologies, and an additional one, echoed at Qumran, "the Tongue"). Like the eschatological sense of the Zadokite exegesis, the eschatological sense of the Hab 2:4 *Pesher*'s "saved from the *Beit ha-Mishpat*" has escaped many commentators. In addition, the *Pesher* retains James' all-important soteriological stress on "works" along with the more familiar one on "belief".

We shall also be able to develop the meaning of other important turns of phrase at Qumran, like "*nilveh*"/"*Nilvim*" in the Nahum *Pesher* and the Damascus Document, which confirm the existence of a cadre of "God-fearers" attached to the Qumran Community. This, in turn, will clarify the decipherment of allusions in the Nahum *Pesher* like the "Simple Ones of Ephraim"—as opposed to those "of Judah", bearing on terminologies like "these Little Ones" and "the First" vs. "the Last" in the Gospels—extant at Qumran with varying signification—the "City of Blood" in the Nahum and Habakkuk *Pesher*s, and the "'*Arizei-Go'im*" in the Ps 37 *Pesher*, not to mention the all-important allusions to "Belial" in the Damascus Document and Hymns—and their probable esoteric variation in the "*balla'* "/"Bela' " usage in the Temple Scroll—almost all in one way or another involving Gentiles. The Temple Scroll refers, as well, to "things sacrificed to idols", a central category of James' directives to overseas communities (later echoed even in *Koran*ic recitations of similar prohibitive categories).

In applying the general theory outlined in MZCQ to the special case of the Habakkuk *Pesher*, we are able to interpret or translate in a meaningful manner almost every passage and turn of phrase in the context of known facts about James' life and doctrines associated with him. This ability to explain key allusions at Qumran constitutes the kind of persuasive evidence the verification of the whole theory of Qumran origins requires. It is as if one were predicting a certain effect, and having predicted it, indeed, finding it in the text. This is the import, in particular, of the reiteration in the Temple Scroll of the Deuteronomic King Law, "thou shalt not put a foreigner over you", not to mention the allied, possible identification in the Temple Scroll of "Bela'" as a circumlocution for *Herodians*. They had to be present, and so they were, closing and clarifying the whole circle of esoteric allusions at Qumran.

Only the paleography and archaeology of Qumran have acted as impediments to the formulations and identifications we propose, but we have discussed these at length in MZCQ. Where the Habakkuk *Pesher*, in particular, is concerned, paleography is not an issue, and the only really serious impediment is the archaeology of Qumran. However, as we shall see, this last is neither strong nor secure enough to rule out an otherwise credible textual theory based on the clear sense of the internal data. Spiritually speaking, it is always more comfortable in Qumran studies to think in terms of indistinct or mythological personalities in the far distant past, not *real* people. It is not, however, the task of the historian to be concerned whether or not others will be pleased with the results that are achieved; his charge is simply to detail the implications of the data at his disposal with as much precision as possible.

Robert Eisenman   Fountain Valley
                                                         June, 1985

I

BACKGROUNDS

In attempting to set forth a new historical framework in which to view the Dead Sea Scrolls, I have noted the key role played by James the Just in later Qumran sectarian documents, but have not delineated this role in any systematic manner.[1] Since the test of any good hypothesis is to introduce it into the materials under consideration, it would be useful to analyze James' role within the context of one of the most important later sectarian documents, the Habakkuk *Pesher*, and see what results can be achieved. Though there has been substantial discussion over the years concerning the Habakkuk *Pesher*, very little in the way of a consensus has been reached concerning identifications of key personalities, events, and chronology. In addition, there has been a hesitancy in, even an animus against, proposing personalities and events touching upon the historical context and ethos of early Christianity (in the case of this study, the members of Jesus' own family and his purported successors in Palestine).[2] In view of the deep emotions likely to be called forth by such proposals, such a hesitancy is not surprising.

The known details regarding James' life and position are not inconsiderable. In many ways we have more independent documentation concerning him than any other New Testament character, except perhaps Paul. The latter, however, functioned very much in relation to the former, and as he documents his own career, provides, often unwittingly, documentation of James' personality and career.[3] James was a Righteous

---

[1] Cf. pp. 17, 31, 61, 110, etc.

[2] See, for instance, J. T. Milik, whose remarks are symptomatic: " ... although Essenism bore in itself more than one element that in one way or other fertilized the soil from which Christianity was to spring, it is nevertheless evident that the latter religion represents something completely new which can only be adequately explained by the person of Jesus himself"; *Ten Years of Discovery in the Wilderness of Judaea*, London, 1959, p. 43. By way of introduction to this statement, he comments on how "Essene influence" almost took over and submerged "the authentically Christian doctrinal element" in the early Church. But still he sees hardly any similarities between "the generation of the Lord and the first disciples" and "the Essenes"; cf. G. Vermes, *The Dead Sea Scrolls in English*, London, 1962, p. 55: "No properly Judeo-Christian characteristic emerges from the scrolls, and unless we are mistaken the Zealots were scarcely a company of ascetics."

[3] See Ga 1:20–2:13. Paul, for instance, in contrast to the Gospels, places James within the framework of resurrection appearances in 1 Co 15:4ff. Though scholarly opinion has usually tried to downplay this testimony considering it a "Jewish Christian" interpolation, we consider the interpolation in this passage to consist rather of the inaccurate "Cephas and the Twelve"—there were only eleven at the time. Vestiges of a resurrection appearance to Jesus' family are, on the contrary, conserved in Luke's Emmaus Road

Teacher-type, and even a casual perusal of the documents at our disposal testifies to the integral connection of the Righteousness-ideal to his person.[4]

The letter associated with his name is saturated with what should be called the works/Righteousness approach, as opposed to more Pauline/Hellenistic "free gift of Faith"/"Grace" doctrines. For the author of James, it is unquestionably Righteousness which—to use the terminology of 1QpHab, viii. 2 and xii.14—"saves", just as it is for the author of 1QpHab and the Qumran Hymns.[5] Filling in from other documents at Qumran and Josephus' description of John the Baptist's *Hesed* and *Zedek* dichotomy, "the Way of Righteousness" is that of the Law and its "acts" or "works" are those of the Law.[6] As the Sermon on the Mount puts

account and confirmed in Jerome's account of the "Hebrew Gospel". When Paul in his introduction of James refers to himself as "specially chosen while still in my mother's womb" (Ga 1:15f.), it is difficult to escape the impression that he does so in competition with the "Holy" or "Nazirite from the womb" claims conserved via Hegesippus in all traditions about James; cf. Eusebius, *E.H.* 2.1 and 2.23; Epiphanius, *Haeres.* 29.3 and 78.13; Jerome, *Vir. ill.* 2; etc. The same claim, i.e., being specially chosen while in his mother's womb, is put forth by the author of the Qumran Hymns—presumably the Righteous Teacher himself.

[4] James' superabundant Righteousness, reflected too in his cognomen, is attested to in all the above traditions; see too Gos Th 12. When the account attributed to Hegesippus refers to James, the epithet "Just One" is applied in place even of his name.

[5] The Habakkuk *Pesher* is acknowledged by all commentators as the paleographic contemporary of Hymns; cf. Cross, *The Ancient Library of Qumran*, New York, 1961, pp. 198f., nn. 118 and 123, calling 1QpHab "early Herodian". S. Birnbaum, *The Hebrew Scripts*, Leiden, 1971, pp. 38–43, dates 1QpHab "about the middle of the first century"; N. Avigad, "Palaeography of the Dead Sea Scrolls and Related Documents", *Aspects of the Dead Sea Scrolls*, Jerusalem, 1958, pp. 72 and 82, notes the very late paleographic characteristics of both 1QpHab and Hymns.

[6] *Ant.* 18.5.2 knows John is a "good man" whose "Way" was that of Righteousness (*Zedek*) and Piety (*Hesed*), i.e. *Righteousness towards men* and *Piety towards God*. This dichotomy of Righteousness and Piety is the basis of Josephus' descriptions of Essenes in both the *Antiquities* and the *War*. In the Slavonic, we are introduced to a John the Baptist-like "Wild Man" who came in "the Way of the Law" "and called on the Jews to claim their freedom." Mt 21:32 identifies John's "Way" as "the Way of Righteousness", and most accounts make it clear that John was zealous for the Law, since he harangues a member of the Herodian family over an infraction of the law of *zanut* ("fornication") until the latter is forced to put him to death as a public agitator.

At Qumran, where the words used to describe John's mission in the New Testament are actually repeated twice in 1QS, viii–ix, the "Way" terminology and "straightening the Way" imagery is omnipresent. In the first exegesis of Is 40:3 in 1QS, viii.15, the "Way" is identified as "the study of the Law which He commanded by the hand of Moses . . . and any man . . . who overtly or covertly transgresses one word of the Law of Moses on any point whatsoever" would be expelled from the Community (cf. Ja 2:10ff. in the

it in the famous "not one jot or tittle" section: "Unless your Righteousness exceeds that of the scribes and Pharisees, you shall in no wise enter the Kingdom of Heaven."[7]

James, too, is the head of a community, often known euphemistically as "the Jerusalem Church", but for our purposes more accurately described as "the Jerusalem Community", and functions, according to all extant early Church testimony, in something of the manner of an "opposition" High Priest. In the light of more recent Qumran evidence suggesting the existence of just such an "opposition" High Priesthood basing itself on the Righteousness doctrine and/or the related "Perfection" ideal (which should therefore perhaps be called "Noachic")—one should be wary of dismissing the implications of these descriptions.[8]

Epiphanius and Jerome, probably basing themselves on Hegesippus, are particularly insistent that James went into the Inner Sanctum or Holy of Holies of the Temple either regularly or, from the sense of the text what appears more likely, at least once in his career, there rendering atonement "until the flesh on his knees became as callused as a camel's".[9] Furthermore, Epiphanius insists that he wore the mitre of the High

context of allusion to the "Poor" vs. the "Rich" and the problem of *zanut*: "You see, if a man keeps the whole of the Law, except for one small point at which he stumbles, he is still guilty of breaking all of it."); in the second in ix.23, the phrase "zealous for the Law" actually occurs. In the introduction of the Damascus Document all these themes, also, come together and "the Way"and its "works" are explicitly identified with those of "the Law".

[7] Mt 5:20. The general Righteousness thrust of the Gospel of Matthew should be self-evident; but the Sermon also includes reference to another fundamental theme at Qumran, *Perfection*. Note how the formulations of Ja 2:5ff. actually appear to underlie those of Mt 5:11ff. and present a more authentically "Palestinian" and, therefore in our view, prior rendering of the same materials.

[8] The exegesis of "the Zadokite Covenant" at Qumran is esoteric. It is to be understood in terms of the concept of "Righteousness" that underlies the root meaning of "Zadok", as much as in terms of any genealogical sense that might be imputed to it. Cf. CD, iv.2ff., where the "Sons of Zadok" are defined eschatologically as "those who ill stand at the End of Days", which is not a genealogical definition at all but an eschatological one ("stand" carrying with it something of the sense of Ezek 37:10). In 1QS, iii.20ff. the phrase "Sons of Zadok" is used interchangeably with the usage "Sons of Zedek" (i.e., Sons of Righteousness), which is not the scribal error many commentators take it for. In 1QS, v.2ff., they are unequivocally defined, following the general thrust in Ezek 44:7ff., as "the Keepers of the Covenant", i.e., the *Shomrei ha-Brit*. Again, this is not a genealogical definition but a qualitative one. In discussing baptism, Jesus too is pictured as pointedly mentioning "the commands of all Righteousness" in Mt 3:15; cf. as well *War* 2.1.2/*Ant.* 17.9.1 for the demands of the insurrectionists in 4 BC for a high priest of "higher purity" and "Piety".

[9] See above n. 3 and n. 13 below.

Priest, and all agree that he wore the priestly linen, a right accorded the lower priesthood in the period in which James held sway in Jerusalem.[10]

One should be chary of dismissing vivid details such as these without carefully considering them. For instance, the Pseudoclementine *Recognitions* are particularly forthcoming in telling us that James broke either one or both of his legs in a riot that erupted on the Temple Mount at the instigation of "an Enemy", clearly intended to represent *Paul*—a riot that has as its counterpart in Acts the events swirling around the attack on "Stephen" (and, one might add, the notice in the *Antiquities* after the stoning of James, about a riot in Jerusalem led by one "Saulus". This

[10] Epiphanius' testimony in this regard, supported by Jerome, has been dismissed as the grossest exaggeration; cf. H.-J. Schoeps, *Paul: The Theology of the Apostle in the Light of Jewish Religious History*, Philadelphia, 1961, p. 67; however, there can be little doubt that some extraordinary kind of activity is being alluded to in these notices about James. See below, pp. 181f, for the interesting link-ups between such an atonement—i.e., in our view a "Zadokite" or "Perfectly Righteous" one—and the *blasphemy* trial against James that led to his execution in 62 CE. Josephus contemptuously calls the right to wear linen (in imitation of James?) won by the lower priesthood shortly after his death, as events moved towards its stopping of sacrifice on behalf of and rejection of gifts from foreigners, "an innovation"; cf. *Ant.* 20.9.6.

The usage "innovation" or "Innovators" has special significance in both the *War* and the *Antiquities*, especially where the "imposters", "deceivers", and "robbers" are concerned and, in particular, that Movement founded by Judas and *Saddok*, which Josephus connects with the destruction of the Temple. Josephus employs the same term in *War* 2.17.2 in describing the decision on the part of the lower priest class to stop sacrifice on behalf of Romans and other foreigners which he describes as beginning the Uprising, even though he knows perfectly well that from Ezra's time and that of Ezekiel's Zadokite Statement, such xenophobia was common. It has particular relevance *vis-à-vis* its reversal when discussing Herod in *Ant.* 15.10.4; see our discussion of this pivotal notice, below, p. 199 and Appendix. These problems over foreigners in the Temple have special relevance not only where the Pauline "Gentile Mission" was concerned, but also Paul's own difficulties in the Temple.

The "linen" theme also appears in an amusingly distorted manner in Josephus' description of "*Banus*" wearing "clothing that grew on trees". *Banus* is a contemporary of and difficult to distinguish from James; cf. *Vita* 2. Note the "bathing" theme in Josephus' account of *Banus*, which also recurs in inverted form in the extant testimonies about James. The "bathing" theme with the same characteristic reversal, i.e., "they preferred being unwashed", also recurs in Josephus' description of the Essenes in *War* 2.8.3. *Talmudic* literature (*Yalqut* Jer 35:12), too, retains a tradition that the sons of the Rechabites were allowed to marry the daughters of the High Priests and do service at the altar. By "Rechabites" we understand "Essenes". There were no longer "Rechabites" as such, the euphemism having to do with the abstention by both from anointing with oil, wine, and a propensity towards life-long Naziritism, all themes prominent in extant testimonies about James. In turn, these correspondences link up very well with the notice about Simeon b. Cleophas (James' "cousin") in Eusebius' version of the stoning of James, i.e., that he was a "Rechabite Priest" (meaning an "Essene" Priest in the Qumran manner).

same Saulus would also appear to be the intermediary between "the Men of Power, the high priests, the principal of the Pharisees, and all those desirous for peace" and Agrippa, whom Josephus also calls Saulus' "kinsman").[11]

James is carried away in a swoon by his supporters to a location *somewhere outside of Jericho*. It is from here that he sends Peter out on his first missionary journey to confront Simon Magus. This confrontation occurs, not in Samaria (as Acts confuses the material with information regarding Simon's Samaritan origins), but in Caesarea, where other material in Josephus shows Simon to have in all likelihood been in the employ of the Herodian family.[12] Detailed accounts such as these are examples of the kind of independent documentation which exists concerning James. While undeniably "lively", it is in the main free of the demonology and fantasizing that often mar parallel New Testament accounts.

We should also pay attention to the motif of a *Yom Kippur* atonement where James' activities on the Temple Mount and possibly in the Holy

---

[11] Ps *Rec.* 1.70ff. Peter recalls the details of James' injury six weeks later on his first missionary journey to Caesarea when he tells Zacchaeus that James was still limping. Details of this kind are startling in their intimacy and one should hesitate before simply dismissing them as artistic invention. It was H.-J. Schoeps who first drew attention to the interchangeability of the attack on Stephen and the attack on James, both coming at precisely the same point in the narratives of Acts and the *Recognitions*; cf. *Theologie und Geschichte des Judenchristentums*, Tübingen, 1949, pp. 408–45. For Saulus, see *Ant.* 20.9.4 and *War* 2.17.3. It is interesting that just as Acts misplaces the stoning of "Stephen", *Antiquities*, where the historiograpy of Acts and the *Recognitions* is concerned, misplaces the riot led by "Saulus". Lk 19:1ff., for instance—the first part of the Acts narrative—presents this "Zacchaeus" incident in somewhat inverted form. Now it transpires in "Jericho"—cf. the Pseudoclementines' "Jericho" theme above—and Zacchaeus is a "Rich" *Chief Tax-Collector*, at whose house Jesus stays. Like the Centurion in Acts' version of the visit of Simon to Caesarea, he gives generously "to the Poor".

[12] Simon's Samaritan origins in Ps *Rec.* 1.72ff. become confused with Acts' confrontation between "Philip and Simon" in Samaria in 8.4ff. Acts is usually treated as superior to the *Recognitions*, but in these sections, anyhow, the sequence in *Recognitions*, which basically parallels Acts, is preferable. It places the confrontation between the two Simons in Caesarea, where it should be, which links up with the key role played by a similar magician called "Simon" in *Ant.* 20.7.2 in arranging Drusilla's legally reprehensible divorce and remarriage to Felix. This is the same Felix who elsewhere in Acts is described as knowing quite a lot about "the Way". Note that the problem as usual is the *fornication* of *Herodian* rulers—in this case illegal divorce. Here Simon is described as "a Cypriot" by birth; cf. the garbled material about Elymas Magus in Acts 13:8 and other individuals described as "Cypriot" in early Christianity. That the *Recognitions* designates "Simon" as originating from "Gitta" in Samaria need not deter us from appreciating the basic similarities in the traditions in question. And note the "Gitta"/"*Kittim*" resonance.

of Holies are concerned. As we shall see, this has particular relevance where the Habakkuk *Pesher* is concerned.[13] The Letter to the Hebrews also gives us something of the ideological perspective for attributing a "Perfectly pure" and Righteous Priesthood to James—language and ideology at the core of parallel "Zadokite" ideologies at Qumran.[14]

In addition, where James' person is concerned, one has the particularly insistent —that is, all sources consistently and emphatically refer to it— and highly revealing sobriquet of "the Just One", i.e., "the *Zaddik*". This epithet should be viewed against notices in the Pseudoclementine *Recognitions* insisting that "the Sadducees" arose in the time of John the Baptist and "withdrew from the community because they thought themselves more Righteous than the others", echoed by notices in both the *Abot de R. Nathan* and Karaite sources about "a split" between "Zadok and Boethus" and the subsequent "withdrawal of the Sadducees".

The *sitz im leben* of these latter notices must be seen as the "split" between "Saddok" and Joezer b. Boethus over both the tax issue and the high priesthood around the time of the death of Herod in 4 BC; and the general implication of these notices when taken together is to make the inception of the "Sadducee" Movement virtually indistinguishable

---

[13] Though the portrait in Eusebius and others via Hegesippus is usually taken as referring to habitual activities on James' part, close evaluation of the notice, as we have noted, will reveal that what is being described is only one particular atonement—the unforgettable simile about James' knees becoming like a camel's vividly describing how he spent the whole day on his knees importuning God on behalf of *the People*. In turn, this testimony links up with materials in 1QpHab below, pp. 181–82, about difficulties on *Yom Kippur* between the Righteous Teacher and his nemesis the Wicked Priest.

[14] See, for instance, Heb 2:10, which refers to "the Sons (being brought) into Glory" and the leader who is "made Perfect through suffering", as well as related notions of adoptionist baptism, i.e., "you are My son; today I have become your Father" in 1:5 and 5:6. These last also are connected to being "a Priest after the order of Melchizedek"; cf. also 3:1ff., 4:14, and 7:1ff. The suffering motif is alluded to in 1QS, viii.1ff. in the same section as that already called attention to in relation to the evocation of the "Way in the wilderness" symbolism. The notion of "Perfection" is highly developed at Qumran in 1QH and 1QS and goes back to the Genesis characterization of Noah as *"ish Zaddik Tamim"*.

Though the precise nature of the usage "Melchizedek" at Qumran is under dispute, 1QMelchizedek does use the phrase "Men of the Lot of Melchizedek" as another terminological euphemism for "the saved of the Last Days" and to denote membership in the community of the Elect of Righteousness. The "new Priesthood", as it is called in Hebrews, was to be based upon the "Perfection" ideal, i.e., "holy, innocent, uncontaminated, beyond the influence of Sinners" (often a euphemism for "Gentiles" and more specifically *Herodians*). These "Perfection" ideas are also expressed in 1QS, viif. about the Community Council, who are themselves an "offering" unto the Lord and "a sweet fragrance of Righteousness".

from that of what Josephus calls "the Fourth Philosophy", that is, the so-called "Galileans" or "Zealots" founded by Judas the Galilean and Saddok.[15] One then has the ideological framework for understanding not only what I believe should be referred to as "the Purist Sadducee" Movement—as opposed to the Phariseeizing and Romanizing Herodian Establishment which might better be termed "Boethusian"—called by most scholars following Josephus' terminology, "Essenes",[16] but also for understanding, following the true thrust of Ezekiel's *qualitative* distinctions, the esoteric thrust of the "Zadokite" usage as it was developed at Qumran.

It has often been missed that the Damascus Document's definition of "the Sons of Zadok" as "the Elect of Israel"—also identified in 1QpHab, v.4 with those who "would execute Judgement at the End of Time", or "the *Kodesh Shonim*", meaning, either the *Rishonim* or the *Anshei Kodesh-Tamim*, but in any event equivalent to Ecclesiasticus' *Anshei-Hesed/Zaddikim*—who "justify the Righteous" and "stand at the End of Time",

---

[15] Cf. Ps *Rec.* 1.53f. It is not incurious that these testimonies link up with New Testament notices concerning the birth of the "Zealot (our "Messianic") Movement" at the time of the coming of John; Mt 11:12 and Lk 16:16. These related materials in both *Talmud*ic and Karaite sources about a split between "Zadok and Boethus" and a consequent "withdrawal" can be seen as a conflation of two separate "splits" or "withdrawals", one early around the time of Judas Maccabee relating to the appearance of the "Hassidaean" Movement—and not uncoincidentally the "Pharisaic"—and a later one relating to the appearance of the "Zealot"/"Messianic" Movement. The clash of "*Saddok*" and "Joezer b. Boethus", not only provides the setting for really serious sectarian strife, and consequently Josephus' discussions of the sects in the *War* and the *Antiquities*, but also for his language of "innovations"/"Innovators", which like his "Zealot" vocabulary, has such relevance to the problem of "the new" or "Herodian Sadducees", by which I mean "Boethusians", and "Purist Sadducees", following an esoteric interpretation of the Zadokite Covenant, in *Maccabees, Zadokites, Christians and Qumran.* By "purist Sadducees" we must include what presently go under the designations "Essenes", "Zealots", "Jewish Christians", "Zadokites", etc.

[16] The identification of the sect as "Essenes" is popularly followed by a consensus of scholars. However, in making such an identification, they still have not identified who the "Essenes" were, nor what links they had, if any, with Hassidaeans, Zealots, and the early Christian Movement in Palestine. In fact, the terminology "Essene" neither appears as such in the New Testament or *Talmud.* It is a specialized terminology used only by Philo, Josephus and their dependents. Josephus constantly confuses Essenes and Pharisees, and even mixes up Zealots to a certain extent with Essenes. The identification of Qumran with "the Essenes" simply says something generically about a movement outside the reigning Pharisaic/Sadducean or "Boethusian" Establishment of the day, an establishment which was put in place by the Herodian family.

is *eschatological*.[17] It is not a normative definition of a priesthood at all; nor is it primarily genealogical. In fact the latter thrust is deliberately broken by the addition of *waw*-constructs in the underlying phraseology of Ezek 44:15.

This exegesis, strikingly enough, also plays on a second usage, "*Nilvim*", which though generally translated as "joined", is applied in Es 9:27 to *Gentiles* attaching themselves to the Jewish community presumably in the manner of converts. We shall see later that a parallel connotation will be discernible in the Nahum *Pesher*, which uses "*nilveh*" and "*nilvu*" relative to those it calls "the Simple Ones of Ephraim", and it will be of the utmost import when finally trying to piece all these troubling euphemisms together. It is impossible to overemphasize such a reference to *Gentile* "God-fearing" auxiliaries attached to the Community in associated status. The exegesis in CD, iv clearly carries an esoteric (or qualitative) sense connected with the notion of Righteousness, which is confirmed too by the presence of material about the "Justification of the Righteous" and word-play centering around the "Sons of Zadok" usage.

When the implications of these ideologies are combined with the original demand by "the Innovators" in 4 BC for a high priest of "higher purity"/"greater Piety" and the notices from Heb 4:14f., 7:26ff., 9:11ff., etc. about a Perfect High Priest "beyond the reach of Sinners", including a variety of references about "Justification", then the reason of a Priest/*Zaddik* like James having to make such a *Yom Kippur* atonement at all becomes clearer. Only an atonement by a Righteous Priest/*Zaddik* could be considered efficacious in terms of ultimate forgiveness for sin and entrance into the Messianic community/Kingdom of Heaven,[18] and

---

[17] CD, iv,4. The word "stand" here has puzzled most commentators because they usually ignore the eschatological sense of the exegesis. Since the usage specifically relates to "the Last Days", one must realize we are dealing with a resurrection of sorts (i.e., of "the Righteous" dead; the Righteous living according to this ideology "will not taste of death", but go directly into the Kingdom; cf. the use of "stand" with precisely this eschatological sense in Dan 12:13, further expanded in *Lam R* ii.3.6), after which there would be "no more express affiliation with the House of Judah". In this context, therefore, "Sons of Zadok" parallels New Testament expressions like "Sons of the Resurrection" or its variations. The exegesis actually seems to refer to two classes of these: "the *Rishonim*" or "*Anshei Kodesh-Tamim*", the recipients in a manner of speaking of "the First Covenant", and the Righteous living, or the *Dor ha-Aharon*, the Last or Last Generation, for whom the rededication of "the New Covenant" comes into play.

[18] This is paralleled in the presentation of Hebrews. In 2:18 this theme of atoning for human sins is expressed. 6:5ff. exactly parallels material in 1QS, viii–ix; 7.3f. parallels

certainly not an atonement made by any members of the Herodian Priestly Establishment. This Establishment and its various families (mostly from the *nouveau riche*), known as "Sadducees" in the New Testament and Josephus, were *inter alia* responsible for the death of James and fanatically opposed by Fourth Philosophy "Innovators" and "Zealot"/ "*Sicarii*" sectaries—the pejoratives are Josephus'.[19]

Qumran criticizes this Establishment over three issues. The first relates to "fornication", a conceptuality playing a prominent role in Acts' description of James' directives to overseas communities and the letter ascribed to his name. By it Qumran specifically denotes "divorce" and "marriage with a niece". These were forbidden as well, according to Karaite historical reconstruction, by "Zadok", Jesus, and Anan. They were also at the root of the beheading of John the Baptist. The Herod who executed John had married his niece Herodias who herself was twice *divorced*—on the illegality of which procedure even Josephus feels obliged to remark, as he does her niece Drusilla's subsequent divorce.[20]

The second of these three "Nets of Belial" is denoted as "Riches".

material about adoptionist sonship in Hymns. 5:14 refers to "the doctrine of Righteousness"; 7:26ff. continues the imagery expressing the need for a Righteous atonement. 8:6ff. speaks of the "First Covenant" of the *Rishonim* and brings into play the notion of the New Covenant speaking of "the End of the Last Age" (9:27), language actually extant at Qumran.

[19] In this period it is edifying to group parties according to their enemies. On this basis, the so-called "Zealots"/"*Sicarii*" have the same antagonists as the "Jerusalem Community" and those responsible for the literature at Qumran. For instance, the high priest, Jonathan, is assassinated in 55 CE by a group Josephus chooses to designate as *Sicarii*, but Jonathan is the brother of the High Priest, Ananus, who is ultimately responsible (together with Agrippa II) for the stoning of James (according to New Testament accounts his father and uncle were involved too in the death of Jesus). When the revolution enters its extremist or "Jacobin" phase, the various members of the priestly aristocracy, including Ananus, are butchered without mercy; cf. *War* 4.5.2.

[20] CD, iv.15ff., directly following the exegesis of Ezek 44:15. See L. Nemoy, "Al-Qirqisani's Account of the Jewish Sects and Christianity", *Hebrew Union College Annual*, 1930, pp. 319–397 for Karaite tradition relating to Zadok's and Jesus' condemnation of divorce and marriage with a niece. These practices were widespread among "the Herodians" and Josephus specifically mentions the illegality of the manner in which Herodias *divorced herself* from her husband: *Ant.* 18.5.4. The same combination of factors also circulates about problems relating to Agrippa II's two sisters Drusilla and Bernice, Herodias' nieces, and once again Josephus specifically comments on the illegality of Drusilla's self-divorce: *Ant.* 20.7.1ff. Note that where Bernice is concerned, Josephus makes special mention of "her Riches", her "fornication" (even reputedly with her brother), and how "she forsook ... the Jewish religion" after being married to *her uncle* Herod of Chalcis (before she took up with Titus); cf. the same combination of charges in CD, viii.5ff., including "fornication", "Riches", and incest ("approaching near kin for unchastity").

It very definitely is connected with the Herodian Priestly Establishment, and we shall demonstrate this in some detail in our analysis of the Habakkuk *Pesher*'s charge against it of "robbing the Poor" (as the Letter of James describes a parallel sentiment, "a burning fire have you Rich stored up for yourselves"). One should also not fail to remark its reflection in Josephus' description of "the Essenes" and Qumran "Poor" appellations.[21]

The third charge is "profanation of the Sanctuary". We shall see that this last will be one of the charges levelled against the Wicked Priest, i.e., "his Abominations" (*To'evot*) with which "he polluted the Temple" (*yetame' et Mikdash-El*) in 1QpHab, xii.8f. It is certainly reflected too in the Phineas-minded lower priesthood's stopping of sacrifice on behalf of and refusing any longer to accept gifts from Romans and other foreigners—referred to as "an innovation" by Josephus—which triggers the Uprising against Rome.

It can also be detected to a certain extent in New Testament notices about the antagonism between Paul's "Gentile Mission" and "the Jerusalem Church" and difficulties both Paul and some of his Gentile converts latterly encounter on the Temple Mount. All of these, however tenuously, are connected with the erection of stone-markers in this period warning Gentiles away from the Temple and the general hostility towards the Herodian family, which is only the special case of these currents. This last is very much in evidence in the erection of the wall in the Temple in the late 50s, the controversies surrounding which in our view lead inexorably and directly to the death of James.[22]

---

[21] Cf. Ja 5:1ff., *War* 2.8.2, and below, pp. 162f and 187ff.

[22] The "Temple Wall" incident, connected as it is with Agrippa II's banqueting habits in *Ant.* 20.8.11, is crucial. Here, the hostility of the lower priesthood to the Herodian family is patent and this hostility must be connected to a plethora of notices in both Acts and the Pseudoclementines about difficulties on the Temple Mount and the conversion "of a large group of priests" and "zealots" (Acts 6:7 and 21:20). Ultimately, Josephus informs us that "the Innovators"—the same ones who stop sacrifice on behalf of foreigners—succeed in having Agrippa II barred from the whole city (*War* 2.17.1). For the crystallization of Agrippa's relations with the High Priest Ananus, see below, n. 32.

The whole is paralleled a generation before in the Simon/Agrippa I episode in *Ant.* 19.7.4. Simon, obviously one of the Temple "Zealots" and "the head of an Assembly" (in Greek, this is literally, "*Ecclēsia*" or "Church"), wishes to bar Agrippa I from the Temple. He is invited to Caesarea to inspect Agrippa I's living arrangements (i.e., the *kashrut* of his house).

It is hardly to be doubted that the episode serves as the original model behind the visit of "Simon Peter" to the Roman Centurion's house in Caesarea. Cornelius, we are told, "gave generously to Jewish causes" (Acts 10–11; cf. the Parallel Lk 19:1ff. above about the "Chief Tax-Collector" Zacchaeus who gives half of what he has *to the Poor*).

Early Church tradition also tells us that James' various titles, i.e., *Zaddik* and *Oblias* ("Protection of the People"/"Bulwark"/"Fortress"), were to be found by searching Scripture, that is, that the followers of James followed a style of esoteric exegesis not dissimilar to that pursued by the sectaries at Qumran in analyzing the life and character of "the Righteous Teacher".[23] The actual words reported via Hegesippus, who lived within about 100 years of the events in question, were: "And the Prophets declare concerning him", i.e., concerning James and his death. Not surprisingly, the text in question, Is 3:10–11, is a *Zaddik*-passage, and the link is directly drawn between the word "*zaddik*" in the underlying biblical text and the fate and person of the *Moreh-Zedek/Zaddik* James in the exegesis. Every exegetical text at Qumran relating to events concerning the life and person of the Righteous Teacher functions in exactly the same manner. This constitutes persuasive testimony that not only was Qumran-style exegesis practiced by the community descended from James, but that such exegesis was current in this period.

If one looks at the ambiance of the Is 3:10–11 passage applied to James' death by these early Church sources, one encounters from about Is 1–5 a general tenor of salvation through Righteousness and allusion

"Peter" in Acts is nothing but the mirror image of this *Simon* and the episode points the way towards deciphering Acts' "historical method", such as it is. Just as Acts conserves an echo of Peter's ultimate—and unexplained—arrest by "Herod" (usually taken to be Agrippa I, but just as likely his brother and son-in-law and the "kinsman" of Josephus' "Saulus"—Herod of Chalcis), the "Temple Wall" episode under Agrippa II can be identified as the ultimate cause of James' arrest and execution. Agrippa II, working through Ananus, exploits his first opportunity in the aftermath of his discomfiture over this issue to deal with the person whom he obviously considers to have been the key to the events we are describing, James the Just. For a further discussion of these matters and their possible reflection in the Temple Scroll, see Appendix.

These real events have their representations in Acts in intimations of confrontations between the Apostles and the Jerusalem Establishment on the Temple Mount, but they find a more insistent echo in the notices about confrontations on the Temple Mount between Christians and the high priest class in *Recognitions* which end up in the riot initiated by the "Herodian" Paul. We call Paul "Herodian" because of the intimations he himself makes (cf. Ro 16:11 relating to his "kinsman Herodion"; "the household of Aristobulus" referred to here is, in our view, most likely that of Herod of Chalcis' son by this same name, later King of Lesser Armenia/Cilicia married to that Salome so celebrated in the Gospels and a close collaborator of Titus') and the general religio-political stance of his "Gentile Mission".

[23] See Eusebius, *loc. cit.* At Qumran without exception, where reference is made in a *pesher* to the Righteous Teacher, the Biblical text being subjected to exegesis is a *Zaddik*-passage; in 1QpHab, i.12 the correspondence is specifically drawn and in CD, i.20 reference to the "soul of the *Zaddik*" actually takes the place of the usual reference to the *Moreh ha-Zedek*.

to the imminent destruction of Jerusalem. The text directly appeals to the *"Beit*-Yaʿacov"—James' Hebrew name—repeated three times, which would doubtlessly have appealed to the practitioners of this kind of exegesis, and amid an atmosphere of oncoming armies and imminent destruction precisely analogous to the Habakkuk *Pesher*, intones: "Jerusalem is ruined; Judea is fallen . . . the Lord is taking away from Jerusalem support of every kind."

These last should be compared with the insistence in early Church sources that James' death was in some way connected to the fall of Jerusalem and Paul's description of the Central Triad of the early Church of "James, Cephas, and John" as "these Pillars". The last in our view incorporates a direct allusion to James' *Zaddik*-nature, which by extension can be seen as a "Zadokite" play—as per the general thrust of Qumran esoteric exegesis and word-play—on the sense of Proverbs' "the *Zaddik* the Foundation of the World".[24] The use of such a style of exegesis explains why the early "Church" felt that the destruction of Jerusalem was inevitable once its "Protection", "Bulwark", or "Pillar" (all allusions having counterparts in the usage of 1QH and 1QS) was removed.

The *Zaddik*-the-Pillar-of-the-World metaphor is also at the root of the allusion to James the Righteous One in the Gospel of Thomas and related materials concerning the disappearance of "Heaven and Earth" in the New Testament "Little Apocalypse".[25] It is the basic thrust behind whatever may be meant by the *"Oblias"* sobriquet which also attached itself to James' person. Though the precise derivation of the latter is unclear, Eusebius/Hegesippus make it clear that it related to James' "support"/"Protection" activities among the mass of Jewish "Poor" (*Ebionim*/*ʿAniyyim*—"the *Rabbim*" of Qumran/Is 53:11 allusion).[26] With all of this data at our disposal, it would not be difficult to imagine the content of a Qumran-style *pesher* on the first four or five chapters of

---

[24] Cf. Prov 10:25 and its telling elucidation in *Zohar*, i.59b on "Noah", including reference to the "Pillar" terminology applied to James and the Central Triad in Ga 2:9. The *Zohar* on "Phineas" also employs a facsimile of the "Protection" terminology in relation to Is 53:11's "Justification" ideology.

[25] Gos Th 11–12 and Mt 24:35ff., including even the note of pre-existence and the reference to "Noah" amid eschatological evocation of "the flood".

[26] "The People" is a quantity associated at all times and in all testimonies with James' activities. Eusebius/Epiphanius via Hegesippus define *Oblias* as "Protection"/"Fortress"/"Shield"/or "Strength of the People". Elsewhere James is alluded to as "Bulwark"; cf. *E.H.* 3.7.8. The terminology is paralleled in Hymns in references to its protagonist—presumably the Righteous Teacher himself—as "Shield" (*Maʿoz*), "Wall", "Fortress" (*Migdal*), "a firm Foundation that will not sway", and the general "building" and "Cornerstone" imagery applied to the Council in 1QS, viii.1ff.—notably including a Central Triad.

Isaiah (including an important oracle which has relevance for controversies regarding the "Pella-Flight" tradition: "to flee into the Rocks and the cave"), so exactly parallel in tone and content to the first few chapters of Habakkuk we will analyze.[27]

What then has primarily held scholars back from looking into the implications of these striking parallels about James' life and person and tying them to actual Qumran events and personalities? On the whole this reluctance has centered on the existence of several references in the Habakkuk *Pesher* and elsewhere relating to the fall of Jerusalem and/or the Temple and describing "the Wicked Priest" as actually having "ruled Israel".[28] These allusions, which we shall treat

---

[27] Cf. "Enter into the rock and hide in the dust ... for the day of the Lord of Hosts shall be on every one that is proud and lofty ... and upon all the cedars of Lebanon that are high and lifted up [a favorite image at Qumran and in early Rabbinic literature for the fall of the Temple in 70 CE; cf. below, pp. 185f.] and they shall go into the holes of the rocks and into the caves of the earth for fear of the Lord and the glory of his majesty when He arises to shake the earth terribly. On that day a man shall cast his idols of silver and his idols of gold ... to the moles and to the bats [cf. Ja 5:2: "your wealth is all rotting; your clothes are all eaten up with moths" and similar imagery at the end of the Habakkuk *Pesher*] in order to go into the clefts of the rocks and into the top of the jagged stones."

Here, the word is *"sela'im"*, which we take to be the possible source of confused data incorporated into the disputed "Pella-flight" tradition of this period; note similar "flight" traditions in 4QD[b] and the actual tradition of a "Jericho" flight centering around James' Jerusalem Community in Ps *Rec* 1.71 above, coinciding with a pronounced rise in Qumran coin distribution during the reign of Agrippa I; cf. as well the parallel flight tradition relating to the *Sicarii* after the stoning of their purported leader "Menachem". For the most recent description of the whole controversy, see G. Lüdemann, "The Successors of Pre-70 Jerusalem Christianity: A Critical Evaluation of the Pella-Tradition", *Jewish and Christian Self-Definition*, i, Philadelphia, 1978, pp. 161–73. Lüdemann generally recapitulates G. Strecker; see also S. G. F. Brandon, *Jesus and the Zealots*, New York, 1967, pp. 208ff.

Not only are these first five chapters of Isaiah seemingly addressed to "the House of Jacob" (2:3, 2:5, 2:6, etc.), but their general *sitz im leben* parallels that of those sections of Habakkuk already subjected to exegesis at Qumran, including an atmosphere of desolation and the burning of cities with fire (1:7), the use of the fall of the cedars of Lebanon, reference to "the proud and the lofty" imagery above, alluding to the redemption of Zion through "Righteousness" and "Faith" (1:26ff., 5:8, 5:16, etc.), combining "fornication" imagery with allusion to "the Judgement of Righteousness" (1:21), evoking the destruction of the city of Sodom in the context of allusions to the removal of the Righteous One (3:9ff) referring to the saving power of "Knowledge" (*Da'at* at Qumran; 5:14), the original behind CD, ii's "justifying the Wicked" and "condemning the Righteous" imagery (5:23ff.), and describing how the "carcasses were mutilated in the midst of the city".

[28] Suggestions about the importance of the "Righteousness" ideal in the delineation of the Zadokite priesthood go all the way back to W. F. Albright (with C. S. Mann),

below, have been combined with some very questionable archaeological and paleographic data, the treatment of which was often affected
by the interpretation of such passages and related historical and
religious preconceptions, to press the provenance of a large share of
Qumran sectarian materials back into the Maccabean age.[29] Most
scholars agree that the scrolls were deposited in the caves in or
around 68 CE, but often mistake this date, as we shall see as well
below, for the *terminus ad quem* for the deposit of the scrolls in the
caves/cessation of Jewish habitation at the site, when it cannot be
considered anything but the *terminus a quo* for both of these, i.e., not
the latest but the *earliest* possible date for such deposit and/or Jewish

---

"Qumran and the Essenes: Geography, Chronology, and Identification of the Sect",
BASOR, Suppl. Studies, 1951, pp. 17ff.; P. Wernberg-Moeller, "*Zedek, Zaddik*, and Zadok
in the Zadokite Fragments (CDC), the Manual of Discipline (DSD) and the Habakkuk
Commentary (SSH)", *V.T.*, iii, 1953, pp. 309–15; and R. North, "The Qumran
'Sadducees' ", *CBQ*, 17, 1955, pp. 164–88; but were never developed in any consistent
manner. Le Moyne's more recent work, *Les Sadducéans*, Paris, 1972, p. 160 is completely
inadequate on this subject.

[29] I have treated the unscientific use of archaeological and palaeographical data in detail
in *Maccabees, Zadokites, Christians and Qumran*. This reference to the Wicked Priest as
actually having "ruled Israel" is exploited by commentators to seek out a time when
priests were rulers, namely, the Maccabean period or before, without noting that High
Priests can always be said to have "ruled Israel" and that there were subsequent times
more in keeping with the plural aspect of the allusion "the Last Priests of Jerusalem"
when priests actually did "rule" Israel, e.g. under the High Priest Ananus in 62 CE and
from 66 to 68 CE. It must be stressed, however, that the reference need not denote a
totally independent secular ruler but simple incumbency in the high priesthood. For
Ananus as an independent ruler, see *Vita* 38 and *War* 4.3.9–5.2.

In addition, archaeological and paleographic reconstructions are set forth on the basis
of precisely such preconceptions. The fact that 1QpHab appears to allude either to the
fall or imminent fall of the Temple is used to press the *sitz im leben* of these references
back 100–200 years in time to 37 BC, 63 BC, or before. For an example of the kind of
ideological preconceptions we are talking about, see Birnbaum, pp. 69–79, 87, 94, and
103, where he calls the Pharisees, in contradistinction to the "Sadducees", "religious
nationalists", uncritically accepts de Vaux's "earthquake" hypothesis in the determination
of "pegs" in his paleographic sequences, and heaps endless abuse on paleo-Hebrew
script, calling it "an artificial revival" and insisting that John Hyrcanus and the Sadducees
"would have been the last people to dig out the old script" (since they were not
"nationalists"). Cf., as well, Milik in n. 1 above and the general propensity on the part
of Qumran scholars to consider the Maccabees suitable candidates for the Wicked Priest,
e.g., F. F. Bruce, *Second Thoughts on the Dead Sea Scrolls*, Exeter, 1956, p. 100: " . . . . in
the eyes of the Qumran community every ruler of the Hasmonean dynasty, not being
a member of the house of Zadok, held the high-priestly office illegitimately and was *ex
officio* a Wicked Priest"; Cross, *The Ancient Library of Qumran*, New York, 1961, pp. 135
and 140, actually calls them "usurpers".

abandonment of the site.[30] The actual *terminus ad quem* for both of these events, however difficult it may be to accept at first, is 136 CE.

Where the Habakkuk *Pesher* itself is concerned, most scholars acknowledge that it exhibits a substantial number of what are considered "late" paleographic characteristics, and its being found (like all *pesharim* at Qumran) in a single exemplar and the manner of its deposit also almost certainly identify it as part of the *current* literature of the sect.[31] Despite these factors and the fact that the military procedures depicted in the Habakkuk *Pesher* appear to be those of *Imperial* Rome, most identifications have still involved a wide assortment of Maccabean (or even *pre-Maccabean*) events and characters. This, in turn, entails the somewhat unrealistic proposition that the sectaries were making intense and idiosyncratic scriptural exegeses about persons as antiquated to them as Napoleon or George Washington would seem today to us, and that in addition, they were ignoring 150–250 years of the most vital and significant Palestinian history, the last installments of which were apparently unfolding at that very moment before their eyes.

Where the problem of "ruling Israel" is concerned, our candidate for "Wicked Priest", James' nemesis Ananus, did rule Israel virtually in an independent manner on two occasions: the first in 62 CE, when he took advantage of an interregnum in Roman rule after the death of Festus to dispose of James; and the second, four years later in the first stages of the Uprising, before he himself was brutally dispatched by Josephus' "Idumaeans".[32]

---

[30] See, for instance, de Vaux, pp. 41 and 138. Note how Birnbaum, p. 27, hardens the import of de Vaux's conclusions considerably: "Archaeological evidence . . . even enables us to arrive at a precise *terminus ad quem*: the year 68 CE, when the Romans put an end to the Qumran settlement." Fitzmyer in "The Qumran Scrolls, the Ebionites, and their Literature", *Essays on the Semitic Background of the New Testament*, Missoula, 1974, p. 446, has turned the actual situation completely around: "The latest possible date for the deposit of the manuscripts is the destruction of Qumran in 68 CE." F. M. Cross, to his credit, realizes that the "absolute *terminus ad quem* for Qumran script types" are the dated documents from the Wadi Murabbaʿat, though sometimes he behaves as if he doesn't; cf. "The Oldest Manuscripts from Qumran", *SBL*, 1955, p. 163.

[31] If we consider that Cave IV was not inhabited and take it to be either a "library", repository, or *genizah*, then caves like Cave I, which were inhabited, where Habakkuk was found so neatly deposited with a selection of other materials, must contain documents that were actually in use at the time the site was abandoned (whenever this was); cf. R. de Vaux, *Archaeology and the Dead Sea Scrolls*, Oxford, 1973, pp. 44ff., 50ff., 107, etc., for habitation in the caves.

[32] See *Ant.* 20.9.1 for the well-known description of the execution of James. Agrippa II's role in these events has not generally been remarked, since Josephus did not directly call attention to it. An inspection, however, of his appointment and removal of the

The notion of applying the "Wicked Priest" appellation to one or another of the Maccabees—time elements apart—is also hardly convincing. The Maccabees, with the single exception of Alexander Jannaeus, seem to have been on the whole rather "popular" rulers, particularly among apocalyptic and xenophobic nationalists of the kind reflected in the literature at Qumran. Even the Nahum *Pesher*, which appears to refer to Alexander Jannaeus, is not particularly hostile to Alexander but rather to the presumable "Pharisees" he crucifies.[33] Where the reference to "the Last Priests of Jerusalem" and the seeming destruction of the Temple in the Habakkuk *Pesher* are concerned, this is an event in progress, not already completed, and from 67/68 onwards with the arrival in Palestine of the main body of Vespasian's troops, the destruction of Jerusalem was a foregone conclusion to any but the most unrealistic observer.[34]

Josephus himself realizes as much and quotes Agrippa to the same effect before the Uprising even began. In addition, there are two known traditions regarding "opposition" groups in this period implying the same point: 1) the "*Sicarii*" followers of Menachem, the descendant of Judas the *Galilean*, who fled Jerusalem to return to Masada in the aftermath of his *stoning*; 2) the "Jewish Christian" supporters of James the Just who shortly before Vespasian's army encircled Jerusalem are said to have fled in response to the mysterious oracle mentioned above.

Scholars, as we have noted, tend to exploit the above kinds of references to press the *sitz im leben* of the Qumran *pesharim* back 100, 150, or even 200 years to a fall of the Temple prior to 70 CE. In doing so, they often cite this same Nahum *Pesher* because it actually appears to mention

Boethusian/son of Kanthera High Priest, Joseph Cabi—whom the Temple "Zealots" seem to have approved of—leading up to his appointment of Ananus and judicial murder of James, indicates that he took the first opportunity he found after the Temple Wall Affair to rid himself of James, and that, therefore, he must have blamed James in some manner for his embarrassment by it. Note that his relations with Ananus appear to have crystallized in the context of previous problems with "Zealot" revolutionaries when Ananus and others had been sent in bonds to Rome in the early 50s and he intervened on Ananus' behalf; *Ant*. 20.7.2f. and *War* 2.12.6.

[33] Milik, for instance, pp. 63f., cannot at all understand Dupont-Sommer's outrage over his suggestion to identify the "heroic and holy" Mattathias with "the man of Belial" (whoever such a "man of Belial" might be), and Cross, pp. 158ff., cannot comprehend why Dupont-Sommer would include Aristobulus II in his list of levitical "saviours". I have treated this subject in some detail in *Maccabees, Zadokites, Christians and Qumran*.

[34] The reference in 1QpHab, ix.4ff. is a general one and relates only to the destruction of the Wicked Priest and "the Last Priests of Jerusalem". From 1QpHab, iii to ix, the coming of the *Kittim* is a background event, against which the main concerns of the *Pesher*—primarily the struggle between the Teacher and his two antagonists, the Wicked Priest and the Lying Spouter—are enacted.

a known foreign ruler—Demetrius, seemingly Alexander Jannaeus' antagonist.

However, a careful literary/historical examination of this text will demonstrate it to be retrospective and historiographical in nature and support the opposite conclusion. Though 4QpNah, i.5 explicitly refers to "the Greeks", the reference is to the past and for it "the *Kittim*"— straightforwardly identified in Daniel as *the Romans*—come *after them* and have already appeared.[35] Presumably the sectaries knew their history as well as Josephus (who more than likely spent time with them).[36] "Demetrius" is mentioned by name because his regime *is* ancient history. Since he is *foreign*, and presumably therefore no longer any threat to those composing the *Pesher*, no hesitation is evinced in overtly speaking about him.

It is quite another matter regarding the sect's *current* enemies. Here the peculiar and by now familiar exegetical code comes into play because the danger is real and palpable. Nor does the condemnation of crucifixion in i.15 include any condemnation, as we have noted, of "the Furious Young Lion" who perpetrates the outrage. Rather, the text's hostility is aimed at those "Seekers after Smooth Things" he crucifies.[37]

---

[35] The stance resembles nothing so much as that of Onias the Just—also "Honi the Circle-Drawer"—in *Ant.* 14.2.1, who, when brought to condemn the Maccabean partisans of Aristobulus II who took refuge in the city inside the Temple before the Roman assault in 63 BC, refuses, for which reason he is promptly stoned by his presumably Pharisaic interlocutors. Textually, which is to say nothing about paleography, the Nahum *Pesher* is a contemporary of the Habakkuk. Its combination of "Tongue" and "Lying" imagery generically parallels similar usages in Ja 3:5ff.

[36] *Vita* 2 documents Josephus' familiarity with a Qumran-style settlement led by a teacher he cryptically refers to as "*Banus*", who is a "Bather". This familiarity borders on obsession and is further reflected in his long description of the sects in *War* 2.8.2ff., which is really nothing but a description of "the Essenes", with the other groups added mostly as an afterword. In *Ant.* 18.1.1ff., where Josephus introduces a new character, "Saddok", and is willing to be more forthcoming about the movement initiated by him and Judas the Galilean, he severely curtails his previous description of "the Essenes", adding material previously included under it to his now expanded description of "the Fourth Philosophy."

[37] The *Pesher* itself is indisputably hostile to "the Seekers after Smooth Things". This party, which in the time of Demetrius was sympathetic both to foreign domination and foreign appointment of High Priests, is none other than that normally referred to as "Pharisees". As time goes on, one must view the usage as generic, referring to all those advocating peaceful compliance with foreign occupation (i.e., "turning the other cheek" and "rendering unto Caesar what is Caesar's"). In the mid-50s of the next century, this would include Pauline Christians. In any event, where foreign policy was at issue, Paul is indistinguishable from Pharisaic teachers like Hillel and Shammai, Rabbi Yohanan b. Zacchai, and Simeon b. Shetach of an earlier era—all recommending a policy of

The commentary itself specifies that it relates to the period in which these last—clearly Pharisees—hold sway in Jerusalem, which must be seen as quintessentially the Herodian, *not the Maccabean*. This is reinforced by the general reference to "High Priests" or "Chief Priests" (plural) to characterize the principal priestly clans of the *Herodian* Period, not the Maccabean. Throughout the former (not before), the Pharisee Party and those "Sadducees" controlled by them were pre-eminent in Jerusalem. Some, as we have noted, even took control under Ananus and Rabban Simeon b. Gamaliel of the first stages of the revolution—Josephus was their commissar in Galilee—attempting thereby to deflect its xenophobic antagonism towards Romans and their Herodian representatives.[38] Quite properly, as it were, the *Pesher* blames these "Seekers after Smooth Things" for inviting foreigners like the Herodians, procurators, and the armies of Vespasian and Titus into the country and cooperating with them, not only in the present but also in the past (the historiographic thrust of the original allusion to Demetrius).[39]

The *Pesher* is not antagonistic to "zealous" Maccabean-style rulers. On the contrary, it is antagonistic to an alliance of "the Seekers after Smooth Things", which we identify with the Herodian Pharisaic/Sadducean establishment, with "those who lead astray"/"lead Many astray" *at the End of Days*. In connection with these last allusions, which below we will

accommodation with Romans and other foreigners; cf. Paul in Ro 13:1ff. See below, p. 172 for the *War*'s reference to how this alignment of those "desirous for peace", when all is lost, *actually invites* the Romans into Jerusalem to suppress the Uprising.

[38] See *Vita* 38 and *War* 4.3.9–5.2.

[39] Cf. *Ant.* 13.13.4f. and *War* 1.4.4f. Josephus' knowledge about the period is obviously confused. Not only does he transpose and interchange Sameas and Pollio, but in placing the "Essenes" side by side with the "Pharisees", he says the same things about Herod's affection for the one as he does about his affection for the other—and for the same reasons; *Ant.* 14.9.3f. and 15.1.1. Continuing the policy of the Pharisees of Demetrius' time, Pollio wins great honor from Herod by advising the citizens of Jerusalem to open their gates to him (Sameas, like "Menachem the Essene", predicted future greatness for Herod when he was a boy). This attitude is hardly distinguishable from that of Yohanan ben Zacchai, who according to *ARN* 4, when Jerusalem was under siege, shot an arrow into Vespasian's camp to inform him he was "one of the Emperor's friends". All effectively employ the stratagem of predicting future greatness or good fortune for foreign rulers or conquerors in order to toady to their egos. Josephus himself employs the same stratagem and Paul's exceedingly cordial relations with Roman governors and Herodians are detailed in the closing chapters of Acts (note, too, the constant reiteration of the theme of "prophets" in New Testament descriptions of early Gentile Christian communities). All the foregoing are important indications of the Pharisaic mentality as we would define it; when Josephus defines opposition leaders like Judas and Saddok as being in all things like the "Pharisees" except for having an inviolable attachment to liberty, he is, according to this view, very close to the mark.

be able to relate to parodies of the proper "Justification" language of Is 53:11, the *Pesher* also employs "Lying" and "Tongue" imagery as per the Letter of James.

In ii.1 it actually makes reference to overseas "messengers" in connection with its "City of Blood" allusion, which we will be able to relate to similar allusions in the Habakkuk *Pesher* where the activities of the "lying Spouter" are at issue. Its thrust is to condemn this alliance together with one of the groups it "deceives", which it designates "Ephraim" or "the Simple Ones of Ephraim".[40] In our view, Ananus appertains to an "Establishment" party which is part and parcel of this general Pharisaic/Herodian alliance. Though called "Sadducee" in Josephus and the New Testament, it is a latterday caricature of Qumran "Sadducees". For the sake of convenience, it is simpler to refer to it as "Boethusian" after the Priest Herod imports from Egypt, as it has nothing whatever in common with Qumran's or James' Righteousness-oriented and eschatological exegesis of "the Zadokite Covenant".[41]

---

[40] Cf. Ja 3:5ff. and 4QpNah, ii.8—also including allusion to "fornication" both as a real circumstance and as imagery; cf. too the allusion "the Simple Ones" tied to this kind of language in iii.7, also referred to in a similarly important context in 1QpHab, xii.4 below. The whole allusion in 4QpNah, ii has particular relevance to the alliance "of all those desirous for peace" signaled in *War* 2.17.3 who oppose the "Innovators" and actually invite the Romans into the city before the Revolt could get started in 66 CE. For more on this connection see below, p. 172. For "the Lying Spouter" and "the city" he *builds upon blood*, see 1QpHab, x.9ff. We will in the course of the analysis below of the Habakkuk *Pesher* be able to relate some of these kinds of allusions and the combinations of individuals to which they refer—that is, "the Men of Violence" and "the Traitors"—to Paul and some of his followers or colleagues, particularly renegade "Herodians" or "Idumaeans", like Silas and Niger of Perea responsible for the death of Ananus. Where the "Ephraim" allusion is concerned in such a context, careful inspection of the Commentary will reveal that it relates like "*Nilvim*" above to non-Jewish believers formerly attached to the community—therefore the signification "Ephraim"; see below p. 188–90.

[41] For detailed enumerations of the various "Herodian" priestly clans, see J. Jeremias, *Jerusalem in the Time of Jesus*, Philadelphia, 1962, pp. 152ff. and 188ff. For Simeon b. Boethus, the eponymous progenitor of the clan, whose daughter married Herod after the latter murdered his Maccabean spouse, see *Ant.* 15.9.3 and 17.4.2. For "Simeon b. Kanthera" (a name possibly distorted into Jesus' *Talmudic* epithet "b. Panthera" and hard to distinguish from the cognomens of two other "sons of Kanthera", Joseph Kami and Joseph Cabi), also a Boethusian, whom Josephus possibly confuses with Simeon b. Boethus and compares to "Simeon the *Zaddik*" two centuries before in the number of his sons doing high priestly service, see *Ant.* 19.6.2ff. Jeremias lists at least seven high priests associated with this family in the first century and connects it, probably correctly, to the famous "Tomb of St James"/*Bene* Hezir Monument. In addition to these, there were several other clans, including "the sons of Ananus" and those of Ananias b. Nebed-

In such a context it is possible to specify with some precision what these "Smooth Things" were that so exercised the community. They are not so much legal trivialities—though these existed—but rather the broad areas of *foreign kingship, foreign appointment of High Priests, foreigners* and *foreign gifts in the Temple, marriage with nieces, divorce*, etc., all in one manner or another involving Herodians or those closely associated with them. This anti-Herodian stance is also very much in evidence in the Temple Scroll, which adds the ban on foreign kings and divorce to the Damascus Document's evocation of the Deuteronomic King Law. Its emphases in later columns on "Abominations" and "pollution" link up with similar concerns in the Habakkuk *Pesher* and Damascus Document, particularly the latter's charges of not observing proper "separation" procedures in the Temple (probably reflected too, albeit esoterically, in the "*balla'* "/"Bela'" and "things sacrificed to idols" materials in 11QT, xlvi–xlvii).

This antagonism to foreigners and "those seeking accommodation" with them is also reflected in the Zadokite/Zealot Covenant of Num 25:7ff./Ezek 44:7ff. directed respectively against *foreigners in the Community* and *foreigners/backsliders in the Temple* and the "not one jot or tittle" approach to the Law of Mt 5:18/Lk 16:17's Jesus, James in Ja 2:10, and at Qumran in 1QS, viii.22/CD, iv.8. It is reflected, too, in the debates in the Temple—refracted in Acts—between James and the High Priests, as reported in the *Anabathmoi Jacobou* and the Pseudoclementines. These debates parallel and can be none other than those in the Temple between "the Innovators" and the Herodian Priestly Establishment concerning barring Gentiles—mainly Herodians, but also Romans and other foreigners—and their gifts from the Temple, which are reported so insistently from the 40s to the 60s CE by Josephus and which trigger the Revolt against Rome.

Both the "pollution of the Temple" and "fornication" charges tied to this last are linked in the Damascus Document to one of "sleeping with women in their periods" (CD, iv.17ff.). Together with its charge of "marrying nieces"—also of concern along with the marital practices of the King generally in the Temple Scroll—this is considered an habitual or

ias. Josephus describes them as "men of little note, whose families were barely those of priests", most notably excepting from this aspersion the Maccabees: *Ant.* 20.10.1. These Herodian Sadducees, for obvious reasons, laid stress on a genealogical interpretation of the Zadokite Covenant as opposed to the Righteousness-oriented one clearly signaled at Qumran, despite the fact that Herod is reported to have jealously destroyed all the genealogical records upon becoming ruler of Palestine: *E.H.* 1.7.13 quoting Julius Africanus.

customary practice, which, as we shall show in our Appendix, can have meaning only within the perceived sexual mores and marital practices of the *Herodian* family and not those of a *Jewish* Priesthood in this period, except derivatively. In line with its theological exigencies—that is to say, the new Pauline/"Petrine" "Christian" community admitting Gentiles, not barring them—the ideological thrust of these debates is *inverted/ reversed* in Acts' portrait of similar debates/problems in the early days of the community in Jerusalem. To make the circle of these allusions complete with regard to such inversions/reversals, one should note the theology in the Pauline corpus—reflected too in the Gospels—of *Jesus as Temple* and the further adumbration of it in Eph 2:2ff. of equality in "Christ Jesus", there being no "aliens" or "foreign visitors" (a further ramification is discernible in the parallel represented by Josephus' concern in the *Jewish War* to absolve the Romans of guilt in destroying the Temple and the contemporary Gospel concern, to absolve them of guilt in destroying the Christ).[42]

This parallel of "Jesus" with "Temple", body, Community, and Community Council is perhaps best illustrated by comparing improper "separation"/"pollution of the Temple" materials involving Belial, "Beliar" (*sic*), "things sacrificed to idols", etc. in CD, ivff., 2 Co 6:4ff., and 11QT, xlvi–xlvii. Amid the imagery of "knowing Christ not according to the flesh", "the Righteousness of God in Him", Truth, "Lawbreaking", "being Poor but enriching Many", and paraphrasing 1QH, ix.35's God as Father to all "the Sons of Truth", 2 Co 6 expounds the charge of "polluting the Temple of God with idols"—a variation of the "Noachic" proscription on idolatry and James' "Jerusalem Council" proscription on "pollutions

---

[42] The same puzzling dichotomy of actual Temple and spiritualized sacrifice and atonement is also present at Qumran, most notably in the Temple Scroll and Community Rule. Though the *Anabathmoi Jacobou* portrays James as complaining against "the Temple and the sacrifices" (Epiphanius, *Haeres.* 30.16), it requires only the smallest shift in conceptuality to envision these complaints in terms of the ongoing ones of "the Innovators" against the Herodian Establishment over "Temple service" and/or the acceptance of gifts/sacrifices from/on behalf of foreigners/backsliding Jews (Ezek 44:9's "uncircumcized in heart and flesh").

Should precise chronological sequencing regarding these approaches be required, this would not be too difficult to provide. When the Community were penitents in the wilderness—because of their perception of Temple pollution—spiritualized sacrifice/atonement was the preferred expression of Piety; when, in control of the Temple, as at various times in the 50s and 60s, e.g., the building of the high wall to block Agrippa II's view of the sacrifices prior to Ananus' assumption of the High Priesthood and James' death and during the last stages of the Uprising, purification of the Temple as per general Temple Scroll parameters (and New Testament portrait) was preferred.

of the idols"—by asking what "has Beliar to do with Christ", "Light with Darkness", and, in effect, "things sacrificed to idols" with the body (for 11QT, xlvi, "Bela'" with "the Temple")?

Completely paralleling the vocabulary of 11QT, xlvi.10f., the Corinthians text proceeds to invoke "separating", "uncleanness", "defiling", and even "fearing God"—connected to the repetition of the "God-fearing" theme appellative of Gentiles evoked in 11QT, xlvi.11 in place of Num 4:20's "seeing"—ending in evocation of the typical Qumran phraseology "Perfection of Holiness" (cf. "*Tamim ha-Kodesh*" in CD, viii.24ff.). As per the imagery of 1QS, viiif. and Paul's 1 Co 2:13ff. prescription about teaching "spiritual things spiritually"—but unlike the exoteric sense of the Temple Scroll—its language is always esoteric; however, there can be no mistaking its relationship to the "Christ"/"body"/"Temple", "Beliar"/"idols"/"Herodians in the Temple" correspondence.

II
HABAKKUK *PESHER* TEXTUAL EXEGESIS

Having set down what some of our ideological and historical parameters ought to be, it now becomes possible to go through the Habakkuk *Pesher* passage by passage and signal its connections to the life and teachings of James the Just. It should be noted, that regardless of one's opinion of their authenticity, the Pseudoclementines *do* place James *with all his Community* in the Jericho area (a notice which can hardly be ascribed to historical interpolation). In turn, this notice corresponds to an impressive rise in coin distribution at Qumran during the reign of Agrippa I. In addition, as wise and comfortably safe as the avoidance of making real identifications may be, we know enough about the personalities and events in this period from the variety of sources—even though some of these have been distorted and obscured by tradition—to require scholars to make *meaningful* and *real* historical identifications.

At the outset of the *Pesher* we encounter a statement in the underlying Habakkuk text (1:4): "the Wicked encompasses the Righteous". This exactly parallels the sense and signification of the Is 3:10 passage which early Church tradition has retained in the Septuagint rendition, i.e., "Let us remove the Righteous One for he is abhorrent to us", which was applied to the death of James. Both are *Zaddik*-passages and both hinge on contrasting the behavior of "the Wicked"—almost always identified with the Wicked Priest—with "the Righteous". Both directly apply the word "*Zaddik*" in the underlying text to the subject of their exegesis,

James and the Righteous Teacher respectively. In the Habakkuk *Pesher* this connection is even *explicitly* drawn: "the *Zaddik* is the *Moreh ha-Zedek*" (i.12).

Though these early passages of the *Pesher* are somewhat fragmentary, their general thrust already relates to "robbing Riches" (i.7), which later will have the specific connotation of "robbing the Poor". This concern is certainly related to the condemnation of the Rich in the Letter of James and Josephus' several notices about the *Rich* Priests robbing the tithes of "the Poor" so that some even perished for want in the early 60s just prior to James' judicial murder.[1] In addition, one encounters the first references to "unfaithfulness", quarrelsomeness, and "rejecting the *Torah* of God" (i.10), with their consonant sense of the perversion of the Righteousness doctrine and the process of Justification which the *Pesher* will develop in such detail where activities of "the Lying Spouter" are concerned.

This *Pesher* has two *bêtes noires*, whose presence along with that of the Teacher's dominate it, and it swings its attention back and forth alternating between them. The first is the Wicked Priest, the mention of whom is usually tied, as we have seen, to references in the underlying text to *Rasha'*/"Evil", and in connection with whom "the Poor" are robbed,

---

[1] Cf. Ja 1:9ff., 2:3ff., 4:7ff. on the humble and the proud (allusions common at Qumran), and 5:1ff. on the final condemnation and destruction of "the Rich", including the phrase "your gold and silver are corroding away" already commented on above. For Qumran, "Riches", "fornication", and "pollution of the Temple"/"idolatry" are important themes—as they are in all materials relative to James—and constitute the three characteristic sins of "the sons of Belial", i.e., the ruling hierarchy. The usage, "*Ebionim*", is a much underestimated title of self-reference at Qumran and is used in 1QH, v.23 in conjunction even with *Hesed*, i.e., the *Ebionei-Hesed*, "the Poor Ones of Piety". For the insistent theme in the period 55–62 CE of robbing the tithes of the "Poor" Priests, see *Ant.* 20.9.8 and 20.10.2 (note the sequence in the latter of the stoning of *James*, the robbing of the Poor Priests, and the attack on "Stephen" parallels similar sequencing in Acts 6–7).

When "the Innovators" finally succeed in stopping sacrifice on behalf of and the acceptance of gifts from Romans and other foreigners at the start of the Uprising in 66 CE, Josephus reports that not only did they rush to burn the houses of the Herodians and Chief Priests, but went directly to burn the debt records in order, as he puts it, "to appeal to the people of the *Poorer* sort": *War* 2.16.6 (italics mine). Agrippa II is at this point barred even from entering Jerusalem and their opinion of him and his sister, the fornicating Bernice, is made abundantly clear (note, Josephus' report above of her Riches and their incest). Imagery relating both to the problem of fornication (i.e., "prostitutes") and table-fellowship ("Sinners", "gluttons", etc.) is turned around in line with the retrospective polemical thrust of the Gospels in order to portray the putative Messiah as being sympathetic to just such classes of people. "Zacchaeus", for instance, in Lk 19:8ff. above is a "Sinner" and "Jesus" proclaims the theology of the Pauline mission.

the Righteous Teacher destroyed, and the city annihilated. The second is "the Man of Lying"/"Pourer out of Lying", who, unlike the Wicked Priest, appears originally to have been a member of the community. He is allied to a group also seemingly inside the community referred to as "the House of Absalom". This last euphemism is tied to allusions to "Traitors" (the *Bogdim*) that explain it—that is, people formerly associated with the community who have "wandered" or been "led astray" and follow the counsel of the Lying Spouter, and to "the Violent Ones"/ "Men of Violence" (*'Arizim*), probably coextensive with this House of Absalom/*Bogdim*.

The portrayal of "the Pourer out of Lying" is graphic. In particular, he is said to have "rejected the Law in the midst of the whole Congregation", or "Assembly", and almost all references to him dwell on his perversion of the Righteous Teacher's proper "Justification" activities— that is, instead of "making Many Righteous", he "leads Many astray" and "wears Many out with worthless service" so that their "*'amal*" (i.e., "works" with eschatological effect) will count for nothing. Together, he and his fellow-traveling "House of Absalom"/"Traitors" and "Violent Ones" are all called "Covenant-Breakers" and "Traitors to the New Covenant", and the animus against them, which focuses on this "Spouter", is so strong that it overwhelms the general background of advancing *Kittim* destroying the land and the debacle being suffered by the people as a whole.[2]

A similar animus can be traced, regardless of paleographic problems, against an individual or genus of individual in the Community Rule, which includes a blanket condemnation of the kind of easy backsliding path that he has chosen.[3] In 1QS, iii.3ff. it is specifically stated that: "He shall not be reckoned among the Righteous, for he has not confirmed the conversion of his life", and his soul is described as detesting "the wise teaching of Righteous Laws". Such an individual or genus of individual is to be barred from the teaching of the Community because he has

---

[2] 1QpHab, ii.1ff., v.7ff., and vii.2–xiii.4. This usage "*Bogdim*" is found throughout the *Pesher* and in the Damascus Document almost always associated with the Liar/Comedian/Spouter/Windbag. The latter's primary failing appears to have been not following the Law and "removing the boundary markers"; cf. 1QpHab, i.3, ii.1ff., v.8ff., x.9ff., and CD, i.12f., viii.4ff., xi.3, etc.; also see 4QpNah, ii–iii. It should also be viewed in connection with allusions in the New Testament to a similar kind of individual and in certain respects, the "Ephraim" usage in the Nahum *Pesher*.

[3] See, for instance, 1QS, vii.13ff. and the extensive references to how to treat such backsliding individuals, who either overtly or covertly transgress the Law; the specific reference to "covert" transgressions is especially important in view of Paul's "Jew to the Jew" and "winning the race" protestations in 1 Co 9:18ff. and consonant behavior.

ploughed "the mud of Wickedness" and returned "defiled" (for purposes of comparison, see Paul's contention in 1 Co 10:23ff. that "for me there are no forbidden things . . . Do not hesitate to eat anything which is sold in the market place. There is no need to raise questions of conscience").

The passage builds to a climax in the baptismal allusions which follow:

> He shall not be justified [i.e., *made Righteous*] by that which his stubborn heart permits, for instead of seeking the Ways of Light, he looks upon Darkness. He shall not be reckoned in the well of the Perfect [note this typical Matthaean allusion]. Nor shall he be purified by atonement, nor cleansed by any waters, nor sanctified by [immersion in] seas and rivers, nor washed clean by any ablution. Polluted, polluted shall he be, all the days that he rejects the Judgements of God [here the word *ma'as* is the same as that of 1QpHab, i.10's "denying the Law" above and 1QpHab, v.11's "rejecting the Law" below] without submitting to the Council of His Community.

In the course of these allusions, one should also note the not insignificant evocation of "the Spirit of Falsehood" and "Holy Spirit"-type baptism in 1Q, iv.26ff. and in v, the stricture to keep away from "table-fellowship" with "the Men of Falsehood who walk in the Way of Wickedness", as opposed, of course, to "those who walk in the Way of Perfection" or "Light", which parallels the use of similar terminology in Acts.[4]

The text lays down that "his words are unclean", and further stresses in vii.17ff. that "whoever has slandered the Community" or "murmured against the authority of the Community shall be expelled and never return". In such a context of "slander" and "murmuring", one should have regard to Paul's "these leaders, these Pillars", "these people who are acknowledged leaders—not that their importance means anything to me" aspersions in Ga 2:6ff. and similar attacks on community leaders in 2 Co 11:23 and in 1 Co 9:5ff. including even "Cephas (Peter) and the brothers of the Lord" (cf. also the reflection of these kinds of difficulties in the symbolic re-enactment of John 7–8 with Jesus taking on the persona of Paul).[5]

---

[4] See "the Way" terminology in Acts 16:17, 18:25f., 19:9 and 23, and 24:22ff.; for "Light" imagery, see 13:47, 22:6ff., and 26:13ff.

[5] Cf. too similar "murmuring" in Lk 19:7 above. It is noteworthy that the punishment for slandering a companion is denial of *table-fellowship*; for slandering the Community as a whole, expulsion. Paul's murmuring against the "Pillar" Apostles or the Jerusalem Church leadership in Ga 2 continues with bitter words about Cephas and is paralleled in Acts 15:38 with unkind remarks directed against "John Mark". In 2 Co 11:5ff., giving vent to his "Tongue", Paul again abuses those people he calls "Arch-apostles", whom he characterizes as "pseudo-Apostles", "*dishonest workmen* disguised as Apostles of Christ"

The Habakkuk *Pesher* presents similar ideas in a more historical context and its exegesis pointedly turns on the allusion to "not believing" in the underlying passage from Hab 1:5:

> Its interpretation concerns the Traitors together with the Man of Lying [note the purposeful linkage of these two categories, later connected to the "House of Absalom" allusion in iv]. For they *did not believe* what the Righteous Teacher told them from the mouth of God [note also the allusion to direct revelation where the Righteous Teacher is concerned, an interesting indication of his exalted status]. And it also concerns the Traitors to the Laws of God and the New Covenant who *did not believe* in the Covenant of God, but instead profaned his Holy Name [italics mine].

This constant reiteration of the word "believe" here, which in effect became the essence of the new Pauline theological position on salvation, as expressed in Romans, Galatians and Hebrews by reference to Hab 2:4 about to be expounded in this *Pesher*,[6] is consistent with the general Qumran predilection for sarcasm, irony, and word-play. Here the point is being strongly drawn by implication, however, that these "Faith" doctrines associated with Paul's new "Grace" ideas violate the stress in Ezekiel's Zadokite Statement on "keeping the Covenant"—picked up as well, including the emphasis on "keeping" as opposed to "breaking", in the Letter of James—upon which the qualitatively precise definition of the "Sons of Zadok" is based in 1QS, v.

The text goes on, confirming its basically eschatological stance, to relate this passage "to the Traitors to the End of Days"—the sect here clearly seeing itself living in the "End Time" of the Gospels' "this generation not passing away until ... ". Using imagery out of the milieu of Ezekiel's "Zadokite Statement", these "Traitors" are identified as "Covenant-Breakers", just as 1QS, following the implied thrust of Ezekiel's

---

and "*the Servants of Righteousness*". Then giving full rein to his Tongue in alluding to "danger from *so-called brothers*" and boasting "*as brazenly as any of them*" (italics mine); he continues: "Hebrews are they? So am I. Israelites? So am I", which makes it unmistakably clear that his interlocutors were Jews; and alluding to reports of his "cunningness" and stressing that he is not "a Liar"—a stress fairly widespread in the Pauline corpus—and doesn't "lie", he concludes that "there is not a thing these Arch-apostles have that I do not have as well."

For the use of '*Ezah*—often "Council" at Qumran, but in this instance "counsel" or what I would otherwise translate as "doctrine" or "approach"—see below n. 14.

[6] In the exegesis of Hab 2:4 below, the Qumran approach turns on the combination of *doing the Law* with restricting the scope of the exegesis only to "Jews" and a stress upon "Faith", which otherwise exactly parallels the familiar Pauline formulations.

Zadokite Statement (particularly Ezek 44:3ff.), identified "the Sons of Zadok" as "the Covenant-Keepers", i.e., "the *Shomrei ha-Brit*".[7]

This kind of language and the contrast of "the Keepers" vs. "the Breakers of the Law", not to mention allusion to the "Righteousness" doctrine, "Light", the Lying "Tongue", etc., dominate the first two chapters of the Letter of James as well, culminating in the quotation of the Righteousness commandment of "loving one's neighbor as oneself" and the references to "keeping the whole Law" and "fornication" (2:8–11). These *Mephirei ha-Brit* (Covenant-Breakers) are described—like "Ephraim" in 4QpNah, ii.3 and ii.8 and "the Simple Ones of Ephraim" in 4QpNah iii.5ff.—as:

> not believing what they heard about all the things that were going to happen in the Last Generation from the mouth of the Priest [the Righteous Teacher] whose heart God illumined with the understanding to expound all the words of His Servants the Prophets, to whom God explained all that was going to happen to His People.

Not only are they to be identified with "the Traitors"/"House of Absalom", but at this point also the "Violent Ones" (*'Arizim*). They were once close enough to the Community—before they *betrayed it* by abandoning the Law and going over to "the Liar"—*to assist* at the Scriptural exegesis sessions of the Righteous Teacher. In addition to his role as

---

[7] 1QpHab, ii.1ff. The stress in ii.5 on "Breakers of the Covenant" is the mirror reversal of the definition of "the Sons of Zadok" in the Community Rule as "Keepers of the Covenant" (1QS, v.2ff.). When in 44:15, Ezekiel defines "the Sons of Zadok", he does so over and against a previous hierarchy that, according to accepted notions of the meaning of the Zadokite Priesthood, must also have been "Zadokite". But for Ezekiel—as well as Qumran thereafter—the distinguishing characteristic of a true Son of Zadok was qualitative, as per 1QS and Ezek 44's "doing their duty in the Sanctuary".

When Ezekiel defines just how the previous hierarchy has "broken the Covenant" (the root he uses in 44:7, *P-R-R*, corresponds precisely with this usage in 1QpHab, ii.5), he does so by leveling the charge that they have "admitted aliens uncircumcised in heart and body to frequent My Sanctuary and pollute My Temple". The "uncircumcised heart" allusion will be used to characterize the Wicked Priest below in x.13. He concludes, "No alien, uncircumcised in heart and body, is to enter my sanctuary, none of these aliens living among the Israelites"—a directive with particular relevance where Paul's difficulties in Jerusalem are concerned and the difficulties of the Herodian family generally with the Temple Wall "Zealots". Not unrelated to both of these, as we have already noted above, were the warning stones put up in the Temple in this period warning foreigners on pain of death against illegally entering the Temple; *War* 6.2.4—*pace* Josephus' complaints against the "Innovators"—whom he blames for every disaster—on the issue of stopping sacrifice for and accepting gifts from "foreigners". For more on this subject and its relationship to concerns expressed in both the Damascus Document and Temple Scroll, see Appendix.

Scriptural exegete *par excellence* and the connected idea that all the events presently unfolding—meaning, in the present "End Time"—had already been foretold by prophets like Habakkuk and Isaiah, the above passage evokes the Righteous Teacher's role as "Priest", i.e., "High Priest".[8] Where James is concerned, we have already discussed above how all early Church sources place particular emphasis on this aspect of his activities.

4QpPs 37 speaks of a group called "the *'Arizei-Go'im*" or "the Violent Ones of the Gentiles". These may or may not be coextensive with the *'Arizim/Bogdim* in the Habakkuk *Pesher*. They were, however, at one time on the same spiritual side as the Community, since 4QpPs 37 makes it clear *they took vengeance for the death of the Righteous Teacher*. In our view they are the force which really triggers the *violent* side of the Uprising— therefore the "Violent" aspect to the circumlocution—and are to be at least partially identified with Josephus' mysterious "Idumaeans" who take vengeance for the killing of James by brutally dispatching Ananus and quite a few other "collaborators".

The "Covenant-Breakers" should include Niger of Perea, "Silas" who was brought up with King Agrippa, possibly "Philip" King Agrippa's bodyguard—whose "daughters" Josephus pointedly mentions in the *Vita*—and Queen Helen's circumcised kinsmen, Monobazus and Kenedaeos, killed along with John the Essene in the early stages of the Uprising. They are what should loosely be referred to as renegade Herodian "Men-of-War"—this last allusion is actually in use in CD, viii—because of the dominance of this element among them (therefore too the "Idumaean" terminology remounting not so much

[8] It is generally conceded that the references to "the Priest" in 1QpHab and 4QpPs 37 carry with them the implied connotation of "the High Priest"; in these contexts, he would appear, also, to be identical to "the Righteous Teacher". Such a correspondence allows us to make sense of the testimony to James in early Church tradition as "High Priest"; cf. Eusebius, Epiphanius, and Jerome, *loc. cit.*, above. The difficulties that emerge between the Righteous Teacher and the Wicked Priest (evidently the official High Priest) over events relating to *Yom Kippur* are referred to below. Such difficulties are not completely irrelevant to the arrest of James on a charge of "blasphemy". Such a charge primarily relates to pronouncing or encouraging others to pronounce the forbidden name of God, which is precisely the procedure of a *Yom Kippur* atonement.

To make extant early Church accounts sensible in this context, it only remains to take the term "Zadokite" in its esoteric sense and to see the atonement, reported of James in these sources, as involving a "Zadokite" *Yom Kippur* atonement or a properly "Righteous" atonement by a Noachic Priest/*Zaddik*; for a fuller treatment, see below pp. 181–82.

to Herod himself, but more particularly his sometimes subversive brother-in-law and Agrippa's cognate ancestor Costobarus[9]).

What follows is the well-known description of the coming of "the *Kittim*" linked to the coming of the Chaldaeans in the underlying text. It is difficult, as we have seen with regard to the Nahum *Pesher*, to escape the conclusion that "the *Kittim*" are the Romans.[10] There has been, of course, much debate on this issue, including detailed analyses of the military tactics of the Romans and Seleucids, but references to their coming "from afar, from the islands of the sea to devour all the peoples like an eagle", marching "across the plain smiting and plundering the cities of the earth", encircling "the Fortresses of the Peoples", "tauntingly deriding them", threshing "the earth with their horses and pack animals", "consume all the peoples", "in the heat of fury, in searing rage, in scorching anger and with livid faces speaking to all the Peoples", "scorning the great and mocking the noble, making sport of kings and princes and ridiculing any large host" can hardly be thought of as relating to the Seleucids, attempts to portray them in this manner notwithstanding. The note about "sacrificing to their standards and worshipping their weapons" in a continuation of this description in vi.3.ff. below, also (as has been argued) certainly reflects the practices of Imperial not Republican Rome.

Nor must such a reference reflect any *specific* sacrifice made by the Romans. The reference is a general one, and certainly does not entail the sacrifice the Romans made on the Temple Mount at the end of the War—the only one Josephus describes—as it is usually taken as doing. The Romans must have made quite a few as they made their bloody way down from Galilee, and Josephus describes the consternation engendered in Jerusalem by the reduction of a series of Galilean strongholds: Gadara, Jotapata, Tarichaeae, Gamala, etc., all the time making continual reference to the "Innovators" as the principal element disturbing the commonweal in Galilee.[11]

It cannot be stressed too often that for the *Pesher* the Roman conquest

[9] For the connection of "Saulus" to other seeming descendants of this "Costobarus", see *War* 2.17.3. Costobarus is the real "Idumaean" in these genealogies, Herod's origins being somewhat more difficult to trace. See also n. 44, p. 184 below.

[10] 1QpHab, ii.12 and 4QpNah, i.5; cf. Dan 11:30.

[11] 1QpHab, vi.3ff. One such sacrifice is, of course, recorded in *War* 6.6.1, but there is absolutely no proof that this was the one hinted at in the Commentary; on the contrary, the notice there is general, not specific. Note that in *War* 3.8.9–10 Josephus gives a long description of the towns around "the Lake of Gennesareth", the locale of the most serious "seditious" activities, in particular naming one "Jesus the son of Shaphat" as "the principal head of the robber band".

is an event *in progress*, not finished. The conclusion some draw from such allusions, in particular one to the destruction of the Temple and/or Jerusalem, that the *Pesher* either would have had to be written after the events of 70 CE—which is archaeologically speaking *not impossible*—or barring this, a century or two earlier, is therefore *not proven*. The conquest and the destruction it entailed, as we have seen, were a foregone conclusion as early as 67 or 68 CE, and, as we have also noted, Josephus and quite a few others were aware of this, as was James' nemesis Ananus[12]. On the contrary, if the notice in iv.10ff. to "the rulers of the *Kittim* in conference in their guilt-ridden house replacing their rulers one after the other and each coming in turn to destroy the earth" refers to "the year of the three Emperors", as it is sometimes taken as doing, then one has a *solid textual* measure for dating the commentary. Again, however, this passage need not refer to a given year such as 68 CE, but to Roman emperors from Caligula to Vespasian. Whatever one's conclusion concerning any or all of these matters, it is clear that the *sitz im leben* of the *Pesher* has little historical relation to any context earlier than this.

Having described these background disasters, the *Pesher* now returns to its favorite topic, the salvation of those who "keep the Covenant"/"the Commandments", and its preoccupation with internecine strife. It contends, somewhat poignantly, that despite the horrors that were transpiring, "God will not annihilate his people at the hands of the Gentiles" (v.3; the use of *Go'im* here as opposed to *Kittim*, is not insignificant as it relates to the *Pesher*'s concern with "Gentiles" generally, in particular that "Judgement" which will be pronounced on them, including the Pourer out of Lying and those of his persuasion, as well as Jewish backsliders in x and xiif.). It insists rather that "God will execute Judgement on all the Gentiles by the hands of His Elect, in connection with which chastisement all the Wicked Ones among his own people, who kept the Commandments only when convenient will also be condemned"—here the employment of the allusion "the Wicked of His People" is important, for it includes Jewish backsliders of the genre of the pro-Herodian "Wicked Priest". There can be no doubt of either the "nationalism" of this insistence or the zeal of its apocalyptic—i.e., these are not "peaceful Essenes"; nor can the era be anything resembling the Seleucid one.

[12] *War* 2.16.4f. and 4.5.2. It is certainly curious that Josephus in the latter notice records of Ananus—whom he scornfully dismisses as corrupt and intemperate in *Vita* and *Ant.*—precisely what early Church tradition insists he said of James in the extant copies of Josephus' works, i.e., that the fall of Jerusalem was directly related to his death and that the Roman armies appeared immediately following his removal; cf. *E.H.* 2.23.18ff. and Origen, *contra Celsum* 1.47 and 2.13 and *Comm. in Matt.* 10.17.

Where backsliding/turncoat Jews are at issue, the stress in the exegesis on the theme of "keeping" is important. It should be noted that CD, iv's exegesis of the Zadokite Covenant identifies "the Sons of Zadok" as "the Elect of Israel" ("who would stand at the End of Days"—i.e., those who would "execute Judgement on all the Gentiles" and backsliding Jews above.) The whole assertion is followed, not incidentally, by an allusion to that same *"zanut"* (fornication—v.7f.) so important to the Damascus Document, the Letter of James, and deadly difficulties with the Herodian family generally.[13] Here it is "the Elect" who "have not lusted after their eyes"—that is, married nieces or divorced illegally— and the allusion to "the Era of Wickedness" is quite simply the Herodian age. One should also note the use of *zanut* imagery along with "Lying lips" and "Tongue" allusions in the "selling *zanut* to the Gentiles" and "leading Ephraim astray" section of 4QpNah, ii.7ff.

This brings us in the text to a dramatic confrontation between "the Liar" and those of his "persuasion" and the Righteous Teacher, the importance of which should not be underestimated. That the confrontation is *verbal*, though it could be otherwise, is given some confirmation by the reference to treachery in the underlying text, interpreted to relate to factional strife within the community, and the usage *"ma'as"* which dominates the actual exegesis, i.e., "rejecting" or "speaking derogatorily against the *Torah*" or "Covenant" as in 1QpHab, i.10 above. Since once again it is the Righteous Teacher who is the subject of the exegesis, the signification being played upon in the underlying text to construct the exegesis is *"Zaddik"*. As so often elsewhere, it is connected with *"Rasha'"*, that is, the Righteous vs. the Evil Ones.

Here the much-vexed turn of phrase "the House of Absalom and the men of their Assembly" or "persuasion" in the exegesis is tied definitively to *"Bogdim"* in the underlying text, thus confirming the figurative sense of the "Absalom" ascription (with the possible additional imputation of treachery within the Messianic family itself). Already linked earlier in the text to "the Covenant-Breakers", "the Man of Lying", and "the *'Arizim'"* (possibly, but not necessarily, linked to the *'Arizei-Go'im* in 4QpPs 37), the House of Absalom (*"Bogdim"*) "remained silent when the Righteous Teacher was being "admonished" or "abused" (i.e. "verbally abused") and did not help him (since we are in an "Assembly" of some kind

---

[13] For an excellent glimpse of the importance of *"zanut"* at Qumran, one should have regard to 1QS, iv.9ff.'s abuse of its genre of "Lying" nemesis who follows "the Ways of Nothingness"—cf. 1QpHab, x.9ff.'s "the City of Nothingness" built by the Liar, etc. below pp. 171f.—who has "a Spirit of fornication", "Lying", and "whoredom", "zeal for lustfulness", "works of nothingness", and "a Tongue full of insults".

involving "the whole community"—possibly of the Pentecost variety in Acts—the meaning is actually "speak up") against the Man of Lying "*who rejected the Law in the midst of their whole Congregation*" or "*Assembly*" (italics mine).[14]

It should be clear that this confrontation is *internal* and that the "Traitors" play some role *within the Community* or as adjuncts to it therefore the "treachery" imputation. For 1QpHab, x.9ff. below, "the Pourer Out of Lying"/"Spouter" (*Mattif ha-Chazav*—identical with "the Man of Lying" and playing as well on the baptismal imagery of CD, i.14ff.'s "pouring the waters of Lying") is also someone inside the community, not outside it. For precisely this kind of ideological dispute, see Ga 2:11ff., where Paul does speak "derogatorily about the Law"—as he probably did in Jerusalem earlier when he went up to put the version of the Gospel as he taught it to the Gentiles fearing that the course he "was adopting or had already adopted would be in vain"—in the process verbally abusing one of the community's most respected leaders and blaming his problems on personal difficulties with James and "the group which insisted on circumcision" in Jerusalem. "Circumcision" was "in the air" in "Asia" in this period—a primary venue of Paul's missionary activities—as its cruciality in the marriages of Herodian princesses in Cilicia, Emesa, and Commagene and the conversion of Queen Helen's son and/or husband in Adiabene attest.

1QS, viii.20ff. gives a picture of the likely Qumran reaction to such remonstrations: "Any man who enters the Council of Holiness walking in the Way of Perfection as commanded by God and, whether overtly or covertly, transgresses one word of the *Torah* of Moses on any point whatsoever [cf. the "not one jot or tittle" allusions in the New Testament], shall be expelled from the Council of the Community and return no more. No Man of Holiness shall associate with him in monetary matters or in approach *on any matter whatsoever.*"

This last by his own testimony is precisely how Paul is treated after the confrontation in Antioch: "The other Jews joined him [Cephas] in this pretense and even Barnabas felt obliged to copy their behavior." In fact, according to the presentation of Acts 15:39, Barnabas, too, parts company with Paul, that is, "after a violent quarrel, they [Paul and Barnabas] parted company and Barnabas sailed off with Mark to Cyprus." From this point Barnabas and the Jewish Apostles have little more to do with Paul, and despite a few isolated references in the corpus

---

[14] 1QpHab, v.7ff. As opposed to Roth and Driver, "the House of Absalom" is to be taken figuratively as implying *betrayal* or *treachery*.

to him, few, if any, *Jewish* Apostles or *Jews*—as opposed to what we would call "Herodians"—appear willing to associate themselves with his "mission".

J. Teicher in the early history of Qumran research developed the position that we are presenting to a certain extent (inspired by G. Margoliouth's early identification of the Cairo *Genizah* Damascus Document as "Jewish Christian"); however, by ignoring James and dwelling too closely on purported difficulties between Paul and Jesus, he vitiated the historicity of his approach and put the entire perspective into ill repute. Since his historical grasp was so unincisive, he did not make sense of any of the "Men of Violence"/"Men-of-War"/"Traitors" terminologies either.

Another, more physical, attack by Paul on James is reported in the Pseudoclementines. On the whole, however, this notice in the Habakkuk *Pesher* must be taken as paralleling a more ideological attack which probably occurred in the context of events relating to the so-called "Jerusalem Council" reported in Acts. We would consider Paul's view of similar events in Ga 2:1–10 to be a more accurate presentation of the progression of these events (if not of how they were perceived by "the Jerusalem Church"). The characterization of "the Man of Lying" as "rejecting" or "speaking derogatorily about the Law in the midst of their entire Community" in v.11 also receives—through the word *ma'as*—generic reinforcement in the Community Rule and the Damascus Document.

The underlying text in question, "the Wicked confounds one more Righteous than he", precisely parallels the sense of other *Zaddik* texts applied to the Righteous Teacher and James. "The Wicked" in v.9 is *not* interpreted in terms of "the Wicked Priest", who emerges later in the *Pesher* in the context of chronologically later, more political, squabbling when the destruction of Jerusalem is imminent. Rather, it is specifically applied to "the Man of Lying", whom along with his fellow travelers "the Traitors" and "'*Arizim*", the *Pesher* has already characterized as being privy to, but "not believing in", the esoteric Scriptural exegeses of "the Priest"/Righteous Teacher. The whole constitutes a perfect representation—including even the incessant theme of verbal derogation of the Community leadership and the earlier ironic allusion to Pauline "Belief" doctrines—of the split between Paul with his more antinomian "free gift of Faith"/"descent of the Holy Spirit" approach and those following the *Zaddik* James insisting both on "works of the Law" and its concomitant in "Perfect Righteousness" (*Tom-Derech* or *Tamim-Derech* at Qumran).[15]

---

[15] It usually goes unremarked that the usage "*ma'asim*" or one of its several variations, "*ma'asei*"/"*ma'aseihem*" (which translate into what we would term "works"), completely

"The House of Absalom" can be, therefore, definitively identified as ideological "Traitors" within the Movement who are willing to go along with the antinomian position of "the Man of Lying"—in our view also referred to by the usage "the Enemy" in the Pseudoclementines. In this, they are connected with the "'*Arizim*", i.e., renegade "Herodians" and those "Men of War" who are reported to have gone over to "the Liar" in the Damascus Document (viii.37; cf, also the use of "*ma'as*"/rejecting, "going astray", "the House of the *Torah*", "Faith", "the New Covenant", etc. in this passage). They are not so different from the more general "Ephraim"/"City of Ephraim"/"Simple Ones of Ephraim" in the Nahum *Pesher* linking up with "city of blood"/"city built upon blood" allusions in it and 1QpHab, x which we shall presently elucidate below.

The drama of this moment should not be lost on any student of early Church history, and its religio-historical implications are far-reaching. If our interpretation is correct, we have in it nothing less than a version of that meeting or confrontation, which is referred to by all commentators as "the Jerusalem Council"—a more likely euphemism in the present context would be "the Assembly of the Jerusalem Community".[16]

---

pervades Qumran usage. So widespread is the usage, beginning in the introduction of the Damascus Document (CD, i.10) and often in conjunction with its ideological opposite *ma'asei-Sheker* and *ma'asei-niddah* associated with the Liar ("Lying works" and "works of Uncleanness"—the "*niddah*" usage also occurs in relation to "pollution of the Temple" charges in CD, viii.13) and the men of his persuasion, that cataloging it is beyond the scope of this study. In this section of the Habakkuk *Pesher* one has to do with a further variation of the usage, the '*Osei ha-Torah* or "Doers of the Torah" (1QpHab, vii.11 and viii.1; cf. Ja 1:22ff. also alluding to "Doers"). A significant ideological counterpart of this usage is the term '*amal*, which also has the signification of "works", but "works" in the most soteriologically efficacious sense—in this case "suffering works" or "travail". Not only is the word '*amal* crucial to the eschatological exegesis Hab 2:4 which is to follow, it is repeated with opposite ideological signification at the end of the *Pesher* in relation to the activities of the Liar. It, too, is based on terminology in the all-important Is 53:11f. proof-text (also a *Zaddik*-passage).

The *Derech*/"Way" terminology is rarely discussed in any detail in Qumran scholarship. The terminology has strong connections with exegetical usages surrounding the mission and activities of John the Baptist and is at the root of allied Qumran usages centering around the root *Y-Sh-R*—meaning "Straightening"/"Upright". The almost total addiction at Qumran to the "Perfection" terminology connected to it, a usage well-known in the New Testament, is also underestimated. For *Tom-Derech* or *Tamim/Tamimei-Derech*, see, for instance, 1QS, i.12ff., v.24, viii.10ff., ix.6ff., x.22ff., xi.2ff., etc. and cf. Mt 5:48's "be Perfect as your Father in Heaven is Perfect" and Mt 19:21, Acts 22:3, 24:22, Ga 3:3, etc.

[16] The allusion "Jerusalem Council" has grown up surrounding the confrontation between Paul and the "Jerusalem Church" leadership, concerning both the advisability and terms of reference of "the Gentile Mission"; cf. Ga 2 and Acts 15. Certainly 1QS, viii.1ff. refers to a central "Council" of the Community which appears made up of twelve

Its point of view, however, is "internal", or "Palestinian"/"Jewish Christian", i.e., that of "the Keepers of the Law" as opposed to those "*Torah-Breakers*" breaking it and those advocating the opposite policy within the early "Church".

As we have noted, too, its connection with Paul's Ga 2:11–14 confrontation with and charges against Peter in Antioch is intrinsic. One should not be too astonished at our linking this seemingly innocuous notice in the Habakkuk *Pesher*—not innocuous in terms of the literary devices of compression, ironic understatement, and parody practiced at Qumran—with the famous "Jerusalem Council". In our view it *is* the actual confrontation as viewed from the point of view of Jerusalem and the supporters of James, not vice versa. That this confrontation made a very

members, of whom "three are Priests" or to which "three Priests are added" (the sense here is tantalizingly obscure, but the dichotomy of priestly and Israelite imagery which follows suggests "the Three" are part and parcel of "the Twelve", not added to it as majority scholarship generally thinks). It is in relation to and following the delineation of this Council that the text evokes the imagery of "atonement by suffering", and it is this Council which is referred to as "a House of Perfection and Truth for Israel" and "a Holy of Holies for Aaron" (note the "Israelite"/"priestly" dichotomy referring to one and the same council). In a further extension of this Pauline-type "spiritualized" Temple and atonement imagery, the Council is referred to as "a sin offering" and "a sweet fragrance". All of this imagery is evoked in relation to the dual citation of "the Way in the wilderness" passage which is used, as already noted, to epitomize the activities of the community.

The usage "Jerusalem Council" has something to do in Acts with an "Assembly" which appears to convene itself in Jerusalem at the time of Pentecost—a time of convocation also important for 4QD^b—probably in reaffirmation of the traditional notion of the descent of the Law associated with this festival. In Acts 2:1ff. this "descent of the Law" is parodied in terms of a more Paulinized "Holy Spirit", which descends together with its Gentile Mission accoutrements of "speaking in Tongues" and doing "mighty works", by which is intended cures, exorcisms, and the like, not "works of the Law" as in James and at Qumran.

Another notice about an opposition "Assembly" or "Church" in Jerusalem appears in *Ant.* 19.7.4 in connection with that "Simon" who wishes to exclude Agrippa I from the Temple as a "foreigner" and his visit to *Caesarea* to inspect the latter's living arrangements (i.e. his household *kashrut*). It should be increasingly clear to the reader that this, in fact, is the authentic and demythologized "Simon" as opposed to his ideological and diametrically opposite mirror image in Acts. Simon in Acts, instead of inspecting the *kashrut* of Agrippa I's household as the Simon in the *Antiquities*, rather visits the household of the Roman centurion Cornelius in Caesarea who is described as "giving generously to Jewish causes", a description which more appropriately suits Agrippa I. He is prepared for this "visit" by a special vision via the always useful "Holy Spirit" mechanism repealing, it would appear, for all of time the normal Jewish dietary regulations. Cf. the parallel here of Jesus' visit to the Rich "Zacchaeus" in Lk 19, developing into a parable about a king not unlike Agrippa (or his grandfather Herod).

lasting impression on the members of the early Community is confirmed not only from Acts' one-sided portrayal of it but also in Paul's version of these events in Ga 2. Along with some other matters of equal import relating to "the Lying Spouter and those of his persuasion", it has made an equally indelible, if ideologically opposite, impression on the authors of the Habakkuk *Pesher*.

Habakkuk was, of course, a very important prophet for the sectaries, as he was for the authors of 2 Macc. One should also note in this regard that Habakkuk, like Phineas, Elijah, Onias the Just (Honi the Circle-Drawer), Hanan the Hidden, and James himself, was a primordial rain-maker. Eschatological notions and the Righteousness ideal associated with rain and rain-making go back to the soteriological activities of the first *Zaddik* Noah.

The *ARN* associates "the bringing of rain" with proper (i.e., "Zadokite") Temple service; drought with its cessation; and rain-making and its associated mechanism of circle-drawing were important attributes in the determination of the true *Zaddik* and eschatological High Priest. Rain-making and "Messianic" rain imagery are integrally related, too, to the parallel imagery of "the Son of Man coming on the clouds of Heaven", and in a sense, all three imageries are combined in the last two chapters of the letter conserved under James' name. The Son of Man coming on the clouds of Heaven, according to Eusebius/Hegesippus' testimony, also comprised the essence of James' Messianic proclamation in the Temple before his death, and, once again, all are to a certain extent invoked in combination with the exegesis of the Messianic "Star Prophecy" in the Qumran War Scroll.[17]

---

[17] For Habakkuk as rain-maker, see the whole narrative relating to Honi and his descendants in *b. Ta'an* 23aff. That James, too, functioned as a rain-maker is confirmed by Epiphanius in *Haeres.* 78.14 (the notice is too original to be simply dismissed as spurious). As such, he is a contemporary of and exhibits suspiciously similar characteristics to another "rain-making" grandson of Honi, Abba Hilkiah. Rabbinic literature unerringly designates Phineas as a rain-maker, anticipating Elijah in this activity, his successor in the *redivivus* tradition, and depicts similar activities on the part of Hanan *ha-Nehba*, another grandson of Honi, who is often identified with John the Baptist.

That the coming of the Messiah in the company of the Host of Heaven "on the clouds" was associated as well with eschatological "rain" imagery is confirmed in 1QM, xi.10ff. It evokes this imagery in connection with its exegesis of Num 24:17, which it purposefully expounds in terms of Daniel's portrait of "the Son of Man coming on the clouds of Heaven"—the favorite metaphor for the hope for a Messianic return. This hope is also expressed following James' condemnation of "the Rich"—whom he blames for the crucifixion of "the Just One"—in connection with his counsel of "patience . . . until the Lord's coming" in Ja 5:7ff. Here, James again ties the allusion to eschatological "rain" imagery and even evokes Elijah, making the connection between the various

The Habakkuk *Pesher* is impressed, not surprisingly, with God's having commanded Habakkuk to "write down" his vision concerning what would happen in "the Last Generation" (2:1f.). However, in it God did not make known to Habakkuk "when the Time of the End would be completed". Rather this information was vouchsafed to the Righteous Teacher in his role as scriptural exegete *par excellence* "to whom God made known all the mysteries of the words of His servants the Prophets" (vii.4ff.). Having said this, the *Pesher* then proceeds to interpret Hab 2:3 (which itself leads to the all-important citation from Hab 2:4: "the Righteous shall live by his Faith") as the Scriptural warrant for what in other vocabularies goes by the name of "the Delay of the *Parousia*".

Nothing could better confirm the overall eschatological thrust of the Habakkuk *Pesher*, evinced whenever notions relating to "the End" or "the Last" are discussed, than this exegesis of Hab 2:3. The declaration that "there shall be yet another vision concerning the End"—which includes not insignificantly an aside about "not Lying"—cf. Paul in Ro 9:1, 2 Co 11:31; Ga 1:20 and *par contra* Ja 3:14—is expounded to mean that "the Final Era would be extended beyond anything which the Prophets foretold".

The very matter-of-factness of this statement is possibly the reason for its having been generally overlooked by most scholarship. Not only do we have in it the explanation—based on the scriptural warrant of Hab 2:3, introducing the all-important materials in 2:4—of why "the End", also so clearly expected in the New Testament, was not going to materialize in this generation, but by implication, too, that such an expectation was part and parcel of the Messianic fervor surrounding the Uprising. Where the latter was concerned, such a delay in the institution of "the Messianic Kingdom" was not surprising in view of its subversion by people like Ananus, Josephus, Agrippa II, and Philo's renegade nephew Tiberius Alexander, responsible for the death of not a few "Messianic" leaders and Titus' *actual* military commander at Jerusalem.

Commenting with perhaps more irony than even it intended, "for the mysteries of God are astonishing", the *Pesher* explains the next sentence: "If it tarries, wait for it, for it shall surely come and shall not be late", in terms of how the faithful should behave in the face of such a "delay". In so doing, it makes its first allusion to "the Doers of the Law" ('*Osei*

allusions and imageries unmistakably clear. In fact, the proclamation of just such a Messianic return forms the substance of James' speech on the Temple stairs at Passover, alluded to in all sources, which either forms the background of the riot on the Temple Mount or events culminating in his judicial murder; cf. as well Paul in 1 Thess 3:13. Jude in 1:12ff. actually explains the imagery.

ha-Torah), which will be one of the cornerstones of its exegesis of 2:4 to follow (as well as its description of "the Simple Ones of Judah" who will be the beneficiaries of the justifying activities of the Community Council and destroyed by the Wicked Priest's "works of Abominations" at the end of the *Pesher*), *viz.* "The Men of Truth who are *Doers of Torah*" are not to "slacken from the service of Truth though the final age is prolonged".

Allusions to "Truth" are common at Qumran from "the Sons of Truth" in 1QS, iv.5 to "the Sons of Your Truth" in Hymns, and to a certain extent may be viewed in the context of those "Lying" allusions predicated of "the Liar".[18] The *Pesher* concludes on an optimistic, if mysterious, note: "all the times appointed by God necessarily come as He has determined them according to the mysteries of His Wisdom."

This expression of the most exalted theological Faith and unwillingness to despair even in the face of overwhelming tragedy, not to mention the pathos of it at this particular historical moment, has also been systematically overlooked in the dating of this *Pesher*. The "doing" or "Doers of the *Torah*" tied to it are the analogue of such important expressions elsewhere in the Qumran corpus like *Shomrei ha-Brit*/"Keepers of the Covenant" or *Nozrei-Brito*/"Keepers of His Covenant". The definition of "the Sons of Zadok", their most perfect embodiment, turns in the Damascus Document on an allusion to "doing"/"works" (both based on the Hebrew root *'-s-h*), in particular, "doing the precise sense of the Law", and the identity of the Habakkuk *Pesher*'s "Law-Doers" and the Damascus Document's "Sons of Zadok" is, therefore, intrinsic.[19]

---

[18] *Emet* is another basic notation at Qumran, which along with usages like *Da'at*, *'amal/ ma'aseh*, *Zedek*, *Hesed*, and *Tom*, must be exhaustively catalogued. "Men of Truth" (1QH, xiv.2) and "Sons of Your Truth" (1QH, vii.29f.—note that God here is the "Father of all the Sons of Truth"; ix.35; x.25; xi.11) are parallel notations of self-designation in use by the sect, like "Sons of Righteousness", "Sons of *Hesed*", "Sons of Light", and "the Perfect of the Way"; cf. 1QS, i.5f., *Brit-Emet* and *Zedek*; iii.6, *'Azat-Emet*; iv.19, *Ruah-Emet*, i.e., "the Holy Spirit"; viii.2, "doing *Emet* and *Zedek* and *Mishpat*"; 1QH, xiii.19, "all your acts are Truth and Righteousness"; xiv.2, "Men of Truth". For "Truth" associated with "the Way of God" in the New Testament, see Mt 22:16, Mk 12:14, John 14:6, 2 Pe 2:2; in connection with "the Spirit", see John 14:17, 15:26, 16:13, 2 Thess 2:13, 1 John 4:65; in connection with "Righteousness", see Eph 5:9; "Knowledge", 1 Ro 2:20, 1 Tim 2:4, Heb 10:26; "Judgement", Ro 2.2; "Lying", "Tongue" imagery, and "the Enemy", Ga 4:10, 1 Tim 2:7, Ja 3:14, 1 John 1:6, 2:4, 2:21, 3:18; with "Children of Light", Eph 4:8; with "walking"—another common Qumran allusion—1 Thess 5:5; and with "Perfection" and "Light", Ja 1:18.

[19] See above for 1QS's definition of "the Sons of Zadok" as the *Shomrei ha-Brit*; the use of the word "service" in this allusion in Habakkuk also echoes the allusions to doing just such "Temple service" in the Zadokite Statement. We shall see it parodied below

CD, iv's definition also turns on the allusion to "justifying the Right-eous and condemning the Wicked", embodying the *"yazdik-Zaddik"* or "Justification" ideology of Is 53:11, which itself has very real connections with 1QpHab, viii.1ff.'s exegesis of Hab 2:4 below.[20] CD, iv.4 also ident-ifies "the Sons of Zadok" with "the Elect of Israel, . . . men called by name to stand at the End of Days" or "men called by name" who in the manner of the primordial *Rishonim* or "Pillar" *Zaddikim*, like Noah in Hebrew Ecclesiasticus, "provide salvation for the earth" (ii.11).[21] The

where the teaching of the Lying Spouter is concerned and further parodied in the esch-atological end of the *Pesher*. The phrase, *Britcha yinzor* (Deut 33:9), "Your Covenant will he keep", actually occurs in the Messianic proof-texts conserved in 4QTest, as does its synonym, *lishmor et chol mizvotai* (Deut 5:26). *Nozrei ha-Brit*, therefore, is simply a variation of the *Shomrei ha-Brit* terminology and the ideological root of the usage "Nazoraean". Further linkage of this phrase with Nazirite oath procedures popular in James' Jerusalem Community (Acts 21:23), life-long Naziritism associated with the persons of John the Baptist, James, and his ideological double *Banus* (which additionally provide the clue as to how the terminologies "Sons of the Rechabites" or "Rechabite" Priests are to be understood in relation to Jerusalem Christianity), and the *Nezer* or "Branch", popular symbolism at Qumran, appealed to the sectarian love of word-play. See also the stress on "Doers" in Ja 1:22f.

[20] This *yazdiku-Zaddik* imagery is inverted when the text has cause to refer to "the Man of Scoffing"/"Lying" who "pours out the waters of Lying on Israel" and "makes them wander astray in a boundariless wasteland" in CD, i.15ff. Both the usages, *nephesh* and "walking in Perfection", are used here relative to the *"Zaddik"*, the former being part of the vocabulary of Is 53:11 upon which all references to the justifying activities of the *Zaddik* are based.

[21] CD, iv.5ff. Note the parallel use in iv.11 of *"Beit-*Yehudah", which will play so important a part in 1QpHab, viii.1ff.'s exegesis of Hab 2:4 below. Iv.9 applies the theme of atonement, applied to the inner priestly elite in the context of spiritualized Temple and sacrificial offering imagery in 1QS, viii.1ff., to the activities of "the Sons of Zadok"/ "Men of the Perfection of Holiness". In all documents we are in the familiar atmosphere of Matthew and Luke's "not one jot or tittle". The reference to "standing in the Last Days" relates to the same eschatological imagery we shall encounter in the exegesis of Hab 2:4 below and is based, at least partly as we have suggested, on "the standing up of the bones" passage in Ezek 37:10 (including the probable sense of resurrection, which is, in fact, the background sense of the entire exegesis of Ezek 44:15 in CD, iv; cf. also "standing" in Dan 12:13 and its exposition in *Lam.R*, ii.3.6 in precisely this vein).

CD, i.16 denotes these primordial "Righteous Ones" by the terminology "the *Rishon-im*", and it is to them the "First Covenant" was addressed, paralleling "the *Aharonim*" of the present generation, to whom "the New Covenant" of "the Last Days" applied (these last presumably to go into the Kingdom *living*). The *Rishonim* are to be identified with the *Anshei-Hesed/Zaddikim* of Hebrew Ben Sira and Wisdom, the list of whom in the first-named work culminates with the *Zaddik* Simeon. It is in legitimation of his "Zadokite" priesthood that Hebrew Ben Sira evokes the Noachic "Covenant of Peace" vouchsafed to all descendants of Phineas (actual or figurative) because of their "zeal". Note the purposeful inversion and/or trivialization of "the First" vs. "the Last" idea, presented in the context of strong atonement imagery, of being "called by name" or "naming names" in CD, ii.11ff. and iv.4ff. further connects all these allusions to the activities of the first *Zaddik* Noah, who was also portrayed in Genesis as "making atonement for the land". These ideas are not a little refracted in the strong emphasis on "name" and "naming" in Acts 2ff.

Having dealt with these preliminary matters, as it were, the text proceeds to its most important exegesis, that of Hab 2:4: "the Righteous shall live by his faith". This famous passage, the exegesis of which is again generally ignored in Qumran scholarship and which in our view is the ultimate *raison d'être* of the entire *Pesher*, is found subjected to parallel, if divergent, exegesis in Galatians, Romans, and Hebrews. In conjunction with Is 53:11 and Ge 15:6 it forms the tripartite exegetical foundation of early Christianity as it has been made known to us, providing, as we have noted, incontrovertible *textual* proof as opposed to archaeological or paleographic that the *Pesher* relates to the 50s and 60s of the common era when such exegesis (however unfamiliar the present context, circumstances, and implications might at first appear) was in vogue. In the absence of an earlier indication of a similar exegesis, particularly prior to Herod's 37 BC conquest of Jerusalem, or even that this style of exegesis (which was in the view of the Habakkuk *Pesher* the seemingly exclusive prerogative of the Righteous Teacher in his role as exegete of "the Last Times") was even practiced to any extent earlier than the mid-first century CE; the burden of proof rests rather upon those who would deny the historical provenance for the Habakkuk *Pesher* as we are setting it forth, not vice versa.

We have already shown that parallel usages and exegesis were employed in relation to the position and person of James in early Church literature. We shall be able to show that exegesis specifically applying the "cedars of Lebanon" imagery to the fall of the Temple in both the Habakkuk and Is^a *Pesher* was also in vogue in Jewish sources regarding the fall of the Temple in 70 CE.

In addition, the exegesis of Hab 2:4 in the Habakkuk *Pesher* provides another interesting example of the basic parallelism between Qumran and New Testament exegetical styles. Not only is a reference to *"Zaddik"* in the underlying text exploited to develop an exegesis about the Teacher/Messiah, but its sense is deliberately reversed, that is, we have

vocabulary in the Gospels, which takes its cue from Paul's allusion to himself as "last" in 1 Co 15:8 ("the First" according to his scheme being the "Jewish" Apostles or the Jerusalem Church leadership; "the Last" are Paul and his new "Gentile Christian" converts).

to do not with "the Righteous" in the Community "living by Faith" as one would expect, but rather with the salvation brought about by this Faith in the Righteous Teacher or Messiah. Put another way, the term *"Zaddik"* in the underlying text is related, not to the individual believer but rather to the object of his belief, as it were, the *Moreh ha-Zedek* or the Messiah. Actually the exposition turning on *"Zaddik"* in the underlying text is double-pronged in both Pauline and Qumran exegesis, signifying at one and the same time both the Righteous Teacher/Jesus and those "saved" by their Faith in him—at Qumran our "Sons of Zadok"/ "Elect of the Last Times", and in Christianity—though in no way as neatly delineated—"the Children of the Promise"/"Community of all the Faithful".

In the Qumran exposition of this passage (viii.1ff.), continuing the theme of the restriction of the provenance of the "Delay of the *Parousia*" materials to "the Doers of the Law" that precedes it, the applicability of "the Righteous shall live by his Faith" is, as it were, deliberately restricted not once, but in a twofold manner. First, as above, to all *"Torah-Doers"* (*'Osei ha-Torah*); and secondly, as if conscious of and completely opposed to the more permissive and cosmopolitan Pauline exposition of the same passage, *only to Jews*. What is left unstated but is nevertheless implied is the negation of its contrary, meaning, it does not even apply to anyone who *does not observe the Law outside the House of Judah*. It is surprising that it has rarely, if ever, been observed that the reference to "the House of Judah" in this passage—and elsewhere—quite simply refers to *Jews* and that the efficacy of this crucial theological proposition is here being restricted only to Jews who are *Doers of the Law*.

Nothing could be closer to what we can assume to have been "the Jerusalem Church" exposition of this passage, opposed as it was, according to all extant testimony, to the extensions via the Gentile Mission's new "free gift of Faith" ideas to "Sinners", that is, all those born *outside the Law* or "born in sin".[22] Here the exegesis is not only "Jamesian" but

[22] The allusion *"Beit-Yehudah"* in all probability goes back to the Jer 31:30f. passage on "the New Covenant". In this context in the Habakkuk *Pesher* it simply means "all Jewry", i.e., the efficacy of the process of "salvation by faith" is deliberately being circumscribed to Jews alone. Gentiles, who had not first associated themselves with "the House of Judah" in the normal manner, are automatically excluded from its provenance. New Testament allusions to Jesus preferring the company of "Sinners"—linking up to the allusion *"Resha'im"* at Qumran, not to mention "prostitutes", "tax collectors", "gluttons", and "winebibbers"—have important ramifications within this context. "Gentiles", who had not been born under the Law and were not therefore, to use Paul's own phraseology, heirs to its "Promise", were automatically regarded as "Sinners" or "born in sin". Paul himself unequivocally makes the linkage between the "Sinner" terminology and

framed seemingly with the express challenge of "the Gentile Mission"/ "the Man of Lying" (who "denied the Law in the midst of the whole Assembly") in mind.[23] In regard to this last, we have already called attention to, in addition to New Testament narratives of problems between Paul and James, the Pseudoclementine account of an actual physical assault by Paul on James, which has via the magic of art probably received its literary transformation into an assault by *the Jews*—inclusive of Paul—on the archetypical *Gentile* believer "Stephen".[24]

The Habakkuk *Pesher* puts the total proposition in the following manner: "God will save those Jews who are *Torah-Doers* [if equivalent to "Covenant-Keepers", "Law-Doers" and "Sons of Zadok" are synonymous] from *the House of Judgement* because of *their works and their Faith* in the Righteous Teacher" (italics mine). Here there can be little doubt that we are in the typically "Jamesian" milieu of works/Righteousness, and where these and the issue of "Faith" are concerned, as in the case of "Jews who were *Torah*-Doers", the *Pesher* would appear to have been framed with the express position of "the Enemy" in mind, that is, a man is not saved by his "Faith" alone, but by "works" working with "Faith" ("Faith" in the effective stewardship of the Righteous Teacher).

What often goes unremarked is that the explicit reference to "'*amalam*", apart from what we shall presently be able to identify as its eschatological thrust, places us (as later in x.12) squarely in the milieu

---

"Gentiles" in Ga 2:15ff.

For Jesus preferring the company of "publicans and Sinners", as opposed to "the Righteous" ("publicans" has interesting ramifications for 1QpHab, ix's "tax-farming" charges below), see Mt 9:10ff., 11:19, Mk 2:15ff., Lk 5:30, 6:32ff., 7:34, 13:2ff., etc. Note that John 9:31 knows very well that according to strict Jewish theory "God does not hear [the prayers of] Sinners", meaning in this context *Gentiles*. For an excellent example of such New Testament inversion, see Mt 21:33's contention that "the tax-collectors and prostitutes believed on" John. But the *Historical John* incontrovertibly lost his life confronting precisely such persons, namely, tax-collectors and harlots!

[23] Cf. above 1QpHab, v.3ff. and the parallel allusion in CD, i.18ff.

[24] Ps *Rec* 1.70. We have already pointed out in passing Paul's perhaps inadvertent application of such a vocabulary to himself in Ga 4:16. Cf. the parallel usages in Ja 4:4 and Mt 13:25's Parable of the Tares, where "the Enemy" (who in Jewish Christian ideology is none other than Paul) sows the evil tares and is finally identified as "the Devil". Paul over and over again shows his concern over the "Lying" accusation; cf. Ro 3:7, 9:1, 2 Co 11:31, Ga 1:20, 1 Ti 2:7, etc. 1 John 1:6, 1:10, 2:4, 2:21ff., 4:20, and 5:10 show the terminology was known to other authors in the New Testament. 1 John 2:4 even places in conjunction the "Liar"-type with the activity of "not keeping his commandments". Ja 3:14f., including an allusion to "Truth", provides the evidence that this kind of terminology was applied to at least one of its ideological opponents. Cf. too Ja 1–2 on "Doers", "Breakers", etc.

and vocabulary of Is 53:11f.[25] It should not simply be translated "suffering" but rather "suffering works", or perhaps even more to the point, "works with soteriological effect". It closely approximates what is translated as "works" in the Letter of James, and we shall encounter it and its companion usages from Is 53 like "*Da'at*" (Knowledge) and "*Rabbim*" ("the Many"),[26] as well as allusions to its analogue "*ma'aseihem*" and its variations, whenever the justifying activities of the Righteous Teacher or their ideological inversion are concerned in Hymns, the Damascus Document, 1QpHab, 4QpNah, etc.[27] One should also note the

[25] The *yazdik-Zaddik* usage is to be found uniquely in Is 53:10ff. in connection with key Qumran terminologies like *Da'at*, *nephesh*, '*amal*, and *Rabbim* (the usage in Is 5:23f. is slightly different, but it too finds an echo in CD, i.19). It is not often remarked that Qumran organization of *Moreh ha-Zedek* and *Rabbim* is itself reflective of Is 53:11's "Justification" ideology, because the basic identity of the *Moreh ha-Zedek/Zaddik*, like the esoteric thrust of the usage "Zadok" related to it, is rarely grasped.

The use of '*amal* in connection with "Faith" in 1QpHab, viii.2, i.e., that "the Righteous" are saved *both* by their Faith and their works, ties up the exegesis of Hab 2:4 with that of Is 53:11 paralleling their same close "tie-up" in "Gentile Christianity". Paul, too, reveals that he was taught such an exegesis of Is 53:11, probably in Jerusalem by the *Jewish* Apostles, in his 1 Co 15:3ff. introduction to his version of the post-resurrection sightings: "I taught you *what I had been taught myself*, namely that Christ died for our sins *in accordance with Scripture*" (italics mine; that Scripture is almost certainly Is 53:12). The interpolation in the order of post-resurrection appearances which follows, can hardly be the phrase, "to James and then to all the Apostles", as it is normally taken to be, but rather the patently inaccurate, "first to Cephas and secondly to the Twelve"—there were only eleven at the time and these must be understood as including "Cephas".

There are numerous references to "Justification" at Qumran, expressed primarily through the *yazdik-Zaddik* terminology, but also through the passive *yizadek*, "to be justified". In this framework, it should be appreciated, "*Zedakah*" differs from "*Zedek*" in that it carries with it something of the sense of the verbal noun "Justification". In addition to *yazdiku* in conjunction with allusion to "Noachic" redeemers in CD, i.19 and the exegesis of "Sons of Zadok" in iv.7, see 1QM, xi.14 (the eschatological "clouds of Heaven" section again) and 1QH, ix.9. For passive usage, see 1QS, iii.2f., 1QH, vii.28, ix.14f., xiii.16f., xvi.11, etc.

[26] "*Da'at*" is used at Qumran as a fundamental conception. Again, it is rooted in the conceptuality of Is 53:11f., that is, not only does the *Zaddik/Moreh ha-Zedek/Maschil* carry out his justifying activities through "suffering works", but also through "imparting Knowledge", i.e., "teaching". As the Pauline "free gift of Faith"/"Grace" doctrines supplanted the original sense of these ideas, the teaching aspects of the Messiah/*Zaddik*'s activities were subordinated to the soteriological ones; but even in the highly refracted portraits in the New Testament, traces of these former still persist. As time went on and the delay of the *Parousia* grew ever more certain, these allusions to "Knowledge" were easily transformed into the more powerful notation "*Gnosis*".

[27] We have already noted the existence of the doctrine of "works", i.e., *ma'asim* and its variations, at Qumran. In this passage and that on "the Delay of the *Parousia*" preceding it, the connection of "works" to "works of the Law" is plain—note the variation of

reiteration of this same "Doers" phraseology in the first two chapters of the Letter of James, accompanied as at Qumran by its ideological opposite "breaking"/"Law-Breakers".

When these aspects of the exegesis are properly recognized and taken in their eschatological sense, then the usage, *"Beit ha-Mishpat"* (which Vermes and other commentators translate quite prosaically as "House of Judgement") and the consonant Hebrew *"yazzilem"*, "He saves them", take on a completely different sense. One does not have here an actual courtroom experience (except figuratively) but an allusion to "salvation" and the believing and commissionary activities required of those waiting for "the Day of Judgement".[28]

This error is fundamental and it has clouded research on the Habakkuk *Pesher* more perhaps than any other. It is certainly remarkable that commentators persist in missing the eschatological sense of references to *"Beit ha-Mishpat"*, *"Yom ha-Mishpat"*, *"'amalam"*, and *"yazzilem"*/*"yazzilum"* in this *Pesher*, just as they persist in missing the eschatological sense of CD, iv.2ff.'s exegesis of the Zadokite Covenant. When this exegesis is viewed in relation to the Pauline exegesis of the same passage, Ja 2:17ff.'s "Faith without works" admonishment of "the Empty Man"/ "Enemy"—which cites *the act* of sacrificing Isaac from the life of Abraham to counter the Pauline ideological position on Ge 15:6—the references at the end of this *Pesher* in x.3ff. and xi–xii to *Beit ha-Mishpat/ Yom ha-Mishpat*, delivered in a milieu of contemptuous reference to "the Spouter's leading Many astray"/"instructing them in Lies so that their *'amal* would be empty", and condemnation of all Gentiles and idolators (including backsliding Jews), then it will be recognized that the exegesis does not refer to some trivial temporal dispute between Seleucids and Maccabeans, or some similar matter, but rather the developing *eschatological and theological framework* of early Christianity. When these matters are properly understood, then it will also be understood that the addition of *'amal* to *amanatam* ("their belief") in viii.2 was neither accidental nor incidental but a direct rebuke to "the Lying Spouter" regarding his

---

it one encounters in the New Testament's "many marvelous works", which entails rather curing, exorcisms, raisings, and the like). The exegesis of "the Righteous shall live by his faith" is restricted to "Doers of the Law in the House of Judah" *only*. Certainly its eschatological thrust was never conceived of as applying to *non-Doers* outside this "house".

[28] 1QpHab, viii.2; cf. 1QpHab, xii.14, where against a background of allusion to *Ebionim* ("the Poor"), "Lying", etc., the same verb, *yazzilum* ("will be saved"), is used, this time in conjunction with the actual expression, *Yom ha-Mishpat* ("Day of Judgement"); the latter recurs in xiii.1ff. In xii.17, Ja 5:3's "gold and silver" is evoked in the context of the same kind of coming "Judgement".

position on the same subject of the genre of that to the Lying "Tongue" in Ja 3:5ff.

Having thus vented its spleen over overriding internal concerns—for which the modern commentator must be grateful—the text now shifts its attention to the second of its two antagonists—this one outside of the actual Community itself and seemingly *directly* responsible for the death of the Righteous Teacher. The *Pesher* is in its *dénouement* stage and moving towards a conclusion. Along with it, the life of the Righteous Teacher is also moving into its final stages, not to mention—in the exegete's view—the history of the people as a whole. The background context, which is ongoing, is still the coming of the Romans and the ultimate destruction of the Jerusalem priesthood. This, it should again be emphasized, is still an event in progress and not necessarily complete. The exegete allows that the Wicked Priest "once enjoyed a reputation for Truth". Since he is very likely Ananus—or, as the two cannot always be safely differentiated, Ananias—one should refer to Josephus' comments about the former in the *Jewish War*. These comments are themselves remarkable, for they accord precisely with what Origen and Eusebius claim was written in the copies of Josephus available to them about Ananus' adversary and opposite number, James.

Later Josephus reveals his true feelings about Ananus in the *Vita*, and these are hardly very flattering. In the process, he also testifies to the fact that Ananus ruled in the manner of an independent ruler.[29] Whether

---

[29] 1QpHab, viii.8ff. Cf. above our comments about contrasting Josephus' portrayal of Ananus in *War* 4.5.2 with his comments in *Vita* 38 and *Ant.* 20.9.1. His account in *War* reads as follows: "He was on all accounts a venerable and very just man [i.e., a *Zaddik*] . . . , who treated even the most humble people [i.e. "the Poor" or Qumran's *'Anayyim* or *Dallim*] with equality. He was a prodigious lover of liberty and admirer of democracy in Government and did ever prefer the public welfare before his own benefit . . ." These are startling words when one considers the parallel virtues accorded James in early Church testimony. In *Vita*, however, Josephus describes Ananus as "being corrupted by bribes" (with Josephus and John of Gischala he was involved in some sort of olive oil racket in the early days of the War in Galilee). In the *Ant.*, where he is most critical of his "breach of the Laws" in dealing with James (i.e., again the "Law-breaking" theme), he describes Ananus as "a bold man in his temper and very insolent".

Having just described in *War* how the common people "went with the greatest zeal" (against the High Priests) and how the "Idumaeans" stood on Ananus' "corpse" and upbraided it because of "his kindness to the People", Josephus nevertheless intones: "I should think it not mistaken to say that the death of Ananus was *the beginning of the destruction of the city and that from that very day may be dated the overthrow of her wall and the ruin of her affairs whereon they saw their High Priest and Procurer of their Preservation slain in the midst of the city*" (italics mine). The resemblance of this testimony to what Origen and Eusebius claim they saw in their copies of Josephus in relation to James' demise is uncanny. Even

or not he did is not really germane, since the notice in the *Pesher* mentioning such rule (viii.9f.) need not relate to his actually "having ruled" in the secular sense but simply to his having occupied the High Priesthood. As we have seen, it is precisely this kind of reference (i.e., "when he ruled Israel, his heart grew arrogant and he abandoned God and *betrayed* the Law", leading directly into the material about "robbing Riches"/"partaking of the Riches of the Gentiles" and the death of the Wicked Priest) which has always been used by scholars to press the provenance of the entire exegesis back into the Maccabean period despite the relevance of almost every allusion in it to events between the 50s and 60s CE. Where the Maccabees, for instance, are concerned, there is absolutely no indication from any source whatsoever that rapaciousness was seen as one of their particularly noteworthy sins, which is *not the case* where the Herodian Priesthood is concerned.

This theme of "stealing Riches" and "gathering"/"taking the Riches of the Gentiles"/"Violent Ones" is extended in ix.4ff. into a condemnation of "the Last Priests of Jerusalem" who "collected Riches and profiteered from the spoil of the Peoples" (attached to a reference to "Gentiles" in the underlying text) generally. The translation of "*beza'*", "profiteered from" or "were greedy about", is very important and sets the tone for appreciating the whole. Josephus tells us how Ananias, and by implication probably Ananus too, piled up Riches for himself by robbing the tithes of the Poor Priests. He also specifically comments on the enormousness of his wealth.[30] That the various Herodian High

allusions like "a very Just Man" and "Procurer of their Preservation" reflect titles applied to James in extant literature like "*Zaddik*" and "*Oblias*" ("Protection of the People").

Josephus concludes: "I cannot but imagine that Virtue groaned at these men's case ("who had but little before worn the sacred garments and . . . were cast out naked and seen to be the food of dogs and wild beasts") and lamented that she was here so terribly conquered by Wickedness"; cf. the opposite sense given the same genre of "Wicked" vs. "the Righteous" scriptural passages applied in 1QpHab, i.11f. to the death of the Righteous Teacher and in early Church history to the death of James, as well as the whole presentation of "the Wicked Priest" destroying the Righteous Teacher, "the Men of his Council" (i.e., "Lebanon"), and "the Poor" in 1QpHab ix.9ff. and xi.4ff.

All of these bizarre turn-arounds can hardly be coincidental and bear heavily on our identification below, pp. 163–70, of these passages in the Habakkuk *Pesher* as relating to Ananus. Josephus himself has, in fact, already shown us the way towards their resolution by the two opposing kinds of things he was willing to say about Ananus; we must assume that he was willing to say the same kinds of opposing things *about James.*

[30] Aside from profiteering charges against Ananus in *Vita*, Josephus specifically calls Ananias "a great hoarder of money" in *Ant.* 20.9.2 directly following his description of James' judicial murder, and here and in 20.8.8 he describes how the High Priests "sent their servants to the threshing floors to seize the tithes . . . so that the Poorer Priests

Priestly clans like "the sons of Ananus" behaved in just such a manner, including "using violence with the people", is also attested to in the *Talmud* in its preservation (despite the Phariseeism of its orientation) of what are referred to as "the Zealot woes".[31] This tension between "Rich" and "Poor" is reflected in Josephus' description in *War* 2.17.6 of how, after stopping sacrifice on behalf of foreigners, "the Innovators" encouraged "the Poor" to rise against "the Rich", and how as a consequence the palaces of Agrippa II, Bernice, and Ananias were burned, as were *the debt records.*

It is also reflected in the sudden appearance of the "Poor" appellations in this period, not only at Qumran, but on into Jewish Christian or *Ebionite* tradition and in Paul's descriptions of his relations with "the Jerusalem Community". These "Poor" terminologies are a concomitant to the second of the two "all Righteousness" commandments, i.e., "Righteousness towards one's fellow man", which Ja 2:8f. calls "the Royal Law according to the Scripture" (it is also cited in the Damascus Document). Nothing could more accord with the condemnation of "the Rich"/"Riches" in James—sometimes echoed in the Gospels—Josephus' descriptions of "Essenes", and CD, iv's condemnation, inter alia, of the "Riches" of the Jerusalem Establishment.

The usage, which is developed in the last chapters of the Habakkuk *Pesher* in the context of the destruction which the Wicked Priest visited upon the Righteous Teacher and the members of his community (note that this "Poor" terminology is inclusive of the Community leadership in contradistinction to "the Simple of Judah" notation which seems only to have applied to the rank and file), is with its two analogues *'Ani/ 'Aniyyim* and *Dal/Dallim*, very widespread at Qumran. In general, all are used synonymously with some of the sect's other manifold forms of self-designation, namely, "Sons of Zadok", "Sons of Truth", "Sons of Light", "Sons of Righteousness", "Sons of Piety", "Men of the Lot of Melchizedek", "Poor Ones of Piety", "Enthusiasts for Righteousness", etc.[32] This struggle between "the Rich" and "the Poor"—the *sitz im leben*

died for want". For "Riches" charges, etc. against Bernice, see *Ant.* 20.7.3 and above, p. 124.

[31] Cf. *b. Pes* 57a and *Tos Men* xiii.21.533. The passage in question knows "the Boethusians, the house of Ananus, Kanthera, Ishmael b. Phiabi", etc. and ends with the lament that "their sons are Treasurers, their sons-in-law are Temple Captains, and their servants smite the People with sticks"; note the stress on the usage "the People" and that the tradition is ascribed to one "Abba Joseph b. Hanin".

[32] While J. Teicher did call attention to the use of the *Ebionim* ("the Poor") terminology, its occurrence at Qumran is much underestimated. Although the parallel usage *'Ani* does

of James, as well as the cessation of sacrifice in the Temple on behalf of foreigners—also punctuates the struggle between the temporizing, more accommodating High Priesthood, compromised as it was by its various Herodian connections, and the "zealous" Lower Priesthood, in which James appears to have played a crucial role.[33]

Where the Wicked Priest, in particular, is concerned, the theme of "abandoning God and betraying the Law" is developed in terms of "stealing Riches and gathering [in the sense of "harvesting" or "collecting"—perhaps even "tax-farming", which sets up interesting resonances with the portrait of "tax-collectors" in the New Testament] the Riches of the Men of Violence, who had rebelled against God" (viii.11ff.). This "Priest" is also described as "rebelling against and *breaking* the Laws of God" (viii.16f.). The occurrence of the root *P-R-R* here, i.e., "breaking" in the sense of Ezek 44:7's "Covenant-Breaking", ties the allusion firmly into the context of the Zadokite Statement's

not appear in Habakkuk until 3:14, the terminology is introduced into the crucial exegesis of xii.2ff. It occurs in similar contexts in 1QM, xi.9ff., xiii.13f, and in 1QH, v. 23 in conjunction with the term *Hesed* and *nephesh* (paralleling *nephesh-Zaddik* in CD, i) in ii.32, iii.24, and v.18, etc. Often it is used interchangeably or in conjunction with *'Ani*, which must be translated as per New Testament usage "the Meek"; cf. CD, v. 21 and xiv.13. Note Mt 5:3's "the Poor in Spirit"—as opposed to the Lk 6:20's "the Poor"—precisely retains the sense of Eusebius' contemptuous references to the *Ebionim* in *E.H.* 3.27.1ff., i.e. they were "Poor" because of the poverty of their Christological conceptions; cf. also Mt 11:5, Lk 4:18 and 7:22, and Paul in Ro 15:26 and Ga 2:10 paralleled by James in Ja 2:2ff.

[33] For James' role among the lower priesthood during this struggle, see S.G.F. Brandon, *Jesus and the Zealots*, New York, 1967, pp. 182ff. We have already seen this same tension between "Rich" and "Poor" reflected above in Josephus' description of how, after stopping sacrifice on behalf of Romans and other foreigners in the Temple, "the Innovators" encouraged "the Poor" to rise against "the Rich" and burn the palaces of Ananias, the Herodians, and destroy all the debt records (*War* 2.17.6).

Where James' custom of wearing only "linen" reported in all early Church accounts is concerned, Josephus pointedly describes how the lower priesthood won this right following his notice about James' death: *Ant.* 20.9.6. Another curious parallel is to be found in the description of Josephus' own Essene/"Rechabite"-style teacher cryptically denoted as *"Banus"* presumably because of his peculiar bathing habits. In *Vita* 2, Josephus tells us *Banus* wore only clothes growing on trees, by which he obviously means "linen". Note that James' bathing habits are also the subject of a good deal of attention in early Church sources (even though the overt sense of these sources appears to contradict this notice in *Vita* about *Banus*). However, this is easily explained by referring to Josephus' description of the Essenes in the *War*, where he specifically notes that these same "Essenes" preferred "being unwashed". He means by this, *not that they never bathed*, but that they did not *anoint* themselves with oil in the Roman style, a constraint pointed out by all sources with regard to James as well. Like the *"Banus"* in Josephus' description, James too condemned "fornication" and was a vegetarian.

prohibition against admitting aliens "uncircumcized in either heart or body" into the Temple and the previous allusion to the *'Arizim/Bogdim, et al.* in ii.6 as "Covenant- Breakers".

Even the "uncircumcized heart" allusion will be *specifically* applied to the Wicked Priest in xi.13. The allusion *"To'evot"*—"Abominations", another key element in the charges in Ezek 44:6ff., and not inconsequentially those of the Temple Scroll, will also be immediately applied to the Wicked Priest making it absolutely clear that this section of the Habakkuk *Pesher* about the Wicked Priest is operating within the context of Ezekiel's "Zadokite Statement". For it, the Wicked Priest, like the guilty establishment in Ezekiel and in contradistinction to the *true* "Sons of Zadok" in the Damascus Document, is here being disqualified from service on the Temple Mount on the basis of Ezekiel's charge of "admitting aliens uncircumcized in heart and uncircumcized in flesh into the Temple" or what elsewhere it will call "unclean pollution" or "polluting the Temple".

The "breaking" charge is also reflected in the "Law-Breaking" one in the Letter of James and its mirror reversal that of "Law-Breaking" *against James* in *Antiquities*' portrait of James' judicial murder. In *War* 2.17.10ff.'s portrait of these events leading up to Ananus' death, Josephus also characteristically reverses this "pollution of the Temple" charge, leveling it instead repeatedly at "the Innovators" or so-called "Zealots" *in the Temple*.

The reference to "Men of Violence"/*"Anshei-(H)amas"* as "rebelling against God" also must relate in some sense to the *Pesher*'s earlier allusion to *'Arizim* or "Violent Ones", not only described in ii.6 as "Covenant-Breakers", but also as being treacherously involved with "the Man of Lying"—for CD, viii.37f. "the Men of War ... walked with" or "turned aside to the Man of Lying". The Habakkuk exegete notes that "he [the Wicked Priest] partook of the riches of the Peoples" thereby "heaping upon himself sinful guilt" (viii.11f.; the resonance of "heaped upon"—*Iosif*—here and "gathering"—*yikboz*—is intentional).

One should see in this allusion two separate processes of rapine both in some way involving Gentiles—therefore the direct and overt accusation of "guilt"—one using violence to plunder the tithes of the lower priesthood (probably via the instrument of "violent Gentiles" like "Saulus" in the *Antiquities* or the other "Saul" in Acts, who has a commission to do violence from the Jerusalem High Priests—following the practice of Qumran and the "Temple Wall Zealots" we include Herodians among "Gentiles"/*"'Amim"*); the second relating to accepting non-Jewish sacrifices and gifts in the Temple. Both are seen as equally "abominable" where his Priesthood is concerned, and as undermining his "good name".

The Wicked Priest's particular personal sins are delineated in viii.12f. as walking in "the Ways of Abominations" (note Ezekiel's "*To'evot*" here linked to an inversion of "the Way" terminology) and "unclean pollution" (*niddat-tum'ah*; viii.12f.). They are meticulously set forth in xii.7ff., which makes it absolutely clear that the first relates to the violence he did "the Poor", including the "destruction" of the Righteous Teacher and his associates for which he will be repaid a full measure of vengeance—as it turns out somewhat ironically by some of these same "Violent Ones"; the second, to "polluting the Temple of God", a charge specifically leveled against him in xii.8f. and which as witnessed by *War* 2.17.10, 4.3.12ff., etc. (including the language of "Abominations", "the Poor", "Traitors", "admission of foreigners", etc.) was "in the air" in this period.

In both 11QT, xlvi.10ff. and CD, v.2ff., this "pollution of the Temple" charge is joined to one of not observing proper "separation" procedures in the Temple. The latter explains this in terms of not properly "separating" from people who "sleep with women in their periods" and "marry their nieces" as a matter of course. As its critique proceeds, including allusions to "removing the boundaries", "walking in windiness" or "pouring out wind", following "the Way of the People(s)" (*'Am*) and "Kings of the Peoples" (*'Amim*—in our view Herodians), reference is made to their "Evil Riches" and "ways of fornication", including even incest (CD, viii.5ff.), not to mention the charge of consonant "pollution . . . of the Temple treasure" (vi.15f.). There was *only one group, and one group only*, in this period that could be thought of as "sleeping with women during their periods" and "marrying nieces" as a matter of course, *Herodians* (see Appendix for more details of these charges).

We have already put forth the view that these "Violent Ones" included an assortment of unruly Herodians and others, as for example Saulus "the kinsman of Agrippa"—the intermediary between the accommodating Jerusalem Establishment "desirous for peace" and the Herodians—and those of more revolutionary sentiment like Silas, Niger, and Queen Helen's "kinsmen", Monobazus and Kenedaeos (in *War* 6.6.4 even their family at the end deserts the revolution and returns to the Roman fold), etc.

While the *Pesher* seems to imply some of these were used by "the Chief Priests" in matters of predation, tax-collecting, and violence, others turn against these very priests and, as so often occurs in such circumstances, devour their former masters. We have already connected the allusion "'*Amim*" in viii.12 and ix.5 to the two problems of "profiteering" operations in which "violence" was used against "the Poor" and receiving gifts from Gentiles in the Temple—cf. the specific underlying reference to *Go'im* in ix.3—but "*'Arizei-Go'im*" (4QpPs 37, ii.19 and iv.10) like Niger and Silas are in turn also among the principals in the early phases of the violent stages of the Uprising at the time of what apparently seemed to be the miraculous discomfiture of the Roman commander Cestius.

In the course of describing the destruction of "the Wicked Priest", the text, as we have already seen, discusses the related fate of "the Last Priests of Jerusalem", who it contends "gathered Riches and profiteered from the spoil of the Peoples". These "profiteering from"/"partaking of" the "spoil"/"Riches of the Peoples" accusations may simply be part and parcel of the kind of war-profiteering/"corruption by bribes" charges Josephus levels against Ananus in *Vita* 38. However it is more likely they imply involvement with Herodians and other violent "Gentiles", i.e., that "the Peoples" are those gathering "the spoil"/"Riches", from which "the Priests" are profiteering.

For 1QpHab, ix.5f., "their Riches together with their booty", i.e., of the "*Chohanei-Yerushalaim ha-Aharonim*" ("the Last Priests of Jerusalem"— note the plural sense here consonant with characteristic Herodian catch phrases like "Chief Priests"/"High Priests") would "in the Last Days be given over to the hands of the Army of the *Kittim*, for they are the Remnant of the Peoples" (*Yeter ha-'Amim*; ix.4ff.) Here the term "*Yeter ha-'Amim*" in the underlying text is specifically applied to the "*Kittim*"/ Romans in the *Pesher*, and there is an additional intended irony where those who advocated a policy of accommodation with foreigners (inclusive of Herodians) are concerned. As these Priests used Gentiles "to rob the Poor" (cf. CD, vi.16) and also enriched themselves by accepting illegal gifts/sacrifices from these or other Gentiles—here the use of the word "*'Amim*" to represent Herodians is pivotal—so too would "additional Gentiles" not part of these original Gentiles devour the illgotten gains and "booty" they had thereby amassed for themselves.

It is virtually inconceivable that this vivid picture could relate to any conquest earlier than 70 CE, in connection with which Josephus in *War* 6.8.3 specifically tells us how the Romans extracted the secret of the whereabouts of the Temple treasure from the last Treasurer, Phineas. This is to say nothing about the portrait's eschatological note about "the Last Times"—compare this with the parallel between "Last Times"/ "Last Priests" and the usage "the Last" generally denoting the Final Generation—and the sense, rendered by the present and future tense of the verbs, of events in progress, not completed. If it relates to any earlier conquest, it is difficult to understand which, as one cannot point to any similar allusions or parallels in any earlier period.

Nor would anyone have thought of applying a plural like "the Last Priests" to the Maccabees, for plural terminologies like the "High Priests" or "Chief Priests" imply an alignment of principal families and cannot in any real way be thought of in terms of the more monolithic Maccabean structure. Nor can there be any doubt, as we have seen, that the Herodian High Priests at this time plundered the tithes of the Poor Priests and accepted Herodian and Roman gifts in the Temple.

The criticism that for the exegete to be discussing these events, they must already have happened is as far from the mark as thinking these "Last Priests" in "the End of Days" could in any sense relate to the Maccabean Establishment, or what is even more far-fetched, a prior one. As we have already noted, any realistic observer, even those on Masada, at Qumran, or in the mysterious "Pella" haven of the Jerusalem Community, would have been quite capable of realizing this end was inevitable. In fact, after 68 CE these "Last Priests" had virtually already been destroyed and it only remained for their wealth to be given over to the Romans—which was in the circumstances an inevitability. The atmosphere of the *Pesher* is so immediate and so tragic that it is hard to escape the impression that it was being set down almost simultaneously with the events it depicts. Still, there is nothing either archaeologically or paleographically which would make its composition after 68 CE an impossibility.

Having described the "sinful guilt" and "Law Breaking" of "the [Wicked] Priest" (meaning here "the High Priest"), his "Abominations" and "unclean pollution" (of the Temple) engendered by his greed, his "skimming" *Gentile* "spoils", and depradations on "the Poor", the text describes the fate that overtook him and the vengeance that was visited upon him. It asserts that the Wicked Priest was "stricken by the Judgements upon Sinning" (ix.1f.). Because this Wicked Priest destroyed "the Righteous Teacher and the men of his Council", or at least committed very grave iniquity against them "dealing so wickedly with His [God's] Elect" (again the synonym for "the Sons of Zadok" through whom "God would *execute Judgement on the Gentiles* and those of His own people *who kept the Law only when convenient*"—italics mine), he would be "delivered into the hands of his enemies that they might scourge him and consume him with bitterness of soul" (ix.9ff.).

Whether or not this accurately portrays Ananus' end or for that matter that of any other known candidate for Wicked Priest cannot be said with certainty. What is clear, however, is that Ananus did deliver James and some of his followers over to be stoned;[34] and, as the Uprising moved into its final phase, was caught by the "Idumaean" supporters of "the Innovators", whoever might be intended by these circumlocutions. He was tortured and "horrible ignominies"—what in modern terms might be called "atrocities"—were inflicted upon his flesh. His enemies, in the *Pesher*'s own words, did in a very real sense "take vengeance upon his lifeless *corpse*", and Josephus specifically informs us that "the Idumaeans" stood over his corpse and "abused" it with jests before declining to bury it and throwing it outside the walls as food for the jackals.

Though the phraseology of this key allusion in the *Pesher* is usually translated somewhat obscurely in a manner similar to Vermes' "they took vengeance upon his body of flesh", the actual translation must run: "they took vengeance upon *the flesh of his corpse*" (italics mine). The word "*geviyyah*" here is also pivotal and certainly in this context has the sense of "lifeless corpse" not "living body". It, along with "*abeit-galuto*" below, relates the events in this *Pesher* directly to Ananus' fate in a way that cannot be claimed for any other candidate for the Wicked Priest. As per Josephus' presentation of the death of Ananus in the *War*—in contradistinction to that which the early Church fathers report concerning the death of James—the description here of the destruction of the Wicked Priest is *immediately* followed by those materials we have outlined above relating to the destruction of Jerusalem and the Jerusalem Priestly Establishment. This sequencing and the allusion to "corpse"/"*geviyyah*", in our view "prove", as much as anything can, the relevance of these references to the extant data and historical context to which we have been linking them.

The expression "Judgements on Sinning" is also important here and links up with the earlier discussion of Hab 2:4 and the climactic finale of "Judgements" which the *Pesher* will go on to delineate. Its plural sense parallels the plural sense of and denunciation implied by "the horrors

---

[34] *Ant.* 20.9.1. Note the description in CD, i.16ff. of the attack on "the Righteous One" also includes reference to an attack on several of his followers, but this probably rather relates to an earlier attack on James recorded in the Pseudoclementine *Recognitions*, in which he was left for dead, but only broke his leg when he fell from the Temple balustrade. Josephus' charge in the *Antiquities* against James of "Law-Breaking" can only have a basis in fact in the context of the *Yom Kippur* atonement on behalf of "the People"—i.e., the '*am*, according to our understanding, a "Zadokite" atonement understood according to the esoteric sense of the term—described in all early Church accounts of his death.

of disgusting pollutions" ("diseases") attached to the description of the violation of "the Priest's" (meaning "the High Priest's") corpse, and both carry with them the very definite implication of "vengeance", i.e., in our view, vengeance for the death of James (ix.1ff.). The latter, in particular, is obscure and need not specifically relate to a person actually having suffered a disgusting physical disease as it is usually taken to mean (though Ananus like anyone else might have been suffering from some disease), a doubtful proposition since such a disease would have disqualified him or any other proposed Wicked Priest from the office of the High Priesthood and nothing is said in any of our sources about such a disqualification. Since it parallels the reference to these divine "Judgements"—the plural sense of which recurs in a more eschatological context in x.12—it is difficult to escape the conclusion that it relates to the disgusting treatment meted out to his corpse and a consonant divine disapprobation attached to this.

Any other reading is, in fact, impossible here, since the plural verbs "inflicted"/"committed" are active not passive and confirm these as *acts done to him, not* diseases. The whole properly reads: "*They inflicted* the Judgements on Evil *by committing upon him* the outrages of Evil pollutions *in taking vengeance* upon the flesh of *his corpse*" (italics mine). In his description of these events in *War* 4.5.2, Josephus makes mention of just such "Impiety", and treatment of this kind, as in the case of crucifixion or beheading, was meant to cast the victim into a sort of divine disapprobation and the public disrepute consonant upon it. While Josephus, good Pharisee that he is, is horrified by the treatment accorded Ananus' corpse, it should be noted that the unknown author of the Habakkuk *Pesher* views the violation of the *body* of the Wicked Priest with equanimity.[35]

---

[35] Cf. Josephus' comments on the beheading of Antigonus in *Ant.* 15.1.2. Such "defilements" were probably also thought to constitute an impediment to resurrection. In *War* 4.5.2 Josephus does not conceal his own repugnance, and it is not without interest that he first makes mention here of the care Jews usually showed in the burial of the dead, that even "those condemned and crucified were taken down and buried before the going down of the sun", a description not lost on Gospel tradition. The phrase, "he rebelled against and betrayed the Laws of God" (viii.17f.), has meaning within Josephus' specific acknowledgement that the "more fair-minded" among the populace thought Ananus had done precisely this in his illegal treatment of James. In addition, as we have seen, this phrase and description would most certainly have been applied by the sectaries to the ongoing confrontation in the Temple over the issue of sacrifices by foreigners, etc., labeled "pollution of the Temple" here and later in this *Pesher*, as well as in CD, iv.18ff.

Where the execution of James is concerned, it should be noted there is a very definite

The eschatological sense of "the Last Times" and "the Last Priests", and the whole emphasis on "Judgements" and vengeful destruction, is given further reinforcement in the next section (x.3ff.) about "the Judgement . . . of fire and brimstone" or "the Judgements of fire" which "God will make in the midst of the many nations". In the process, precise definition is given to the "*Beit ha-Mishpat*" terminology so crucial to the earlier exegesis of Hab 2:4. Vermes, who previously rendered it "House of Judgement"—and who rendered "*geviyyah*" above "body of flesh"— now renders it "the condemned house" ("whose judgement God will pronounce"), but the phrase is *eschatological*. It is discussing "the Judgement . . . of fire and brimstone" which God will make "in the midst of many Nations" (4ff.), and the theme of such a coming eschatological *Judgement* will dominate the *Pesher* until its conclusion. It must be translated as "the Judgement that God will make when he comes to execute Judgement among the nations", and understood in terms of that "Judgement" which the *Pesher* has already insisted will be the prerogative of and executed by "His Elect" (that is to say, "the sons of Zadok").

causality in the events leading up to his death, and from it, to the fall of the Temple (as per early Church versions of Josephus). First, Josephus' so-called "*Sicarii*" murder the former High Priest Jonathan, brother of the Ananus presently under consideration and brother-in-law to Caiaphas (*Ant.* 20.8.5). There follows the "Temple Wall" Affair centering around the attempt by the Temple "Zealots" to block Agrippa II's view of the sacrifice while he was lounging, presumably in the Greek manner, at dinner (*Ant.* 20.8.11; if Agrippa was not keeping Jewish dietary law, but rather eating in James' words "things sacrificed to idols", the insult would be all the more grievous). This triggers a Paul-style appeal to Nero on the part of "the Innovators". Almost immediately thereafter Agrippa II and Ananus take advantage of an interregnum in Roman governors to accomplish the judicial murder of James (*Ant.* 20.9.1). Shortly thereafter, Josephus undertakes his puzzling mission to the Empress Poppea to obtain the release of certain "Essene"-type Priests still imprisoned in Rome. There follows the fire in Rome blamed by Nero on what are considered to be "Christians", after which the repression in Judea mounts to fever pitch, finally provoking the Revolt that is proclaimed by the lower priest class who halt sacrifice on behalf of Romans and other foreigners. It is this last, it should be noted, which Josephus condemns as "an innovation", even though it was not, and which, he informs us elsewhere, in a moment of presumable inadvertence, was inspired by the Messianic "Star Prophecy".

One is entitled to ask what was behind this series of events. Certainly the same agitation is behind the visit of Simon to Caesarea in 44 CE to inspect Agrippa I's household arrangements that is behind the "Temple Wall" Affair, which ultimately leads to Agrippa II's being barred from Jerusalem and the Temple altogether and the stopping of sacrifice in the manner demanded in Ezek 44:7ff. on behalf of Romans and other foreigners. Our answer, provable or not, is that Agrippa II and Ananus certainly considered they were removing the symbolic center of this agitation when they removed the incarnate "Righteous One" (*Zaddik*), "Pillar", and popular leader of his generation, James the Just.

The underlying text now moves directly on to an allusion to "building a city with blood and erecting a town on Falsehood" (Hab 2:12f.), and the *Pesher* exploits this and the eschatological note leading up to it to return to its favorite topic and seemingly overriding concern, its ideological battles with "the Man of"/"Spouter of Lying". In particular, the expression "Falsehood" in the underlying text is connected to its complaints about "the Pourer out of Lying", i.e., the *Mattif ha-Chazav* (x.6ff.).

The allusion to "Pourer" here (x.9, instead of the earlier "Man of Lying" in v.11), testifies to the basic interchangeability all of these terminologies. The additional implied parody it carries of baptismal procedures associated with this ideological adversary—continued in x.14ff., though the text is defective, moving on into further eschatological reference to "the Day of Judgement" and "Judgements by fire"—is made even more explicit in the Damascus Document's parallel allusion (about an attack on the *Zaddik*: CD, i.10ff.). There, the *Ish ha-Lazon* ("the Man of Jesting"/ "Scoffing"/"Comedian") "pours out (*hittif*) on Israel the waters of Lying" (*maimei-Chazav*) and "leads them astray in a trackless waste without a Way" (note the play on "Way" and "wilderness" allusions, the whole relating to "removing the boundary markers" of the Law). From 1QpHab, x.10ff. to xii.11, another of these interchangeable usages, *"Sheker"* ("Lying"), is introduced into the *Pesher*, though it is not found in the underlying biblical text, and combined with reference to the *Mattif ha-Chazav* who "leads Many astray ... instructing them ['the Many'] in *ma'asei-Sheker*" (that is, "works of Lying").

In 4QpNah, ii.7ff. these kinds of "Lying" and "deceit" allusions are linked to "Tongue" imagery—as they are in 1QS, iii—which also forms the background of allusion to the brazenness of the ideological adversary in Ja 3:5ff. (as we shall see, the "Empty Man" allusion in Ja 2:20 linking up with the "empty" *'amal* allusion in x.10 below). In 1QH, ii.31 and iv.9f. the expression *"Malizei-Chazav"*—best translated as "the Lying Deceivers"—completes the circle of these various parallel allusions and demonstrates them to be basically variations on the same or similar themes.[36]

---

[36] Often these kinds of allusions are viewed in conjunction with another expression, *Remiyyah* ("Deceit"); cf. how this last expression is used in relation to the expulsion of backsliders from the sect and to the "Way in the wilderness" allusions of 1QS, vii.5f., viii.22, ix.8, x.23, etc., after already having been employed in the same document relative to baptismal allusions in iv.9 and 23. 4QpNah, ii.1ff. even understands the allusion "City of Blood" in terms of "walking in Lying and Falsehood", which in turn is connected to an allusion to "the Seekers after Smooth Things at the End of Days". This "Lying" imagery together with "fornication", "Tongue", "lips of Deceit", and "leading the Many

In its attempt to expound this allusion to "building a city with blood and erecting a town on Falsehood", the *Pesher* provides an esoteric exposition of such surprising content that its meaning has eluded many commentators. When Paul's teaching "spiritual things spiritually" thesis is properly taken into account and when it is understood that the "building"/"foundation"/"erecting" imagery employed here parallels the kind of imagery he uses in 1 Co to develop his ideas on "Holy Communion", then it can be expounded. Beginning with a parody of the Righteous Teacher/*Zaddik*'s proper Justification activity of "making Many Righteous", it contends, as we have seen, that "the Spouter of Lying ... led Many astray in order to build a worthless city on blood and to raise an Assembly on Lying." The addition of the allusion "worthless", the shift from "erect" in the underlying biblical text to "raise", and from "town" to "congregation" or "Assembly on Lying" (since *'Avlah* does not mean precisely "Lying") are all significant. We have already identified the "leading astray" imagery, used in CD, i.15 in conjunction with "the Liar's" "boundary-removing" activities, as the ideological opposite of the "keeping the Covenant"/"Law" and "Justifying" activities of the true "Sons of Zadok". There, it also carried an implied parody of both Is 53:11's "*yazdik-Zaddik*" ideology and Is 40:3's "Way in the wilderness" imagery. The parody of the former is consolidated in this particular passage by the pointed employment several times of the term "*Rabbim*", also used in Qumran organizational documents to describe communal membership.

This inversion of the "*Rabbim*" terminology is repeated in the very next sentence, this time in relation to "the Liar's tiring out Many with worthless work"—here expressed as "*'avodah*" or "work" in the sense

astray" allusions is further developed with regard to a group called "Ephraim" or "the Simple Ones of Ephraim" in ii.7ff. and iii.4ff. In these passages about "Ephraim"/"City of Blood", as well as those about "leading Many astray"/"tiring out Many with a worthless service", the possible hint of what were seen as illegitimate Pauline activities abroad by the Jerusalem Community—or the one at Qumran—should not be ignored.

For our exposition of these puzzling usages, together with their link-up with "the Pharisees" and all "those seeking accommodation with foreigners at the End of Days", see below, p. 173f. The *sitz im leben* of these allusions is also clear and constitutes the retrospective historical perspective of the Nahum *Pesher*. Josephus provides it in *War* 2.17.1ff., when he links "all those desirous of peace" with "the Men of Power (i.e. the Herodians), the High Priests, the principal of the Pharisees" and one "Saulus", who had already led a riot in Jerusalem and who was the actual go-between to Agrippa II, who was residing outside the city because he has been barred from it by "the Innovators". Not only did this alliance object to stopping sacrifice on behalf of Romans and other foreigners by "the Innovators", but Josephus describes it as *actually inviting* the Roman soldiers into the city to suppress the Insurrection.

of "mission" or "service"; (x.12). It is immediately followed by the employment of another key term from Is 53 Justification theorizing, *'amal*, already encountered in the exegesis of Hab 2:4 above. Both will be followed up in x.14 by the use of a third such usage from the vocabulary of Is 53:11, "*Da'at*" or "Knowledge", which, as we noted above, will be related to what appears to be an evocation of either Spirit or water baptism.

Before, we identified "*'amal*" as the distinguishing characteristic (along with "*Torah*-Doing") of the "Jamesian" or Jerusalem Church exposition of Hab 2:4, defined it as "works" (more precisely "suffering works"), and connected it with the Letter of James' insistence that "Faith without works is dead". Here the *Pesher* contends that "their works (*'amalam*, i.e., the "works" of the Community that was built on "blood" and raised on "Lying", not "on the Law") would be empty", i.e., "empty" of soteriological content and inefficacious. Not only should the implicit rebuke here to Pauline faith doctrines be obvious, but, in particular, there is the implied rebuke to Paul's exposition of Ge 15:6 that Abraham's "Faith counted for him as Righteousness", i.e., "Faith without works" in this eschatological scheme "counted for nothing".

In what must be seen as yet another strong verification of our presentation, Ja 2:20 at this point actually applies the word "empty", which the Habakkuk *Pesher* uses to describe the soteriological efficacy of those "works" emanating out of "the Liar's" teaching, to the very person of its interlocutor, that is, "Empty Man" or "Man of Emptiness", implying thereby that just as the "Faith" he taught was "dead", the "works" predicated upon it were "empty" or "of emptiness".

The addition of the word "worthless" (*shavo*) to the underlying "City on blood" phraseology which we have already remarked above, like the subtle shifting of the underlying "Falsehood" to "Lying" in the exegesis, is also purposeful. This reference to "worthless" (*shavo*) is repeated in the next sentence, where "the Liar's" "work—*'avodah* as opposed to "works", *ma'asim*/*'amal*—is characterized as "worthless". "*Shavo*"/"*shaveh*" is also to be found in the Qumran Hymns (1QH, ii.22, vi.4f., and vii.34) in the context of allusions to similar "laying the Foundations" and "congregational" activities.

It should be noted that where 4QpNah, ii.1ff.—in our view hostile to both Herodians and Pharisees—uses the imagery of "walking in Lying and Deceitfulness", it is also expounding the notation "City of Blood". Not only does it do so, not coincidentally, in connection with an allusion to *overseas messengers*, it ties the notation to another puzzling notation, "Ephraim"/"city of Ephraim". 4QpNah, ii.9 goes on to expound the latter allusion in terms of "the Tongue of their Lies" and selling "forni-cation to the Gentiles", which it interprets in terms of "leading Ephraim astray"/"leading Many astray"—note again the telltale vocabulary of 1QpHab here and the extremely pregnant allusions to "Lying lips" and "Deceitful teaching". If one interprets 4QpNah's "Seekers after Smooth Things at the End of Days" in terms of "seeking accommodation with foreigners"—in the context of which both Pauline and Pharisaic cooper-ation with what was seen as the "fornication" of the Herodian family was pivotal—then the "Ephraim" allusion can be seen inter alia as inclus-ive of Pauline missionary activities overseas (cf. its use in just such a context and with just such effect when the hope is expressed in iii.5ff. that "the Simple Ones of Ephraim . . . will forsake those who misled them and *join themselves* to Israel"—italics mine).

In such an ideological framework, the usage "city" or "community" is not difficult to elucidate; nor is the constant recourse to "building" or "laying the Foundations" in this *Pesher*, 1QS, and Hymns. Mt 5:14f. in the Sermon on the Mount makes oblique reference to the community as "city" both in the context of "Light" imagery and allusion to "works"; and in Ga 4:26 Paul—responding to the "Enemy" charges—refers to "the Jerusalem above", interpreting it to include those "born in the Spir-it" and "free", not those "zealous" slaves who "wished to be under the Law".

Heb 12:12ff. even uses citizenship imagery to describe this "Heavenly Jerusalem", calling everyone in it "a firstborn son and a citizen of Heav-en".[37] Even more germane for our purposes, in 1 Co 3:9ff. Paul uses the kinds of "building" and "laying the Foundations" imagery the *Pesher* uses when he describes his Community as "God's building" and refers to himself as "the architect". He finally concludes with a picture of his followers as "the Temple of God".

This latter must be seen as generically related to both the "Heavenly Jerusalem" and "building" imageries. With regard to it and in the context of discussing James' directives on "fornication" and "food sacrificed to idols" and his own notion of "Communion with the blood of Christ" in 1 Co 10:16ff., Paul develops a portrait of the members of his Com-munity as one body in contrast to "the other Israel" (i.e., 1QpHab, viii.1's "House of Judah"). He continues this spiritualized "body" imagery in 1 Co 12:12ff., where he designates them not only as the Temple but

---

[37] For more on Paul's view of adoptionist sonship, see his discussion of "the Children of the Promise" in Ro 9:7ff., which grows out of his discussion of spiritual sonship in Ro 8:14ff.

straightforwardly as "the body of Christ"—this of course connects with the famous saying in the Gospels linking Jesus' body, after the resurrection, with the Temple. Eph 2:16ff. elaborates on this "single body" metaphor while at the same time denying there are any "aliens or foreign visitors", an allusion patently directed against those problems concerning foreigners in the Temple we have already analyzed above. This imagery, it should be appreciated, is all "spiritualized" in the manner recommended by Paul in 1 Co 2:13 and includes both "spiritualized" body and "spiritualized" Temple imagery. Like Hebrews, Ephesians calls its congregationalists "citizens like all the Saints and part of God's Household". Using Paul's "building" imagery, it summarizes the position by describing them as "part of a building with the Apostles and Prophets for its Foundations and Christ Jesus himself, the Cornerstone. As every structure is aligned on him, all grow into one Holy Temple in the Lord and you too in him are being built into a house where God lives in the Spirit."

Precisely the same genre of terminological approach and imageries are being employed—but in an atmosphere of "keeping the Law", not "breaking" it—in 1QS, viii.1ff. Here "Cornerstone" and "laying the Foundations" imagery are invoked in conjunction with allusions to "the Council" as a spiritualized "Temple"/"Holy of Holies" and "a sin offering"/"sweet fragrance" of Righteousness (cf. in particular the strong allusion here to "the Cornerstone not swaying on its Foundations" and even the ideas of "keeping faith in the land" and "atoning for sin" by "suffering afflictions"). We have already called attention to this imagery of the Community Council as Temple and spiritualized sacrifice/atonement in connection with the parallel "pollution of the Temple of God with idols" themes in 2 Co 6:16ff., CD, iv, and 11QT, xlvif. at the end of the "Backgrounds" section above.

The notion of Communion built on some form of a "blood" compact appears to have been put forth very early on by Paul and those following his ideological "approach". In particular, one should note in this regard 1 Co 10:16, 11:25ff., and 15:50, as well as Ro 5:9, Eph 2:13, 1 Pe 1:2 and 1:19, 1 John 1:7 and 5:6ff., etc. That abstention from "blood" was part and parcel of James' "Jerusalem Council" directives is made clear in Acts 15:20ff. and 21:25. That from 1 Co 6:12 to 10:33, beginning with the typically Pauline proclamation, "for me all things are lawful", the terms of these directives are being discussed, including "fornication", "blood", "things sacrificed to idols", etc., should also be clear. The discussion rises to fever pitch in conjunction with the "building" imagery and the first reference to "Communion with the blood of Christ" when

Paul pronounces in 10:25: "Do not hesitate to eat anything that is sold in the market place. There is no need to raise questions of conscience" (for Paul, a euphemism for "questions of the Law").

The horror with which these ideas, in particular that of the mystery-religion-oriented "Community built upon blood", would have been greeted at Qumran can be measured by CD, v.5ff.'s ascription of the cutting off of the children of Israel in the wilderness to the consumption of "blood". The very idea that a Community could be "built", even figuratively, on the consumption of "blood" would have been greeted in the circles represented by Qumran and the Jerusalem Church with just the kind of contemptuous condemnation we find in 1QpHab's characterization of the Lying Spouter as:

> leading Many astray in order to build a worthless city on blood and erecting a Congregation [or "Church"] on Lying; and for self-Glorification tiring out Many with Worthless Service [*'Avodah*] and instructing them in Lying works [*ma'asei-Sheker*] so that their *'amal* would be empty [or "count for nothing"] when they were brought to those [same] Judgements of Fire concerning which they themselves had vilified and insulted the Elect of God.

Where Paul's relationship with the Jerusalem Church is concerned, the notes about "self-Glorification" and "tiring out Many with a worthless service" have particular import. We have already distinguished the word *'avodah* from "works" as expressed by *ma'asim* or *'amal*. *'Avodah*, which is also the subject of some speculation in relation to the genre of lying nemesis in the Community Rule,[38] is rather to be associated with the kind of "work" or "service" Paul takes to "boasting about" and "glorifying" in 2 Co and can in some contexts even be translated as "mission".

For the *Pesher*, those persons instructed in this manner, or part of this "building", "Church", or "city", also "insulted and hurled abuse at the Elect of God"—in our view James and the "Jerusalem Church" leadership, or precisely those "Pillars" so strikingly and enviously evoked in Ga 2:9.[39] These "insults" or "abuse" would, inter alia, appear to involve

---

[38] See above n. 36 and CD, viii.30 and 1QS, ix.8, where the postulant is urged not to cooperate with such an individual in "work" and "finances", and where reference is made in parallel context to "the *Anshei-Remiyyah*", their "work" being the opposite of *'avodat-Zedek* ("the service of Righteousness") and *'avodat-Emet* ("the Service of Truth"; cf. Paul in 2 Co 11:15 on "the Servants of Righteousness"). Note that in Ga 4:16 Paul's actual words are: "So your Enemy have I become by speaking Truth to you."

[39] The defamation of the Jerusalem Leadership in the Pauline corpus proceeds in almost a drumbeat fashion. It is most evident in Ga 2:5ff., 1 Co 9:2ff. (where Paul calls his communities his "work in the Lord" parallel to the meaning we have to the Hebrew

'*avodah* above), and 2 Co 11:2ff. and 12:12ff. In conjunction with these murmurings against and slanders of the leadership, he often announces his view of the Law and Salvation by Faith, which is diametrically opposed to the Qumran position above and the Letter of James; cf. Ga 2:15ff.: "Though we were born Jews and not pagan Sinners, we acknowledge that what makes a man Righteous is not obedience to the Law, but Faith in Jesus . . . no one can be justified by keeping the Law"; Ga 2:21ff.: "If the Law can justify us, there is no point in the death of Christ . . . Are you foolish enough to end in outward observance what you began in the Spirit"; Ga 3:11ff. interpreting Hab 2:4 to mean "the Law will not justify anyone in the sight of God" and playing on this further in Ro 1:16f. by interpreting "Righteousness" to mean "God saving all who have faith—Jews first, but Greeks as well"; Ro 3:20ff. in almost a direct riposte to James: "No one can be justified in the sight of God by keeping the Law; all the Law does is to tell us what is sinful . . . a man is justified by faith and not by doing something the Law tells him to"; and summing up in Ro 9:30ff.: "From this it follows that the pagans who were not looking for Righteousness [how pregnant this saying now appears and how true] found it all the same, a Righteousness that comes of faith; while Israel looking for a Righteousness derived from the Law failed to do what that Law required . . . Brothers, I can swear to their [the Jews'] zeal for God, but their zeal is misguided." (Here, of course, is the ultimate play on Josephus' "Zealot" terminology and the true thrust of the combination of these terminologies becomes clear; for James in an opposite vein, see inter alia Acts 21:21.)

Qumran makes its criticism of the type of position expressed here clear, as we have already seen, in the section preceding its description of the Community Council as "a Holy of Holies for Aaron . . . that Precious Cornerstone whose foundations shall neither rock or sway in their place . . . a sweet fragrance": "Any man who enters the Council of Holiness to walk in the way of Perfection as commanded by God and who overtly or covertly [here the Hebrew is "*Remiyyah*", which Vermes mistranslates as "negligence", but the word is "Deceit"] transgresses one word of the *Torah* of Moses on any point whatsoever shall be expelled from the Council of the Community and shall return no more; no man of Holiness shall associate with him further either in monetary affairs or in approach." This whole position is preceded by the directive: "Whoever has gone about slandering his companion shall be excluded from the pure meal of the congregation for one year and do penance [i.e., "table-fellowship"; cf. Paul's "Nazirite"-style penances in Acts 18:18 and 21:26] . . . Whoever has murmured against the Community Leadership shall be expelled and shall not return" (1QS, vii.15ff.).

Ja 2:9 puts the same position in the following manner: "If a man keeps the whole of the Law except for one small point at which he stumbles, he is still guilty of [breaking] it all", concluding in 2:21: "Do you realize you Empty Man that Faith without works is useless?" Its author shows his familiarity with the problem of "Lying": "But if at heart you have the bitterness of jealousy, or a self-seeking ambition, never make any claims for yourself or cover up the Truth with lies [cf. also "Doers" against a critique of "Tongue", "deceit", "fornication", and "Riches" in 1:2ff.]. Principles of this kind are not the Wisdom that comes down from above; they are only earthly, animal and devilish" (3:14f.; cf. 1QS, iii.1ff.). He, also, demonstrates his familiarity with the "Enemy" terminology well known to Jewish Christian tradition and alluded to as well in the Gospels (Mt 13:25ff.): "Don't you realize that making the world your Friend is making God your Enemy? Anyone who chooses the world for his Friend turns himself into God's Enemy

... Brothers, do not slander one another. Anyone who slanders a brother or condemns him is speaking against the Law and condemning the Law. But if you condemn the Law, you have stopped keeping it and become a judge over it" (4:5ff.; for Paul's "making the world" his friend, see 2 Co 9:19ff.: "I made myself a Jew to the Jews to win the Jews ... To those who have no Law I was free of the Law myself ... I made myself all things to all men ... That is how I run intent on winning; that is how I fight, not beating the air").

In Ro 10:12 and elsewhere, Paul announces his desire to found a community that would "make no distinction between Jew and Greek". In our view this is precisely the kind of ambitions which characterize the Herodian family, particularly Agrippa I and his brother Herod of Chalcis, but also his son Agrippa II and very likely the latter's son "Aristobulus" (cf. Ro 16:11) in Northern Syria, Cilicia, and Lower Armenia. In Ro 13.1ff. Paul lays out his political philosophy, such as it is: "You must obey the governing authorities. Since all government comes from God, the civil authorities were appointed by God [here Paul attacks "the Zealots" on their own "philosophical" ground] and so anyone who resists authority is rebelling against God's decision ... Good behavior is not afraid of magistrates [the witnesses to the crucifixion of Jesus would have been interested in this point, as would the author of Ja 5:6ff.]; only criminals have anything to fear ... The State is there to serve God for your benefit ... This is also the reason why you must pay taxes [Paul's view of the "tax" issue which so exercised the "Innovators" from 4 BC to 70 CE], since all government officials are God's officers. They serve God by collecting taxes" (this last point has particular relevance to the Gospel portrait of Jesus' "table-fellowship" with *tax-collectors*).

Doubtlessly my presentation of Paul's position on these matters will not be a popular one, but I believe the strong links between the Pauline approach and Herodian family ambitions are not difficult to appreciate. Paul's Roman citizenship is easily comprehended in such a context. Herodians had married into the Cilician Royal House and, in addition, Paul hints at his own "Herodian" roots in Ro 16:11 above. The massive fear displayed at Qumran over the power of an individual of the "Pauline" genus and Paul's ready access into the circles of Jerusalem power as described in Acts also become comprehensible within such a framework. The reticence of the Letter of James and its meticulous avoidance of the same kind of slander that Paul permits himself in more unguarded moments, as well as James' seemingly endless indulgence of him, are also made comprehensible in such a context.

As we have seen, 4QpNah, ii.1ff. interprets "the City of Blood" in terms of "walking in Lying" and "Deceit", which in turn is connected to an allusion to "the Seekers after Smooth Things". If we see this as alluding at Qumran to all those seeking accommodation with the governing authorities, Roman or Herodian, which was true as much of "Gentile" Christians as it was of Pharisees and so-called "Herodians", then we put ourselves into a more realistic historical framework for grouping "the Man of Lying" in such a company. In any event, Paul, like Josephus, made no secret of his "Pharisaic" orientation. Both he and Josephus mean the same thing by this, i.e., accommodating themselves to the powers-that-be and foreigners, and this orientation has retrospectively been assimilated into the portrait of Jesus in the Gospels, to all intents and purposes vitiating its historicity.

calling down on the Communal Leadership precisely those curses—i.e., that of the coming "Judgements of Fire"/"Day of Judgement"—that the *Pesher* here and in its finale calls down upon them (and "Gentiles" and "Idolators" generally). Viewed in its simplest terms, the allusion, therefore, threatens those "instructed" in the Liar's "works" with that same "Judgement"/"House of Judgement", which the *Pesher* earlier insisted would be executed via the hands of this "Elect of God"—CD, iv.3f.'s "Sons of Zadok". However it is viewed, these kinds of allusions, at least where the Liar is concerned, have little or nothing to do with the violent or "bloody" construction of an actual "city", but are almost always completely esoteric and ideological in nature.

For good measure, our commentator has added the condemnation on "instructing them in Lying works" (*ma'asei-Sheker*), which relates to that "Church" or "Congregation on Lying" which the Liar is "raising" and is, ideologically speaking, precisely the opposite kind of activity of that predicated of the Righteous Teacher. It is in connection with these "Lying works" that he invokes the "*'amal*" usage we have discussed above (and defined as "works with soteriological effect"). Had these "works" been full, not "empty", they might have saved them from these same "Judgements of Fire"/"Last Judgement".

Exploiting a transition in the underlying text where reference is made to "water . . . filling the earth with the Knowledge of the Glory of God" (Hab 2:14), the *Pesher* now moves back to events relating to the Wicked Priest, the death of the Righteous Teacher, and the destruction of the Temple and/or Jerusalem, all easily paralleled in events relating to James the Just's life and surviving traditions connecting his death to the fall of Jerusalem. So incensed is Origen over this last, which he claims to have seen in the version of Josephus available to him, a claim supported by Eusebius, that he cannot resist castigating Josephus for not connecting the fall of Jerusalem to Jesus' death, not James'![40]

The *Pesher*, while poorly preserved at this point, first relates these "waters" to the "Lying" activities presumably of "the Pourer"/"Spouter".

---

[40] Origen's outrage is probably not a little connected with the notice's disappearance in *all* extant versions of Josephus; however, once again, we have historical elements relating to James' death assimilating themselves retrospectively into the narrative of Jesus' death; cf. Origen, *Contra Celsum* 1.47, 2.13, and *Comm. in Matt.* 10.17 and Eusebius, *loc. cit.*; also Josephus' parallel comments in the extant *War* 4.5.2 in n. 35 above. See, too, how in the total portrayal of these events Josephus turns the "pollution of the Temple" charge back upon "the Zealots"/"Innovators" finally blaming them for the destruction of the Temple and Jerusalem just as in our view the Habakkuk *Pesher* blames Ananus, "the Liar", and such genre of individuals.

However, seizing on the reference to "knowing the Glory of God" noted above, it goes on to delineate this "water" imagery in terms of an ideologically opposite "revelation" of saving "Knowledge". The "*Da'at*" it invokes—also translatable as "*Gnosis*"—is a fundamental concept at Qumran. We have already signaled its relationship to the vocabulary and ideology of Is 53:11 when taken according to its literal sense, not to its superficial one, that is, "through the '*amal* of his soul ... and by his Knowledge (*Da'at*) will my Servant the Righteous One justify Many." The *Pesher* pictures this "Knowledge" as flowing over earth's creatures like "waters over the seas", imagery not unrelated to New Testament pictures of baptismal-like "descents of the Holy Spirit"—language not completely alien to the vocabulary of Hymns and the Community Rule.[41] It should be seen, too, as related to a certain extent to "Messianic" water imagery, itself associated with rain-making, "the Son of Man coming on the clouds of Heaven",[42] "raining Judgement on all the evil ones", (in Mt 5.45 "on the Just and Unjust" alike), and the Noachic-style destruction that was going to overwhelm these last—though the relationship here is indirect, not intrinsic.

The text now returns to its final description of the destruction of the sect's leadership by its second nemesis the Wicked Priest and the coming ultimate eschatological Judgement. It refers to a mysterious angry or

---

[41] 1QpHab, xi.1ff. CD, i.1 addresses itself to all those who "know Righteousness and understand the works of God" (cf. CD, ii.3ff.) and we encounter the same combination of "the Foundations of Knowledge and Wisdom" in 1QS, ii.3ff. The latter usages progress through baptismal imagery in iv.6ff. and iv.22 until the final passages in viii–x of such interest to us (in particular, viii.9, ix.17, x.9f., 13, and 25f.). Reference to "Knowledge" combined with baptismal and "Holy Spirit" allusions is omnipresent also in Hymns. For 1QpHab, xi.1ff. above, contrasting with "the waters of Lying" spouted by "the Deceiver" in the Damascus Document, this "Knowledge" will be revealed to the right-guided members of the Elect of the last times "like waters of the sea in overflowing abundance", imagery which moves easily into the *Gnosis* of succeeding centuries.

[42] We have called attention to this imagery in 1QM, xi.7ff. and Ja 5 above. For the combination of the themes of Noachic destruction by flood and the Judgement coming on the clouds of Heaven, see Mt 24:37 comparing the coming of the Son of Man to the days of Noah. This is further alluded to in 24:17, Mk 13:15, and Lk 17:27ff. and 21:21, ending with the allusion from Daniel of "the Son of Man coming in clouds with great Power and Glory". Mt adds: "And he shall send forth his angels with a great sound of a trumpet and gather together his elect from the four winds ... " The statement that "this generation shall not pass away till all these things be accomplished" has relevance, as we have seen, to the expression of the disappointment of such hopes in 1QpHab, vii.10ff.'s exposition of Hab 2:3. Mt 24:36's avowal that "Heaven and Earth shall pass away but my words shall not pass away", is developed with more precision in Mt 5:18 about "not one jot or tittle of the Law" passing away, and relates to Gos Th 11f., which itself is tied up with the pre-existent nature of "the Zaddik" of Pr 10:25—developed so straightforwardly in both Hymns and *Zohar*, i, 53b's discussion of "Noah".

violent confrontation between the Wicked Priest and the Righteous Teacher. This confrontation relates to or is presented in conjunction with problems surrounding *Yom Kippur* observances. Because of its language, it has never adequately been explained by any theory of Qumran origins.

It would not be surprising if this confrontation was simply anonymous and not documented in the sources available to us. However, even here elements do link up, however tenuously, to traces of events conserved in our sources. As we have seen in our Introduction, early Church sources are unanimous in testifying to James' Atonement activities on the Temple Mount. Both Epiphanius and Jerome make it clear that these appear to have transpired in the course of a single day and in some manner involved James' entering the Holy of Holies. If accurate, they must be seen as relating to *Yom Kippur* devotions of some kind, sectarian or otherwise.

Continuing this catalog of known information regarding James in this crucial period, Epiphanius also pictures James as *kneeling* to make an Atonement of some kind—before God's Presence—until "his knees became hard as camel's hide". Eusebius conserves the "kneeling" and "camel's hide" elements of this testimony, but prefers the more general reference to "Temple" or "Sanctuary". These astonishing notices, despite their vividness, have been dismissed as pure fantasy, as we have seen. For his part, Josephus testifies that James was tried before a Pharisaic/Sadducean Sanhedrin on a charge of blasphemy, that is, pronouncing or causing others to pronounce the forbidden name of God. Together with some of his colleagues (the plural note is important for the presentation of events in the Habakkuk *Pesher*), he was stoned.

In our view, this judicial murder was connived at by *both* Agrippa II and Ananus—a position which will receive some support, even if oblique, in the *Pesher*—and it is related to earlier confrontations in the Temple, confrontations also discernible through the highly refracted presentations of both the Pseudoclementine *Recognitions* and Acts surrounding the matters we have been following in this study, most notably the "Temple Wall" incident and attempts to bar both Agrippa I and Agrippa II from the Temple *as foreigners*. In our view, James' entry into the Holy of Holies, however improbable it might at first appear, constituted a proper "Zadokite" Atonement based on his "Noachic" nature, i.e., a "Man *Zaddik Tamim*" or "Perfectly Righteous in his generation", and at least makes the "blasphemy" aspect of this charge more comprehensible.[43]

---

[43] Cf. *Ant.* 20.9.1f. The narrative in Eusebius, Jerome, etc., *loc. cit.*, about James falling from the balustrade or pinnacle of the Temple, only to be stoned outside the walls, is

The *Pesher*, which turns on the reference to "Wrath" and "feast days" in the underlying text, discusses how "the Wicked Priest pursued the Righteous Teacher to confound" or "destroy him with his angry wrath at the house of his retreat" (or "at the house where he was discovered"; xi.4ff.). The usage "*leval'o*" (xi.5) does not appear in the underlying text, but it indicates strong action, and as it is used in a seemingly violent context, signifies "destroy", not "confuse" as some render it. When linked to the esoteric understanding of Belial/Balaam as "consumer of the People" (developed in the Appendix), this signification is dramatic. It triggers the much vexed reference to "*abeit galuto*" which, while defective, is usually translated as "House of his Exile".

The latter notice, in particular, is obscure, probably the most obscure in the *Pesher*. If, nevertheless, we attempt to fit it into the events we are discussing, it can be thought of with little difficulty as referring to a physical "exile" or "retreat" outside of Jerusalem as at Qumran. However, since the evocation of it is followed by a parallel allusion to "a rest period" associated with *Yom Kippur* observances, and since all of these events appear to transpire "in Jerusalem" (xii.7), it can with equal merit be thought of as simply referring to a *Yom Kippur* retirement of some kind, i.e., that the Wicked Priest pursued him "in order to destroy [or consume] him with his furious wrath at the house where he retired" (to observe the fast) or "was concealed". Taken in this sense, it need not refer to a physical locale outside of Jerusalem at all.

But when taken according to another of its root meanings, i.e., "uncovering" or "discovering", it could with even more sense be read to refer to "the house where he was discovered". This, in fact, is how in the first instance we thought to read it, i.e., as relating in some manner to James' arrest (as we shall see below, if the *juridical* sense of the usage "*zamam*", which follows in xii.6, is taken into consideration and the various "his"/*o*'s attached to *Beit-Galut* carefully analyzed, then the expression can be thought of as referring not only to James' arrest, but also to his *trial* which follows). We shall see in the article on "Interpreting

---

a conflation of two separate attacks on James, one by "the Enemy" in the 40s—perhaps related to the attempt by "Simon" to have Agrippa I barred from the Temple as a foreigner—and the other by Ananus (our "Wicked Priest") in the 60s, which did result in James' stoning. The first, as reported in Ps *Rec* 1.70f., did involve a "fall" from the Temple stairs in which James broke either one or both of his legs (such vivid details are not ignored with impunity; cf. the suspiciously similar "fall" "Judas Iscariot" takes in Acts 1:25f.). The detail about a "fuller" smashing James' skull would appear to relate to material in *M. Sanh* 9.6 concerning the similar punishment reserved for a priest serving at the altar "in a state of uncleanness".

Abeit-Galuto", this idea of a judicial trial of James will actually be found in the expression itself and reinforced by similar notices about "the High Priest's House" in the Gospels and the Sanhedrin in the *Talmud*.

The note about "appearing to them during the period of their *Yom Kippur* observance to consume them and cause them to desecrate the fast day of their sabbath rest" (xi.7f.) relates to the plural "them"/"their" and may or may not involve the same events as the pursuit and attack on the Righteous Teacher preceding it above, though the use of "*leval'o*"/ "*leval'am*" is common to both. The confusion surrounding these references to "Sabbath"s, "Feast"s, "*Yom Kippur*", etc. has given rise to considerable discussion about calendrical differences between Qumran and Jerusalem. As in the instance of the "disgusting" or "horrible contagions" allusion, since the notices are obscure, their meaning will probably never be completely known to us. Where "*abeit-galuto*", however, is concerned, two clear themes do emerge: that of some kind of confrontation probably involving the arrest and leading to the destruction of the teacher and some of his comrades, and that of a desecration of the sect's *Yom Kippur* observances (whether different from those of the Wicked Priest or the same).

Strengthening our view of an arrest and consonant destruction—not simply verbal "confusion"—the theme of "destruction" is further developed in the conclusion of the *Pesher* where "the Simple of Judah doing *Torah*"/"the Poor" are the subject (and where it is expressed quite straightforwardly as "*lechalah*"/"*lechalot*" and linked to the "*zamam*" we noted above, i.e., "intrigue"—even *judicial intrigue*; xii.2ff.). However, even before this in xi.15, it can be readily ascertained from the manner in which "*teval'enu*" is turned around and applied to *the fate of the Wicked Priest* instead of that of the Righteous Teacher and his companions, that our initial description of "*leval'o*"/"*leval'am*" as connotative of "destruction", not "confusion"/verbal confrontation, was correct. The exegesis in xi.11ff. turns on the reference "to the Cup of the Lord's right hand" in Hab 2:16. In this context, the *Pesher* also accuses the Wicked Priest of "not circumcizing the foreskin of his heart" (xi.13). As we have seen above, this allusion from the context of "the Zadokite Covenant" in Ezek 44:9 relates to the barring of *both* "those uncircumcized in heart and those uncircumcized in body" from the precincts of the Temple. When applied to a *Jewish High Priest*, it not only has the force of disqualifying him from Temple service in specifically "Zadokite" terms, but is of the utmost import *vis-à-vis* the difficulties and confrontations between "Innovators" and Herodians in the Temple and elsewhere at the root of the problems we have been discussing throughout this study.

The force of these allusions to "his wrath" (cf. how "*hamato*" is tied to "*abeit-galuto*" in xi.6 above), "Cup", and "destroying him" (*teval'enu*) is turned against "the Wicked Priest" in xi.14f. Since the thrust of the allusion to the Lord's "Cup of Wrath" is one of Divine Vengeance and retribution for the destruction of the Righteous Teacher[44] (as the *Pesher* itself puts the proposition in the next section referring to the destruction of "the Poor": "as he himself criminally conspired to destroy the Poor, so will God condemn him to destruction"/"he shall be paid the reward which he himself tendered the Poor"), the sense of "*teval'enu*" here, and as a consequence that of "*leval'o*"/"*leval'am*" earlier, is certainly that of "destruction"—in this instance Divine Destruction.

In xi.13f. the phrase "walking in his Way of satiation" or "in the Way of drinking his fill" is usually translated in terms of alleged "drunkenness" on the part of the Wicked Priest. But the allusion has nothing whatever to do with "drunkenness" except figuratively (in the sense of "drinking the cup of his own" or "the Lord's wrath"—a mistake typical of the approach of Qumran research to these matters). Rather it parodies the proper "Zadokite" stress on "walking in the Way of Uprightness" or "Perfection of the Way" and relates to the "Cup" and "Wrath" imagery in the underlying text in continuation of the theme of violent retribution. It expresses how the Wicked Priest, in "sating" his "own wrath" upon the Righteous Teacher (xi.5f.) would himself taste from the "Cup" of the Lord's Divine "Wrath" (xi.14; cf. Rev 14:10 on "His Cup of Anger" in precisely this vein).

The idea that the Wicked Priest "*criminally* conspired to destroy the Poor" (italics mine—"*zamam lechalot Ebionim*") adds a more indirect or "judicial" dimension, as we have noted, to these "*leval'o*"/"*leval'am*" charges—therefore perhaps their seeming obscurity. We have already placed James at the center of difficulties in the Temple between "Zealots"—cf. Acts 21:20 on the majority of James' "Jerusalem Church" supporters—and "Herodians", particularly where so-called "gifts from foreigners" were concerned. The meaning of "*zamam*" is completely in

---

[44] Cf. 4QpPs 37, ii.12ff. and iv.7ff. Note that here the '*Arizei-Go'im* take vengeance for the Righteous Teacher who has already been violently done to death by the Wicked Priest. As noted, we identify these '*Arizei-Go'im* (who are not necessarily the same as the '*Arizim* in the *Pesher*) with those renegade Herodian "Men-of-War" like Silas, Niger of Perea, and Philip son of Jacimus, all formerly intimates of Agrippa II, who first support the Uprising and are later either consumed by or desert it. One should also note that in this *Pesher* the Man of Lying once again "leads Many astray with words of Lying" (*Sheker*; i.18f.), God executes Judgement (*Mishpat*) on the Wicked Priest through "the hands of the Violent Ones of the Gentiles" (ii.21; in our view identical with Josephus' mysterious "Idumaeans"), and "Lebanon" imagery also occurs (iv.13).

keeping with that conspiracy we mentioned above between Agrippa II and Ananus to effect the removal of James.

But it also carries another more "judicial" sense relating to "bearing false witness" or "perjury", which brings us back to Josephus' picture of the Sanhedrin proceedings Ananus pursued against James and his companions and is particularly appropriate to Josephus' report that "the most equitable citizens" protested against the "breach of the Law" implicit in them. If we now view the phrase "*be-cha'as hamato abeit-galuto*" ("with *his* angry wrath at *his* house of exile"—italics mine) in the context of these proceedings, apply it *to Ananus, not James* (i.e. "the *beit*-expletive" of Ananus), the "*abeit-galuto*" can be seen as an insulting circumlocution relating to these proceedings which the sectaries would not dignify with the title of either a "*Beit-din*" or "*Beit-mishpat*". The whole then translates more logically: "The Wicked Priest ... pursued the Righteous Teacher to destroy him in *his* hot anger in *his* guilty trial" or "in *his* guilty house" (italics mine). It is certainly remarkable that, when the obscurity surrounding such notices is parted only a little, so much good sense can be made of them in the context even of *known* historical events and traditions relating to James. We will see this completely borne out in the "*Abeit-Galuto*" article later in this book.

The text now draws to a close with an analysis that turns on references to "the Violence done to Lebanon", "the destruction of the dumb beasts", and "the Violence done to the land" in the underlying text (Hab 2:17). The allusion to "Lebanon" also is to be found in the ambiance of the Is 3:10–11 materials applied to James' death in early Church tradition. In fact, as we shall also see, these materials are actually employed in the *Pesher* to describe how the Righteous Teacher and his followers among "the Poor" *dumb beasts* are "destroyed" by the Wicked Priest. It is subjected to exegesis in several other Qumran documents, most notably 4QpIs[a] on Is 10:33f.[45] In Qumran exposition, it almost always carries an esoteric sense connected to a play on the root meaning of "white" relating either to the Community Council or the Temple—according to 1QS metaphor and to a certain extent Paul in 1 Co above these are, in effect, the same.

This play on words parallels that already encountered in the Qumran exegesis of "Zadok"/"*Zaddik*" and its further extensions in "*Moreh*

---

[45] Cf. 1QpHab, xii.2ff. with 4QpIs[c] on 14:8ff. and on Zech 11:11/Is 30:1ff., 4QpNah, i.7, and 4QpIs[a] on 10:33f. That in these various Qumran contexts the expression "Lebanon" is interpreted to variously mean, the Community Council, the Temple, etc., should not be too surprising in view of the identification of the Council with the Temple in the context of spiritualized atonement imagery in 1QS, viii.1ff.

ha-Zedek" and "Melchizedek". Here, however, the text unhesitatingly—as in the case of *Zaddik* with *Moreh ha-Zedek* at the beginning of the *Pesher*—identifies "Lebanon" as "the Council of the Community" (xii.4f.). Not only does this mean the one at Qumran, but in our view that of "the Jerusalem Church" as well. In 4QpIs^a, although the text is somewhat damaged, "Lebanon" appears to represent the Temple and/or Priestly Establishment, but there also appears to be some mention of the community in the form of "the Poor" (here *Dallim/'Anayyei-Arez*) amid a barrage of Messianic imagery.[46] In 4QpIs^c on Is 14:8, "Lebanon" again appears to be the Community Council, while on Zech 11:11/Is 30:1–5 we have a parallel to one of the classic *Talmudic* references to the 70 CE fall of the Temple.[47]

---

[46] The allusion to "Lebanon" in Is 10:34 is followed by the famous "Messianic" material in 11:1ff. This is interpreted in strict Messianic manner as relating to "the Branch of David who will arise at the end of days", smite the earth with the rod of his mouth, and judge all peoples with his sword. "Arise", here, is a translation of the Hebrew, *ha-'amod*, "who will stand up". If we are correct in considering this usage to carry something of the sense of "be resurrected" in the Damascus Document, then this exegesis coincides even more closely with parallel notions known to early Christianity. An alternative translation would, therefore, run something like: "At the End of Days, the Branch of David will be resurrected and judge the Poor and the Meek with Righteousness, etc." In addition to *Lam. R*, ii.3.6, see xxiv of the prologue applying this very word *'amod* to the "Messianic" return of Moses.

[47] See *ARN* 4, where in the context of delineating R. Yohanan's attempt to recommend himself as a "friend" to the Emperor (note the similar legend, "friend of Caesar" or "friend of the Romans", on the coins of Herod of Chalcis and his son Aristobulus the husband of Herodias' daughter Salome in this period—Agrippa I even published himself, not without a little hyperbole, as "King Agrippa Great Lover of Caesar"), "Lebanon" is emphatically interpreted in terms of the fall of the Temple in 70 CE. The two passages cited in this regard, Is 10:34 and Zech 11:1, both find their parallels in extant Qumran materials; cf. 4QpIs^c on Zech 11:11/Is 30:1ff.

For additional *Talmudic* references of this nature, see *b. Gitt* 56a including Is 10:33f. and *b. Yoma* 39b including Zech 11:1 and Nah 1:4. For more general references see *b. Yoma* 21a. There is no indication that these passages were ever applied to a fall of the Temple prior to 70 CE. Curiously, it would appear that 4QpIs^c on Is 14:8ff. was also about to refer to Zechariah, but Allegro did not attempt a reconstruction. There also appears in Is 30:3 a reference to "*Ma'oz*" ("Strength" or "Fortress"), a title used in 1QH to refer to the redeeming activities of its author—probably the Teacher himself—and probably not unrelated to James' title of "*Oblias*", again in early Church literature "Protection of the People" or "Bulwark". Here, too, however, the *Pesher* is missing. Is 14:30 makes the ritual reference to the "*Ebionim*" and "*Dallim*", but the exegesis here is also missing. "*Ebionim*", "*Zaddik*", "*ma'asim*" ("works"), "*beit-Ya'acov*" ("House of Jacob"; cf. materials surrounding the "*Zaddik*"-passage in Is 3:10–11 that early Church literature applied to the death of James referring to "*beit-Ya'acov*" and "Lebanon") etc. also appear in another fragment of 4QpIs^c on Is 29:19ff.

Not only is it implied that the Wicked Priest destroyed the Community Council, i.e., "he shall be paid the reward which he himself tendered to the Poor", for which "God would condemn him [the Wicked Priest] to destruction"—here expressed quite straightforwardly as "*lechalah*"; xii.2ff.—but the ambiance is also that of the earlier "robbing the Poor of their substance" (xii.10). Not only did "the Wicked Priest" "criminally conspire to destroy the Poor" (including the note of "juridical intrigue" and/or "criminal conspiracy" discussed above), he is even said to have polluted the *Temple of God*".

Here, too, the actual words of Is 3:10–11 passage, applied to the death of James in early Church literature, "Woe unto the Wicked . . . the reward of his hands will be paid him", are incorporated into the *Pesher* on these passages from Hab 2:15–17, even though they nowhere appear in the underlying text. In all my work I have looked for these passages from Is 3:10–11 at Qumran. To find them reflected here at this critical juncture of the Habakkuk *Pesher* to describe the "reward that would be paid the Wicked Priest" for what he did to "the Poor" or "*Ebionim*" *proves*, as little else can, the identity of these Scriptural *milieu*s being applied both in the early Church to *the death of James* and at Qumran to *the Wicked Priest's destruction of the Righteous Teacher*.

As with regard to the problems circulating about the person of James, to which it is related, we have already placed this notice about "polluting the Temple" within the context of the controversy over admitting Herodians into the Temple and accepting gifts from foreigners and noted the constant reiteration of a parallel theme in the sections of the *War* leading up to Josephus' description of the demise of Ananus.[48] As one of the two main sins—the second is "*To'evot*"—the "Abominations" of his treatment of the Righteous Teacher and "destruction of the Poor"—for which the Wicked Priest is condemned, it cannot be underestimated. It is also reflected in the Damascus Document's "Three Nets of Belial" charges against the Jerusalem Establishment (the other two, it should be remembered, were *Riches* and *marrying nieces/divorce*, all with particular relevance where Herodians were concerned). It also relates to the "separation"/"pollution of the Temple" materials, invoking "*balla'*" or "Bela'" in 11QT, xlvif.

There can be little doubt that in this section of the Habakkuk *Pesher*, as in quite a few elsewhere in the *Pesharim*, the term "*Ebionim*", applied in

---

[48] See *War* 4.2.3ff. particularly 4.3.2, 4.3.7ff., 4.3.11, 4.3.13, 4.4.3, 4.5.2, etc. One should appreciate that the imagery, which also includes reference to "Traitors" and the like, as one would expect and parallel to the methodology of the New Testament, is usually inverted.

early Church usage to "Jewish Christians"—and by Paul to the Jerusalem Church—is specifically being applied by the Community to itself. Punctuating the point, it is employed *three times* in this section, though it nowhere appears in the underlying text of Habakkuk.[49] Once again, we can only consider this usage to be purposeful and further enhances the proofs or correspondences between the materials relating to the destruction of James in early Church sources and the materials relating to the destruction of the Righteous Teacher and his followers among "the Poor" here in the Habakkuk *Pesher*.

However *'Ani*, one of its parallels, probably best translated by the New Testament's "the Meek", does appear in Hab 3:14 and occurs in close proximity to the Is 3:10–11 passage which early Church testimony applies to the circumstances of James' death. *'Ani/'Anayyim* also appears together with another parallel *Dallim* in the Is 10:33f. "Lebanon" passage above. Like *Ebion/Ebionim* it is widespread in Qumran usage and sometimes even coupled with *Ebion*.[50] In this section of the *Pesher*, the *Ebionim* are identified with another group called "the Simple Ones of Judah doing Torah" ("*Peta'ei*-Yehudah *'oseh ha-Torah*").

This latter euphemism not only should be understood in terms of expressions in the New Testament like "these Little Ones" and "the *'Anayyei-Arez*" in 4QpIs[a] 15 above, but it occurs not insignificantly twice in an environment of familiar allusions to being "misled"/"led astray" and "joining" in 4QpNah, iii.5 and 7. In the first it is connected with the "Ephraim" circumlocution, i.e., "the Simple Ones of Ephraim [note the significant omission of xii.4f.'s "*'oseh ha-Torah*"/"doing *Torah*" when speaking about these "*Peta'ei*-Ephraim"] will forsake . . . those who mislead them and join themselves [*nilvu*] to Israel."

The reference to "*nilvu*" is crucial and clinches the entire presentation. Not only is it linked to the use of the parallel expression "*Nilvim*" in Es 10:27 as expressive of Gentiles "attaching themselves" to the Jewish Community (cf. the use of "*ger-nilveh*" carrying this sense in 4QpNah, ii.9) and in the *esoteric* exegesis of the Zadokite Covenant in CD, iv.3, but once again it brings all these imageries full circle providing definitive

---

[49] 1QpHab, xii.3 (again in conjunction with allusion to "Lebanon"), xii.6, and xii.10.

[50] See Hab 3:14; cf., as well Zech 11:7 and 11:11—the actual passage subjected to exegesis in 4QpIs[c], Is 3:14f. in proximity to the Is 3:10 passage above, and Is 14:29f. already noted in 4QpIs[c] above. See also Is 10:21ff. in 4QpIs[c] on "the remnant of Jacob", which includes references to "the Poor" and "Lebanon"; cf. as well, similar combinations of *Ebion* and *'Ani* in CD, vi.21 and xiv.13. For "*nephesh-Ebion*" and "*nephesh-'Ani*", both synonyms for the term "*nephesh-Zaddik*" in Is 53:11 (and CD, i.20), see 1QH, ii.32ff., iii.25, and v.18ff.

confirmation of the correctness of our original identification of "Ephraim" as Gentile God-Fearers "misled"/"led astray" by a more anti-nomian Pauline teacher. By linking these "Simple of Ephraim" with "the Seekers after Smooth Things . . . at the End of Time", the Nahum *Pesher* also provides support for our other historical thesis concerning the generic thrust of the latter usage as implying all "those seeking accommodation with foreigners", and that originally Qumran sectaries saw so-called "Pharisees" and "Pauline Christians" as part and parcel of the same alliance. Such evidence from a third independent textual context (in addition to that of 1QpHab and CD) provides important verification of what might have appeared on the surface a speculative suggestion and confirms as nothing else can the accuracy of our categorization of the "Ephraim" usage as relating inter alia to Pauline Christians.

Returning to the context of the Habakkuk *Pesher*, one can specify with a fair degree of precision that "the Poor" and "the Simple Ones" ("of Judah", not Ephraim), as used in xii.3ff., are more or less coequal appellations, except "the Poor" is a little more general and meant to include the Community Council or leadership as well. Conversely, "the Simple of Judah doing *Torah*", like the parallel "'*Osei ha-Torah*" in vii.11 and viii.1, probably was not meant to include the leadership as such, but rather only the rank and file—the beneficiaries of the justifying activities of the Council/Central Triad/Righteous Teacher in 1QS,viiiff. and 1QpHab, viii above. For the *Pesher*, "the dumb beasts" who are destroyed in the underlying text are "the Simple of Judah doing *Torah*". By implication, too, as in the exegesis both of Hab 2:3 and 2:4 above, the exegete wants us to understand that *they are not* "the Simple Ones" (cf. the term "Little Ones" in the New Testament) not of "Judah", i.e., *not non-Jews*—in the terms of the Nahum *Pesher*, not "the Simple Ones of Ephraim" unless they had in some prior manner specifically "joined" themselves to "Israel" or "the House of Judah" (cf. "'*Am 'im ger-nilveh*" in 4QpNah, ii.9).

This theme of "destruction" in the underlying text is applied in the exegesis to "the Poor", including and not exclusive of the Community Leadership, for which the Wicked Priest was to be specifically "condemned (by God) to destruction" (xii.5ff.). Not only does this last reference link up with language of Is 3:9–11, it also links the exegesis directly with that of the "Cup" of Divine Retribution and the plural destruction of the Righteous Teacher and some of his followers in xi preceding it, already considered above.

As used in xii.4f. above, "the Simple of Judah *doing Torah*" (italics mine) establishes a perfect and purposeful contrast with xii.8's description of the "acts" or "works" of the Wicked Priest as "*ma'asei-To'evot*" ("works of Abominations"). Since the latter usage is attached to the notice about "polluting the Temple of God" (xii.9), which we have also considered above, it is meant to be recapitulative of the earlier "Ways of *To'evot* . . . in all unclean *tum'ah*" in which the Wicked Priest acted "to heap guilt on himself" in viii.12f. The *Pesher* also relates this usage to "the Violence done to the land", etc. in the underlying text, which it will now proceed to interpret in terms of "robbing the Poor" in the villages round about Jerusalem and the destruction of the Teacher and some members of his Council. As noted above, we have already encountered the expression "doing *Torah*" ('*oseh ha-Torah*) in the exposition of Hab 2:4, where those who "*would be saved*" by their Faith in the "*Zaddik*"/"*Moreh ha-Zedek*" were specified as "*Torah*-Doers in the House of Judah" (meant also, as we can now see, to contrast with the "House of Ephraim"). In the exegesis of Hab 2:3 on "the Delay of the *Parousia*" preceding it, these "*Torah*-Doers" were instructed to wait patiently. Ja 5:7 (which earlier in 1:22ff. had thrice addressed itself to these same "Doers") counsels a similar eschatological patience under similar circumstances, and James 5:3's note about "gold and silver . . . in the last days" will now reappear in the underlying text from Hab 2:19f. about to be expounded in the concluding eschatological exegesis about the "Day of Judgement" in xiii.1ff.

For xii.7f. the Community Council is actually functioning in this period in Jerusalem, not Qumran, since "Jerusalem" is straightforwardly designated as the locale "where the Wicked Priest committed his Abominable works" against it (as well as "polluting the Temple"). Consequently, this "'*Azat ha-Yahad*" must be considered virtually indistinguishable from what goes in other contexts by the name of either "the Jerusalem Council" or "the Jerusalem Church". This is also the gist of what emerges in the Psalm 37 *Pesher* where "the Congregation" or "Assembly of the Poor in Jerusalem", which can also be referred to by the term "Church" or "*Ecclesia*", is also repeatedly evoked.

Again these kinds of "Abominable works" are meant to contrast with those "Righteous" ones or "*ma'asei-Torah*" predicated of the Righteous Teacher and so much a part of the ideological approach of the Letter of James. To summarize: "As he himself criminally conspired to destroy the Poor", that is, "in Jerusalem where (he) . . . committed his works of Abomination" and in "the cities of Judah where he robbed the Poor of their sustenance"[51]; so too would the Wicked Priest "be paid the reward

---

[51] 1QpHab, xii.9f. See above, pp. 138 and 161f. for how the servants of the High Priests robbed "the Poor" among the lower priests of their tithes and the reflection of this in the so-called "Zealot woes".

which he paid the Poor" and "be condemned (by God) to destruction."[52] Here too, then, is the incorporation of the language of Is 3:10–11, described above applied to the death of James in early Church literature.

That what is implied here is nothing other than the reward the Wicked Priest paid the Righteous Teacher and the members of his Council is also clear in the passage from Hab 2:17 underlying the exegesis:

> For the Violence done to Lebanon shall overwhelm you and the destruction of the dumb beasts shall terrify you because of the Blood of Man ["Adam"] and the Violence done to the township, and all its inhabitants.

Here, "Lebanon" is specifically identified as "the Community Council"; "the Violence done to Lebanon" is the stoning of James and some of his associates in 62 CE as reported in Josephus and variously reflected in early Church sources as we have seen above—the "whitening" imagery purposely evoking the *white linen they wore* and their purported sinlessness; "the dumb beasts" are "the Simple Jews" or "the *Ebionim* of Jerusalem" variously referred to as "Jewish Christians", "the Jerusalem Church", and referred to in Ro 15:26, 16:18, Ga 2:10, Ja 2:2ff. etc.; "the Blood of Men"—here the allusion is real and is overtly so designated in the *Pesher* because we are speaking about the rapine and murder remounting *directly* to the Wicked Priest, not the Spouter of Lying—refers once again to James and his associates on the Community Council (cf. ix.9ff. above); and "the Violence done to the land", etc., is the "polluting the Temple" both with the violence done to James and others and by admitting and accepting gifts from *Herodians* and other foreigners along with the concomitant robbing of the tithes of the Poor Priests in the cities of Judea outside Jerusalem, so vividly described in Josephus' several references.[53]

---

[52] 1QpHab, xii.5ff.; the "abominable works" (*ma'asei-To'evot*) of the Wicked Priest referred to in xii.8 are the counterpart of the "Righteous" ones, or the "*ma'asei-Zedek*" of the teacher whom he destroys; cf. how the same terminologies, "Abomination" (relating to his "Violence") and "pollution" (relating to his Temple desecration), are reflected in the earlier description of "the Ways" of the Wicked Priest in viii.12f. These themes of "*To'evot*" (Abominations) and "*tum'a*" (pollution) also dominate the Temple Scroll.

[53] It is clear from the context that some of the members of the Council—referred to as well here as "the Poor"—share the fate of the Righteous Teacher; cf. *Ant* 20.9.1 where James and some others close to him are all condemned to death. This was, of course, stated explicitly in ix.9ff. The whole exegesis is paralleled in 4QpPs 37, which also combines repeated allusions to the "*Zaddik*"/"*Zaddikim*" with the repeated allusions to "the Congregation" or "Church of the Poor", '"*Anavim*", "*Ebionim*", "*Tamimim*", Lebanon, "*Ma'oz*", etc. As in 1QpHab, the Community Council is described as "doing the Law" ('*oseh ha-Torah*, with an accent on "doing"; ii.22), and it is clear that they (referred to as well as "the Community of the Poor") share to a certain extent the fate of the teacher—here, also, referred to as "the Priest", meaning, "the High Priest".

Where the "Lebanon shall fall by a mighty one" allusion is concerned in 4QpIs[a], one encounters many themes even in the extant text paralleling those of Hab 1–2, including the conquest by oncoming *Kittim*, the allusions to "the Meek", "Downtrodden", etc., together with an additional one, "the rising of David at the End of Days"—including the use of the telltale "'*amod*", i.e., "standing up"—in a similar, if albeit fragmentary, exegesis. Even more significantly, however, as in the case of the exegesis of Hab 2:4, we have incontrovertible evidence from independent sources—in this instance *Talmudic*—that this "Lebanon" passage in Is 10:33f. *was* being subjected to exegesis in the latter part of the first century and *was* applied to the fall of the Temple in 70 CE. The same is true of Zech 11:11/Is 30:1–5.[54]

The sentence, "the Wicked watches out for the Righteous and seeks to slay him", in 4QpPs 37, ii.12 and iv.7 is completely paralleled by 1QpHab, i.11f., CD, i.20f. (note that at this point the Damascus Document is stringing together materials from Is 30 and a "*Zaddik*"-allusion from Ps 94:21), and Is 3:10. In so far as the "'*Arizei-Go'im*" ("Violent Ones of the Gentiles") in 4QpPs 37, ii.21 and iv.10 are to be identified with the "'*Arizim*" in the Habakkuk *Pesher*, they also must be connected, as we have seen, with the Lying Spouter and "Covenant-Breaking". In 1QpHab, ii.6 the "'*Arizim*" are described "as not believing what they heard from the mouth of the Priest" concerning the Last Times, that is, they were privy to his exegeses.

As we have seen in n. 44 above, they are to be identified with quite a few Herodian Men-of-War, including "Niger", "Silas", "Philip", even Queen Helen's relatives, Monobazus and Kenedaeos, who along with "John the Essene" are among the uprising's bravest military commanders; cf. *War* 2.20.4 and 3.2.1. Niger of Perea is an important leader of Josephus' "Idumaeans" (according to our interpretations, pro-Revolutionary "Herodians") who are seen by the exegete as the instruments of God's retribution on Ananus. Niger is finally caught up in factional division and undergoes public execution at the hands of the Revolutionary crowds, the atmosphere surrounding which (perhaps not completely coincidentally) is very similar to that portrayed in the New Testament surrounding *the execution of Jesus.*

[54] In the fragment relating to Is 14:8–30, once again one has "Lebanon" mentioned in the context of a reference to "the *Dallim*" and "*Ebionim*" which seems to have so appealed to the sectaries. In fact if one makes a list of the incidences of these kinds of words in the Prophets and Psalms, one will find that one has probably inadvertently stumbled on the actual method used by Qumran exegetes in choosing scriptural texts. "Lebanon" is to be found in Is 2:13 (in proximity to the 3:10–11 material applied to James' death), 10:34, 14:8, 29:17, 33:9, 35:2, 37:24, 40:16, 60:13, Nah 1:4, Zech 10:10, 11:1, and Hab 2:17. The words, "Poor" and "Meek", either represented by "*Ebion*", "'*Ani*", or "*Dal*", are to be found in Is 3:14f., 10:2, 10:30, 11:4, 14:30f., 25:4ff., 29:19, 32:7, 41:17, 58:7, 66:2, and Zech 11:7ff. Almost every one of these passages where the two usages have been found in conjunction has been subjected to exegesis in extant materials at Qumran. If we include the Is 3:10 passage above, known to have been subjected to exegesis with regard to the events of James' life, then the passages where such correspondences occur are virtually exhausted.

Whether the exegesis of these passages parallels the *Talmudic* in *every* respect is not the crucial issue—nor is it where Pauline exegesis of Hab 2:4 is concerned—and impossible to say in all cases because of the imperfect preservation of some *pesharim*. What is, however, important is that "Lebanon" imagery *was being* associated with the fall of the Temple in 70 CE. There is not the slightest evidence from any other source that exegesis of this kind was applied to any previous fall of the Temple, or, as we have emphasized, that such exegesis was even being practiced prior to about 30 CE in any systematic manner, that is to say, roughly the time of the appearance of the Messianic Movement and the last stage of Period II of Qumran habitation. In the face of such persuasive historical and textual evidence for the *sitz im leben* of the Habakkuk *Pesher*, one must be able to present substantive evidence from another source to controvert it, but this cannot be done (nor should one expect in the face of the numerous connections to events and proof texts of this period we have already been able to show that it could be done).

The *Pesher* ends poignantly—in view of the historical circumstances which form its *sitz im leben*—and appropriately enough, in terms of the ideological concerns and internecine disputes which characterized its previous subject matter, with an outright and fulsome condemnation of all "Gentiles" (*Go'im*) and "the idols they serve" (xii.12ff.). We are to understand that these "idols" include not only those "served" by the present destroyers of Jerusalem and the Temple, i.e., the Romans (including their omnipresent standards), but also that "idolatry" implicit in the Spouter's "Lying" activities and in the acceptance of sacrifices and gifts on behalf of Herodians (considered here as Gentiles) and other foreigners in the Temple. These "idols" would "not be able to save them on the Day of Judgement" (*Yom ha-Mishpat*). The use of the verb, "*yazzilum*" here is purposeful. It parallels the use of "*yazzilem*" in the earlier Hab 2:4 exegesis reversing its signification because it is now talking about *idolatrous Gentiles* not "*Torah*-Doing Jews". It also provides absolute confirmation that our initial characterization of the earlier use of "*yazzilem*" in the *Pesher* (and by implication the use of the mysterious "*Beit ha-Mishpat*" connected to it) as *eschatological* was correct, because in the present textual context the use of "*yazzilum*" and the "*Yom ha-Mishpat*", to which it is tied, are undoubtedly eschatological. Just as in viii.1ff. it was only "the Doers of *Torah*" in "the House of Judah" whom God "would save" from "the House of Judgement", here all idolatrous "Gentiles" are being condemned—as well as, as we shall see in xiii.4, "backsliding Jews".

The use, too, of the word "*le'ovdam*", "to serve them" in xii.13 and its slightly varied repetition in xiii.2's "served" and xiii.3's "Servants", is also not without a touch of irony. It is of particular import where the presumed idolatrous "City built upon Blood" by the Lying Spouter who "tires out Many with worthless work [service, *'avodat-shavo*] and teaches them works of Lying" in x.11f. is concerned, and the implications of such usage are fully set forth in the portrait of "the Spirit of *'Avlah* . . . and slackness in the service of Righteousness" in 1QS, iv.9ff. As with the implied parallel between the use of "gold and silver" in the underlying text from Hab 2:18 and the "gold and silver" in the eschatological Judgement section of James 5:3 above, the underlying text from Hab 2:19 also contains a somewhat obscure note about "Lying" (*Sheker*, variously rendered as "Teacher of Lying", "Lying images", or the like) which links up with the "*ma'asei-Sheker*" ("acts" or "works of Lying") aspect of the above references.

The allusion to "*Yom ha-Mishpat*"/"Day of Judgement", is repeated in the repetition of the condemnation on "all the Gentiles" in the conclusion of the *Pesher* (xiii.1ff.) and, because of the parallelism of its language and the sense of the exegesis, completely validates our earlier translation of the phrase "House of Judgement" as synonymous with this "Day of Judgement" (while the former has more the connotation of the actual *decision* of "Judgement"; the latter is more connotative of the event itself). The vision of this "Judgement" is broadened to include "idolators" generally, i.e. "the Servants of Graven Images"—cf. Paul's contempt for "the Servants of Righteousness" in 2 Co 11:15—and "Evil Ones" generally (*Resha'im*), which must be seen as inclusive of Jews like the paradigmatic "*Chohen ha-Rasha'*" who "deserted the Law" and/or "Covenant" or who served it "only when convenient".

Here the verb used to express this hope for the rendering of such eschatological Judgement in xiii.3, "*yechaleh*", is the same as that "*lechalah*"/"*lechalot*" used in xii.5f. to express the vengeance that God would visit upon the Wicked Priest for his "destruction of the Poor". The inclusion in this "Judgement" of these "*Resha'im*"—meaning primarily backsliding *Jews*—in addition to "idolatrous Gentiles", completely parallels that "Judgement" which God would pronounce "by the hand of His Elect" on both "the Gentiles"—primarily those *Kittim* presently destroying the land and their "Pauline"/Herodian confrères—and "*the Wicked of His Own People* who kept the Law only when convenient" in v.3ff. (italics mine; here too the verb employed to express the withholding of *complete* "destruction" from "His Own People" is the usual "*yechaleh*").

The text ends, as with the Letter of James it so much resembles and the earlier discussion of "the Delay of the *Parousia*", on a pious note of quiet confidence, which could not contrast more with the debacle occurring at the present moment, a debacle itself the ostensible reason for its composition. Delivered in exposition of Hab 2:20's equally pious underlying sentiment, "The Lord is in His Holy Temple; let all the earth be still before Him", it expresses the apocalyptic and—given the *sitz im leben*, poignantly optimistic expectation that "on the Day of Judgement God will destroy from off the earth all those serving idols and all the Evil Ones".

III
THE ARCHAEOLOGICAL EVIDENCE

We can, as should by now be clear, account in our theory for almost every allusion, every sentence, even almost every turn of phrase in the Habakkuk *Pesher*. We can, in addition, put them into real historical settings relating to real and important people contemporary with the fall of the Temple about 70 CE when the scrolls were supposed to have been put into the caves and when parallel exegeses were circulating relating to Hab 2:4 and "Lebanon" imagery in Prophets and Psalms. There is no other theory of Qumran origins or identifications which can achieve as much. The verification of any good scientific theory is that it can elicit more from the data than was previously known without it. This is certainly the case with the desecration of the Wicked Priest's "corpse", the discussion of the two terms, "House of Exile" and "House of Judgement", and the incorporation of the language of Is 3:9–11—applied to James' death in early Church literature—into the *Pesher* on Hab 2:15–17 on the destruction of the Righteous Teacher and "the Poor".

What then holds or has held scholars back from arriving at such identifications? Since, where the Habakkuk *Pesher* is concerned, paleography is not an important issue, aside from an ideological predisposition *not to arrive at such results*—in some instances even a "psychological" one or spiritual one—the only real impediment has been the archaeology of Qumran. Even though it, too, was based on many of these same psychological and ideological predispositions, many scholars adhered to this archaeology as if it presented an insurmountable barrier.

If, even accepting the validity of Qumran archaeological theory as it presently stands, one were required to account for the whole expanse of Qumran literature on the basis of our presentation, it would not be difficult. It is possible to identify a series of martyred *"Zaddikim"* beginning with Onias the son of Simeon the *Zaddik*. Judas Maccabee,[1] Honi the Circle-Drawer,[2] his grandson Hanan the Hidden,[3] John the Baptist (if not identical to Hanan the Hidden),[4] Jesus,[5] James, etc., are all identified in one way or another as "*Zaddikim*" in the extant literature. However, in the particular instance of the Habakkuk *Pesher*, recourse to the broader implications of such theorizing is not necessary because the identifications we propose fit very comfortably into the present confines of Qumran archaeological and paleographic theory and the internal data.[6]

[1] I have covered the subject of Judas as *Zaddik* in MZCQ (Chapter 1), pp. 13f., 32f. and 57–61.

[2] We have already discussed Honi the Circle-Drawer above in relation to rain-making, Josephus, calling him "Onias the Just", identifies him (in our view definitively) as a *Zaddik*/"Righteous Man" in *Ant.* 14.2.1. Cf. also *b. Ta'an* 23a.

[3] We have also discussed Hanan *ha-Nehba* above in relation to rain-making. The "Hidden" theme associated with his person was also an element in Josephus' description of his grandfather Onias. This theme is also discernible in Lk 1:24's description of John the Baptist's mother "Elizabeth" who "hid herself" and in the Protevangelium of James 18:1, where Elizabeth "hides" John in a mountain cave when Herod tries to destroy him. For the *Zohar*, i, 63a and 67b, Noah "was hidden" by God in the ark in order to escape both someone it calls "the Adversary" and the impending eschatological Flood. "Cave-dwelling" is also an important theme of both the "*redivivus*" and "rain-making" traditions.

[4] John, of course, is identified as a "Righteous One" who "came in the Way of Righteousness" in Mt 21:32 and Mk 6:20; in these accounts it is always foreigners, Herodians, or Roman Governors who properly recognize "Zaddikim". Josephus, too, in his capsule description of John's baptism and death in *Ant.* 18.5.2, implies that John enjoyed such a status. For Josephus, John is teaching what Justin Martyr calls the "all Righteousness" doctrine (cf. Mt 3:15), characterized by the dichotomy of "*Hesed*" and "*Zedek*", i.e., the Piety commandment of "loving God" and the Righteousness commandment of "loving one's neighbor as oneself", the latter evolving into notions of economic equality and poverty. Justin Martyr treats these matters in *Dial.* 23, 47 and 93. Not only do they form the backbone of Josephus' long description of "Essene" doctrine in *War* 2.8.2ff., but also his short note about Essenes in *Ant.* 15.10.5. Josephus also applies these categories to the person of Simeon the *Zaddik* in *Ant.* 12.2.5. They are also presented as forming the essence of Jesus' teaching in Mt 22:34ff. and Mk 12:28ff. and are set forth in no uncertain terms as "the two Ways" in the first section of the *Didache* 1.1.

[5] Acts refers to Jesus repeatedly as "the Just One" or "*Zaddik*". Paul, as we have seen, in 1 Co 15:3, introducing his version of post-resurrection appearances, reveals his familiarity with the "Justification" ideal based on the ideology of Is 53:11f. and implies that he learned it in *Jerusalem*. More importantly, Ja 5:4 in discussing matters relating to the Messianic return and the condemnation of "the Rich" leading up to its evocation of eschatological "rain" imagery, knows that "the Just One" was done to death. But unlike Paul in 1 Thess—who blames the Jews—it, probably more accurately, *blames the Rich* for this murder.

[6] Milik, p. 64, categorically placed 1QpHab in the mid or late first century CE, insisting it "could not come from any part of the first century BC". We have already noted the range of opinion concerning its "secure" Herodian dating above. On internal data alone,

Since the advance, as we have emphasized, of "the *Kittim*" and the imminent destruction of "the Last Priests of Jerusalem" were for the *Pesher* events in progress, not necessarily completed, there is no reason why it could not have been written in 68 CE.

Even more germane to our purposes, most scholars have arrived at a date for the fall of the monastery on the basis of their interpretations of coin data, a fragile tool under the best conditions. The date, however, at which they have arrived for the fall of the monastery and the deposit of the scrolls in the caves—which they envision as simultaneous events—is 68 CE. But this is not the latest possible date for either of these two events, but simply the earliest one, that is, it is not a *terminus ad quem* but a *terminus a quo*—unless these two *termini* are identical which is, of course, the implication of their theories. In particular, if we are talking only about "the fall of the monastery", this date says nothing about the cessation of *Jewish* habitation around the area of the site.[7]

For these purposes, it is important, as we have shown, to distinguish between cessation of habitation *at* or *around* and the destruction of buildings *on* a given site. Though the buildings at Qumran may have been destroyed in 68 CE, or even some years later, habitation in the area, particularly at Ein Feshka, did not come to an end until after the Bar Kochba Uprising in 134–36 CE. The actual *terminus ad quem*, therefore, for the deposit of the scrolls in the caves at Qumran—if not the *destruction* of its buildings—is 136.

R. de Vaux, who along with his colleagues J. T. Milik and F. M. Cross, did more than anyone else to establish the consensus that presently surrounds these issues, was sometimes (though not often) willing to admit these technicalities.[8] Despite this, many of his conclusions were rather

---

however, including its exegesis of Hab 2.4, its presentation of what generally goes by the name of "the Delay of the *Parousia*", its use of the terminology of Is 53:11 in its eschatological exegesis of Hab 2:4, its reference to "the Last Priests of Jerusalem" in the context of its discussions about the death of the Righteous Teacher, its use of "the Poor" terminology to refer to his community, and its eschatological use of the language of "the Last Times" and "the Day of Judgement", one can assert with a fair degree of certitude that *Habakkuk is late*.

[7] This has particular relevance when groups are following a "Rechabite" or "wilderness" life-style as at Qumran.

[8] De Vaux, to his credit, states, p. 41: "It is perfectly true that strictly speaking the coins only provide a *terminus post quem*"; but sometimes he drops his diplomatic approach and states categorically, as on p. 112: "The community installed itself at Qumran in the second half of the second century BC. It abandoned the site for a period of some thirty years during the reign of Herod the Great, and definitively left the area in 68 CE." No wonder the greater part of his followers take this for a *terminus ad quem* and not the *terminus post quem* he admits it is above. Here Cross in "The Oldest Manuscripts from Qumran", *SBL*, 1955, p. 163, has accurately understood that the "absolute *terminus ad*

routinely employed to develop paleographic sequences which were themselves then used to date documents—in some cases even in an *absolute manner*. Where these sequences and the absolute dates derived from them were concerned, a precision came to be claimed in relation to individual documents in some cases down to within twenty-five years of the theoretical date of production of that document.[9]

But de Vaux's own work was not always so precise. Sometimes it was even extremely problematic. In his enthusiasm for his proposal of a 68 CE *terminus* for the simultaneous destruction of the monastery and the deposit of the Scrolls in the caves, he announced that he had found a coin bearing the countersign of the Tenth Roman Legion.[10] But this proved to be inaccurate and later he had to admit that it was not a coin of the Tenth Roman Legion as he had thought and that "such a coin never in fact existed". His retraction, delivered only in a footnote however, never made the same popular impression as his original announcement.[11]

He was also in large measure responsible for propounding the famous "earthquake hypothesis" to explain the destruction by fire and a seeming interruption of Qumran settlement during the Herodian period. However, natural phenomena like Josephus' 31 BC earthquake are not sufficient to explain this destruction and relative abandonment, for if the sectaries could have returned in 4 BC (as most commentators theorize), they could also have returned in 30 or 29 BC, and there must have been *other* factors—in our view political ones—coinciding with Herod's reign

quem for Qumran script types" are the dated documents from the Wadi Murabba'at (though sometimes he behaves as if he doesn't.) As opposed to this, see Birnbaum, p. 27, quoted above: "Archaeological evidence confirms the post-Christian era part, and even enables us to arrive at a precise *terminus ad quem*: the year 68 CE, when the Romans put an end to Qumran settlement." Having said this, he then proceeds to plug this date into all his "equations"—such as they are—as the *absolute* upper pole limit for Qumran script types.

[9] See, for instance, Birnbaum, pp. 115ff., where he is willing to project dates down to actual years, corroborates one set of dates by others, and projects new dates on the basis of his previous projections without a word about margins of error.

[10] R. de Vaux, "Fouilles au Khirbet Qumrân", *Revue Biblique*, 61, 1954, pp. 232f.; he reiterated this claim in *RB*, 63, 1956, p. 567, where he typically treats the conquest and occupation of the site "by the soldiers of the Xe Legion" as a proven fact. See also Cross, pp. 62ff., particularly n. 18, for detailed analyses of the movements of this legion; also de Vaux, pp. 38ff. For the opposing view, see C. Roth, "Did Vespasian Capture Qumran", *Palestine Exploration Quarterly*, pp. 122ff.

[11] De Vaux, p. 40: "Recent discussions refer to the existence of a coin with the countersign of the Tenth legion, which, so it is held [by whom?], was found at Khirbet Qumran and which I have in fact recorded . . . The mention of this was unfortunate for this coin does not exist."

in Palestine which made habitation at Qumran difficult, if not impossible.

In fact for the perspicacious observer, Josephus explains these quite straightforwardly in *Ant.* 15.10.4 (in the same notice where he discusses Herod's cordial relation with "Pollio the Pharisee and Sameas and their community of scholars"). Noting that Herod "greatly guarded against those malcontents" who objected to "the practices he had introduced into their religion to the dissolution of their customs" (note how Josephus here reverses the language of "Innovators" and "innovations" which he will presently apply to those unalterably opposed to the Herodian monarchy), Josephus describes how Herod relentlessly persecuted such persons because they "could in no way be reduced to acquiesce to his regime". Aside from a ban on public and communal meetings, he set "spies everywhere, both in the city and on the roads, who watched those that met together". He "watched everything they did, and when any were caught they were severely punished and many were brought to the citadel Hyrcania [not far from Qumran] both openly and in secret and there put to death".

This is all presented in the context of his first description of any consequence of both "Pharisees" and "Essenes". What Josephus has done, by placing in conjunction parallel notices about Herod's equal regard for these two groups, as we have suggested elsewhere,[12] is confused them with each other. The *real* political stance of those "Essenes" responsible for the Qumran corpus may be surmised from his earlier notes about "malcontents . . . opposing the dissolution of their customs" which introduces these details and is in every way consonant with what we know of Qumran.

This *simple historical error* led to quite a few derivative ones which have prevented Qumran commentators from accurately approaching the materials before them. Primarily it gave rise to the notion that "Herod held these Essenes in such honor that he thought higher of them than their mortal nature required"—the group Josephus really intends here are "Pharisees" not "Essenes", i.e., Herod held *the Pharisees* in high regard, not *the Essenes*, which is true. This, in turn, has given rise to the common impression that so-called "Essenes" were peace-loving and a rather retiring group with little or no political interests, an impression that has no relationship, as should be obvious, to the apocalyptic spirit and lust for vengeance against political and religious opponents which, as we have seen, permeates the Habakkuk *Pesher*. The practitioners of 1QpHab's "Day of Judgement" (on "all Gentiles", "idolators", and "backsliders")

---

[12] MZCQ (Chapter 1), pp. 23f, 39, 42–43, 48. etc.

and "Judgement executed at the hands of God's Elect"—resembling nothing so much as the spirit of militancy one encounters in the *Koran* with its parallel and derivative pronouncements against "idolators" and "backsliders" and its use of the very same "Day of Judgement" terminology throughout—were completely and by definition *anti-Herodian*.

The note about Herod's "innovations to the dissolution of their customs" precisely corresponds to Josephus' later accusations against "Innovators" and the "innovations" sought by those who wished to *ban foreigners from the Temple Mount*—which, as we noted, Josephus typically *reverses*, much as the New Testament *reverses* the ideological orientation and historical drift characterizing Qumran documents in constructing its portrait of similar events. The "innovations" in question are made quite clear in the Damascus Document's ban on *divorce* and *marrying nieces*, as well as its complaints about *pollution of the Temple* already dealt with above. In our view, these were unquestionably aimed directly and unerringly at "Herodians". If the Damascus Document were the second (even the third century) BC document most commentators claim—which we dispute categorically (on *textual* grounds not *paleographic*)—this would make Herod's esteem for purported "Essenes" all the more incomprehensible. In fact, the so-called "Essenes" at Qumran—despite these citations in Josephus—*never* approved of "Herodians", which is precisely the reason for both the New Testament's and Josephus' parallel ideological and historical surgeries. It is these historical confusions, misconceptions, and inaccuracies which have, more than anything else, sapped the work of both paleographers and archaeologists in Qumran studies.

S. Steckoll (whom de Vaux contemptuously dismissed as "this Sherlock Holmes of archaeology")[13] questioned even whether there was evidence of earthquake damage at Qumran. That an earthquake could have caused the kind of complete conflagration that seems to have occurred at Qumran is not very convincing. Even de Vaux's own colleague Milik, who questioned the former's evidence for a total abandonment of the site between 31 BC and 4 BC, admitted that the evidence of a conflagration was of such magnitude as to suggest "an intentional destruction of Qumran".[14] In any event, since the sectaries do not appear to have inhabited *the buildings* at Qumran, an earthquake—whether it

[13] De Vaux, p. 48. Cf. S. Steckoll, "Marginal Notes on the Qumran Excavations", *Revue de Qumran*, 7, 1968, pp. 34ff.

[14] Cf. Milik, pp. 51ff. Even de Vaux in his last work took a much more conciliatory stance on the subject: "The question remains open, therefore, and my *real reason* for *believing* that the fire coincided with the earthquake of 31 BC is that this solution *is the simplest* and that there are *no positive arguments to contradict it*" (*sic*—italics mine).

damaged them or not, cannot be used as a measure for the date of the abandonment of the site (the same point applies to the destruction of these *buildings* by Roman soldiers).

There are very good reasons for the abandonment of the site coinciding with the period of Herod's reign in Palestine—or at least a severe diminution in the numbers of persons residing there, as we have seen—but in order to appreciate them one must firm up one's *historical* grasp and not be deceived by Josephus' portrait of the Essenes as pro-Herodian. Simply put, the sect was vehemently, even violently, *anti-Herodian*, and the site was most likely destroyed in 37 BC *by Herod himself* on his way up to invest Jerusalem.[15]

Milik and de Vaux have also disagreed with each other on whether the ruins of a wall and the broken dishes which appear to be connected to it appertain to the mid-first century BC or the destruction in the later part of the first century CE.[16] Despite the fact that their disagreement in dating such a relatively large piece of masonry amounts to a difference of approximately 100 years, Qumran stratigraphers regularly claim a precision where dating is concerned that comes down in some instances to the month and year, a confidence paralleling that of Qumran paleographers to which, of course, it is related.[17] Where coins are the issue, one is entitled to say certain kinds of general things based on the general trends of Qumran coin distribution, like the Community was founded around the time of John Hyrcanus, or there seems to have been an

---

[15] See for instance Josephus' account in this period of the "Zealot" suicide of the "old man" and his seven sons—whom Josephus refers to as "robbers" 100 years before Masada—in Qumran-type terrain not far from the Jordan Valley: *Ant.* 14.15.4f. This episode would appear to have had a certain amount of importance since it has received its fictional refurbishment in the "Eleazar" and the "Seven Brothers" stories in 2 and 4 Macc, which are further refined via *Gematria* in the "*Taxo*" materials in As. Mos. 9:1ff. The "Resurrection" ideal, so important to these materials, has received its ultimate parody in Mk 12:20ff./Lk 20:29ff./Mt 22:25ff. That this suicide ideal in this period was part and parcel of the recommendation to "make a pious end" *is confirmed* in the "Razis" material in 2 Macc 14:37ff. See also Appendix on the "Three Nets of Belial".

[16] See Milik, pp. 51ff., in particular, p. 55, n. 1, and de Vaux, pp. 24ff.

[17] Cf. R. North's criticism of de Vaux in "Qumran and its Archaeology", *CBQ*, 16, pp. 426–37 and Milik above. Where stratigraphy is concerned, we are speaking of small coins purportedly suspended between stratigraphic layers. It is dubious if our archaeologists' work was precise enough to determine a one- or two-year difference in stratigraphy regarding these. North also subjected de Vaux's pottery typology to severe criticism. Cf. as well Cross' testimony in "Scripts", p. 190, n. 9, on how he wavered back and forth between de Vaux and Milik on the matter of the bowl graffiti (related to the problem of the wall and broken dishes), finally dutifully following the former against his original judgement.

increase in habitation during the time of Agrippa I, and an even greater one during the Revolt, but one is not permitted to make the kinds of precise dating claims that are common to this field. For instance, even if the sect's communal buildings were destroyed in 68 CE, one cannot be sure that habitation in the area of the site then completely ceased or that the Romans in fact garrisoned the location at this time and not several years later.

De Vaux, Cross, *et al.* point to the non-Jewish coins found at the site overlaying the layer of destruction which they presume to be 68 CE.[18] However, finding a certain coin at a particular site, as they well know, says nothing about the identity of the person who dropped it there, or for that matter the precise date on which it was dropped, only that it could not have been dropped *before* the date on the coin. Neither does it say anything about the even more important subject of habitation in *the caves* and when they were abandoned, since the inhabitants, as we have noted, do not seem to have lived in the actual buildings of the monastery but in *Rechabite*-style huts or in the caves themselves.

Nor do they appear to have carried any coins on their persons, as no coins of any kind have yet been found in any of the caves.[19] Nor can it say anything, in these circumstances, about when a given cave like Cave I, where the Habakkuk *Pesher* was so neatly deposited, was ultimately abandoned.[20] In any event, after the fall of Jerusalem Jewish coins would

---

[18] See de Vaux, pp. 41ff., 66ff., and 123, recapitulated in E. M. Laperrousaz, *Qoumrân L'Établissement Essénien des bords de La Mer Morte*, Paris, 1976, pp. 61f.

[19] For evidence of habitation in some forty caves, see de Vaux, pp. 44ff., 50ff., 56ff., and 107. Cross agrees, p. 64, n. 20. There is even evidence of habitation in mere crevices or "depressions" in the cliff walls, and on p. 107, de Vaux admits that pottery types also appear to be of later date than the outside limits he himself set for the life of the community; see also Laperrousaz, p. 91 for the pottery found in these caves.

[20] Even Cross admits that the finding of an all-important commentary like Habakkuk so neatly placed in a jar along with other similar materials in Cave I implies that it was actually in use at the time of the fall of the monastery and, therefore, comprised part of the current literature of the sect. Both the evidence of some habitation and the careful appearance of the deposits in Cave I, despite some breakage, contrasts markedly with the disorder and completely disrupted state of Cave IV, where it is obvious that people of hostile intent did disturb the manuscripts.

Since Cave IV is located in such close proximity to the settlement, it is not surprising that it should have been disturbed at the time of the investment of the actual settlement; however it is certainly more likely that such disturbance occurred in 136 rather than in 70 CE. In view of the sheer magnitude of the materials found there, it is not surprising that some have taken it for a "library" (see Cross, p. 25, n. 29); on the other hand, if the helter-skelter disorder of the cave characterized its state before the fall of the community, then, aside from the evidence of deliberate mutilation, it would not be surprising if the cave was already being used as "a *genizah*" before the fall of the Community.

no longer have been considered legal tender and no one would have been using anything but pagan coins.[21]

It is just as likely that the Romans, in destroying the settlement, simply burned the buildings and then proceeded on to their siege of Jerusalem.[22] Though coin evidence indicates habitation after 68 CE, it is impossible to say who inhabited the site from 68–73 CE. Inhabited caves (as opposed to book repositories like Cave IV) show no evidence of having been disturbed by the Romans. Though habitation at Qumran seems to have come to an end sometime in the 70s or 80s, evidence of not insubstantial habitation does continue at Ein Feshka, and this cannot really be separated from Qumran.[23] For our purposes, where issues of this kind and the cessation of habitation at Qumran generally are concerned, it is sufficient to prove that there is nothing in the available evidence that

---

[21] Cf. de Vaux in *RB*, 60, 61, and 63, 1953, 1954, and 1956, pp. 93ff., 229ff., and 565ff.; in *Archaeology*, pp. 18ff., 33ff., 64ff., and 70f.; also Laperrousaz, pp. 30, 85, and 90.

[22] Groups could easily have filtered back to the site in the ruined conditions engendered by war or for that matter continued living in the caves up until the time serious operations got under way against Masada in 72–73 CE. In this terrain pursuit was almost futile, as the higher up the cave-punctuated cliff-face the pursuit progressed, the higher any party could also retreat to escape—even as high as the Bethlehem plain itself. As long as any stragglers, refugees, or holdouts remained quiescent at Qumran and refrained from harassing the Jericho Road—the importance of which Cross, p. 75ff., has rightly pointed out—the Romans probably would not have bothered them to any extent. To use for the purposes of illustration a parallel example, even the Masada sectaries do not appear to have taken a very active role in the final stages of the Uprising after their leader Menachem was killed (*War* 2.17.8). For these purposes, their mass suicide does not indicate a particularly aggressive resistance.

We have already noted the flight of the early "Christians" from Jerusalem in this period in response to a mysterious "oracle" not unlike those familiar to us in Qumran scriptural exegesis. The resemblance of traditions regarding this "Pella flight of the Jerusalem Church" to the Masada flight of "the *Sicarii*" is strong. Even the stonings of their respective leaders, which trigger the two events, are to a certain extent parallel. Between the years 100 BC to 100 CE, the only stoning Josephus records, aside from those of James and his rain-making predecessor "Onias the Just", is that of this Menachem the son or grandson of "Judas the Galilean". Josephus' pejorative "*Sicarii*" need not be taken too seriously. In both Hippolytus' and Origen's work it appears "*Sicarii*" more relates to "those who circumcize" and the *Lex Sicarion* related to this. For their suicide as presaged by earlier ones in 37 BC and 2 and 4 Macc, see above n. 15.

[23] That this habitation was Jewish and not Roman cannot be doubted. That non-Jewish coins may have been found here is not particularly relevant, since, as we have already noted, until the Bar Kochba period nothing but non-Jewish coins would have been in circulation. As against this point, see de Vaux's critique of the hypotheses of Driver and Roth in *NTS*, xiii, 1966–67, p. 102 about a "hoard" of later coins found in the Jericho area. This hoard consisted of five silver shekels from the Fourth Year of the Revolt, but the exception proves the rule, and it was just this, a hoard.

can be said with certainty, and which, therefore, warrants discarding otherwise credible *textual* theories. Nothing more.

Even as things presently stand, a not insubstantial number of coins from the third year of the Jewish Revolt, 68–69, have already been found at Qumran and more at Ein Feshka, and it is surprising that after the encirclement of Jerusalem as many coins as this escaped.[24] De Vaux claims that there was sufficient time between April (his presumed, but by no means proven, date for the beginning of minting) and June (the date he contends *Jewish* habitation at Qumran came to an abrupt end) for such a large number of Jewish coins to have made an appearance at Qumran. But we are well into the year 68–69 as it is. There is also a substantial number of coins too oxidized to read, and as long as these exist, doubt must persist.[25] All such matters must be carefully examined when attempting to say anything final on the basis of coin data regarding habitational *termini* at Qumran.

Neither has a satisfactory explanation yet been given for Pliny's contention that there was an "Essene" settlement "above Ein Gedi" (in such a context, "above" probably means "north of") when he was writing after the fall of Jerusalem. Though this might be the anachronism many scholars take it for, it cannot simply be dismissed as misinformed or

---

[24] Though rare coins from the year 70 CE were also found at Masada, as in the case of the Jericho hoard above, these coins were probably the product of the final flight to Masada after the fall of Jerusalem across the Bethlehem plain past Herodion; cf. Y. Yadin, *Masada: Herod's Fortress and the Zealots' Last Stand*, London, 1966, pp. 108f. and 170f. and de Vaux in *NTS* above, pp. 102f. and 126. If commentators are correct in claiming the buildings at Qumran had already been destroyed (its caves being indestructible), the refugees probably would have preferred (as well as in the circumstances found it easier) to flee to Masada.

[25] De Vaux argues that after 68–69 CE no further *Jewish* coins were found at the site until the Bar Kochba period. But no coins have yet been found, for instance, from the Fourth Year of the Revolt on the Temple Mount (cf. B. Mazar, "The Archaeological Excavations near the Temple Mount", *Jerusalem Revealed: Archaeology in the Holy City 1968–1974*, ed. Y. Yadin, Jerusalem, 1976, p. 32). Are we to assume that the Temple then fell in 69 and not 70 CE? Likewise, no coins have yet been found from the First Year of the Revolt at Qumran. Does this mean that the sectaries were, therefore, absent at this time? These are, to be sure, nonsense questions, but they illustrate the kind of logic being applied and the kind of precision claimed by archaeologists at Qumran on these and similar issues. Suppose de Vaux had missed a single coin or gone on to dig a little further! With regard to the existence or non-existence of Roman arrowheads outside the settlement, he responds, "Was I supposed to dig up the whole hillside?"; *NTS*, p. 101. Where *precision* in matters as tenuous as coin data is at issue, I for one would be tempted to reply in the affirmative.

tendentious without some explanation.[26] Certainly James' successor and reputed "cousin", the "Rechabite Priest" Simeon bar Cleophas, must have subsisted somewhere outside of Jerusalem with his community until his execution under Trajan (and by this, one does not mean at "Pella").

Where questions such as these are concerned it must be concluded that after the period so meticulously documented by Josephus our sources are just too sketchy to say anything with precision about the continuation or absence of habitation at Qumran or its environs. What can be agreed upon is that the site was at some point inhabited by partisans of Bar Kochba before they retreated further into the Wadi Murabba'at or the Nahal Hever after the collapse of their Uprising. Any fairminded observer has to acknowledge this as the *absolute terminus ad quem* for both *the cessation of habitation* at Qumran and the deposit of the Scrolls in the caves.[27]

If the Scrolls were deposited before this time, additional questions emerge. Why were they left relatively undisturbed during the period when we know that the site was occupied not only by Romans but also by Bar Kochba's partisans? How can one account for the fact that they, not to mention the jars, etc.—which even materially were surely not without value—were not disturbed even more than they were during these various occupations leading up to the final abandonment of the site? How are we to account for the fact that a cave like Cave I shows no signs of disturbance at all during this period? Is it conceivable that no curious inhabitants ever went up to inspect a location like Cave I, particularly when the whole area appears to have been used as a defensive perimeter of some kind by Bar Kochba's men (cf. the reference to the "*Mezad ha-Hassidin*" or "the Fortress of the Hassidaeans" in Bar Kochba's correspondence[28])? Certainly there is evidence of disorder and

---

[26] *Hist. Nat.* 5.17.4. Pliny is most insistent here, but de Vaux, pp. 134ff. and Cross, pp. 15 and 70ff., while willing to make use of this testimony to support their identifications of the sect as "Essenes", dismiss his chronology. Cf. the hint of such a settlement in Mur 45.6 below.

[27] For the Nahal Hever finds, see Y. Aharoni, "Expedition B—The Cave of Horror"; Y. Yadin, "Expedition D"; and "Expedition D—The Cave of Letters", *Israel Exploration Journal*, 12, 1962, pp. 186–99; 11, 1961, pp. 36–52; and 12, 1962, pp. 227–57. Here, too, the evidence shows that Bar Kochba's people occupied the site. They probably abandoned it in the face of superior force, but they could not have remained unaware of Cave IV.

[28] Cf. in *DJD*, ii.xlv.6. The phrase, as it is used here, is a geographical place-name, which in all probability refers to Qumran or some place very much like it. The reference implies habitation at the site, and in the process ties groups from Judas Maccabee's "*Hassidim*" to Bar Kochba's partisans to the locale.

destruction in Cave IV (a cave that could not have been missed by anyone living in the "ruins" of Qumran), but how are we to account for the fact that it was not disturbed even more than it was, and why were the materials it contained simply left as they were between 68 and 136 CE?[29]

Regardless of how all these numerous questions will finally be answered, and satisfactory solutions will certainly never be found to all of them, 68 CE is nothing but the *earliest* possible date for the *deposit* of the Scrolls in the caves, not the latest. There is absolutely *no finality* on these matters, not even a presumption of one. In particular, as we have already stressed, such results cannot be used to rule out theories intrinsically better than the methodologies upon which they are themselves predicated. This is particularly true when the detailed theory we have presented can fully account for almost the whole of the historical *sitz im leben* of, as well as almost every allusion and turn of phrase in, the Habakkuk *Pesher*—and as a consequence, of most of the other *pesharim* at Qumran—and where contrariwise opposing theories are hardly even able to render such data sensible.

In this case, *meaningful* textual analysis which can make *real* sense out of internal data must take precedence over the kind of archaeological and paleographic evidence which exists at Qumran. Problems centering about this paleographical evidence, where there is hardly an absolute "peg" except the Queen Helen lapidary work—which says little about manuscripts[30]—and the Bar Kochba documents, are based on many of the same archaeological and historical preconceptions we have already

[29] See our remarks concerning these caves in nn. 19–20 above.

[30] Though Cross claims "a series of absolute dating" pegs "at intervals throughout the Herodian Age"—by which he means Birnbaum's "ossuaries", including those of Uzziah, at Beit Schur, Ein Roghel, and Wadi Sali'a, which the latter treats as a *single* "peg" even though "the Herodian period" endures by their definition approximately 125 years, the only really secure "peg" he has is Queen Helen's funerary monument which we would date in the 50s or 60s CE. He and Avigad exhibit substantial differences over the Dominus Flevit ossuaries.

Where the Beni Hezir inscription is concerned, he ("Scripts", pp. 174, 198, and 199; in "Oldest Manuscripts" he confidently termed it *"a terminus ad quem"* for first-century BC scripts) and Albright ("A biblical Fragment from the Maccabean Age: the Nash Papyrus", *SBL*, 56, 1937, p. 159) agree on a date of about the beginning of the Christian era. However, the names of the priests on the plaque and the unfinished condition of the monument (as well as that of adjoining ones) can as well relate to "the sons of Kanthera" in the 50s and 60s CE as to those "Boethusians" at the end of the first century BC. The last of these former, Joseph Cabi, was very much connected with events relating to the death of James, whose name tradition also attaches to this monument. Certainly this plaque cannot be considered a secure *terminus ad quem*, at least *not a precise one*, for first-century BC scripts.

discussed above.[31] But where the specific problem of the Habakkuk *Pesher* is the issue, paleographic evidence, as we have noted, is not a significant factor. Where relevant to the Qumran corpus as a whole, I have treated it in detail above.[32]

[31] See pp. 128ff. above. Almost all paleographers uncritically accept de Vaux's "earthquake" hypothesis using it as a *terminus* to date the end of period I of Qumran habitation (cf. Birnbaum, pp. 127ff. and 149, and Cross, "Scripts", pp. 133ff., 173, and 199, and "Oldest Manuscripts", pp. 147f.). This, in itself, does not overly distort the chronology since the proper *terminus* (if there was a total abandonment at Qumran and not simply a diminution in habitation) is Herod's final assumption of power in Palestine in 37 BC; but almost all, as well, uncritically accept his determination of 68 CE for the cessation of *Jewish* habitation in the region of Qumran, and, therefore, for the deposit of the scrolls in the caves—a precarious thesis at best. In addition, most of the usual historical and sociological assumptions behind such determinations are the warp and woof of their general textual and historical approach.

[32] MZCQ (Chapter 1), pp. 80–95.

APPENDIX: THE "THREE NETS OF BELIAL" IN
THE DAMASCUS DOCUMENT AND *"BALLAʿ"*/
"BELAʿ" IN THE TEMPLE SCROLL

Directly upon its exegesis of Ezek 44:15, the Damascus Document raises the "Three Nets of Belial" charge against the Jerusalem Establishment. These, it contends, were erected by "Belial" as "three kinds of Righteousness" in order to ensnare Israel. It enumerates these as *"zanut"* (fornication), *"Hon"* (Riches), and *"teme' ha-Mikdash"* (pollution of the Sanctuary). While one or another of these charges could relate to any establishment in any time or place, taken together, they concretize the general thrust of the critique as anti-Herodian. ("Belial" in such a context has interesting connotations where Josephus' description of the new practices introduced by Herod are concerned, and one should also note its relation to the *"ballaʿ"*/"Belaʿ" esotericisms below and the language of *"levalʿo"*/*"levalʿam"* in the Habakkuk *Pesher* we have already delineated above.)

Though usually taken as directed against the Jerusalem Priesthood, "priests" are nowhere mentioned as such. Rather these accusations are accompanied by ongoing evocation of a Pauline-type adversary, who is referred to as a "Windbag"/"Spouter" and connected from CD, iv to viii with allusions to "Lying" prophets crying "peace when there is no peace" (Ezek 13:10ff.; note that Josephus' "Saulus" is the intermediary between "all those desirous of peace" and Agrippa II), a "blaspheming Tongue", "pouring out Lies", "daubing upon the wall", "departing from the Way" (in CD, i–ii, "leading astray in a trackless waste without a Way" and "removing the boundary-markers"; note the inversion here of "wilderness"/"Way" imageries), and "the Way of Traitors".

The "Riches" charge, which recurs throughout these sections, is usually accompanied by the imagery of "fornication". It carries the general meaning of the Habakkuk *Pesher*'s "robbing the Poor", "gathering Riches", and "profiteering from the spoils of the Peoples", and even includes an allusion to "keeping away (*lehinnazer*—the same root as the word "Nazirite") from the polluted Evil Riches . . . of the Temple Treasury (CD, vi.16). The allusion to "Peoples" both here and in the Damascus Document concretizes the kind of "profiteering" (CD, viii.7) being envisioned, linking it directly to *Herodians* and "Violent Gentiles" generally.

The "fornication" charge, however, is crucial for determining the historical provenance of the critique. It is explained in terms of taking a second wife while the first is still living, in support of which "two by two" and "male and female" quotations from Genesis are invoked. Where the Ruler is concerned, it is treated here and in the Temple Scroll as a variation of the Deuteronomic "not multiplying wives unto himself" and clearly involves *both* polygamy and divorce. The Temple Scroll makes the "divorce" aspect to the charge concrete and generalizes it further at the end in lxvi.8ff. where the seduction of a virgin is at issue and the ban on *marrying nieces* is enunciated. It is safe to say that though Rabbinic Judaism in theory permitted polygamy and divorce, these practices were nevertheless rare. More importantly, there is no indication whatsoever that Maccabeans indulged in either to any extent. The opposite can be said of Herodians.

Consonant with its length and greater systematization, the Temple Scroll also goes into more detail than the Damascus Document concerning the "Deuteronomic King Law", adding the all-important stricture, *"thou shall not put a foreigner over you"* (italics mine; Deut 17:15ff.). There is no doubt that the recommendation against foreign Kings has little relevance to any period *except the Herodian*; not even the Seleucid or Persian—certainly not the Maccabean. Had it not been specifically evoked in 11QT, lvi.15, we would have had to postulate it. Also where "the King" is concerned, the Temple Scroll further develops the Damascus Document's not taking another wife during the lifetime of the first and "not multiplying wives" to include not taking a wife except from among Israelites and taking one wife, and one wife only during her lifetime and *never divorcing* (11QT, lvii.17f.). These recitations are so forced as to make their purpose almost certain, and their anti-Herodian flow, both as regards Herodian Kings and Herodian Princesses (cf. CD, v.10), should be clear. More narrowly, they are always directed against persons connected in some way with the families of Agrippa I and Agrippa II who indulged in these practices promiscuously and as a matter of course. To be much plainer Qumran would have had literally to *name* its respondents.

We have already noted the "pollution of the Temple" charge in the Habakkuk *Pesher*, where together with the theme of "Abominations"—as per the imagery of Ezek 44:6ff., where it is directed against the admission of those "uncircumcised either in heart or body" into the Temple—it is directed against the disqualification in "Zadokite" terms of the Wicked Priest ("who did not circumcise the foreskin of his heart"). In 11QT, lxvi.14f. the Habakkuk *Pesher*'s "Abominations"/"*To'evot*" is linked to the two matters of "divorce" and "marrying nieces", and elsewhere to other matters involving Gentiles. For its part, the Damascus Document, following upon its discussion of "fornication", "Riches", and the Deuteronomic King Law, introduces the theme of "separation", i.e., "separation from impure things", to explain this charge of "Temple pollution". The *separation* referred to is the sort described in 11QT, xlvi.10 and at the root of the Temple Wall incident directed against Agrippa II, i.e., the separation of the Temple from the city and the separation from the Temple of unclean groups like lepers, menstruating women, etc. (including Herodians, as the concrete charge of "sleeping with women during their periods" in CD, v.7 and the curious play on the word "*balla*'" in the Temple Scroll make plain), not only from the Temple, but also from the area around the Temple.

This theme of "pollution of the Temple" permeates the fabric of the Temple Scroll—cf. particularly 11QT, xlv–lii—when it comes to the separation of impure persons from the Temple and separating the Temple from the city (11QT, xlv–vi—matters echoed in CD, vi.12ff.'s "barring" the door of the Temple and separating from "the sons of the Pit . . . and polluted Riches": cf. Acts 21:28ff. on Paul's disbarment from the Temple including both the notes about "polluting the Temple" and "barring the door").

Where the theme of "separation" in the Damascus Document is concerned, the relationship of such allusions to *Herodians* is made explicit. Some translators actually place a "because" between the charge of "polluting the Temple" and "sleeping with women in their periods", but there is no "because" in the text, only the conjunction "and"—the first being the general charge; the second, only one of its several aspects. The guilt of the Jerusalem Priesthood, as is made clear in CD, v.14f., is guilt by association. The Priests have polluted the Temple by associating with and accepting gifts or sacrifices from such classes of persons, namely, "Rich" Herodians and other foreigners or people in touch with such persons (the problem of the pollution of the Temple Treasure). The text is not saying that Ananus or other priests "slept with women during their periods"—any more than it is saying in the next sentence that *they married their nieces*—only that by associating in various ways with people who did, they brought upon themselves and the Temple the general pollution.

Of course, one can be fairly confident that no *Jewish* Priesthood, whatever corruptions or pollutions imputed to it, Maccabean, Sadducean, Boethusian, or some other, ever indulged in "sleeping with women in their periods", and no accusation of such is on record—most certainly not where Maccabeans are concerned—nor is there any record in regard to them of undue *divorce, marriage with nieces,* or *Riches.* The sexual behavior

Presumed bust of the Jewish historian
Josephus
© Robert Eisler, *The Messiah Jesus and
John the Baptist*, New York, 1931

The western wall of the Herodian
temple—the only wall left standing
after the destruction in 70CE
© Robert Eisenman

Greek warning block in the temple warning foreigners not to enter inner
precincts on pain of death
© Robert Eisenman

Mar Saba, one of the oldest Christian monasteries in the Kedron Valley on the way to Qumran and the Dead Sea
© Robert Eisenman

The St George Monastery in Wadi Kelt, a very old Christian monastery in the Judean wilderness
© Robert Eisenman

Columns VIII–IX of the Community Rule, twice alluding to Is. 40:3—'make a straight way in the wilderness'—and applying it to the activities of the Community in the wilderness
© John Trevor

Herodian artificially built-up fortress at Herodion with sumptuous circular
palace on the way to the Dead Sea and Masada
© Robert Eisenman

Herodian winter palace at Jericho where the last Maccabean high priest
claimant, Jonathan, was drowned in a pool in 36 BC
© Robert Eisenman

Qumran cave 4 marl terrace where
the bulk of the Qumaran documents
were found
© Robert Eisenman

Qumran artificially hollowed-out
water channel, the basis of the
Community
© Robert Eisenman

Bathing pool at Qumran, presumably for ritual immersion, with steps
© Robert Eisenman

A view of the ruins of the settlement at Qumran, with the Dead Sea in the distance
© Robert Eisenman

Radar groundscan conducted by the California State University expedition, 1992, which disproved de Vaux's 'earthquake hypothesis'
© Judean Desert Explorations Project, CSULB

Crack in the stairs leading to bathing pools—the basis of the 'earthquake hypothesis'—which radar groundscan proved was only a local displacement at the ground rather than a fault
© Robert Eisenman

Hot springs at Callirhoe across the
Dead Sea in Perea, near where John
the Baptist was undoubtedly arrested
© Robert Eisenman

Machaeros, Herodian fortress across
the Dead Sea in Perea, where John
the Baptist was taken and executed
© Robert Eisenman

The legendary tomb of James the Just in the Kedron Valley beneath the
Pinnacle of the temple, with the so-called 'Tomb of Zechariah' next to it
© Robert Eisenman

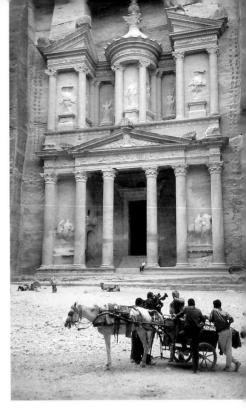

Left Jerash of the Hellenistic cities across the Jordan in the Decapolis
© Robert Eisenman
Right Petra, capital of Aretas' Arabian kingdom; Paul probably fled here, or
further east, after his Damascus-road experience
© Robert Eisenman

Palmyra in the Syrian Desert on the route to the Kingdom of the Edessenes and
Adiabene in Northern Syria and Iraq
© Robert Eisenman

Left The Herodian Step Palace at Masada with the Dead Sea in the distance
© Robert Eisenman
Right Hot baths at the Herodian Palace at Masada of the kind wilderness-
dwelling ascetics like Banus and James probably abjured
© Robert Eisenman

Pella, across the Jordan, where the Jerusalem Community of James the Just was
reported to have fled after his death
© Robert Eisenman

of Agrippa I and Agrippa II cannot be determined with any precision from the material available to us, though both were brought up in Rome and both would have been seen as guilty by association. One can be fairly certain, however, that neither Titus nor the infamous Felix observed Jewish scrupulousness over sexual relations during a woman's menstrual flow. For Qumran this charge precisely reflects how Agrippa I, Agrippa II, Herodias, Bernice, Drusilla, and others, with their easy-going Hellenized ways, would have been seen. In this regard, too, one should not forget the rumor conserved by Josephus of Bernice's incest with her brother Agrippa (a charge echoed very specifically in CD, viii.6f. where the "fornicating ways and Evil Riches" of "the Princes of Judah" were at issue—in viii.10 "the Kings of the Peoples"/"'*Amim*", in this context very definitely alluding to Herodians). One can be fairly confident, too, that these condemnations were part and parcel of the reasons why Agrippa II and Bernice were ultimately barred from Jerusalem by "the Innovators" and their palaces burned.

That this fornication during menstruation charge was directed against Herodians is verified in the next sentence, where the specific claim is raised that "each man marries the daughter of his brother or sister". It is clear from the phraseology of the latter that we have to do with *frequency of occurrence* and *habituality*. To be sure there are examples in the *Talmud* of marriage with nieces, but as with polygamy, these are noteworthy rather for the testimony they provide of the infrequency of the practice. As with polygamy and divorce, there is *no* evidence that the Maccabees indulged in the practice to any extent, if at all. Only *one group, and one group only*, can be said to have done this *habitually* or as a matter of course—Herodians. They married their nieces and close cousins *regularly* as a matter of seeming family policy. When persons who did, in fact, pollute themselves in such a manner entered the Temple and were not properly "separated" from it—the essence of the improper "separation" charge—then, of course, a general pollution ensued.

The references to a "Tongue full of insults" and the "Abominations of the vipers" run on until the treatment of the "serpents" and the condemnation of "the Windbag and the Lying Spouter's spouting" in CD, viii.13. One should note that at this point the Damascus Document is speaking in terms of the "New Covenant", language which links up in this period absolutely with Josephus' discussions of "Innovators"/ "innovations" and problems relating to accepting gifts and sacrifices from or on behalf of foreigners in the Temple, as well as the admission into the precincts of the Temple of persons "uncircumcized in heart or body" as per the vocabulary of Ezek 44:7 and 1QpHab, xi.13—"the New Covenant" or "innovations" having to do with envisioning precisely the opposite set of circumstances.

All of these matters are concretized in some detail in the Temple Scroll, as we have seen, including the ban on marriage with a niece, divorce, foreign kings, the demand for proper "separation", etc. In turn, they are systematically *inverted* in the New Testament with its *retrospective* portrait of the "Hellenized" Christ *preferring* the company of just such classes of persons, namely, "Sinners", "prostitutes", "tax-collectors", people not observing Jewish dietary regulations, etc. This portrait of Christ "eating" with "Sinners", "tax-collectors", etc., has particular relevance within the ideological framework of the presentation of Jesus as "Temple" elsewhere in the New Testament and Eph 2:11ff.'s insistence on there being no "aliens" or "visiting foreigners" in Christ Jesus (the Temple).

With regard to innovations of the opposite kind, namely those "set up by Belial as three kinds of Righteousness" in CD, iv.12ff. above and Herod in *Ant.* 15.10.4, the language of 11QT, xlvif. on "separating" unclean classes of persons from the Temple—the essence of the Temple Wall Affair involving Agrippa II above and the related incident directed by "Simon" against his father Agrippa I—concentrates the focus of all these matters on a single issue. Pursuant to a notice about "the Children of Israel . . . entering My Temple" (7f.) and playing on the language of "swallowing", so characteristic of attacks at Qumran on the Herodian Establishment from Belial in CD, iv to *leval'o/leval'am/teval'enu* in 1QpHab, viii–ix; it reads: "Make a barrier around the Temple one hundred cubits wide [high?] in order *to separate* the Holy Temple from the city and should not come (plural) *balla'*/Bela' into My Temple, nor violate it" (italics mine). The passage varies Num 4:20's "*che-valla'*" dropping the "*che*" and Job 20:15's "*hayil bala'*", "swallowing Riches".

In its second part it employs the "pollution"/"violation of the Temple" vocabulary of Lev 21:12, Ezek 22:26, 22:39, and most importantly Ezek 44:7. It closes with an imprecation which plays on "seeing" from Nu 4:20 (the actual point of conflict in the Agrippa II affair) to produce "fearing", itself having interesting repercussions *vis-à-vis* "God-Fearers" (though the citation could be read, "nor see into My Sanctuary", not "fearing"). Although "*balla'*" might simply be obscure here, what appears to have been reproduced in this passage is "Bela'", not "*balla'*".

Whether these things are deliberate cannot be determined with any certainty; nor can the meaning of "*heil*" in the above context—whether a barrier or high wall of some kind, or a Job 20:15-like esotericism—

but in view of the evocation of the name of the father of both Bela'
and Balaam, "Be'or", in the constant reiteration in the next column of
"in skins sacrificed to idols", bearing on the issue of gifts and/or other
offerings to the Temple probably either Gentile or Herodian and the
association of the parallel "pollution of the Temple with idols" and eating
"food sacrificed to idols" with "Beliar"/"Balaam" in 2 Co 6 and Rev
2:14 below; in our view it *is* purposeful. We have discussed the correspondence of these "pollution of the Temple"/"pollution of the body"/
"Christ" and "Beliar" materials above, pp. 135–37.

"Bela'" is the name of the first Edomite King in the Old Testament
(cf. Ge 14:ff.—the Five Kings of the Plain, Ge 35:31, 36:32f., and 1
Chron 1:43f.). His father is "Be'or"—making the name indistinguishable
from its variation "Balaam the son of Be'or" (cf. the evocation of the
latter in 2 Pe 2:15 below). A second "Bela'" is the firstborn son of
Benjamin in Ge 46:21, Num 26 and 1 Chron 7–8, which sets up interesting
resonances with Paul's claim to be of "the Tribe of Benjamin". For Ju
19–20 "the Sons of Belial" are also Benjaminites, inhabitants of Saul's
Gibeah, and their reprehensible *sexual* acts make their name a byword
(for 2 Sam 16:7, 20:1, and 2 Chron 13:7, the usage is often applied to
Benjaminites in close association with "Saul" opposing the Davidic king
line in some manner; and for 1 Ki 21:13, two "Sons of Belial" are directly
involved—at the instigation of *Jezebel*—in the stoning of Naboth for
blasphemy and *opposing the King*).

Seen in these senses, it is possible to read the letters *B-L-'* as a *circumlocution for Herodians*—an identification already independently arrived at in
relation to the "Belial" usage in the Damascus Document when considering euphemisms like "sleeping with women in their periods" and "marrying nieces". That "Bela'"—the name of an Edomite king and "Balaam"
interchangeable with it—is intended as a circumlocution for Herodians
is reinforced as well by the plural usages that accompany it throughout
the citation. If this is true, then not only, therefore, would the "Bela'"
esotericism be a variation of the "Belial" terminology, but it provides
possibly further confirmation of the historical provenance of these matters as relating integrally to the exclusion of Herodians and other foreigners from the Temple in the mid-first century CE, as we have developed
it from our analysis in a third independent textual context, that of the
Habakkuk *Pesher* (cf. too the same set of allusions relating to "the Sons
of Belial" in 1QH, iv.10ff., including "Scoffers of Deceit"/"Scoffers of
Lying", "Tongue", "lips", etc. Note the common vocabulary it shares
with 4QpNah, ii and 2 Pe/Jude below. 1QH, iv even hints at the
relationship of these "sons of Belial"/Herodians to the "conspiracy"

("*zamam*"/"*zammu*") of the Wicked Priest to remove the Righteous Teacher, not surprisingly also containing the foregoing intimations which in our view hint at the role of a genre of persons like Josephus' "Saulus" or the New Testament's "Saul" as part and parcel of these events). Yet another confirmation of the correctness of the historical provenance we have specified for these materials is 11QT, xlvi.11's use of "*yehalluhu*", which cannot be divorced from the central role this same usage plays— amid the language of "Covenant-Breaking", "*To'evot*", "the Sons of Zadok", etc.—in Ezek 44:7ff.'s ban on "bringing strangers uncircumcized in heart or flesh into My Temple *to pollute it*" (italics mine).

In particular Job 20:15 above could not have helped appealing to the sectaries, referring as it does to "swallowing Riches", "stealing from the Poor", the "Tongue", and "the poison of asps"—cf. CD, viii.19ff., relating this last usage to "the Kings of the Peoples" (that is, Herodians) and ultimately "Gehazi", a favorite circumlocution in Rabbinic literature for persons connected with early Christianity like Paul. This "Gehazi" allusion is invoked in CD, viii.21 following directly upon the allusions to "preaching wind and the Lying Spouter's spouting" and "rejecting the commandments of God and abandoning them in stubbornness of heart".

The subject of these last has to do with "the Kings of the Peoples" and "the builders of"/"daubers upon the wall", relates to Ezek 13:10ff. where it has the specific sense of "Lying prophets" crying "peace when there is no peace" (cf. that "Saulus" above who is the intermediary between "all those desirous of peace" in Jerusalem and Agrippa II outside it—the "peace alliance" ultimately inviting the Romans into the city to suppress the Revolt). The "Gehazi" reference is followed in CD, viii by allusion to "betraying the New Covenant in the land of Damascus" and the reference to the "*standing up* of the Messiah of Aaron and Israel", which we have already interpreted in terms of a Messianic return. All these references to "standing" or "standing up" should be viewed in relation to "the Standing One" of Ebionite/Jewish Christian ideology, itself part and parcel of the "Primal Adam" theorization.

Balaam and Gehazi were two of four commoners Rabbinic literature repeatedly insists would have no share in the world to come and no portion among the Righteous. Directly upon its play on Balaam as "swallower of the people" and Be'or as "*be'ir*", that is, "animal" in 105a–*b*. *Sanh* 106b applies Job 20:15 above to Do'eg, a third of these "Enemies"/ "Scoffers" (cf. Do'eg the *Edomite* over Saul's bodyguard, called "Benjaminites" in 1 Sam 22, who betrays David and slaughters eighty-five priests in "linen ephods"; in particular, note Ps 52 connecting him, in the context of "swallowing" imagery, to the "Tongue", "doing deceit"/"*oseh*

Remiyyah"—as opposed to "speaking Righteousness", "Lying"/"*Sheker*", "the deceitful Tongue loving words of swallowing"/"*balla'* ", "Riches", etc.).

B. San 106a links Balaam, Job ("the Enemy"; cf. too 1 Pe 5:8 linking "the Enemy" with "swallowing"), and Jethro (the latter being further linked to Cain and Kenites); and 109bf. takes up Korah, another of those who "will have no share in the world to come", who contended with Moses. Jude 11 specifically evokes three of these "Enemies", Cain, Balaam, and Korah in the same verse. The Letter of Jude is replete with the Qumran-style language of "fornication", "Darkness", "pollution", a person with "a mouth full of boasts", "the Day of Judgement" (cf. 1QpHab, xii.114–xiii.2), "Fire" (x.5), rain imagery, "the Lord coming with his tens of thousands of Holy Ones" (1QM, xif.), and "murmurers, complainers walking in their own lusts ... for the sake of gain" (cf. 1QH, iv.7–22 on "the Sons of Belial" and 1QpHab, v.7f). Even more strikingly, Jude 10, introducing these allusions to "the way of Cain, profiteering from the error of Balaam, and perishing ["being swallowed"] in the contentiousness of Korah", makes pointed reference to "animals", which in this context can only be seen as a play on the name of "Be'or" in the manner of that of *b. San* 105a above.

Preceding its evocation of this *be'ir*/"animal" theme, *b. San* 105a further identifies Be'or with "Cushan-Rishathaim and Laban". In Ju 3:4ff., the former is related to having a Gentile king put over the Israelites because of fornication and intermarriage with foreigners. In Ge 31:23f., the latter relates to how Laban "pursued after" ("*radaph aharei*") *Jacob*. This last phrase is, in turn, identical with and probably at the root of the language employed by 1QpHab, xi.6—itself culminating in "swallowing" imagery—to describe the destruction of the Righteous Teacher, i.e., "the Wicked Priest pursued after the Righteous Teacher to swallow" or "destroy him"—or varying the allusion slightly, "to *Bela'* him", that is to say, to do the things the Herodian Establishment characteristically did, "consume the People". As in Is 2:5 preceding Is 3:10, the further resonance of "Jacob" with the name James provides an additional correspondence should one choose to regard it. (Cf. too CD, i.21's use of "*yirddephu*" to describe the assault by "the Lying Scoffer", "the Seekers after Smooth Things", and those "breaking the Law" (*yapheiru-Hok*) on "the Righteous One", which we would identify with an earlier assault on James, the one by Paul described in Pseudoclementine tradition, refracted to a certain extent in Acts; cf. too the parallel note of violent pursuit in both traditions.)

No less important in continuation of this theme of avoiding "pollution of the Temple" and having regard to the "separation" of "clean" and "unclean" things in the Temple—a dichotomy alluded to esoterically by Paul in exposition of James' directives to overseas communities in 2 Co 6:14ff.—11QT, xlvii.13ff. specifically raises the issue of "food" or "things sacrificed to idols". This is always attached to the Hebrew "*be'orot*", which literally means "in skins", producing a solecism, i.e., one cannot speak of "skins sacrificed to idols", only "beasts" or "animals" (a secondary root meaning of *B-'-R*, *yod* and *waw* being generally interchangeable in Qumran epigraphy; cf. too "things immolated to idols" in the *Koranic* redaction below, also related to this root).

Since unclean vessels were considered to render the foodstuffs within them unclean, not to mention their bearers (cf. *b. Hull* 129a), it is proper to ask who was bringing such "skins" into the Temple and from where? Since, in addition, skins were considered to lead to the spoilage of grain (*b. Pes* 45b) and were hardly a fit vehicle for oil, this would leave them as useful containers only for water and perhaps wine. The point about skins, however, was that they were valuable (being used for such things as parchment, aprons, shoes, cushions, bed coverings, rugs, etc.) and that *the High Priests were allowed to keep them* (*M. Shek* 6:6).

11QT, xlvii's exaggerated concern over "skins", then, can be seen as an aspect of its more general one over Gentile gifts in the Temple and the consumption of "things sacrificed to idols" (and idolatry in general), and the "pollution" connected to both—compare with James' proscription on "the pollutions of the idols . . . " (Acts 15:20), which, in fact, would include this narrower proscription on "skins sacrificed to idols". In this context, a reference to "polluted" offerings of some kind entering the Temple—or for that matter the body—most likely relates to the kinds of things that were being said about Herodians and those priests or "Violent Ones" associated with them.

However these things may be, it is the "pollutions of"/"things sacrificed to idols", which produced the resonances that so interested the Community especially where gifts from overseas were concerned. The category of "food"/"things sacrificed to idols", as should be clear, is a key element in James' directives to overseas communities (also using the language of "keep away from" or "abstain" of the Damascus Documents' *lehinazzer lohhazir* above), as conserved for us in Acts 15:29 and 21:25 and reflected in 1 Co 8:1ff., 10:19ff., 2 Co 6:16 (note the specific reference to "Belial" and "Light" and "Dark" imagery here), and Rev 2:14ff. (Note here the attribution of the license to consume such "food" to Balaam and the reiteration of the typical "nets" and "fornication" themes, i.e., he "taught Balak *to cast a snare before the sons of Israel, to eat things sacrificed to idols and commit fornication*"—italics mine. Cf. too the parallel accusation in 2 Pe 2:15 that "Balaam", described as "loving Unrighteousness", led Israel "astray from the Right Way", surrounded by the intense imagery of "fornication", "pollutions", "licentiousness", "Darkness", "Day of Judgement"/"End of Days", "scoffing", and echoed in Jude 11 above amid the kindred imagery of "murmuring", "walking in their own lusts", "scoffers in the last times", "greed", and "Judgement" executed by God's Elect.)

Not only is James' ban on "food sacrificed to idols", which appears in few other known contexts, a common concern of all these documents (note its reappearance accompanied by allusion to "blood", "carrion", and "strangled animals" in Muhammad's instructions to a more recent *Ummah* in *Koran* 2:172, 5:3, 16:115, etc.)—it takes on new meaning in the context of the allusions signaled above in the Temple Scroll and what one can surmise to have been the behavior of Herodians and their consorts in regard to it, particularly those from "Asia"—not to mention that of other "*Nilvim*"/"'*Amim*"/"'*Arizei-Go'im*". In this regard the evocation of the Jamesian position on this issue in an "Asian" context in Rev 2:14ff. and in the context of reference to "the Three Nets of Belial" is particularly revealing. The evocation of a variation of this proscription in the Temple Scroll ties concerns evinced in it directly to concerns associated by tradition with the Historical James. That both "Be'or"— the father at once of both Bela' and Balaam—and "Do'eg" are Edomite names provides further scope for known Qumran predilection for word-play, setting up additional resonances with the Bela'/Balaam/Belial circle of language above.

The usage "pollute"/"violate" in 11QT, xlvi.11 above provides additional insight too into our decipherment of "the Judgements of Evil" material tied to the "vengeance taken upon *the corpse* of the Wicked Priest" in 1QpHab, ix.1ff. (cf. the parallel allusion to "*kin'at Mishpatei-Zedek*"/"Zeal for the Judgements of Righteousness" in 1QS, iv.4f.), that is, we have to do not with "illnesses", but "pollutions", that is "*they inflicted* the Judgements on Evil by committing the scandals of Evil pollutions *on him*" in taking vengeance upon the *flesh of his corpse*" (Again the plurals "they inflicted" and "committed upon him" confirm that we have to do with something being "done" by others "to him"—not a disease— namely, the brutal and outrageous violations "*they* inflicted" upon "his corpse"(italics mine).

PART TWO

CHAPTER 3

The Jerusalem Community of James the Just and the Community at Qumran[*]

In Qumran research, the Jerusalem Community of James the Just and its relationship to the Community at Qumran has been seriously under-valued. Both communities are led by a man of pre-eminent Righteous-ness: in the one he is described as "the Righteous One"; in the other as "the Righteous Teacher" or "Teacher of Righteousness". In both instances the leader or "Teacher" appears to come to a violent end at the hands of the Establishment High Priest of the time, alluded to at Qumran under the term "the Wicked Priest".

Both are leaders in a Community of strict hierarchical organization. Both appear to follow a regime of extreme asceticism and poverty, for which they and their followers are often known by others and themselves as "the Poor". Both exhibit an extreme "zeal for the Law", which expresses itself in a "not one jot, not one tittle" approach—i.e., he who is guilty of breaking one small point of the Law is guilty of "breaking" it all. In both communities the language of "keeping" or "breaking" the Law predominates.

Aside from the Wicked Priest, or the Establishment High Priest who appears to be responsible for the Teacher's demise, both have an ideo-logical "Enemy" within the Community itself. Whereas both James and the Teacher preach a doctrine of Salvation by "works working with Faith", the ideological adversary—known as "the Liar", "the Scoffer"/ "Comedian" or "the Pourer out of Lying"/"Spouter of Lies"—preaches a more antinomian doctrine of Salvation. In both communities, generi-cally similar "Tongue" imagery and contrasting "Lying" and "Truth" ter-minologies are used to typify these differences.

At Qumran, not only does "the Liar" preach a version of Salvation

* Paper given to the Mogilany Conference in Poland, 1987.

that includes "removing the boundary-markers which the ancestors have set down" and "leading astray in a trackless waste"—undoubtedly an allusion to the Law—he is said to have "rejected the Law in the midst of the entire community" and led an assault on the Teacher, either verbally or physically.

All of these details can be linked to events in and known aspects of the relationship of Paul to James (however painful these may be to the commentator to enumerate). At Qumran, the correspondence of these events to the life and doctrinal position of Paul are made stronger not only by the evocation of language fitting perfectly into the known vocabulary of both the Pauline corpus and the Letter of James, but also by the characterization of the Liar's mission as "leading the Many astray with works of Lying" and teaching others "to perform worthless service" or "mission"—as opposed to the proper "Justification" activity of the Righteous Teacher in "making the Many Righteous". In addition, the Liar's soteriological works are regarded as "of emptiness" directly echoing the "Empty Man" allusion in the Letter of James uses when referring to its ideological adversary (Ja 2:20).

But the parallels can be drawn much closer even than these. Not only is the "Righteousness" doctrine, as based on a "not one jot, not one tittle" adherence to the Law—whatever may be meant by "the Law" in these circumstances—the central concern and doctrinal emphasis of both communities; but it can be shown that in every exegetical text at Qumran in which the activities and personality of the Righteous Teacher are evoked, the underlying biblical text being subjected to textual exegesis invariably turns out to be a *"Zaddik"* passage—so much so that the methodology used by the sectaries in choosing these texts can be demonstrated by setting forth, *inter alia*, the totality of such texts.

It can be shown furthermore that the Jamesian exegesis of Hab 2:4 is actually present in the *Pesher* on this text at Qumran and restricted in a manner evocative of the well-known dispute between the adherents of Paul and those of James on this matter: first the text is restricted "only to the House of Judah"—that is, to *Jews only*—and second, among these Jews its efficacy is further restricted only to "Doers of *Torah*". Against this ideological background of "Doers", "Breakers", and "Keepers" of the Law, the repeated emphasis in the opening passages of the Letter of James on the term "Doer" should not be overlooked.

In view of these striking convergencies, what has held researchers back from arriving at such results? Primarily it has been the archaeology and paleography of Qumran, and the adherence to a genre of research in these areas that would not have gone so easily unchallenged in other fields of scholarly research. I have criticized this form of research at length in my *Maccabees, Zadokites, Christians and Qumran*, Leiden, 1983 (Chapter 1 of this book). Simply stated, the problem is this: given the present consensus in archaeological and paleographical studies, no real sense can be made out of the internal textual material at Qumran, and vice versa. That is, when real sense is indeed made out of the historical and textual allusions in the Qumran corpus, it is rejected because it does not fit the presumed archaeological and paleographical parameters. In my view this is a faulty way of putting things together, and I have stated as much.

As far as I am concerned, archaeological and paleographical data—impressive as they may be—can in no case be used to rule out an otherwise convincing historical and textual reconstruction based on the clear sense of the internal information. This is true for the matters outlined above, as it is on the subject of the "Three Nets of Belial" in the Damascus Document and "*balla'*"/"Bela'" in the Temple Scroll (which forms the focus of the Appendix to Chapter 2 in this book). To put it another way, the archaeological and paleographical data that has been analyzed is not secure enough to rule out an otherwise convincing internal analysis that falls roughly within Qumran habitational *termini*. The paleographical reconstructions at Qumran are particularly subjective and, when analyzed, circular: i.e., the sequences assume from the first what they set out to prove.

A particularly important piece of internal data in the total puzzle is the "Three Nets of Belial" allusion in the Damascus Document, the whole circle of "*balla'*"/"B-L-'" language at Qumran and, especially, the parallel allusion to "*balla'*"/"Bela'" in the Temple Scroll. This language is used not only to relate to the death or destruction of the Righteous Teacher and other members of his Community in several Qumran documents, but it has strong links with "Beliar", "Balaam", "nets", "swallowing", and "animal" imagery in New Testament and *Talmud*ic literature.

The conjunction of "nets" and "Belial" is symptomatic. This is how the allusion is made in the Damascus Document and Hymns, and this is how it is echoed in Revelation 2 Peter, and Jude. The allusion in the Damascus Document is pivotal for determining the historical provenance of crucial Qumran texts on internal not external grounds. It is perhaps the only *clear* historical allusion in the whole Qumran corpus that can be analyzed with precision on the basis of the internal textual data that accompanies it. As stated in the Chapter 2 Appendix, when the results of paleographical and archaeological research are set aside as secondary, it allows an unambiguous dating of Qumran texts on internal textual evidence alone.

The "Three Nets" in question are those of "Riches", "fornication", and "pollution of the Temple". The charge of "Riches", while also central to the scheme of the Letter of James—as indeed "fornication" is—and all subsequent "Ebionite" history, is not crucial to the analysis, because it can presumably be leveled against any establishment by its adversaries in any time or place. In the case of James' criticism of the Establishment, however, it is a central thesis. And in relation to the Herodians, to whom the high priests owed their appointment, the theme of their excessive "Riches" is equally persistent.

"Fornication" is precisely, if tendentiously, defined at Qumran and relates to two key matters: *marriage with nieces* and *divorce*. In this context, the marital practices of the contemporary ruling elite were a particular irritant. In the Qumran critique, the former practice, if not the latter, was considered *habitual,* that is, "every man marries the daughter of his brother or sister". There was *one elite and one elite only* of which this could be said: the Herodian. It certainly cannot be said of the Maccabean—and probably not of any earlier elite or ruling family either.

These charges are further enlarged upon in the Temple Scroll, so much so that they appear to be aimed specifically at the one Establishment: the *Herodian.* The Damascus Document rails against the Ruler "multiplying wives unto himself"—Herod had ten—and the Temple Scroll introduces a significant section on *polluting the Temple* and *polluted offerings in the Temple* with the Deuteronomic King Law, "Thou shalt not put a foreigner over you." If we had not found this commandment reiterated at Qumran, we would have had to postulate it.

But it is the conjunction of the criticism of these sexual mores with the charge of "pollution of the Temple" that is crucial for determining the historical provenance of the corpus at Qumran. The Damascus Document, in passing from the charge of "niece marriage" to "pollution of the Temple", makes the additional accusation that "they sleep with women in their periods". In our view this cannot have been said about Maccabeans, or for that matter about any *Jewish* priesthood. Rather, it is precisely how Herodians like Agrippa I and II—who were brought up in Rome—with their easy *Hellenized* ways, would have been seen at Qumran. Certainly daughters and sisters like Drusilla, who married Felix, and Bernice, Titus' mistress, would have been seen in this way—not to mention that Herodias responsible for the death of John the Baptist and her various sexual and marital infractions, all involving what is called "fornication" at Qumran.

So, this is the final problem: *polluted persons* and *polluted gifts and sacrifices in the Temple.* These same difficulties echo throughout the early Christian corpus. They also constitute the impulse behind the Uprising against Rome in 66 CE, which involved the barring of sacrifices and gifts from or on behalf of foreigners in the Temple, and the banning of Herodians not only from Temple, but from all of Jerusalem as well, and the burning of their palaces.

CHAPTER 4

*Paul as Herodian**

There are materials in the New Testament, early Church literature, Rabbinic literature, and in Josephus which point to some connection between Paul and "Herodians" (Mt 22:16 and pars.—or members of or supporters of the Herodian family). These materials provide valuable insight into problems related to Paul's origins, his Roman citizenship, the power he conspicuously wields in Jerusalem when only a comparatively young man, and the "Herodian" thrust of some of his doctrines—and as a consequence those of the New Testament—envisioning a community in which both Greeks and Jews would enjoy equal promises and privileges.

By "Herodian" we mean a religio-political orientation not inimical to the aims of the Herodian family as a whole, not only in Palestine but also in Asia Minor and even Rome—possibly even implying a genealogical connection as well. Examples of the effect of such an orientation, expressed with retrospective historical effect in the Gospels, would include the curious thematic repetitions portraying a Jewish Messiah desiring table-fellowship with "Sinners" (for Paul in Ga 2:1 such "Sinners" are "Gentiles"), "publicans" (i.e., "tax-collectors", or persons fitting comfortably into the political philosophy enunciated by Paul in Ro 13: 1–7, for whom presumably Jewish dietary regulations were of little consequence), and "prostitutes" (in our view, a euphemism for "fornicators" as per Jamesian/Qumran allusion).

In addition to these would be a whole genre of other allusions such as "the First shall be Last", "these Little Ones"/"Simple Ones", the Messiah as "winebibber"—presumably therefore distinguished from such well-known, life-long Nazirite-types as Jesus' brother James, John the Baptist, the wilderness teacher who wore only clothing of vegetable

* This paper was first given to the Society of Biblical Literature in 1984.

origin and bathed regularly in cold water that Josephus calls *"Banus"*, and probably the Righteous Teacher at Qumran.

In recent work, I have not only argued for the precedence literary and historical evidence must take over archaeological and paleographic evidence of the kind which exists for Qumran, but have also attempted to concretize the basic political, and by consequence religious, orientation of Qumran as *anti-Herodian*. The last allows us to arrive at a proper textual and historical dating of Qumran documents (see, for instance, my arguments in "The Historical Provenance of the 'Three Nets of Belial' Allusion in the Damascus Document", summarized in an Appendix to JJHP) and has important ramifications for Gospel research. Underestimating it, I believe, is one of the most serious defects of Qumran research.

I have also redefined "Pharisees" generically in terms of "seeking accommodation with foreigners". The reasons for this were twofold: first, to take into account important self-professed "Pharisees", like Paul and Josephus, and second, to relate such persons and others to the well-known Qumran circumlocution "the Seekers after Smooth Things", found in documents like the Nahum *Pesher* and the Damascus Document. By this I mean that we should not simply call "Pharisees" those whom the *Talmud* or Josephus might so identify, but those so identifiable because of an accommodating attitude towards foreign rule generally and some of its important ramifications like *acceptance of gifts* or *sacrifices on behalf of foreigners in the Temple, Herodian* or *foreign appointment of High Priests*, etc.

This is something of a new way of looking at Pharisees, who in Jewish tradition have generally always been looked upon as the "heroic" saviors of the Jewish people. Taken within parameters such as these, however, they look very much like collaborators, and this would have been very much how they were regarded by their more extremist "Zealot" opponents. In several documents and contexts, Qumran presents a basic alliance or *modus vivendi* between groups it variously refers to as "the Traitors"/"Congregation of Traitors" (*Bogdim*), "the Seekers after Smooth Things", "the Man of Lying"/"Comedian"/"Pourer out of Lying", "the Violent Ones of the Gentiles"/"Men of War", "the House of Ephraim", etc.

The last allusion, which is found in the Nahum *Pesher* in the context of various problems relating to the period in which *"the Seekers after Smooth Things"* held sway in Jerusalem, is also linked to a "Lying Tongue", who "leads Many astray"—including a group denoted as "the Simple Ones of Ephraim"—problems with overseas messengers, and allusion to the

"City of Blood", which in the Habakkuk *Pesher* relates to *ideological* problems with "the Liar", and through the use of the expression "*nilvu*" (i.e., "joining"—see also "*Nilvim*"/"Joiners" in the Damascus Document, an expression Es 9:27 applies to non-Jews attaching themselves in some manner to the Jewish Community), is also linked to Gentiles.

It also contrasts with other expressions found, for instance, in documents such as the Habakkuk *Pesher* like "the Simple Ones of Judah doing *Torah*", "*Torah*-Doers in the House of Judah", "the Poor" (*Ebionim*), "the Meek", and "the Downtrodden", and "the Many", on behalf of whom the Teacher of Righteousness carries out his proper Justifying activity of "making Many Righteous" as opposed to "Lying", "leading Many astray", and "wearing out the Many with a worthless service for the sake of his Glory" and "works that count for nothing".

In MZCQ (Chapter 1), I identified at least those indicated under the circumlocution "Violent Ones of the Gentiles" with renegade Herodian Men-of-War, some of whom at first support the Uprising and then desert it. These are said in another *Pesher* from Qumran, that on Psalm 37—a "*Zaddik*" text like Hab 1:4 and 2:4—to have taken vengeance on the Wicked Priest for what he did to the Righteous Teacher. They can also perhaps be partly identifiable with those Josephus calls "Idumaeans", who are at first the allies of those he starts to call at this point "Zealots" and support the Uprising, then desert it.

Along with John the Essene, these "Violent Gentiles" are among the Revolution's bravest military commanders in the early days, and would appear to take their war policy even further than "Zealots" or "*Sicarii*". Among these I would include Queen Helen's kinsmen Monobazus and Kenedaeos, who were killed in the attack on the Roman reinforcements at the Pass at Beit Horon; Niger of Perea from across Jordan, a leader of Josephus' Idumaeans, who ultimately died a death at the hands of "the Zealots" suspiciously similar to that predicated of Jesus in Scripture; Silas, also close to the Herodian family, possibly brought up with Agrippa I and in the final analysis a deserter from Agrippa II's army; and perhaps even Philip the son of Jacimus, "the *Strategos*" or Head of Agrippa II's bodyguard in Caesarea.

At the same time, some of these last were probably on intimate terms with a person Josephus calls *Saulus* "a kinsman of Agrippa". This "Saulus" was probably the descendant of the Idumaean Costobarus, the husband of Herod's sister Salome and the real *Idumaean* in Herodian genealogies. His descendant Saulus some two generations later was a principal member of the pro-Roman "peace" coalition and the go-between in 66 CE, before he was sent to Corinth on a mission to Nero, for Agrippa II and "all those desirous for peace". This is the Alliance which actually invites the Romans camped outside the city to send their soldiers into Jerusalem to suppress the Revolt. In turn, it was the failure of this attempt that encouraged the crowd in Jerusalem and their extremist leaders to think they could defeat the might of Rome.

Paul's basic attempts to found a community where both Greeks and Hebrews—or as he puts it sometimes "Jews first, but Greeks as well" — enjoy equal promises and privileges—spiritual or otherwise—and consonant soteriological equity, are well documented (Ro 3:22, 1 Co 12:13, etc.). This cosmopolitanism is based on a more easygoing attitude towards the Law, as opposed to Qumran's and James' strict constructionist "not one jot or tittle" approach, the ideal of Justification by Faith alone (as opposed, for instance, to 1QpHab, viii's insistence upon "doing the *Torah*" as a prerequisite for Justification), and an open hostility to circumcision, which undoubtedly found a sympathetic response from such "Asian" rulers as Antiochus of Commagene, Monobazus' mother Helen of Adiabene further east, Azizus of Emesa—modern Homs in Syria—who married Drusilla after he had specifically agreed to circumcize himself only to have her divorce him, and Polemo of Cilicia, whom Bernice divorced after he too had had himself circumcized, which Josephus tells us he did on account of her great "Riches". It also included an easygoing approach to dietary matters.

As Paul puts this last in 1 Co 9:19ff., in his discussion of the terms of James' "Jerusalem Council" directives, despite somewhat disingenuous protests about not wishing to be the cause of his brother's "stumbling": "Do not be afraid to eat anything sold in the market place; there is no need to raise questions of conscience"—"conscience" in his view being a euphemism for "the Law" (cf. his allusion to vegetarianism like James' as "weak"—Ro 13:2, echoed in 1 Co 8:13). Sometimes in allusions, such as being a "Jew to the Jews", "running the race to win", etc. (1 Co 9:19ff.), he almost seems to turn this proposition around to Greeks first, but Jews as well.

When he turns Ja 5:6's accusation against "the Rich" for killing "the Just One" into 1 Thess 2:14f.'s accusations against "the *Jews*", as killing the Lord Jesus and turning themselves into "the Enemies of the whole human race", he virtually closes the doors against Jews. This accusation, which parallels the thrust of the inversion of imagery above (where "harlots" (i.e., "fornicators"), "tax-collectors", and "Sinners" are pictured as being on intimate terms with the Messiah) was retrospectively assimilated into the historical fabric of the New Testament—not to mention the later *Koran*—thereby vitiating it.

Paul's traveling companions and closest collaborators after his break with the Jewish Apostles are usually Judeo-Greeks, such as Timothy (Titus?), "whose mother was a believing Jewess" (Acts 16:1—the same expression Acts 24:24 applies to the Herodian Princess Drusilla), of the Herodian type and who like Paul carried Roman citizenship, the mysterious Silas (Silvanus?), etc. This mix is typical of second-generation "Herodians", at least those descending from Herod's original Jewish wife, the Maccabean Princess Mariamme, and her replacement, Mariamme II, the daughter of the High Priest Herod imported from Egypt to become a mainstay of the Herodian "Sadducean" Priesthood. The Jewish blood of third-generation Herodians like Agrippa I, his brother Herod of Chalcis (a Roman princedom in Syria), and sister Herodias, was even further diluted—not to mention that of "Jewesses" like Drusilla above in the fourth.

The "Christian" Community in Antioch, where according to Acts 11:26, Christians were first called Christians—a suitable locale for the crystallization of this terminology—comprises even according to Acts' historical reckoning, various persons of this "Herodian" mix (Acts 13:1). Among these, one should include the curious Niger, Lucius of Cyrene (very likely identifiable with Paul's famous traveling companion "Luke"), and "Manaen who was a foster-brother of Herod the Tetrarch".

Though the last-mentioned description is probably garbled or purposefully dislocated—that is, we are probably speaking about Paul's other famous associate, Ananias of Damascus, and it is Paul himself who was most probably the *foster-brother of Herod the Tetrarch*—at the very least it testifies that among those in the early Community in Antioch—where Christians "were first called Christians"—*there were Herodians*. Silas, another traveling companion of Paul, goes unmentioned, but we have already noted above one or two namesakes of his in Josephus, the elder of whom having actually been *brought up* with Agrippa I as well.

According to Josephus the latter was executed by Herod of Chalcis after he had been in prison for acting too familiarly or in a rebellious manner towards Agrippa (d. 44 CE). Silas the Younger—if he really can be distinguished from the elder—miraculously materializes with Niger as one of the heroes of the Jewish Revolt along with John the Essene and Queen Helen's kinsmen, Monobazus and Kenedaeos. He is the type of the Gentile/Idumaean/Herodian "Men-of-War", who desert the Uprising when all is lost and whom I have identified above with the Psalm 37 *Pesher's* "*'Arizei-Go'im*" or "Violent Ones of the Gentiles", who take vengeance on the Wicked Priest for what he did to the Righteous Teacher.

Where the composition of the Antioch Community is concerned—
or possibly that of Edessa, which was also called "Antioch" at this time
("Antioch by Callirhoe" as opposed to "Antioch on the Orontes")—
Acts adds the name of "Saulus" directly after describing Manaen as being
"the foster-brother of Herod the Tetrarch". Aside from noting the
resemblance of this Herod to Herod of Chalcis above—who succeeded
his brother Agrippa I in 44 CE around the time of the death of Theudas
and the arrest of "Simon Peter"—it is tempting, as we have seen, to
turn the positioning around and consider that the notice about fosterage
relates to *Saulus*, not "Manaen", which is defective, anyhow.

Josephus/Josippon tradition, for instance, knows a "Mannaeus", the
son or nephew of Lazarus or Seruk, who deserted with Josephus to
Titus; and Acts 21:16 knows a "Mnason", who accompanies Paul on his
last trip to Jerusalem because he has a house there, though Acts calls
him a "Cypriot". However, the most plausible identification of this
"Manaen" from among Paul's close associates is the quasi-anagram
Ananias, whom Acts portrays as greeting Paul when he comes to Damascus (9:17) and who is curiously missing from the Antioch group.

It is noteworthy that Josephus, too, knows a propagandist named
"Ananias"—whom he calls "a merchant"—active in these eastern regions
in the upper and lower Tigris at this time. He gets in among the women
of Adiabene and converts the Queen, Helen, while taking a patently
"Pauline" line on the issue of the circumcision of her son. In this episode
Josephus also mentions a colleague of Ananias following the same
approach, but declines to name him. It is in opposing him and deciding
to circumcize himself that Helen's son Izates, and following him Monobazus, are converted to Judaism. While these points are not decisive, they
are nevertheless edifying.

Where the political aims of individuals of this Herodian mix are con-
cerned, Herodian incursions via marriage and other means into "Asia
Minor" (i.e., Cilicia, Northern Syria, Commagene, and the like) and
"Lower Armenia" were certainly on the increase in the first century. For
instance, the first Herodian ruler of Armenia proper was a grandson of
Herod, again via his Maccabean wife Mariamme, called Tigranes. Other
Herodians were married to the King of Cilicia, denoted in Acts as Paul's
place of origin. There is also a note of conspiratorial activities against
Rome where Agrippa I and Antiochus of Commagene are concerned.
This is not the case for Agrippa I's son Agrippa II or his brother Herod
of Chalcis (44–49 CE) after this, who were perfect Roman civil servants.

Antiochus, who blamed Rome for the death of his son, ultimately did
lead a revolt in the wake of the Jewish War. Herod of Chalcis' son

Aristobulus, who like Agrippa I proudly proclaimed his pro-Roman sentiments on his coinage, made himself very useful to the Romans in helping to suppress this Revolt. It is possible we have a reflection of him in Paul's reference to "the household of Aristobulus" preceding the one to his "my kinsman Herodion" in Ro 16:10–11. Many of these areas in Asia Minor and northern Syria, too, are the scenes of Paul's most aggressive early missionary work.

Aristobulus must be seen as one of the inner circle around Titus— along with Tiberius Alexander, Josephus, Bernice, and Agrippa II. It is he who is married to Herodias' infamous daughter Salome (whose picture, along with himself, he proudly displays on his coinage as "great lovers of Caesar"), considered responsible with her mother Herodias in the New Testament for the death of John the Baptist. In fact it was not Herodias who was married to "Philip" (as the Gospels would have it), but rather Salome herself —Herodias being married to another uncle named "Herod", the son of the second Mariamme mentioned above *This* "Philip", Josephus specifically tells us, "died childless".

While the subsequent marriage of Aristobulus to Salome—she was the daughter of his father's sister Herodias—is not strictly speaking an instance of "marriage with a niece", so frowned upon at Qumran and practiced by Herodians as a matter of seeming family policy, it is the closest thing. But connections of this kind with close family cousins were in any case also condemned as "fornication" and "incest" in the Damascus Document at Qumran, "niece marriage" being considered but a *special* case of them.

It is also interesting to consider Herodian links with the Hellenized Alabarch in Alexandria. In the generation we are examining, the family of the latter not only produced the famous Jewish philosopher Philo of Alexandria, but was considered the "Richest" in Egypt, controlling the all-important granaries there and commerce in the Red Sea ports. It was also instrumental in Vespasian's rise to power in Rome.

One of its scions Tiberius Alexander, Philo's nephew, who became Procurator in Palestine during the reign of Herod of Chalcis (44–49 CE), ultimately re-emerged as Titus' military commander during the siege of Jerusalem after Vespasian went to Rome to become Emperor. Josephus, who understood these matters well, specifically called attention to Tiberius Alexander's defection from Judaism, as he did Bernice's, who ultimately became Titus' mistress. Bernice's second sister, also named Mariamme—presumably after her grandmother—divorced her first husband Julius Archelaus, himself the son of the Herodian Temple Treasurer and a putative kinsman of Saulus above, in order to marry someone even

Richer, seemingly another member of the family of the Jewish Alabarch of Alexandria.

Agrippa I's third daughter Drusilla, after contemplating marriage with the son of King Antiochus of Commagene in northern Syria, married Azizus King of Emesa because "he had agreed to circumcize himself"— as Antiochus' son, who later led a group of stalwarts called the "Macedonian Legion" on the Roman side at the siege of Jerusalem, had not. Displaying that cynical opportunism so typical of Herodians, Drusilla thereafter divorced Azizus on her own initiative—even though he had had himself circumcized specifically to marry her—to marry the Roman Governor Felix (52–60 CE). This marriage seems to have been connived at in Caesarea by someone very much resembling the infamous Simon Magus (like its quasi-anagram *Mnason* above, in Josephus, he too is a "Cypriot"). Simon's singular service to Felix appears to have been to convince Drusilla *to divorce Azizus and marry Felix*.

In this episode many themes emerge which are of the utmost importance for dating Qumran documents like the Damascus Document on the basis of internal evidence and understanding the true gist of their critique of the Establishment. Even Josephus, who is usually so accommodating on such matters—later finding Herodian practices congenial, he too divorces his wife, an action that would have been condemned according to Qumran doctrine—describes Drusilla's self-divorce from the King of Emesa as contrary to "the Laws of her Forefathers". As mentioned above, he makes a similar comment about the divorce by her aunt Herodias of her husband "Herod" in the previous generation, the root of the problems relating to the death of John the Baptist in both Josephus and the New Testament.

These divorces were anticipated two generations before this by the divorce of Herod's sister Salome from the Idumaean Costobarus, so important in the genealogy of Saulus mentioned above. They are also reflected in the divorce by Mariamme III (Drusilla's sister) from Julius Archelaus, the marriage of whose father Helcias the Temple Treasurer— also a descendant of Herod's sister Salome—to Cypros, Saulus' sister, consolidated the overlap between these two lines of "Idumaeans".

Salome's divorce at Herod's insistence to marry the first Helcias (Alexas), one of Herod's close friends and the first in this line of Temple Treasurers, is paralleled by similar ones by Mariamme above and by Bernice herself, from Polemo of Cilicia, to take up with Titus. Qumran, obviously, knew whereof it spoke in heaping fulsome condemnation on these practices.

At least from its perspective and from the one in Revelation, Bernice would almost singlehandedly be the "whore of Babylon" (an expression also incorporating an additional play on the "Belial"/"*ba-la-'a*" imagery so widespread in the Qumran corpus). It is instructive to contrast such insults with the more accommodating picture of Jesus in Scripture as preferring table-fellowship with "tax collectors", "Sinners", and/or "prostitutes"—which in the context delineated above would be symbolic euphemisms for Herodians or their hangers-on. In Bernice's case, what we have sketched would involve her in a twofold denunciation at Qumran, not to mention her "Riches" and the rumor of her incest with her brother Agrippa II—also mentioned by Josephus in relation to her divorce from Polemo.

Therefore, in her case, where practices condemned at Qumran are concerned, we have niece marriage, divorce, Riches, incest, and finally *abandonment of Judaism altogether* to take up with Titus, the destroyer-to-be of Jerusalem. According to the view we are presenting, the burning of the Temple at Jerusalem has not a little to do with the burning of her palace and that of her brother earlier by the insurgents, and she and her brother, no doubt played a role in urging Titus at the end to destroy it.

Paul, too, shows his knowledge of these kinds of divorces in discussing James' "Jerusalem Council" directives—in particular "fornication", in 1 Co 7:9f.—but does not condemn them as fulsomely as at Qumran. Rather he merely slaps the wrists of the offending woman by recommending that she abstain from further marriage, and specifies no additional punitive procedures.

It is important to understand that Qumran in general condemns divorce. The disapproval there is linked to the proscription on polygamy and based on references in the Damascus Document to "male and female He created them" and "two by two they went into the ark", both citations from Genesis. Where the Ruler is concerned, it is combined in good Deuteronomic style not only with "not multiplying wives", but in the Temple Scroll with the proscription on putting "a foreigner over you" and the additional ban on marrying foreigners, all with important consequences in respect of Herodians, as should be clear from what we have already described. At the end of the Temple Scroll these matters are developed more fully and introduce the proscription on marriage with nieces.

In many of the above examples, where a direct correspondence can be adduced regarding Herodian behavior norms, "niece marriage" forms an integral part of the problem. Herodias marries not one but *two* uncles, while at the same time incurring condemnation for divorce at least once. New Testament speculation notwithstanding, "levirate marriage" probably had nothing to do with problems relating to her, though she did marry two half-brothers by Herod's two High-Priestly and therefore demonstrably "Jewish" wives, Mariamme I and Mariamme II. However this may be, it is not "Philip" whom Herodias divorces, as we saw, but another uncle named Herod.

Not only is Paul's pro-Roman—and by extension pro-Herodian—political philosophy clear from the general tenor of his missionary activities in Acts, it is made explicit in the enunciation of this philosophy in material like that found in Ro 13:1ff. A more anti-"Zealot" passage could not be imagined. Setting forth what can only be thought of as a deliberate contradiction of the "Zealot" political position on almost every point, including the *tax question, obeying overseas rulers, armed resistance*, etc., it is also anti-Jamesian, e.g., "Good works have nothing to fear from magistrates" (13:4). Ja 2:6 states the exact opposite position: "Is it not the Rich who are always dragging you before the courts?" Certainly, "good works" taken in their Palestinian sense, meaning "works of the *Torah*", could have quite a lot to fear from magistrates, as even the crucifixion of Jesus would have demonstrated; and the "good works" being alluded to here would appear to be more those sensible in a Greco-Roman sphere. But Paul even goes beyond that here, going on in Ro 13:8 to quote in support of such "good works", and, in particular, *paying your taxes to Rome*, the all-important "all Righteousness Commandment", "love your neighbor as yourself", which Ja 2:8 calls "the Royal Law according to the Scripture".

Acts portrays Paul as speaking felicitously in Caesarea on several occasions at some length with many of the above *dramatis personae*—Bernice, Agrippa I, Drusilla their sister—identified in Acts 24:24, somewhat tendentiously, as we also saw, as simply "a Jewess" with no mention of her relationship to Bernice and Agrippa—and her husband the infamous Felix. Who were his additional contacts in Rome is not treated by our documents. At one point Paul is pictured as saying to Agrippa in the presence of the great fornicator and future apostate Bernice, "I know that you believe." King Agrippa, nothing loath, replies, "A little more and you would have made me a Christian." Then Agrippa goodnaturedly pronounces the judgement (Acts 26:27ff.) which, via the miracle of art, has been retrospectively assimilated into the portrait of Herod and Pilate in the Gospels: "This man has done nothing to deserve death or imprisonment."

It is not very likely that Paul could have made the miraculous escapes he does without the involvement of some combination of these powerful Herodian/Roman forces. Nothing less is conceivable under the circumstances of the attack on Paul in the Temple and his rescue by Roman soldiers witnessing these events from the Fortress of Antonia. This episode, too, makes mention of a nephew and possibly a sister of Paul—identities otherwise unknown—resident in Jerusalem, but also presumably possessed of Roman citizenship. According to the above *dramatis personae* related to Josephus' "Saulus", they could very well be Julius Archelaus, whom Josephus mentions as one of the avid readers of his *Antiquities* later in Rome—and Julius Archelaus' mother Cypros, mentioned above and Saulus' probable sister, married to the Temple Treasurer Helcias (Alexas).

Whatever one may finally conclude about these relationships, it is they who warn him of a plot by Nazirite "Zealots" of some kind, who have taken "an oath not to eat or drink"—i.e., a Nazirite-style oath to abstain from "eating and drinking"—until they have killed Paul" (Acts 23:12). Without this kind of intervention, Paul could never have enjoyed the comfortable protective custody he does in Caesarea, where he stays, under restraint or otherwise, in Agrippa II's palace (23:35). Nor could he have been packed off in relative security to Rome, where Felix and Drusilla preceded his arrival. Felix it should be remarked, was the brother of Nero's favorite freedman, Pallas.

Paul had arrived in Jerusalem in the first place with funds gathered overseas from many of the areas into which these same Herodians expanded, where circumcision had become such an issue, partly because of the marital practices of Herodian Princesses. In fact, it could even be theorized that Paul stopped earlier at Philip's house in Caesarea (Acts 21:8—"the Evangelist" or "the *Strategos*"?) to lay the groundwork for precisely such an intervention, having been warned in advance of the dangers that awaited him in Jerusalem (Acts 21:4 and 12). In this context Paul can be seen as a "stalking horse" for Herodian family interests in the Temple testing the ban on Greco-Jews, such as the Herodians, and their gifts by those of a more "Zealot" frame of mind.

But where Paul is concerned, one can go even further. As remarked above, Paul speaks in a unguarded moment in Ro 16:11 of his "kinsman Herodion" or "the Littlest Herod". Though the name could relate to any person by this name anywhere, names like "Herod" and its derivatives—note the parallel with the name of Caesar's son Caesarion—are uncommon. Nor is there any indication that the passage is an interpolation—rather the opposite, for so original and startling is it that its authenticity is virtually assured. If it were indicative of actual familial relationships with Herodians, as we consider it is, then by itself it explains the hint of Herodian activity in the early Christian Community in Antioch.

It also very easily explains the matter of Paul's Roman citizenship, which is such an important element in these escapes. It will be recalled that Josephus records that Herod and his father—the first Roman Procurator in Palestine after the original storming of the Temple by Pompey's forces in 63 BC—were granted citizenship in perpetuity, along with all their heirs, for conspicuous service rendered in the cause of Rome. As it turns out, this Roman confidence was not ill-placed.

In turn, it helps explain why Paul is always so convinced of his own Jewishness, while others seem to have misgivings concerning it, and it throws considerable light on the peculiar manner in which he chooses to exercise this Judaism. Paul's claim to being of "the Tribe of Benjamin" may relate to a general genre of such claims in the *Diaspora* (as it does in the War Scroll, i.3, at Qumran), but it also illustrates the superficial ease with which such claims could be passed off on credulous and relatively unschooled audiences. It is more likely that Paul derives the claim to "Benjaminite birth" (Phil 3:5 and Acts 13:21) not from any actual genealogical link but from the simple fact that his Hebrew namesake "Saul" was *of the Tribe of Benjamin.*

There is, also, a third somewhat more esoteric possibility. This has to do with the biblical description of the Benjaminites as "sons of Belial" (Ju 19:22 and 20:13). In addition, it relates to an anomaly in biblical genealogies, that the name Bela' in Genesis—from the same Hebrew root as "Belial" and "Balaam" ("Balaam", for instance, is the son of Be'or, just as Bela' is; Ge 36:32)—is both the first Benjaminite Tribe and the name of the *first Edomite* King (Ge 46:21): that is, there are terminological overlaps in the Bible between the genealogy of the Edomites and the Benjaminites, as a result of which *Herodians really might* have considered themselves and made the claim of being "of the Tribe of Benjamin". If Herodians, as Greco-Arab Edomites, in addition to considering themselves "Children of Abraham"—another favorite area of allegorical speculation in Paul—were also making "Benjaminite" claims, this really would be a component of Paul's use of the term, not to mention Qumran's inversion of it in its "Belial" accusations.

Paul's reputed description of himself as a "Pharisee the son of a Pharisee" (Acts 23:6) is also readily explained by his Herodian pedigree, and I have been at some pains to set forth the Pharisaic connections of the Herodians in MZCQ (Chapter 1) and in another paper given to the Society of biblical Literature in 1983, "Confusions of Pharisees and

Essenes in Josephus". These connections are perhaps best illustrated by the anti-Maccabean tendencies of the Pharisee Party in general and the cry, conserved in *M Sot* 7:8 of those assembled—presumably Pharisees— when Agrippa (whether I or II is not specified, probably I), when coming to read the Deuteronomic King Law, "Thou shalt not put a foreigner over you, who is not your brother" (Deut 17:5—already mentioned as having been evoked in the Temple Scroll above), begins to weep: "You are our brother! You are our brother! You are our brother!"

For the purposes of "Zadokite" history in Palestine, the mirror reversals of this episode are the attempt by Simon—"the Head of an Assembly" (*Ecclésia*) or "Church" of his own in Jerusalem—to bar Agrippa I from the Temple as a foreigner in the 40s, and the wall built by Temple "Zealots" in the next generation to bar Agrippa II's view of the sacrifices—not to mention this Agrippa's ultimate expulsion with his sister Bernice by these same "Zealots" from all of Jerusalem not long afterwards.

It is this wall, built around the year 61–2 CE, that would appear in this context to be the immediate cause of *James' stoning*. The Temple Scroll, as we saw, makes the Qumran interest in these matters palpable, not only delineating the building of such barriers (column xlvi, also curiously alluding to the usage "*balla'*" or "Bela'" in Hebrew), but even evoking the Deuteronomic King Law and going into the marital practices of the King, insisting that in addition to *not multiplying* or *taking foreign wives, he keep the same wife his whole life*—all matters relevant to the general "fornication" charge leveled by Qumran and perhaps by James against Herodians.

Paul's Herodian links might even explain how as a comparatively young man he could have wielded such powers when he first came to Jerusalem and been authorized by "the High Priest" to search out "Christians" in areas as far afield as "Damascus" (Acts 9:1–2)—whether we are dealing with the "Damascus" settlement of Qumran allusion or an actual settlement of "Jews in Damascus" is impossible to tell from the sources. They readily explain his easy entrance into Jerusalem ruling circles, all matters that have never adequately been explained.

The reference, noted above, immediately preceding the one to "Herodion" in Ro 16:10, to a certain "household of Aristobulus", consolidates these suspicions even further. Though Aristobulus may have been a common name, still it is most prominent among Herodians; there were in fact two or three Aristobuluses from different Herodian genealogical lines living at the same time, the most interesting of whom was the son of Agrippa I's brother Herod of Chalcis, already remarked above. In addition, it was this Aristobulus who had a son called "Herod", that is, "Herodion", "the littlest Herod".

So far our evidence is all inferential—but there is a surprising notice from another quarter which straightforwardly makes the charge we have been implying. Epiphanius, who conserves many traditions found in Rabbinic literature—including, for instance, the one about Jesus being the son of a Roman legionnaire called "Panthera" found in the *Talmud*—conserves a tradition about Paul's background. According to it, Paul was *a non-Jew who came up to Jerusalem* and converted to Judaism because he *wanted to marry the High Priest's daughter* ("the Priest", as per *Haeres* 30.16.9, is usually used at Qumran and in Rabbinic tradition as denotative of "the High Priest"). Disappointed in this design, Paul defected from Judaism and "turned against circumcision and the Law".

Epiphanius attributes this notice to the *Anabathmoi Jacobou* (*The Ascents of James*), a lost work about the debates of James with the High Priests and the Pharisees on the Temple stairs—from which presumably it takes its name, also finding refraction in the Pseudoclementine *Recognitions*—the gist of these debates, as summarized in Epiphanius' citation from the *Anabathmoi*, is that James "*complained against* the Temple and the sacrifices" (italics mine). It only takes the slightest lateral translation to make these intelligible in this period in terms of the way *Temple service was being carried out by the Herodian Priesthood* and the associated problem of the *acceptance of Gentile gifts and sacrifices in the Temple*.

We have no way of knowing if the traditions conserved by Epiphanius are true. While the *Anabathmoi Jacobou* would appear to have been "Jewish Christian" or "Ebionite" and, therefore, hostile to Paul, this is not cause for dismissing *a priori* the tradition Epiphanius conserves from it. On the contrary, when one comes upon a tradition of such surprising content, it is often worthwhile paying close attention to it.

One famous "convert" of sorts, who did aspire to marry the High Priest's daughter—*in fact he married two*—was Herod himself. Seen in this light, it is possible that the tradition, conserved in the *Anabathmoi*, preserves an echo of valuable historical data not necessarily about Paul, but about his *family origins*. If we now retranslate this tradition in terms of the points made above, we can understand it not in terms of Paul himself being a "convert"—which he may have been—or of Paul's wanting himself "to marry the High Priest's daughter" (though he might have), but that he was descended from someone who actually did wish to do these things and did so—someone *who was a convert to Judaism* and *aspired to marry the High Priest's daughter—Herod*! Once again, interpreted in this manner, it would then be a tradition not about Paul but about his *Herodian* origins.

In our view, it is just these Herodian origins that explain Paul's peculiar view of Judaism, his inferiority complex and defensiveness where Jews were concerned, his patent jealousy of them, even of his own Jewish Leadership in the "Church" at Jerusalem—in fact, his "anti-Semitism" generally—and finally his extremely lax and (from the Jewish view)—utterly unconscionable view of the Law.

It is hard to believe that a native-born Jew, comfortable in his identity, could have indulged in the kinds of insults Paul so gratuitously makes concerning circumcision, circumcizers, and those keeping dietary regulations generally (often he calls them "weak"), or adopted the curious approach towards the possibility of simultaneously being a "Law-Keeper to those who keep the Law" and a "Law Breaker to those" who did not, in order, as he puts it, "to win . . . not beat the air" (1 Co 9:24–26), or imagined that by avoiding circumcision one could avoid the demands of the Law, which in some manner he saw as "a curse" (Ga 3:13). In 2 Co 3:6, for instance, he regards the Tablets of the Law as "killing", and in 3:7–13, following this, portrays the Law-giver, Moses himself, as a kind of charlatan deceiving the people by putting a veil over his head to disguise the fact that the light of the Law had gone out, when in fact Jewish tradition portrays him as wishing to avoid irradiating the people.

This theme of a Gentile/foreigner/outsider with ambitions toward the High Priesthood undergoes a curious transformation in *Talmudic* traditions in a celebrated episode involving Hillel and Shammai, where a presumptuous outsider wishes to know the whole of the *Torah* "while standing on one foot". Shammai dismisses the interloper with a blow, but Hillel is willing to quote the "all Righteousness" Commandment to him—called, as we saw, in Ja 2:8 "the Royal Law according to the Scripture"—"love your neighbor as yourself". This last, in turn, is alluded to with similar import not only in the Gospels and the Letter of James but also in the Damascus Document and, as we also saw by Paul in Ro 13:9.

Paul actually quotes the commandment in the context of allusion to "Darkness and Light", "Salvation", "fornication", "jealousy", etc., and, it will be recalled, as verification of his anti-"Zealot" philosophy in Ro 13:9, (note that following this in 14:1f. Paul characterizes as "weak" people [like James] who "eat only vegetables").

In succeeding material relating to this presumptuous outsider in the *Talmudic* version of these matters, it is stated he actually wished to *become High Priest*. When viewed in the context of Paul's own reported insistence that he was a student of Hillel's grandson Gamaliel (Acts 5:34 and 22:3—this in addition to actually characterizing himself as "according to the

Law, a Pharisee" in Phil 3:9), the tradition takes on additional resonances. One is not unjustified in considering that the individual in question is a type of Pauline outsider, and that the theme of *wishing to become High Priest* is simply a variation on that of *wishing to marry the High Priest's daughter* in Epiphanius, itself relating to Paul's non-Jewish, quasi-Jewish, or Herodian origins. When one considers Hillel's own rather cordial relations with Herod, as reported in Josephus, the connection receives additional reinforcement.

From a different quarter, too, evidence emerges which concretizes and sums up, albeit unwittingly, all the tendencies we have been discussing, providing us with an example of just the kind of person we have been describing. As we have signaled above, there are descriptions in Josephus of a member of the Herodian family—and a clear contemporary of Paul—named "Saulus", not a common name in this period. Saulus plays a key role in the events leading up to the destruction of Jerusalem and the Temple. Not only is he the intermediary between "the Men of Power [the Herodians], the principal of the Pharisees, the Chief Priests, and all those desirous for peace" (i.e., peace with the Romans), he is also a *"relative of King Agrippa"*.

In the references to him, too, he is always associated with a brother, Costobarus and another relative, Antipas, quite clearly a member of the Herodian family, who elsewhere in Josephus is identified as the Temple Treasurer—for which he seems to have been murdered by the "zealots" just prior to their 68 CE takeover and butchering of the Rich High Priests—and an offspring of that Helcias mentioned above, the first Herodian Temple Treasurer and a crony of the original Herod. It will be remembered that it was his namesake, Herod Antipas, who was responsible for the death of John the Baptist.

This association with Costobarus and Antipas gives us additional valuable insight into Josephus "Saulus'" genealogy. In this sense Antipas would be a relative, perhaps even a brother or cousin, of the Julius Archelaus mentioned above, Mariamme III's first husband and the man who read Josephus in Rome. He would also be a relative of Saulus' sister Cypros, all probably going back in one way or another to the original Idumaean, the first Costobarus and the husband of Herod's sister Salome.

Together with Costobarus and Antipas, and probably a fourth Herodian, Philip the son of Jacimus, the Head of Agrippa II's bodyguard, mentioned above, in Caesarea, Saulus was in Agrippa II's palace in Jerusalem (as Paul in Acts seems himself to have been in Caesarea) when it was besieged and forced to surrender at the beginning of the Uprising. At this point, the whole garrison was butchered except for its commander, who agreed to "circumcize himself"!

It was after these events that Saulus clearly slipped out of Jerusalem and led the delegation to Agrippa II that wished to invite the Romans into the city to suppress the Uprising—Agrippa II having sometime before been barred from Jerusalem along with his sister Bernice by those Josephus calls "Innovators". The patently anti-Herodian "innovation" of these last had been an unwillingness any longer to accept gifts or sacrifices on behalf of foreigners, including of course Herodians—perceived as foreigners by the extremists—and the Roman Emperor.

The description of Saulus as an intermediary here between the Chief Priests and principal Pharisees, the Herodian King, and the Romans is interesting in the parallel it provides with material in Acts relating to Saul's commission a quarter century before from the High Priest to go and arrest "Christians". Directly following the Temple Wall Affair, too, and James' stoning in 62 CE, Josephus had pictured his Saulus and Costobarus as leading a band of thugs in rioting in Jerusalem, which, in particular, would seem to have involved stealing the tithes of the Poorer Priests on behalf of these same Rich High Priests, so that many of the former died from want. In this episode we have a further echo of possible compromising relationships with the High Priests.

Finally, like Paul in Acts, Josephus' Saulus also seems to have sent or made an appeal or been sent to Nero. Whereas Paul's appeal in Acts comes in approximately 60 CE just before or around the time of the Temple Wall Affair directed against Herodians, which climaxed in the stoning of James and his elimination from the scene, the "Saulus" in Josephus goes to see Nero six years later in 66 CE in Corinth—also a favorite locale of the New Testament Paul's activities—to debrief him on the situation in Palestine and the events described above. It is this report that finally causes Nero to dispatch the best Roman General, Vespasian, from Britain to Palestine to put down the Revolt and, of course, the epoch-making events following upon this. Here, both Josephus and Acts fall silent on their respective "Saulus"s.

It is curious the *Antiquities* places this picture of the riot its Saulus leads in Jerusalem immediately after its two descriptions of the plundering of the tithes of the Poor Priests by the Rich Chief Priests and the stoning of James. For its part, Acts refers to the riotous behavior in Jerusalem of the man it, too, is calling "Saulus" (8:3), but it places this event after problems over the distribution of collection monies (6:1), the conversion of *a large group of Jewish Priests* (6:7), and this stoning of "Stephen" (6:8–

7:60). The sequencing in both narratives is virtually the same, as it is in the Pseudoclementine *Recognitions*. The German scholar, H.-J. Schoeps, was the first to remark the resemblance of the stoning of Stephen to this stoning of James, and the more one examines it, the more the convergence of the two episodes becomes absolute, including the vision both have of "the Son of Man standing on the right hand of Power" (for James he is "sitting") and the words both are reported as uttering before dying. The overlap here is just *impossible to deny*.

The Pseudoclementine *Recognitions* present a third version of these events. In it, Saulus did lead a riot in the 40s and *did* attack James, but James did not die in the attack. He was only injured and instead was carried down by his followers to the Jericho area, from where he lived to send out Peter on his *first missionary journey to Caesarea*. It is curious that whereas Acts may have transposed the stoning of James in the 60s with the stoning of Stephen in the 40s (when the *Recognitions* claims Paul *did lead an attack on James* in the Temple—Josephus may have done just the opposite, i.e., transposed Saul's riotous behavior in Jerusalem in the 40s with its analogue, the riot led by Saulus in the 60s *after the stoning of James*.

It will probably never be possible to sort out the facts concerning this tangle of events in our triangle of sources and what transpositions occurred, if any. However, in order to contend that Saulus and Paul are identical, one would have to assume that Paul, after his appeal to Nero, did return to Jerusalem. This is not as implausible as it may appear at first impression because, as we saw, our sources fall uncharacteristically silent on the subject of Paul's last years and, for instance, the matter of his proposed trip to Spain alluded to in Ro 15:28—not to mention the fates of all important leaders, such as Peter, James, and Paul.

Where Saulus is concerned, aside from his defection to the Romans and last trip to debrief Nero in 66 CE, we know nothing about his ultimate fate either—only that both he and the other Saulus disappeared from the scene at approximately *the same time* and both seem to have entered relations with Nero or those on his staff.

Regarding these last and Paul, not only does it emerge from a careful consideration of his various contacts but it is actually boldly stated at the end of one letter, Philippians. Here, Paul speaks about a colleague of his, Epaphroditus, in terms virtually duplicating those of the Qumran Community Rule, of "being an odor of a sweet smell and an acceptable sacrifice well-pleasing to God" (Phil 4:18), after which he sends greetings from "all the Holy Ones ("Saints") and especially those of the household of Caesar" (4:22), by which he seems to mean he is sending greetings from Epaphroditus and others *in Nero's own household*—to say nothing of calling such persons "Saints".

But this Epaphroditus, who according to Philippians is Paul's "comrade-in-arms" and one of his *closest* associates, is hardly to be distinguished from Nero's secretary and Josephus' publisher by that name, a man who was involved in Nero's last moments and who himself was ultimately executed by Domitian in 95 CE because of it, despite the fact that he had acted as Domitian's secretary as well. This was also around the time of Josephus' own disappearance from the scene. It is hard to imagine that there were several such persons called "Epaphroditus" (a portrait sculpture known to be of him also exists) moving in the same circles at the same time, though some might argue this.

At an earlier point in Philippians, Paul refers to this "Epaphroditus" as "my brother, co-worker, and fellow soldier, but your apostle and minister of my need" (2:25). We feel that this is the Epaphroditus in question, and Josephus does refer to his rich experience of events. In any case, the presumption is very strong. If true, then Paul's contacts—like those of his younger contemporary Josephus thereafter—went *very* high up in Nero's household indeed.

It is certainly possible to conceive that after Paul's first appeal to Nero, he did enter his service in some manner or other, just as his close associate Epaphroditus did—this borne out by the allusion to contacts high up in Nero's household in connection with reference to Epaphroditus in Phil 4:22 above—if he had not been in this service all along. This, too, is what is implied by the existence of the apocryphal correspondence between Paul and Seneca, Nero's Chief Minister, whether fictional or based on something more real, and the more than cordial relations Paul obviously enjoyed with *Seneca's brother* Gallio—*also in Corinth*—in Acts 18:12–17. Of course, all of this is circumstantial and may or may not prove anything, but it certainly adds to the presumption.

It should be remarked that Josephus, whom, as we saw, ultimately became very close to someone called "Epaphroditus" as well, also entered Roman service in some manner or other after an early trip to Rome and interview with Nero's wife, Poppea, around 64 CE, which he documents quite straightforwardly in his *Vita*, and which led directly to his ultimate betrayal of his people. This, too, seems to have occurred in the aftermath of the Temple Wall Affair and James' stoning. However this may be, it is certainly possible to conceive—and this in the author's view is the more likely and the gist of the notices in Josephus—that after a decent amount of time Paul returned to Palestine to involve himself in its affairs in the manner sketched out with regard to Saulus above, as he had in younger days a couple of decades before.

As for Epaphroditus, he certainly had relations with persons at the highest level of Nero's household and was very likely a member of it himself. The historical Epaphroditus even seems to have helped Nero commit suicide or been accused by some, like Domitian, of having assassinated him. Where the man Josephus is calling "Saulus" is concerned, he, too, in some manner certainly seems to have entered Nero's service. Where Paul is concerned, one can only cite his cordial relations with Roman Governors and Herodians generally, plus the notices at the end of Romans and Philippians.

Whatever the conclusion here, the parallels—including the names themselves—are very striking and the coincidences broad. Though none of this information is precise or secure enough to draw any final or firm conclusions, it does nonetheless raise interesting questions and opens new directions not heretofore explored. We do not deny that Paul *considered himself Jewish*, whatever his definition of this might have been. So did Herodians generally, though this confidence does not seem to have been shared by the populace at large and certainly not by the extremists.

This is precisely the point of departure of the so-called "Zealot Movement", i.e., it is "Zealot" in the manner of Phineas, Ezekiel, and Ezra, in terms of removing foreigners from the Israelite camp, Temple, or Community. In Ezek 44:3–15, this idea is expressed prior to defining who the "Sons of Zadok" were—so important for the exegetes at Qumran—i.e., the previous Priesthood had *polluted itself by admitting foreigners into the Temple*. Ezekiel even sets forth requirements so stringent that they are applicable to backsliding Jews as well as foreigners—i.e., no one "uncircumcized in heart or body" shall be admitted into the Temple.

Not only is this the phraseology applied to the "Wicked Priest" in the Habakkuk *Pesher* when discussing the problem of *pollution of the Temple* and his *disqualification from Temple service* (i.e., using the imagery from Ezekiel above, "he did not circumcize the foreskin of his heart"); it is also the imagery seized upon by Paul when he compares his teaching with the teaching of the Law in 2 Co 3:3 above: viz., "You are *Christ's letter, served by us*, not written with ink, but with the *Spirit of the Living God*, not on tablets of stone [meaning, like the Ten Commandments] *but on the fleshy tablets of the heart*" (italics mine).

These themes of *disqualification from the Temple* and *pollution* are also picked up in the Temple Scroll, where their ramifications are delineated amid long passages about what was expected of the King. They are also to be found in the Damascus Document, where they are related to the problem—as we have seen—of improper "separation" of clean and unclean in the Temple. In our view this theme of "improper separation" includes the one of foreigners, a theme directed *inter alia* against Herodians and the "pollution" engendered by association with them—"anyone who approaches them not being free of their pollution" in column vi of the Damascus Document—either by receiving the Priesthood from them or the consonant reception of their *gifts and sacrifices in the Temple.*

Those we have called "Nazirite Zealots", who mob Paul in the Temple and unceremoniously deposit him outside—it should be remarked that preceding this in Acts 21:20 James' followers are called "all Zealots for the Law"—like Phineas and the practitioners of the "not one jot or tittle" approach to the Law in Ja 2:11 and at Qumran, do not "seek Smooth Things", namely, *they do not seek accommodation with foreigners* on the key issues we have been signaling, foreign kingship, foreign appointment of high priests, divorce, marriage with nieces, sacrifice *and* gifts from foreigners in the Temple, etc.

It is in a context of this kind that Paul takes on something of the character of the "stalking horse", we have mentioned above, we have mentioned above, for the Herodian family. In our view, what he is doing in his last trip to Jerusalem, despite warnings not to go, as Acts depicts it (21:4 etc.), is testing *the ban on various classes of foreigners*—particularly Herodians—*in the Temple* and their other relationships to the Temple. Though matters such as these are not really capable of proof to everyone's satisfaction, still no other explanations *better* explain the combination of events we are witnessing.

One thing cannot be denied: Paul's Herodian connections make the manner of his sudden appearances and disappearances, his various miraculous escapes, his early power in Jerusalem while still a young man, his Roman citizenship, his easy relations with Herodian Kings and Roman Governors, and the venue and terms of his primary missionary activities in Asia Minor and then in Corinth and Rome, comprehensible in a manner no other reconstruction approaches. When it comes to linking the thrust of these testimonies and allusions to the political life-setting of later Qumran sectarian texts and the references to the genre of "Lying Spouter" contained in them, much good sense can also be achieved; but this is perforce beyond the scope of our present treatment in this paper.

CHAPTER 5

Interpreting Abeit-Galuto *in the* Habakkuk *Pesher:* Playing on and Transmuting Terms*

In *James the Just in the Habakkuk Pesher*, Leiden, 1986 (Chapter 2 in this book), I adopted an approach unusual in Qumran Studies but often followed in the physical sciences: working backwards from the particular indicator to establish the general theory. Since no theory of Qumran origins has won general approval and, in fact, the subject is very much up in the air (even more so than in the early days of research), this was as good a way as any of proceeding—perhaps the only way.

To put the proposition differently, if a given theory can explain hitherto puzzling or inexplicable details in the internal evidence of a particular document, then this is good reason for taking that theory more seriously. Even more so, if in explaining these details, further unexpected information can actually be elicited which could not be explained in any other manner, then this adds to the presumption of its validity. In the physical sciences, theories are rarely considered absolutely certain, only that they explain the larger part of the data and, additionally, through them, hitherto marginally understood materials come to be clarified. When this kind of data mounts up, then there is reason for thinking the theory works better than another.

Take the widely held "Essene Theory" of Qumran origins, which was hurriedly promulgated in the early days of Qumran research and which has since more and more come under attack. We have no way of knowing who, in fact, these mysterious "Essenes" were—whether they are

---

* This paper was presented at the Groningen Conference in Holland in 1989. It was rejected from the publication of these papers in the *Revue de Qumran* and finally published in Poland.

the same as or different from Qumran sectaries, we are still no further advanced. The same is true in the case of "Zealots", if in fact these can be separated to any extent from "Essene" and other "opposition" or "Fourth Philosophy" groups (the term is from Josephus)—even "Christians".

Then there was the troubling paleography and archaeology in Qumran studies, which ended up explaining very little and only added to the confusion.[1] For instance, if "*abeit-galuto*" can be explained in terms of a first-century CE life-setting, how are the Qumran paleographers or archaeologists going to deal with such a conclusion? Usually they ignore it, as they have other troubling *internal* pointers from the beginning, such as "the Star Prophecy", demonstrably current in the first century CE across a wide range of sources,[2] *Holy Spirit*-baptism,[3] "making a Way in the wilderness",[4] the anti-Herodian thrust of a large swath of Qumran materials, etc. The trouble with their reconstructions is that, though they claim to be based on initial observations of script types or stratigraphic levels, once promulgated they have a tendency to become inflexible: The theories do not "bend" to accommodate new data; rather, the new data must be bent to accommodate the theories.

This is also true in relation to an expression like "*abeit-galuto*".[5] Explaining expressions like this does not interest Qumran paleographers or archaeologists to any extent because, on the whole, they are not much concerned with whether the theories they develop have any connection with historical materials or textual data. Most early theories of Qumran origins simply ignored expressions like this because they were too puzzling or obscure. The reasoning seems to have run something like this: since this usage was esoteric or defective anyhow, nobody could pretend to know what it meant, so why bother about it? In JJHP, I took every allusion, every turn of phrase, and every sentence in the Habakkuk *Pesher* and explained it in terms of known events and circumstances in the life of James the Just. I was, therefore, obliged to deal with this expression.

At first, however, I could make very little sense of it. Following general wisdom on the subject, I took the allusion and the material surrounding it to relate to some kind of confrontation with the Righteous Teacher "at the House of his Exile". Most scholars in Qumran studies had from the beginning surmised that "the House of his Exile" was where the Righteous Teacher was exiled outside Jerusalem, either in the wilderness of Judea, further afield in the wilderness of Damascus, or even overseas.[6] None of this was very enlightening and only added to the general obscurity surrounding the expression. Since we had no idea who the "Righteous Teacher" might be, we had no idea where this purported "House of his

Exile" or "his Exiled House" might be either, or what the circumstances were surrounding his taking up residence there.

Associated with this allusion and the place where the Righteous Teacher was thought to be residing, hiding out, or "exiled", there was a confrontation of some kind relating to *Yom Kippur* observances of the group following the Righteous Teacher—*Yom Kippur* observances which, because the sectaries normally associated with Qumran seemed to be following a calendar different than Jerusalem circles, had something to do with the possibility that the *Yom Kippur* of the one was not the same as that of the other or that recognized by the Wicked Priest in his capacity as Establishment High Priest.[7] As I inspected these materials, it came to look as if the underlying biblical text itself, Hab 2:15–16, had been deliberately transmuted to produce an exegesis relating to a problem centering about *Yom Kippur* observances. This I shall clarify below.[8]

Associated with this confrontation was an element of violence, for the expositions succeeding it related to "vengeance" and "destruction". The normal exposition is very well represented by Vermes' translation, which goes something like "the Wicked Priest . . . pursued the Teacher of Righteousness to the house of his exile" to "consume him with his venomous fury".[9] Vermes translates *leval'o* as "confuse him", but, as I have argued in the Appendix to *JJHP* (Chapter 2), the root *B-L-'* has to do with a circle of language connected to "Belial"/"Balaam" imagery and plays on these names and other matters.

The notice here in the Habakkuk *Pesher*, in particular, involves *destruction* and nothing so vague or innocent-sounding as "confuse". Out of these kinds of translations—or mistranslations, as the case may be—the picture that emerged to the general public was that the Wicked Priest "pursued the Righteous Teacher" to Qumran to interrupt his *Yom Kippur* observances, holy to the one and not to the other, and either have a *verbal* confrontation of some kind with him and desecrate these observances, or at worst arrest him and return him to Jerusalem. In any event, the key phrase in this whole series of reconstructions was the puzzling and clearly defective "*abeit-galuto*".

Initially I too followed these reconstructions, so dominant in the minds of most second-generation Qumran scholars obliged to rely—for lack of real access themselves to original materials—on the work of their peers and predecessors. I took the phrase to mean that the Wicked Priest had "pursued the Righteous Teacher" to the headquarters of the Community, whether at Qumran or someplace further afield.

This was followed by a notice relating to the difficulties over *Yom Kippur* observance, which involved the plural "them", not "him". But I could do little more with the sense of these allusions than this, admitting that it was one of the impediments to developing a clear exposition of Habakkuk *Pesher* materials—this together with the purported "drunkenness" of the Wicked Priest, which I shall be able to clarify at the conclusion of this paper.[10] Because I was looking at materials relating to James, in JJHP I proposed considering the expression in terms of the arrest of the Righteous Teacher, i.e., "he pursued him to his place of concealment", deriving a meaning for the allusion of "where he was hiding". This, in any event, allowed one to consider that we could be in a Jerusalem milieu as easily as one outside it.

Then, considering the facts of James' life and paralleling these with the Righteous Teacher's, the real decipherment of the "House of his Exile" became clear to me. It could only be grasped *when the details of James' life were superimposed on the data*—i.e., we were reasoning backwards from the particular event to the general theory. We could not grasp the meaning of ambiguous phrases like this by considering them alone. Outside events had to be superimposed on them for a clearer meaning to emerge. In turn, if this interpretation could be validated, the basic strength of the general theory was also increased. With it, too, a whole range of other meanings developed, as we shall see at the conclusion of this paper.

The same had happened when I looked at a usage two columns earlier—what translators in English often refer to as the meaningless "his body of flesh" ("flesh of his body"?) based on the Hebrew expression "*geviyyat-besaro*". Since we are dealing with a *punishment* being inflicted upon the Wicked Priest presumably for his Evil deeds—particularly, it would seem, for what he had done to the Righteous Teacher/Priest (i.e., these were "the Judgements upon Evil/Sinning" inflicted by those who "took vengeance" on his flesh)—the real meaning of this term emerged only when comparing it with particular external events and applying them to the internal data. In turn, this elucidated what was meant by the obscure "they inflicted the Abominations of Evil diseases upon him", i.e., upon "his body of flesh", or, as the case will emerge, "*the flesh of his corpse*" (italics mine).

Such insight could only be achieved when looking at the biography of a particular person, in this instance James the Just, and looking at the fate of the Wicked Priest—in these circumstances, Ananus the son of that Ananus prominent in the Gospels (Acts 4:6, Jn 18:13, and Lk 3:2). Originally Josephus referred to this Ananus in honorable style (in the *Vita*, however, he changed this, castigating him for a nefarious olive-oil cartel with John of Gischala), that is, he had both "ruled Israel" and been "called by the name of Truth".[11]

In an extremely pregnant account in the *War*, Josephus describes Ananus' death at the hands of those he calls "Idumaeans" (cf. the Psalm 37 *Pesher*'s "Violent Ones of the Gentiles", also described as taking vengeance on him, paralleling "the Judgements on Sinning" vengefully inflicted by unnamed parties upon the flesh of the Wicked Priest's "body" in this section of the Habakkuk *Pesher*[12]). He tells us how these violent Idumaeans stood over his *corpse*, probably defiling it in some manner, and berated it (for the death of James?), before flinging it outside the city without burial as food for jackals.[13]

Examining the Habakkuk *Pesher*, therefore, in the light of this *sitz im leben*, otherwise vague or baffling usages became clarified. "The diseases" they inflicted "upon the flesh of his corpse" are no longer "diseases" but rather "pollutions"—since *diseases* are not inflicted by people and *pollutions* are—or those indignities or "violations" inflicted upon his "corpse" to render it utterly unclean. (It is curious that at this point in his narrative Josephus refers to Ananus in exactly the same manner he is reputed to have referred to James in early Church literature, that it was because of his death that *Jerusalem fell*.[14])

Here the puzzling redundancy "flesh of his body" is clarified too. Properly, "*geviyyah*" actually does mean "corpse", not "body". In one stroke the meaning of the allusion is enhanced and clarified. We are not dealing with "Evil diseases", but rather "unclean pollutions", namely those inflicted upon "the flesh of his corpse" by the actions of "the Violent Ones of the Gentiles"/"Idumaeans"—to combine data from the Psalm 37 *Pesher* with the Habakkuk *Pesher* 37 and Josephus—and the choice becomes clear. Do we prefer the obscure redundancy of the normative translation, "his body of flesh", or does a finer meaning emerge from a consideration of the biography of James, leading to hitherto unsuspected and better constructions? Certainly the idea that "*they inflicted the abominations of disgusting pollutions in taking vengeance upon the flesh of his corpse*" would appear to be preferable to the redundant "they inflicted the horrors of Evil diseases and took vengeance upon his body of flesh".

Now let us also look at the "*abeit-galuto*" passage in the light of known facts from the biography of James. In the first place, the term "*radaph ahar Moreh ha-Zedek*" which introduces the phrase "*leval'o be-cha'as hamato abeit-galuto*", is often found in biblical contexts having to do with Israel or Jacob. In the story of Jacob, the expression is almost always used in conjunction with the note of "the sword"—they "pursued him with the sword", as it is in CD, i.21, also describing an attack on "the Righteous One" and his followers. That is, the expression usually involves intent to *kill* or *destroy* the object of the pursuit.[15] These usages are recapitulated in Amos 1:11's accusation that Edom "pursued his brother with the sword". The constant reiteration of the name "Jacob" in these allusions could not have failed to appeal to Qumran textual exegetes if James—whose Hebrew and Greek name *is* "Jacob"—were the subject of the exegesis. What is clear in almost all these contexts is that "the pursuit" in question is mortal and carries with it the intent to "*kill*" or "*destroy*".

In these passages in the *Pesher* the pursuit is linked to a peculiar Hebrew root *B-L-ʿ*, which I have repeatedly connected to the Herodian family (and to a certain extent to Benjaminites), i.e., Belaʿ was both the first Edomite King and a Benjaminite ancestor. Since I have also linked Saul/Paul to the Herodian family (cf. his reference to his "kinsman Little Herod" and "the household of Aristobulus" in Ro 16:10–11 and note his possession of Roman citizenship), one should, also, not forget *his pursuit* of Peter or the Jerusalem Community as far as *Damascus* (Acts 9:2), also referred to in evocation of "the Enemy" terminology in Ebionite/Pseudoclementine tradition.[16]

I have also linked this phrase to Herodian collusion in the removal of James—i.e., it was Agrippa II who took advantage of an interregnum in Roman governorship to appoint Ananus High Priest in 62 CE, whose only noteworthy act in his short first period of "rule" before the arrival of the Roman Governor Albinus was the removal and stoning of James. In my view, this is hinted at by the peculiar usage "*zamam*"/"*zammu*" ("conspired"—often carrying a judicial connotation) in two places in the known Qumran corpus, once in 1QpHab, xii.6, "*zamam lechalot Ebionim*"—"he conspired to destroy the Poor" or "the Ebionites". In 1QH, iv.7f., the same term is used in conjunction with the language circle of "nets", "Belial", "Scoffers of Lying", etc., which I have linked in other work to the innovations introduced by Herodians and their hangers-on. The relationship between Ananus and Agrippa II is specifically signaled by Josephus and was, interestingly enough, *concretized in Rome*.[17]

In this pregnant passage in the Habakkuk *Pesher* all the key components of the language circle are present. If the circumstances surrounding James' death could be considered a possible *sitz im leben* for this allusion, then the expression "*abeit-galuto*" would not have to relate to any particular "Exile" *per se* or even an arrest. Ananus had destroyed James and *several* of his associates by bringing them before a Sanhedrin Trial for blasphemy. The notice is from Josephus, reiterated in early Church literature and linking up with similar plural notices in the Qumran literature, i.e., the plural notation *vis-à-vis* the peculiar *Yom Kippur* confrontation connected to the allusion to "swallowing"—which we shall analyze further below, the plural object in "conspired to destroy *Ebionim*" mentioned above, and the plural sense in the attack upon the "soul of the *Zaddik* and all the Walkers in Perfection" at the end of the first column of the Damascus Document.

In all these contexts, too, there can be little doubt that the object of the various attacks was mortal. Since Ananus' attack on James and several of his associates took the form of a judicial trial before the Sanhedrin on charges of blasphemy, a process and charge which were clearly designed to end in his destruction, then the term "*abeit-galuto*" could be seen as indicative of these events. Following this line of argument, in JJHP I suggested it was possible to see it as an expletive for the "*Beit-Din*" or "*Beit-Mishpat*" (judicial proceedings) "pursued by the Wicked Priest"—where James at of issue, in collusion with the Herodian Establishment) against the Righteous Teacher, which the authors of this document would not dignify by describing it as an actual court process. Seen this way, it could be considered a derogatory characterization of these proceedings, that is, not his "*Beit-Din*" or "*Beit-Mishpat*", but rather his "*Beit-Galut*". At the time I considered this just one of many solutions, not realizing there was overwhelming information from another source to confirm it.

Admittedly in some quarters this might have been considered a speculative suggestion, but certainly no more speculative than some of the other interpretations of internal data abroad in Qumran studies; for instance, the purported "drunkenness" of the Wicked Priest or seeing the Copper Scroll as an exercise of overly fertile imaginations.[18] The term "*Beit ha-Mishpat*" had already been evoked in the Habakkuk *Pesher* with eschatological signification involving judicial proceedings "in the Last Days"—in some circles known as "the Last Judgement"—and would appear to relate to the actual decree of divine Judgement delivered in the course of this process.[19]

In the parallel represented by *abeit-galuto*, I suggested we had a derogation of the language signifying a *Beit ha-Mishpat*—the judicial process pursued in the Sanhedrin where capital punishment was at issue. The *Talmud*ic rules concerning judicial procedure in capital offenses are extensive, but certainly part of the procedure, *particularly when "blasphemy"* was at issue, involved trial before the Sanhedrin. Much is made of this in the attempt to portray Jesus' trial in such manner in the New Testament. In fact, what makes this even more plausible, the Gospel of Luke even uses the word "House" in regard to these proceedings and actually seems to think the Sanhedrin trial for blasphemy of Jesus took place at "the *High Priest's House*" (22:54). The other Gospels rather speak of this as "the Court of the High Priest" (Mt 22:58, etc.), but once again the parallel is illustrative and we have direct testimony in the Gospels, if such were needed, that this type of language was circulating about procedures relating to *High Priestly judicial activities*.

In James' case there can be little doubt that something of this kind did transpire. Stripped of its mythological elements, it is reported to us rather prosaically in Josephus, where aside from telling us that James was not alone in the proceedings, Josephus supplies the additional information that "those among the populace that cared most for Justice and not breaking the Laws disapproved of what was done" to James. As I have explained, Agrippa II was almost certainly involved in these proceedings as well, the aim of which was to remove "the *Zaddik* of the Opposition Alliance" post-haste. When viewed in this manner, the defective "*a*" introducing the phrase can be given a meaning of "with" or "in", i.e., "with his guilty trial" or "in his guilty judicial proceedings"— even better where the latter is concerned, "in his *guilty House*" (italics mine).

Immediately, another aspect of the usage is clarified. Now the adjectival modifier "*o*"/"his" refers not to the Righteous Teacher, which is the normative translation in most works about Qumran, but as is more logical from the context, to *the Wicked Priest*. There are three such *o*'s, i.e., *hims* or *hises*, in this sentence in quick succession: *leval'o* ("swallowed him"), *be-cha'as hamato* ("in his hot anger"), and *abeit-galuto* ("to" or "in his House of Exile"), and these are what have caused all the problems. To my knowledge, no one ever thought of applying the last one to the Wicked Priest and not the Righteous Teacher.

The first, "*leval'o*", obviously refers to the Wicked Priest's attack on or pursuit of the Righteous Teacher, however one views this. The second, "*be-cha'as hamato*", "his hot anger" or "furious rage", just as obviously refers to the Wicked Priest's emotional state (once the third is clarified, this will probably have a more esoteric meaning too).

But the third, "*abeit-galuto*", the subject of our discussion, is not so obvious. So firmly entrenched in researchers' minds was the preconception that the Righteous Teacher had been "exiled" from Jerusalem for some reason, it has always been conceived of, as explained, as relating to *the Righteous Teacher's place of abode* or *location*. This would make the sequence of *o*'s read as follows: the first to the Righteous Teacher, the second to the Wicked Priest, and the third to the Righteous Teacher. Here, therefore, we have the fairly illogical grammatical shift of going from the Righteous Teacher to the Wicked Priest and back to the Righteous Teacher again.

If we take the reading according to our new suggestion, this illogicality disappears and we now have one reference to the Righteous Teacher followed by two succeeding references to the Wicked Priest. Then "*Beit-Galuto*" no longer refers to the Righteous Teacher's whereabouts or has anything to do with the Righteous Teacher, but rather the Wicked Priest's whereabouts or behavior, i.e., "his House" or the illegal or illegitimate trial "he pursued" against the Righteous Teacher in it. The logic of this, however, only emerged *after* we tried to fit data relating to James' life and death into this sequence of allusions, *not before*. This is what we meant by insisting that when material from an outside event can elucidate in a meaningful manner an otherwise obscure passage, a convincing case for the theory it is based upon gradually develops.

The root *B-L-ʿ* in both expressions referred to above—*levalʿo*, meaning "swallowing the Righteous Teacher" (xi.5), and *levalʿam*, meaning "swallowing the Men of his Community", identified as "the Poor" or "*Ebionim*" in the allusion that follows (xi.7)—carries the signification "destroy" and not "confuse" or "confound", as one sees it in most translations of Qumran documents (see our translation in Part Three of this book)—incorrectly as it turns out and missing the sense of the circle of allusions depending on this root. In this instance, the "destruction" is wrought by the Herodian Establishment, who—as per the sense of the Edomite King name "*Belaʿ*" (also a derivative of the underlying root as we explained above)—"swallow him".

"Balaam", for instance—another adumbration of this root or terminology and often alluded to in the New Testament and elsewhere (in particular 2 Pe 2:15 and Rev 2:15)—is given the meaning in *Talmud*ic discussions of "swallowing" or "consuming the People". In this sense, we could now interpret this phraseology in the Habakkuk *Pesher* to mean "the Wicked Priest pursued after the Righteous Teacher to *belaʿ* him", i.e., "to swallow him" or what Herodians characteristically did to the People—particularly Messianic and apocalyptic leaders like James— "swallow them".[20]

If we were to leave the argument at this point, we would already have broken new ground, but not achieved anything approaching certainty. But further evidence can be developed, also as it turns out from *Talmud*ic sources, that can be seen as clinching the case for this reading. This data emerges from puzzling allusions in *Talmud* and *Midrash* relating to the Sanhedrin and, not insignificantly, *Sanhedrin trials carrying a capital penalty*. The notices in at least three Tractates in the *Talmud* and one section of

Genesis *Rabbah* are so repetitive as to occasion surprise. Seen in the context we wish to place them in, they approach persuasiveness.

They tell us that in the period prior to the fall of the Temple, "the Sanhedrin *was exiled*" from its normal place of sitting—i.e., in the Chamber of Hewn Stone on the Temple Mount—to a new location outside the Temple Mount altogether, which they refer to as *"Hanut"*. As we have already implied above, and as we shall see below, this place-name will probably have additional meaning when the further implications of the Habakkuk *Pesher* are finally grasped. In every embodiment of the tradition, as it emerges in these *Talmudic* sources, the reference invariably is to *"galtah"*/"exiled"—in two, variations occur; one incorporating the usage *nigli*, that is, "let us be exiled", and one, the more interesting perhaps for our purposes, actually using the word *"Galut"*, in this sense meaning "House of Exile".

In every one—and this is again the important point for our purposes—the peculiar root *G-L-H* used in the Habakkuk *Pesher* in its discussion of the Wicked Priest's behavior towards the Righteous Teacher, is used to discuss *the Sanhedrin's Exile from the Temple Mount*, and in the view of these sources, from Divine Favor, in the years *prior to the fall of Jerusalem*, the period of the stoning of James. In addition, these references are associated in several places with both the illegality of imposing the death sentence in capital trials because of this "exile" and, not insignificantly where the presentation of the trial and death of James in early Church sources is concerned, *the fall of the Temple* and/or *departure of God's presence from the Temple*.

Particularly in the Tractates *Sanhedrin* and *'Avodah Zarah*, the usage refers to the *illegality of passing the death sentence* under such circumstances. This has particular resonance when one realizes that in James' case the passing of a death sentence was considered in all early Church sources a monstrous miscarriage of justice. Again, we find additional resonance of this with the notice in Josephus *vis-à-vis* the death of James that "the more Righteous among the population and those most worried about breaking the Law" objected to what was done to James. Though the *Talmudic* references are talking about the impropriety of imposing any death sentence at all when the Sanhedrin was sitting outside its normal place of meeting in the Stone Chamber on the Temple Mount in the years when it was sitting in its *"Beit-Galut"*—that is, its "House of Exile" or "Exiled House"—the specific case of sentencing to death by reason of *blasphemy* must be reckoned among these.

Equally striking about these *Talmudic* traditions is that in most of the references, the word *"Bayit"* or "House" occurs in close proximity to the verb or noun derived from the root *G-L-H*. In other words, the mention of "Exile" usually appears in direct reference to the word "House", just as it does in the passage before us here in the Habakkuk *Pesher*. In these *Talmudic* citations the meaning is, of course, the Temple—it was "exiled from the Temple"—but it is the proximity of the two usages which is striking.

The tradition incorporating these usages is also attested to in two places in Tractate *Rosh Hashanah*. In every case in the *Talmud*, the second part of the construct *Beit ha-Mikdash*, i.e., "the Temple", is invariably missing, leaving just the word *"Bayit"* or "House" (cf. similar *Koranic* allusions to "House", meaning the *"Ka'bah"*[21])," producing the curious resonance with the usage *"Beit-Galuto"* in the Habakkuk *Pesher*.

That the matter of the Sanhedrin's "Exile", as persistent as it is, must come down and be rooted in some important oral tradition seems clear, but an oral tradition of so insistent and peculiar a kind that the words employed are always the same: *"galtah"*/*"Galut"*, *"Bayit"*, and *"Hanut"*. This is powerful evidence indeed of the basic homogeneity of all these traditions and, once again, the point of departure is James' life. If we had not examined the life of James, we would not have thought of applying a "Sanhedrin Trial" to the events being portrayed at this point in the Habakkuk *Pesher*, nor considered applying the *"o"* in the curious and defective *"abeit-galuto"* to the Wicked Priest and not the Righteous Teacher.

Let me take the gist of these *Talmudic* allusions in turn. The first and fullest occurs in Tractate *Rosh Hashanah*. Here there are two references to *"galtah"* and one to *"Galut"*. The tradition is mainly concerned with "the Exiles" or "Banishments" of the Sanhedrin from the Chamber of Hewn Stone on the Temple Mount and not the judicial implications of this "Banishment", which constitute the main thrust of the notices in *Sanhedrin* and *'Avodah Zarah*.

In 31a, the allusion is to *"galtah"*/"exiled" and issues from a discussion of *the departure of the Divine Presence from the Temple* in anticipation of its destruction—a theme, equally as persistently, always connected to the stoning and death of James in all early Church versions of these materials. Also dealt with are the supposed "ten stages" of the Sanhedrin "Exile" from its "House" on the Temple Mount in the years just before the fall of Jerusalem to a place outside it called *"Hanut"*. This reference to "stages", too, has a decided echo to known traditions about James' life in the lost book described by Epiphanius, supposedly incorporating his teachings on the Temple stairs, the *Anabathmoi Jacobou/Ascents of Jacob* or, as is equally possible, his "Mystic Ascents".

The tradition, as we have it here in *Rosh Hashanah* is ascribed to R. Yohanan and is followed in 31b by a fuller statement, this time including a notice about how the Divine Presence "tarried in the wilderness six months waiting for Israel to repent". "*Repent*" is repeated twice and the conjunction of it with the notation "wilderness"—which evokes related traditions about Jesus' temptation in the wilderness in the Gospels—and another reference to R. Yohanan are themselves noteworthy. The note, too, about the departure of the Divine Presence from the Temple before its destruction is reminiscent of Josephus' description of the departure of the Divine Presence from the Temple in the context of his discussion of "the Star Prophecy" at the end of the *Jewish War* as the chief cause encouraging the Jews to revolt or the Uprising against Rome.[22]

The second reads: in the years prior to the fall of Jerusalem and the departure of the Divine Presence from the Temple and Israel, "the Sanhedrin was exiled (*galtah*) . . . from the Chamber of the Hewn Stone to *Hanut*". Both specifically note that the Sanhedrin's "Exile" from its original home on the Temple Mount was an event known to and preserved "in Tradition". The third reference, also found in 31b, ascribed this time to R. Eleazer, revolves around an exegesis of two passages from Isaiah, 29:4 and 26:5, reminiscent of Qumran expositions of similar biblical passages—many also from Isaiah.

The citations refer to "the Lofty Ones falling" or "being brought low", in this case meaning the fall of the Cedars of Lebanon, but interpreted allegorically to refer to the "fall" of the Temple—presumably because it was built of cedar—and the "Banishment"/"Exile" of the Sanhedrin from it, i.e., just as the Divine Presence left Israel, so the Sanhedrin was "exiled" from its Temple location. Qumran *pesharim* like the one on Is 10:29ff., discussing the fall of Jerusalem (presumably, as per Josephus and the *Talmud* above, that of 70 CE), also evoke "the fall of Lebanon" and "the tallest trees being felled". They play on the themes of "whiteness" and "loftiness" to denote the fall or destruction of the Temple or the Priesthood.

Sometimes this "falling" imagery is applied to the destruction of the Community Council, and here we have the further adumbration of the general symbolism in the Scrolls and Paul of "the Council" or "Community" as Temple. Is 10:34 and similar "falling" passages like Zech 11:1ff are interpreted in exactly the same style in the *Abbot de R. Nathan* and elsewhere in the *Talmud*, but in these instances they are specifically designated as referring to the fall of the Temple in 70 CE, not earlier![23]

This is extremely persuasive evidence of the chronological *sitz im leben* of all of these references—70 CE and not before.

In these passages in *Rosh Hashanah*, there are six "Exiles" or "Banishments" of the Sanhedrin corresponding to the states of degradation in Is 29:4. It is at this point that the word *"Galut"*, used to describe the High Priest's "pursuit" of the Righteous Teacher in the Habakkuk *Pesher* above, is actually employed in exposition of these passages about the "fall of the Lofty Ones", namely, "the Exile" or "Banishment of the Sanhedrin" from the Temple precincts. The relationship of the constant connection of these "Banishments" with the departure of the Divine Presence and the fall of Jerusalem to the similar causality emanating from all the early Church traditions about the death of James, as already noted, should not be missed—a relationship that will be further concretized in the condemnation of the judicial proceedings connected with these "Banishments" below.

The same language is repeated in Tractate *Sanhedrin* 41a, where the subject is the *Mishnaic* number of witnesses required for conviction in capital cases, and the procedures for conviction or acquittal in the instance of close votes. Again R. Yohanan is connected to the tradition (this time specifically identified as *Yohanan ben Zacchai*). The tradition, however, is not ascribed to him, only to the events of his life. Again it states that "before the destruction of the Temple ("the House"), the Sanhedrin was exiled (*galtah*) and took up its sitting in *Hanut*". The ambiance of the discussion relates to the authority or lack of authority *to try capital cases*, the polemical conclusion being that outside the Chamber of Hewn Stone *such authority was rescinded*. The importance of this conclusion in relation to the Sanhedrin proceedings the High Priest Ananus "pursued" against James cannot be overestimated.

Tractate *'Avodah Zarah* 8b twice repeats the tradition with similar emphases, the first instance recapitulating the above redaction almost verbatim: ". . . before the Temple was destroyed the Sanhedrin was exiled [this time we have *"ha-Bayit galtah"* in direct conjunction] and began sitting in *Hanut*". It is hard to escape the conclusion that there would seem to be some verbal tradition behind the persistence of all these conjunctions of *"Galut"/"galtah"* and *"Beit"/"Bayit"*.

The context is directly linked to Roman perfidiousness and subsequent dominion over Israel, together with chronological determinations related to these. The second reference picks up the theme of "being exiled" (*nigli*), as noted above, in the sense of "let us be exiled from place to place". Again the theme of "Stages" or "Ascents" is strong—a theme, as we saw above, with a known context in James' life—but the thrust has to do directly with the cessation of the authority to *try capital cases as a result of this Exile.*

The last incidence of this reference I have found, which occurs in *Gen R* on 49:13, reproduces the theme of the Sanhedrin being "exiled" (*galtah*) from place to place, in this instance from Jerusalem to Galilee, applying *Jacob's* blessing upon Zebulon to this phenomenon. But this time, in another interesting variation, *the destruction of the Temple* is prophetically foreseen by *Jacob* in his blessings enumerated in Ge 49, particularly the shift from Judah to Zebulon. Here again we have just the slightest touch of Gospel presentations of Jesus moving from Judea to Galilee.[24]

In my view, this is very powerful evidence confirming that the suggestion that this ambiguous and difficult allusion to "*abeit-galuto*" in the Habakkuk *Pesher* does not relate to the *Righteous Teacher's* theoretical "Exiled House", as it is normally taken to mean, but rather that of the Sanhedrin's "Exiled House" or "Place of Banishment", in this period outside the Temple Mount, and the proceedings before it—considered, even as in these *Talmudic* reflections, completely illegitimate and reprehensible by the authors, presumably because they ended up in the illegal and unconscionable condemnation of "the Righteous Teacher" or James. To my mind, nothing else could account for the striking coincidence—and I do not consider it accidental—of the same language being used in the Habakkuk *Pesher* as in *Talmudic* allusions to refer to the *Exile of the Sanhedrin from the Temple Mount* and the consonant illegality of any capital judgements there.

Nor, as stated, would I have thought of looking into these parallels if I had not investigated the insistent description of an *illegal Sanhedrin Trial for blasphemy* in relation to the life of James. In this instance, therefore, judging by the internal data of the texts themselves, the theory about James begins to satisfy the several, necessary conditions of verification: 1) it explains otherwise incomprehensible aspects of the data, and 2) it leads to new and hitherto unsuspected information not explainable by any other theory—nor even previously suspected—that could not have been anticipated without recourse to it. Again, the second is even more impressive than the first, because I would not have thought to look into these connections had I not first considered the theory of the identity of James with the character called "the Righteous Teacher" from Qumran—and this, despite any sorts of external determinations like archaeology, paleography, or even carbon testing.

PLAYING ON AND TRANSMUTING WORDS

But in considering the rest of these passages about the destruction of the Righteous Teacher and several of his colleagues at the hands of the Wicked Priest, one can go further still. In particular, this will relate to the characteristic Qumran word-play—for instance, the very *"hamato"*/ "his anger", we mentioned above, connected with the allusion to *"abeit-galuto"*, and its relation to the *Talmud*ic allusions to *"Hanut"*. This even leads to a kind of esoteric key to the passage.

For this we must look at columns viii–xii of the Habakkuk *Pesher* and see how Qumran exegetes change words in a consistent pattern in favor of a desired exegesis. Taken as whole, these columns are concerned with "the Chastisement" or "Judgement" that will be inflicted on the Wicked Priest "because of the Evil he did to the Righteous Teacher and the Men of his Council" (ix.9f.), which is probably recapitulated in additional descriptions of "the Violent Ones of the Gentiles" in the Cave IV Psalm 37 *Pesher*, mentioned above as well.

In the Habakkuk *Pesher*, these notices are also concerned with that *eschatological Judgement* that is inflicted upon all backsliding Jews and Gentile idolators generally, with which the *Pesher* ends. In the particular notice just cited, it should be noted that the allusion to "Evil" is introduced by the same *"be"* preposition that seems to introduce the allusion to *Beit-Galuto* in xi.6, and that the two usages are more or less interchangeable—i.e., "Evil" in the one can be substituted for "with" or in his *"Beit-Galut"* in the other.

It is curious that many commentators miss the eschatological dimension of the phrase being used in at least two places in the *Pesher* to denote this kind of Judgement, *"Beit ha-Mishpat"* or "House of Judgement", despite the fact that the key column viii.2 exegesis of the all-important Hab 2:4, "the Righteous shall live by his Faith", alludes to *"being saved"* or "Salvation" in connection with it.

In column x.2ff., where the usage occurs again, it clearly means that "Judgement"—or, if one prefers, "Decree of Judgement"—which God will pronounce "in the midst of many nations". For some reason, G. Vermes of Oxford, whose works until recently comprised the most widely disseminated English translation, changes the second translation of this construct phrase to read "Condemned House", having already translated it in the first instance as "House of Judgement". Not only is this second rendering virtually meaningless, but it is inconsistency of this kind in Qumran translations that the non-specialist reader must necessarily find confusing—even misleading—as he or she will think that there are different Hebrew words underlying this. There are not.

Finally, in columns xii.14 and xiii.3, the "Judgement" under discussion is definitively designated as "the Day of Judgement" so familiar to readers of the *Koran*, which also includes the telltale allusions to "burning" and the like mentioned in relation to it in this passage.[25] Here, the real thrust of this kind of phraseology emerges—what in common parlance in the West is often referred to as "the Last Judgement".

There can be little doubt that we are to assume that the Righteous Teacher was *done to death* by the Wicked Priest in the course of "*his Beit-Galut*"—in our view "Sanhedrin Trial"—since in describing both the destruction of "the Poor"/"Lebanon"/"the Council" and the reciprocal one of "the Wicked Priest", the term used is actually "*lechalot*", which literally means "destroy", not the more ambiguous "swallow"/"consume". Early Church sources persistently tell us that directly following James' death, the Roman army appeared, and Jerusalem and the Temple fell. In fact, this even becomes a bone of contending ideologies when Origen, followed by Eusebius, objects to the fact that in his version of Josephus, he read that the greater part of the Jews blamed the fall of Jerusalem on the death of James. For Origen, Josephus should have said the death of Jesus!

In these passages in the Habakkuk *Pesher* there are two sets of basically overlapping materials leading up to the allusion to "the Day of Judgement" or "Last Judgement" mentioned above. One picks up the materials relating to the exegesis of Hab 2:4 on "the Righteous shall live by his Faith" from viii.1–x.5 and ends up in the description of "the Judgement which God would pronounce in the midst of many Nations" described above, including also the description of the death of the Wicked Priest. The second, recommencing in column xi.4, includes the allusion to "*abeit-galuto*" just discussed, and ends up with the two evocations of *the Day of Judgement on all backsliders and idolators* with which the *Pesher* closes.

In the first of these sets, the death of the Wicked Priest and presumably that of the Righteous Teacher, is followed by a description of the destruction of "the Last Priests of Jerusalem . . . whose Riches and booty [which they collected via the hand of the Violent Ones] would be given over to the hand of the Army of the *Kittim*" (ix.4ff.)—self-evidently the Romans and the destruction of 70 CE, because Josephus specifically tells us that the Romans *did not take any booty* after the two stormings of the Temple in the previous century, the one in 63 and that in 37 BC. Rather, he makes it completely plain that they refrained, the first time because at that stage Pompey wanted to show his magnanimity and, in any event, had been backed by the Pharisees and so declined to do so. In the second instance, it was out of deference to Herod whom, Josephus tells us, out of regard for his future subjects, *paid the Roman legionnaires out of his own pocket*. In any event, one would not normally be speaking of "the Last Priests of Jerusalem" in the first century BC, and even less so at the time of the Maccabean Uprising before this.

In the second, the *ba-la-'a* allusions of column xi.5ff.—including the one connected with "*abeit-galuto*" above—specifically describe the destruction of the Righteous Teacher and end up once again with the destruction of Jerusalem "where the Wicked Priest acted out his works of Abomination and polluted the Temple of God". As I have explained in MZCQ (Chapter 1) and JJHP (Chapter 2), this "pollution of the Temple" probably involved acceptance of the "spoils" and/or "polluted" gifts from Herodians and other non-Jews, a process repeatedly referred to in these columns and in columns v–viii of the Damascus Document.

This is particularly the case when the allusion "he did not circumcize the foreskin of his heart" is evoked to disqualify the Wicked Priest from Temple service according to the parameters set forth in Ezek 44:7–16's "Zadokite" Statement".[26] His polluted "works" are presumably to be contrasted with the *Righteous/Salvational* ones of the Righteous Teacher. As noted above, too, it is interesting that Josephus describes the death of this same Ananus as the beginning of the destruction of the city, asserting that he could have saved it.

One has, in effect, here in the Habakkuk *Pesher*, regarding the death of the Righteous Teacher, the same narrative sequence as in early Church sources: the death of the Righteous Teacher, leading inexorably to the destruction of the Temple and the fall of Jerusalem. There is evidence, as we have seen, in some of these allusions from this *Pesher* and that on Psalm 37 that the destruction of Jerusalem was seen as punishment for what the Wicked Priest and his confederates had done to the Righteous Teacher—at least it is a direct effect and inevitable consequence of these actions.

Tying these together, a last insight emereges in this *pesher* having to do with the pursuit of the Righteous Teacher by the Wicked Priest "in his House of Exile" or "with his guilty trial". This has to do with his supposed "drunkenness", mentioned above, which emerges in the interpretation of Hab 2:15–16 in column xi, out of which the exegesis is constructed. The Qumran text of Hab 2:15 underlying the *Pesher*, which differs from the normative biblical one, as we shall see first alludes to something verging on an idea of "drunkenness" in the sense of causing one's fellow men "to drink fully of his dregs [possibly also "skin"] that he might gaze on their Festivals". This is not the reading of the Bible as we now have it. Here, the word "Festivals" (*Mo'adeihem*) has seemingly purposefully been added, and transmutes the Massoretic/Septuagint reading of "nakedness" or "privy parts" (*me'oreihem*) by substituting the Hebrew letter *daleth* for *resh*. Instead of *me'oreihem* it, thus, conserves *Mo'adeihem.*

Here, too, where the usage "*hamat*"/"anger" or "fury" is at issue—which will be important when interpreting its resonance with the reference to "*Hanut*" in the *Talmud*ic notices we considered above—the underlying thrust of the normal Bible reading, as noted, would appear to be "strong dregs"/"skin" that make drunk, rather than the "fury", into which the *Pesher* transmutes it in order to describe the Wicked Priest's attitude towards the Righteous Teacher.[27]

This transmuting of consonants, vowels, and even meanings is exactly the same as would have occurred if "*hamat*" were also a *play* on "*Hanut*" mentioned so persistently in our sources, or vice versa. Not only here but elsewhere, the exegetes at Qumran did not hesitate to play on readings in this manner in the interests of a desired exegetical construction.[28] Similar liberties are taken in New Testament Scripture.

Here in the underlying text from Habakkuk, the "drunkenness" or "drinking to satiation" imagery continues into Hab 2:16, where it becomes "the Cup of the Lord's Right Hand shall come around to him"—meaning quite explicitly "Vengeance", i.e., just as he (the Wicked Priest) "poured out" for others—namely the Righteous Teacher and his colleagues, called "the Poor"—to drink to satiation or drunkenness, so too would he drink his fill.

The "drinking" in question here has nothing whatever to do with any "drunkenness" on the part of the Wicked Priest. On the contrary. Nothing could be further from the truth and shows how poorly many Qumran commentators handle literary allusion. Rather, it has to do with "*the Cup of the Wrath of God*"—a tremendously forceful metaphor through the whole of biblical Scripture.

Since the whole biblical text from Habakkuk—at least the Masoretic and Septuagint if not the Qumran version—has been dealing with *nakedness* or *privy parts* (with some liberties taken in the Qumran reading of the text to develop the exegesis about the *Yom Kippur* confrontation), the theme of "not circumcizing the foreskin of his heart" is evoked in the exegesis, demonstrating in the process that the exegetes at Qumran probably knew the original sense of the underlying biblical passage and were playing on it to develop a *pesher* more in keeping with the events as they saw them. This, in turn, relates to the disqualification in the *Pesher* of the Wicked Priest from the Temple and Temple service according to the parameters of the Zadokite Statement enunciated in Ezek 44:7's "not circumcizing the foreskin of his heart". This is further concretized in the additional transmuting between "*Chos*" and "*Cha 'as*" ("Cup" and "Anger") and "trembling" and "foreskin", also discernible in these lines.

This "Priest"—almost certainly the Establishment High Priest of the time and, as I have attempted to demonstrate elsewhere, probably *Herodian*—does not walk "in the ways of drunkenness that he might quench his thirst" (as some render this translation, while others move further afield *to have him killed at a banquet*, because they misunderstand the thrust of the imagery). Rather "*he walks in his way of satiety so that he will drink his fill*" (italics mine). The meaning here is unmistakable, exploiting the various plays and transmutations in the underlying text, as well as the direct thrust of the imagery, to produce the desired exegesis about Vengeance, not drunkenness! Nor does it have anything whatever to do with *drunkenness* or *banqueting*, so disseminated in the field as to become almost proverbial, but *Divine Vengeance* that, as we have already shown, is being referred to throughout these sections and in parallel allusions in the Cave IV Psalm 37 *Pesher*.

The confirmation of this proposition comes in the next sentence: "And the Cup of the Wrath of God shall swallow him" (*teval'enu*—xi.15). Again the imagery being used to produce the exegesis is the *B-L-'*- imagery of "swallowing" or "consuming", also related to "Belial" or "devilishness", which is now turned around to relate to the Wicked Priest not the Righteous Teacher. This plays on the basic *ba-la-'a* circle of language, even though this language nowhere appears in the underlying text—i.e., just as the Wicked Priest "swallowed" or "consumed" (*leval'o*) the Righteous Teacher and "swallowed" or "consumed" (*leval'am*) those observing their "*Yom ha-Kippurim*" fastday, so too would he himself be "swallowed" or "consumed" in turn (not, for instance, Vermes' "*confuse*" or Gaster's "*confound*"). God did not want to "confound" or "confuse" the Wicked Priest (more likely these two translators are "confused"!). God wanted to *destroy him*.

This is made absolutely clear in the next column: "so too would God condemn him to destruction". The "Cup" imagery being used here in evocation of God's Divine Wrath "is not new. It is widespread in both Old and New Testaments and has deeper and deeper levels of meaning the more one delves into it. It is only strange that so many Qumran specialists have failed to grasp it or misconstrued it.

As Is 51:21, perhaps the original root of the usage, expresses it quite straightforwardly: "You have been afflicted and drunken, but *not with wine*" (italics mine). This could not be more straightforward and is the key to how the expression is used at Qumran as well. In fact, "*Chos-Hamato*"/"the Cup of His divine Anger", the usage as it appears here in the Habakkuk *Pesher*, is referred to three times in this passage from Isaiah in terms of the destruction of Jerusalem and another equally famous allusion—"*Chos ha-Tar'elah*"/"the Cup of Trembling"—is added twice in Is 51:18 and 23f.

Not only must one pay attention to the ongoing play in the exegesis between "*Chos*" and "*Cha'as*"/"Cup" and "Anger" in the underlying biblical citations and the *Pesher*, but this helps us to understand the additional play and transmutation taking place in the background to the text between "*he'arel*"/"foreskin" and "*hera' el*", "tremble"/"stagger" (which can also carry an underlying sense of "poison"—also *ra'al*: "*Poison*"—, here, for instance, resonates with the imagery of "*hemah*"/ "*Hamat*" or "hotness"/"Wrath", which can also mean "poison" because of the "stinging" connotation involved, and the "poison" imagery generally, used against the Establishment in later columns of the Damascus Document).

The Qumran text shows its knowledge of these intertwining, homophonic idioms by playing on the underlying "privy parts"/"foreskin" imagery originally present in the normative biblical version of these lines from Habakkuk; though the first, it will be recalled, it replaced with "Festivals" and the second, with "tremble"/"stagger" in the interests of the interpretation it wished to develop. This produced "'*orlat-libbo*" in the exegesis, "the foreskin of his heart" symbolism relative to the perceived disqualification of the Wicked Priest from service in the Temple because of his "works of Abomination"—"'*orlah*" in the exegesis playing on "*hera'el*" in the underlying citation about "drinking" and "staggering" in the Qumran version of Hab 2:16.

Not only does this reintroduction of the "foreskin" material—now in the exegesis—play off the disqualification of "those of uncircumcized heart and uncircumcized flesh" ("'*arlei-lev*" and "'*arlei-basar*"), who are "polluting the Temple" and "breaking the Covenant" with their "Abominations" in Ezek 44:7's "Zadokite Statement" (favorite language, as we have just seen, in the Habakkuk *Pesher* too); but in doing so, it shows that it probably appreciated that the sense of the normal biblical reading was probably originally present in the underlying text and it had been *purposely* changed to produce the desired exegesis.

In the process, too, the evocation of the theme of Divine Vengeance is also continued, that he—the Wicked Priest—would be forced to drink and that this would "swallow" him too. The same "Cup of Fury" imagery is utilized in Jer 25:15ff.'s "take the Wine Cup of His fury ("*Chos Hemah*" here) out of my hand and cause the Nations . . . to drink of it" (cf. Ezek 23:31–33 to the same effect).

Nor is the New Testament unfamiliar with this kind of "Cup" imagery, relating to "drinking the Cup" as used here in apocalyptic and eschatological contexts of the Habakkuk *Pesher* in the sense of "drinking the Cup of Divine Vengeance" or, on the other side of the coin, *being martyred.* This is certainly the thrust of Jesus' discussions with his Apostles (Mt 20:22–23/Mk 10:28–29/John 18:11). But even more to the point, the most vivid presentation of it is to be found in Rev 14:9–10, repeated in 16:19 and 18:6: they "who gave the whole world the wine of God's Anger to drink . . . will be made to drink the wine of God's Fury, which is ready, undiluted in His Cup of Anger in fire and brimstone".

Nothing could better recapitulate the Qumran usage of this imagery than this. *The correspondence is exact,* including even the allusion to "fire and brimstone", which forms an intrinsic part of the "Decree of Judgement" *God makes in the midst of Many Nations* in 1QpHab, x.5 above. Rev 16:17 emphasizes the retributive nature of this imagery, i.e., "God made her [the whore of Babylon, or, as the case may be, Rome—another variation on the "Belial/Balaam" imagery mentioned above] drink the full wine Cup of His Anger . . . She must be paid double the amount she exacted. She is to have a doubly strong Cup of her own mixture." Rev 18:6 adds an allusion to "the End" to this imagery, also found here in these last columns of the Habakkuk *Pesher.*

But the New Testament also knows another variation on or adumbration of this imagery, which is central to Pauline Christianity as it has devolved upon us, and that is, "the New Covenant in the Cup of (his) blood, which was poured out for you" (Lk 22:20 and 1 Co 11:25–27). This leads to a wholly different series of images and spiritualized usages centering on the word "Cup" and the decipherment of the peculiar Qumran usage, "the New Testament in the Land of Damascus", referred to in this document, but at greater length in the Damascus Document. It should be appreciated that "Damascus" in Greek epigraphy is a partial homophone for the Hebrew words "*dam*"/"blood" and "*Chos*"/"Cup". This can be appreciated by the phonetically aware reader, though it is not present in the Hebrew, since "Damascus" in English only comes through the Greek transliteration.

However this may at first appear, the relationship of this Qumran "Damascus" (taken according to its Greek orthography) with the New Testament "Cup of blood" does, therefore, have a linguistic basis, which means that the language of "the New Covenant in the Land of

Damascus" in the Hebrew of the Qumran Scrolls is related to the language of The New Testaments' "the Cup of the New Covenant in (his) blood", and this relationship is probably not simply accidental. This is an astonishing proposition, which would then relate the two "Covenant"'s and about which I have more to say in my forthcoming *James the Brother of Jesus* (Faber, 1996), mentioned above.

Furthermore, the additional adumbration of this imagery, "the Cup of the Lord", enunciated by Paul in these same passages from 1 Co 10:21 and 11:27—also amidst "body" and "blood" imagery—is reflected in a tradition about a first post-resurrection appearance by Jesus not to Peter and the other Apostles—whoever these may have been and if any sense of these appearances can ever be made—but in the Gospel of the Hebrews as preserved by Jerome to James. It is, however, not clear what the sense of this allusion is, whether spiritualized, as in Paul's or in Gospel versions of *Last-Supper* scenarios; or otherwise, as in Mt 20:22–23/Mk 10:38–39's and Synoptic parallels—the *two brothers* having to "drink the Cup" that Jesus would drink. There is no doubt that this has to be seen as martydom, and brings us back full circle again to the "Vengeance" aspects of the usage, we find here at Qumran.

It is also possible, as just noted above, that *"cha'as-hamato"/*"his hot anger" also plays on the "exile to *Hanut*" notices found in *Talmud*ic materials, transmuting words in the same clearly discernible pattern as "Festivals" (*Mo'adeihem*) for "privy parts" (*me'oreihem*), "trembling" (*ra-'el*) for "foreskin" (*'arel*), and similarly playing "*Chos*" (Cup) on "*Cha'as*" (Anger). In such a context, it is possible to see "*hamat*" here in the Qumran text as a play on "*Hanut*" in parallel *Talmud*ic reporting of similar events, the one relating to the Wicked Priest's fury during and, the other, to the location of the Sanhedrin proceedings he pursued against James, and both relating to the perception of their illegitimacy.

There is one final suggestion that can be related to all these plays-on-words and esoteric transmutations. This mysterious "*Hanut*" has also been identified as an esotericism for the "House" or "Chamber of the sons of Hanan"[29], that is, "the sons of Ananus", the very Highly-Priestly family involved in all these executions of James and supposedly of Jesus. If this correspondence is true and can be borne out, then all these allusions come full circle and we have still another indication of the relationship of these usages to the events we are considering here.

Though it is recognized this can never be proven, there can be no mistaking the import of these *Talmud*ic passages, nor their relationship to this powerful formulation in the Habakkuk *Pesher*, concretizing the milieu of the Wicked Priest's destruction of the Righteous Teacher as being in "his *Beit-Galut*"—in our view, a *Sanhedrin Trial*. "His hot anger", redundant in any case, would then play off the place of this infraction, that is, "the House of Exile" or "his Exiled House" of the Sanhedrin now sitting at "*Hanut*" in this period, not on the Temple Mount. And according to the sense of these *Talmud*ic passages, no trial should have been held there—certainly *not one carrying the death penalty*. The whole proceedings were illegal.

The underlying text from Hab 2:15, as reproduced in the Habakkuk *Pesher*, also substitutes a "his" for a "your" in the normative reading of the underlying biblical text from Hab 2:15 in the interests of the exegesis it wishes to develop *vis-à-vis* "*hamato*". It then carries the sense of "his poison"—a secondary meaning of the word "*hemah*", as we have seen—rather than "your powerful dregs" or "your wineskin" as per Masoretic/ Septuagint reading—another transmutation. Not only, therefore, does this correspondence between "*hamat*" and "*Hanut*" hint at a further code no more fantastic than these other transmutations, but it further concretizes the *sitz im leben* thrust of the other language couplets here in these closing lines of the Habakkuk *Pesher*.

Again considerations relating to James and the peculiar usages implicit in the "*Beit-Galuto*" allusion brought us to these insights in the first place. Nor we would otherwise have suspected them. But once the materials relating to James are inspected, then these are the determinations that emerge. Nor are more familiar theories helpful in elucidating these kinds of allusions. On the contrary, they rarely even consider them and if they do, often get them wrong. It is evidence of this kind that provides the build-up necessary to the general theory: the identity of James and the Righteous Teacher, and the congruence of the Jerusalem Community of James the Just with the last stages of the evolution, represented Qumran.

[1] For criticisms of these, see P.H. Davies, "How not to do Archaeology: The Story of Qumran", *Biblical Archeaologist*, December, 1988, pp. 203–207, *Maccabees . . .*, pp. 17ff., 28ff., 32ff., and 71–93.

[2] See *War* 6.312ff.; Tacitus, *The Histories*, 2.78ff. and 5.13; Suetonius, *The Twelve Caesars*, 10.4; *b. Git* 56b.; *ARN* 4, etc., all with a first-century milieu. Josephus applies this prophecy to Vespasian, as does R. Yohanan.

[3] 1QS, ii.1–iv.26 (particularly iv.21), viii.12ff., xi.1; 1QH, vii.6f., xii.11f., xiv.2., etc.

[4] This is referred to twice in key exegeses in 1QS, ix.13 and x.18ff.

[5] 1QpHab, xi.6.

[6] See, for instance, J.T. Milik, *Ten Years of Discovery in the Wilderness of Judaea*, London, 1959, p. 67f.; F.M. Cross, *The Ancient Library of Qumran and Modern Biblical Studies*, New York, 1958, p. 153; and others.

[7] See both Milik and Cross above; A. Jaubert, "Le calendrier des Jubilés et de la secte de Qumran: Ses origines bibliques", *VT* 3, 1955, pp. 250–64; S. Talmon, "The Calendar Reckoning of the Sect from the Judaean Desert" in *Aspects of the Dead Sea Scrolls*, Jerusalem, 1958, pp. 162–99.

[8] See discussion below on 1QpHab, xi.3 and the Qumran reading of Hab 2:16 "*Mo'adeihem*"/"their Festivities" for the Masoretic "*me'oreihem*"/"their privy parts". Showing the shift probably to be deliberate, the Masoretic (followed by the Septuagint) *is played upon* to produce an important usage below in the Commentary.

[9] See Vermes, *The Dead Sea Scrolls in English*, 3rd ed., Baltimore, 1987, p. 289; T. H. Gaster, *The Dead Sea Scriptures*, 3rd ed., 1976, has "confuse" on p. 324, but uses "confound" on p. 325 when the usage is turned against the Wicked Priest in xi.15.

[10] Cross, pp. 151ff., is particularly weak in this regard, but Milik, p. 69f. is better. See also discussions like F.F. Bruce's *Second Thoughts on the Dead Sea Scrolls*, Exeter, 1966, p. 105 dependent on them.

[11] See *War* 4.318ff.; but cf. *Vita* 39 and *Ant.* 20.9. Ananus actually "ruled" Israel twice, at the time of the execution of James and in the first stages of the Uprising against Rome. Properly speaking, though, any high priest can be said to have "ruled Israel".

[12] 4QpPs 37, ii.19f. and iv.9ff. That we are in a framework of "Judgement" and that this is "recompense" for what he had done to "the Righteous One"/"Righteous Teacher" is made clear, as it is in the language of 1QpHab. The language here actually incorporates that of Is 3:9–11 about "*gemul*"/reward applied to the death of James in early Church literature.

[13] See *War* 4.316.

[14] See Origen, *Contra Celsum* 1.47, 2.13, and *Comm. in Matt.* 10.17; also Eusebius, *E.H.* 2.23.17ff.; cf. also 3.7.8.

[15] This is also the theme in Ex 14 (repeated in Deut 11:4 and Joshua 24:6) and the interesting case of Saul's pursuit of David "into the wilderness" in 1 Sam 23:25.

[16] See Ps *Rec* 1.70f. This "Enemy" terminology is known in the palpably anti-Pauline "Parable of the Tares"; Mt 13:25ff. It is also used in the all-important Ja 4:4. Paul shows some consciousness of the appellation as applicable to himself in Ga 4:16.

[17] *Ant.* 20.6 Cf. JJHP (Chapter 2) pp. 182ff., 208 and 215.

[18] See, for instance, Cross' long note in this regard, pp. 23ff. For "drunkenness" see n. 13 above and my further discussion below.

[19] See 1QpHab, x.3, preceded by a more difficult reference in viii.2. Vermes translates x.3 as "condemned House", whatever this may mean; Gaster does better, grasping its eschatological character.

[20] I have discussed this usage and the circle of language related to it in JJHP (Chapter 2), pp. 208 and 216f. For the reference to Balaam as "consuming the people", see *b. Sanh* 105a. For the anti-Herodian tenor of these usages, see pp. 182ff and 208–17.

[21] The use of "House" is widespread in the *Koran*; cf. 2:125, 2:127, 3:96, etc., referring to the Ka'bah. But most important of all, see the reference to the Sanhedrin trial of Jesus at the "House of the High Priest".

[22] This discussion introduces his discussion of the "Star Prophecy"; *War* 6.288–300. It begins not with the star over Bethlehem, but with the star over the Temple as a portent to its destruction. Josephus introduces a rough peasant (prophet?), "Jesus ben Ananias", who "four years before the war" from around the time of the death of James continually proclaims the destruction of the city and the Temple, even to Albinus for the next seven years. That there is some connection between this and the notice in early

Church literature tying the destruction of the Temple and the fall of Jerusalem to the death of James should be clear. It is also interesting that in this passage Josephus identifies the "Star Prophecy" as the moving force behind the Uprising against Rome.

[23] See *ARN* 4 above, which makes it clear that this kind of "falling" imagery relates to the destruction of the Temple in 70 CE. See also *b. Git* 56a referring to Is 10:33f., and *b. Yoma* 39b referring to Zech 11:1 (4QpIs^c combines Is 30 with Zech 11. Note our discussion below of 1QpHab's use of the imagery of Is 29:9: "they are drunk but not with wine") and Nah 1:4 (4QpNah begins with Nah 2:1). This is definitive evidence that Qumran passages of this kind apply to the fall of the Temple in 70 CE and not to an earlier fall as has been widely suggested to support given identifications or theories.

[24] A similar kind of symbolism is present in Gospel exegeses of "Zebulon"/"Naphtali"; cf. Mt 4:14ff. referring to Is 8:23ff. Just as *Talmud*ic exegeses of these "exiles" of the divine presence, as embodied by the Sanhedrin, refer to a shift from Judah to Galilee, so too the coming of Jesus (also pictured as an embodiment of the divine Presence—even sometimes the Temple itself) to Galilee is pictured similarly. Both exegeses signal a transfer of favor from Judah to Zebulon.

[25] Cf. *Koran* 2:39, 2:126, 2:174f. (including palpably Jamesian dietary regulations), 3:185, 73:12, 74:26 (note "Day of Judgement" in 46), 82:15 (with "Day of Judgement"), 84:12, 92:14, etc.

[26] See Ezek 44:7ff., and the pivotal exegesis in CD, iv. The "uncircumcized heart" allusion forms the backdrop of the disqualification of the former Priesthood. See my discussion in JJHP (Chapter 2), pp. 208–11. It is curious that Josephus in *War* 2.408ff. describes this rejection of gifts and sacrifices from foreigners, which triggered the Uprising against Rome, as an "innovation", with which the ancestors before were unacquainted. But is unequivocally set forth in these passages in Ezekiel. This makes the Qumran *Pesher* on Ezek 44:15 all the more important. Throughout the Habakkuk *Pesher*, it is clear that the Wicked Priest enriches himself by illegally receiving gifts from the "spoils" of Violent People and "robbing the Poor". Receipt of gifts such as these is described as "polluting the Temple treasury" in CD, vi.15f. I have sketched an ambiance for these in JJHP (Chapter 2), pp. 162ff and 187ff.

[27] The wine here is very strong, as will be the retribution corresponding to it. Cf. the "vinegar" given Jesus in Mt 27/Mk 15/Lk 28/John 19 based on Ps 69:21.

[28] In addition to the examples cited above, see the all-important CD, iii.21–iv.2 citing Ezek 44:15 where *waw*-constructs seem to be deliberately inserted between "Priests *and* Levites *and* Sons of Zadok" (italics mine) to produce a given exegesis—i.e., "Priests" are "penitents", "Levites" are "Joiners" (probably Gentile God-fearers as in Esther 9:27; cf. "*ger-nilveh*" in 4QpNah, ii.9), and "Sons of Zadok" the eschatological "Elect".

[29] The *Babylonian Talmud*, vol. iii, *Sanhedrin*, London, 1935, p. 267.

CHAPTER 6

Eschatological "Rain" Imagery in the War Scroll and the Letter of James[*]

In appraising eschatological themes and imagery at Qumran, surprising constructions emerge. Themes develop, when pursued, that provide new clues for ideas and motifs hitherto unsuspected or previously unknown. One of these themes is "rain" and eschatological "rain" imagery. When this theme is pursued, using Qumran imagery as a focus, a new set of ideologies emerges relating to the imagery of the Son of Man/Messiah "coming on the clouds of Heaven", first alluded to in Daniel and picked up as a central construct in theology relating to the Gospel portrait of Jesus.[1] Another persistent theme that finds linkage to this cluster is the one of primordial rain-maker, rain-making being clearly a procedure associated with the whole apocalyptic complex of eschatological "rain" and "rain" imagery.

There are in the literature of this period several such primordial rain-makers. The first immediately recognizable one is Elijah, which links the rain-maker concept to *redivivus* notions centering about his person, thereby tying the tradition to activities related to those of John the Baptist.[2] In fact, both Josephus and the *Talmud* are acquainted with the rain-making tradition, as is in its own way the medieval *Zohar*.[3] In these, the notions of rain and Judgement are also linked to eschatological Flood and the Noah tradition.[4] One possible ancestor of John the Baptist—or at least a parallel tradition line—is to be found in the person of Josephus's Onias the Just or the *Talmud*'s Honi the Circle-Drawer.[5] This, in turn, links the tradition to "the Just"/"Just One" notation, which has interesting overtones with the relation of this tradition to the person of James the Just in early Church literature, bringing this complex of themes full circle.[6]

The method of this discussion will be literary-critical, for it is only

[*] *Journal of New Eastern Studies* 49, no. 2 (1990), University of Chicago.

through a literary-critical analysis and evaluation of relevant texts that the main lines of these various and interlocking eschatological notions emerge. There is no guidebook to these ideologies or, for that matter, to the terminologies related to them. In fact, the tradition may be a figment of the modern critic's imagination; however, the interlocking themes and notations are there, and through an analysis of their parallels and connections, a reconstruction may be achieved which comes to look something like an ideology.

According to Rabbinic literature, Phineas was also linked to a *redivivus* tradition, and here, too, there is an allusion to rain-making, i.e., closing the Heavens and opening them.[7] Both are important motifs. Not only is it all but indistinguishable from the *redivivus* tradition associated with Elijah above, but it links the above complex of themes to the "Zealot" Priestly tradition and that "zeal" which has become proverbial where Phineas' behavior is in question.[8] Elsewhere, I have associated this with the "Zadokite"—and possibly the "*Zaddik*ite"—tradition,[9] a tradition which has strong links with the *redivivus* one alluded to in the presentation of John the Baptist in the Gospels.

Both the Phineas and the Elijah *redivivus* traditions are priestly with some association with rain-making. Elijah was also a miracle-worker. As such, he was taken up to Heaven alive in a kind of prefiguration of later "Messianic" ideology. Once again this ascent has strong links with "the Son of Man on the clouds of Heaven" theme, first evoked in Daniel and echoed, as we shall see, in materials present in the War Scroll from Qumran. The New Testament, too, associates the theme of primordial Flood with the signs of the End, and such a Flood, of course, has to be associated with Noah, again one of the first, if not *the* first, in the quasi-rain-making tradition, but also an archetypical personality in the tradition of "*Zaddik*" theorizing.[10]

I have dealt with this "*Zaddik*" tradition to a certain extent elsewhere. Noah is perhaps the first identifiable Priest/*Zaddik*. It is his sacrifice that ends the period of primordial Flood and allows mankind, once again, to begin the consumption of flesh (with the provision that it be *free from blood*).[11] The "*Zaddik*"tradition is, of course, strong in *Kabbalah* and picked up in *Zohar* tradition, i.e.,

> Noah was a Righteous One. Assuredly so after the Heavenly pattern [here the "Primal Adam" ideology intrudes]. It is written, "the Righteous One is the Foundation of the world", and the Earth is established thereon, for this is the Pillar that upholds the world. So Noah was called "Righteous" below . . . and acted so as to be a true copy of the Heavenly ideal . . . an embodiment of the world's Covenant of Peace (59b on "Noah").

That this *Zaddik*-tradition was known in the Second Temple period is, also, hardly to be doubted, judging by its use in the New Testament's portrait of its Messiah, not to mention its use as a cognomen within the Messianic family itself, primarily relating to James the Just.[12] The implications of the "*Zaddik*" terminology for the person of James is set forth in Eusebius/Epiphanius/Jerome exposition, probably based on Hegesippus.[13] In all cases, some extreme purity regulations were associated with it, as was a terminology having to do with "Fortress" and/or "Protection of the People", if these two can be reckoned as separate designations.[14] In addition, the idea, first encountered in Proverbs that "the Righteous One is the Pillar of the world" (as well perhaps as the *lamed-waw* tradition in Rabbinic/Kabbalistic literature on the number of Righteous Men necessary to uphold or keep the world in existence) is to be associated with James' role as "Pillar" of the Jerusalem Community as in the Pauline allusion (Ga 2:8) and related materials associating his removal with the destruction of Jerusalem.[15]

The implication here, unlike the normal implication of early Church tradition, that of punishment upon the Jews,[16] is rather different—i.e., as in the *Zohar* evocation of "the *Zaddik*-the-Pillar-of-the-world" above, to a certain extent echoed in the Gospel of Thomas[17]—once the Shield ("*Ma'oz*" at Qumran) was removed, the city could no longer remain in existence (like Sodom and Gomorrah at the time of the second "*Zaddik*" in Genesis presentation, Lot, and the world at the time of the Flood—here Noah's role as first "*Zaddik*" should not be overlooked).

"Rain-making" itself is not unassociated with the theme of eschatological flood. One of the most interesting characters in the "rain-making" tradition, aside from Elijah and the *redivivus* tradition associated with his person, is Honi the Circle-Drawer or, as Josephus refers to him, "Onias the Just". Not only does the person of Honi bring the tradition down to the Second Temple Period, it also associates it with what we are signaling as the developing "*Zaddik*"-tradition, "the Just" being a cognomen usually associated with certain priestly individuals in this line from the saintly Simeon the Righteous in Ben Sira and Rabbinic tradition to James, the subject of this discussion.

For these purposes, James' priestly attributes are not inconsequential, nor are those of the Righteous Teacher at Qumran, another "*Zaddik*". Here it emerges that rain-making involved some characteristics perhaps associated with Noah's original primordial Priesthood/eschatological function as a quasi-rain-maker, that is, the Flood appeared against the backdrop of his soteriological "Perfection" and "Righteousness". "Perfection" and "Righteousness" are two very basic Qumran doctrines, as they are to a certain extent in Matthew's presentation of Jesus—another of these soteriological *Zaddik*s with priestly functions according to Hebrews' presentation.[18]

One might add that in *ARN* 4:4, one of the concomitants to proper "Temple service" is rain coming in its season. Such an allusion cannot help but have links to what goes under the name of "the Zadokite Covenant", also associated with a "Covenant of Peace" attached to Phineas' name in Ben Sira and 1 Maccabees, the Zadokite Covenant as in Ezekiel's presentation having to do with proper Temple service.[19] Elsewhere, we have already associated the Priest/*Zaddik* tradition with an esoteric understanding of the Zadokite Covenant of the kind delineated to a certain extent at Qumran.

Onias' position is not unlike the position of James. Just as James would seem to have been stoned to death in 62 CE just prior to the fall of the Temple, so Honi/Onias the Just was stoned just prior to Pompey's assault on the Temple in 63 BC. Onias prefigures James in other ways, not the least of which being that a fall of the Temple followed their individual deaths—again the *Zaddik*-tradition involving "Protection of the People" (one of James' epithets) would appear to be operative to some extent here. If early Church accounts are to be credited, in both instances Establishment figures send representatives to the two "*Zaddik*"s asking them to condemn a seemingly seditious situation and, in both cases, their refusal culminates in their stoning. In addition, there is the "rain-making" tradition attached to their persons.

"Circle-drawing", of course, is one of the mechanisms of rain-making. There is some indication that the followers of Josephus' "*Banus*" or his "Essenes" followed a variation of this mechanism on the Sabbath, since they were unwilling to go outside a certain perimeter even for defecation.[20] Furthermore, we hear in *Talmud*ic accounts that two grandchildren of this Onias, one referred to as "Hanan" or "Hanin *ha-Nehba*'", i.e., "the Hidden", also appear to be associated with the "rain-making" tradition, a connection which, therefore, would appear to have been carried down by Honi's descendants. This Hanan or Hanin has sometimes been associated with John the Baptist and, if nothing else, there is also a "Hidden" tradition associated with both John the Baptist and Jesus.[21]

The "Hidden" tradition is another interesting one, which in some way appears to have resurfaced in Shi'ite Islam in association with another doctrine, the "Primal Adam", known among the Ebionites and perhaps before. It, too, has some *redivivus* characteristics, this one linked to Jesus' own person, i.e., Jesus was "the Second Adam" (cf. 1 Co 15:45). The *Koran*, for its part, is very much aware of the "Primal Adam" tradition and knows the doctrine that Jesus is "the Second Adam"—what we will also associate presently with the terminology of "the Son of Man".[22] One should note that for Shiʿite (and even Sunnit) Islam, Jesus and "the *Mahdi*"—in Twelver Shiʿism the *Mahdi* is the last "*Imam*"—are *both* expected to return at the end of time. Nothing could better illustrate the Shiʿite notion of "the Hidden '*Imam*'" than this.

Also associated with Honi's heirs is a "Rip van Winkle" tradition which finds expression in another grandson of Honi, "Abba Hilkiah", who in fact appears to have been active *around the time of James*. This individual, too, whoever he may have been, was a rain-maker, and the stories about him sound vaguely like the stories associated with James in Epiphanius' curious retelling, i.e., children are sent by the Jerusalem Establishment to him to ask him to make rain. In both stories, such Establishment representatives are treated very gruffly by the putative rain-maker. Of course, the theme of being requested to do things by the presumably Pharisaic/Sadducean/Herodian Establishment is a motif in all traditions associated with James—as earlier too the person of Honi.[23]

This brings us to the core of my presentation of the two references to eschatological "rain" in both the letter associated with the name of James and the War Scroll at Qumran. Where the latter is concerned, this moves into imagery, first evoked in Daniel, of the Messiah "coming on the clouds of Heaven", which cannot be separated from the use made of this imagery in New Testament presentations of "the Son of Man". Seen in this way, "the Son of Man" is another variation of "the Second Adam" ideology so important in Ebionitism or Jewish Christianity— "Man" and "Adam" presumably being interchangeable. This leads us into James' reported proclamation in the Temple of the imminent return of "Jesus" or "the Messiah"—"the Second Man"—at the behest of Establishment representatives, reported variously in all early Church traditions (including the Pseudoclementines), which provokes the riot ending in James' death—another basic element in all early Church accounts.

Epiphanius tells us that James was a rain-maker, a most peculiar bit of information, whether a figment of his imagination or real—since rain-making, as we have seen, was associated with the "*Zaddik*" tradition. James is also, of course, a "*Zaddik*", and the terminology is prominent among his cognomens. Eusebius through Hegesippus appears to use this epithet as a substitute even for James' name itself (see allusions such as "Justus is praying for you", etc.—in this context, it should be remarked that in Roman catacombs "Justus" and "Zadok" are synonymous appellations). The material leading up to the allusion to rain-making in the Letter of James—allusion to which is also to be found not uncoincidentally in no other New Testament letter or document—follows the condemnation of the individual or process being referred to as "the Tongue" (3:5ff.). I have already remarked that the use of this genre of condemnation is generically parallel to similar Qumran condemnations of adversaries of the "Righteous Teacher"/"*Zaddik*" at Qumran—for example, the "Spouter", "Comedian", or "Liar".[24]

There follows the condemnation of "fornication", so often associated with James' name and a favorite theme at Qumran (4:4), as well as "making the world your Friend", which I have elsewhere identified as anti-Pauline.[25] The "Friend" terminology is extremely important in the light of the emphasis on Abraham as "the Friend of God" in Ja 2:23 and CD, iii.2ff., an emphasis which continues on into Islam, presumably transmitted by the Ebionites.[26] This is explained in terms of "the Enemy", terminology also important in Jewish Christianity, presumably applying to Paul; in Islam "the Enemy of God" is similarly dubbed "the *Dajjāl*"—"the Joker" or "the Comedian".

He precedes the return of Jesus and "the *Mahdi*", i.e., just as the unnamed interlocutor makes the world "his Friend", so he will be considered "the Enemy of God" (4:4). The implication is clear and harks back to the earlier description of Abraham as "the Friend of God", itself coupled with aspersions on "the Empty Man" who presumably also cited Abraham to justify his Salvation-by-Faith doctrine, i.e., Abraham exemplifies his "Friendship" with God in being willing to sacrifice his principal son. Ja 2:21 ff. cites this as the example *par excellence* of "Faith working with works". It is striking that this peculiar example of works finds a parallel expression in Josephus' description of the last stand of the extreme "Zealots"/*Sicarii* on Masada, who are willing to sacrifice *their children*.[27] That this "Enemy" terminology was already current in Paul's lifetime and was not unknown to him can be inferred from his use of it in Ga 4:16 (paralleling New Testament evocations of the same terminology in the anti-Pauline "Parable of the Tares"; Mt 13:26ff.).

Here follows in Ja 4:7 the evocation of the Greek "Diabolos", which not unlikely has some linguistic relationship to the Hebrew "Belial", so common in Qumran usage and corrupted in Paul's "Beliar" (2 Co 6:15). Also of interest here in this linguistic circle of words is the Islamic "Iblis", used in the *Koran* in conjunction with allusions to a supernatural Adam. Leading up to the evocation of being a "Doer of the Law"—at the heart of the key interpretation of Hab 2:4 in the Habakkuk *Pesher* and important in discussions of Faith in Paul (and probably Ja 2:5ff.)—is the condemnation of slandering a brother (Ja 4:11—another activity

Paul indulges in rather promiscuously in Acts, Galatians, Corinthians, etc.). This theme is a strong one in the Community Rule, and the punishment for it set forth there is expulsion from "table-fellowship" and non-cooperation with such an individual in "work and purse".[28]

In the Letter of James, the emphasis on "doing" continues, again paralleling the Habakkuk *Pesher*, leading into the condemnation of "the Rich" and "Riches". As with the condemnation of "fornication", the condemnation of "the Rich"/"Riches" is another of "the Three Nets of Belial" in CD, iv–v and a known theme in James' life. In this all-important presentation in CD, iv–v, the third "net" is "pollution of the Temple", which is an important element of Paul's evocation of "Beliar" in 2 Co 6:16—a passage with unmistakable doctrinal connections to Qumran. Elsewhere, I have linked this "pollution" theme to James' condemnation of "food"/"things sacrificed to idols", another strong theme in Paul's Corinthians correspondence, strong too in the Temple Scroll in relation to "pollution of the Temple" (xlvi–xlvii), and later appearing once again in *Koran*ic dietary regulations, along with another Jamesian element repeatedly reported in Acts, "abstention from blood".[29]

Not only is this condemnation of "the Rich" the climax of the Letter, it is linked to a condemnation of those who killed "the Just"/"Just One"/"Righteous One". This, of course, is the Jamesian riposte to the Pauline aspersion in 1 Thess 2:14 that "the Jews killed the Messiah"; in James, more appropriately, it is "the Rich", a pregnant allusion, too, in relation to James' own death and probably that of the Righteous Teacher in 1QpHab and 4QpPs 37. It has important implications where the High Priests and Herodians in this period are concerned.[30] At this point, the eschatological "coming of the Lord" is proclaimed in Ja 5:7f. and linked to the coming of "rain". This will have strong overtones with the presentation of the coming of the Messiah in Judgement together with all the Heavenly Host in columns xi f. and xix in the War Scroll below, where the all-important evocation of eschatological "rain" also occurs.

This allusion in James also has strong links to the proclamation associated with his person in the Eusebius/Hegesippus presentation of the events leading up to his death, i.e., "Why do you ask me concerning Jesus the Son of Man ["the Second Adam"]. He is now sitting in the Heavens on the right hand of great Power and is about to come on the clouds of Heaven" (here again, "cloud" imagery from Daniel is linked to evocation of eschatological Judgement). The stoning of James and the fall of Jerusalem follow (i.e., "the *Zaddik*-the-Pillar-of-the-world" ideology echoed in Origen's insistence that Josephus stated that Jerusalem fell because of the death of James, not of Jesus).[31]

Ja 5:7 cautions "patience until the coming of the Lord" and equates this coming with the coming of "rain". This theme of "patience" is also strong in the Habakkuk *Pesher* preceding the pivotal "Jamesian" exposition of Hab 2:4 in what I have elsewhere identified as the "delay of the *Parousia*" (this in exposition of Hab 2:3 related, as here in the Letter of James, to "doing the Law" or "doers of the Law"). The Habakkuk *Pesher*, too, ends on a similar note of hopeful *patience* and expectation of an eschatological "Last Judgement" on all idolators and evildoers on the earth. This is exactly the position of *b.San.* 96b on Hab 2:3, "waiting for" the Messianic Era, and the "thirty-six Righteous Ones" related to this.

This theme of patience in expectation of divine Judgement continues throughout the remainder of Chapter 5 of the Letter of James until the evocation of Elijah's rain-making miracle in the course of an allusion to the efficacy of the prayerful supplication of "the Righteous One" in 5:17. Of course, just this kind of prayerful supplication is referred to in the Eusebius/Jerome/Epiphanius/Hegesippus presentation of all the supplication James as "Righteous One" did in the Temple asking for forgiveness on behalf of the People until, unforgettably, "the skin on his knees turned to camel's hide". I have discussed this allusion and tied it to a *Yom Kippur* atonement James may have made in his role as High Priest of the Opposition Alliance.[32]

Here Elijah, a predecessor in the Priestly *Zaddik/redivivus* tradition—and a man with "the same kind of feelings" as James and his Community—Ja 5:17f.—is portrayed as being of such power that his prayer could both cause rain to cease and then fall again. The implication of this to the power attributed to James in his role as Priest/*Zaddik* is obvious. The interval between these two events is denoted as the pregnant one of three and a half years (5:17), a period important also for Daniel's eschatological framework. It should be noted, when discussing eschatological notions of chronology and final apocalyptic events, that this was also the approximate interval between James' death in 62 CE and the outbreak of the Uprising against Rome in 66 CE, which was, no doubt, seen in some circles as the beginning of this process of final eschatological Judgement.

The evocation of Daniel's Messiah "coming on the clouds of Heaven" at this point in Hegesippus/Eusebius is, in this context, crucial, as is Josephus' claim of the import of the Messianic "Star Prophecy" to the Uprising against Rome—this last picked up by Roman historians and important to Vespasian's pretensions and those of the Flavian line, as it was to become in probably not unrelated Christian presentations.[33]

The evocation of eschatological "rain" in the War Scroll at Qumran also grows directly out of citation of "the Star Prophecy" and in evocation of final Judgement, *the coming of the Heavenly Host on the clouds of Heaven*.

If we turn to the passages relevant to this theme in the War Scroll, we find ourselves in a similar—if for the modern mind somewhat alien—environment. The relevant materials are to be found in column xif., recapitulated and repeated in column xix and in a number of allusions and images in columns leading up to these. After movement from "the camp in the Desert of the Nations" (see Mt 2:22's "Galilee of the Nations") to "the camp in the Desert of Jerusalem" and the outlining of battle order and slogans (columns i–vii), we come to a central doctrine in the War Scroll's presentation of purity, that is, no boy or woman or person who is blind, crippled, afflicted, blemished, etc. will be allowed in the camps (similar preoccupations are represented in the Temple Scroll where the city of the Temple is at issue, the "camps" being a possible wilderness and/or tabernacle prelude anticipating the process of purification of the Temple). We are told that only the "Perfect in Spirit" prepared for "the Day of Vengeance" (the Day of Judgement) will be accepted[34]—no one "who is impure . . . for the Holy Angels are together with their hosts" (vii.6). This need for absolute ritual purity in the camps is, therefore, necessary because the final apocalyptic War against all the Evil Ones on the earth was to be effected with the intervention of the Heavenly Host. Thus the stringent purity regulations in the camps, so they will not incur earthly, human pollution.

Since it is "the battle of God" which is being fought, "the priests shall trumpet at a distance, so as not to approach the slain and become polluted with impure blood . . . They shall not desecrate the anointment of their priesthood with the blood of the nations of vanity." In the camps, they shall be "kept from all pollution and Evilness", for "God goes with you to fight for you against your enemies so as to deliver you" (x. 4; Deut 20:2–4 repeated in Num 10:9).

The reference to "save" or "deliver" is important, particularly, as we shall see, when weighed with other persistent evocations of "*Yesha‘*"/ "*Yeshu‘a*" variations.[35] Evoking "works and mighty works" (the analogue to similar language in the New Testament) and Daniel's "*Kedoshim*"/ "Saints", i.e., "the Saints of the Covenant", the War Scroll makes its first reference to the Heavenly Host, namely, "the Angels of Holiness", "the Spirits [parallel to "*Jinn*" in Islam] and the dominion of the Holy Ones". These images are connected with an evocation of "clouds", presumably anticipating specific reference to the Heavenly Host coming on the clouds of Heaven later in the text. Here occurs another of these all-important evocations of "Adam" (x. 14, presumably "the Primal Adam"), and, by implication—if the two can be differentiated—the parallel ideology of "the Son of Man" also associated with proclamations related to James. This leads into the Messianic imagery of column xi.

Alluding to the "Name" ("Name" and "naming" are particularly important in key columns of CD, as they are in Acts, *Kabbalah*, etc. As the *Koran* would have it, probably through Ebionitism and the "*Primal Adam*" ideology, "God taught Adam all the names")[36] and David (xi. 2—important as a forerunner/progenitor of the Messiah), we encounter a variation of the Pauline "Salvation by Grace" ideology, i.e., "Salvation"/"Deliverance" ("*Yeshu'a*"—again the Hebrew links to the name "Jesus" should not be overlooked) has been "through thy Grace (*Hesed*) and not through our works" (xi. 3).

Allusion to "Grace" against the backdrop here of the usual Qumran emphasis on "works" requires explanation. Presumably the situation of divine intervention in apocalyptic Holy War engendered a more reverential approach. Unlike parallel New Testament ideologies, however, the allusions here are always physical and actual, not spiritualized, he New Testament reversing Qumran doctrine in a systematic and clearly discernible fashion—whereas at Qumran the apocalyptic final war is immediate and real; in Pauline variations—this is transformed into intimation of personal and heavenly salvation.

Evoking "Power" (cf. parallel New Testament allusions such as "the right hand of Power"—Mt 22:29, 24:30, 26:64, 28:18, etc.) and, once again "works and mighty wonders"; since this is a "Messianic" passage, the "Star Prophecy" is now cited in its entirety to be expanded upon at length in the quasi-*pesher* to follow. This "Star Prophecy" is cited upwards of three times in the extant Qumran corpus, testimony to its overwhelming importance there. Just as the Habakkuk *Pesher* can be seen as revolving around an exegesis of Hab 2:4, so the War Scroll can be seen as a long discourse revolving around the climactic evocation of Num 24:17–19 at this point in column xi.

Josephus cites this Prophecy, as we have seen, as the moving force behind the Uprising against Rome, thereby providing it with a *firm* 60–70 CE *sitz im leben* (having already alluded to it previously in his designation of Vespasian as Messiah). *Talmudic* sources testify to a similar currency, again claiming that Yohanan ben Zacchai (not Josephus) applied it to Vespasian. Roman authors also pick up the allusion, testifying to its currency in this period.

Here we are provided with the all-important Qumran exegesis of this critical prophecy. If there was any doubt that in the minds of the exegetes this prophecy related to Messianism and the Messiah, Qumran confirms it by following it up immediately with an exposition using the words, "by the hand of your Messiah" (it is unclear if the allusion here is plural or singular). This develops into an evocation of eschatological "rain" where final apocalyptic Judgement is invoked. Not surprisingly, "Belial", too, is directly invoked (as we have had "Diabolos" at this point in the Letter of James, "Iblis" in the *Koran* in the context of a *Primal Adam*-like ideology, and "Beliar" amid a flood of Qumran-type allusions in 2 Co 5–6). To this Messianism in the War Scroll is tied the language—familiar from the Sermon on the Mount—of "the Poor" and "the Poor in Spirit", not to mention the use of this terminology in Ebionite tradition and probably following this, the tradition emerging in the medieval *Zohar*.[37]

Here, as in the *Zohar*, "the Messiah" places himself among "the Meek" and "the Poor" (in this section "the Poor in Spirit" and "those bent in the dust"). The miracle that will be wrought is likened, as in Is 43:16f., to what was done to "Pharaoh and to the captains of his chariots in the Red Sea". The language of "kindling" and "burning" is used, as in parallel New Testament passages about John the Baptist: "You shall kindle the Poor in Spirit and they shall be a flaming torch in the straw to consume Uprighteousness and never cease till Evil is destroyed" (cf. Mt 2:10f.: "the fire is in the fan and the straw ready for the burning").

That this is something equivalent to the "Last Judgement" or "the House"/"Decree of Judgement", referred to variously in the Habakkuk *Pesher*, particularly in the course of *eschatological* exegesis of Hab 2:4, is hardly to be doubted.[38] Here and in the Habakkuk *Pesher*, this "Judgement" is to be rendered/pronounced by "the Elect", identified in CD. iv.2 in exposition of the key Ezek 44:15 passage, with "the Sons of Zadok" and here connected to repeated evocations of "the Poor" (also prominent in parallel sections of the Habakkuk *Pesher*). The enemies, too, at this juncture—as in these parallel sections of the Habakkuk *Pesher*—are "the *Kittim*", once again demonstrating the basic circularity of all these accounts.

This great Judgement is pictured throughout the remainder of column xi into column xii and with it the Noachic/Phineas "Covenant of Peace" (also important in the *Zohar* materials cited above). Again "Name" imagery is evoked in conjunction with allusion to "the Elect of the Holy People"—i.e., CD. iv's "Sons of Zadok"—coupled with an allusion to "the Elect of Heaven". Now consciously utilizing allusions from crucial eschatological sections in Daniel, "the *Kedoshim*" are grouped with "the

Angels . . . mighty in battle" in a perfect exposition of this final apocalyptic Judgement. Referring to actual divine or Messianic intervention, the text continues: "You shall fight with them from Heaven . . . the Angelic Host are numbered with our Assembly ("Church") . . . the Spirits [Islamic "*Jinn*" again] are with our footmen and horsemen".

At this point the imagery shifts to "cloud" imagery because the ambiance is that of Daniel's "Son of Man coming on the clouds of Heaven"—note that the passage began with evocation of the Messianic Prophecy and that this would be accomplished by "no mere Man" (*Adam*), —and in this context eschatological "rain" imagery is now used. In this case, the framework is definitively that of Daniel, which is emphasized with the words, "they [the Heavenly Host with the Messiah] are as clouds of dew over the earth, as *a shower of rain shedding Judgement* on all that grows on earth" (emphasis mine). This eschatological allusion to "rain", tied as it is to evocation of "the Last Judgement" and "the Son of Man coming on the clouds of Heaven" is pivotal. It clarifies and is a key to a whole complex of apocalyptic imageries.

It is followed by the allusion, "Arise Mighty One [possibly even "be resurrected"],[39] smite the Nations, thine adversaries and devour the flesh of the Sinner with your sword [certainly the Messiah here] . . . Sovereignty shall be to the Lord and everlasting dominion to Israel." Six more columns follow, recapitulating the imagery already encountered and adding to it, including allusion to "Belial", "Light", "Darkness", "works and mighty wonders", "Judgements", "Your Salvation" (note the linguistic connection again to the name "Jesus"), "the Poor in Spirit", "the Perfect of the Way", "the Day of Vengeance", "the Saints of the People", "the *Kittim*", "the Power of God", "the burning" (cf. the extensive *Koran*ic use of this language), "Everlasting Light", "Righteousness", "Truth", "Knowledge", the Jamesian "keeping the Covenant", "the Kingdom of Michael in the midst of the gods and the realm of Israel in the midst of all flesh" (cf. Pauline and Kabbalistic notions of Heaven above and Jerusalem below), and "the Gates of Salvation".

This last allusion has particularly strong relevance to the question asked of James in early Church tradition, as reported by Eusebius/Hegesippus: "What is the *gate to Jesus*?" (emphasis mine) and the response: "He is coming on the clouds of Heaven with all the Mighty Ones." Once again, the intrinsic relationship of such materials to Daniel and these passages in the War Scroll is inescapable.

These sections culminate in a second evocation of eschatological "rain":

Our Sovereign is Holy and the King of Glory is with us . . . they are *as clouds, clouds of dew covering the earth* and *a shower of rain shedding Judgement* on all that grows there (emphasis mine).

Here we find the crystalization of all these kinds of eschatological rain, Flood, and Final Judgement imagery. At Qumran, it is tied not only to the all-important "Star Prophecy" so intrinsic to events having to do with 66–70 CE and perhaps beyond, but also to Daniel's "Son of Man" (so important in New Testament exposition as well) "coming on the clouds of Heaven" to render final eschatological Judgement on all the sons of men.

In Ja 5's evocation of "rain-making", paralleled too in early Church accounts of James as a rain-maker and describing his "Messianic" proclamation in the Temple as well, we probably have an allusion to the intercession of "the *Zaddik*" (alluded to probably pejoratively in Josephus' aspersions on "imposters"/"deceivers"/"magicians")[40] in his role as "rain-" and "Judgement"-making forerunner setting this final eschatological process in motion.

[1] Mt 24:30; Mk 13:26, 14:62; Dan. 7:13 f.; also note that *Pseudo-Epiphanius* 100 links this last to Zech 12:10 about the descent of the Holy Spirit.

[2] Mal 4:5; Mt 11:14, 16:14, 17:10; Mk 6:15, 8:28, 9:11ff; Lk 1:17 and 9:8ff.

[3] *B. Ta'an* 23a–b on *M. Ta'an* 3:8 (in fact, much of the tractate is concerned with it), *j. Ta'an* 66b, *Ant.* 14.22ff., and *Zohar*, i,10a, 63a, and 67b.

[4] Cf. Mt 24:37ff.: "As with the days of Noah, so shall be the coming of the Son of Man", referring as well to the important motif evoking the "passing of Heaven and Earth".

[5] *Ant.* 14.22ff.; *b. Ta'an* 22b–23a.

[6] For James, see Eusebius, *E.H.* 2.23.2ff.; Epiphanius, *Haeres.* 29.3ff. and 78.14; and Jerome, *Vir. ill.* 2.

[7] The Chronicles of Jerahmeel 59.17/Ps Philo 48.1; cf. the twelve miracles associated with him in *Sifre* Numbers 131.

[8] Cf. Num *Rabbah* 21.3 and Num 26:6ff.; also *Zohar*, iii, 214a.

[9] See MZCQ (Chapter 1), pp. 74ff, 107f, and passim; note for Numbers *Rabbah* 21.4, Phineas too is a "*Zaddik*" as is Honi/Onias in *Ta'an* and Josephus.

[10] 2 Ki 2:11; cf. Lk 24:51 and Mk 16:19—in the latter his place in Heaven is described as "on the right hand of God", an allusion to coming Judgement. For Noah as the first *Zaddik*, see Ge 6:9, coupled with an allusion to the "Perfection" notation so important at Qumran and in the New Testament. Hebrew Ben Sira 44:17 starts its enumeration of "Pious Men" with "Noah the Righteous", anticipating succeeding such individuals in the "*Hesed*" and "*Zedek*" tradition; cf. the *Zohar*, i,66b comparing him to Elijah and Phineas and mentioning the "Covenant of Peace" associated with his name and 68b referring to him as "*Zaddik*".

[11] Ge 8:20, 9:4ff., particularly 9:44ff. referring to "clouds", rain, rainbow, etc. The

"blood" motif is particularly important where any associations with James are concerned, "abstention from blood" being an element in "Jamesian" rulings and their reflection in 1 Co below and the *Koran*; cf. also in CD, iii.6 and other "blood" imagery at Qumran. Cf. too the allusion to Noah's promordial sacrifice in *Zohar* i, 70a.

[12] See Acts 3:14, 7:52, and 22:14 on Jesus and Mt 27:19, 24; cf. Joseph as "Just" in Mt 1:19 and Lk 2:25 and also Ja 5:6. For Mt 5:49 in pursuance of biblical themes, the rain falls on the Just and Unjust alike. For James as "the Just One", see testimonies delineated above.

[13] Eusebius, *E.H.* 2.23.8ff. and Epiphanius, *Haeres* 78:7–14.

[14] Prov 10:25; Eusebius, *E.H.* 2.23.7 and 3.7.8; Epiphanius, *Haeres* 29.4; cf. *Zohar* on Phineas, iii, 218a–b, where the "Protection of the People" mentioned in Eusebius/Hegesippus is alluded to.

[15] For "Pillar" in *Zohar*, see i, 59b and iii, 222a; cf. an assortment of related allusions in 1QH, i.11, ii. 5, iii. 37, iv. 3, vi. 17ff., vii. 8ff., viii. 22ff., ix. 28f., etc., including "Foundations", "Fortress" (*Migdal*), and "Strength" (*Ma'oz*).

[16] Eusebius, *E.H.* 1.1.2, 2.6.4, 2.6.8, and passim.

[17] Gos Th 12, including the telltale "Pillar"-type reference to "Heaven and Earth", also in *Zohar* allusions, the New Testament above, and *b. Ta'an* on Is 45:8 below.

[18] This soteriological approach to Jesus is based on Is 53:11 (also a *Zaddik*-text) and "Justification" theorizing based on it in combination with texts such as Hab 2:4 and Ge 15:6. For the Priestly implications, see Heb 5:1ff., 7:11ff., 7:22ff., and variously coupled with "Perfection" ideology, see 9:11 and 12:24.

[19] Ben Sira 45:23f. and 1 Macc 2:26, 53; cf. also *Zohar* 66b. For *b. Ta'an* 22b the Prophet Habakkuk is one of these primordial circle-drawers/rain-makers! Cf. too James' vow not to eat, or presumably do anything else, until he "sees Jesus" in Jerome below.

[20] *War* 2.147f.; *Vita* 11.

[21] *B. Ta'an* 23af./*j. Ta'an* 66b (including a Rip van Winkle tradition relating to one of Honi's heirs). Lk 1:24, Protevangelium of James 18:1, and *Koran* 19:22; cf. also Noah in the *Zohar*, i, 63a and 67b.

[22] *Koran* 2:31ff., 3:33ff., and 3:59 (cf. 6:86 designating Jesus, John, Zechariah, and Elias as "Righteous"). See also Paul in 1 Co 15:22, 45 and Epiphanius in *Haeres* 30.3 for the "Ebionite" presentation of this key notation.

[23] Cf. *Ant.* 14.22f. with *Haeres* 78,14 and *b. Ta'an* 23a–23bf. Also see *E.H.* 2.23.10 for the Scribes and Pharisees coming to James; Mt 3:7, to John.

[24] See MZCQ (Chapter 1), pp. 16–17 and JJHP (Chapter 2), pp. 133, 173–74.

[25] See again JJHP (Chapter 2), pp. 177–78.

[26] *Koran* 4:125, etc.

[27] *War* 7.340ff. and 386ff.

[28] 1QS, vi. 15ff. and viii. 20ff. There are different degrees of murmuring and slandering—the worst being against the authority of the community.

[29] Chapter 2, pp. 209–14f; Acts 15:20, 15:29, 21:25—also in 1 Co 8:1ff., 10:19ff; 2 Co 6:16; Rev 2:14f.; cf. *Koran* 2:172, 5:3, and 16:115.

[30] The problem of "Rich"/"Riches" is strong in *Ant.* 20.7.3, 20.9.2, 20.9.4, and *War* 2.427 (on turning "the Poor against the Rich" and burning the debt records).

[31] *Contra Celsum* 1.47, 2.13, and *Comm. in Matt.* 10.17.

[32] MZCQ (Chapter 1), pp. 20, 110 and Eusebius, *E.H.* 2.23.6 and *Haeres* 29.3 and 78.13. Jerome in *Vir. ill.* parallels Epiphanius with James actually in the Holy of Holies!

[33] *War* 6.312ff. following on an earlier allusion to a "star" (289); cf. New Testament

variations in Mt 2:2ff. When Josephus presumably applies the Prophecy to Vespasian in 3.400ff. he actually seems to call himself a "messenger of good tidings". Cf. Suetonius, *The Twelve Caesars*, 10.4 and Tacitus, *The Histories*, 2.78ff. and 5.13.

One should note that in describing the signs and portents relating to this prophecy and the fall of the Temple, Josephus mentions Jesus b. Ananius, who prophesied the fall of Jerusalem around the time of Albinus' Governorship and continued doing so for seven and a half years. This is not without relevance to the tradition connecting James' death with the fall of Jerusalem in Origen, related to a Jewish Christian oracle connected to "the Pella-Flight" tradition. The seven and a half years mentioned here is the *exact* length of time between James' death and the fall of Jerusalem. In fact, Jesus seems to have begun his mournful cry exactly following the *death of James*.

[34] Vii. 5f.; cf. Lk 21:22, Ro 12:19, 2 Thess 1:8, etc. and numerous parallel *Koranic* allusions.

[35] X.4. The term is also evoked at critical junctures of the Damascus Rule; e.g., viii. 43 and 57; cf. Josephus' description of the false prophet proclaiming "the token of their *Deliverance*"—the *precise* words of the Scroll at this point—preceding the destruction of the Temple in *War* 6.286 above (italics mine).

[36] *Koran* 2:31ff.; cf. Acts 2:21, 38, 3:6, 16, 4:7, 10, 12, 17f., etc., and CD, ii. 11ff. and iv. 4ff. "Name" usage is very strong throughout the War Scroll; cf. xi. 3 and xii. 2.

[37] Mt 5:3/Lk 6:20, Ro 15:26, and the famous Ga 2:10 (cf. Ja 2:2ff.). In *Zohar*, iv, 195 on Numbers (i.e., "the Star Prophecy"), King David/the Messiah "placed himself among the Poor ... the Pious ... and ... those who are ready to sacrifice themselves ... for the sanctification of God's Name" (note evocation of "the Name" again).

[38] Cf. 1QpHab, v. 4, viii. 1f. (in exegesis of Hab 2:4), x. 3, xii. 14, and xiii. 2f. Jerome, for instance, to pursue this theme of "clouds", "rain", "Deliverance", and Judgement/ "Son of Man coming on the clouds of Heaven", reads Is 45:8 relating to "the clouds pouring down Righteousness" and "*Yesha'* "/salvation (cf. CD, viii. 43 above), as "let the clouds *rain down the Just One*". For him in *Vir. ill.* 2, James makes a vow not to eat or drink till he will "see Jesus"; these are basically the same words of the last sentence of the exhortative section of the Damascus Rule (viii. 55ff.): " Your Judgements be upon us ... who have listened to the voice of the Righteous Teacher and have not abandoned the Laws of Righteousness; they shall rejoice and their hearts shall be *strengthened*, and *they shall triumph over all the sons of the earth*. God will *forgive them* and they shall *see His Salvation*, because they took refuge in His Holy *Name*" (emphasis mine).

For *b. Ta'an* 6a–6b, also evoking Is 45:8, "the day on which rain falls is as great as the day on which Heaven and Earth were created" (note the evocation of "Heaven and earth" again) or "the *Torah* was given". "No rain falls unless the sins of Israel have been forgiven" (with relevance to the twin motifs connected to James' person of "rain-making" and an atonement for sin). But more interesting, *b. Ta'an* 5b evokes the word "*yoreh*" in pursuance of this theme, meaning former or "spring rain" (not "torrential"). But this is *exactly* the allusion used to refer to "the Teacher" in CD, vi. 10f. and viii. 36f. above, which has long troubled scholars. Here, then, we not only have a play on "teaching"—meaning that knowledge that comes down from above—but also on "rain".

[39] The use of this root *'-M-D* at Qumran is a curious one. It is used in the course of eschatological exegesis of Ezek 44:15's "Sons of Zadok" in CD, iv. 4 and iv. 11f. relating to former and present generations at "the end of time". It is used in reference to the three famous evocations of "the Messiah of Aaron and Israel" in viii. 24, xii. 23f., xiv. 18, and "the *Yoreh ha-Zedek*" in vi. 10 above. Certainly in Ezek 37:10 the reference is to

resurrection. This is true, too, in Dan 12:13, which uses "the Last Days" exactly as in CD, vi. 10 above, and is almost an exact parallel for this reference. But it is also true in Lamentations *Rabbah* ii. 3.6 and *Zohar*, i, 62b in exposition of Dan 12:13. *Zohar*, iii, 222a on "Phineas" expanding Ezek 37 also uses "stand" in precisely this vein.

[40] *War* 2.258f., 264, 6.288ff. and *Ant.* 20.167ff.

CHAPTER 7

Interpreting some Esotericisms:
The Kings of the Peoples, the Princes
of Judah *and* Gehazi *in the*
Damascus Document*

Because I have the impression that arguments relating to paleographic and historical assumptions in Qumran studies are just not heard and that current general knowledge of historical detail is somewhat superficial, let me cover a few wider points first before turning to more detailed ones. We cannot approach the subject of little-noticed esotericisms in later columns of the Damascus Document until we have addressed the issue of paleography.

If we are to be bound by the present paleography of the Damascus Document, little new can be said about most of these puzzling usages. Indeed, the reason so little of substance has emerged in analyzing the Damascus Document over the years is that internal data cannot be harmonized within the parameters and assumptions of Qumran archaeological and paleographic theorizing. (We can now also add to this, carbon testing.) As far as later columns of the Damascus Document are concerned, therefore, we are to all intents and purposes at the beginning, with little or no understanding at all. Virtually no attempt has been made within prevailing theories of Qumran origins to render them intelligible, and so the present situation is likely to continue.

This in itself is a criticism of present consenses on Qumran origins and chronology. If a given theory—and everything said on this subject so far is no more than that—cannot render internal data in key documents intelligible, then in what way can it be considered either useful or, for

---

* Given to the Society of Biblical Literature in 1989.

that matter, viable? Nor does glossing over a given subject in silence, the preferred method of dealing with difficult subjects in this field, relieve a scholar of the necessity of explaining abstruse matters like these. Conversely, if a theory, however improbable it might at first appear according to received doctrine and prevailing assumptions, can within the parameters of Qumran habitational *termini*, actually explain some esotericisms, this is good reason for taking it more seriously. Indeed, the accumulation of such explanations begins to approach a proof.

The paleographic situation of the Damascus Document parallels that of the Temple Scroll, to which it has a doctrinal relationship as well: one or two so-called "older" fragments—whatever in such a context is meant by "*older*"—as opposed to a cluster of so-called "newer" or more recent ones. The "older" fragments are uncritically and almost always automatically assumed to determine the date. Where the Damascus Document is concerned, the existence of these "older" fragments has been used to arrive at a second- to first-century BC dating—even earlier—and rule out a first-century CE date, even though early commentators, using the Cairo *Genizah* versions of the Document and, relying on internal data only, tended towards a later dating.

The argument against paleography is simple. Suppose it were possible to identify the chronological origins of a given script style—a dubious proposition at any time or place, and one that certainly should not be used *a priori* to rule out interesting theories based on the clear thrust of the internal data—can we then be sure, given the conservative atmosphere prevailing in the Community at Qumran, that a particular scribe actually used this script at that time and not some other, regardless of the earliness or lateness of its supposed origin? It should be kept in mind that, where the Damascus Document is concerned, we are talking here about one or two divergent fragments of manuscripts, not clusters of fragments.

This is the "leap of faith" demanded by Qumran paleographers and those relying on their typological sequences. As long as there was no "internal" data to counter-indicate these, then perhaps it could be justified as a working hypothesis—but "book hands" (i.e., formal scribal styles) in conservative religious communities such as the one at Qumran are notoriously stubborn, despite the accepted dogma among paleographers of the Second Temple Period about *rapidly developing scripts in this period.*

In fact, we cannot be sure whether what seem to observers to be innovations are not simply regressions, or that a given scribe had simply not learned his lessons very well. The situation is somewhat analagous to that of coin data in archaeology, where the only thing that is sure is that the coin was not dropped before the date appearing on the face of the coin. Nothing more. Obviously a given hand could not have been used *before it developed*, but when really did it develop, and how much later after it developed—even if such could be fixed with any accuracy—did a given scribe actually employ it? The answer is mute.

To be sure, Qumran typological paleographic sequences have mostly developed in a vacuum with insufficient, securely-dated manuscripts used for control to make the kinds of sweeping judgements that are routinely made on their behalf. (Similar arguments apply to more recent AMS carbon-14 testing, where despite a facade of *seeming* accuracy, there is interpretation.) As long as these determinations did not present a problem nor conflict with the internal data, they were, perhaps, of some use. But when they did conflict with the internal data, then they must be looked upon simply as one of many tools in helping to evaluate Qumran textual and historical data. Despite the closed nature of the debate, there is no certainty in these matters, not even the presumption of any.

A theory can, therefore, be open to debate as long as it falls roughly within the parameters of Qumran habitational *termini*, which are themselves not completely fixed, some commentators insisting on a second-century BC to 68 CE range, while others extend this to a 136 CE *terminus ad quem* ("terminus up to which"). In that the theorizing we outline here falls between both of these sets of *termini*, the earlier and the later, we feel justified in proceeding.

In MZCQ (Chapter 1) and JJHP (Chapter 2), I insisted that certain allusions in column iv of the Damascus Document, carrying over to column v, place us not in the Maccabean Era—and certainly not in any earlier age as some more recent theories of Qumran origins have suggested (perhaps realizing the absurdity of Maccabean-era identifications, but not willing to acknowledge the implications of this)—but in *the Herodian*. The key allusions that lead one to make these determinations on the basis of the *internal textual data*—not the external—are those occurring in the discussion of the "Three Nets of Belial".

I have connected these allusions to similar ones found in the New Testament to "Balaam"—a variation on the root producing *Belial* and derivative usages relating to "swallowing", and "the nets" associated with his name in Rev 2:15, which in turn gives one a chronological and historical context within which to view this material. Nor is there any indication of any earlier parallel context, certainly not one going back to the third century BC that can be delineated. Rather I have focused on charges of "fornication", "polygamy", "divorce", "sleeping with women during their periods", and "niece marriage"—all made in the crucial "Three Nets of Belial" section of the Damascus Document—as being critical ones for determining the historical ambiance of the text.

This is particularly true of the attack on niece marriage directed against a Jerusalem Establishment not only here, but elsewhere at Qumran. The authors of the Damascus Document are well aware of the innovative nature of their legal exegeses. This is clear from the apologetic at the beginning of column v of the Damascus Document, attempting to exonerate David for having transgressed the new construction forbidding marrying more than one wife that they have just enunciated, which insists that this new law was "hidden" until the "rising" or "standing up of Zadok".

The use of the word "rising" or "standing up" here is important. Depending on the context, it can mean "coming"—the usual translation one sees—but this is not necessarily correct here. Later columns of the Damascus Document also use it with respect to a figure referred to as "the Messiah of Aaron and Israel", and his "arising" or "standing up" (despite some theorizing about plural messiahs, the usages here are *all singular*). This expression can mean, as it does in Ezekiel and Daniel, "to be resurrected", a connotation which would change the sense appreciably. It is an open question whether it means this or a combination of both. If the former, then it links up with the Jewish Christian, "Ebionite" doctrine of the "Standing One".

Where these exegeses go, it is also useful to catalog the references in Josephus to "Innovators" and "innovations", from the time of the appearance of the movement founded by "Judas and *Saddok*" at the beginning of the first century CE—called by some "Zealot", but referred to only in Josephus as that of the "Fourth Philosophy"—to the outbreak of the Uprising against Rome some seventy years later.

The allusion here to "*Saddok*" or "Zadok" is puzzling, as well, and most have always found it so in Qumran studies. The question has always been whether one is talking about the Zadok of David and Solomon's time—the proverbial first High Priest of the First Temple in the eleventh century BC, an unlikely proposition—or the "*Saddok*", just mentioned, who together with Judas the Galilean founded a new Movement at the beginning of the first century. Josephus often refers to the followers of this movement as "loving innovation", but for lack of a better designation it might simply be referred to as "the Messianic Movement", as we have done in MZCQ (Chapter 1).

A "Zadok", like the one pictured in column v of the Damascus Document or in Josephus at the beginning of the first century CE, is known to medieval Jewish Karaite tradition, where both his teaching, and that of Jesus, *whom it says followed him*, is characterized as consisting of banning *polygamy, divorce,* and *niece marriage*—just the points we find condemned in columns iv–vi of the Damascus Document. Even the picture of Jesus one gets in the Sermon on the Mount in Mt 5:32 includes the *pro forma* attacks on "fornication" and "divorce". If we were to add to these an additional attack on "niece marriage" here, we would have an almost perfect convergence of themes with Qumran. For its part, Ja 2:11, mentioning adultery, also hints at these things.

Even the picture one gets of John the Baptist condemning Herodias for marrying Herod Antipas, and presumably "fornication", can be explained as easily on the bases of the charges one finds here at Qumran as on the more arcane one of "levirate marriage" posited in the Gospels. Herodias, for instance, married not one, but *two uncles*. Plus, she *divorced* one of them, all matters condemned in the Damascus Document and the Temple Scroll (and by Josephus as well).

Actually the Philip of the New Testament, who is pictured as Herodias' *first* husband, was probably not "Philip" at all, but rather another of her uncles, also confusingly named "Herod". Like Antipas his half-brother, this *real* Philip was also a "Tetrarch" and married to Herodias' *daughter*, Salome, not Herodias. In any event, even Herodias seems to have earned Josephus' reluctant condemnation by divorcing a husband on her own initiative, a thing he remarks as being contrary to Jewish law, by which—where this matter is concerned—he clearly means to include Pharisees as well.

But divorce in general was forbidden at Qumran, as it was in early Christianity thereafter. What always seems to be at issue in these condemnations at Qumran are the *marital practices of Herodians*—our candidates for "the Princes of Judah" in CD, viii.3—who *divorce at will, marry nieces as a matter of course,* and *rarely hesitate to marry non-Jews*—all specifically condemned where "the King" is concerned in the Temple Scroll. These aspects of the "fornication" charge at Qumran also include Herod's own earlier wide-ranging *polygamy*.

If we add to these condemnations the involvement in Caesarea of the man, designated in the *Antiquities* as "Simon Magus", bearing on the affair of Herodias' niece Drusilla's self-divorce and remarriage to the Roman Governor Felix, then we have a substantial pool of data to link events of this kind to what Qumran was calling "fornication" and only mentioned in these Gospel accounts of John via esoteric innuendo.

Here, it is important to note that if the Qumran materials are indeed "Essene", then it is inconceivable that Herod and the Essenes could have been on such terms of conviviality, highlighted in Josephus' discussion of "Essenes". I have discussed this matter in detail in MZCQ (Chapter 1) and in "Confusions between Pharisee and Essenes in Josephus", a paper given to the Society of biblical Literature in 1983. The "confusions" highlighted there were based on the pro-Herodian stance of both parties, the Pharisees as presented in Josephus, but also "the Essenes" too, giving rise to what only can be seen as a contradiction or substantial overlap in the two descriptions.

Where these succeeding columns of the Damascus Document go, the reference to the "wall" and the "daubers on it" in CD, iv.19, picked up again in CD, viii.12ff. (Text A), certainly relates to another condemnation of the Establishment. At the Cairo *Genizah*, there are two overlapping texts of the Damascus Document. Text B has this on xix.31ff. CD, viii.12ff. is also a passage about the "Lying Spouter's" activities, referred to early in the document and spoken about in terms of "walking in wind" or "windiness". This also can be seen as a play on the ideology of "the Spirit", "*wind*" and "*spirit*" being the same word or homonyms in Hebrew.

The sense of the prophetical contexts behind these allusions from Ezek 13 and Mic 2–3, forming the background to these two allusions to "daubing on the wall", is the coming destruction of the Temple and of Jerusalem. In particular, in these biblical passages, these allusions are connected to references to "Lying" prophets "crying peace when there is no peace". It is difficult in the extreme to link any reference to "Lying prophets crying peace when there is no peace" to a Maccabean Establishment.

Not only does the term "prophets" in these passages echo Acts' constant evocation of "prophets" in the original Church at Antioch, but there is also a relationship—however tenuous—to an alliance Josephus describes just prior to the fall of the Temple in Jerusalem of "all those desirous for peace", including principal Pharisees, Chief Priests ("Sadducees"), the Men of Power ("Herodians"), and a mysterious but powerful outsider described as a relative of King Agrippa, who was the intermediary between this Establishment and the Roman army outside the city.

Josephus calls this individual, "Saulus" or "Saul", and he seems to have been in King Agrippa's palace, together with Philip the son of Jacimus and other Herodians, like Saulus' brother Costobarus and cousin Antipas, when it surrendered to the Revolutionaries. Subsequent to these events in 66 CE, he was sent by Agrippa II to see Nero, then in Corinth— a favorite provenance of the activities of Paul—to personally debrief him on the situation in Palestine. It was this interview which seems to have ended up in Nero's decision to send his most successful Roman military commander, the future Emperor Vespasian, to Palestine. Afterwards this "Saulus" is heard from no more in Josephus.

It is important to grasp that this same Herodian King Agrippa II already seems to have been banned not only from the Temple, but all Jerusalem as well, because of the complaints made against him by "the Innovators" on issues relating to foreign kingship and his sexual and marital mores. He was accused of incest with his sister Bernice, who appears with him in Acts talking congenially to Paul (Acts 25:23–26:32), and whom Josephus calls the "Richest" woman in Palestine.

The antagonism to him on the part of "Zealot Innovators" seem not only to relate to his close relations with Roman officials and persons perceived as having been involved in illicit sexual relations with foreigners—namely his sisters—but also to the illicit sexual and marital behavior of Herod's family generally. It is this motif which would seem to have been at the root of the improper "separation" charges earlier in columns iv–v of the Damascus Document, namely, *not separating pure from impure in the Temple* and *sleeping with women in their periods.*

These kinds of things, which also seem to be the crux of the "pollution of the Temple" charge in the "Three Nets of Belial" accusations being delineated in these columns, are probably not unrelated to the *stopping of sacrifice* and *rejection of gifts from foreigners in the Temple*, which Josephus himself specifically labels an "Innovation"—itself the signal for the outbreak of the War against Rome in 66 CE. Not only is the matter of incest or illicit sexual relations with close family relatives also specifically raised in CD, viii.6f., Bernice's "Riches"—"Riches" also being part and parcel of the "Three Nets of Belial" charges—seem to have been the source of her attractiveness (and probably that of her aunt Herodias before her) to various lovers.

Bernice, too, was involved in marriage with her father's brother Herod of Chalcis and several divorces on her own recognition. In addition, she was engaged or married to several foreign kings, ultimately ending up as Titus' mistress, a liaison which in our view—along with the presence of Philo of Alexandria's nephew, Tiberius Alexander the Roman commander at the siege of Jerusalem—had not a little to do with the final decision the Romans seem to have taken (despite Josephus' attempts to conceal it) to destroy the Temple.

These passages evoking Ezek 13 and Mic 2–3 on "Lying prophets spouting", are also the root of the "Lying"/"Spouting"/"Scoffing" vocabulary applied to the ideological adversary of the Righteous Teacher at Qumran. In CD, viii.13, continuing this kind of imagery, the allusion, "walking in wind" is added—perhaps meaning "Windbag", but also possibly playing on the ideology of the "Holy Spirit" (*wind* and *spirit* in Hebrew being, as we have just seen). This is directly followed by the usual theme of rejecting the Commandments of God, part and parcel of the Habakkuk *Pesher*, Psalm 37 *Pesher*, the Nahum *Pesher*, and columns i–ii earlier in the Damascus Document, where the activities of the "Man of Lying" or "Lying Spouter" are at issue.

The phrases used to describe these include "leading astray", "rejecting the *Torah* in the midst of their whole Assembly"—cataloging the usage "*ma'as*" or "reject" in these contexts is always illustrative—"pouring out on Israel the waters of Lying" (an allusion seemingly playing on "pouring"/"spouting" and, even possibly, baptismal, imagery), etc. In the face of the homogeneity of descriptions of this kind, it is difficult to separate the Damascus Document from the *Pesharim*, regardless of paleographic or other kinds of external indicators. That all these notices are generically related—belying a trend in recent Qumran scholarship to deny the homogeneity of the documents—should also be clear.

To elucidate the charge of "pollution of the Temple" in column iv, related to the charge of improper "separation" of pure from impure, Holy from profane, in the Temple in column v, the charge of "sleeping with women in their periods" is made. This is related not only to the charge of "*fornication*" in the "Three Nets of Belial" triggering it, but also to the one of having commerce or intercourse with Gentiles. Commentators generally have rarely tried to make sense of this charge of "sleeping with women in their periods" where Maccabeans are concerned, nor probably could they. When the focus is shifted to the Herodians, it is relatively easily explained and can, therefore, be related to the desire on the part of those Josephus designates as "Innovators" in the first century CE to bar Herodians from the Temple as foreigners.

Not only do "the Innovators" bar Agrippa II and his sister Bernice from all Jerusalem prior to the Uprising—presumably on account of their incest—but afterwards they also burn their palaces. Later, so are those of the principal High Priests, who are then brutally butchered by those Josephus is calling "Zealots" or "*Sicarii*". From the visit of Simon, the head of an "Assembly" (*Ecclēsia* or "Church") of his own in Jerusalem in the 40s, to the rejection of gifts and sacrifices on behalf of Gentiles in the Temple in the 60s—which triggers the War against Rome—this theme is a constant one. But in Qumran studies so strong is the fixation on the Maccabean Period and earlier, it is hardly ever remarked.

The overall hostility towards Herodians on these counts can be viewed as but an aspect of the hostility towards foreigners and foreign gifts and sacrifices in the Temple generally (also forming the background to Ezek 44:15 underlying the exegesis of "the Zadokite Covenant" in column iv). Where receipt of gifts from Herodians is concerned—to say nothing of Romans or even, for example, the contributions of Paul's overseas communities to "the Jerusalem Community"—the ultimate effect is the "pollution of the Temple Treasury" referred to in column vi.15f., where the "improper separation" language is, once again, also evoked.

In the matter of Paul's gifts to the Jerusalem Community, one should note that in Acts 21:24, James instructs Paul to pay for "Nazirite" oath-style procedures in the Temple for four others out of such funds. This, even according to Acts, triggers the rioting in the Temple and all over Jerusalem against the way Paul teaches about the Law. Curiously, Acts 21:30 even uses the language of CD, vi.12f., about "barring the door to the Sons of the Pit"—i.e., "they barred the doors behind him"—in describing this riot, which was touched off by the report that Paul was *introducing Gentiles into the Temple.*

Foreigners, like Paul's traveling companion Timothy, are actually of the Herodian genre, with Jewish mothers and Greek fathers (Acts 16:1–2), and are presumably representative of Paul's attempts to found a community of "Greeks and Jews together" where, as Eph 2:19 puts it, there should be "no foreign visitors or resident aliens." Whether we find noting them pleasing or not, verbal correspondences of this kind, involving parallel thematic motifs and linguistic commonalities, do exist from the first century CE in a way that cannot be said for previous centuries.

To sum up: the Damascus Document uses material relating to the "fornication" charge to expound the charge of "pollution of the Temple", the point being, as can be seen from the note about "every man marrying his niece" that follows in column v as well, that pollution of the Temple and fornication are inextricably related, and sleeping with women in their periods explains the charge of not observing proper separation in the Temple. Since from column iv onwards, we have been speaking about the Establishment, it should be clear that this relates to Herodians with their easy-going Hellenized ways, many of whom were educated in Rome—and those who acquired their pollution by relations with them—not any Jewish priests *per se.*

The charge that "each man marries the daughter of his brother or sister" that then directly follows, further clarifies this; namely, it is Herodian behavior which is at issue, particularly Herodian sexual and marital practices, because it is the Herodians who married their nieces and close cousins—a point also then condemned in CD, v.7–11 and viii.6–7. The behavior of the Establishment Priesthood in Jerusalem is only a derivative issue, because they took their appointment from Herodians and accepted them as co-religionists. It should also be clear that what is at issue here is not some incidental or aberrant behavior, but rather the customary practice of the whole ruling elite. *This cannot be Maccabeans.*

Since it would be impossible to cover all the allusions in columns v–viii of the Damascus Document, I will not dwell too long on more familiar ones like those to "the Land of Damascus", "the New Covenant", "the Messiah of Aaron and Israel", etc., but turn to those which are directly explainable in a Roman/Herodian context and never really explained in any other. These columns are replete with images relating to the same themes, namely "keeping the Law" and *not* "breaking it"—paralleled in Ja 1–2—"stubbornness of heart", "polluted Riches", etc., and brim with Messianic imagery.

In column v.11, one encounters an important allusion generically related to the "Lying" and "Spouting" imagery always applied to the Liar in Qumran documents, that of "the Tongue"—in this case a "blaspheming Tongue against the Laws of the Covenant of God". Its applicability to "the Lying Spouter" becomes clearer when considering the clause attached to it, that "at the time of the desolation of the land there arose removers of the bound who led Israel astray". This clearly recapitulates the earlier references to the Scoffer "pouring over Israel the waters of Lying" and "removing the boundary-markers" in the first column of the Document as found in Cairo. It also relates to similar imagery found in the Habakkuk *Pesher* in relation to the "Lying Spouter".

This genre of "Tongue" imagery is also to be found in the Nahum *Pesher* and the Community Rule. That parallel imagery occurs in Chapter 3 of the Letter of James, where it is used to describe a troublesome internal adversary, is fraught with significance—in Qumran studies it is rarely, if ever, remarked. The "Tongue" imagery in the Letter of James, which is of the same genre as the "spouting" imagery here at Qumran, also probably refers to "the Empty" or "Foolish Man" which precedes it in Chapter 2, who misreads the significance of how Abraham is justified—note the allusion to Abraham as "Friend of God" occurs in both Ja 2:23 and CD, iii.2.

Following this reference to "opening their mouth with a Tongue full of blasphemies against the Laws of the Covenant of God", column v of the Damascus Document now draws on two biblical quotations from Is 50:11 and 59:5 to further attack the Establishment. The references used are to "Fire" and "the eggs of vipers", allusions familiar from presentations of John the Baptist's curses on the Sadducees and Pharisees at the beginning of the Gospels (Mt 3:7–12 and Lk 3:7–17). The text now makes it clear how the guilt of this Establishment and its pollution is communicated—by association: "no man that approaches them shall be free of their pollution unless he was forced".

When looked at in terms of the Priesthood sponsored by the Herodians, the kind of association envisioned would, no doubt, have to do with acquiring the High Priesthood at their hands, accepting sacrifices and gifts in the Temple on their behalf and on behalf of foreigners generally, and, in general, treating them as *bona fide* Jews. We have already seen a good example of this in the *Talmud* (presumably compiled on the basis of Pharisaic tradition). When Agrippa (I or II is immaterial—probably I) comes to read the Deuteronomic King Law in the Temple on *Succot* and begins to weep—presumably because extremist groups like "the Zealots" do not consider him a Jew—the Pharisees around him cry out, "You are our brother, you are our brother, you are our brother" (*M. Sota* 41a).

The repetition of this cry three times brings to mind Peter's denying Jesus three times on his trial night in the Gospels or the voice from Heaven crying out to Peter three times on a rooftop in Jaffa in Acts 10:14–16, abrogating Jewish dietary regulations and teaching him "not to call any man profane". One could not imagine the "Zealot" Simon in Josephus, the head of an "Assembly" of his own (literally *Ecclēsia* or "Church") in Jerusalem, who wants to bar Agrippa I from the Temple as a foreigner, crying out or paying attention to any such things.

The reference to "vipers' eggs" is reprised three columns later in viii.9f. in the references to "asps" and "serpents", where we hear about their "poison" in relation to allusions about "the Princes of Judah", "the Kings of the Peoples", and "the Spouter's spouting". The imagery accompanying it in column v, referring to such persons as "kindlers of fire and lighters of firebrands" also echoes that in John's attack on "the offspring of vipers" and the Pharisaic/Sadducean Herodian Establishment above as "kindling the chaff". It also occurs in the extremely important exposition of the Messianic "Star Prophecy" in columns xi–xii of the War Scroll, where we hear about this same "kindling", amid allusions to the "no mere Adam", "the rising of the Meek", and "the Poor".

Regardless whether one denies corresponding exegetical intent in these allusions, parallel imagery is present. Even an allusion like "this is the time for the preparation of the Way in the wilderness", applied to John in the Gospels, is twice evoked in columns viii–ix of the Community

Rule and rather applied to the activities of the group responsible for these writings. Parallel imagery of a similar genre in an era earlier than the Herodian has yet to be described.

There now follows in column v an additional reference to "Belial", this time relating him to "Jannes and his brother", echoing the well-known reference to "Jannes and Jambres" in 2 Tim 3:8. In column v it is followed by the usual allusions to "leading Israel astray", "rebellion", "removing the bound", and ultimately, "the Lying Spouter's spouting". In 2 Tim 3:8, as here in the Damascus Document, Jannes and Jambres are described as "rebelling against Moses" and in Rabbinic literature they are generally usually presented as "Enemies of God". They are known, too, in Greco-Roman contexts and even later *Zohar.*

This is not the place to go into the whole literature of the "Jannes and Jambres" legend, but it cannot be denied that on the whole it relates to the first century, and afterwards, and has to do—at least in Jewish contexts—with opposing the Law and moving "Aaron" (the Priesthood) towards idolatry. Usually, too, it is associated in some manner with "Balaam"—just as here in CD, v.18 it is associated with "Belial".

In general, Jannes and Jambres are considered magicians and disciples of Balaam. Like the Damascus Document, Pliny and Apuleius name only Jannes. Both know, along with Origen and Eusebius, of his association with magic. In 2 Tim above, the context is replete with Qumran language, paralleling that of 2 Pe 2:15 on "Balaam the son of Be'or", Rev 2:15 on how "Balaam taught Balak to cast a net before Israel", and Jude 1:11 mentioning "the error of Balaam"—not to mention Paul in 2 Co 6:15 on "Beliar". Again the general *sitz im leben* of all these references is first century and beyond, not before.

In column vi, the references "to preaching rebellion" and "prophesying Lies" continue. Picking up the earlier theme of Ezek 13 of "daubing upon the wall"—this clearly the effect of *prophesying Lies*—these end in an allusion to "digging the well" (Num 21:18), which now turns more Messianic. Just as "the Way in the wilderness" in column viii of the Community Rule is linked to "the study of *Torah*", the "well" here is interpreted as the *Torah*. The "*Mehokkek*" or "Staff" also plays on the underlying meaning of "Law" and clearly has something to do with the Teacher of Righteousness. In the same manner, the "well" imagery has something to do with "bathing" or "baptism" and will be refined further in column viii when it comes to describing just what "the New Covenant in the Land of Damascus" really is.

Not only are those who dig it, like those who "prepare the Way in the wilderness" in 1QS above, "studying the Law"; as in the exegesis of

Ezek 44:15's "Sons of Zadok" in column iv, they are called "the Penitents of Israel". And just as in this earlier exegesis these last were "the
Priests who went out from the Land of Judah", now they are described
as "going out from the Land of Judah to dwell in the Land of Damascus". All are now called "Princes" since they are described as "seeking
after" God and after the *Torah*. This sets up a purposeful apposition two
columns later in viii.3 to the allusion "the Princes of Judah" who, like
"the Liar" above are also said "to remove the bound".

These allusions from column v move directly into the allusion to "barring the door" in vi.12f., echoing Acts 21:30's description of Paul's uncer-
emonious ejection from the Temple. Even this passing allusion in Acts
includes the themes of "teaching against the Law" and "polluting the
Holy Place by bringing Greeks into the Temple". It is noteworthy that
Acts 21:24's reference to "walking regularly and keeping the Law", preceding this and ascribed to James, also echoes formulations to the same
effect both in the Scrolls and James 2:8–10.

Coupling now *Riches* with *pollution*, and again picking up the theme of
"separation from the Sons of the Pit", complaints against the Establishment are, once again, being aired in these lines in the Damascus Document from column vi.14–vi.18. These include distinguishing "between
Holy and profane"—just the opposite of what Peter is pictured as learning in Acts 10:15 above—"polluting the Temple Treasury", and "robbing
the Poor". These themes are also discernible throughout the Habakkuk
Pesher (viii.5, ix.5ff., and xii.8ff.) and have an easily discernible first-
century *sitz im leben*.

One should also note the references to "keeping" in CD, vi.14 and
vi.18, culminating in vi.20f. in the citation of what we have elsewhere
called the all-Righteousness Commandment—the Royal Law according
to the Scripture in Ja 2:8: "each man shall love his brother as himself".
Under other headings, as for instance Josephus' descriptions of John
the Baptist's teaching and that of the "Essenes", this is expressed as
"Righteousness towards one's fellow man".

In James 2:8, the Righteousness Commandment is quoted following
references to "the Poor" and condemnation of "the Rich", emphases
reflected in these sections of the Damascus Document as well. As James
puts it, "Keep the Royal Law according to the Scripture: You shall love
your neighbor as yourself." Whereas in James, reference to "the Poor"
directly precedes the citation of this Commandment, in the Damascus
Document it directly follows it.

These references to "keeping" and "breaking", found at this point in
James, are familiar Qumran categories and bear on the precise definition

of "the Sons of Zadok" in the Community Rule as "Keepers of the Covenant". In James, following upon the quotation of the all-Righteousness Commandment, they develop into the quintessential "whoever keeps the whole of the Law, but stumbles on one small point, is guilty of [breaking] it all" (2:10). Here "keeping the whole Law" follows upon "keeping the Royal Law according to the Scripture". This develops into the attack on "the Empty Man" in 2:20ff.—whose understanding of the "Justification" process with regard to the Faith of Abraham is so defective—and on "the Tongue" in Ja 3:5ff.

In the Damascus Document, the "keeping" involved is keeping the Sabbath, the Festival Days, and the Day of Fasting, "according to the precise letter of the Law", that ends in citation of the all-Righteousness Commandment. As noted above, "the Righteousness Commandment", along with "the Piety Commandment" ("loving God"), are the essence of John the Baptist's teaching in Josephus. Needless to say, they are both presented in the New Testament and Justin Martyr as the essence of Jesus' teaching as well. They are also the basis of Josephus' description of the categories of Essene doctrine.

Finding "the Righteousness Commandment"—if one looks carefully, one will also be able to discern "the Piety" one as well—at this juncture of the Damascus Document coupled with the second reference to "the New Covenant in the Land of Damascus" and three successive references to *keeping the exact letter of the Law* (vi.15, 18, and 20), only adds to the presumption of a first-century CE date for this document—based on the internal evidence, not the external.

"Keeping the Covenant", as set forth in Deut 7:9, is also one of the main themes of column vii of the Damascus Document, where the references to "separation" continue (vii.3 and vii.4). Now the followers of "the Way" are referred to as "walking in the Perfection of Holiness according to the Covenant of God". The promise in Deut 7:9 to those who "love God"—the second of the two "*Love Commandments*", just enumerated above, thus completing the basic parallelism of all these texts—and "keep" His Commandments of living "for a thousand generations", is now presented as implying resurrection or eternal life.

This allusion to "Perfection of Holiness" to characterize "the Assembly" (or "Church") is later repeated three times in CD, viii.25–30. But once again, here too we come upon a precise first-century parallel. Paul uses this precise formulation at the end of the crucial imagery in 2 Co 5:21–7:1, already called attention to above, a section replete with Qumranisms, like "Beliar", "Light and Darkness", "pollution of the Temple", "Poor", "Truth", and even the words clearly paralleling those at this point in the Damascus Document, "come out from among them and be separated" (2 Co 6:17, quoting Is 52:11).

Paul's reference to "fearing God", in this passage too, will also find an echo in words we shall encounter in column viii.43f. of the Damascus Document below. One should, as well, note the common motif in the words in 2 Co 7:1, introducing the reference to "Perfection of Holiness", and here in CD, vii.4, "polluting one's Holy Spirit". The very same expression occurred earlier in CD, v.13 in relation to the "Tongue blaspheming the Laws of the Covenant of God". The conclusion is simple— at this point, CD, vii.4 and 2 Co 7:1 are using both corresponding sequencing and precisely parallel vocabulary (though the sense in Paul always *reverses* that in the Damascus Document and Qumran generally).

The references to "the Assembly (or "Church") of the Men of Perfect Holiness" and "interpreting the *Torah* according to its precise letter" in column viii.25–30 follow upon a string of notices about someone or a genre of person like "*the Liar*" the text regards as either a backslider or an internal adversary. The themes of "betraying the New Covenant in the Land of Damascus" (which parallels similar notices about "Traitors to the New Covenant" connected to "the Liar" and his violent associates at the beginning of the Habakkuk *Pesher*), of exclusion from the Community's baptismal procedures, expulsion, (also evoked in CD, vii.1–5), and non-cooperation with him in purse or work, are also developed.

This expulsion from the Community (for "straying to the right or left of the *Torah*") is actually the subject of the last column of the Damascus Document (*The Dead Sea Scrolls Uncovered*, Element Books, 1992). In these kinds of notices, non-cooperation in "work" is expressed by means of the Hebrew word "*'avodah*" (not "*ma'aseh*"), connotative of what is understood in English as "mission" or "service". This is equivalent to the "mission" or "work" or "toil" Paul refers to so often in 1 Co 3, 9, 15, 16, and elsewhere, not the soteriological *works* referred to in James, here in the Damascus Document, and elsewhere at Qumran.

First-century parallels bunch up to such an extent at this point in the Damascus Document that vocabulary chains and circles of argument are discernible. In vii.17f. it is stated that "the Tabernacle of the King" of Amos 5:26f. is "the Books of the Law" and that "the King is the Assembly" ("Church"). This can be paralleled in Paul's discussions in 1 Co 12:12ff. and elsewhere on Jesus (or his body) as the Community, and both being, then identified as the Temple—refracted in Eph 2:19ff., denying there are any "foreign visitors in Christ Jesus" (meaning "in the Temple").

Column vii ends in lines 19f. with evocation of the famous "Star

Prophecy" from Num 24:17. This Prophecy, as noted above, is also quoted in the War Scroll in the crucial context mentioning the burning of the chaff, the Messiah, Judgement executed by the Poor and the Meek, and Messianic "rain" imagery relating both to Daniel's "Son of Man coming on the clouds of Heaven" and paralleling "rain" and "Judgement" imagery in James 5:7–18.

The "Star Prophecy" is quoted three times in the known corpus from Qumran: once in the War Scroll, once in the compendium of Messianic proof-texts, and once here in the Damascus Document. Clearly it constitutes an important moving ideological force for the texts represented there. As we have shown, in a little remarked passage at the end of the *Jewish War*, Josephus also presents it as *the moving force behind the Revolt against Rome*, calling it the thing that most moved the Jews to revolt, despite what he considers to be the self-evident foolhardiness of doing so.

This picture of the currency of "the Star Prophecy" in the mid-first century CE receives indirect support in the *Talmud*, where Rabbi Yohanan ben Zacchai is portrayed as applying it to Vespasian at the time of the Uprising. Josephus concomitantly portrays himself as applying it to Vespasian, as well, explaining in the *Jewish War* how mistaken the Jews were in applying it to one of their own, but how the Prophecy was actually fulfilled by Vespasian himself, who came out of Palestine to rule the world.

The Prophecy also seems to have had some relationship to the Bar Kochba Revolt in 132–136 CE, as the name "Kochba" (the Hebrew for "Star") implies. In the *Talmud* and in recently-found letters signed in Bar Kochba's name, it is clear that the name of this leader was really "Bar Kosiba", Bar Kochba being only its more symbolic reformulation. Regardless of one's interpretation of these matters, there can be no doubt about the central role of "the Star Prophecy" in events in the first century, culminating in the stopping of sacrifice on behalf of and rejection of gifts from foreigners in the Temple. Nor can one show its currency at any earlier time. This too is the gist of the use of "Star" imagery in the Gospel of Matthew. In our view, these matters are reflected in one way or another in these later columns of the Damascus Document.

In column viii of this document, we come to what is perhaps the most important allusion for determining its historical *sitz im leben*. Again the material is introduced by evocation of "Belial", further concretizing the relationship of this expression to Herodians. Using Hos 5:10 about how "the Princes of Judah have removed the bound" and "Wrath", therefore, "being poured out upon them" (note the "pouring" imagery here), CD, viii.3 specifically denotes the Establishment as the "Princes of Judah", and, in particular, evokes their *Law-Breaking* ways.

This expression, "the Princes of Judah", as noted, stands in a contrapuntal relationship to the "Princes" mentioned earlier in column vi, the "Penitents in the wilderness who went out from Judah to dig the well" and "sought God in the Land of Damascus". Here in column viii, not only is the thrust of the allusion—like that to the "Three Nets of Belial" earlier—completely anti-Establishment, it is directed now not against a Priestly Establishment *per se*, but against a seemingly more secular one. It is seriously to be doubted if such an expression was ever applied to Maccabeans, since for all intents and purposes it ignores their sacerdotal role.

In column viii, familiar themes like "removing the bound", "Law-breaking", "rebellion", "fornication", "Evil Riches", and the "incest" charge (viii.6—possibly inclusive of "niece marriage") are once more recapitulated. Taken together, these must be seen as what is meant in viii.16 by the expression "the Way of the People (as we shall see, this is possibly 'Peoples') which the Penitents of Israel departed from". The same matters are being alluded to with reverse signification in viii.8's "not keeping away from the People", not to mention viii.4f.'s "not departing from the Way of Traitors" and "the Ways of fornication". The strong antagonism to *fornication* and *Riches* of the "Three Nets of Belial" charges in iv–vi continues.

It should be remembered that in column iv.2 in Ezek 44:15's Zadokite Covenant, the "Priests", described as "Penitents of Israel", "went out from the Land of Judah", and in vi.5, now identified as Num 21:18's "Princes", they "dwell in the Land of Damascus". The theme of "Traitors" is integral, as we saw, as well to the Habakkuk *Pesher* and the conceptuality there of "the New Covenant"—here in the Damascus Document, "the New Covenant in the Land of Damascus".

In the Habakkuk *Pesher*, these "Traitors to the New Covenant" are identified with "the Violent Ones", also described as "Covenant-Breakers", with some association with "the Liar" (not to mention the Righteous Teacher). In turn, these "Violent Ones" and/or "Men of War" also form part and parcel of the background to these events in the Damascus Document. For another *pesher*, the Psalm 37 *Pesher*, these "Violent Ones" are Gentiles who take vengeance on the Wicked Priest for his destruction of the Righteous Teacher.

The use and evocation of the word "People"/"Peoples" moves in column viii.8f. into the quotation from Deut 32:33 about "wine", "serpents", "venom", "poison", and "asps". The venom of these serpents is interpreted as "the Kings of the Peoples and their ways"—plural. In Deuteronomy, this passage declares that "vengeance is Mine" and over and over again refers to "the Rock" and the destruction of the people. It characterizes the paternity of "the Princes of Judah" as "the vinestock of Sodom, the groves of Gomorrah, whose grapes are poisonous, clusters bitter", but only the phrase "whose wine is the poison of serpents and the cruel venom of asps" is actually quoted here. Other words like "the Enemy" and "the deceitful brood", are actually referred to earlier in CD, v.17.

The usage "'*Am*"/"'*Amim*" ("People"/"Peoples") at Qumran has several meanings which should be cataloged. Sometimes the meaning is positive, normally where the "People" generally are at issue, as, for instance, in Hymns. Here in the Damascus Document, the sense is usually pejorative, with hints of the *Am ha-Arez*, well-known as a pejorative in the *Talmud*. But this is not the complete sense in these lines in the Damascus Document. The term is used, particularly in the plural "'*Amim*", to describe the Establishment and identified in some way with "the Princes of Judah removing the bound" and "the wine of their ways".

In the Habakkuk *Pesher*, this usage "'*Amim*"/"Peoples" appears together with another, "*Yeter ha-'Amim*"/"the Additional Ones of the Peoples", to produce a very important exegesis. In column viii.5 of the Habakkuk *Pesher*, "'*Amim*" in the underlying text from Hab 2:6 has the clear sense of "Gentiles" or "the surrounding Nations"—in fact, the direct translation into Greek would be "*Ethnē*" as in Paul's "Mission to *the Gentiles* or "*Peoples*". The term is exploited there to produce an exegesis which characterizes the Wicked Priest's exploitation of "the Riches of Violent Ones" and the "Riches of the Peoples" as "walking in the ways of Abominations and all unclean pollution" (viii.11–15).

In column ix.4ff, the subject is reprised again, and "'*Amim*" and "*Go'im*" in the underlying text from Hab 2:7–8 are exploited to produce an exegesis relating to "the Riches of the Last Priests of Jerusalem", who "profiteered from the spoils of the Peoples". This use of the word "*beza*'", "profiteer from" or "exploit illegally", is pivotal, because the same usage appears in these critical lines from the Damascus Document in column viii.7 as part of the charges being directed against the activities of "the Princes of Judah"/"Kings of the Peoples"! Not only does this demonstrate the basic circularity between these discussions, but it makes the correspondence and overlap between them undeniable.

In the Habakkuk *Pesher* and Damascus Document, therefore, we are in the same universe of *corruption*. That it is also part and parcel of what must be understood as "the way of the People", from which the *Penitents in the Land of Damascus* are instructed "to separate" and "depart", should also be clear. In addition, in the Habakkuk *Pesher*, these Gentiles, who at first glance appear behind this corruption, are, in fact, being exploited by the "High Priests" (plural). That is, the High Priests in the manner of the *plural* Priestly clans of the Herodian period—not the *singular High Priest* of the Maccabean period—are enriching themselves with the help of or by exploiting persons perceived as Gentiles, in fact, "Violent Gentiles". This is the chain of meaning behind *Gentile gifts and sacrifices polluting the Temple Treasury*—themselves based on illgotten gains and gathered illegally.

Such a situation, including this charge, can patently only relate to the period of the Pharisaic/Sadducean Establishment of the first century, where the notices about such enrichment grow evermore shrill the closer they are to the final rejection of gifts and sacrifices on behalf of Gentiles in the Temple in 66 CE, the signal for the war against Rome. There are no notices about this in any previous period—certainly none relating to the highly nationalistic and normally xenophobic Maccabeans.

The Damascus Document exegesis of the phrase "Kings of the Peoples" above reprises the earlier "viper"/"poison" imagery in column v.13, directed against the Establishment, where an earlier passage from this section of Deut 32:28 was also quoted and "Belial" and "Jannes and his brother" evoked. Here then the exposition of Deut 32:33 becomes clear: "*The serpents* are the Kings of the Peoples and *their wine* is their ways."

"*The Kings of the Peoples*" relates exactly to what we have said of "the Princes of Judah" above, namely, *the Herodians and their ways*—by many, particularly of the more Zealot or extremist frame of mind, such Herodians were *not even considered Jews*. Even such an expression as "King of the Jews", as the New Testament so vividly illustrates, did not have to refer to someone who was Jewish at all. Rather it was simply a term used by the Romans to refer to one or another of their appointees. This is the thrust of the usage "Kings of the Peoples" parallel to it in this exegesis. Not only did it relate to the perceived non-Jewish origin of Kings such as these, but also to the fact that they actually *were* kings and styled themselves as such.

According to the Pharisees and Establishment Sadducees of the first century, they could be reckoned as Jews. But to others, like the "Zealot" Simon above, who wanted to bar them from the Temple as foreigners, they could not—not by any stretch of the imagination. Their "Ways", being delineated here, were those of *fornication, Riches, approaching near kin for bodily connection, niece marriage*, and *incest*. There is no indication in any source that the Maccabeans did any of these things in a consistent manner, whereas for the Herodians they were a matter of studied family practice and policy.

That reference, "the cruel venom of asps", interpreted to relate to "the Head of the Kings of Greece" or "Grecian" or "Greek-speaking Kings", does not present a problem in this context. In the first place the word "*rosh*"/"poison", as in "the poison of asps" in the underlying text, is being played upon to produce the variant meaning "Head". In the second place, the word "wine"/"*yayin*" is being played on to produce the virtually homophonic usage "*Yavan*"/"Greece", both together producing the homonymic "the Head of the Grecian Kings".

In fact, the Roman Emperor *really was* the "Head" of such a confederation of Greeks or Greek-speaking kings in the Eastern Empire, particularly in Asia Minor and Syria, including Commagene, Armenia, Lesser Armenia, Cilicia, Emesa (modern Homs), Chalcis, etc. The Romans followed a different policy in the East from their policy in the West, leaving these petty, Greek-speaking, puppet kings in power as little more than tax-farmers and satraps. Among these, as Josephus graphically illumines, the Herodians played a significant part—not only in Palestine, but also in Armenia, Lesser Armenia, Chalcis, Cilicia, and Commagene.

Finally—and this perhaps clinches the exposition—this term, "Kings of the Peoples" *really was* being used in Roman administrative parlance to refer to peoples and their rulers in outlying provinces of the Roman Empire, particularly in "Asia". A.N. Sherwin-White, *The Roman Citizenship*, Oxford, 1939, pp. 269ff., in discussing the extension of Roman citizenship to the provinces, discusses the terms in Latin, "*omnes Gentes*", and in Greek, "*ta Ethnē*", showing that both were used in the first and second centuries CE to denote just these kinds of "Peoples" and their "Kings". In fact, Paul and his "Mission to the Gentiles" or "Peoples" in just these regions provides additional clear verification of this, because he means by this expression largely Greek-speaking, Gentile peoples in the East.

For Cicero, the Roman people—not to mention the Emperor—were "*Princeps Gentium*"/"Lord of Peoples". Josephus himself uses the term to refer to Quirinius' role in Syria in *Antiquities* 18.1, and Paul, not without moment, uses it to refer to his own Apostleship and developing Mission in Ro 11:13. By the first and second centuries the term "*ta Ethnē*" was being used by Greek writers to refer to "the Peoples" in the outlying provinces newly incorporated into the Empire. Stronger proof of the provenance and currency of the expression "Kings of the Peoples" to denote provincial Kings in the Eastern provinces in the Roman Period—like Herodians—could not be offered.

In the view of the writer, this is indeed proof of the Herodian histori-cal provenance of this crucial usage in the Damascus Document—paleo-graphy, archaeology, imprecise or questionable carbon testing, or what-ever external measure employed, notwithstanding. Furthermore, in this passage, the "Kings of the Peoples" seem to be distinguished from the other "Greek Kings" as actually having power and influence in Judea proper. The conclusion is inescapable: they are *Herodians*. Certainly they cannot be thought of as Maccabeans. Nor can "*'Amim*" be considered appropriate to describe Maccabeans.

In the Habakkuk *Pesher* a similar conundrum emerges. Whereas "*'Amim*", as it is used, seems, as explained, to relate to the Herodian Establishment enriching itself in various forms of illicit "profiteering" and "violent" and "polluting Abominations", "*Yeter-'Amim*", from Hab 2:8 in the underlying text, is specifically identified with "the Army of the *Kittim*", which at the End of Days will co-opt "the booty" and "polluted Treasure" that "the Last Priests of Jerusalem amassed" in the Temple by "profiteering from the plundering operations of the Peoples". The "Last Priests of Jerusalem", as argued above, are simply that—the alliance of High-Priestly clans during the Herodian Period, taking control particularly towards its end under an assortment of Roman Governors. In the New Testament and other contexts, these are denoted under the heading of "Chief Priests" or "High Priests"—plural.

As noted, it would be absurd to apply this terminology "Last Priests"—"Priests" here clearly connoting "High Priests"—to Macca-beans, for they were monolithic, ruled for life, were not plural, and were in no way "the Last" (whatever one's interpretation of this, eschatological or otherwise). Nor was the Maccabean period normally considered to be "the Last Times" or "the End Time"—unless one takes the consensus interpretation of the Scrolls literally.

A further proof of this proposition comes in the all-important col-umns v–vi of the Habakkuk *Pesher* in exposition of Hab 1:15–16 about "burning incense to his dragnet" and "his portion is fat and his eating plenteous", interpreted, once again, to refer to "the Kittim". Not only do we have here the actual description of the *Kittim* as "sacrificing to their standards and worshipping their weapons of war", but in pursuit of the exegesis of their "portion being fat" and their "eating plenteous", they ("the *Kittim*") are said to "parcel out their yoke and their taxes" (i.e., *tax-farming*), "eating all *the Peoples* year by year".

These "Peoples" are also linked in this exegesis in column viii.47 of the Damascus Document to a group called "the Men of War, who deserted to the Liar" during the Period of Wrath. Elsewhere we have

linked this expression to Gentile or Herodian *"Men-of-War"*, exploited
by the High Priests to carry out predatory activities described at the end
of Book Nineteen of the *Antiquities* and continuing into descriptions in
Book Twenty surrounding the death of James. In our view, this is the
true sense of the idea of "they profiteered from the spoils of the Peoples", developed in the Habakkuk *Pesher*, viii.5–11 and ix.5 and reflected
in CD, viii.8, 16, and 47 above. In other work, we have linked these kinds
of usages to *"Violent"* "Herodians", including Niger of Perea, Philip b.
Jacimus, Antipas, Costobarus, and the individual denoted in Josephus as
"Saulus".

These references in column viii of the Damascus Document to "the
Kings of the Peoples" and "the poison of asps" are immediately followed, just as those about "the Men-of-War walking with the Liar" later,
by reference to the "daubers upon the wall" of Ezek 13:10, "to whom
the Spouter of Lying spouted" or "poured out". In previous work, too,
we suggested an identification of Paul for this ideological adversary of
the Righteous Teacher, who "poured out the waters of Lying on Israel",
"removed the boundary-markers which the Ancestors had laid down
causing them to wander astray in a trackless waste", and "rejected the
Law in the midst of their whole Assembly".

In these references in Ezek 13:7 and Mic 2:11 about "the spouting"
or "visions of Lying prophets", the "Lying Spouter's" spouting is also
compared, as we saw, to "blowing", "pouring out", or "spouting wind",
or if one prefers, "the Windbag". However, one could interpret this as
well, in terms of "teaching about the Spirit", "wind" and "Spirit", as
already noted above, being homonyms in Hebrew. Again we have powerful textual links firming up correspondences with a Pauline "Adversary".
However one wishes to view this identification, and the further one with
the Herodian "Man-of-War" Saulus, this "pouring out upon them"—
another possible play on "Holy Spirit" baptism—is now said "to kindle
the Anger of God upon his whole Assembly" (if one prefers, "his
Church"; CD, viii.13).

From viii.13–22 there follow the now standard references to "stubbornness of heart", "rejecting the Commandments of God", so typical of the
language used in the Habakkuk *Pesher* in describing the Spouting Liar's
activities, "rejecting" or "betraying the New Covenant", and *par contra* being
rejected from the proper baptismal procedures of the Community of "the
New Covenant in the Land of Damascus". As these charges and counter-
charges proceed, we are also presented with a variation on Pauline notions
of "Grace"—namely, it was not because of your "Righteousness and
Uprightness, but because God "loved the fathers" (Deut 7:8 and 9:5) or, to

rephrase this, it was because God "loved the First" (the Forefathers) that he *would love those* who came after them.

This is something of the way Paul develops his ideology of the "Saving" Faith of Abraham in Romans and Galatians. Still, it is difficult to believe that the authors, here, did not have a variation of something resembling Paul's "Grace" notions in mind when framing this position. Whether the combination of these passages from Deuteronomy at the end of column viii in the Damascus Document would be the original scriptural warrant for this developing ideology would be difficult to say.

These allusions culminate in evocation of Elisha's rejection of "Gehazi" (viii.20–21). Elisha's rebuke of Gehazi (2 Ki 4–5) is of the same genre as allusions to "Belial"/"Balaam" and "Jannes and Jambres" earlier. It is not without moment that it should directly follow these allusions to the "Lying Spouter surely spouting" and (his "pouring out wind" Adversary of the Pauline genre). It directly precedes more information about "betraying the New Covenant in the Land of Damascus", the rejection from the "living waters" (i.e., the baptism of the Community), and the "rising" or possible resurrection of "the Messiah of Aaron and Israel" (again, all the surrounding verb usages here are singular).

Material about "Damascus" does relate to the Elijah and Elisha cycle of stories and the usage "Desert of Damascus" first appears in relation to the former in 1 Ki 19:15. The rebuke at this point may relate to an episode in which Gehazi was unable—presumably because of his impurity—to perform a resurrection for Elisha (2 Ki 4:31). More likely it relates to Gehazi's having *taken payment from the King of Syria* for the cures Elisha has been doing (2 Ki 5:20–27; cf. Paul in 1 Co 9:5ff. and 1 Tim 5:18)—enough to make him a "Rich" man. For this Elisha turns him leprous as snow. The direct relation of this to accusations against Paul should be clear (cf. 1 Co 9:5ff. and 1 Tim 5:18).

Early this century, Travers Herford identified allusions to "Gehazi" of this kind in Rabbinic literature with Paul (*Christianity in Talmud* and Midrash, London, 1903, pp. 97ff.). This shows amazing prescience with regard to these notices in the Damascus Document. I have nothing to add to his arguments. If nothing else, we have here another correspondence of the material before us with allusions thought in their Rabbinic context to have related to "Enemies" like Paul. However these things may be, the fixing upon characters like "Jannes", "Balaam", "Gehazi", "Korah", "Do'eg", and others, to relate to doctrinal disputes is a known literary phenomenon in the first century CE and afterwards. There is no indication of such exegesis earlier (unless it be in these Scrolls), though it may have existed.

In this section of *b. Sanhedrin* or these "Enemies of God" (104a–107b), immediately following that on Hab 2:3 and the Messianic "delay" (97–99a), Gehazi is directly connected to "the family of Benjamin" (99b). It is also made very clear that Gehazi's sin was "calling his master by Name".

A last point: Gehazi is certainly a servant to Elisha, as Baruch in the same passage is to Jeremiah. Baruch's service seems to have related to delivering Jeremiah's vision of the destruction of Jerusalem to the Ruling Authorities. The allusions in question do appear to relate to precise internal problems or events within the Community. For his part, Paul does labor over the issues of taking monetary remuneration at some length in 1 Co 9:7–9 and, in addition, alludes to the fact of his suffering from some disfiguring disease that makes it unpleasant for others to see him or have him visit them (2 Co 10:10, etc.). Some have even suggested this was leprosy. If he did suffer from a kind of leprosy—this, the essence of Elisha's rebuke of Gehazi above—then, of course, the correspondence is even more precise. But these are matters incapable of proof. What is interesting is how much good sense can be made of such notices even with the data at our disposal.

In closing, it is important to note that at the end of these narrative sections of column viii of the Damascus Document (Cairo version, Text B, column xx), before the enumeration of specific legal points that follow in the rest of Text A, there are references to "*Yesha'*" and "*Yeshu'ato*", "Salvation" and "His Salvation" (viii.43 and 57). These come in the particularly sensitive doctrinal summations at the conclusion of Text B, where "fearing God and worshipping His Name" and "God showing Grace to those that love Him [the "Piety" Commandment again] and watch for Him for a thousand generations", are mentioned. The first is epitomized by the phrase "when Salvation (*Yesha'*) and Justification (*Zedakah*) shall be revealed to those that *fear God*".

We have already noted this phrase "fearing God" above and it is widespread in the Scrolls, as for instance in column xlvi of the Temple Scroll in connection with blocking the view of the Temple to various classes of polluted persons, including an allusion to "*balla'*"/"swallowing" or "Bela'", the name of the first Edomite King in the Bible. Paul, too, in 2 Co 7:1 above on "the Perfection of Holiness" and "Beliar" and other Damascus Document-style allusions like "being consecrated" or "separated", links these to the allusion "in the fear of God".

This kind of allusion continues in the closing statement of this section of the Damascus Document:

> However, all those who hold fast to these Laws ... listening to the voice of the Teacher of Righteousness, confessing before God, "we have sinned" ... who have not deserted the Laws of Righteousness ... they shall rejoice and their hearts shall be strengthened ... God will make atonement for them and they shall see His *Salvation* (*Yeshu'ato*), because they took refuge in His Holy Name.

Not only do we have "Name" and "naming" symbolism of the sort that one encounters in the New Testament regarding "the name Jesus", but it is possible to imagine a situation where expressions like these became personalized in overseas Gospels created expressly for external purposes.

This is the kind of exposition one can achieve on the basis of internal data once the parameters of paleography (and now carbon testing) are relaxed. Here we encounter identifiably first-century CE themes and usages which one would be hard pressed to relate to any previous century. This is what is meant by paying attention to the internal usages and allusions. We need to require Qumran specialists to toe the line on important internal usages of this kind. Avoiding or passing them over in silence will not do. Do they have an alternate explanation of them? If not, the choice facing Qumran scholarship is clear: cleave to the exact parameters of paleographic typology in texts like the Damascus Document and make no sense of the internal textual evidence, or admit the layer upon layer of textual commonality with known first-century themes, as encountered in the Pauline corpus and elsewhere—as for instance, James and early Christian documents like the Pseudoclementines.

CHAPTER 8

Joining/Joiners, 'Arizei-Go'im, *and the* Simple of Ephraim *Relating to a Cadre of Gentile* God-Fearers *at Qumran*[*]

A much underestimated question in the study of Qumran documents is the role of a cadre of Gentile "God-Fearers" at Qumran. "God-Fearer" has generally been acknowledged to be a term applied to non-Jewish outsiders interested in Judaism or attached in some kind of associated status to Jewish synagogues in principal cities in Asia Minor and Greece.

The Book of Acts uses the term in this manner and twice applies it to the conversion of the archetypical Gentile convert, the Roman Centurion Cornelius at Caesarea and all his household (10:2 and 10:35). It also applies it to the "wonders and miracles done through the Apostles" (2:43) and to the Jews and Greeks at Ephesus after the discomfiture of "the seven sons of the Jewish High Priest Sceva" ([*Sceva* obviously being a corruption of the number *sheva'* or "seven" in Hebrew] 19:17). Acts 9:31 speaks of "the Assemblies [or "Churches"] in Judea and Samaria walking in fear of the Lord" and depicts Paul as speaking to the Israelites and "God-Fearers" at Antioch in Asia Minor (13:16).

Paul himself refers to it—sometimes negatively or as part of his anti-nomian polemic—in Ro 8:15 (*par contra*, see Ro 3:18). One particularly cogent occurrence of it is to be found in his exhortation "to separate" and "purify oneself of all unclean pollution" in 2 Co 6:14–7:1 in the context of reference to "Beliar", "Light" and "Dark" imagery, and plural divine sonship, culminating in the key evocation of "Perfecting Holiness in fear of God". This is also the gist of like allusions in Eph 5:21 and 1 Pe 2:17. But 1 John 4:18, using the "casting" and "Perfection" language so important in Qumran ideology, reverses it again. Playing on the all-

---

[*] Paper presented at the Society of Biblical Literature, 1991.

important "love" motif (i.e., the two "Love" Commandments of "loving God" and "loving your fellow man"), it reiterates that "Perfect love *casts out* fear" (Greek *ballei*—italics mine).

The notion of "fear of"/"fearing God" is widespread in the Qumran corpus as well. The reference to it is, once again, framed as a positive injunction in the all-important culmination of the narrative section of the Damascus Document, which alludes on three separate occasions (like Paul in 2 Co above) to "the Perfection of Holiness", addressing itself to "the Assembly [or "Church"] of the Men of the Perfection of Holiness".

This exhortation in the final column of the narrative portion of the Damascus Document begins with an allusion to "the New Covenant in the Land of Damascus", "the *standing up* of the Messiah of Aaron and Israel", and even to how the Penitent's "works" should be "in accordance with the precise interpretation of the *Torah* in which the *Men of the Perfection of Holiness* walked" (italics mine—CD, viii.21–30).

Following this and following another reference to "loving one's brother" (the second of the two "Love" Commandments and the second in the document, the first having been two columns earlier in the context of reference to "the New Covenant in the Land of Damascus" and "setting aside the Holy Things according to their precise letter"—vi.17–21); God-Fearers and "fearing God's Name" are twice mentioned (viii.42–43). The context is exactly that in 1 John above, of "loving one's neighbor", "being built up" or "fortified", and "Perfection", albeit with the reverse signification of being for "the *Torah*" instead of antinomian.

In this exhortation in the Damascus Document, the "Penitents from sin" are encouraged to love their neighbors and "fortify their step in the Way of God". At this point, it is reiterated:

> A "Book of Remembrance" will also be written out for those God-Fearers that reckon His [God's] Name, until God will reveal *Salvation* [*Yesha'*] and *Justification* [*Zedakah*] to those that *feared His Name* (italics mine).

Not only is the reference to "*Yesha'*"/"Salvation" interesting here, because it is the Hebrew root of the name "Jesus", but the term "reckon" is the same verb that occurs in the Ge 15:6 passage both Paul and James refer to, namely, "Abraham's Faith was reckoned to him as Righteousness" (or, as this is sometimes expressed in the Greek, "justified him").

Moreover, this promise is immediately followed by the quotation of Ex 20:6 about "God's *Hesed*" or "Piety" (in this case "Loving-kindness" or "Grace") to those that love Him and keep Him "for a thousand Generations" (viii.21–22). "Loving God" here is the first part of the "Piety"/"Righteousness" dichotomy of "Piety towards God" and

"Righteousness towards one's fellow man"—the two "Love" Commandments which the Gospels claim were the fundamental essence of "Jesus'" teaching (Mt 22:37–39 and pars.)

For Josephus, they are the essence of John the Baptist's doctrine as well and the practices of those he is calling "Essenes" are delineated in terms of these two categories. They are also the twin doctrines of James' teaching as presented in all early Church sources and the traces of them are easily discernible in the first two chapters of the New Testament letter ascribed to his name. This means that this fundamental promise to "God-Fearers" or those "who Fear His Name" in the last column of the narrative portion of the Damascus Document is framed or, as it were, circumscribed by allusion to the two "Love" Commandments or the "Righteousness"/"Piety dichotomy" as well.

This section of the Damascus Document also ends on the culminating note of "not deserting the Laws of Righteousness", "strengthening the hearts" of the Penitents, who will ultimately "be victorious over all the sons of earth", and "God making atonement on their behalf [or "through them"] and their seeing His Salvation ("*Yeshu'a*"), because they took refuge in His Holy Name" (viii.55–57). In this presentation, it becomes very clear that these "God-Fearers" are coequal with or come under the same salvational scheme as those being called elsewhere "the Disciples of God" or "the House of *Torah*" (viii.27 and 36).

Another very striking incidence of the notion of "fearing God" at Qumran occurs in the all-important passage about the classes of persons being barred not only from the precincts of the Temple but even seemingly from "seeing" it, in column xlvi of the Temple Scroll (note how in certain verbal constructions "seeing" and "fearing" can be homonyms). One should also remark the curious conjunction of allusion to the term "*balla'*" ("swallowing") or "Bela'" (the name of the first Edomite King in Genesis and the father of Balaam in Numbers and elsewhere—in Hebrew there is no difference in writing "*balla'*" or "Bela'") with this ideology of barring classes of unclean persons not only from the Temple, but also even from seeing it.

In turn, this kind of usage is part of the *B-L-'* circle of language that includes the references to the "Three Nets of Belial" in the Damascus Document and the nets "Balaam taught Balak" in Revelation, which I have attempted to relate to how the reigning Establishment, particularly *Herodians*—but certainly *not Maccabeans*—were viewed by their opponents.

This language cluster would also include the language of "*swallowing*" applied in the Habakkuk *Pesher* to the death of the Righteous Teacher, and thereafter to the reward God paid to the Wicked Priest, as it includes *casting down* language generally in Greek, in particular as related to the death of James in early Church literature and references to "the *Diabolos*" or "the Devil" (cf. 1 John 3:7 and 10 above), another variation on this language.

Certainly, too, there are Greek texts at Qumran which, while not proving the existence of a cadre of Gentiles in some form of associated status with the Community, could be viewed as additional evidence pointing in that direction. But one doesn't need these to prove the proposition, for there is already enough evidence in the widely published texts from Qumran to, at least, raise the question of whether there were Gentiles at Qumran in some form of associated status like that of the Gentile "God-Fearers", who so freely appear to have associated themselves with Jewish synagogues in Asia Minor and elsewhere in the Hellenistic world.

But what kind of status might this have been—a status of full conversion or some intermediate one? If there was a Community of them at Qumran (Prof. Golb notwithstanding) would they have been part of it physically, or would they have been associated elsewhere in peripheral towns and villages in some manner? These questions are unanswerable on the basis of the data before us. Certainly where Qumran is concerned, following the letter of the "*Torah* of Moses" is repeatedly reiterated as a *sine qua non* of the documents. But was this simply a formal requirement or were there other (perhaps "hidden") requirements as sometimes seems to be implied in the documents?

It is interesting that on introducing the exegesis of "the Zadokite Covenant" from Ezek 44:15 at the beginning of column iv, the Damascus Document states that:

> God in his marvelous Mysteries atoned for their sin and pardoned their transgression, *building for them a House of Faith*, the likes of which had never stood in Israel from ancient times until now. And for them that hold fast to it there will be *Eternal life* ["life Victorious"] and *all the Glory of Adam* [the Ebionite *Primal Adam* ideology] will be theirs (CD, iii.18–20).

Following this and an exposition of the role of the true "Sons of Zadok", and just prior to enunciation and exposition of the "Three Nets of Belial", the Damascus Document concludes:

> And all those coming after them ["the First Men of Holiness"] are to *do* [note the Jamesian emphasis on "doing" here] according to the precise letter of the *Torah* which the First ["the Ancestors" or "Forefathers"] transmittted, until the Completion of the Era of these years. According

to the Covenant which God made with the First to atone for their sins, so too would God make atonement for them. But with the completion of the Era of these years, there will be *no more joining to the House of Judah* [i.e., no more Jews], but rather each man will *stand on his own watchtower* (italics mine—iv.7–12).

There would appear to be a mistake in the transcription of this last word. The text has "*mezudo*"/"his net" instead of "*mezoro*"/"his watchtower", but the meaning is clear. This last would be the same "watchtower" spoken of in the Habakkuk *Pesher* (Hab 2:1), where the Prophet Habakkuk looks out and sees that "the Last Era would be extended beyond anything the Prophets have foretold"—in Christian parlance, "the Delay of the *Parousia*". Interestingly, Josephus pictures the revolutionaries in the last days on the Temple Mount before the final Roman assault as avoiding the necessity of following the strictures of the Law—this, collaborating backslider that he is, of course, comes in for his vociferous condemnation.

Josephus also provides a picture of a wild, forced circumcision of Gentiles by the Revolutionaries in the period of the 66–70 CE Uprising. Not only does the Roman Commander of the Citadel in Jerusalem—the same level of commander who seems to have rescued Paul from the crowd in Acts 21–22—accept circumcision to save his life at the beginning of the Uprising, but Josephus provides other examples of the Zealots forcibly circumcizing Gentiles in the course of the Uprising, particularly on *the other side of the Jordan*.

Hippolytus, the third-century Church historian, who conserves a version of Josephus' description of "Essenes" more detailed even seemingly than Josephus', pictures *two* groups of "Essenes": one the traditional one, but another more "Zealot", whom he actually calls "Zealot Essenes". This fits more into our notions of what the Qumran sectaries, given their eschatology, were really like. Hippolytus, presumably following Josephus, also pictures them as *forcibly circumcizing Gentiles on pain of death*. In fact, providing the clue to unraveling some of the little-understood terminologies, Hippolytus tells us that this party of "Essenes"—whom he also calls "Sicarii"—should they hear anyone discussing "God and His Laws", will forcibly circumcize that person; and Origen, in a little-remarked passage, also insists that "the *Sicarii*" were forcibly circumcizing people—thereby violating the Roman "*Lex Cornelia de Sicarius*", specifically aimed at forbidding this.

"Circumcision" is clearly the key issue in a series of confrontations, variously and sometimes contradictorily portrayed in both Acts and Paul's letters, between the Jerusalem Leadership of the early Church in

Palestine and Paul. Acts focuses on this issue of "circumcision" in the run-up to its picture of the famous "Jerusalem Council"—fictional or real—when it says, "Some, who came down from Judea [to "Antioch"] taught the brothers that unless you are circumcized according to the tradition of Moses, you cannot be saved" (15:1).

These are presumably the same "some from James" whom Paul in Galatians, probably more accurately and realistically, depicts as coming down from Jerusalem to Antioch and opposing table-fellowship with Gentiles. Paul specifically identifies them as "of the circumcision" or the party "insisting on circumcision", to whom even Peter and Barnabas must defer—what Paul surprisingly and insultingly refers to as "their *hypocrisy*" (Ga 2:12–13).

The language of "keeping apart from" and "separating himself" that Paul uses here to describe Peter (2:11–12) also permeates the language of the Damascus Document at Qumran. The latter both calls on its adepts "to separate" (also echoed by Paul in 1 Co 6:14 above), and repeatedly stresses "keep apart from polluted Riches" and "polluted things" generally, including those whom it calls derogatorily "the Sons of the Pit". The "Disciples of God" or "Men of the Perfection of Holiness", who follow "Perfection of the Way", are urged to "keep away [*lehazzir*] from fornication" and "separate the Holy from the profane" (vi.15, vii.1, and viii.9).

The verb used here, *linzor* or *lehinnazer*, is based on the same tri-letter Hebrew root *N-Z-R*, "to keep apart from"/"avoid", that the well-known term "Nazirite" is. This conjunction is hardly accidental and gives the Damascus Document the appearance of an excursus on a "New Covenant" or "Community" based on a new "Naziritism", absolutely concerned—unlike Paul—with "setting aside the Holy Things", including "Holy persons" and purity.

The attitude of these extreme "Zealot Essenes" or "*Sicarii*", who wish forcibly to circumcize Gentiles, seems to have been in the extreme circumstances engendered by war—as in Islam—circumcision or die. Niger of Perea, who, as his epithet implies, came from across Jordan where John the Baptist had been active baptizing one or two decades before, is a leader of those Josephus is calling "Idumaeans". Whoever they are, they certainly participated in the War against Rome and were close allies of those Josephus now begins calling "Zealots".

Though seemingly a convert of some kind and an early leader of the Revolt, even Niger ultimately falls foul of such extremists and was executed. Two events from his life, as recorded in Josephus, resemble events recorded of the life of Jesus in the Gospels. One occurs in the initial period of the Uprising, when his followers give him up for dead; he suddenly re-emerges from the earth after being seemingly buried *for three days*! A second takes place toward the end of the Uprising, when he is forced to walk through a large and hostile crowd on the way to his execution outside Jerusalem—an eerie preview of the literary recreation of "Jesus'" death in Gospel narratives.

There were other Gentiles in the Uprising or, better yet, converts—though one man's "convert" was another's "Gentile"—as the name "Simon bar Giora" implies, also active in Idumaea, later executed in Rome at the conclusion of Titus' victory parade. Queen Helen of Adiabene's two sons, Izates and Monobazus, are very famous converts and constitute additional examples of the conversion of this kind of foreign "Man-of-War". And, of course, there was Queen Helen's own conversion.

The real issue behind these conversions, as Josephus makes clear, was circumcision. As I will show in my forthcoming book on *James the Brother of Jesus* (Faber and Faber, 1996), Helen miraculously reappears in the episode in Acts about the conversion to Christianity of the "Ethiopian Queen Kandakes' eunuch" (8:27—here the malevolent and somewhat ribald pun on circumcizing will be straightforwardly delineated). Not only is the overlap between the episode of the conversion of Queen Helen's Law-abiding son, Izates, who circumcised himself, and the "eunuch" of this "Ethiopian Queen" a key to separating out Acts' historical method, such as it is, but there is also a touch of Hellenistic racism here, as there was no conversion of *real* "Ethiopians" at this point in Christian history and no queen called "Kandakes". Here Acts is rather implying that to its author and its readership, all "Arab queens" were like "Ethiopians" (the slur, of course, is intentional).

In any event, the speech Josephus puts into the mouth of the "Zealot" teacher of Helen's son Izates miraculously reappears in the speech to "the Treasurer of the Queen" Acts puts into the mouth of its "Philip" (8:30–38). Two other sons or "kinsmen" of Queen Helen, a second Monobazus and one Kenedaeos—no doubt the real name behind Acts' "Kandakes" above—also die, not insignificantly, in the first battle of the Uprising, fighting the Romans as they retreated from Jerusalem at the legendary Maccabean stronghold astride the Pass at Beit Horon.

Another "Philip", the Herodian "Philip the son of Jacimus, the *Strategos*" or "Head" of Agrippa II's army, was possibly another of these converts. In Acts, "Philip the Evangelist" ends up in Caesarea after meeting "the Ethiopian Queen's eunuch" and is "the father of four virgin daughters who could prophesy" (Acts 21:9). In Josephus, "Philip the *Strategos*" also has daughters, who miraculously escaped the Zealot suicide at Gamala in the Golan Heights (Judas the Galilean's place of origin) and a home in Caesarea. This Philip is another of these Herodian Men-of-War, like Niger of Perea and another of Philip's colleagues Josephus calls "Silas" (there seem to have been two Silases, one older and the other younger). Helen's two sons also fit this "Men-of-War" typology, as does another of Niger's colleagues and revolutionary commander—like Helen's two kinsmen, killed in the early fighting—whom Josephus calls "John the Essene"!

Speaking of "Herodians", are we to consider them Jews, converts, or Gentiles? Much depended on how you looked at it. This is certainly a pivotal issue in Josephus' picture of the visit—again to Caesarea—of another "Simon". Josephus describes this Simon as "the Head of an Assembly [literally *Ecclēsia*/"Church"] of his own in Jerusalem", and he wants, in around 44 CE, to bar the Herodian King Agrippa I from the Temple *as a foreigner* or as one of the classes of polluted person alluded to above in the Temple Scroll.

This is certainly a very crucial episode in the *Antiquities*, which Josephus omits in the *Jewish War*. It is a doublet for the visit of the "Simon" the New Testament calls both "Peter" or "*Cephas*", who in Acts visits *the Roman Centurion Cornelius in Caesarea* (10:24–25—another case of probable New Testament refurbishment), after being the recipient of a "tablecloth" vision in which he learned not to call "any man profane or unclean" (Acts 10:28)—or any food (10:14–15). This is the very opposite of the position we have just seen enunciated in the Damascus Document above. Once appreciated, such reversals of "Zealot" and Qumran positions can be seen to be part and parcel of the New Testament *modus operandi*.

It is types of individual of this kind whom I have identified as "the *'Arizei ha-Go'im*" in Qumran texts—as I have expressed it—often "Violent", sometimes pro-revolutionary, *Herodian* "Men-of-War". This last is another term found in the last narrative column of the Damascus Document (viii.37). There, "the Men-of-War" are said to have "walked with the Man of Lying". Whether these were Jews, Gentiles, or even *bona fide* converts, would very much depend on one's point of view—"Pharisee", Zealot, Nazirite, or some other.

Certainly there are allusions to such persons in the Qumran corpus, and the agitation against foreigners, foreign customs, and ultimately foreign gifts or sacrifices in the Temple is a constant theme of the period from the days of Judas Maccabee to the agitation ending in the Uprising against Rome. This is particularly true, as Josephus repeatedly makes clear, at the time this agitation rose to its zenith in the 50s and 60s, the period in which James held sway in Jerusalem. In fact, the stopping of sacrifice on behalf of Romans and other foreigners in the Temple was the actual issue on which the War was finally proclaimed by the "Zealot" Lower Priesthood in the Temple, probably the same Priests among whom James had been active (Acts 6:7 and 21:20).

The very idea of "Zealot", whether in the early or last days of this Movement, very much bears on this attitude towards foreigners. The High Priest Phineas, the prototypical "Zealot" in Num 25:11–13, had his High-Priestly warrant bestowed on him and his heirs in perpetuity for having killed people marrying foreigners and mixing with or bringing them into the Community. Even the context of "the Zadokite Covenant" of Ezek 44:15, subjected to such crucial exegesis in column iv of the Damascus Document above, was the stricture about barring Gentiles from the Temple (Ezek 44:7). As Ezek 44:9 puts it:

> No foreigner *uncircumcized in heart or uncircumcized in flesh* shall enter My Temple or any foreigner [living] among the Sons of Israel (italics mine).

The "uncircumcized heart" allusion here is a key phraseology too. Paul understands its significance in 2 Co 3:3, when in parodying his opponents *within the Church* and the written letters of recommendation they seem to have (no doubt from personages like *James*), he raises the issue of the "fleshy tablets of the heart" and "writing" on these "not with ink but with the Spirit of the Living God"—meaning his own "Gentile Mission"-style Christianity. Poetic licence notwithstanding, this would no doubt have been profoundly shocking not only to those at Qumran but also to "the Elders and teachers of *the Jerusalem Assembly*" (italics mine).

Especially shocking would have been Paul's then going on to compare the "fleshy tablets of the heart" to "the service of death" represented by the written letters cut into the tablets of stone on Sinai, while at the same time, intoning "the letter kills, but the Spirit gives life" (2 Co 3:6–7). Again, his meaning here is unmistakable and the issue is arguments about written Apostolic certification *within* the early "Church" not *outside it*. The allusion to "uncircumcized heart" from Ezek 44:7–9 is also clearly applied to the Wicked Priest "who did not circumcize the foreskin of his heart" in the Habakkuk *Pesher* (xi.13). It is the reason for his disqualification from Temple service on account of all the "Abominations he committed"—including presumably destroying the Righteous Teacher.

Josephus' allusions to "Idumaeans" led by this "Niger" and others are themselves curious. It should be noted that Acts has someone called

"Niger" as a founding member of the Pauline Community in Antioch, where according to it, "Christians" were first "called Christians" (11:26), including someone even Acts acknowledges was *the foster brother of Herod the Tetrarch*" (the man responsible for the murder of John the Baptist— 13:1)! These "Idumaeans" suddenly materalize in a later phase of the Uprising and clearly are on the same side as the most extreme "Zealots". In fact, Josephus starts using both the terms "Idumaean" and "Zealot" at around the same time.

They have a particular enmity towards Herodian or Establishment High Priests—that is, priests owing their appointment to Herodian kings or Roman governors—and play a principal part in the elimination of them (presumably because of their willingness to use *Violence*), in particular Ananus, the son of the Ananus in the Gospels. Not only is this "younger" Ananus the brother of Jonathan, whose death in 55 CE at presumably "Zealot" or "*Sicarii*" hands is also recorded by Josephus in the run-up to the Uprising; he is the High Priest responsible for the death of James in 62 CE.

How can we say these Gentile Idumaeans—for certainly they seem to be Gentiles—are on the same side of the Uprising as "Zealots" (note that in Acts 21:20, the greater part of James' "Jerusalem Assembly" supporters are described as "Zealots for the Law"). I prefer another term Josephus uses, "innovators", because, as the late Morton Smith of Columbia has pointed out, the Movement we are speaking of cannot simply be called "Zealot" until the last days of the Uprising. Here, too, the term is really only applied to those who take vengeance on Ananus—vengeance for the death of James?—and the later "Zealot" band under Eleazar who *actually occupy the Temple*. In other work, I have called this "the Messianic Movement" and for various reasons believe this term to be the more accurate.

These Idumaeans have a particular animus against Ananus—but why? And if they have this animus towards High Priests, how then do they differ from that group designated as "*'Arizei-Go'im*" ("the Violent Ones of the Gentiles") in the Psalm 37 *Pesher*? It is not even clear if this category of "Idumaeans" in Josephus is not a circumlocution, signifying not a whole national entity but only perhaps pro-revolutionary Herodians—"Idumaeans" clearly being one possible circumlocution applicable to Herodians.

"*'Arizei-Go'im*" is used in at least two places in the Psalm 37 *Pesher* (ii.20 and iv.9). In both, whatever group is intended by this circumlocution, the context has to do with the vengeance taken by "the Violent Ones of the Gentiles" (and presumably these *are* Gentiles) on those who attacked "the Priest"/"Righteous Teacher"—referred to in the first instance (ii.18) as "the Wicked of Ephraim and Manasseh" and in the second, as "the Wicked Priest" (iv.8).

In the Nahum *Pesher* we encounter some of the same terms, but there the sense is "the Simple Ones of Ephraim", obviously meant to parallel in some manner "the Simple Ones of Judah doing *Torah* " in the Habakkuk *Pesher*. The two groups of "Wicked Ones" in the Psalm 37 *Pesher* are evidently meant to correspond to another group called "the Violent of the Covenant in the House of Judah" (ii.14 and iii.12), terminology that parallels material in the Habakkuk *Pesher* and references simply to " *'Arizim*" ("Violent Ones") there.

In the second context, starting with the identification of "the Priest" (i.e., the "Opposition" High Priest) with "the Teacher of Righteousness" at the end of the third column of the Psalm 37 *Pesher*, the events referred to are more specifically tied to the Wicked Priest *per se*. As in the Habakkuk *Pesher* references to "swallowing" and "drinking the Cup of the Lord" (or *Divine Vengeance*), once again, he is given his proper reward by these "Violent Ones of the Gentiles" who "execute Judgement upon him".

Where the fate of the Wicked Priest is in question, the Habakkuk *Pesher* is of similar import, even similar vocabulary ("they [unspecified] inflicted upon him the Judgements of Evil"—ix.1). Whoever these Violent Gentiles may be, in the Psalm 37 *Pesher* they are certainly on the same side as "the Priest" (identical with "the Righteous Teacher"), "the Men of his Council", "the Doers of *Torah* " and "the Poor"—also referred to as "the Assembly of the *Ebionim* of Jerusalem" (this last closely paralleling what often goes by the phraseology "the Jerusalem Church" in early Christianity)—again, all terms with parallels in the Habakkuk *Pesher*.

Whether these " *'Arizei-Go'im*" in the Psalm 37 *Pesher*, who "take vengeance" on the Wicked Priest, can be identified with Josephus' "Idumaeans" cannot be proven and will largely depend on one's identification of key personalities. However, if the expression does not refer to them, one would be hard-pressed to find a specific group which fulfills these criteria better, particularly in Maccabean times. The identification with James—also a "Priest" and a "Teacher of Righteousness" in all early Church tradition—may be questioned, but those who do so would themselves find it difficult to provide the name of another who fits such a description from the Maccabean Period. It is easy to criticize others without being required to produce better identifications oneself.

The identification of these " *'Arizei-Go'im*" in the Psalm 37 *Pesher* depends on one's interpretation of the text in question. But the term "*'Arizim*" also appears elsewhere in the published Qumran corpus, most notably in the Habakkuk *Pesher* (ii.6). Whether in the Habakkuk *Pesher* references these are supposed to be "Gentiles" or not cannot be determined from the context (we have already noted two groups of "Violent Ones"—both "Gentiles" and "of the Covenant" in the Psalm 37 *Pesher*); but there is no reason to believe, in view of the other parallels implicit in the commentaries, that the term is very different from the parallel one in the Psalm 37 *Pesher*.

In the Habakkuk *Pesher*, the "*'Arizim*" or "Violent Ones" are allied in some way with "the Liar", "the Covenant-Breakers", and "the Traitors to the New Covenant" (1QpHab, ii.3–6). Confirming the basic parallelism of these two contexts, there is also a reference to "the Liar" in the Psalm 37 *Pesher*, directly following the passage about the vengeance taken on the Wicked Priest by "the Violent Ones" (i.26 and iv.14). The passage in the Habakkuk *Pesher* seemingly refers to some internal struggle within the Community itself, and these various groups of persons are even portrayed as *attending the Scriptural exegesis sessions* of "the Priest"/"Righteous Teacher"—interpretations of biblical writ he is said to get from "the Mouth of God" Himself (1QpHab, ii.3–10 and viii.4–8).

In the course of these or other like confrontations, "the Liar" is said to "reject the *Torah* in the midst of their whole Assembly" and attacks the Righteous Teacher verbally (1QpHab, v.12). That this would appear to be an internal matter within the Community is reinforced by the note that the parties concerned were privy to the internal Scriptural exegesis sessions of the Righteous Teacher. Though the words "their Assembly" ["Church"] are indeterminate here, if it is the Righteous Teacher's "Assembly", we have in these confrontations something very much resembling what goes by the name of "the Jerusalem Council" in early Christianity. I have discussed this point in some detail in JJHP (Chapter 2). Whatever the conclusion, this is further evidence supporting *some association* of persons, called "the Violent Ones"—"the Violent Ones of the Gentiles" in the Psalm 37 *Pesher*—with the Community, even if at this point they are "walking with" or following the ideological opponent of the Teacher—called "the Man of Lying" or "the Spouter" or "Pourer out of Lying," within this Community.

The same categories or groups are encountered in the Nahum *Pesher*, including the reiteration of the theme of "Lying" again. Elsewhere I have identified this theme of "Lying" with a Paul-like teacher. Paul himself in extant correspondence is clearly aware of this accusation as applying to him, and vigorously protests at key junctures that he "does not lie" (cf. Ga 1:20 on his first meeting with James and 2 Co 11:31 on his escape from Damascus in a basket). In Galatians he also shows knowledge of the "Enemy" terminology, so well attested in early Christianity and applied in *Ebionite* Christianity to Paul, and connecting with the issue of "telling the Truth" (4:16).

Though most attention with regard to the Nahum *Pesher* has been focused on the first column (more recently reconstructed as the *second* column—the first dealing with torrential rain and what is clearly a scenario of final "Judgement" of some kind) and the well-known allusions there to "the Furious Young Lion", "(Deme)trius", "the Greeks", "the *Kittim*", and the like; for our purposes the third column is more interesting. Beginning with an allusion to "Messengers" in Gentile countries (in Greek, "Apostles") and a reference to "the City of Ephraim", tied to an allusion to "those who Seek Smooth Things at the End of Days" and "walking in Lying", there is an allusion to "City of Blood", also tied to an allusion to "the City of Ephraim" (4QpNah, ii.1–2). In my view, the "*Blood*" and "*Lying*" imagery both have to do in some manner with the Qumran character known as "the Man of" or "Spouter of Lying".

The repeated description of the great heaps of corpses with "no end to their total", taking off from a vivid description of the destruction of Jerusalem by the Babylonians in the underlying text from Nah 3:1–3, is hardly to be associated with a fall of Jerusalem less important than the one of 70 CE. Only the fallacious interpretation of Qumran archaeological and paleographical evidence could make one think differently.

If we understand "Seekers after Smooth Things" according to its normative interpretation of "Pharisees" then, once again, we are really in the first century CE, because "the Seekers after Smooth Things" did not really "hold sway in Jerusalem" at any period prior to the Herodian or Roman Period. This really cannot be said for the Maccabean, except in the imaginations of those who feel it is legitimate to present the Maccabeans as "Wicked Priests" of some kind—as opposed to Herodian High Priests. But, in addition, the first column tells us that "the *Kittim*" come after "the Greeks", "Demetrius", *and* "Antiochus" Epiphanes (ii.3); thus making it crystal clear that we are in the Herodian Period, not any period previous to this, and that "the *Kittim*" *are* the Romans.

The interesting allusion to "Ephraim" in the third column is connected also to "being led astray by" someone (iii.7). "Leading astray" is also the characteristic activity of "the Lying Spouter" or "Liar" in the documents at Qumran. This kind of imagery is also present in the Psalm 37 *Pesher* and to be found in the Damascus Document and Habakkuk *Pesher* as well, once again, attesting to the homogeneity of the literature and belying any attempt—whether by carbon dating or otherwise—to date these at widely varying periods of origin. Though the offenders are plural in the Nahum *Pesher*, the imagery is the same as that in the Habakkuk *Pesher*, where it is singular and unequivocally applied to

> the Spouter of Lying, who leads Many astray to build a Worthless City upon Blood and erect an Assembly [or "Church"] on Lying, tiring out Many with a Worthless Service for the sake of his Glory and instructing them in works of Lying, so that their works would count for Emptiness (x.9–12).

The import of this passage speaks for itself.

In the Nahum *Pesher*, following the sense of the underlying text from Nah 3:4, the idea of *"ger-nilveh"*—"resident alien" or "convert"—is specifically evoked in relation to these "Many"/"Simple Ones of Ephraim", i.e., "the *ger-nilveh*" or "stranger *who joins them*" (italics mine—iii.9). There can be little doubt about the meaning of the allusion to "join" or "joining" in this context, and the idea of such "joining" or "being attached" in some manner to the Jewish Commonweal is incorporated too into the next column of the *Pesher* (iv.5). We will see in our interpretation of the all-important term, *"Nilvim"*, as it occurs in exposition of Ezek 44:15 in the Damascus Document below, that the "Nilvim"/"Joiners" carries the connotation one finds here in columns iii–iv of the Nahum *Pesher*, namely of Gentiles or converts specifically "joining" or "attaching themselves" to Israel.

Here in the Nahum *Pesher*, the imagery is again that of "Falsehoods", "Lying"/"Lies", and "Deceit" (ii.7–8). These allusions are tied to additional key images like "lip", important in the Community Rule, and "Tongue", a crucial allusion that will appear again and familiar in the letter of James (3:5–10). "Tongue" imagery there is generically parallel to the imagery of "Spouting" or the "Lying Spouter who will surely spout" at Qumran.

In JJHP (Chapter 2)—I have tied this "City built upon Blood" imagery—when connected to "the Lying Spouter . . . leading Many astray with works of Lying" and "erecting a City upon Blood"—with building a Community on *the Blood of Christ* or *"Communion"*, as it is developed by Paul in 1 Co 10–11. This is the same "Man of Lying" who in connection with "the Violent Ones", "Covenant-Breakers", and "Traitors to the New Covenant", "rejected the Law in the midst of their whole Assembly" and led a verbal assault upon the Teacher in the Habakkuk

Pesher. This analysis can either be accepted or not. But, if it is accepted, it leads to an indisputable connection between the "City of Blood" and "Ephraim" imagery and a teacher of this kind.

Without involving themselves in complex analyses such as these, some confidently assert that "Ephraim" represents the Pharisees; and "Manasseh"—in the Nahum *Pesher* (iii.9 and iv.3)—the Sadducees. This is, of course, an unproved assumption of the kind normal in Qumran research since the 1950s. One colleague, particularly enamored of such a view, having read "*MMT*", recently *discovered* that Qumran was "Sadducean", something set forth in MZCQ (Chapter 1 in this book) without benefit of "*MMT*" almost a decade ago. Not only does he not acknowledge his indebtedness to this work (while appropriating many of its ideas), he has only the most simplistic ideas of early Christianity and no comprehension whatever of what "anti-Establishment", "Opposition", or "Messianic Sadducees" of the kind represented by the literature at Qumran might be (and has the temerity to call *others* "plagiarists").

On the basis of the evidence in the Nahum *Pesher* alone, it is not possible to say with any finality who or what "Ephraim" is—to say nothing of "Manasseh"—except to say that the "*ger-nilveh*" and "joining" imagery must be reckoned with it and seen as a component of whatever one means by it. Besides, there are different kinds of allusion to "Ephraim", namely, "the City of Ephraim", "the Wicked of Ephraim", and "the Simple Ones of Ephraim"—paralleling "the Simple Ones of Judah *doing Torah*" in the Habakkuk *Pesher* (xii.4–5)—and all these categories do not necessarily represent or mean the same thing.

As this imagery moves into column iii of the Nahum *Pesher*, "the Seekers after Smooth Things" are still the subject of the exposition, as is the eschatological nature of the time (that is, "the Last Days" or "the End Time"—iii.2 and iv.3). There is no way of knowing from the presentation here either what the meaning of "Ephraim" and "Manasseh" is, nor the "*Beit*" or "House of *Peleg*" that is now mysteriously joined to the latter at the beginning of column iv. There "Manasseh" seems as much the King by that name as anything else, and I would venture a guess that we are dealing with "Herodians" once again.

How some would derive "Sadducees" from this is incomprehensible—but if Sadducees, we certainly do not have to do here with Qumran or "Messianic Sadducees" but rather Herodian or Establishment ones, whom Josephus tells us were dominated at this time in all things *by the Pharisees*. I have covered the difference between these two kinds of Sadducees in MZCQ (Chapter 1). One thing that does emerge even in the Nahum *Pesher*: the group being called "the Wicked of Ephraim" (iv.5) is certainly different from "the Simple Ones of Ephraim" (iii.5). The latter is complimentary, the former is not; and, as noted, the latter must be seen as a counterpart to "the Simple Ones of Judah doing *Torah*" in the Habakkuk *Pesher*.

And another thing that clearly emerges: in column iii.5 of the Nahum *Pesher* also, the term "Simple Ones of Ephraim" is linked to the Glory "of Judah", i.e., "when Judah's Glory is revealed [a term in the Damascus Document usually associated with God or "His Messiah" "*visiting*" the earth], the Simple Ones of Ephraim will flee from the midst of their Assembly [presumably that of "the Seekers after Smooth Things" or, as I have put it elsewhere, "those accomodating themselves to foreign rule" and forsake those who *lead them astray* [here, our telltale imagery again repeatedly associated with "the Spouter spouting Lies to them"] and *join themselves once more to Israel*" (italics mine). This "joining" imagery, now expressed in terms of the verb "*nilvu*", is a key allusion and links up with that to "*ger-nilveh*" and "joining" in the previous column.

In my view all of these allusions are more complex than generally acknowledged. Even the term, "Seekers after Smooth Things", probably doesn't mean "Pharisees" in the normative sense of the term. Rather, as used in this *pesher* anyhow, it probably represents a more general collection of persons "*seeking accommodation with foreigners*", which, of course, would *include Pharisees*. But it also includes others—namely persons of the mindset of a Paul, especially as this reveals itself in sections of his letters, such as Ro 13:1–10 in interpretation of Jamesian "works" and "loving your neighbor as yourself". For Paul, "loving your neighbor" is *paying taxes to Rome*!

Speaking of the first century CE if not the second century BC, it is even possible to identify what these "Smooth Things" were that so agitated the protagonists of our documents. These were not small, picayune problems but broad general themes. These I have identified as: *accommodation with foreign kings* (the probable root of the "Manasseh" imagery above and certainly that centering about the *B-L-ʿ* language cluster I have elsewhere alluded to), *foreign appointment of High Priests, divorce, polygamy, marriage with nieces, Riches*, and, most notably in the context of what we have been discussing here, *gifts and sacrifices on behalf of foreigners in the Temple*, interpreted in the Damascus Document as "pollution of the Temple"—even pollution of "the Temple Treasury" (CD, iv.17 and vi.16).

Under such a broad definition of "Seekers after Smooth Things", Pauline Christians can certainly be included. One should also note in this regard the New Testament's insistence that Paul was a "Pharisee of the

Pharisees" (Acts 23:6, echoing Phil 3:5). The use of "Ephraim,", too, at least the term "the Simple Ones of Ephraim", in some of these contexts is not very different from that of "Samaritan" in the Gospels—for all intents and purposes a parallel nomenclature.

We are now in a position to approach the all-important *Pesher* on Ezek 44:15, "the Zadokite Covenant", at the beginning of column iv of the Damascus Document (iii.21–iv.12), by way of introducing the equally pivotal "Three Nets of Belial" charges ("fornication", "Riches", and "pollution of the Temple") at the end of that column (iv.13–19). *Waw*-constructs have seemingly been purposely added to the original biblical passage underlying the *pesher*—originally, "the Priests, who are the *Beni-Zadok* Levites"—to produce the now fairly widely known "the Priests *and* the Levites *and* the Sons of Zadok" (iv.1).

This prepares the way for the interpretation of "Priests" as "the Penitents of Israel, who departed from the Land of Judah"—not the customary definition of "Priests" (note the dichotomy between "Israel" and "Judah", also part and parcel of the Nahum *Pesher* approach). The *Pesher* now, again seemingly purposely, leaves out the expression "the Levites" altogether, replacing it with "and the *Nilvim*"/"Joiners with them" in the exegesis, before going on to give an eschatological exposition of the term "the Sons of Zadok" as "the Elect of Israel" who would "*stand*"/ *stand up* at the End of Time . . . justifying the Righteous and condemning the Wicked" (italics mine).

"*Nilvim*" is, of course, based on the same root in Hebrew as "Levites", which is the connection the *pesher* is building on, and wishes to draw, but it is *not the same word*. Our exegetes were surely aware of this. Nor is this a normative definition of "the Sons of Zadok" either, which is why I have elsewhere termed it "eschatological", meaning that the exegesis is more than just an interpretation, it is an *eschatological* interpretation dealing with "Last Things"/"Last Times".

It is also esoteric, as is the exposition of "Priests" that precedes it. Defining "Priests", which normally means "High Priests", as "Penitents" who have "gone out" into the wilderness and "departed from the Land of Judah"—in column vi they are said to "dwell in the Land of Damascus" (vi.5)—is certainly not a normal definition of "Priests" either, nor is it genealogical, at least not superficially. However, it is *esoteric*.

But what of the words "and the *Nilvim* with them", meant not as an explanation of something "Levites" do but as a play on or actual stand-in for the term—and perhaps something more. If the approach we are pursuing here is correct and these expositions are indeed esoteric, then so is this allusion to "the *Nilvim* with them". The hint for its exposition is already supplied in the "Simple Ones of Ephraim"/"*ger-nilveh*" allusions in the Nahum *Pesher* above. But it is clinched by the single use of this term in a biblical context: Esth 9:27.

There, playing once more on the "joining" imagery as utilized as well in the Nahum *Pesher* above, it clearly denotes *non-Jews* or *Gentiles attaching themselves to the Jewish Community in some form of associated status*. We are, therefore, right back to where we were at the beginning of this discussion. This specific sense of the term "*Nilvim*", as set forth in Es 9:27, the only biblical book missing from Qumran (the book is, but the term "*Nilvim*" is not), has been completely overlooked in all interpretations of this curious, yet fundamental, allusion in the Damascus Document.

This would seem to me to be for two reasons: one, the esoteric and actually eschatological nature of the exegesis has not usually been acknowledged or appreciated; and two, it has generally been assumed that the words "the Levites" are not missing from the exposition, though they are. Most translators in English have, therefore, simply taken the liberty of writing them in. But this is a mistake. They *are* missing, of course. As in all such exegeses in Qumran documents, this is purposeful. There is very little that is *not purposeful* in Qumran documents and this *lacuna* must be respected as such. This is the meaning I would give it in this all-important exegesis in the Damascus Document, that is, foreigners in a kind of associated status or what we began in our discussion by calling "God-Fearers".

When this esoteric sense of the text is understood, the term "the Sons of Zadok" that follows it turns out to have an esoteric sense as well– something to do with either the Resurrection at the End of Time or a Judgement of the Heavenly variety, or both. In fact, this is the way the idea of God's "Elect"—in the Damascus Document, "the Elect of Israel" and part of the definition of "the Sons of Zadok"—is used in the Habakkuk *Pesher*, that is, they participate with God in *the Judgement on all the Nations*—normally termed "the Last Judgement" (1QpHab, v.4). The term "Sons of Zadok" too is, therefore, not normative; in fact, it would appear to actually have a "supernatural" meaning and its esoteric sense comes out to mean something very much like "the Sons of Righteousness" or "the Sons of God".

In turn, these several esoteric senses have interesting implications when re-applied to the passage about "Ephraim" and "joining" in the Nahum *Pesher* above and the whole gamut of allusions—we have just reviewed—to Gentiles cooperating in some manner or being involved in the affairs either of the Community or the early Church. If the relationship of phrases, such as "leading astray" and the like "to the

Liar"'s activities is properly grasped, then "the Simple Ones of Ephraim", who have been "led astray" by "fraudulent teaching", "deceitful lips", and "a Lying Tongue" will have much to do with a Paul (or even Simon Magus)—like teacher. These will "when Judah's Glory is revealed", "forsake those who have misled them and once more join themselves to Israel".

In my view, there is much to recommend an interpretation, here, of "Pauline Christians" or Gentile "God-Fearers" in some form of associated status being misled by an antinomian Pauline-type teaching or teacher, returning by way of true conversion to a proper observation of the Law or, as it were, *Torah*—if you will, a "Jamesian" interpretation of it—before the promises of the Covenant could be thought of as being truly available to them.

CHAPTER 9

The Final Proof that James and the
Righteous Teacher are the Same*

For some time now, as many know, I have been looking for the proof
or unproof of the proposition that James and the Righteous Teacher are
the same. One of the reasons I involved myself in the struggle for freedom of access to the Dead Sea Scrolls in the first place was that, as a
historian, my needs were not being met by the philologists and gram-
marians, who acted as if we had lifetimes to go through all the data. As
I have repeatedly stressed, a historian needs all materials at his or her
disposal now. He or she cannot wait while philologists go through what
may indeed be labors of love, but while they are laboring, life is drifting
away. Open archives and unrestricted freedom of access were the only
answer to this problem.

As it turned out, however, the proof I was looking for could have
been done on the basis of the already published, not the unpublished
texts—though these last did help in sharpening one's focus and further
appreciating the "Jewish Christian" and/or "Zealot" nature of the texts.

It is interesting that even in the New Testament there are Hebrew
words incapable of translation into Greek, which have, therefore, to be
transliterated directly from the Hebrew. One is "Nazoraean", which for
some, through further transliteration, comes out "Nazarene"; for others
"Nazareth", even perhaps "Nazirite"—though these words are not all
based on the same Hebrew root. "Cananaean"—"Cananite" to some—
for "Zealot", and most likely "Iscariot" for "*Sicarios*" are two others; but
there is also "Beliar" in Paul (2 Co 6:15), and even "Beelzebul" in the
Gospels—variations of "Belial" in the Scrolls. They show indisputably
that at least some of the authors responsible for the New "Cananite"

* Paper presented at the Society of Biblical Literature in 1994.

Testament knew Hebrew. Paul, too, shows some of the same knowledge in his numerous wordplays and allegorizing.

But more than that, some of these Greek authors not only knew Hebrew, but—however incredible it may at first appear—were taking allusions and language clusters from the Hebrew and moving them directly over into Greek, and *changing the meaning*. This does not seem to have mattered to them as long as the main letters remained the same, *as if the basic epigraphic cluster had a meaning all its own*. At Qumran, there are several such language clusters, to which I have repeatedly called attention. Two of the most obvious are *"Zaddik"* and *"Rasha'"*/"Righteous" and "Evil". These go through a variety of adumbrations in the literature, including words like "justify" and "condemn".

Perhaps the most interesting of these is the one centering around the Hebrew letters, *ba-la-'a*, or "swallowing" and its multitudinous variations. These give rise to a whole series of usages fundamental to the material before us: for instance "Belial", but also the related "Balaam", and another related personal noun with importance where Herodians are concerned (and even perhaps Paul), "Bela'", the father in the Old Testament of both the Edomites and one clan of Benjaminites—these, not to mention Paul's defective reference to "Beliar" in 2 Co 6:15 above.

Not only is "Balaam" in the Old Testament listed, for instance, as "the son of Be'or", but so too is "Bela'". Clearly we have some genealogical overlapping here. As well, these names sometimes even seem to have an esoteric meaning associated with them. For instance, in the *Talmud*, "Balaam", playing on the root meanings of "swallow" and "People", is "he who devours" or "swallows the people". "Be'or", playing on *"be'ir'* in Hebrew, is "animal" or "beast". Similar usages appear in the Letter ascribed to "Jude the brother of James". For 2 Peter 2:15, a letter replete with Qumranisms, which even contains this "beast" allusion for "Be'or" "Balaam the son of Besor [*sic*]", "loved the reward of Unrighteousness" and led people astray from "the Straight Way". One doesn't have to be an expert to see the linguistic relationships here, despite the erroneous spelling "Besor"!

In Revelation, a repository in Greek for esotericisms of this kind, we come upon the extremely interesting allusion that "Balaam taught Balak to cast down [*balein*—this will turn out to be a fundamental usage] a net before Israel to eat the things sacrificed to idols and commit fornication" (Rev 2:14). Again, it doesn't take a genius—though sometimes it seems it does—to see the relationship of this to the parallel allusion in the Damascus Document and the famous "Three Nets of Belial" section in column iv, thus increasing the points of contacts between early

Christianity and the Scrolls; yet, as far as I am aware, *no one has ever pointed it out.*

As this is presented in the "Three Nets of Belial" section in the Damascus Document, it comes in interpretation of Is 24:18, one of the most militant and aggressive passages in Prophecy, which insists that the earth is polluted because the Covenant has been broken and the Law violated, condemns Traitors, and avers, therefore, that the earth is put under a curse. The famous exegesis in the Damascus Document, which basically plays off a reference to "snare" or "net" in the underlying passage from Is 24, reads:

> Its interpretation concerns the Three Nets of Belial ... with which he ensnares Israel, transforming them into three kinds of Righteousness. The first is fornication, the second Riches, and the third, pollution of the Temple. Whoever escapes the first will be caught in the second, and whoever eludes the second is caught in the third.

The relationship of this passage to the one in Revelation above should be clear. Though the latter uses "Balaam" instead of "Belial", the effect is the same.

In addition—and this is significant—the passage in Revelation uses the categories of James' directives to overseas communities, as reported in three versions in Acts ("abstain from blood, fornication, things sacrificed to idols, and strangled things"—Acts 15:20, 15:29, and 21:25), in particular, "things sacrificed to idols", in place of the basically parallel allusion to "pollution of the Temple" in the Damascus Document. This is an absolutely fundamental shift, especially when attempting to evaluate James' role as Righteous Teacher and Paul/James disputes generally.

For the moment it must suffice to point out here not only the emphasis on "nets"—an emphasis running through the whole of the Qumran corpus, as it does the New Testament—but also the presence of the root of this allusion to "Balaam" or "Belial" ("Beliar" in Paul—"Beelzebul", too, in further New Testament word-play on this fundamental root, not to mention, "Babylon", in "whore of Babylon" also in Revelation), *ba-la-ʿa* meaning, as noted above, to "swallow" or "consume" in Hebrew. When used with regard to the destruction of the Righteous Teacher at Qumran by the Wicked Priest, which it is three times in almost as many lines in the Habakkuk *Pesher*, it clearly means "consume" or "destroy"— in the event, probably implying his death.

I was unaware of all these symbolisms and their thematic variations, until I pursued the study of James the Just and his relationship to the Righteous Teacher from Qumran. Pursuing such a study led me to understand the importance of the key reference to "pursuing the Right-eous Teacher" in the Habakkuk *Pesher* either "to", "with", or "in" his *Beit-Galuto*/"his House of Exile" or "Exiled House"—any of these prep-ositions is arguable, since the *alef* introducing it is defective—in a way that I could not have understood it before. In fact, I did not even under-stand it fully at the time I published *James the Just in the Habakkuk Pesher* in 1986 (Chapter 2 of this book), which is why I wrote the paper I did on this subject (also published in this volume as Chapter 5) for the Groningen Conference in 1989 thereafter and the one on the other "Eso-tericisms" in columns v–viii of the Damascus Document the next year (Chapter 7).

What I began to realize was that the ambiguous "his" in the construct phrase "his House" did not necessarily have to relate to the Righteous Teacher's "house", as it was usually automatically and routinely inter-preted. On the contrary, it could relate to the Wicked Priest's "House"—meaning in this instance, the Temple (a normal usage in Hebrew) or the Sanhedrin. The idea is actually picked up in the Gospel of Luke, where, in the picture of Jesus' trial for "blasphemy", the Sanhedrin is actually pictured as convening in "the High Priest's House" (22:54), a usage prob-ably based on the one we have in the Habakkuk *Pesher* above.

I first suggested this in JJHP. But events of consulting the events of James' life and the fact of his *Sanhedrin Trial* by a latterday embodiment of the "Wicked Priest", that had led me to consider this possibility in the first place. It was by plugging the known details from James' trial and stoning—also supposedly for "blasphemy"—into allusions in the Scrolls that this understanding emerged. This is the way scientific proof is developed. Nor would I have thought of this alternative way of looking at the passage otherwise and a much deeper understanding of the passage itself also emerged.

This in itself was powerful proof of the identity of James and the Righteous Teacher, because if a hypothesis not only helps to explain the data, but—as any student of science would know—in addition, is able to elicit *new information from that data* that was not apparent or could not have been suspected previously without it, it is very strong proof of its validity or, at least, its usefulness. This is induction, through which scien-tific proofs are built up by a process of data accumulation—by a process of gradually approaching certainty. Certainty is rarely arrived at in a single instant.

This was just the point I made in the "*Abeit-Galuto*" paper included in this volume—but this was the paper my colleagues from the École Biblique in Jerusalem who edit the *Revue de Qumran* and the International

Scrolls Editorial team, who appear to have been involved to some degree in the organization of the Groningen Conference, rejected in the final publication of the papers from that conference, despite assurances to the contrary. So much for free scholarship and honoring an opponent's views in Qumran Studies, where these niceties do not appear to count for much and are obviously not observed. Many of these same colleagues agreed to the publication of their papers in that journal following this conference knowing that these elemental assurances and fundamental courtesies were not being honored.

Aside from the matter of the *"abeit-galuto"* allusion in the Habakkuk *Pesher*'s description of the destruction of the Righteous Teacher and its relationship to the Sanhedrin's "exile from the House"/*"galtah min ha-Bayit"*—*"galtah"* and *"Galut"* both meaning "exile" in Hebrew—in the period of the stoning of James from its normal place of sitting in the Stone Chamber on the Temple Mount to a place called *Hanut* outside it as recorded in numerous *Talmud*ic sources; I also examined a whole series of fundamental word-plays in that *Pesher*, like *"Chos"* and *"Cha'as"* ("Cup" and "Wrath"), *"me'oreihem"*/*"Mo'adeihem"* ("privy parts"/ "Festivals") and *"'arel"*/*"ra'al"* ("foreskin" and "trembling" or "poison"), to my knowledge never remarked by anyone else. In the latter two instances, the play on words and love of homophones and hom-onyms in this passage about what the Wicked Priest did to the Righteous Teacher and the members of his Council—called "the Poor"—and the vengeance that God would take for what he did even went so far as *reversing letters* in words like "foreskin" and "Festival", above.

I also discussed how—approaching this genre of literary symbolism in a way not previously remarked—the episode about "drinking the Cup of the Lord" had to do not with "drunkenness"—as many "Consensus" scholars had insisted earlier—but with *the Cup of the Lord's Divine Anger* and *Vengeance* in the manner one finds it in almost word-for-word repli-cation in Revelation—namely, the Vengeance the Lord would take on the Wicked Priest, "who had not circumcized the foreskin of his heart", for what he had done to the Righteous Teacher (here too "circumcized foreskin" played on another allusion from Is 51:17–22, "Cup of Trembling"). Just as the Wicked Priest "swallowed him"—meaning, gave the venomous cup of "his angry wrath" to the Righteous Teacher—so too would "the Cup of the Lord's Divine Wrath" come around to "swal-low him" and "he would drink his fill".

It was this last phrase that was interpreted as the Wicked Priest's "drunkenness" in Qumran Studies previously, which in preferring the more easy-to-understand results of external parameters, such as paleography and carbon testing, had shown a distinct inability to come to grips with internal ones like this. The sense of the literary metaphor here is perhaps best illustrated in the words of Revelation—referring as well to "the whore of Babylon", another variation of the basic *ba-la-ʿa* homophonic symbolism alluded to above—giving "the wine of the Fury of her fornication to all Nations to drink":

> He also shall drink of the wine of the Wrath of God, which is poured out [one should note the "pouring" usage as well here] full strength into the Cup of His Anger. And he shall be tormented in Fire and brimstone [all imagery known to the Habakkuk *Pesher*] before the Holy Angels and the Lamb (Rev 14:8–10).

As with the repetitive "nets" attributed to Balaam and Balak above, the fit here is perfect.

The conclusion I arrived at, both in JJHP (Chapter 2) and the "*Abeit-Galuto*" article in Chapter 5, was that there was no *drunken* Wicked Priest at Qumran—usually expressed in Establishment theorizing in terms of one or other of the first-generation Maccabees dying at a banquet *because they were drunk*—only "the Cup of the Anger of the Lord", from which he (the Wicked Priest) "would drink his fill".

To return to these "nets of Balaam"/"Belial" and this basic *ba-la-ʿa*-language circle, it was not until I came to understand that in Greek all of these usages involving the words "casting down" (*ballō*) were based on a variation of the same phonetically parallel root letters *b-l*, i.e., *kataballō*/"cast down", *ekballō*/"cast out", *einballō*/"cast in", and other variations (in Josephus, for instance, in the description of how the corpse of James' destroyer the Wicked Priest Ananus was "cast out" of the city without burial, even *paraballō*) that I came to understand that the proof I had been looking for had been staring me in the face from the beginning, even in the already published documents from Qumran.

In the process, so was an aspect of the exegetical method, or rather linguistic inventiveness, of the New Testament. This involved not only word-play—sometimes even malevolent—but spin-offs and variations that moved towards Philo's and the Pauline literary method of allegorization. So widespread was this in the Gospels that at times these documents even took on the appearance of playful divertimentos on the Greek cluster of letters embodying the meaning of "casting" or "throwing down".

These things had to do with the fact that in the Greek the usage "casting down" associated with Balaam in Rev 2:15—and by extension even "the Diabolos", not to mention the name "Balak" added to it in

Revelation—and always, as at Qumran, involving "nets", was also based on a similar homophonic linguistic configuration in the Greek *ballō*/"cast down" and its variations. In linguistic theory two consecutive consonants or separated vocalic sounds are considered sufficient to establish a linguistic connection or loan. A good example would again be "Beliar" in 1 Co 6:15, and even the corrupt *"Besor"* in 2 Peter mentioned above. Another would be Muhammad's use of *"Iblis"* in Sura 2 of the *Koran* in connection with, it should be remarked, the Ebionite "Primal Adam" ideology—a fundamental ideology in Pseudoclementine descriptions of the doctrines of the Jerusalem Community of James and the first Christians.

But the final point, which is perhaps crucial, is that in all early Church presentations of attacks on or the death of James, these are always also expressed—and this pointedly—in terms of the Greek root *ballō*/"being cast down", e.g., *kataballō*, as if the *B-L* part of the root had some primordial or archetypical significance all its own, whether in either the Greek or the Hebrew. This is true no matter which account one consults—Clement of Alexandria, Eusebius, Epiphanius, Jerome or the source of many of these individuals and, like Epiphanius, a Jewish Christian convert from Palestine, the second-century Church historian Hegesippus. It is also completely true of the Two Apocalypses of James in the Nag Hammadi corpus. It is true in spite of the fact that James probably did not die in the manner he was said to have died in all these accounts, but rather, as Josephus probably more accurately records at the end of the *Antiquities*, as the result of a Sanhedrin stoning, though, of course, the two processes may have some common elements.

This is very solid proof indeed: the same linguistic symbolism centering on the same root consonants, having to do in both Greek and Hebrew with "the Devil" or "Devilishness" (the "Devil" or "Diabolos" too being based on these same phonetic root consonants) was being used to express the deaths of James—the Leader of the Jerusalem Assembly—and the Righteous Teacher at Qumran. This constitutes a last and final proof, aided and abetted by a host of additional linguistic, textual, historical, and ideological ones I have been presenting over the years, of the identity of James and the Righteous Teacher.

In sum, I had already called attention in all my works to the fact that the destruction of the Righteous Teacher by the Wicked Priest in the Habakkuk *Pesher* was being expressed in terms of "swallowing": first, the Wicked Priest *"swallowing" the Righteous Teacher*—this expressed both in terms of the Wicked Priest wishing to "swallow him" or "them"—the Poor")—but also, God ultimately "swallowing" the Wicked Priest for what he had done to the Righteous Teacher and the Men of his Council (this pointedly using *ba-la-ʿa/*"swallowing" imagery, in turn, related to "Belial" symbolism).

This is followed up in the next episode in the Habakkuk *Pesher* in terms of "the *Ebionim*"—the designation in early Church history for the Community of James, i.e., the *Ebionites*—"he himself would be *paid the reward which he paid to the Poor*", or even more pointedly, "as he himself plotted to destroy the Poor, so too would God condemn him to destruction" (italics mine). Not only this, but as we saw in JJHP, the *Pesher* on Hab 2:17 is demonstrably using the vocabulary of Is 3:9–11 to express this, the specific scriptural passage applied to the death of James in all early Church literature.

One cannot get more explicit than this. But this "swallowing" is related as well to the sins of the Establishment—which as everyone by now knows—I identify for various reasons with the Herodian—paleography and even more recent carbon-14 testing notwithstanding. In other words, this "*ba-la-ʿa*" or "swallowing"/"consuming" symbolism is related to the sins of the Establishment. These, in turn, are expressed in the Damascus Document in terms of an additional variation on this language and the same concept of *Devilishness*, "Belial", not to mention his "nets"!

This last goes directly into the Greek as either "Balaam" or the "Diabolos", and from there into English as "the Devil". What I had not understood previously is how in the fertile mind of such sectaries, linguistic symbolism functioning in one language could with slight modification simply be moved over to function in a homonymic or homophonic manner in the other, just so long as the basic root symbolism behind the linguistic cluster—in this case having to do either with "the *Devil*" or "*Devilishness*"—as if imbued with some mystical significance, remained the same.

To again summarize: I had been looking for years for the final proof of the identity of James and the Righteous Teacher, which previously I only suspected because of parallels in their lives and the principal doctrines attributed to both. Primarily this was because of the emphasis on the notions of "Righteousness", "Righteous One", and "Righteous works" attached to both. But I had not realized that the proof existed in the material I already had.

Let me give examples of how this works in early Church texts, the basic presentation of which comes from a very early Palestinian historian and theologian, Hegesippus (c.100–180 CE), a mature individual, thus, only a little more than a half-century after the events in question. His testimony is preserved in Eusebius and Epiphanius in the fourth century, and by the latter's younger contemporary, Jerome, in the fifth. Western early Church writers, other than those who came from and went to Palestine, do not seem to know his work—or, at least, do not generally use it, again testifying to the *Palestinian* nexus of its contents.

Hegesippus describes how James is brought to the Temple by the Scribes and the Pharisees to quiet the Passover crowd hungering after the Messiah. For his part, James fans the flames of Messianism, proclaiming the imminent coming of the Messiah. As Hegesippus describes these events, the Scribes and the Pharisees cry out:

> "We did wrong to provide Jesus with such a testimony. Let us therefore go up and *cast him down* [italics mine—here is our "*kataballō*" in Greek] that they may be afraid and not believe him." And they cried out, saying, "Oh. Oh. Even the Just One [*Dikaios*, this used in place of James' very name itself] is led astray." And they fulfilled the Scripture written in Isaiah [3:10], "Let us remove the Just One for he is abhorrent to us" [this according to the Septuagint; the Masoretic is different], for they shall eat the fruit of their works.

Not only are these words absorbed into the description of the destruction of the Wicked Priest in return for what he had done to "the *Ebionim*" in the Habakkuk *Pesher*, but one can immediately see this is a typical Qumran-style exegesis, now being applied to the death not of "the Righteous Teacher" but of James the *Righteous One*. Just as in *peshers* on passages in Habakkuk and Psalm 37 at Qumran, evoking the destruction of the Righteous Teacher; it is always a "*Zaddik*"-passage—James' cognomen—which is being played upon to produce the desired exegesis.

The text continues:

> So they went up and threw down [again *kataballō*] the Just One [*Dikaion*].

Then they stoned him, bashing in his brains with a laundryman's club—the "laundryman" and the "club" both have additional implications which will be further explained in *James the Brother of Jesus* (Faber and Faber, 1996).

Bloodthirsty as this presentation may be, this is basically the same testimony Epiphanius and Jerome preserve. Eusebius quotes Clement of Alexandria (c.150–215 CE), a younger contemporary of Hegesippus—passages from his *Hypotyposes* which, again, have not survived—to the effect that:

> James the Just was cast down [*blētheis*] from the Pinnacle of the Temple and beaten to death with a laundryman's club.

This episode reappears in the Synoptics as the Temptation of Jesus in the wilderness—at least in Matthew and Luke—by "the Devil". This same dichotomy between the Devil (*Diabolos* in Greek) and Satan in one and the same context one encounters here in the Gospels occurs to some degree in Qumran texts, as it does in Revelation—and, seemingly following these, even in the *Koran*.

As everyone knows, here too, the Devil tempts Jesus "to cast himself down from the Pinnacle of the Temple" (*balē*/"cast" and *katō*/"down" in Mt 4:6 and Lk 4:9, both using "Diabolos" in the narrative but with Jesus replying in terms of "Satan"). We here have vivid indication that this tradition about James, true or false, has been retrospectively absorbed into stories about Jesus and that, therefore, these Gospel accounts are no older and, in fact, probably later than these traditions recorded about James in Clement and Hegesippus, whatever their age of origin might be. Mark, who uses "Satan" throughout, abjures this aspect of the Temptation narrative, probably advisedly.

In the First and Second Apocalypses of James at Nag Hammadi we encounter the same scenario—this time perhaps in an even more primitive version. While our texts are fragmentary, we still have continual allusion to "casting"—sometimes even "casting aside the Cup of Bitterness", which is important where the Habakkuk *Pesher* at Qumran is concerned—but most importantly "casting out", as Luke in Acts has Stephen being "cast out" (*ekbalontes*).

Finally at the end of the Second Apocalypse, the Priests find James *standing* beside a *Pillar of the Temple* beside the *mighty Cornerstone*—here the *pro-forma* allusion to "standing" again, so important in Pseudoclementine tradition where "the Primal Adam" ideology is concerned, not to mention "Pillar" and "Cornerstone" imagery generally. We shall note the constant repetition of this imagery as we proceed—"and they decided to *throw him down* from the height and they *cast him down*" (italics mine), adding even more bloodthirsty details perhaps in accord with *Talmud*ic stoning descriptions or vice versa, to wit, they "stretched him out and placing a big stone on his belly", cried out, as in the Hegesippus tradition above which it largely overlaps, "You have erred, you have erred".

It is clear these are variations of the same basic tradition, all using one form or another of the basic Greek phraseology, "*ballō*" (as, for instance, in Diabolos), even though James *probably didn't die in precisely this manner*. This is just the way, because of linguistic considerations, the authors felt obliged to express it.

In the Pseudoclementines this scenario is varied slightly and, in the writer's view, more realistically, but the effect is the same. Book One of the *Recognitions*—but not the *Homilies*—describes an earlier attack in the 40s CE on James by Paul (referred to as "the Enemy") as a result of which *James was only cast down from the steps of the Temple*. It is clear this is a representation of Paul because following this "Enemy" gets letters from the High Priest in Jerusalem to pursue Christians all the way to Damascus (Ps. *Rec* 1.69–71). James is debating with the Temple Authorities on the steps of the Temple when the "Enemy" bursts in with some ruffians, takes a faggot or firebrand from the altar, and *casts James down headlong from the top of the steps* (here our "casting down" language again)—an account probably representing the truth of the matter.

Supposing him dead, "the Enemy" (Paul) cares not to inflict any further violence upon him. But James does not die in this attack; rather *he simply breaks a leg*—details of such intimacy are not to be dismissed with impunity. From thence, they carry James away to an unknown location outside Jericho, that is, not far from Qumran, to where the whole Community, numbering some 5,000, flee.

In previous work, taking a cue from H.-J. Schoeps, I have shown how this attack has been replaced in Acts by the attack on Stephen, which now uses the same "casting out" language (*ekbalontes*) but applying it to Stephen's stoning, not James'. In *James the Brother of Jesus* I also show how Jerome provides the clue to how to separate out the conflation involved in these *two separate accounts*, for there is conflation—the stoning of James in the 60s in early Church accounts (confirmed by what is found in Josephus) and this one, presumably in the 40s—to form the single narrative we now have.

Interestingly, this would make both the traditions preserved in these narratives, as noted—the one in early Church accounts and the one in the Pseudoclementines—at least in their earliest form, older than the stories about Jesus' temptation in the Gospels of Matthew and Luke, which I think really is true, since in the Gospel accounts the conflation has already occurred. But even more interesting—and this indisputably—*the same homophonic language is being used in Greek to apply to the attack on or death of James the Just as is being used in the Hebrew to apply to the death of the Righteous Teacher at Qumran*, albeit with a different meaning dependent on the language involved.

In fact, both traditions—the one in the Hebrew and the one in the Greek—are also using the language of "the Devil" or "Belial casting down his nets", but even the word "Devil" in Greek—*Diabolos*—is based on the same linguistic root, *ballō*. For its part, "Belial" is clearly based on the same language of "swallowing" found at Qumran. Before doing these studies on James I never realized the connection between "Diabolos" in Greek and "Belial" in Hebrew—not to mention the relationship of both to the Arabic derivative "Iblis" in Muhammad's *Koran*.

Let us see how this language reverberates through the whole of the New Testament, where these linguistic symbolisms are sometimes actually quite funny and always very playful, branching out into "casting down" or "fixing" *fishermen's nets*, when Jesus chooses his Apostles or, later in John, reappears to them along the Sea of Galilee, or "casting" *hooks into the sea*, as Peter does in the Gospels of Matthew and Luke, *to catch a fish which has a coin in its mouth* to pay the Roman tax. Mark, rather, has "a millstone cast into the sea" and, immediately thereafter, one's eyes "being cast into Gehenna"—all of these again using the Greek root phoneme "*ballō*" meaning "to cast".

The use of this root then metamorphoses into that of the Apostles *casting themselves into the sea*, as Peter also does in the post-Resurrection episode in the Gospel of John, or even a "Poor widow casting her coins into the Temple Treasury" in the Gospel of Mark—her now proverbial "two widow's mites". This also finds its variation in Judas Iscariot's casting his *thirty pieces of silver into the Temple Treasury*, a particularly interesting allusion, though here the "*ballō*"/"casting" language is missing and the episode is framed in terms of a synonym in Greek, but the meaning is the same.

Sometimes, as in the Parable of the Tares—"the tares", paralleled by "all the Evil Ones", being "cast into a furnace of fire"—it is quite frightening. In some Gospel presentations these become a bunch of rotting fish "cast into the fire". The language is always the same, bordering even on the obsessive. Sometimes it relates to individuals like the fictional Stephen who is "cast out of the city" after having a vision, like James in the early Christian presentation of "the Son of Man standing on the right hand of Power" before he is viciously stoned (note the "standing" imagery here, not to mention that of the "Power").

Sometimes, as we saw, it is Jesus who is tempted by the Devil (*Diabolos*) to "cast himself down" from the Pinnacle of the Temple. Finally, there is the permission Jesus gives his Apostles "to cast out Evil demons" (*ekballō* now), an authority or "power" Jesus too, is said to possess. Again, the language is the same, and all of these essentially vary the "casting"/*ballō* usage.

Let us look at Jesus' post-Resurrection appearances along the Sea of Galilee in John first. This particularly humorous account is a fairly lengthy one using both the language of "nets"—i.e., the *Three Nets of Belial* of the Damascus Document and *the net* "Balaam taught Balak to cast down before Israel" in Revelation—and "casting down" language generally. Here the Disciples, Simon Peter, Didymus Thomas, the sons of Zebedee and two other unnamed ones—unnamed individuals are always important—are *casting out nets* (again the usage is *ekballō*—John 21:1–2). Suddenly they see Jesus *standing on the shore*—allusion to "standing", so much a part of Jewish Christian/Ebionite ideology, as already noted above, whether accidental or real, is always important—and he instructs them to "*cast* [*balete* now] the net to the right side of the boat".

At this point Simon Peter, who "was naked", feels obliged for some reason to "put on his clothes in order to *cast himself* [*ebalon*] into the sea" (italics mine; 21:7). None of this, of course, makes any sense. This is the third mention of "casting down" in as many lines. Again this is joined to the omnipresent imagery of "net"/"nets" repeated *four times* in just six lines (John 21:6–12).

I think we are on familiar ground here and can say we have heard this vocabulary before in less cartoon-like contexts. Unlike the famous episode in Mt 14:24–36, where Peter, emulating Jesus, tries to walk out on the waters to the others who are "in their boats", this time Peter does not sink, *but swims*, "dragging *the net* full of 153 large fishes to land" (italics mine). For good measure the text adds that "though there were so many, the net did not tear". We are, of course, not in the realm of historical reality here, but sardonic word-play on the twin themes of "nets" and "casting". We shall see the significance of the "*not tearing*" allusion momentarily.

Meanwhile, as the story progresses, the other Disciples are also dragging their "net of fishes" to land—whether the same one or different from the one Peter is dragging is not made clear—and we become dizzy from all this "casting" and "net" imagery, as one imagines did the authors of all this as well. Clearly then, as noted above, they were fascinated to the point of obsession by this "casting down" and "net" imagery.

Jesus then invites his Apostles in the usual manner to "come and eat" (the theme of "breaking bread and eating" will also be expounded more fully in *James the Brother of Jesus*). "Taking the bread, he gave it to them", the text now adding in light of its previous subject matter, "and the fish too". One is tempted to remark, "Yes, and a big one too—perhaps the biggest of all big-fish stories." For his part John laconically remarks, as if there was nothing odd in this and it was all simply routine, "This was now *the third time that Jesus was manifested to his Disciples after having been raised from among the dead*" (21:14—italics mine).

In the Synoptics this episode by the Sea of Galilee occurs much earlier and is attached to Jesus' calling of the Four at the *beginning* of his earthly ministry, not *after* his resurrection (Lk 5:4ff. and pars.). In one of the most beloved episodes in Gospel narrative, Peter and Andrew are "casting a net into the sea" (the "casting nets" imagery again—Mk 1:16), while the sons of Zebedee are "mending their nets" further along the shore (Mt 4:21).

Luke, paralleling John above, repeats this word "net" *four* times in as many lines. In his version, Jesus is now out with Peter *in Peter's boat and teaching the people from it.* (One should note here the parallel in Josephus of one Jesus ben Sapphias, the insurgent leader of the Galilean boatmen around Tiberias, whom Josephus also has out *on a boat teaching the people* in the 67 CE disturbances around the Sea of Galilee. These end up with everyone being butchered by the Romans, so that "the whole sea turned red with their blood").

In Luke's version of the episode, it is at this point that Jesus, who is in Peter's boat, tells Peter to "let down" his net (Lk 5:4). However, instead of the 153 large fishes that he dragged ashore in the post-Resurrection episode in John above, this is put as follows: having "worked through the whole night, *their net was breaking* [in John above, Peter's net is characterized as "not tearing"], and they filled two ships *almost to sinking*". Here again we have the allusion to "sinking" now connected not to *Peter's sinking* but to the *boats almost sinking*. In Mt 14:24–36, it will be recalled, it is the Apostles who are in the boats and Peter, trying to repeat Jesus' miracle of walking on the waters, "begins to sink" for lack of "Faith". For its part, Mark adds the charming little detail that Zebedee had "hired servants" in his boat (1:20)!

In any event, in all the Synoptics all the Apostles then "leave their nets", whereupon Mark and Matthew add Jesus' famous words—since become proverbial—that he will make them "fishers of men" (Mk 1:17 and Mt 4:19). In Luke this is "catching men" (5:10), "nets" repeated here for the umpteenth time! That we are in a universe of multiple literary variations on a theme—and the theme is the one in the Damascus Document and the Book of Revelation in the New Testament of "*Belial*" or "*Balaam casting down his net to deceive Israel*", and the related one using the language of "swallowing" in all these variations in the Habakkuk *Pesher*'s picture of the death of the Righteous Teacher—this in turn related to early Church versions of the death of James—is hardly to be denied. It is this that is causing the endless stream of obfuscating variations.

Matthew, again, returns to this theme of "casting a net into the sea [*blētheise*] and gathering together every kind" of fish in the famous series of parables relating to "the Tares" (13:1–53). These are really the only pro-Jewish and anti-Gentile Mission or, if one prefers, *Jewish Christian* parables in the whole New Testament. All others are pro-Pauline. As one would expect, these mention "the Enemy"—here identified with "the Devil" or *Diabolos*—but in Jewish Christianity, Paul.

On the other hand, they come right after Jesus rejects his *mother and his brothers* in words that have also now become proverbial, "Who is my mother and who are my brothers?" (Mt 12:46–50)—this episode, of course, anti-Jewish Christian. Significantly, these family members are also described as "*standing outside* waiting to speak with him", who *could not get to him because of all the crowds* (italics mine—more loaded play on the critical Jewish Christian/Ebionite "standing" notation, not to mention Gentile Christian jibes against the family leadership of the Palestinian "Jewish Christian" Church).

Again, as Jesus begins these parables here in Matthew, he is portrayed as *teaching from a boat* (13:2) and explaining in a quite militantly "Palestinian Christian" manner "the Kingdom of Heaven". Just after picturing how the tares sown by "the Enemy" are to be "cast into the furnace of fire" (now *balousin*) and how "the Righteous shall shine forth as the sun in the Kingdom of their Father" (13:43—more, perfect Palestinian or, if one prefers, "Jewish Christian" imagery totally in harmony with Qumran), he compares this whole situation to "*a large net cast* [*blētheise*] into the sea" catching all different kinds of fish—our "net" and "casting" imagery again.

Though this begins by looking something like a Gentile Christian overlay, it ends on what can only be considered a patently uncompromising Jamesian or Palestinian Christian conclusion. This is expressed as follows: coming to the shore, instead of breaking bread with the Disciples, as in the Gospel of John, the bystanders now "gather the good fish into containers and the rotting" or "polluted ones they cast away" (*ebalon*—13:48, a new variation of this *ballō*/"B-L usage).

This is now followed by the words: "So shall it be at the Completion of the Age ["Completion of the Age" being a typical Qumran usage]. The Angels will go out and *separate the Evil from among the midst of the Righteous* and *cast them* [*balousin*] *into the furnace of the Fire*" (13:49—italics mine). This is pretty heady stuff and, as anyone familiar with the Qumran mindset will appreciate, for a change quite in tune with its approach— probably one of the few *authentic* native Palestinian parables. In this regard, one should also note the allusion to "separating the Righteous" and "casting the Evil into the furnace of fire" typical of Qumran, where the ideas of *separating from polluted persons* and *the Fire* are particularly strong.

Another variant on this vocabulary, "casting out" (*ekballō*) receives further refurbishment in the lexicon of the Gospels in the "Authority" Jesus supposedly gives his Apostles to "cast out Evil spirits"—as for instance, in the opening appointment episode in Mk 3:15, "and he appointed Twelve . . . to have authority to cast out demons" (*ekballein*). This, of course, is a trivialization of the underlying Jewish Christian/ "Essene" concept of "expelling backsliders" or "expulsion", *par excellence* and another play on the "casting" language originally found in the Belial episode in the Damascus Document and the "Balaam"/"Balak" episode in Revelation—refracted in the early accounts in the death scenario of James.

These make it clear that all these traditions—those of the early Church, Qumran, and the New Testament—are operating within the same "*ba-la-'a*"/"*ballō*", "Nets" and "Belial" parameters. These and the language of the death scenario of James are being played on, altered, and overwritten, whether in the Synoptic or Johannine tradition, sometimes in an extremely playful and often even patently malevolent manner.

The kind of vocabulary implicit in the "casting out"/"*ekballō*" language also re-emerges in Acts in the Stephen episode, mentioned above and itself a variation of the death scenario of James. This is expressed in Acts 7:58 in terms of "having cast him out of the city [*ekbalontes*], they stoned him", and also plays on and, of course, reverses more native Palestinian plays on two additional occurrences of this same formulation provided for us by Josephus: one the "casting out" of the body of James' nemesis, the High Priest Ananus—the man responsible for James' stoning (notice the reversal of this implicit in the Stephen episode)—from the city without burial as food for jackals (also a key episode for the exposition of curious usages in the Habakkuk *Pesher* about the violation of the Wicked Priest's "corpse", alluded to above and elucidated in JJHP—(Chapter 2).

The second has to do with Josephus' descriptions of how the Essenes "cursed" and "cast out" backsliders from the Community (*ekballō*). This kind of expulsion, and the cursing accompanying it, are also pregnant with meaning regarding the mutual cursing and threats of excommunication going on in the Letters of Paul and the Qumran corpus, as I have expounded them in my discussion of the last column of the Damascus Document in DSSU.

For Acts' transformation and reversal of the gist of this episode, Stephen is "cast out" of the city by a mob of *vicious Jews*, who then stone him. His last words and the vision attributed to him, as he kneels down and prays to God to forgive them (Acts 7:56–60), are exactly those of "the Son of Man *sitting on* the right hand of *Power*" in Eusebius' account based on Hegesippus, of James' stoning and death at the hands of the Jewish mob (only in Acts, as we saw, it is "*standing on* the right hand of God"—italics mine).

This also includes the "standing" imagery of "the Son of Man standing at the right hand of God" and praying for the forgiveness of the mob and, of course, "the Standing One" ideology applied to Jesus in Jewish Christian Ebionite/Elkasite ideology, not to mention that of the "Hidden" or "Great Power" associated with it. Again the conclusion is—however difficult it may be to appreciate—that these traditions about James, whatever their original form, pre-date their subsequent reformulations in the documents of the New Testament as we presently have them and are part and parcel of the recasting and subversion of material relating to him and his marginalization proceeding from this.

Where the other story we have noted with overtones of the James story above is concerned—that of Jesus' "Temptation by the Devil", first in the wilderness and then to "throw himself down from the Pinnacle of the Temple"—aside from its patently mythological aspects, anyone who knows the tradition of James being "cast down from the Pinnacle of the Temple" in all second-century early Church tradition will immediately recognize this as simply a restrospective reformulation of it. This too—or at least the source it was, based on—as we have remarked, has to be seen as earlier than the Gospel refurbishments found in Matthew and Luke. What does this tell us about the Gospels? Or vice versa, about the earliness of these traditions about James, however conflated?

Another variation of the tradition of the kind of "casting" allusions embodied in Matthew's Parable of the Tares can be seen in Mk 4:26–32, where once again—perhaps for the fourth time—Jesus is pictured as *teaching the people from a boat*. Now the "casting" of the seeds on the ground becomes something quite different. The fiercely indigenous Palestinian attitude inherent in the "fiery furnace" version of such things is reversed and pacified into a haze of Hellenizing spiritualization, and the whole exercise becomes one supporting the Gentilizing process of the Pauline Mission, not vice versa.

Two other examples of the "Authority" Jesus gives his Apostles "to cast out demons" follow Jesus' Transfiguration before the Central Three in Mt 17:1–8. Coming down from the mountain, Peter, James, and John "his brother"—here in the style of a shell game, the "brother" language is now applied to John not James—are pictured as being *unable even to cure a demonic*! They, therefore, ask, "Why were we not able *to cast out*?" (*ekbalein*—italics mine; 17:19). The answer they get, as in the case of Peter *sinking into the Sea of Galilee* because his Faith was weak, is—Jesus now employing the language and critique of Paul even against his core Aspostles—"because of your unbelief" (17:20—for this "weakness" language as applied to the Jerusalem Leadership or core Apostles, see Paul in 1 Co 8–11, 2 Co 11–13, etc.).

In another funny adumbration, we have already noted above of the way this kind of "casting out"/"casting down" language is transformed, the Gospels now have Peter "casting (*balē*) a hook into the sea" to get the coin to pay the Roman tax, presumably because he was unwilling to pay it himself or in good "Essene" style did not carry coins on his person. However this may be, Jesus concludes, "the Sons are truly free" (Mt 17:26–27). Though the overt meaning here is freedom from Rome or foreign oppression, this also carries with it the additional, not so subtle suggestion of Pauline "freedom from the Law".

Another particularly humorous example of this kind, "the widow's mites" already noted in Mk 12:41–44 above, has to do with the "pollution of the Temple", or more precisely, the "pollution of the Temple Treasury"—charges, as we have seen, part and parcel of the "Three Nets of Belial" accusations in the Damascus Document and what follows them. Here *the Poor widow* (one should always note any allusion to "Poor" in these texts—"*Ebion*" in Hebrew, the name of the group that followed James) "casts her last two mites into the Temple Treasury". In this pericope the usage *ebalen*/"cast in" and its variations occur *seven times in just four lines*!

These insistent repetitions certainly cannot be considered either accidental or normal and demonstrates the fascination with this language in the Gospels. This too, of course, has a "Gentile Christian" cast, going further even than the Damascus Document at Qumran—which only appears to attack the Herodian Establishment—in implying the disqualification of the Jewish People as a whole from the Temple.

Her contribution, too, is pointedly compared by Jesus to what was cast in by "the Many" (12:42)—"the Many" being at Qumran the name used to designate the rank and file of the Community—but even more significantly, to what "the *Rich*" do, a major theme in the Damascus Document's "Three Nets of Belial" accusations and the Letter of James' attacks on the Establishment. This episode, as well, is but a further variation on Matthew's parallel one about Judas "casting the thirty pieces of silver" he received for betraying Jesus "into the Temple Treasury" (Mt 27:3–10)—more scurrilous transmutation we shall treat in greater detail in *James the Brother of Jesus*.

One final, very humorous, example of this kind of word-play is the allusion to "*Beelzebul*" (in some versions "*Beelzebub*") just preceding Jesus' rejecting his mother and his brothers and the *"Tares"* Parables in the Gospel of Matthew. Here, in further flights of fancy, a *demon-possessed* man is brought to Jesus and Jesus heals him. Not only does this episode end in the evocation of forgiving every kind of "blasphemy"—the evocation of which is again not without significance, because this is the charge for which James was stoned according to all sources—except "blasphemy against the Holy Spirit", the basis of the Pauline approach to Jesus and its extension in the Gentile Mission; but it again plays on the contradiction between *"Belial"*/*"Diabolos"* and *"Satan"* language in these episodes we have called attention to above—a dichotomy which certainly would have puzzled outsiders.

Here the play on this *"ekballō"*/*"expulsion"* language, as well as *Belial casting down his net*, continues. The Pharisees are made to complain that one "does not cast out [*ekballei*] demons except by Beelzebul" and there are *four allusions* to "casting out" in as many lines (Mt 12:24–27 and Lk 11:15–19). Again one should remark the abnormality of this amount. These references are, once again, intertwined with several accompanying allusions to "standing", the importance of which in Jewish Christian/ Ebionite ideology we have called attention to on several occasions above. Playing on the Authority given the Apostles to "cast out demons", "Beelzebul"—clearly an elaboration on the "Belial" terminology at Qumran— is now called "the Prince of Demons". Using the famous *"house divided cannot stand"* metaphor and the Greek version of "Belial", "Diabolos", Jesus now responds with the purposely abstruse statement, "If Satan *casts out Satan* (*ekballei*) against himself, he is divided. How then will his Kingdom *stand*?" (Note, once again, the recurrence of the Ebionite/Jewish Christian "standing" imagery here. This, too, begins to seem no longer accidental.)

Clearly much fun is being had here with the mix-up in vocabulary between "Satan" and "Belial". Jesus responds to his own question with the nonsense question, "so how could Satan *cast out* Beelzebul? ", or vice versa—"Satan" and "Belial" being the same. Then in response to his own rhetorical question—once again expressed in the Gentile Christian framework of "casting out Evil spirits"—"by whom does he cast out demons, Beelzebul or the Spirit of God", he concludes portentously, "if the latter, then the Kingdom of God has come" (Mt 12:28).

I think this should suffice to show the obsession of New Testament narrative with the *"Belial"*/*"casting"*/*"nets"* vocabulary, not to mention the kind of allusion to "casting" found in all accounts of the death of James. The method of the Gospels here, as well as that of Acts, should be clear. Important usages in Palestinian Christianity and the Dead Sea

Scrolls are being played upon, reversed, and basically reduced to nonsense.

Nor could we have arrived at these insights without looking into the "Three Nets of Belial" allusions in the Damascus Document and the scenario for the death of James in early Church literature. I have looked at these passages in the Gospels and in Acts literally hundreds of times, as many others no doubt have, without ever having noticed any of these relationships. It is only when looking at the testimonies regarding James' death, incorporating aspects of the usage of the Greek "*ballō*", and connecting them, in turn, with the "Balaam"/"Belial" word-play in Hebrew and *ba-la-ʿa*/"swallowing" imagery generally relating to the death of the Righteous Teacher at Qumran or, in Greek, to how James was *cast down from the steps* or *Pinnacle of the Temple*—as the case may be—that the *modus operandi* of these New Testament thematic accretions and word-play approaching the level almost of caricature became clear to me. This is very powerful verification, indeed, mounting up almost to certainty.

The conclusion is that these seemingly innocuous episodes in the Gospels about "casting down" and "nets" yield completely unexpected results about the whole "Belial"/"Diabolos"/"casting down" language circle generally, the New Testament variations on the Apostles "casting down" their nets or being granted Authority "to cast out demons", or the more native Palestinian version of this vocabulary, how *the tares of the Enemy*—in Jewish Christian literature "the Enemy" is usually considered to be Paul—or Evil persons generally would be "cast into a furnace of Fire" at the Last Judgement. "Judgement" allusions like this last, which incorporate the idea of Divine retribution, do parallel the Qumran description of how the Wicked Priest, after "swallowing" *the Righteous Teacher*, would "drink the Cup of the Wrath of God" and "be swallowed" or "consumed".

In the face of powerful textual evidence of this kind, external indicators like carbon-14 testing or like-minded paleographical arguments—themselves subject to multiple pitfalls and inaccuracies—are insufficient. In fact, the kind of arguments being put forth here are themselves perhaps the most potent argument against external data of this kind. The final conclusion is that the same language formulae with slight variations are being used in parallel traditions in both Greek and Hebrew to refer to the deaths or destructions of James and the Righteous Teacher—and the two are, therefore, identical.

PART THREE

CHAPTER 10

The Damascus Document
(CD)[1]

Column I

1 And now hear, all (you) Knowers of Righteousness, and comprehend the works of

2 God, because He has a dispute with all flesh and will *do Judgement*[2] on all those who insult Him [possibly also "blaspheme Him"].

3 Because they rebelled when they forsook Him, He hid His face from Israel and from His Temple

4 and *delivered them up to the sword*.[3] But because of his memory of the Covenant of the First,[4] He left a remnant

5 for Israel and *did not deliver them up* to be destroyed. And in the Era of Wrath, three hundred and

6 ninety years after He *delivered them into the hand* of Nebuchadnezzar, King of Babylon,

7 He *visited them* and caused a Root of Planting [the usage here is singular][5] to grow from Israel and from Aaron, to inherit

8 His land and to prosper on the good things of His earth. And they understood their sinfulness and knew that they were

9 guilty men [or "Sinners"]. And they were like blind men and groped for the Way[6]

10 for twenty years. And God *considered their works*, because they sought Him *with a whole heart*

11 and He raised up for them a Teacher of Righteousness to guide them in the Way of His heart. And he made known

12 to the Last Generations[7] what he would do in the Last Generation to the Congregation [also possibly "Assembly" or "Church"] of Traitors,

13 those who were Turners-Aside from the Way. This is the time about which it is written, "Like a straying heifer,

14 thus did Israel stray" [Hos 4:16]. And when the Man of Scoffing ["Man of Jesting" or "Comedian"] arose, who *poured over Israel*

15 *the waters of Lying*[8] and caused them to wander astray in a trackless waste with no Way, bringing low the Everlasting Heights, abolishing

16 the Pathways of Righteousness and removing the boundary (markers), which the First had marked out as their inheritance, for which reason

17 He called down on them the curses of His Covenant[9] and *delivered them up to the avenging sword of Vengeance*

18 *of the Covenant.* For they sought Smooth Things and chose illusions, watched out for

19 breaks ["loopholes"—Is 30:10–13], and chose the fairest neck [meaning, "the easiest way"], and they Justified the Wicked[10] and condemned the Righteous,

20 and they transgressed the Covenant and broke the Law, and they banded together against the soul ["life"/"being"] of the Righteous One and against all the Walkers

21 in Perfection, execrating their soul ["being" or "whom they loathed"]. And they pursued them with the sword and attempted to divide [or "rejoiced in the division of"] the People. And the Wrath

Column II

1 of God was kindled against their Congregation, devastating all their multitude, for their works were unclean [or "polluted"] before Him.

2 And, now, listen to me all who enter the Covenant and I will unstop your ears concerning the Ways of

3 the Wicked. God loves Knowledge and Wisdom, and good counsel He places before Him.

4 Discernment and Knowledge minister to Him. His is long-suffering patience and abundant forgivenesses

5 to atone for the Penitents of Sin. But Power, Might, and overwhelming Wrath with sheets of Fire,[11]

6 in which are all the Angels of Destruction, are upon the Turners-Aside

from the Way and the Abominators [or "Despisers"—even "Blas-phemers"] of the Law. There shall be no remnant

7 or survivor for them. Because before the world ever was God chose them not, and before they were established He knew

8 their works and abominated their Generations *on account of blood*[12] and hid His face from the earth

9 until they were consumed. For He knew the years of their Standing and the number and precise determination of their Eras ["Times" or "Ends"] for all

10 Eternal Being and existences, until that which would come in their Eras for all the years of Eternity.

11 And in all of them, He raised up for Himself men called by Name[13] so that a remnant might remain in the land and fill

12 the face of the earth with their seed. And He made known to them by the hand of His Messiah [singular] His Holy Spirit,[14] and he [or "it"] is

13 Truth, and in the explanation of His [or "its"] Name their names (are to be found).[15] And those whom He hated He led astray.

14 And now, my sons, listen to me and I shall uncover your eyes, so that you may see and understand *the works of*

15 *God,*[16] so that you may choose that which pleases (Him) and reject that which He hates, in order that you may walk in Perfection

16 in all His Ways and not follow after the thoughts of a sinful imagin-ation or fornicating eyes. Because Many

17 have gone astray in these things and mighty warriors stumbled in them from ancient times until now.[17] Because they walked in stubbornness

18 of their heart, the Watchers of Heaven fell. They were caught in them, because they did not *keep the Commandments of God.*[18]

19 And their sons, whose height was like the height of cedars and whose bodies were like mountains, also fell.

20 All flesh which was on dry land also perished and they were as if they had never been. And in *their doing* according to

21 their own will, they did not *keep the Commandments of their Maker.* Therefore His Wrath was kindled against them.

Column III

1 In these things, the Sons of Noah, together with their families, went astray (and) because of them, *they were cut off.*[19]

2 (But) Abraham did not walk in them and he was made *a Friend of God, because he kept the Commandments of God* and did not choose

3 the will of his own spirit [cf. Ja 2:21–23]. And he transmitted (them) to Isaac and Jacob, and they kept (them) and were inscribed as *Friends*

4 *of God and the Heirs* ["*Possessors*"] of the Covenant forever. The Sons of Jacob strayed in them and were punished according to

5 their errors. And their sons walked in the stubbornness of their heart in Egypt, complaining against

6 the Commandments of God, each man doing what was right in his own eyes. And *they ate blood*

7 *and their males were cut off in the wilderness.* He (spoke to them) in (the wilderness) of Kadesh: "Go up and possess (the land" [Deut 9:23]. But they did according to) their own spirit and did not listen to

8 the voice of their Maker, the Commandments of their teachers, but rather murmured in their tents. And *the Wrath of God was kindled*

9 *against their Assembly* and their sons perished. And because of it their Kings were cut off, and because of it their Mighty Ones

10 perished, and because of it their land became desolate. Because of it the members of the Covenant of the First ["the Ancestors" or "Forefathers"] sinned and *were delivered up*

11 *to the sword, because they deserted the Covenant of God* and chose their own will, following after the stubbornness

12 of their heart, each man doing according to his own will. But as for those who held fast to the Commandments of God—

13 those who remained of them—God established his Covenant with Israel Forever, revealing

14 to them the Hidden Things, concerning which all Israel went astray, and He opened for them [in the sense of "revealed"] His Holy Sabbaths and His Glorious Festivals,

15 the testimonies of His Righteousness and the Ways of His Truth, and the wishes of His will, which

16 a man [literally, "the Adam"] *must do in order to live through them.* And they dug a well rich in waters,

17 but those rejecting them[20] shall not live. But they immersed themselves [or "wallowed"] in punishable sin and the Ways of uncleanness [or "pollution"].

18 And they said that "it [this "Way" or "sin"] is ours". But God, in His marvelous mysteries, atoned for their sin and forgave their iniquities.

19 And He *built for them a House of Faith in Israel* [see Paul in 1 Co 3:9–12], the likes of which has *never stood from ancient times until*

20 *now.* And for them that hold fast to it, there will be Victorious Life, and *all the Glory of Adam will be theirs* [again the Ebionite "Primal Adam" ideology here—cf. 1 Co 14:22–15:58], which

21 God established for them by the hand of the Prophet Ezekiel, saying: "The Priests and the Levites and the Sons of

Column IV

1 Zadok, who kept the service of the Temple, when the Sons of Israel strayed

2 from Me, will offer Me the fat and the blood" [Ezek 44:15[21]]. "The Priests" are the Penitents of Israel,

3 who went out from the Land of Judah and "the Joiners" with them ["*Nilvim*" in Hebrew, a play on the term "Levites" in the underlying Ezek 44:15]. And "the Sons of Zadok" are *the Elect of*

4 *Israel, called by Name, who will stand up* [or "go on standing"] *in the Last Days.*[22] Behold this is the exact exposition

5 of their names, according to their Generations and the Eras of their Standing and the number of their trials [or "sufferings"] and the years of

6 their existence, and precise exposition of their works. (They are the Fi)rst (Men of) Holiness, for whom [or "through whom"]

7 God made atonement. *And they justified the Righteous and condemned the Wicked.* And all those coming after them

8 are *to do*[23] *according to the precise letter of the Torah*, which the First ["the Ancestors"[24]] transmitted, until the Completion

9 of the Era of these years. According to the Covenant which God made with "the First" to atone

10 for [or "forgive"] their sins, so too would God make atonement for [or "through"] them. And with the Completion of the Era of the number of these years,

11 there will be *no more joining to the House of Judah*, but rather *each man will stand on*

12 *his own net* [the word here is rather the "watchtower", referred to in the *Pesher* on Habakkuk 2:1 below[25]]: "The fence is built and the Law far removed" [Mic 7:11]. And in all these years

13 Belial was sent against Israel, as God foretold by the hand of the Prophet Isaiah, the son of

14 Amoz, saying: "Panic and snare and net are upon you, O inhabitant of the land" [Is 24:17]. Its interpretation concerns

15 "the Three Nets of Belial", about which Levi the son of Jacob spoke,[26]

16 by means of which he catches Israel, transforming these things before them into *three kinds of*

17 *Righteousness. The first is fornication, the second is Riches, and the third is*

18 *pollution of the Temple.* He who escapes the first is caught in the second, and he who eludes the second is caught

19 in the third. "The builders of the wall" [see Ezek 13:10 in columns vi and viii below], who followed So (and So. He is "the Spouter",

20 about whom it was said, "He will surely spout" [Mic 2:6]), are caught in two (of these): in fornication, because they take

21 two wives in their lifetimes, whereas the Foundation of Creation is "male and female he created them" [Ge 1:27].

Column V

1 And (regarding) those entering the ark: "two by two they went into the ark" [Ge 7:9]. And as for the Ruler ["the *Nasi*" or "Prince"], it is written:

2 "He shall not multiply wives unto himself" [Deut 17:17]. But David had not read the sealed Book of the *Torah*, which

3 was in the Ark [of the Covenant—probably Deuteronomy], since it was not opened in Israel from the day of the deaths of Eleazar

4 and Joshua and the Elders who served Ashtarte. And they hid it

5 and it was not revealed until Zadok arose [again literally, "stood up"]. And the works of David rose up [i.e., "in his favor"], except for the blood of Uriah.

6 And God counted them to him. And (secondly), they ["the builders of the wall"] also pollute the Temple, because

7 they *do not separate* as (prescribed by) *Torah* [meaning the "separation" of clean from unclean in the Temple], but rather *they lie with a woman during the blood of her period,* and *each man takes* (to wife)

8 *the daughter of his brother and the daughter of his sister.* But Moses said: "You shall not

9 approach your mother's sister. She is your mother's near kin" [Lev 18:13]. But while the Law of incest

10 was written for males, it likewise applies to females. Therefore, if the
daughter of a brother uncovers the nakedness of the brother of

11 her father, he is near kin. Also *they pollute their Holy Spirit*

12 *and open their mouth with a Tongue full of insults* ["blaspheming Tongue"] *against the Laws of the Covenant of God*, saying,
"They are not certain." They speak an Abomination [or
"blasphemy"]

13 concerning them. "All of them are kindlers of Fire and lighters of
firebrands" [Is 50:11]. "Their webs

14 are spiders' webs, and the eggs of vipers are their eggs" [cf. John in
Mt 3:7 and pars.]. *Whoever approaches them*

15 *cannot be cleansed.* Like an accursed thing, his house is guilty—unless
he was forced. For in former times

16 *God visited their works* and His Wrath was kindled by their actions. "It
is a people without discernment" [Is 17:11].

17 They are a nation devoid of counsel, because there is no intelligence
in them" [Num 21:18]. But in former times,

18 Moses stood up along with Aaron by the hand of the Prince of
Lights, while Belial[27] in his guilefulness raised up Jannes and

19 *his brother at the time of the first Salvation of Israel.*

20 And in the Era of desolation of the land, the Removers of the Bound
stood up and led Israel astray,

21 and the land was decimated, because *they spoke rebellion against the Commandments of God* (as given) by the hand of Moses and also against

Column VI

1 His Holy Messiah [again *the usage is singular*, though the most widely
used English translation renders this "His holy annointed ones"].
They prophesied Lying to turn Israel aside from

2 God. But God remembered the Covenant of the First ["the Forefathers"] and raised up from Aaron, men of discernment and from
Israel, (men of)

3 Wisdom, and made them listen. And they dug the well, "the well
which the Princes dug, which

4 the Nobles of the People dug with the Staff" [*Mehokkek*—Num 21:
18]. "The Well" is the *Torah*, and its "Diggers" are

5 the Penitents of Israel, *who went out from the Land of Judah to dwell* [or
"*sojourn*"] in the Land of Damascus,

6 for which reason, God called them all "Princes", because they sought him, and their honor was questioned

7 by no man. And "the Staff" [*Mehokkek*], he is the Interpreter of the *Torah*, of whom

8 Isaiah said: "He creates an instrument for His works" [Is 54:16]. And "the Nobles of the People" are

9 those who came *to dig the well with the staves* [playing on Laws: *Hukkim*— the Hebrew for "Laws" and "Staves" being the same basic root], in which *the Staff* [*Mehokkek*] decreed [*hakak*]

10 (they should) walk during all the Era of Evil and without which, they would not persevere, *until the Standing up of*

11 *he who Pours Down* ["teaches"²⁸] *Righteousness at the End of Days.* But all who have been brought into the Covenant

12 shall not enter the Temple to kindle its altar in vain. Rather they shall be the Barrers of

13 the Door, just as God said: "Who among you will bar its door? Nor should you light My altar

14 in vain" [Mal 1:10—see also Acts 21:30]. If they do not keep (the Commandments), *to do according to the precise letter of the Torah* in the Era of Wickedness, *to separate*

15 *from the Sons of the Pit, to keep away from* [the verb here, "*lehinnazer*", is based on the same root, from which the term "Nazirite" is derived] *polluted Evil Riches* (acquired either) by vow or ban

16 and (to keep away) from the Riches of the Temple and robbing the Poor [literally " '*Aniyyei*" in the sense of "the Meek"] of His People,²⁹ (from) making widows their spoil

17 and murdering orphans. But, rather, to *separate between polluted and pure, and to distinguish between*

18 *the Holy and profane* [compare this with what "Peter" learns in Acts 10:15 and 10:28], and to keep the Day of the Sabbath according to its precise letter, and the Festivals,

19 and the Day of Fasting, according to the Commandment of those entering *the New Covenant in the Land of Damascus:*

20 *to set up the Holy Things according to their precise specifications, to love each man his brother*

21 *as himself* ["the Royal Law according to the Scripture" in Ja 2:8], to strengthen the hand of the Meek ['*Ani*], the Poor [*Ebion*], and Convert [*Ger*], for each man to seek the welfare

Column VII

1 of his brother and not uncover the nakedness of his near kin, to *keep away from* ["*lehazzir*", again based on the same root as "Nazirite" above] *fornication*

2 according to Statute, to reprove each man his brother according to the Commandment and to bear no rancor

3 from day to day; *to separate* [here "separate" and "keep away"/"*nazar*" are synonyms] *from all pollutions, according to their Statute.* And no man should defile

4 his Holy Spirit, which God separated for them. Rather all should *walk in*

5 *these things in Perfect Holiness* [cf. Paul in 2 Co 7:1] *on the basis of the Covenant of God in which they were instructed, Faithfully promising them*

6 *that they would live for a thousand Generations* [Manuscript B adds: "Promising them they would live for a thousand generations, as it is written, keeping the Covenant and the Grace (promised to) those who love and keep My Commandments for a thousand generations"—Deut 7:9]. And if they are living in camps, as per the "Rule of the Land" [Manuscript B: "as per the Laws of the Land as they were of old"], and they take

7 wives and they beget sons, they shall walk in accordance with the *Torah* and according to the Statute

8 they were instructed in as a Rule of the *Torah*, which speaks about "Between a man and his wife, and between a father

9 and his *son*" [Num 30:17]. But all *those rejecting* (the Commandments) *will be paid the reward on Evil Ones,*[30] *when God* visits the earth,

Manuscript A	Manuscript B (Column XIX)
10 when there will come to pass the Word, which is written in the words of Isaiah, son of Amoz, the Prophet,	when there shall come to pass the word, which is written
11 which say: "There shall come upon you and upon your people and upon the House of your father,[31] days the like of which	by the hand of Zechariah the Prophet, "Awake, O sword, against
12 have (not) come since the day Ephraim departed from Judah" [Is 7:17]. When the	My shepherd and against the man who is My companion", says God, "Strike the shepherd

two Houses of Israel separated,

13 Ephraim departed from Judah, *and all those who turned back were delivered up to the sword.* But those who held fast [or

14 "were steadfast"] *escaped to the Land of the North.* As He [God] said: "I will exile the Tabernacle of your King

15 and the bases of your statues from My tent of Damascus" [Amos 5:26–27]. The Books of the *Torah*, these are "the Tabernacle

16 of the King", as He [God] said, "I will establish the Tabernacle of David, which is fallen" [Amos 9:11]. *The "King"*

17 *is the Community*,[32] and "the bases of the statues", they are the Books of the Prophets

18 whose words Israel despised. *And "the Star" is the Interpreter of the Law,*

19 *who came to Damascus*, as it is written: "A Star shall go forth from Jacob, and a Sceptre shall rise

20 out of Israel" [Num 24:17]. The "Sceptre" is the Prince [*Nasi*] of the whole Congregation, and with his standing up [or "with his arising"], "he shall utterly destroy

21 all the Sons of Seth" [Num 24:17]. *These escaped in the Era of the First Visitation*

and scatter the flock,

and I will stretch My hand over the Little Ones" [Zech 13:7].[33] The *"Keepers of Him" are the Meek of flock.*[34]

These shall escape in the Era of the Visitation, but the rest shall be given over to the sword with the coming of the Messiah of Aaron and Israel,[35] as it was *in the Era of the First Visitation*, concerning which (God) said by the hand of Ezekiel, "To put a mark on the foreheads of those who cry and weep" [Ezek 9:4].

But the rest shall be given over to the avenging sword of the Covenant

Column VIII

1 *while the Backsliders were given up to the sword.* And this also will be the Judgement on all those who entered His Covenant, who

2 did not hold fast to these (Laws and Statutes). *Their Visitation [or "command"] will be for destruction by the hand of Belial.*[36] This is the Day

3 which God commands [or "in which God visits";[37] Manuscript B adds: "As He said",] "The Princes of Judah are those who are Removers of the Bound, upon whom Wrath shall be poured out" [Hos 5:10],

4 For they have become diseased without a cure,[38] and He will exterminate them, since all of them are Rebels and [Manuscript B adds: "since they came to the Covenant of Repentance, but"] have not turned aside from the Way of

5 Traitors. Rather they have immersed themselves [or "wallowed in"] the ways of fornication and Evil Riches. *They have been vengeful and a man has borne malice*

6 *against his brother, each man hating his brother* [that is, "not loving him"].[39] *And each man has sinned against the flesh of his own flesh* [that is "near relatives"],

7 *approaching them for fornication. And they have used their power for Riches and profiteering,*[40] each man doing what was right in his own eyes

8 and each choosing the stubbornness of his heart, for they did not keep apart from the People [possibly "Peoples"—again the root of "keeping apart", *N-Z-R*, here is the same as that of "Nazirite"] and have knowingly sinned,

9 walking in the Way of the Evil Ones, about whom God said: "Their wine is the venom of vipers,

10 and the cruel poison of asps" [Deut 32:33].[41] *The "vipers" are the Kings of the Peoples and "their wine"*

11 *is their Ways, and "the poison of asps" is the Head of the Kings of Greece* [in our view, "Greek-speaking" or "Grecian Kings", "Greece"/"Yavan" playing on the word "wine"/*yayin* in Hebrew in the underlying text—*rosh*/"poison" also being a homonym for *Rosh*/"Head"], who comes to execute

12 vengeance upon them.[42] But all this "the Builders of the Wall" and "the Daubers with plaster" [see Ezek 13:10 above] have not understood, because

13 one of confused wind [*Ruah*—also possibly "Spirit" in the sense of "Holy Spirit"—*wind* and *spirit* being homonyms in Hebrew. This can possibly even be "Windbag". Manuscript B has "walking in the Spirit", probably correct and the actual quotation from Mic 2:11,

upon which the whole passage is based[43]] and the *Spouter of Lying, spouted to them, which kindled God's Wrath on all his Congregation* [or "Church"].

14 Nor (do they understand) what Moses said, "Not for your Righteousness or the Uprightness of your heart are you going to possess

15 these Nations" [Deut 9:5], but "because of His love for your fathers and keeping the oath" [Deut 7:8].

16 And this is the Judgement upon the Penitents of Israel, who turned aside from the Way of the People. *Because God loved*

17 "*the First*" [or "the Forefathers"], *who testified on His behalf* [Manuscript B has: "testified on behalf of the People for God"], *He loved those coming after them,* because theirs is

18 the Covenant of the Fathers. And because of His hatred for "the Builders of the Wall", His Anger was kindled [Manuscript B: "against them and against all those walking after them"]. *And this is the kind of Judgement that*

19 *will be upon all those who reject the Commandments of God and forsake them,* turning away in the stubbornness of their heart.

20 This is the word which Jeremiah spoke to Baruch the son of Neriah and Elisha

21 to Gehazi his servant. *All the Men who entered the New Covenant in the Land of Damascus*

22 [Manuscript B, column xix, line 34], *but turned back and betrayed and turned aside from the Fountain of Living Waters,*

23(35) will not be reckoned in the Foundation [also "Secret"] of the People and, in its book ["register"] shall not be inscribed, from the day of the gathering

[What follows till the end is actually column xx of Manuscript B, lines 1–34]

24(1) of the Teacher of the Community until the standing up [or "arising"] of the Messiah from Aaron and from Israel [again this is *definitely* singular[44]]. And this is the Judgement

25(2) on any member of the Assembly [or "Church"] of the Men of Perfect Holiness, [or "the Perfection of Holiness"—again, see Paul in 1 Co 7:1], who hesitates to do [note the Jamesian emphasis on "doing" again here] the Commands of the Upright ["Straight"].

26(3) He is the man who is melted in the Furnace [Ezek 22:21–22]. *According to the appearance of his works shall he be expelled from the Assembly* ["Church"],

27(4) *like someone whose lot had never fallen among the Disciples of God.* According to his rebelliousness, the Men

28(5) of Knowledge shall punish him until the day he returns to stand in the presence [the imagery of "standing" again] of the Men of Perfect Holiness

29(6) and his works are revealed according to the letter of the interpretation of the *Torah*, in which

30(7) the Men of Perfect Holiness walk. Nor shall anyone *cooperate with him in purse* ["Riches"] *and work* [this is "*'avodah*" in the sense of "service" or "mission"⁴⁵—again, see Acts 15:38 above],

31(8) *for all the Holy Ones of the Most High have cursed him.* And this is the Judgement, too, which will be upon all those who reject [the *Torah*] among "the First"

32(9) and "the Last" [here our "First"/"Last" language in the Gospels with a vengeance], who have put idols on their heart and walked in stubbornness of

33(10) their heart [compare with Paul in 1 Co 8:4–7]. *They shall have no share in the House of the Torah.* They shall be judged according to the Judgement on their companions, who turned aside

34(11) with the Men of Scoffing ["Men of Jesting" or "Comedians"], because *they spoke mistakenly about the Laws of Righteousness and rejected*

35(12) *the Covenant and the Compact* [literally "the Promise" or "the Faith"], *which they raised in the Land of Damascus—and this is "the New Covenant"—*

36(13) *And neither they nor their families shall have a share in the House of the Torah* [a variation of line 33 above]. And from the day

37(14) of the gathering in of the Guide [here again "*Yoreh*", as in v.10–11, instead of "*Moreh*"/"Teacher" in lines 23–24 above] of the Community, until the end of all the Men-of-War, who walked

38(15) with the Man of Lying, approximately forty years. And in that Era, the Wrath

39(16) of God will be kindled against Israel, as it was said, "There is no King, no Prince, no Judge, none to

40(17) rebuke with Righteousness" [Hos 1:4]. But the Penitents from Sin in (Ja)cob [James?⁴⁶] kept the Covenant of God.⁴⁷ Then each man shall speak

41(18) to his neigh(bor, each man strengthening) his brother to support their step(s) in the Way of God. And God harkened to

42(19) their words and heard, and a Book of Remembrance was written before Him for God-Fearers⁴⁸ and for those considering ["reckoning"]

43(20) *His Name, until God shall reveal Salvation* [*Yesha'*]⁴⁹ *and Justification to those fearing His Name* [again the "God-Fearers" of line 42]. "Then you shall return and see the difference between the Righteous

44(21) and the Wicked, between the Servant of God and he who does not serve Him" [Mal 3:18]". For He does Mercy [literally "Grace" or "Piety"] to (thousands) of them that love Him [the definition of "Piety"—cf. Ja 2:5 on "the Kingdom promised to those that love Him" and "the Poor"].[50]

45(22) and to His Keepers for a thousand generations" [Ex 20:6]. But (all the Men of) the House of Peleg ["the House of Separation"], who went out from His Place of Holiness

46(23) and *relied upon God during the Era of Israel's rebellion and pollution of the Temple*, but turned aside from God

47(24) among the People [here, too, possibly "Peoples"] in things that were for them of little importance, they shall be judged—each man according to his Spirit—in His Holy

48(25) Council. And with the appearance of the Glory of God to Israel, all among the members of the Covenant, who transgressed the boundary of the *Torah*,

49(26) *shall be cut off from the midst of the camp*, and with them all the Evil Ones of

50(27) Judah in the days of its trials ("tribulations"). However, all those who hold fast to these Statutes, coming

51(28) and going in accordance with the *Torah*, and listened to the voice of the Teacher and confessed before God: "We have sinned,

52(29) We have been Wicked, we and our fathers, because they walked contrary to the Laws of the Covenant.

53(30) But Your Judgements upon us are Truth. Nor will we lift up (our) hand *against the Holiness of His Laws and the Righteousness of His*

54(31) *Judgements and the Testimonies of His Truth*. Rather (we) have been instructed in the Statutes of the First, in which

55(32) the Men of the Community were judged." And they shall listen to the voice of the Teacher of Righteousness and not desert

56(33) the Laws of Righteousness. But rather, when they hear them, they shall exult and rejoice, and *their heart(s) will be Strengthened, and they shall prevail*

57(34) against [or "be Victorious over"] *all the Sons of the Earth*. And God will make atonement for [or "through"] them, and they will see His Salvation [*Yeshuʿa*], *because they took refuge in His Holy Name*.[51]

NOTES

[1] The first eight columns of the longer version and the two columns of the shorter version found by Solomon Schechter at the Cairo *Genizah* in Egypt in 1896. The transription we provide is based on the transcription provided at that time by Solomon Schechter. See p. 428 at the end of the Glossary for a general note on translations.

[2] One should note all references to "doing" throughout this text—in Hebrew the basis of the word "works" in English, which we generally identify as "Jamesian".

[3] In this language of "delivering up" one should note the possibly inverted play represented by the constant reiteration in the Gospels of Judas *Iscariot* "delivering up" Jesus.

[4] Here one should note the parallels with "the First" vs "the Last" language in the Gospels.

[5] See Paul in Ro 11:18–26 and 1 Co 3:6–9.

[6] One should note the parallel represented by "the Way in the wilderness" language associated with the mission of John the Baptist and "the Way" terminology generally as a name for early Christianity in Acts.

[7] Here "the Last" terminology of "the Last Days" or " Times".

[8] Note the parallel with "the Spouter of Lying" in the Habakkuk *Pesher*, literally "the Pourer Out of Lying" in the sense of "pouring out the waters of Lying".

[9] See Paul in Ga 1:8–9 and 3:13 on such "curses" or "cursing".

[10] Possibly also "Sinners"—the opposite of "justifying the Righteous and condemning the Wicked" on the part of the true Sons of Zadok in column iv above.

[11] This is definitely a vision permeating the *Koran* in Islam.

[12] If this is a correct translation, this issue of the consumption of *blood*, banned in James' directives to overseas communities in Acts, is very important.

[13] Later applied to "the Sons of Zadok" in column iv. In the New Testament, transformed *vis-à-vis* Jesus into, "called by this Name", that is to say, Christ's "Name".

[14] In the most popular English translation this is translated as "His annointed ones"—but the pronominal and verbal usages surrounding it are singular, as they are in other similar contexts in this document and in the War Scroll from Qumran. What is more, the usage here is clearly *singular*.

[15] The most common English translation inexplicably *discards this sentence altogether* without explanation. Again, note the singular usages here, transformed by many translations into plurals! In fact, this conflict between supposedly plural "anointed ones" and singular "His Name" was probably the reason for the omission in the first place.

[16] Here the "he who has eyes let him see, ears, let him hear" of New Testament variation.

[17] This language of "stumbling" is also found in Ja 2:10 and Paul in 1 Co 8:9 and 13.

[18] "Keeping the whole of the Law" is also found in Ja 2:10 above.

[19] Here our language of being "cut off" again; cf. Paul in Ga 5:12, using the same language to lewdly parody circumcision.

[20] The typical verb *"ma'as"*, meaning "reject" and applied to the activity of "the Spouter of Lying" in Qumran literature, namely, *rejecting the Law* or *Covenant*.

[21] This is a paraphrase, since *waw*-constructs or "ands" are purposely added between "Priests", "Levites", "the Sons of Zadok" in favor of developing a desired exegesis.

[22] Or "at the End of Days". The "standing" here and throughout this document not only appears to relate to the notion of being resurrected (in Ezek 37:10, "they stood up"), but also the "Standing One" ideology as a name for the resurrected Christ among

Jewish Christian groups like the Ebionites or Elkasaites of northern Syria and northern and southern Iraq.

[23] Note the Jamesian emphasis on "doing" again here.

[24] Again *the First* vs *the Last* of New Testament allusion.

[25] The difference here is actually the difference between the Hebrew *mezudo*/"net" and *mezuro*/"rampart" or "watchtower" of Hab 2:1.

[26] This is from the Testament of Lev 14:5–8. But see the same attributed to Balaam— a variation on "Belial"—in Rev 2:14, including now the category of "things sacrificed to idols" from James' directives to overseas communities in Acts 15:20, 15:29 and 21:25.

[27] For some reason Vermes insists on translating "Belial" throughout as "Satan". But at Qumran and in Rev 2:10–15 above, for instance, the two are different usages.

[28] "*Yoreh ha-Zedek*" instead of the usual "*Moreh ha-Zedek*"/"Teacher of Righteousness".

[29] We shall find the same usage "they robbed the Riches of the Poor" (*Ebionim*) in the Habakkuk *Pesher*, xii.10, below.

[30] This is the same usage in the Habakkuk *Pesher*, ix.1 about inflicting the Judgements upon Righteousness on the corpse of the Wicked Priest below. Also note again that the verb here is "*ma'as*"/"reject", mentioned above as always applied to the characteristic activity of "the Liar" at Qumran.

[31] One should compare this with the sayings attributed to Jesus in the Gospels that "a Prophet is not without honor except in his own country and among his own kin and in his own house" (Mk 6:4 and pars.)

[32] Notice the parallel here to Paul's doctrine of Jesus as the Community and his members being "the members" of the body of Christ (1 Co 12:12–27), including even the specific allusion to "the feet" and "the Prophets".

[33] Note the parallel here to "these Little Ones" in the New Testament.

[34] Here, of course, we have the parallel with the definition of "the Sons of Zadok" in the Community Rule, v.2 and v.9 below, as "Keepers of the Covenant". Again note the usage "*'Anayyim*" for "Meek" in the New Testament, paralleling the "*Ebionim*" or "Poor".

[35] Again this is definitely *singular*. The most widely known English translator, obscures this with the nondescript and indefinite "the Anointed of Aaron and Israel".

[36] Here too he translates "Belial" as "Satan".

[37] In the *Koran* 82:19, this is expressed as, "On this day the command is Allah's".

[38] In the *Koran* 2:10, this is "in their hearts, there is a disease".

[39] The opposite of "the Royal Law according to the Scripture" in the Letter of James and here, "each man loving his brother".

[40] "*Beza'*"—this is the same word as in the Habakkuk *Pesher* ix.5 below, which also refers to "gathering Riches", about "the Last Priests of Jerusalem profiteering from the spoils of the Peoples"—"Peoples" in our view being Herodians.

[41] This is the same as the "generation of vipers" metaphor ascribed in the Gospels to both John the Baptist and Jesus. But here the "vipers" are identified. They are "the Kings of the Peoples" or, in our view, Herodians. However this is interpreted, "the Kings of the Peoples" *cannot be* the Maccabeans.

[42] This is the same view of the role of the Roman Army as in the New Testament and Christian theology dependent on it.

[43] In this sense—if Paul is "the Spouter"—it is a play on his doctrine of "Holy Spirit" baptism. Mic 2:11 also has "Spouter of the People", reproduced in Manuscript B as "the Spouter of Adam". Manuscript B also adds "weigher of storms", probably mistaking

"weighing"/*shakal* for "Lying"/*Sheker*. Still the sense of all this is clear and it is probably one of the most important passages in the documents at Qumran.

[44] Here Vermes at last agrees the usage *is singular*.

[45] The other kind of works, "*ma'asim*", the Jamesian kind, is based on the root in Hebrew for "doing".

[46] The word "Jacob" here is unsure, but if it is the "Jacob" from Is 59:20, then *Jacob* goes with *Penitents*, not "the sin of Jacob" as in most translations but rather "the Penitents from sin *in* Jacob".

[47] Compare with the famous statement in Ja 2:10 above on "keeping the whole Law" and the definition of "the Sons of Zadok" as "Keepers of the Covenant" in column v of the Community Rule below.

[48] This is a very important use of the "God-Fearing" terminology and illustrates that there probably was a cadre of Gentile *God-Fearers* or "*Nilvim*"/"Joiners" associated in some manner with Qumran.

[49] This is a very important use of the term "*Yesha'* "/"Salvation", the basis of the name "Jesus" in Greek and English. The usage is also reprised in the last line of this text— there attached to an allusion to "seeing"—and elsewhere at Qumran.

[50] In Ja 2:5 this fundamental Commandment on "loving God" precedes the citation of the Royal Law according to the Scripture, the second "Love" Commandment. Paul quotes this Commandment in 1 Co 8:3 above, when attacking James' directive in Acts prohibiting "things sacrificed to idols" for overseas communities. In Ja 2:23 and the Damascus Document above, this is further refined into "the Beloved" or "Friend of God".

[51] One should note the triumphant exultation of this ending, almost exactly the same as in the Habakkuk *Pesher* below. In addition to the usage of "seeing *Yeshu'a*", with which it ends, one also should note that of "being strengthened"—the meaning of the curious nickname "*Oblias*" applied to James in early Church literature, "Strength" or "Fortress of the People".

Column I

1	ועתה שמעו כל יודעי צדק ובינו במעשי
2	אל כי ריב לו עם כל בשר ומשפט יעשה בכל מנאציו
3	כי במועלם אשר עזבוהו הסתיר פניו מישראל וממקדשו
4	ויתנם לחרב ובזכרו ברית ראשנים השאיר שארית
5	לישראל ולא נתנם לכלה ובקץ חרון שנים שלוש מאות
6	ותשעים לתיתו אותם ביד נבוכדנאצר מלך בבל
7	פקדם ויצמח מישראל ומאהרן שורש מטעת לירוש
8	את ארצו ולדשן בטוב אדמתו ויבינו בעונם וידעו כי
9	אנשים אשימם הם ויהיו כעורים וכימגששים דרך
10	שנים עשרים ויבן אל אל מעשיהם כי בלב שלם דרשוהו
11	ויקם להם מורה צדק להדריכם בדרך לבו ויודע
12	לדורות אחרונים את אשר עשה בדור אחרון בעדת בוגדים
13	הם סרי דרך היא העת אשר היה כתוב עליה כפרה סוררה
14	כן סרר ישראל בעמוד איש הלצון אשר הטיף לישראל
15	מימי כזב ויתעם בתוהו לא דרך להשח גבהות עולם ולסור
16	מנתיבות צדק ולסיע גבול אשר גבלו ראשנים בנחלתם למען
17	הדבק בהם את אלות בריתו להסגירם לחרב נקמת נקם
18	ברית בעבור אשר דרשו בחלקות ויבחרו במהתלות ויצפו
19	לפרצות ויבחרו בטוב הצואר ויצדיקו רשע וירשיעו צדיק
20	ויעבירו ברית ויפירו חוק ויגודו על נפש צדיק ובכל הולכי
21	תמים תעבה נפשם וירדפום לחרב ויסיסו לריב עם ויחר אף

Column II

1	אל בעדתם להשם את כל המונם ומעשיהם לנדה לפניו
2	ועתה שמעו אלי כל באי ברית ואגלה אזנכם בדרכי
3	רשעים אל אהב דעת חכמה ותושויה הציב לפניו
4	ערמה ודעת הם ישרתוהו ארך אפים עמו ורוב סליחות
5	לכפר בעד שבי פשע וכוח וגבורה וחמה גדולה בלהבי אש
6	בו כל מלאכי חבל על סררי דרך ומתעבי חק לאין שארית
7	ופליטה למו כי לא בחר אל בהם מקדם עולם ובטרם נוסדו ידע
8	את מעשיהם ויתעב את דורות מדם ויסתר את פניו מן הארץ
9	מי עד תומם וידע את שני מעמד ומספר ופרוש קציהם לכל
10	הוי עולמים ונהיית עד מה יבוא בקציהם לכל שני עולם
11	ובכולם הקים לו קריאי שם למען התיר פליטה לארץ ולמלא
12	פני תבל מזרעם ויודיעם ביד משיחו רוח קדשו והוא

אמת ובפרוש שמו שמותיהם ואת אשר שנא התעה 13
ועתה בנים שמעו לי ואגלה עיניכם לראות ולהבין במעשי 14
אל ולבחור את אשר רצה ולמאוס כאשר שנא להתהלך תמים 15
בכל דרכיו ולא לתור במחשבות יצר אשמה ועני זנות כי רבים 16
תעו בם וגבורי חיל נכשלו בם מלפנים ועד הנה בלכתם בשרירות 17
לבם נפלו עידי השמים בה נאחזו אשר לא שמרו מצות אל 18
ובניהם אשר כרום ארזים גבהם וכהרים גויותיהם כי נפלו 19
כל בשר היה בחרבה כי גוע ויהיו כלא היו בעשותם את 20
רצונם ולא שמרו את מצות עשיהם עד אשר חרה אפו בם 21

Column III

בה תעי בני נח ומשפח[ותי]הם בה הם נכרתים 1
אברהם לא הלך בה ויע[שה או]הב בשמרו מצות אל ולא בחר 2
ברצון רוחו וימסור לישחק וליעקב וישמרו ויכתבו אוהבים 3
לאל ובעלי ברית לעולם בני יעקב תעו בם ויענשו לפני 4
משגותם ובניהם במצרים הלכו בשרירות לבם להיעץ על 5
מצות אל ולעשות איש הישר בעיניו ויאכלו את הדם ויכרת 6
זכורם במדבר להם בקדש עלו ורשו את רוחם ולא שמעו 7
לקול עשיהם מצות יוריהם וירגנו באהליהם ויחר אף אל 8
בעדתם ובניהם בו אבדו ומלכיהם בו נכרתו וגיבוריהם בו 9
אבדו וארצם בו שממה בו חבו באי הברית הראשנים ויסגרו 10
לחרב בעזבם את ברית אל ויבחרו ברצונם ויתורו אחרי שרירות 11
לבם לעשות איש את רצונו ובמחזיקים במצות אל 12
אשר נותרו מהם הקים אל את בריתו לישראל עד עולם לגלות 13
להם נסתרות אשר תעו בם כל ישראל שבתות קדשו ומועדי 14
כבודו עידות צדקו ודרכי אמתו וחפצי רצונו אשר יעשה 15
האדם וחיה בהם פתח לפניהם ויחפרו באר למים רבים 16
ומואסיהם לא יחיה והם התגוללו בפשע אנוש ובדרכי נדה 17
ויאמרו כי לנו היא ואל ברוי פלאו כפר בעד עונם וישא לפשעם 18
ויבן להם בית נאמן בישראל אשר לא עמד כמהו למלפנים ועד 19
הנה המחזיקים בו לחיי נצח וכל כבוד אדם להם הוא כאשר 20
הקים אל להם ביד יחזקאל הנביא לאמר הכהנים והלוים ובני 21

Column IV

צדוק אשר שמרו את משמרת מקדשו בתעות בני ישראל 1
מעליהם יגישו לי חלב ודם הכהנים הם שבי ישראל 2
היוצאם מארץ יהודה והנלוים עמהם ובני צדוק הם בחירי 3

4   ישראל קריאי השם העמדים באחרית הימים הנה פרוש

5   שמותיהם לתולדותם וקץ מעמדם ומספר צרותיהם ושני

6   התגוררם ופירוש מעשיהם   [הם אנשי] הקודש   [הרא]שונים אשר כפר

7   אל בעדם ויצדיקו צדיק וירשיעו רשע וכל הבאים אחריהם

8   לעשות כפרוש התורה אשר התוסרו בו הראשנים עד שלים

9   הקץ השנים האלה כברית אשר הקים אל לראשנים לכפר

10   על עונותיהם כן יכפר אל בעדם ובשלום הקץ למספר השנים

11   האלה אין עוד להשתפח לבית יהודה כי אם לעמוד איש על

12   מצודו נבנתה הגדר רחק החוק ובכל השנים האלה יהיה

13   בליעל משולח בישראל כאשר דבר אל ביד ישעיה הנביא בן

14   אמרץ לאמר פחד ופחת ופח עליך יושב הארץ   פשרו

15   שלושת מצודות בליעל אשר אמר עליהם לוי בן   יעקב

16   אשר הוא תפש בהם בישראל ויתנם פניהם לשלושת מיני

17   הצדק הראשונה היא הזנות השנית ההון השלישית

18   טמא המקדש העולה מזה יתפש בזה והניצל מזה יתפש

19   בזה בוני החוץ אשר הלכו אחרי צו הצו הוא מטיף

20   אשר אמר הטף יטיפון הם ניתפשים בשתים בזנות לקחת

21   שתי נשים בחייהם ויסוד הבריאה זכר ונקבה ברא אותם

Column V

1   ובאי התבה שנים שנים באו אל התבה   ועל הנשיא כתוב

2   לא ירבה לו נשים ודויד לא קרא בספר התורה החתום אשר

3   היה בארון כי לא נפתח בישראל מיום מות אלעזר

4   ויהושע ויושע והזקנים אשר עבדו את העשתרות ויטמון

5   נגלה עד עמוד צדוק ויעלו מעשי דויד מלבד דם אוריה

6   ויעזבם לו אל וגם מטמאים הם את המקדש אשר אין הם

7   מבדיל כתורה ושוכבים עם הרואה את דם זובה ולוקחים

8   איש את בת אחיהם ואת בת אחותו   ומשה אמר אל

9   אחות אמך לא תקרב שאר אמך היא ומשפט העריות לזכרים

10   הוא כתוב וכהם הנשים ואם תגלה בת האח את ערות אחי

11   אביה והיא שאר   וגם את רוח קדשיהם טמאו ובלשון

12   גדופים פתחו פה על חוקי ברית אל לאמד לא נכונו ותועבה

13   הם מדברים בם כלם קדחו אש ומבערי זיקי קורי

14   עכביש קוריהם וביצי צפעונים ביציהם הקרוב אליהם

15   לא ינקה כהר ביתו יאשם כי אם נלחץ כי אם למילפנים פקד

16   אל את מעשיהם ויחר אפו בעלילותם כי לא עם בינות   הוא

17   הם גוי אבד עצות מאשר אין בהם בינה כי מלפנים עמד

משה ואהרן ביד שר האורים ויקם בליעל את יחנה ואת 18

אחיהו במזמתו בהושע ישראל את הראשונה 19

ובקץ חרבן הארץ עמדו מסיגי הגבול ויתעו את ישראל 20

ותישם הארץ כי דברו סרה על מצות אל ביד משה וגם 21

Column VI

במשיחו הקודש וינבאו שקר להשיב את ישראל מאחר 1

אל ויזכר אל ברית ראשנים ויקח מאהרן נבונים ומישראל 2

חכמים וישמעם ויחפורו את הבאר באר חפרוה שרים כרוה 3

נדיבי העם במחוקק הבאר היא התורה וחופריה הם 4

שבי ישראל היוצאים מארץ יהודה ויגורו בארץ דמשק 5

אשר קרא אל את כולם שרים כי דרשוהו ואל הושבה 6

פארתם בפי אחד והמחוקק הוא דורש התורה אשר 7

אמר ישעיה מוציא כלי למעשיהו ונדיבי העם הם 8

הבאים לכרות את הבאר במחוקקות אשר חקק המחוקק 9

להתהלך במה בכל קץ הרשע וזולתם לא ישיגו עד עמד 10

יורה הצדק באחרית הימים וכל אשר הובאו בברית 11

לבלתי בוא אל המקדש להאיר מזבחו ויהיו מסגירי 12

הדלת אשר אמר אל מי בכם יסגיר דלתו ולא תאירו מזבחי 13

חנם אם לא ישמרו לעשות כפרוש התורה לקץ הרשע ולהבדל 14

מבני השחת ולהנזר מהון הרשעה הטמא בנדר ובחרם 15

ובהון המקדש ולגזול את עניי עמו להיות אלמנות שללם 16

ואת יתומים ירצחו ולהבדיל בין הטמא לטהור ולהודיע בין 17

הקודש לחול ולשמור את יום השבת כפרושה ואת המועדות 18

ואת יום התענית במצא . . באי הברית החדשה בארץ דמשק 19

להרים את הקדשים כפירושיהם לאהוב איש את אחיהו 20

כמהו ולהחזיק ביד עני ואביון וגר ולדרוש איש את שלום 21

Column VII

אחיהו ולא ימעל איש בשאר בשרו להזיר מן הזונות 1

כמשפט להוכיח איש את אחיהו כמצוה ולא לנטור 2

מיום ליום ולהבדל מכל הטמאות כמשפטם ולא ישקץ 3

איש את רוח קדשיו כאשר הבדיל אל להם כל המתהלכים 4

באלה בתמים קדש על פי כל יסורו ברית אל נאמנות להם 5

לחיותם אלף דור ואם מחנות ישבו כסרך הארץ ולקחו 6

נשים והולידו בנים והתהלכו על פי התורה וכמשפט 7

היסורים כסרך התורה כאשר אמר בין איש לאשתו ובין אב 8

לבנו וכל המואסים בפקד אל את הארץ להשיב גמול רשעים 9

עליהם כבוא הדבר אשר כתוב בדברי ישעיה בן אמוץ הנביא 10

אשר אמר יבוא עליך ועל עמך ועל בית אביך ימים אשר 11

באו מיום סור אפרים מעל יהודה בהפרד שני בתי ישראל 12

שר אפרים מעל יהודה וכל הנסוגים הסגרו לחרב והמחזיקים 13

נמלטו לארץ צפון   כאשר אמר והגליתי את סכות מלככם 14

ואת כיון צלמיכם מאהלי דמשק   ספרי התורה הם סוכת 15

המלך כאשר אמר והקימותי את סוכת דוד הנפלת המלך 16

הוא הקהל וכינוי הצלמים וכיון הצלמים הם ספרי הנביאים 17

אשר בזה ישראל את דבריהם   והכוכב הוא דורש התורה 18

הבא דמשק כאשר כתוב דרך כוכב מיעקב וקם שבט 19

מישראל   השבט הוא נשיא כל העדה ובעמדו וקרקר 20

את כל בני שת   אלה מלטו בקץ הפקודה הראשון 21

Column VIII

והנסוגים הסגירו לחרב וכן משפט כל באי בריתו אשר 1

לא יחזיקו באלה לפוקדם לכלה ביד בליעל הוא היום 2

אשר יפקד אל היו שרי יהודה אשר תשפוך עליהם העברה 3

כי יחלו למרפא וידקמום כל מורדים מאשר לא סרו מדרך 4

בוגדים ויתגוללו בדרכי זונות ובהון רשעה ונקום וניטור 5

איש לאחיו ושנוא איש את רעהו ויתעלמו איש בשאר בשרו 6

ויגשו לזמה ויתגברו להון ולבצע ויעשו איש הישר בעיניו 7

ויבחרו איש בשרירות לבו ולא נזרו מעם ויפרעו ביד רמה 8

ללכת בדרך רשעים אשר אמר אל עליהם חמת תנינים יינם 9

וראש פתנים אכזר   התנינים הם מלכי העמים ויינם הוא 10

דרכיהם וראש הפתנים הוא ראש מלכי יון הבא לעשות בהם 11

נקמה ובכל אלה לא הבינו בוני החוץ וטחי תפל כי 12

מבוהל רוח ומטיף כזב הטיף להם אשר חרה אף אל בכל עדתו 13

ואשר אמר משה לא בצדקתך ובישר לבבך אתה בא לרשת 14

את הגוים האלה כי מאהבתו את אבותך ומשמרו את השבועה 15

וכן המשפט לשבי ישראל סרו מדרך העם באהבת אל את 16

הראשנים אשר העירו אחריו אהב את הבאים אחריהם כי להם 17

ברית האבות   ובשונאי את בוני החוץ חרה אפו   וכמשפט 18

הזה לכל המואס במצות אל ויעזבם ויפנו בשרירות לבם 19

הוא הדבר אשר אמר ירמיה לברוך בן נרייה ואלישע 20

לגחזי נערו   כל האנשים אשר באו בברית החדשה בארץ דמשק 21

Column XIX
(Manuscript B)

נאמנות להם לחיותם לאלפי דורות כב שומר הברית והחסד	1
לאהבי ולשמרי מצותי לאלף דור ואם מחנות ישבו כחוקי	2
הארץ אשר היה מקדם ולקחו נשים במנהג התורה והולידו בנים	3
ויתהלכו על פי התורה וכמשפט היסודים כסרך התורה	4
כאשר אמר כ'"ן'איש לאשתו ובין אב לבנו וכל המאסים במצות	5
ובחקים להשיב גמול רשעים עליהם בפקד אל את הארץ	6
בבוא הדבר אשר כתוב ביד זכריה הנביא חרב עורי על	7
רועי ועל גבר עמיתי נאם אל הך את הרעה ותפוצינה הצאן	8
והשיבותי ידי על הצוערים והשומרים אותו הם עניי הצאן	9
אלה ימלטו בקץ הפקדה והנשארים ימסרו לחרב בבוא משיח	10
אהרן וישראל כאשר היה בקץ פקדת הראשון אשר אמר יחזקאל	11
ביד יחזקאל ו+ה+ת+ב+ לההתות התיו על מצחות נאנחים ונאנקים	12
והנשארים הסגרו לחרב נוקמת נקם ברית וכן משפט לכל באי	13	*(1)
בריתו אשר לא יחזיקו באלה החקים לפקדם לכלה ביד בליעל	14	(2)
הוא היום אשר יפקד אל כאשר דבר היו שרי יהודה כמשיגי	15	(3)
גבול עליהם אשפך כמים עברה כי באו בברית תשובה	16	(4)
ולא סרו מדרך בוגדים ויתעללו בדרכי זנות ובהון הרשעה	17	(5)
ונקום ונטור איש לאחיהו ושנא איש את רעהו ויתעלמו איש	18	(6)
בשאר בשרו ויגשו לזמה ויתגברו להון ולבצע ויעשו את	19	(7)
איש הישר בעיניו ויבחרו איש בשרירות לבו ולא נזרו מעם	20	(8)
ומחטאתם ויפרעו ביד רמה ללכת בדרכי רשעים אשר	21	(8-9)
אמר אל עליהם חמת תנינים יינם וראש פתנים אכזר התנינים	22	(9)
מלכי העמים ויינם הוא דרכיהם וראש פתנים הוא ראש	23	(10)
מלכי יון הבא עליהם לנקם נקמה ובכל אלה לא הבינו בוני	24	(11)
החיץ וטחי תפל כי הולך רוח ושקל מ+ו+פ+ה סופות ומטיף אדם	25	(12)
לכזב אשר חרה אף אל בכל עדתו ואשר אמר משה	26	(13)
לישראל לא בצדקתך וביושר לבבך אתה בא לרשת את הגוים	27	(14)
האלה כי מאהבתו את אבותיך ומשמרו את השבועה כן	28	(15)
משפט לשבי ישראל סרו מדרך העם באהבת אל את הראשנים	29	(16)
אשר העידו על העם אחרי אל ואהב את הבאים אחריהם כי להם	30	(17)
ברית אבות ושונא ומתעב אל את בוני החיץ וחרה א+ף אפו בם ובכל	31	(18)
ההלכים אחריהם וכמשפט הזה לכל המאס במצות אל	32	(19)
ויעזבם ויפנו בשרירות לבם כן כל האנשים אשר באו בברית	33	(20)
החדשה בארץ דמשק ושבו ויבגדו ויסורו מבאר מים החיים:	34	(21-22)
ל[א] יחשבו בסוד עם ובכתבו לא יכתבו מיום האסף י+ו+ר+ מ+ו+ר+ה	35	(23)

Column XX
(Manuscript B)

מורה היחיד עד עמוד משיח מאהרן ומישראל   וכן המשפט 1 (24)

לכל באי עדת אנשי תמים הקדש ויקוץ מעשות פקודי ישרים 2 (25)

הוא האיש הנתך בתוך כור   בהופע מעשיו ישלח מעדה 3 (26)

כמו שלא נפל גורלו בתוך למודי אל כפי מעלו את יזכירווהו אנשי 4 (27)

מעות עד יום ישוב לעמד במעמד אנשי תמים קדש אשר אין 5 (28)

גורלו בתוך ובהופע מעשיו כפי מדרש התורה אשר יתהלכו 6 (29)

בו אנשי תמים הקדש אל את יאות איש עמו בהון ובעבודה 7 (30)

כי אררוהו כל קדושי עליון וכמשפט הזה לכל המאס בראשונים 8 (31)

ובאחרונים אשר שמו גלולים על לבם וישימו וילכו בשרירות 9 (32)

לבם אין להם חלק בבית התורה   כמשפט רעיהם אשר שבו 10 (33)

עם אנשי הלצון ישפטו כי דברו תועה על חקי הצדק ומאסו 11 (34)

בברית ואמנה אשר קימו בארץ דמשק והוא ברית החדשה 12 (35)

ולא יהיה להם ולמשפחותיהם חלק בבית התורה   ומיום 13 (36)

האסף יורריה היחיד עד תם כל אנשי המלחמה אשר הלכו 14 (37)

עם איש הכזב כשנים ארבעים   ובקץ ההוא יחרה 15 (38)

אף אל בישראל כאשר אמר אין   מלך ואין שר ואין שופט ואין 16 (39)

מוכיח בצדק ושבי פשע י[עקב] שמרו ברית אל אז נד[ברו] איש 17 (40)

אל רע[הו להחזיק איש] את אחיו יתמך צעדם בדרך אל ויקשב 18 (41)

אל אל דבריהם וישמע ויכתב ספר זכרן לפניו ליראי אל לחושבי 19 (42)

שמו . עד יעלה ישע וצדקה ליראי אל ושבתם וראיתם בין צדיק 20 (43)

ורשע בין עבד [א]ל לאשר לא עבדו   ועשה חסד לאלפים לאוהביו 21 (44)

ולשמריו לאלף דור   מביתפלג דור אשר יצאו מעיר הקדש: 22 (45)

וישענו על אל בקץ מעל ישראל וטמאו את המקדש ושבו עד 23 (46)

אל   נסיך העם בדברם מעט....לם אי⟨ש⟩ לפי רוחו ישפטו בעצת 24 (47)

קדש   וכל אשר פרצו את גבול התורה מבאי הברית בהופע 25 (48)

כבוד אל לישראל יכרתו מקרב המחנה ועמהם כל מרשיעי 26 (49)

יהודה בימי מצרפותיו   וכל המחזיקים במשפטים האלה לצאת 27 (50)

ולבוא על פי התורה וישמעו לקול מורה ויתודו לפני אל [חט]אנו 28 (51)

רשענו גם..אנחנו גם אבותינו בלכתם קרי בחקי הברית 29 (52)

ואמת משפטיך בנו   ולא ירימו יד על חקי קדש ומשפט 30 (53)

צדקו ועדוות אמתו   והתיסרו במשפטים הראשונים אשר 31 (54)

נשפטו בני אנשי היחיד והאזינו לקול מורה צדק   ולא ישיבו 32 (55)

אל חקי הצדק בשמעם אתם ישישו וישמחו ויעז לבם ויתגברו 33 (56)

על כל בני תבל וכפר אל בעדם וראו בישועתו כי חסו בשם קדשו 34 (57)

CHAPTER 11

The Community Rule (1QS)*

Column I

1 For (the Guide, in order to teach all the Holy) Ones ["Saints"] to li(ve according to the Ru)le of the Community, to seek

2 God (with a complete heart), *to do* what is Good and Upright before Him, as

3 *commanded by the hand of Moses* and all His servants the Prophets, *to love all*

4 *He chooses and to hate all He rejects*, to distance oneself from all Evil

5 and to hold fast to all the works of Goodness, and *to do Truth and Righteousness, and Judgement*

6 on the Earth, and no longer to walk in blameworthy stubbornness of heart and fornicating eyes,

7 doing all Evil, and to be admitted into the Covenant of Grace [literally "Piety"/*Hesed*] of all those volunteering *to do the Laws of God*,

8 to be a part of the Council of God and to walk before Him in the Perfection of all

9 that has been revealed concerning their appointed Festivals, and *to love all the Sons of Light*, each man

10 according to his allotted place in the Council of God, and *to hate all the Sons of Darkness*, each according to his just desert of

11 God's Vengeance. And all the Volunteers for His Truth will bring all their Knowledge, their Strength,

12 and their Riches into the *Community of God*, that they may clarify their Knowledge with the Truth of God and refine their Power

13 in the Perfection of His Ways, and all their property [literally

* The first nine columns.

"Riches" again] into the *Council of His Righteousness*, and not straying in anything

14 from all the words of God concerning their Eras, for they shall not advance the times of these, nor delay

15 any of their commemorations. *Nor shall they depart from the Laws of His Truth, to walk either to the right or to the left.*

16 And all those who enter in the Rule of the Community, undertaking the Covenant before God *to do*

17 *all that He commanded*, should not turn aside from Him out of any fear, dread, or mortal

18 torment during the Dominion of Belial. And upon their undertaking the Covenant, the Priests

19 and the Levites shall bless the God of Salvations (*Yeshu'ot*) and all the works of His Truth, and all

20 those entering the Covenant shall repeat after them, "Amen, Amen."

21 And the Priests shall tell of *the Righteous Acts of God in His triumphant works*,

22 and declare all His merciful Grace [literally "Pieties"] to Israel. And the Levites shall recount

23 the sins of the Children of Israel and all their guilty transgressions and their sinfulness during the Dominion of

24 Belial. And after them, those entering the Covenant shall confess, saying: "We have transgressed,

25 (we are guilty, we have si)nned, we have been wicked, we and our fathers before us, in that we walked [cf. Mt 27:4 and 25]

26 (counter to the Laws) of Truth and Righteousness (and may the God of Salvations execute) His Judgement upon us and upon our fathers

Column II

1 and bestow His merciful Grace upon us forever and ever." And the Priests shall bless all

2 the men of the lot of God, those who walk Perfectly in all His Ways. And they shall say: "May He bless you with all that is Good,

3 and keep you from all that is Evil. May He illumine your heart with life-giving intelligence and comfort you with Eternal Knowledge.

4 May He raise up His face full of Grace ["Pieties"] towards you in Eternal peace." Then the Levites shall curse all the Men

5 of the lot of Belial and say: "Cursed be you because of all your guilty works of Evil. May God *deliver you up to torment*

6 *at the hand of all the avenging Avengers. And May you be commanded to destruction by the hand of all the Payers of*

7 *Rewards.* Cursed be you without mercy, because of the Darkness of your works. Be damned

8 in the netherworlds of Everlasting Fire. *May God not comfort you when you call out to him, nor forgive you by pardoning your sins.*

9 On the contrary, may He raise up His angry countenance to take vengeance upon you, and may you enjoy no peace." As for all those who hold fast to the Fathers

10 And *all those who undertake the Covenant, they shall say after the blessings and cursings, "Amen, Amen."*

11 And the Priests and the Levites will continue, saying: "Cursed be he who enters this Covenant with

12 idols upon his heart, setting before himself the stumbling block of his sin to cause him to backslide [cf. Paul in 1 Co 8:4–13 and Ja 2:8–10],

13 and, hearing the words of this Covenant, blesses himself in his heart, saying, "Peace be upon me,

14 even though I walk in the stubbornness of my heart." Rather, his spirit, wracked with hunger, shall be obliterated without

15 forgiveness. *God's Anger and zeal for His Judgements will burn him in Everlasting damnation.* All the curses

16 of this Covenant will cleave to him and God will set him aside for Evil [admonishment], and he shall be *cut off from among all the Sons of Light because of his backsliding*

17 *from God* [cf. Paul in Ga 5:12]. Because of his idols and the stumbling-block of his sin, his lot shall be among the Eternally accursed [cf. Ga 3:13].

18 And all those entering the Covenant shall respond after them and say, "Amen, Amen!"

19 This is what they shall do year by year (during) all the days of the Dominion of Belial. The Priests shall enter

20 in the Order first according to their spirits, one after the other, and the Levites shall enter after them,

21 And third, all the people will enter the Order, one after another, in their thousands, hundreds,

22 fifties, and tens, so that *every man of Israel in the House (of God) will know his rank [literally "standing"] in the Community of God*

23 *according to Eternal design. And no man of the House (of God) shall move down from his standing or up from his allotted rank.*

24 Because all are part of the Community of Truth with self-effacing Goodness and love of Piety and the thought of Righteousness,

25 each man towards his neighbor in the Council of Holiness, the Sons of the Eternal Foundation. And he who rejects entering

26 (the Covenant of Go)d to walk in the stubbornness of his heart, shall not (enter the Com)munity of His Truth, because

Column III

1 *his soul detests the Foundations of the Knowledge of the Judgements of Righteousness. Therefore, he will not be reckoned among the Upright, because he was not steadfast in the conversion of his life.*

2 Nor shall his Knowledge, his Power, his Riches be brought into the Council of the Community. Whoever ploughs the mud of Wickedness returns defiled

3 *And he will not be justified by what his stubborn heart permits, because he looks upon Darkness instead of the Ways of Light.* In the spring [or "eye"] of the Perfect Ones,

4 he shall not be counted. *Nor shall he be cleansed by atonements, nor purified by cleansing waters, nor sanctified by seas*

5 *and rivers, nor purified by any waters of ablution.* Polluted! Polluted, shall he be all the days that he rejects the Judgements

6 of God, without submitting to the Council of His Community. For in the Spirit of the Council of Truth of God will the ways of man and all

7 his sins be atoned for, so that he may *look upon the Living Light. And he shall be cleansed of all his sins by the Holy Spirit, joining him to His Truth,*

8 And by a Spirit of Uprightness and Humility shall his sin be forgiven, *And by humble submission of his soul to all the Laws of God will his flesh*

9 *be washed by purifying waters and sanctified by cleansing waters.* Let him then order his steps so as to walk Perfectly

10 in all the Ways of God, as He [God] commanded concerning His appointed Festivals, neither straying to the right or the left, nor

11 infringing on one of His words [compare with Ja 2:11]. Thus will he be *acceptable as pleasing atonement before God and he will be for Him as a Covenant*

12 *of the Eternal Community.*

13 For the Guide, in order to communicate and teach all the Sons of
   Light the history of all the Sons of Man,

14 according to all the kinds of their spirits, the signs concerning their
   works and their generations, and *the Visitation of their punishments and*

15 *the Eras of their reward.* From the God of Knowledge comes all that
   ever was and will be. Before ever they existed, He prepared their
   whole mentality.

16 And when they are permitted to come into being in accord with His
   Glorious design, they are to fulfill all their tasks without changing
   anything. In His hands

17 are the Judgements on all things and He provides them with all their
   wishes. He created Man [*Enosh*] to govern

18 the Earth, and placed in him two Spirits in which to walk until the
   Era of His Visitation. They are the Spirits of Truth and of
   Unrighteousness,

20 And in the hand of *the Prince of Lights is the Government of the Sons of
   Righteousness [Zedek]* walking in the Ways of Light. And in (the hand
   of) the Angel

21 of Darkness is the whole Government of the Sons of Unrighteousness, and they walk in the Ways of Darkness. And because of
   the Angel of Darkness,

22 *all the Sons of Righteousness [Zedek] are led astray,* and all their sins, their
   iniquities, their transgression, and the infractions of their works are
   under his Dominion

23 according to the Mysteries of God until the End (Time). And all
   their punishments and the periods of their sufferings are by the
   malevolence of his Dominion.

24 and all the spirits (in Islam, "*jinn*") of his lot cause the Sons of Light
   to stumble. *But the God of Israel and the Angel of His Truth help all*

25 *the Sons of Light.* And He created the Spirits of Light and of Darkness
   and upon them based all (His) works

26 (and on their W)ays, all (human) activity (was established . . .). God
   loved the former for all

Column IV

1 the Eternal Ages and takes pleasure in all of its actions forever. But
  the latter's Foundation He abominates, hating all its Ways unto
  Destruction.

2 And these are their Ways in the world: *to illumine the heart of man that*

all the Ways of Righteousness and Truth may be made Straight before him, and instill in his heart the fear of the Judgements

3 of God, a Spirit of Meekness, long-suffering patience, abundant Mercy, Eternal Goodness, intelligence, understanding, Majestic Wisdom *having Faith in all*

4 *the works of God* and *leaning on His abundant Grace* ["Piety"]. (It is) a Spirit of Knowledge in every rational work, of *Zeal for the Judgements of Righteousness, of thoughtful*

5 *Holiness with imperturbable steadfastness and abundant Grace and Glorious purity on all the Sons of Truth,* detesting all the idols of pollution. (It is) modest behavior

6 wary of all and *concealing the Truth concerning the Mysteries of Knowledge* ["Gnosis"]. These are the Foundations [or "Secrets"] of the Spirit for the Sons of Truth of the world. And as for *the Visitation* [or "Reward"] *of all who walk in it, it is healing,*

7 *abundant peacefulness in long life, fruitful seed with all blessings forever, everlasting joy in Life Victorious, and a Crown of Glory*

8 *with majestic raiment in Eternal Light* [cf. 1 Co 15:51–58].

9 But (the Ways of) the Spirit of Unrighteousness (are): greediness of soul, stumbling hands in the Service of Righteousness [cf. 2 Co 11:15], Wickedness and Lying, pride and proudness of heart, duplicitousness and Deceitfulness, cruelty,

10 abundant ill temper, impatience, much folly, and *Zeal for lustfulness, works of Abomination in a Spirit of fornication and Ways of uncleanness in the service of pollution,*

11 *a Tongue full of blasphemies,* blindness of eye and dullness of ear, stiffness of neck and hardness of heart in order to walk in all the Ways of Darkness and Evil inclination. And the Visitation ["Reward"]

12 of all who walk in it will be immeasurable punishments [this is the same word used in the Habakkuk *Pesher* to describe what was *done to* "the Wicked Priest's *corpse*"] at the hands of all the Angels of Destruction, for Eternal damnation by the burning Wrath of the God of Vengeance, Everlasting torment and endless admonishment,

13 with shameful extinction in the Fire of the Netherworlds. And all the Eras of their Generations they shall spend in mournful weeping and bitter Evils in the Abysses of Darkness until

14 their annihilation without remnant or survivor.

15 In the (two Spirits) is the history of all the Sons of Man, and in

their (two) kinds, all the Hosts inherit a share according to their Generations and walk in their Ways, and all the works

16 they do are in their (two) divisions. *And a man shall be rewarded for all the Eternal Ages according to the division of all their works,* whether lesser or greater. Because God has apportioned them equally until the Last

17 Times. And He has placed Eternal hatred between their divisions. Truth abominates the acts of Unrighteousness and Unrighteousness abominates all the Ways of Truth. Zeal for

18 division (infuses) all their Judgements, because they do not walk in unison. God, in the Mysteries of His Intelligence and the Wisdom of His Glory, has put an End to all Unrighteous being and *at the Time*

19 *of the Visitation, He will destroy it forever.* Then Truth, which has wallowed [or "lain immersed"] in the ways of Wickedness during the Dominion of Unrighteousness

20 until the Time of the Appointed Judgement, will emerge Victorious in the world. *Then God will refine with His Truth all the works of man and purify for Himself the Sons of Man, Perfecting all the Spirit of Unrighteousness within*

21 *his flesh, and by means of the Holy Spirit, purifying it from Evil actions. He will pour upon him the Spirit of Truth like baptismal waters (washing him) of all the Abominations of Lying,* and he shall be immersed in

22 the Spirit of Purification that (He may) cause the Upright to understand the Knowledge of the Most High and the Wisdom of the Sons of Heaven, to teach the Perfect of the Way, whom God has chosen as an Everlasting Covenant.

23 *And all the Glory of Adam will be theirs* [here, of course, the Ebionite/ Elkasaite/Sabaean "Primal Adam" ideology permeating all baptist groups in northern Syria and southern Iraq] and there will be no more Unrighteousness and all the works of Deceitfulness will be put to flight. Until now the Spirits of Truth and Unrighteousness have struggled in the hearts of Man

24 and they have walked either in Wisdom or Unrighteousness. And according to a man's inheritance in Truth and Righteousness, so will he hate Unrighteousness. And according to his inheritance of the lot of Unrighteousness, so he will behave wickedly through it

25 and abominate Truth. Because God has put (the two Spirits into the world) equally until the appointed End and the New Creation. He knows the actions of their works for all the Eras

26 (of Ti)me, and He has given them as an inheritance to all the Sons
of Men to know Good (and Evil. He has ap)portioned the lots
of all living beings according to his Spirit (on the Day of the)
Visitation.

Column V

1 And this is the Rule for the Men of the Community, those freely
volunteering to turn aside from all Evil and hold fast to all He
commanded according to His will. *And they shall separate from the
Assembly*

2 *of the Men of Unrighteousness in order to be a Community of Torah and common
possessions* ["Riches"] *under the authority of the Sons of Zadok,* the Priests
who are Keepers of the Covenant and the multitude of the Men

3 of the Community, who hold fast to the Covenant. They will make
their decision on the basis of lot concerning every matter that has
to do with *Torah,* property ["Riches"], and Judgement, in order to
do Truth together with humility

4 *Justification, Judgement, the love of Piety, and modesty in all their Ways,* so that
no man will walk in stubbornness of his heart, to go astray after
his heart,

5 his eyes, and lustful inclination. On the contrary, in the Community
*he will circumcize the foreskin of his desire and stiff-neckedness in order to
lay a firm Foundation of Truth for Israel (and) for the Community of the
Everlasting*

6 *Covenant,* in order to make atonement on behalf of all the Volunteers
for the sake of Holiness in Aaron [later "a Holy of Holies for
Aaron"] and a House of Truth in Israel and the Joiners ["*Nilvim*",
again a play on "Levites"] for a Community and for struggle and
for Judgement,

7 *to condemn all Law-Breakers.* And these shall be the essence of their
Ways concerning all these Laws for those joining the Community.
Anyone entering the Council of the Community,

8 coming into Covenant of God under the eyes of all the Volunteers
(for Holiness) shall *swear upon his soul with a binding oath to return to
the Torah* of Moses in everything that it commanded with all (his)

9 *heart and with all* (his) *soul,* according to all that was revealed concerning
it to the Sons of Zadok, who are the Priests, the Keepers of the
Covenant and the Seekers after His will, and according to the
majority of the Men of their Covenant,

10 the Volunteers of the Community for His Truth, in order to walk in His will and that which *he swore upon his soul by the Covenant, to separate from all the Men of Unrighteousness* walking

11 in the Way of Evil. For they are not to be reckoned in His Covenant, since they have not asked concerning or *studied His Laws to know the Hidden Things, in which they have gone astray*

12 *to their own guilt* and because they did the Revealed Things with contempt, *kindling the Wrath for Judgement and for the Avengers of the Vengeance of the curses of the Covenant to execute upon them the majestic*

13 *Judgements of Eternal destruction without a remnant.* He shall not enter the water in order to touch the Purity [the Communal meal] of the Men of Holiness, for they *shall not be cleansed*

14 *even if they turn away from their Wickedness, because all Breakers of His Word are polluted.* Therefore, no one should cooperate with him in his work [in the sense of "service" or "mission"] or his purse ["possessions" or "Riches"], lest he contract his

15 guilty Sinfulness. Rather he should distance himself from him in every thing, as it is written: "Keep away from all things that are Lying" [Ex 23:7—so much for "Peter's" tablecloth vision in Acts 10–11]. Therefore *no man among the Men*

16 *of the Community shall acquiesce to their authority in any (matter of) Torah or Judgement. He shall not eat anything by (means of) their purse, or drink or take anything from their hands whatsoever* [Ga 2:12–13],

17 except for payment, as is written: "Keep away from the man whose breath is in his nostrils, for what is he reckoned?" [Is 2:22], since

18 one should *separate from all those not reckoned in His Covenant—(separate) from them and from all that is theirs* [cf. 2 Co 6:16–17]. No Man of Holiness should contract any unclean work,

19 for unclean are all those who do not know His Covenant. And anyone who has contempt for His Word will be eradicated from the world, because all his works are unclean

20 before Him and *all his possessions* ["Riches"] *are polluted.* And when someone enters the Covenant to do according to all these Laws [again note the emphasis on *doing*] to become one with the Holy Assembly [or "Church"], they shall examine

21 his spirit in the Community, one man towards his neighbor, with respect to his mentality and his works of the *Torah*, on the testimony of the Sons of Aaron, the Volunteers in the Community to erect

22 His Covenant and *to command all the Laws which He commanded (them) to do*, and upon the testimony of the Many of Israel, the Volunteers turning aside unto the Community (supporting) His Covenant.

23 And they shall inscribe them in the Order, one after another, according to his intelligence and his works, *so that each man will obey his fellow, the man of lower rank (obeying) the higher.*

24 And they shall examine their spirit and their works year after year, so that a man can be advanced according to his intelligence and the Perfection of his Way, or lowered according to the infractions (he has committed). Each man should admonish

25 his neighbor in Truth, Meekness, and love of Piety towards the man. One should not speak to his brother angrily or abusively,

26 or stub(bornly or with animus or) an Evil spirit. One should not hate another (because of his uncircumcized) heart, but rather reprove him the very same day, so as not

Column VI

1 to bring sin upon oneself. And, in addition, a man should not bring something he has against his neighbor before the Many, which he did not (first) reprove him for before witnesses.

2 *In these (rules) they shall walk wherever they dwell, each man towards his neighbor and the lower is to obey the higher in work and purse ["Riches"] wherever they find themselves. They shall eat in common,*

3 *pray in common, and deliberate in common.* Wherever there are ten men from the Council of the Community, there should not be lacking among them a man

4 who is a priest. And each man shall sit before it [the Council] according to his rank, and they shall be asked their outlook on everything. And it shall be when they prepare the table to eat and the new grapes

5 to drink, the Priest shall stretch out his hand first to bless the first fruits of the bread or the new grapes [this may not include extremely fermented or alcoholic beverages in general—see Jesus too on "new wine in old wineskins" (Mt 9:16–17 and pars.)].

6 [The text repeats itself here.] And in the place where ten are present, there shall never lack a man to study the *Torah* day and night,

7 always, a man taking the place of his brother. And the Many shall *keep vigil together for a third of all the nights of the year,* to read in the Book and to seek Judgement,

8 and pray together. *This is the Rule for the Assembly of the Many,* each

according to his rank: the Priests will sit down first and the Elders second [in Christianity, "the Presbyters"], *and the remainder of*

9 *all the People will sit down, each according to his rank.* And in this manner they shall be examined with regard to any Judgement, any opinion, or any matter concerning the Many, so that each can impart his Knowledge

10 to the Council of the Community. A man shall not start speaking during the speech of his neighbor until his brother has finished speaking. Nor shall he speak ahead of someone ranked

11 ahead of him. Rather the man questioned shall respond in his turn. In the session of the Many, a man shall not say anything without the permission of the Many, and indeed (without the permission) of

12 the Overseer ["Bishop"] over the Many. And any man who has something to say to the Many, but is not of the rank ["standing"] of someone who can question the Council of

13 the Community, let that man stand upon his feet and say, "There is something I have to say to the Many." If they permit him, then let him speak.

14 And the Man Commanding, the Head over the Many, shall examine any Volunteer from Israel (wishing) to join the Council of the Community with regard to his mentality and his works and, if he meets the qualifications, he shall admit him

15 into the Covenant, to turn aside to Truth and turn away from all Unrighteousness. And he shall inform him about all the Judgements of the Community. And after this, when he comes to stand before the Many, they shall consider

16 all his words. And on the basis of the result of the casting lots by the Council of the Many, he shall either be included or excluded. If he draws near the Council of the Community, he shall not touch the Purity ["Pure Food"] of

17 the Many until they *examine him as to his spirit and his works until one full year is completed*; neither shall he mix (his) property ["Riches"] with (that) of the Many.

18 And when he completes one full year within the Community, the Many shall examine (him) as to his words with regard to his outlook and his works of the *Torah*, and if the result of the casting of lots

19 by the Priests and the multitude of the Men of the Covenant is that he enter the Foundation ["Secret"] of the Community, they shall also admit his property ["Riches"] and his belongings into the hand of the Man who is

20 the Overseer [*ha-Mebakker*] of the property of the Many, and it shall be written in the ledger to his account, and the Many shall not be able to withdraw it. But he shall not touch the drink of the Many until

21 he has completed the second full year among the Men of the Community. And when he has completed the second year, he will be examined by the Many, and if

22 *the casting of lots results in his being (finally) brought into the Community, they shall enter him into the Order according to his rank* among his brothers for *Torah*, Judgement, and Purity. His belongings ["Riches"] shall be merged (with theirs) and his counsel will be (merged with)

23 the Community, as will his Judgement.

24 And these are the Judgements upon which they shall judge his words in the investigation by the Community: if a man is found among them who knowingly lied

25 concerning (his) property ["Riches"], they shall separate him from the Purity of the Many for one year and he will do penance with a quarter of his bread. (If) he answers

26 his brother rudely or speaks to him impatiently, insulting his honor and disobeying the authority of a fellow inscribed (in the ledger) ahead of him,

27 or (if he) has raised his hand against him, he will do penance for one whole year (and shall be excluded . . . If any man), utters the Glorious Name, in a bl(asphemous manner)

Column VII

1 whether in jest or as a result of some reversal, or for any other reason—even if while reading the Book or praying—he shall be expelled [literally "separated"]

2 and return no more to the Council of the Community. *And if he speaks to one of the Priests inscribed in the Book in anger, he shall do penance*

3 *for one year and be separated on pain of death from the Purity of the Many.* And if he spoke unintentionally, he will do penance for six months. And whoever has deliberately lied,

4 he shall do penance for six months. And whoever deliberately insults his fellow without cause will do penance for one year

5 and be separated. And whoever speaks to his fellow deceptively or knowingly behaves deceitfully with him shall do penance for six months. And if

6 he has been negligent with his fellow, his penance is three months. And if he has been negligent with the property of the Community causing loss, he shall repay it

7 in full.

8 And if he is unable to repay it, he shall do penance for sixty days. And whoever has unjustly borne malice against his fellow shall do penance for one year.

9 And likewise, anyone who has taken physical vengeance for any reason whatsoever. And whoever utters idiocy with his mouth, three months penance; and for talking in the middle of his neighbor's words,

10 ten days; and for falling asleep during the session of the Many, thirty days penance. And the same for whoever leaves the session of the Many

11 without permission up to three times in one sitting—ten days penance. But if he gets up

12 and leaves (completely), thirty days penance. And if he unnecessarily walks around naked before his brother, three months' penance.

13 And if a man spits in the midst of a session of the Many, he shall do penance thirty days. And whoever is so carelessly attired that when he takes his hand from under his cloak,

14 his nakedness becomes visible, thirty days penance. And if someone guffaws out loud so foolishly that his voice can be heard, thirty

15 days penance [many of these same points are covered in column xiv of the Damascus Document]. And whoever raises his left hand and gesticulates with it, ten days penance. And whoever goes around slandering his brother

16 shall be excluded from the Pure (Food) of the Many and do penance for one year, but whoever goes about slandering the Many, he shall be expelled from among them

17 and never return. And the man who murmurs against the Foundation [or "Secret"] of the Community shall be expelled and return no more, but if he has (only) murmured against his fellow

18 without justification, six months penance. However if the man returns, whose spirit is so changeable regarding the Foundation of the Community as to betray the Truth

19 and walk in the stubbornness of his heart, two years penance. In the first year he shall not touch the Pure (Food) of the Many,

20 and in the second he shall not touch the drink of the Many and only be seated after all the Men of the Community. And with the completion

21 of two full years, the Many shall examine his words, and if they permit him to enter, he shall be inscribed according to his rank and after this, questioned regarding Judgement.

22 And any man who has been in the Council of the Community for ten full years

23 and whose spirit backslides so as to betray the Community, departing from the presence of

24 the Many to walk in the stubbornness of his heart, he shall never more return to the Council of the Community. And any man of the Men of the Community who mixes

25 with him with regard to table-fellowship and common purse ["Riches"] in a manner not authorized by the Many, the Judgement on him will be the same as the first's. He shall be ex(pelled from among them. And there shall be)

Column VIII

1 in the Council of the Community twelve men and three priests, *Perfect in all that has been revealed about the whole*

2 *Torah, doing Truth, Righteousness* [literally "Justification"], *Judgement, loving Piety, and humility, each man to his neighbor* [cf. Ja 2:8–10],

3 *to keep Faith in the land with a steadfastness and humble spirit and to atone for sin by doing Judgement* [again the emphasis is on "doing"]

4 *and suffering affliction.* And (they) shall walk with everyone according to the standard of Truth and the essence of the Time. With the existence of these in Israel

5 *the Council of the Community shall be established upon Truth like an Eternal Plantation, a House of Holiness* ["Temple"] *for Israel* [cf. 1 Co 3:9–12] *and the Foundation of the Holy of*

6 *Holies for Aaron,* witnesses of the Truth for Judgement and the Chosen [or "Elect"] of (His) Will, to *make atonement for the land and to pay*

7 *the Wicked their reward. It will be a Tested Rampart, a Precious Cornerstone,*

8 *the Foundations of which will not shake or sway in their place* [Is 28:16]. *It will be a dwelling of the Holy of Holies*

9 *for Aaron with everlasting Knowledge of the Covenant of Judgement, offering up a pleasing fragrance, a House of Perfection and Truth in Israel,*

10 *to establish an Everlasting Covenant of Laws. And they* [the Community Council] *will be an acceptable free will offering to atone for the land and render Judgement on Evil. And there will be no more Unrighteousness.* When

these have been confirmed in Perfection of the Way for two whole years by the Foundation of the Community,

11 they will be set aside as Holy within the Council of the Men of the Community [i.e., "Consecrated Ones" or "Nazirites"], and the Guide will not hide from them

12 any matter revealed by him, but hidden from Israel out of fear of the spirit of heresy. And with the existence of these for a Community

13 in Israel and according to these regulations, *they shall separate from the midst of the habitation of the Men of Unrighteousness to go into the wilderness to prepare the Way of the Lord,*

14 *as it is written: "Prepare in the wilderness the Way of the Lord. Make straight in the desert a Pathway for our God"* [Is 40:3].

15 This is the study of the *Torah*, which He commanded by the hand of Moses, to do [again the emphasis on "doing"] all that has been revealed from Age to Age,

16 and which the Prophets have revealed through His Holy Spirit. And *any man of the Men of the Community of the Covenant,*

17 *who deliberately turns aside from any of the Commandments on any point whatsoever is not to approach the Purity of the Men of Holiness,*

18 and he shall know none of their doctrine until his *works have been washed clean of all Unrighteousness and he, once more, walks in Perfection of the Way.* Only then may he approach

19 the Council by the Authority of the Many according to his rank. And this Judgement will apply to all who join the Community.

20 And these are the Judgements in which the Men of Perfect Holiness are to walk, each towards his fellow,

21 all coming into the Council of Holiness to *walk in Perfection of the Way* [here, therefore, we are definitely dealing with a Community of "Nazirites"] *in the manner commanded.* Any man of them

22 who *breaks one word of the Torah of Moses, whether overtly or covertly, shall be expelled from the Council of the Community*

23 *and return no more.* And no man of the Men of Holiness shall mix (with him) in purse ["Riches"] or doctrine in any

24 thing whatsoever [cf. Ga 2:11–13 and Acts 15:38]. But if he did so by accident, he shall (only) be excluded from the Pure (Food) and the Council, and they shall examine him for Judgement,

25 meaning, (they) shall not judge a man or ask his view (on anything) for two whole years. But if he (then) Perfects his Way,

26 he may return to study and to the Council (under the authority of the Many), as long as he does not err inadvertently again until such time that he has completed two full years (of penance).

Column IX

1 But for an additional unintentional infraction, he shall do penance for two (more) years. However, if he acted intentionally, he shall return no more.

2 Only the inadvertent Sinner shall be tested for two (more) years, so that his Way and his perspective may be Perfected under the authority of the Many. And afterwards he shall be inscribed according to his rank in the Holy Community.

3 With the existence of these in Israel according to all these regulations, the *Holy Spirit shall then be established upon Truth*

4 *Forever. They shall atone for the guilt of sin and rebellious transgression and be a pleasing sacrifice for the land without the flesh of burnt offerings and the fat of sacrifices. And prayer rightly offered*

5 *from the lips will be for Judgement like the sweet smell of Righteousness and Perfection of the Way, an acceptable free will offering.* At such time, the Men

6 of the Community—the Walkers in Perfection—will be *separated as a House of Holiness* ["Temple"] *for Aaron in order to be the Community of the Holy of Holies and the House* ["Temple"] *of the Community for Israel.*

7 But the sons of Aaron alone will rule in (matters of) Judgement and purse ["Riches"], and upon their authority based on lot will every regulation concerning the Men of the Community

8 and the Riches of the Men of Holiness who walk in Perfection be set forth. Nor should their Riches be mixed with the Riches of the Men of Deceit, who have

9 not washed their Way in order to separate from Unrighteousness and walk in Perfection of the Way [cf. 2 Co 7:1 above]. Nor shall they turn aside from

10 any counsel of the *Torah* to walk in any stubbornness of their heart, and they shall be Judged according to the Judgements of the First ["the Forefathers"], in which the Men of the Community were instructed

11 until the Prophet [the "True Prophet" of Ebionite, Jewish Christian ideology] and the Messiah of Aaron and Israel [the usage, though idiomatic here, should be seen as singular] come.

12 These are the Laws, in accordance with which the Guide is to behave [literally, "to walk"] with all living things, according to the essence of time as time and the standard of man as man.

13 He shall do the will of God in accord with everything that has been

revealed from Age to Age and study all the learning that has been discovered according to the Ages and

14 the Law of that Age, to separate and evaluate the Sons of the *Zaddik* ["Sons of the Zadok"? Here now, we do have plural "Righteous Ones"] according to their spirit, and fortify the Elect of the Age according to

15 His Will as He commanded, and thus to do His Judgement on each man according to his spirit. And each man shall draw near in accordance with whether he has clean hands and is advanced in his intelligence;

16 and, thus, shall be His love together with His hatred. Nor should he admonish or argue with the Men of the Pit,

17 *but rather he shall conceal the counsel of the Torah from the Men of Unrighteousness* and (only) admonish (with) the Knowledge of Truth and Judgement of Righteousness the Elect

18 of the Way, each man according to his spirit according to the rule of the Age. He shall comfort them in Knowledge and thus illumine them in the marvelous Mysteries and Truth amid

19 the Men of the Community, *to walk Perfectly, each with his neighbor, in all that has been revealed to them, for this is the time of "making a Way*

20 *in the wilderness". Therefore, he should instruct them in all that has been revealed that they should do in this time, to separate from any man who has not turned his Way away*

21 *from all Unrighteousness.* And these are the rules of the Way for the Guide in these Times, relating (both) to his loving together with his hating: *everlasting hatred*

22 *for the Men of the Pit in a spirit of secrecy*, to leave them to their Riches and the toil of their hands, like a servant to his master or the Meek One before

23 the individual dictating to him. Rather *he shall be as a man zealous for the Law and His Time, (a man zealous for) the Day of Vengeance. To do (His) will in all the work of his hands*

24 *and in all His Dominion as He commanded.* And he should freely delight in all that happens to him, but other than by God's Will, nothing should please (him).

25 And he should delight in all that has been said by His mouth, but *he should not desire anything He does not command. And he should always be mindful of the Judgement of God*

26 . . . *to bless his Creator, and no matter what occurs . . . bless Him with his lips.*
   [The document continues more in the nature of a psalm for some two more columns.]

Column I

1 ל[משכיל ללמד את כל הקדו]שים לחיו[ת כפי סר]ך היחד לדרש
2 אל [בלב שלם ... ול] עשות הטוב והישר לפניו כאשר
3 צוה ביד מושה וביד כול עבדיו הנביאים ולאהוב כול
4 אשר בחר ולשנוא את כול אשר מאס לרחוק מכול רע
5 ולדבוק בכול מעשי טוב ולעשות אמת וצדקה ומשפט
6 בארץ ולוא ללכת עוד בשרירות לב אשמה ועיני זנות
7 לעשות כול רע ולהבי את כול הנדבים לעשות חוקי אל
8 בברית חסד להיחד בעצת אל ולהתהלך לפניו תמים כול
9 הנגלות למועדי תעודותם ולאהוב כול בני אור איש
10 כגורלו בעצת אל ולשנוא כול בני חושך איש כאשמתו
11 בנקמת אל וכול הנדבים לאמתו יביאו כול דעתם וכוחם
12 והונם ביחד אל לברר דעתם באמת חוקי אל וכוחם לתכן
13 כתם דרכיו וכול הונם בעצת צדקו ולוא לצעוד בכול אחד
14 מכול דברי אל בקציהם ולוא לקדם עתיהם ולוא להתאחר
15 מכול מועדיהם ולוא לסור מחוקי אמתו ללכת ימין ושמאול
16 וכול הבאים בסרך היחד יעבורו בברית לפני אל לעשות
17 ככול אשר צוה ולוא לשוב מאחרו מכול פחד ואימה ומצרף
18 נהיים בממשלת בליעל ובעוברם בברית יהיו הכוהנים
19 והלויים מברכים את אל ישועות ואת כול מעשי אמתו וכול
20 העוברים בברית אומרים אחריהם אמן אמן
21 והכוהנים מספרים את צדקות אל במעשי גבורתום
22 ומשמיעים כול חסדי רחמים על ישראל והלויים מספרים
23 את עוונות בני ישראל וכול פשעי אשמתם וחטאתם בממשלת
24 בליעל [וכול] העוברים בברית מודים אחריהם לאמר נעוינו
25 [פשענו חט]אנו הרשענו אנ[ו] ואב[ו]תינו מלפנינו בהלכתנו
26 [קרי חוקי] אמת וצדק ...] עשה] משפטו בנו ובאבותינו

Column II

1 ורחמי חסדו [ג]מל עלינו מעולם ועד עולם והכוהנים מברכים את כול
2 אנשי גורל אל ההולכים תמים בכול דרכיו ואומרים יברככה בכול
3 טוב וישמורכה מכול רע ויאיר לבכה בשכל חיים ויחונכה בדעת עולמים
4 וישא פני חסדיו לכה לשלום עולמים   והלויים מקללים את כול אנשי
5 גורל בליעל וענו ואמרו ארור אתה בכול מעשי רשע אשמתכה יתנכה
6 אל זעוה ביד כול נוקמי נקם ויפקוד אחריכה כלה ביד כול משלמי
7 גמולים ארור אתה לאין רחמים כחושך מעשיכה וזעום אתה
8 כאפלת אש עולמים לוא יחונכה אל בקוראכה ולוא יסלח לכפר עווניך

9 ישא פני אפו לנקמתכה ולוא יהיה לכה שלום בפי כול אוחזי אבות

10 וכול העוברים בברית אומרים אחר המברכים והמקללים אמן אמן

11 והוסיפו הכוהנים והלויים ואמרו ארור בגלולי לבו לעביר

12 הבא בברית הזות ומכשול עוונו ישים לפניו להסוג בו והיה

13 בשומעו את דברי הברית הזות יתברך בלבבו לאמור שלום יהי לי

14 כיא בשרירות לבי אלך ו[נ]ספתה רוחו הצמאה עם הרווה לאין

15 סליחה אף אל וקנאת משפטיו יבערו בו לכלת עולמים ידבקו בו כול

16 אלות הברית הזות ויבדילהו אל לרעה ונכרת מתוך כול בני אור בהסוגו

17 מאחרי אל בגלוליו ומכשול עוונו יתן גורלו בתוך ארורי עולמים

18 וכול באי הברית יענו ואמרו אחריהם אמן אמן

19 ככה יעשו שנה בשנה כול יומי ממשלת בליעל הכוהנים יעבורו

20 ברשונה בסרך לפי רוחותם זה אחר זה והלויים יעבורו אחריהם

21 וכול העם יעבורו בשלישית בסרך זה אחר זה לאלפים ומאות

22 וחמשים ועשרות לדעת כול איש ישראל איש בית מעמדו ביחד אל

23 לעצת עולמים ולוא ישפול איש מבית מעמדו ולוא ירום ממקום גורלו

24 כיא הכול יהיו ביחד אמת וענות טוב ואהבת חסד ומחשבת צדק

25 [אי]ש לרעהו בעצת קודש ובני סוד עולמים וכול המואס לבוא

26 [בברית א]ל ללכת בשרירות לבו לוא [יבוא בי]חד אמתו כיא געלה

Column III

1 נפשו ביסודי דעת משפטי צדק לוא חזק למשיב חיו ועם ישרים לוא יתחשב

2 ודעתו וכוחו והונו לוא יבואו בעצת יחד כיא בסאון רשע מחרשו וגאולים

3 בשובתו ולוא יצדק במתיר שרירות לבו וחושך יביט לדרכי אור בעין תמימים

4 לוא יתחשב לוא יזכה בכפורים ולוא יטהר במי נדה ולוא יתקדש בימים

5 ונהרות ולוא יטהר בכול מי רחץ טמא טמא יהיה כול יומי מאסו במשפטי

6 אל לבלתי התיסר ביחד עצתו כיא ברוח עצת אמת אל דרכי איש יכופרו כול

7 עוונותיו להביט באור החיים וברוח קדושה ליחד באמתו יטהר מכול

8 עוונותו וברוח יושר וענוה תכופר חטתו ובענות נפשו לכול חוקי אל יטהר

9 בשרו להזות במי נדה ולהתקדש במי דוכי ויהכין פעמיו להלכת תמים

10 בכול דרכי אל כאשר צוה למועדי תעודתיו ולוא לסור ימין ושמאול ואין

11 לצעוד על אחד מכול דבריו אז ירצה בכפורי ניחוח לפני אל והיתה לו לברית

12 יחד עולמים

13 למשכיל להבין וללמד את כול בני אור בתולדות כול בני איש

14 לכול מיני רוחותם באותותם למעשיהם בדורותם ולפקודת נגיעיהם עם

15 קצי שלומם מאל הדעות כול הווה ונהייה ולפני היותם הכין כול מחשבתם

16 ובהיותם לתעודותם כמחשבת כבודו ימלאו פעולתם ואין להשנות בידו

17 משפטי כול והואה יכלכלם בכול חפציהם והואה ברא אנוש לממשלת

18 תבל וישם לו שתי רוחות להתהלך בם עד מועד פקודתו הנה רוחות

19 האמת והעול במעון אור תולדות האמת וממקור חושך תולדות העול

20 וביד שר אורים ממשלת כול בני צדק בדרכי אור יתהלכו וביד מלאך

21 חושך כול ממשלת בני עול ובדרכי חושך יתהלכו ובמלאך חושך תעות

22 כול בני צדק וכול חטאתם ועוונותם ואשמתם ופשעי מעשיהם בממשלתו

23 לפי רזי אל עד קצו וכול נגיעיהם ומועדי צרותם בממשלת משטמתו

24 וכול רוחי גורלו להכשיל בני אור ואל ישראל ומלאך אמתו עזר לכול

25 בני אור והואה ברא רוחות אור וחושך ועליהון יסד כול מעשה[ו]

26 [ועל דרכי]הן כול עבודה [ועל דרכיהן כול עב]ודה אחת אהב אל לכול

Column IV

1 עדי עולמים ובכול עלילותיה ירצה לעד אחת תעב סודה וכול דרכיה שנא לנצח

2 ואלה דרכיהן בתבל להאיר בלבב איש ולישר לפניו כול דרכי צדק

אמת ולפחד לבבו במשפטי

3 אל ורוח ענוה ואורך אפים ורוב רחמים וטוב עולמים ושכל ובינה וחכמת

גבורה מאמנת בכול

4 מעשי אל ונשענת ברוב חסדו ורוח דעת בכול מחשבת מעשה וקנאת

משפטי צדק ומחשבת

5 קודש ביצר סמוך ורוב חסדים על כול בני אמת וטהרת כבוד מתעב כול

גלולי נדה והצנע לכת

6 בערמת כול וחבא לאמת רזי דעת   אלה סודי רוח לבני אמת תבל ופקודת

כול הולכי בה למרפא

7 ורוב שלום באורך ימים ופרות זרע עם כול ברכות עד ושמחת עולמים

בחיי נצח וכליל כבוד

8 עם מדת הדר באור עולמים

9 ולרוח עולה רחוב נפש ושפול ידים בעבודת צדק רשע ושקר גוה

ורום לבב כחש ורמיה אכזרי

10 ורוב חנף קצור אפים ורוב אולת וקנאת זדון מעשי תועבה ברוח זנות

ודרכי נדה בעבודת טמאה

11 ולשון גדופים עורון עינים וכובד אוזן קושי עורף וכיבוד לב ללכת בכול

דרכי חושך וערמת רוע ופקודת

12 כול הולכי בה לרוב נגיעים ביד כול מלאכי חבל לשחת עולמים באף

עברת אל נקבות לזעות נצח וחרפת

13 עד עם כלמת כלה באש מחשכים וכול קציהם לדורותם באבל יגון ורעת

מרורים בהייות חושך עד

14 כלותם לאין שרית ופליטה למו

15 באלה תולדות כול בני איש ובמפלגיהן ינחלו כול צבאותם לדורותם

ובדרכיהן יתהלכו וכול פעולת

16 מעשיהם במפלגיהן לפי נחלת איש בין רוב למועט לכול קצי עולמים כיא
אל שמן בד בבד עד קץ

17 אחרון ויתן איבת עולם בין מפלגותם תועבת אמת עלילות עולה ותועבת
עולה כול דרכי אמת וקנאת

18 ריב על כול משפטיהן כיא לוא יחד יתהלכו ואל ברזי שכלו ובחכמת כבודו
נתן קץ להיות עולה ובמועד

19 פקודה ישמידנה לעד ואז תצא לנצח אמת תבל כיא התגוללה בדרכי רשע
בממשלת עולה עד

20 מועד משפט נחרצה ואז יברר אל באמתו כול מעשי גבר וזקק לו מבני איש
להתם כול רוח עולה מתכמי

21 בשרו ולטהרו ברוח קודש מכול עלילות רשעה ויז עליו רוח אמת כמי נדה
מכול תועבות שקר והתגולל

22 ברוח נדה להבין ישרים בדעת עליון וחכמת בני שמים להשכיל תמימי דרך
כיא בם בחר אל לברית עולמים

23 ולהם כול כבוד אדם ואין עולה והיה לבושת כול מעשי רמיה עד הנה
יריבו רוחי אמת ועול בלבב גבר

24 יתהלכו בחכמה ואולת וכפי נחלת איש באמת וצדק וכן ישנא עולה
וכירשתו בגורל עול ירשע בו וכן

25 יתעב אמת כיא בד בבד שמן אל עד קץ נחרצה ועשות חדשה והואה ידע
פעולת מעשיהן לכול קצי

26 [...] וינחילן לבני איש לדעת טוב [ורע והואה ה]פיל גורלות לכול חי
לפי רוחו ב[...] ה[פ]קודה

Column V

1 וזה הסרך לאנשי היחד המתנדבים לשוב מכול רע ולהחזיק בכול אשר
צוה לרצונו להבדל מעדת

2 אנשי העול להיות ליחד בתורה ובהון ומשובים על פי בני צדוק הכוהנים
שומרי הברית ועל פי רוב אנשי

3 היחד המחזקים בברית על פיהם יצא תכון הגורל לכול דבר לתורה ולהון
ולמשפט לעשות אמת יחד וענוה

4 צדקה ומשפט ואהבת חסד והצנע לכת בכול דרכיהם אשר לוא ילך איש
בשרירות לבו לתעות אחר לבבו

5 ועיניוהי ומחשבת יצרו כ]י[א אם למול ביחד עורלת יצר ועורף קשה ליסד
מוסד אמת לישראל ליחד ברית

6 עולם לכפר לכול המתנדבים לקודש באהרון ולבית האמת בישראל והנלוים
עליהם ליחד ולריב ולמשפט

7 להרשיע כול עוברי חוק ואלה תכון דרכיהם על כול החוקים האלה בהאספם
ליחד כול הבא לעצת היחד

8   יבוא בברית אל לעיני כול המתנדבים ויקם על נפשו בשבועת אסר לשוב
אל תורת מושה ככול אשר צוה בכול

9   לב ובכול נפש לכול הנגלה ממנה לבני צדוק הכוהנים שומרי הברית
ודורשי רצונו ולרוב אנשי בריתם

10   המתנדבים יחד לאמתו ולהתהלך ברצונו ואשר יקים על נפשו להבדל
מכול אנשי העול ההולכים

11   בדרך הרשעה, כיא לוא החשבו בבריתו כיא לוא בקשו ולוא דרשהו
בחוקוהי לדעת הנסתרות אשר תעו

12   בם לאשמה והנגלות עשו ביד רמה לעלות אף למשפט ולנקום נקם
באלות ברית לעשות בם שפטים

13   גדולים לכלת עולם לאין שרית   אל יבוא במים לגעת בטהרת
אנשי הקודש כיא לוא יטהרו

14   כי אם שבו מרעתם כיא טמא בכול עוברי דברו ואשר לוא ייחד עמו
בעבודתו ובהונו פן ישיאנו

15   עוון אשמה כיא ירחק ממנו בכול דבר כיא כן כתוב מכול דבר שקר תרחק
ואשר לא ישוב איש מאנשי

16   היחד על פיהם לכול תורה ומשפט` ואשר לוא יוכל מהונם כול ולוא ישתה
ולוא יקח מידם כול מאומה

17   אשר לוא במחיר כאשר כתוב חדלו לכם מן האדם אשר נשמה באפו כיא
במה נחשב הואה כיא

18   כול אשר לוא נחשבו בבריתו להבדיל אותם ואת כול אשר להם ולוא ישען
איש הקודש על כול מעשי

19   הבל, כיא הבל כול אשר לוא ידעו את בריתו וכול מנאצי דברו ישמיד
מתבל וכול מעשיהם לנדה

20   לפניו וטמא בכול הונם וכיא יבוא בברית לעשות ככול החוקים האלה
להיחד לעדת קודש ודרשו

21   את רוחום ביחד בין איש לרעהו לפי שכלו ומעשיו בתורה על פי בני אהרן
המתנדבים ביחד להקים

22   את בריתו ולפקוד את כול חוקיו אשר צוה לעשות ועל פי רב ישראל
המתנדבים לשוב ביחד לבריתו

23   וכתבם בסרך איש לפני רעהו לפי שכלו ומעשיו להשמע הכול איש
לרעהו, הקטן לגדול ולהיות

24   פוקדם את רוחם ומעשיהם שנה בשנה להעלות איש לפי שכלו ותום דרכו
ולאחרו כנעוותו להוכיח

25   איש את רעהו בא[מ]ת וענוה ואהבת חסד לאיש   אל ידבר אל אחיהו באף או בתלונה

26   או בעורף [קשה ...] רוח רשע ואל ישנאהו [...]לבבר כי ביומו יוכיחנו
ולוא

Column VI

1. ישא עליו עון וגם אל יביא איש על רעהו דבר לפני הרבים אשר לוא
   בתוכחת לפני עדים באלה

2. יתהלכו בכול מגוריהם כול הנמצא איש את רעהו וישמעו הקטן לגדול
   למלאכה ולממון ויחד יואכלו

3. ויחד יברכו ויחד יועצו ובכול מקום אשר יהיה שם עשרה אנשים מעצת
   היחד אל ימש מאתם איש

4. כוהן ואיש כתכונו ישבו לפניו וכן ישאלו לעצתם לכול דבר והיה כיא
   יערוכו השולחן לאכול או התירוש

5. לשתות - הכוהן ישלח ידו לרשונה להברך בראשית הלחם או התירוש
   לשתות הכוהן ישלח ידו לרשונה

6. להברך בראשית הלחם והתירוש ואל ימש במקום אשר יהיו שם העשרה
   איש דורש בתורה יומם ולילה

7. תמיד עליפות איש לרעהו והרבים ישקודו ביחד את שלישית כול לילות
   השנה לקרוא בספר ולדרוש משפט

8. ולברך ביחד   זה הסרך למושב הרבים איש בתכונו הכוהנים ישבו
   לרשונה והזקנים בשנית ושאר

9. כול העם ישבו איש בתכונו וכן ישאלו למשפט ולכול עצה ודבר אשר
   יהיה לרבים להשיב איש את מדעו

10. לעצת היחד אל ידבר איש בתוך דברי רעהו טרם יכלה אחיהו לדבר   וגם
    אל ידבר לפני תכונו הכתוב

11. לפניו האיש הנשאל ידבר בתרו ובמושב הרבים אל ידבר איש כול דבר
    אשר לוא לחפץ הרבים וכיא האיש

12. המבקר על הרבים וכול איש אשר יש אתו דבר לדבר לרבים אשר לוא
    במעמד האיש השואל את עצת

13. היחד, ועמד האיש על רגלוהי ואמר יש אתי דבר לדבר לרבים אם יומרו
    לו ידבר וכול המתנדב מישראל

14. להוסיף על עצת היחד ידורשהו האיש הפקיד ברואש הרבים לשכלו
    ולמעשיו ואם ישיג מוסר יביאהו

15. בברית לשוב לאמת ולסור מכול עול ויהבינהו בכול משפטי היחד ואחר
    בבואו לעמוד לפני הרבים ונשאלו

16. הכול על דבריו וכאשר יצא הגורל על עצת הרבים יקרב או ירחק ובקורבו
    לעצת היחד לוא יגע בטהרת

17. הרבים עד אשר ידרושהו לרוחו ומעשו עד מולאת לו שנה תמימה וגם
    הואה אל יתערב בהון הרבים

18. ובמולאת לו שנה בתוך היחד ישאלו הרבים על דבריו לפי שכלו ומעשיו
    בתורה ואם יצא לו הגורל

19   לקרוב לסוד היחד על פי הכוהנים ורוב אנשי בריתם יקרבו גם את הונו
ואת מלאכתו אל יד האיש

20   המבקר אל מלאכת הרבים יכתבו בחשבון בידו ועל הרבים לוא יוציאנו אל
יגע במשקה הרבים עד

21   מולאת לו שנה שנית בתוך אנשי היחד ובמולאת לו השנה השנית יפקודהו
על פי הרבים ואם יצא לו

22   הגורל לקרבו ליחד יכתובהו בסרך תכונו בתוך אחיו לתורה ולמשפט
ולטוהרה ולערב את הונו ויהי עצתו

23   ליחד ומשפטו

24   ואלה המשפטים אשר ישפטו בם במדרש יחד על פי הדברים אם
ימצא בם איש אשר ישקר

25   בהון והואה יודע ויבדילהו מתוך טהרת רבים שנה אחת ונענשו את רביעית
לחמו ואשר ישיב את

26   רעהו בקשי עורף ודבר בקוצר אפים ל[פר]ע את יסוד עמיתו באמרות את
פי רעהו הכתוב לפנוהי

27   [והו]שיעה ידו לוא ונענש שנה אח[ת ... וא]שר יזכיר דבר בשם הנכבד
על כול ה[...]

Column VII

1   ואם קלל או להבעת מצרה או לכול דבר אשר לו   הואה קורה בספר או
מברך והבדילהו

2   ולוא ישוב עוד אל עצת היחד ואם באחד מן הכוהנים הכתובים בספר דבר
בחמה ונענש שנה

3   אחת ומובדל אל נפשו מן טהרת רבים ואם בשגגה דבר ונענש ששה
חודשים ואשר יכחס במדעו

4   ונענש ששה חודשים והאיש אשר יצחה בלי משפט את רעהו בדעה(א) ונענש שנה אחת

5   ומובדל ואשר ידבר את רעהו במרים או יעשה רמיה במדעו ונענש ששה חודשים ואם

6   ברעהו יתרמה ונענש שלושה חודשים ואם בהון היחד יתרמה לאבדו ישלמו

7   ברושו   [the actual text skips 7 lines here]

8   ואם לוא תשיג ידו לשלמו ונענש ששים יום ואשר יטור לרעהו אשר לוא
במשפט ונענש שנה אחת

9   וכן לנוקם לנפשו כול דבר ואשר ידבר בפיהו דבר נבל שלושה חודשים
ולמדבר בתוך דברי רעהו

10   עשרת ימים ואשר ישכוב וישן במושב הרבים   שלושים ימים וכן לאיש
הנפטר במושב הרבים

11   אשר לוא בעצה והנם, עד שלוש פעמים על מושב אחד ונענש עשרת ימים ואם יזקפו

12   ונפטר ונענש שלושים יום ואשר יהלך לפני רעהו ערום ולוא היה אנוש
ונענש ששה חודשים

13 ואיש אשר ירוק אל תוך מושב הרבים ונענש שלושים יום ואשר יוציא ידו מתוחת בגדו והואה

14 פוח ונראתה ערותו ונענש שלושים יום ואשר ישחק בסכלות להשמיע קולו ונענש שלושים

15 יום והמוציא את יד שמאולו לשוח בה ונענש עשרת ימים והאיש אשר ילך רכיל ברעהו

16 והבדילהו שנה אחת מטהרת הרבים ונענש ואיש ברבים ילך רכיל לשלח הואה מאתם

17 ולוא ישוב עוד והאיש אשר ילון על יסוד היחד ישלחהו ולוא ישוב ואם על רעהו ילון

18 אשר לוא במשפט ונענש ששה חודשים והאיש אשר תזוע רוחו מיסוד היחד לבגוד באמת

19 וללכת בשרירות לבו אם ישב, ונענש שתי שנים ברשונה לא יגע בטהרת הרבים

20 ובשנית לוא יגע במשקה הרבים ואחר כול אנשי היחד ישב ובמלואת

21 לו שנתים ימים ישאלו הרבים   על דבריו ואם יקרבהו ונכתב בתכונו ואחר ישאל אל המשפט

22 וכול איש אשר יהיה בעצת היחד   על מלואת עשר שנים

23 ושבה רוחו לבגוד ביחד ויצא מלפני

24 הרבים ללכת בשרירות לבו לוא ישוב אל עצת היחד עוד ואיש מאנשי היח[ד אשר ית]ערב

25 עמו בטהרתו או בהונו אש[ר לוא על פי] הרבים והיה משפטו כמוהו לש[לחהו מאתם ויהיו]

Column VIII

1 בעצת היחד שנים עשר איש וכוהנים שלושה, תמימים בכול הנגלה מכול

2 התורה לעשות אמת וצדקה ומשפט ואהבת חסד והצנע לכת איש עם רעהו

3 לשמור אמונה בארץ ביצר סמוך ורוח נשברה ולרצת עוון בעושי משפט

4 וצרת מצרף ולהתהלך עם כול במדת האמת ובתכון העת בהיות אלה בישראל

5 נכונה עצת היחד באמת   למטעת עולם בית קודש לישראל וסוד קודש

6 קודשים לאהרון עדי אמת למשפט ובחירי רצון לכפר בעד הארץ ולהשב

7 לרשעים גמולם   היאה חומת הבחן פנת יקר בל

8 יזדעזעו יסודותיהי ובל יחישו ממקומם   מעון קודש קודשים

9 לאהרון בדעת כולם לברית משפט ולקריב ריח ניחוח ובית תמים ואמת בישראל

10 להקם ברית לחוקות עולם והיו לרצון לכפר בעד הארץ ולחרוץ משפט רשעה ואין עולה בהכון אלה ביסוד היחד שנתים ימים בתמים דרך

11 יבדלו קודש בתוך עצת אנשי היחד וכול דבר הנסתר מישראל ונמצאו לאיש

12 הדורש אל יסתרהו מאלה מיראת רוח נסוגה   ובהיות אלה ליחד

13 בישראל בתכונים האלה יבדלו מתוך מושב אנשי העול ללכת למדבר לפנות שם את דרך הואהא

14 כאשר כתוב במדבר פנו דרך .... ישרו בערבה מסלה לאלוהינו

15 הואה מדרש התורה [אשר] צוה ביד מושה לעשות ככול הנגלה עת בעת

16 וכאשר גלו הנביאים ברוח קודשו וכול איש מאנשי היחד ברית

17   היחד אשר יסור מכול המצוה דבר ביד רמה אל יגע בטהרת אנשי הקודש

18   ועל ידע בכול עצתם עד אשר יזכו מעשיו מכול עול להלך בתמים דרך וקרבהו

19   בעצה על פי הרבים ואחר יכתב בתכונו וכמשפט הזה לכול הנוסף ליחד

20   ואלה המשפטים אשר ילכו בם אנשי התמים קודש איש את רעהו

21   כול הבא בעצת הקודש ההולכים בתמים דרך כאשר צוה כול איש מהמה

22   אשר יעבר דבר מתורת מושה ביד רמה או ברמיה ישלחהו מעצת היחד

23   ולוא ישוב עוד ולוא יתערב איש מאנשי הקודש בהונו ועם עצתו לכול

24   דבר ואם בשגגה יעשה והובדל מן הטהרה ומן העצה ודרשו המשפט

25   אשר לוא ישפוט איש ולוא ישאל על כול עצה שנתים ימים אם תמם דרכו

26   במושב במדרש ובעצה [על פי הרבים] אם לוא שגג עוד עד מולאת לו שנתים

27   ימים

Column IX

1   כיא על שגגה אחת יענש שנתים ולעושה ביד רמה לוא ישוב עוד אך השוגג

2   יבחן שנתים ימים לתמים דרכו ועצתו על פי הרבים ואחר יכתוב בתכונו ליחד קודש

3   בהיות אלה בישראל ככול התכונים האלה ליסוד רוח קודש לאמת

4   עולם לכפר על אשמת פשע ומעל חטאת ולרצון לארץ מבשר עולות ומחלבי זבח
     ותרומת

5   שפתים למשפט כניחוח צדק ותמים דרך כנדבת מנחת רצון בעת ההיאה יבדילו אנשי

6   היחד בית קודש לאהרון להיחד קודש קודשים ובית יחד לישראל ההולכים בתמים

7   רק בני אהרון ימשלו במשפט ובהון ועל פיהם יצא הגורל לכול תכון אנשי היחד

8   והון אנשי הקודש ההולכים בתמים אל יתערב הונם עם הון אנשי הרמיה אשר

9   לוא הזכו דרכם להבדל מעול וללכת בתמים דרך ומכול עצת התורה לוא יצאו ללכת

10   בכול שרירות לבם ונשפטו במשפטים הרשונים אשר החלו אנשי היחד לתיסר בם

11   עד בוא נביא ומשיחי אהרון וישראל

12   אלה החוקים למשכיל להתהלך בם עם כול חי לתכון עת ועת ולמשקל איש ואיש

13   לעשות את רצון אל ככול הנגלה לעת בעת ולמוד את כול השכל הנמצא לפי העתים ואת

14   חוק העת להבדיל ולשקול בני הצדוק   לפי רוחום ובבחורי העת להחזיק על פי

15   רצונו כאשר צוה ואיש כרוחו כן לעשות משפטו ואיש כבור כפיו לקרבו ולפי שכלו

16   להגישו וכן אהבתו עם שנאתו   ואשר לוא להוכיח ולהתרובב עם אנשי השחת

17   ולסתר את עצת התורה בתוך אנשי העול ולהוכיח דעת אמת ומשפט צדק לבוחרי

18   דרך איש כרוחו כתכון העת להנחימם בדעה וכן להשכילם ברזי פלא ואמת בתוך

19   אנשי היחד להלך תמים איש את רעהו בכול הנגלה להם היאה עת פנות הדרך

20   למדבר ולהשכילם כול הנמצא לעשות בעת הזואת והבדל מכול איש ולוא הסר דרכו

21   מכול עול ואלה תכוני הדרך למשכיל בעתים האלה לאהבתו עם שנאתו שנאת עולם

22   עם אנשי שחת ברוח הסתר לעזוב למו הון ועמל כפים כעבד למושל בו וענוה לפני

23   הרודה בו ולהיות איש מקנא לחוק ועתו ליום נקם לעשות רצון בכול משלח כפים

24   ובכול ממשלו כאשר צוה וכול הנעשה בו ירצה בנדבה וזולת רצון אל לו יחפץ

25   [ובכו]ל אמרי פיהו ירצה ולוא יתאוה בכול אשר לוא צוהו ולמשפט אל יצפה תמיד

26   [...נ]היה יברך עושיו ובכול אשר יהיה יס[פר ...] שפתים יברכנו

CHAPTER 12

The *Habakkuk* Pesher
(1QpHab)*

Column I

1 (*The Vision which Habakkuk the Prophet saw: How long, O Lord, shall*) *I cry out for help and You not*

2 (*hear?* [1:2a]. Its interpretation concerns the be)ginning of the Last

3 (Generation . . . and what is com)ing to them.

4 (*I cry out to You, "Violence!" and You do not deliver me* [1:2b] . . .

5 *Why do you show me Evil and cause me to lo)ok upon suffering,*[1]

6 *because robbery and violence are before me* [1:3a]. Its interpretation concerns those who rebel against) God with oppression and Treachery

7 (. . . th)ey rob Ri(ches. There) *is strife*

8 (*and division roused up* [1:3b]. Its interpretation is because of this *str*)*ife* and . . . *because of this the Torah falls into disuse,*

9 (*and Judgement does not go forth triumphantly* [1:4a]. The interpretation) is that they rejected the *Torah* of God

10 (. . . *because the Wicked encompas*)*sed the Righteous* [1:4b].

11 (Its interpretation is *the Wicked* is the Wicked Priest and *the Righteous*) is the Righteous Teacher,

12–13 (. . . *because*) *of this Judgement goes forth* (*perverted. See the Nations and behold, marvel and be astonished, for I*

14–15 *will work a wonder in your days, which you will not believe even if it*)

---

* This is a *new* translation, so there will be usages and translations in it beyond what is to be found in MZCQ and JJHP. But we have chosen to leave these books as they were to preserve their original form.

Column II

1 *is told you* [1:5]. (Its interpretation concerns) the Traitors with the Man
2 of Lying, because they did not (believe what the) Righteous Teacher
   expounded from the mouth
3 of God. (And it concerns) the Trai(tors to the Laws of God and the
   New Covenant), since they
4 did not believe in the Covenant of God (and defiled His) Holy Name.
5 Likewise the interpretation of the passage (concerns the Trai)tors to
   the
6 Last Days. These are the Vio(lent Ones and the Covenant-Brea)kers,
   who did not believe
7 all that they heard that was (going to happen to) the Last Generation
   from the mouth of
8 the Priest, (in whose heart) God put (the intelligence) to interpret all
9 the words of His Servants the Prophets, (through whom) God foretold
10 all that was coming to His people . . . *For behold, I raise up the*
11 *Chaldeans, a (cruel and aggressive) Nation* [1:6a].
12 Its interpretation concerns the *Kittim,* w(ho ar)e swift and strong
13 in war, causing many to perish (by the sword and all the world to
    fall under) the Dominion
14 of the *Kittim* . . . and the Evil Ones . . . they do not believe
15 in the Laws of (God . . . *who march to the ends of the earth*
16 *to take possession of populated places which are not their own* [1:6b]. Inter-
    preted, this means . . .

Column III

1 And they march across the plain, smiting and plundering the cities of
   the earth.
2 For this is what is meant by *taking possession of populated places, which are
   not their own. They are frightening*
3 *and terrible, for their Judgement and Majesty proceed from themselves* [1:7].
4 Interpreted, this concerns the *Kittim,* the fear and dread of whom is
   upon all
5 the Nations. And in their Council, all their Evil plotting is planned in
   advance. They deal with all Peoples with cunning and deceitfulness,
6 *Their horses are swifter than leopards and more swift than*
7 *wolves at night. Their horsemen ride and hurl themselves from afar,*

8 *and they swoop down like an eagle anxious to eat. All come to do violence and the breath*

9 *of their faces is like the East wind* [1:8–9a]. (Its interpretation) concerns the *Kittim*, who

10 trample the earth with their horses and pack animals.

11 And they come from afar, from the islands of the sea, to consu(me[2] a)ll the Peoples *like an insatiable eagle.*

12 And they speak to all the Peoples with anger, ill-will, fury, and livid

13 faces, for this is what is

14 meant by *the breath on their faces is like the East wind, and they gather captives like sand* [1:9b]

15 ... its interpretation ...

Column IV

1 *They scoff at Kings and they ridicule Leaders* [1:10a]. Its interpretation is that

2 they jeer at the mighty and sneer at honorable men. They deride

3 kings and ministers, and they make light of large armies.

4 *They laugh at fortified cities, and they batter down earthworks and capture them* (1:10b).

5 Its interpretation concerns the Leaders of the *Kittim*, who despise

6 the Fortresses of the Peoples,[3] laughing at them contemptuously.

7 With a mighty host, they encircle and capture them, and through terror

8 and fear, they surrender (them) into their hands, and they destroy them because of the sins of their inhabitants.[4]

9 *Then the wind shifts and passes by, and he makes of this, his power*

10 *for his god* [1:11]. Its interpretation concerns the Leaders of the *Kittim*,

11 who, in their guilty Council House["the Senate"], pass by one man

12 following another. Their Leaders come one after the other

13 to despoil the ea(rth. Th)is is *his power for his god.*

14 Its interpretation ... (t)o the Peoples ... (*Are You not from Everlasting,*

15 *O Lord my God, my Holy One. We shall not die. O Lord, you have*)

Column V

1 *ordained them for Judgement. O Rock, for chastisement You have established them. Your eyes are too pure*

2 *to view Evil and You cannot look upon iniquity* [1:12–13a].

3 The interpretation of the passage is that God will not destroy His people by the hand of the Nations.

4 But rather by the hand of His Elect, God will execute Judgement on all the Nations, and with their *chastisement,*

5 all the Evil Ones of His (own) people, who kept His Commandments only when convenient, will be punished.

6 For this is what He meant when He said: *Your eyes are too pure to look*

7 *upon Evil.* Its interpretation is that they did not lust after their eyes during the Era

8 of Evil. *Why do you stare, O Traitors, and remain silent when the Wicked swallowed*

9 *one more Righteous than he* [1:13b]? Its interpretation concerns the House of Absalom

10 and the Men of their Council who were silent at the time of the *chastisement* of the Righteous Teacher

11 and did not aid him against the Man of Lying, who rejected

12 the *Torah* in the midst of all their Assembly ["their Church"]. *And You deal with man like the fish of the sea,*

13 *like creeping things, to rule over him. All of them he takes up with a fishhook, catching them in a net*

14 *and collecting them (in a dragnet. This is why he sacrifices to his net.) This is why he rejoices*

15 (*and celebrates, and burns incense to his dragnet, since by them*) *his portion is fat*

16 (*and his eating is plenteous* [1:14–16]. Its interpretation concerns the Evil Ones of the Rulers)

Column VI

1 of the *Kittim,* who collect their Riches with all their booty

2 like *the fish of the sea.*[5] As for what was said about *thus sacrificing to his net*

3 *and burning incense to his dragnet,* its interpretation is that they

4 sacrifice to their standards and worship their weapons of war,

5 since it is because of them *his portion is fat and his eating plenteous.*

6 Its interpretation is that they parcel out their yoke and

7 their taxes,[6] consuming [literally "eating" or "devouring"] all the Peoples[7] year by year,

8 giving many countries over to the sword. *Therefore, his sword is always unsheathed*

9 *to decimate the Nations mercilessly* [1:17].

10 Its interpretation concerns the *Kittim*, who destroy Many by the sword,

11 Young men, grown-ups, and old people, women and children, and *have no pity* even on the fruit of the womb.

12 *But I will stand up upon my watchtower*

13 *and take my stand upon my fortress*[8] *and spy out to see what He will say*

14 *to me, and wh(at I shall ans)wer when I am reproved* [2:1]. *And the Lord answered*

15 *(and said, "Write down the vision and make it pla)in on tablets,*[9] *so that*

16 *he may read it on the run* [2:2].

Column VII

1 And God told Habakkuk to write what was going to happen

2 to the Last Generation, but He did not inform him when the Age would end.

3 And concerning what He said about *reading* and *running*

4 Its interpretation concerns the Righteous Teacher, to whom God made known

5 all the Mysteries of the words of His Servants the Prophets. *For there shall yet be a vision*

6 *of the Appointed Time, and it will speak of the End and will not Lie* [2:3a].

7 Its interpretation is that the Last Era will be extended and shall exceed all

8 that the Prophets have foretold, since the Mysteries of God are aston- ishing [the "Delay of the *Parousia*" in Christian theology].

9 *If it tarries, wait for it, for it will surely come and not*

10 *delay* [2:3b]. Its interpretation concerns the Men of Truth,

11 the Doers of the *Torah*, whose hand will not slacken from the service

12 of Truth,[10] though the Final Age be prolonged before them. Because

13 all the Eras of God will come to their Appointed End, as He determined

14 them in the Mysteries of His Intelligence. *Behold his (soul) is puffed up*[11] *and not Upright*

15 *(within him* [2:4a]). Its interpretation is that their sins will be doubled upon them,

16 and they will not be pleased with their Judgement.

17 *And the Righteous shall live by his Faith* [2:4b].

Column VIII

1 Its interpretation concerns all the Doers of the *Torah* ["*Torah-Doers*"] in the House of Judah [that is, *all Jews*], whom

2 God will save from the House of Judgement because of their works and their Faith[12]

3 in the Righteous Teacher. *And furthermore the arrogant man is betrayed by Riches which*

4 *cannot comfort, but rather he opens his mortal soul as to Hell and like death cannot be satisfied.*

5 *But rather all the Nations are gathered to him and the Peoples are collected unto him.*

6 *Do they not all satirize him and make up sayings against him.*

7 *And they say, "Woe to the man who multiplies unto himself that which is not his. How long will he continue to burden himself*

8 *with debts* [2:5–6]?" Its interpretation concerns the Wicked Priest, who

9 at the beginning of his Office [literally "Standing"] was called by the name of Truth. But when he ruled

10 in Israel, his heart became *puffed up* and he deserted God and betrayed the Laws for the sake of

11 Riches. And he stole and collected the Riches of the Men of Violence, who rebelled against God.

12 And he took the Riches of the Peoples, heaping upon himself guilty Sinfulness,

13 and he acted in the Ways of Abominations of all unclean pollution. *Will not suddenly*

14 *Your torturers arise and your tormenters awake? You will be their spoils,*

15 *since you spoiled many Nations, all the Remainder of the Peoples will plunder you* [2:7–8].

16 (Its interpretation con)cerns the Priest [meaning, "the *High Priest*"] who rebelled

17 (and bro)ke the Laws of (God . . .)

Column IX

1 They afflicted him with the Judgements upon Evil and inflicted upon him the outrages of Evil pollutions[13]

2 in taking Vengeance upon *the flesh of his corpse* [not the redundant "body of his flesh" one often sees here]. As for

3 the words, *since you spoiled many Nations, all*

4 the Additional Ones of the Peoples will plunder you, its interpretation concerns the Last Priests of Jerusalem,

5 who gathered Riches and profiteered from the spoils of the Peoples[14].

6 But in the Last Days, their Riches, together with their booty, will be given over to the hand of

7 the Army of the *Kittim*, because they are *the Additional Ones of the Peoples* [*Yeter ha-'Amim*[15]].

8 *Because of the Blood of men and the violence done to the land, the township, and all its inhabitants* [2:8].

9 Its interpretation concerns the Wicked Priest, whom, as a consequence of the Evil he did to the Righteous

10 Teacher and the Men of his Council, God delivered to the hand of his enemies to afflict him

11 with torturing (and) to consume with bitternesses of soul, because he condemned[16]

12 His Elect. *Woe to the profiteer's profiteering, Evil unto his house, who places his nest*

13 *high up to escape the power of Evil. You have devised shame*

14 *for your house by cutting off many Peoples and sinned against your soul. For*

15 *the stones will shout from the walls and the beams of wood will answer it* [2:9–11].

16 (The interpretation of the passage) concerns the (Priest), who ...

Column X

1 *Its stone* will be for oppression and *its beams of wood* for stealing. And concerning what

2 it says, *cutting off many Peoples and the sins of your soul,*

3 its interpretation concerns the House of Judgement,[17] which God will deliver in

4 (rendering) His Judgement in the midst of many Peoples, and He will arraign him [literally, "lead him"] there

5 and condemn him in their midst and judge him with Fire and brimstone.[18] *Woe*

6 *unto him who builds a City on Blood and establishes a township on Unrighteousness. Behold, does*

7 *this not come from the Lord of Hosts, that the Peoples labor for the sake of Fire*

8 *and the Peoples tire themselves out for the sake of Nothingness* [2:12–13]?

9 The interpretation of the passage is about the Spouter of Lying, who leads Many astray,[19]

10 in order to build a Worthless City upon Blood and erect an Assembly
   [even possibly "Church"] upon Lying,[20]

11 for the sake of his Glory, tiring out Many with a Worthless Service
   and instructing them

12 in works of Lying, so that their *'amal* ["suffering works"][21] will be
   of Emptiness [or "count for nothing"—cf. the famous "Empty
   Man" allusion in James 2:20]. And they will be brought

13 to the (same) Judgements of Fire, with which they insulted [even
   possibly "blasphemed"] and vilified the Elect of God.

14 *For the earth will be filled with the Knowledge of the Glory of the Lord like
   waters*

15 *covering the s(ea* [2:14]). The interpretation of the passage is that

16 in their return (to Go)d ... (The Spouter)

Column XI

1 of Lying, and afterwards this Knowledge, like *waters of the sea,* will be
   abundantly revealed to them.

2 *Woe to the one who causes his neighbor to drink, pouring out*

3 *his fury unto drunkenness* [also, possibly "to make them drunk"] *in order
   to look upon their Festivals* [2:15—in the received Habakkuk, this is
   "look upon their privy parts"].

4 Its interpretation concerns the Wicked Priest, who

5 pursued after the Righteous Teacher *to swallow him* in his hot
   ["venomous"]

6 anger in ["with"] his House of Exile [or "Exiled House"]. And at the
   completion of the Festival of Rest

7 of the Day of Atonements, he appeared to them *to swallow them,*

8 causing them to stumble [literally "and cast them down"] on the Fast
   Day, the Sabbath of their Rest. *You are satiated more*

9 *with shame than Glory. Drink also and stagger* [in the received version, this
   is "Let your foreskin be uncovered"]!

10 *For the Cup of the Right Hand of the Lord* [playing on "the Cup of
   Trembling"] *will come around to you and shame*

11 *shall cover your Glory* [2:16].

12 Its interpretation concerns the (High) Priest, whose shame was
   greater than his Glory,

13 Because he did not circumcize the foreskin of his heart [here the

"foreskin"/"privy parts" imagery, but now harking back to "the Zadokite Covenant" of Ezek 44:7–9] and walked in his Way of

14 satiety, in the way of drinking his fill.

15 But the Cup of the Wrath of God will swallow him,[22] adding to (*his shame* and *dis*)*grace, and the pain* . . .

16 (*Because the violence of Lebanon shall overwhelm you and the destruction of the dumb beasts*)

Column XII

1 *shall terrify you, because of the Blood of Man* [literally, "Adam"[23]] *and the violence to the land, the township, and all its inhabitants* [2:17].

2 The interpretation of the passage concerns the Wicked Priest. He will be paid

3 the reward which he rewarded the Poor [*Ebionim*],[24] because *Lebanon*

4 is the Council of the Community and *the dumb beasts* are the Simple Ones of Judah doing

5 the *Torah* [here the language of "doing"/"Doer" of vii.11 and viii.1 above]. Just as he conspired to destroy the Poor [*Ebionim*],[25]

6 so too God would Judge him [the Wicked Priest] to destruction. And as to the saying, *because of the Blood*

7 *of the township and the violence of the land*, its interpretation is: *the township* is Jerusalem.

8 where the Wicked Priest committed his works of Abominations [or "Abominable works"], polluting

9 the Temple of God. *The violence of the land* relates to the cities of Judah, where

10 he stole the sustenance ["Riches"] of the Poor.[26] *Of what use are graven images, whose makers formed*

11 *a casting and images of Lying, in whom, the craftsman puts his trust when he*

12 *creates dumb idols* [2:18]. The interpretation of the passage concerns all the

13 idols of the Nations, which they create in order to serve and bow down

14 to them. These will not save them on the Day of Judgement.[27]

15 *Wo(e, to anyone saying) to pieces of wood, "Awake!" and to dumb (stone), "Arise!"*

16 *This can guide? Behold, it is covered with gold and silver,*

17 *and there is no spirit at all within it. But the Lord is in His Holy Temple,*

Column XIII

1 *be silent before him, all the world* [2:19–20]. Its interpretation concerns all
   the Nations,
2 who serve stone and wood. But on the Day
3 of Judgement God will destroy all the Servants of idols
4 and Evil Ones from off the earth.[28]

NOTES

[1] The first use of "'*amal*'/"suffering" or "works", which will become so important later in the document *vis à vis* the ideologies of the "Righteous Teacher" and "the Liar".

[2] The verb here is literally "eat", important in terms of the predatory activities of Herodians and Romans.

[3] Since we identify "the Peoples" as a circumlocution for Herodians, these would be Herodian Fortresses like Cypros, Hyrcania, Machaeros, etc.

[4] This, of course, is the *mea culpa* cry, turned against the Jews in New Testament theology, as for instance in Mt 27:25.

[5] Here, a variation of the "nets"/"fishermen" imagery applied in the Gospels to Jesus' Apostles.

[6] An overt clear allusion to Roman "*tax-farming*", which we interpret to apply to Herodians.

[7] Again, "eating" used seemingly to describe Roman conquests.

[8] This is the explanation for the curious passage in the Damascus Document (iv.10–12): "And with the Completion of the number of these years, there will be no more joining to the House of Judah. But rather a man will stand up upon his own watchtower", where "*mezudo*"/"net" has been mistakenly transcribed instead of "*mezoro*"/"watchtower" as here in Hab 2:1.

[9] The same "tablets" reappear in Paul's "fleshy tablets of the heart" attack on the Jerusalem Leadership of the Church in 2 Co 3:3–6. In attacking written credentials, not the Apostleship by the Holy Spirit, Paul states that on these "fleshy tablets of the heart", one writes not "with ink, but with the Spirit of the living God, not on stone . . . not on the letter, but the New Covenant of the Spirit". He then goes on to assert, in an attack not calculated to win him many friends in Jerusalem, "for the letter kills, but the Spirit gives life".

[10] See Ga 4:15, where, as Paul sees it, he is reckoned "the Enemy" by his communities for telling them "Truth", i.e., he "does not lie", also reiterated elsewhere in the Pauline corpus. This "Enemy" terminology is generally reckoned as having been applied to Paul by "the Ebionites" or "Jewish Christians".

[11] Paul uses this same terminology, "being puffed up", in 1 Co 4:18 and 8:1. The latter is extremely important, because it occurs in the context of criticizing those whose

"consciences are so weak" they will not eat "food sacrificed to idols" and are *vegetarians*—an attack on the Jamesian Leadership of "the Jerusalem Church".

[12] Cf. the Letter of James 2:22. Literally the word "works" here is that "*'amal*" found in Is 53:11—in this context "suffering works".

[13] We translate this "pollutions" not "diseases", because of the verb "they inflicted upon him" connected with it. Diseases are not "outrages", nor are they "inflicted" by anyone on anyone.

[14] In our view, Herodian "tax-farming". Again, that the "Chief Priests" profiteer from these activities proves the point.

[15] Here the definite article "*he*"/"the" is deliberately added. This concretizes the parallel between "the Peoples"/Herodians and "the Additional Ones of the Peoples"/Romans.

[16] As in ix.1 above.

[17] This is the same "*Beit ha-Mishpat*"/"House of Judgement" as in the exposition of Hab 2:4 in viii.2 earlier, which makes it clear that the meaning is eschatological and akin to the decision of Judgement.

[18] I.e., "the Last Judgement".

[19] "Leading astray" is the opposite of the proper "justifying" activity "making Many Righteous" of the Righteous Teacher.

[20] Here the meaning of "Blood" is esoteric and symbolic, because the "Spouter of Lying" is being described.

[21] Now this "*'amal*" or redemptive works are those taught by the Liar, which are "Empty" of saving efficacy. See also the allusion to the individual, who teaches Salvation by Faith as the "Empty Man" or "Man of Emptiness" in Ja 2:20. The "works" this individual teaches are "Empty" ones just like here in the Habakkuk *Pesher*.

[22] See Rev 14:6 and 16:9.

[23] The actual Hebrew here is "Adam" which some could have seen as having to do with "the Blood" of the Messiah and a possible covert or esoteric reference to the "Jewish Christian" or Ebionite "Primal Adam" ideology.

[24] The language here is taken directly from Is 3:9–11, applied in all early Church literature to the death of James.

[25] The note of "conspiring against the Poor" is very important. There is conspiracy here.

[26] Because this has to do with "the Wicked Priest" and not "the Spouter of Lying" and his ideology, the "Blood" here now is real again. This is the "stealing Riches" and "plundering" we heard about earlier.

[27] Now we really have the "Day of Judgement" referred to. Compare this with the *Koran* 82:17–19, also on the "Day of Judgement".

[28] Again, as in Islam, "Servants of Idols" are "idolators". The allusion to "Evil Ones" probably refers to backsliders, accommodators, and "Traitors" among non-idolators or Jews. Josephus, Paul, Rabbi Yohanan ben Zacchai (the proverbial founder of Rabbinic Judaism), the Herodian Agrippa II (if he was even considered to be Jewish, which is doubtful), his sister Bernice (Titus' mistress), and Philo's nephew Tiberius Alexander (whom even Josephus says, deserted the religion of his fathers), Titus' military commander at the siege of Jerusalem, would be good examples of these from a Qumran perspective.

Column I

1 [...עד אנה יהוה] שועתי ולוא

2 [תשמע   פשרו על מ]חלת דור

3 [אחרון...ועל הבא]ות עליהם

4 [אזעק אליך חמס ... נזע]קו על

5 [החמס למה תראני און וע]מ[ל תב]יט

6 [ושוד וחמס לנגדי   פשרו כי מרדו ב]אל בעשק ומעל

7 [נגד יהוה] יג[זו]לו ה[רון ויה]י ריב

8 [ומדון ישא   פשרו כיא מר]יבה ... על כן תפוג תורה

9 [ולוא יצא לנצח משפט   פשרו] אשר מאשו בתורת אל

10 [לא נשפטו כמשפט כיא רשע מכתי]ר את הצדיק

11 [פשרו הרשע הוא הכהן הרשע והצדיק] הוא מורה הצדק

12-13 [...ע]ל כן יצא המשפט

14-15 [מעוקל...כיא פעל פעל בימכם ה]לוא ת[אמינו כיא]

Column II

1 יסופר   [פשרו על] הבוגדים עם איש

2 הכזב כי לוא [האמינו את אשר פשר] מורה הצדק מפיא

3 אל ועל הבוג[דים בחוקי אל ובברית] החדשה כיא לוא

4 האמינו בברית אל [ויחללו] את ש[ם ק]ודשו

5 וכן   פשר הדבר [על הבו] גדים לאחרית

6 הימים המה ערי[צים מפיר הברי]ת אשר לוא יאמינוא

7 בשומעם את כול הב[אות על] הדור האחרון מפי

8 הכוהן אשר נתן אל ב[ל]בו בינ]ה לפשור [את] כול

9 דברי עבדיו הנביאים [אשר על] ידם ספר אל את

10 כול הבאות על עמו ו[...כ]יא הנני מקים את

11 הכשדאים הגוי ה[מר והנמהר]

12 פשרו על הכתיאים א[שר המ]ה קלים וגבורים

13 במלחמה לאבד ... בממשלת

14 הכתיאים ורשעים ... ולוא יאמינו

15 בחוקי [אל ... ההולך למרחבי ארץ]

16 ל[רשת משכנות לוא לו   פשרו...]

Column III

1 ובמישור ילכו לכות ולבוז את ערי הארץ

2 כי הוא אשר אמר לרשת משכנות לוא לו איום

3   ונורא הוא ממנו משפטו ושאתו יצא

4   פשרו על הכתיאים אשר פחדם ואמתם על כול

5   הגואים ובעצה כול מחשבתם להרע וב[נ]כל ומרמה

6   ילכו עם כול העמים וקול מנמרים סוסו וחדו

7   מזאבי ערב   פשו ופרשו פרשו מרחוק

8   יעופו כנשר חש לאכול כולו לחמס יבוא מגמת

9   פניהם קדימ   [פשרו] על הכתיאים אשר

10   ידושו את הארץ בסוס[יהם] ובבהמתם וממרחק

11   יבואו מאיי הים לאכו[ל] את כ[ו]ל העמים כנשר

12   ואין שבעה ובחמה וב[קצף ובח]רן אף וזעף

13   אפים ידברו עם [כול העמים כי]א הוא אשר

14   אמר מ[גמת פניהם קדים ויאסוף כחו]ל שבי

15   [...פשרו...במלכים]

Column IV

1   יקלס ורזנים משחק לו   פשרו אשר

2   ילעיגו על רבים יבזו על נכבדים במלכים

3   ושרים יתעתעו וקלסו בעם רב והוא

4   לכול מבצר ישחק ויצבור עפר וילכדהו

5   פשרו על מושלי הכתיאים אשר יבזו על

6   מבצרי העמים ובלעג ישחוקו עליהם

7   ובעם רב יקיפום לתפושם ובאמה ופחד

8   ינתנו בידם והרסום בעוון היושבים

9   בהם אז חלף רוח ויעבר וישם זה כוחו

10   לאלוהו   פשר[ו ע]ל מושלי הכתיאים

11   אשר בעצת בית אשמתם יעבירו איש

12   מלפני רעיהו מושלי[הם וז]ה אחר זה יבואו

13   לשחית את הא[רץ ז]ה כוחו לאלוהו

14   פשרו ... [א]ל העמים ... [הלוא אתה מקדם

15   יהוה אלהי קדושי לוא נמות יהוה]

Column V

1   למשפט שמתו וצור למוכיחי יסדתו טהור עינים

2   מראות ברע והבט אל עמל לוא תוכל

3   פשר הדבר אשר לוא יכלה אל את עמו ביד הגוים

4   וביד בחירו יתן אל את משפט כול הגוים ובתוכחתם

5   יאשמו כול רשעי עמו אשר שמרו את מצוותו

בצר למו כיא הוא אשר אמר טהור עינים מראות   6

ברע   פשרו אשר לוא זנו אחר עיניהם בקץ   7

הרשעה למה תביטו בוגדים ותחריש בבלע   8

רשע צדיק ממנו   פשרו על בית אבשלום   9

ואנשי עצתם אשר נדמו בתוכחת מורה הצדק   10

ולוא עזרוהו על איש הכזב   אשר מאס את   11

התורה בתוך כול ע[ד]ם ותעש אדם כדגי הים   12

כרמש למשל בו כו[לה בחכ]ה יעלה ויגרהו בחרמו   13

ויספהו [במכמרתו על כן יזבח] לחרמו על כן ישמח   14

[ויגיל ויקטר למכמרתו כיא בהם שמן] חלקו   15

[ומאכלו בראה   פשרו על רשעי מושלי]   16

Column VI

הכתיאים ויוסיפו את הונם עם כול שללם   1

כדגת הים ואשר אמר על כן יזבח לחרמו   2

ויקטר למכמרתו   פשרו אשר המה   3

זבחים לאותותם וכלי מלחמותם המה   4

מוראם כיא בהם שמן חלקו ומאכלו ברי   5

פשרו אשר המה מחלקים את עולם ואת   6

מסם מאכלם על כול העמים שנה בשנה   7

לחריב ארצות רבות על כן יריק חרבו תמיד   8

להרוג גוים ולא יחמל   9

פשרו על הכתיאים אשר יאבדו רבים בחרב   10

נערים אשישים וזקנים נשים וטף ועל פרי   11

בטן לוא ירחמו על משמרתי אעמודה   12

ואתיצבה על מצורי ואצפה לראות מה ידבר   13

בי ומ[ה אשיב ע]ל תוכחתי ויענני יהוה   14

[ויאמר כתוב חזון ובא]ר על הלוחות למען ירוץ   15

הקורא בו   [פשרו]   16

Column VII

וידבר אל אל חבקוק לכתוב את הבאות על   1

(על) הדור האחרון ואת גמר הקץ לוא הוד(י)עו   2

ואשר אמר למען ירוץ הקורא בו   3

פשרו על מורה הצדק אשר הודיעו אל את   4

כול רזי דברי עבדיו הנבאים כי עוד חזון   5

למועד יפח לקץ ולוא יכזב   6

פשרו אשר יאריך הקץ האחרון ויתר על כול 7

אשר דברו הנביאים כיא רזי אל להפלה 8

אם יתמהמה חכה לו כי בוא יבוא ולוא 9

יאחר   פשרו על אנשי האמת 10

עושי התורה אשר לוא ירפו ידיהם מעבודת 11

האמת בהמשך עליהם הקץ האחרון כיא 12

כול קיצי אל יבואו לתכונם כאשר חקק 13

ל[הם] ברזי ערמתו הנה עופלה לוא יושרה 14

[נפשו בו]   פשרו אשר יכפלו עליהם 15

[חטאתיהם ולא י]רצו במש[פ]טם 16

[וצדיק באמונתו יחיה] 17

Column VIII

פשרו על כול עושי התורה בבית יהודה אשר 1

יצילם אל מבית המשפט בעבור עמלם ואמנתם 2

במורה הצדק ואף כיא הון יבגוד גבר יהיר ולוא 3

ינוה אשר הרחיב כשאול נפשו ו[ה]וא כמות לוא ישבע 4

ויאספו אליו כול הגוים ויקבצו אליו כול העמים: 5

הלוא כולם משל עליו ישאו ומליצי חידות לו 6

ויומרו הוי המרבה ולוא לו עד מתי יכביד עלו 7

עבטט   פשרו על הכוהן הרשע אשר 8

נקרא על שם האמת בתחילת עומדו וכאשר משל 9

בישראל רם לבו ויעזוב את אל ויבגוד בחוקים בעבור 10

הון ויגזול ויקבוץ הון אנשי [ח]מס אשר מרדו באל 11

והון עמים לקח לוסיף עליו עון אשמה ודרכי 12

ת[וע]בות פעל בכול נדת טמאה הלוא פתאום ויקומו 13

[נושכ]יך ויקיצו מזעזעיכה והיתה למשיסות למו 14

כי אתה שלותה גוים רבים וישלוכה כול יתר עמים 15

[פשר הדבר ע]ל הכוהן אשר מרד 16

[ויפי]ר חוקי [אל...] 17

Column IX

נגועו במשפטי רשעה ושערוריות מחלים 1

רעים עשו בו ונקמות בגוית בשרו ואשר 2

אמר כי אתה שלותה גוים רבים וישלוכה כול 3

יתר עמים   פשרו על כוהני ירושלים 4

האחרונים אשר יקבוצו הון ובצע משלל העמים 5

ולאחרית הימים ינתן הונם עם שללם ביד 6

חיל הכתיאים   כיא המה יתר העמים 7

מדמי אדם וחמס ארץ קריה וכול יושבי בה 8

פשרו על הכוהן ה[ר]שע אשר בעוון מורה 9

הצדק ואנשי עצתו נתנו אל בידי אריביו לענותו 10

בנגע לכלה במרירי נפש בעבור אשר הרשיע 11

על בחירו   הוי הבוצע בצע רע לביתו לשום 12

במרום קנו לנצל מכף רע יעצתה בשת 13

לביתכה קצוות עמים רבים וחוטי [נפ]שכה כיא 14

א[בן מ]קיר תזעק וכפיס מעץ יעננה 15

[פשר הדבר] על ה[כוהן] אשר ... 16

Column X

להיות אבניה בעשק וכפיס עיצה בגזל ואשר 1

אמר קצות עמים רבים וחוטי נפשכה 2

פשרו הוא בית המשפט אשר יתן אל את 3

משפטו בתוך עמים רבים ומשם יעלנו למשפט 4

ובתוכם ירשיענו ובאש גופרית ישפטנו הוי 5

בונה עיר בדמים ויכונן קריה בעולה הלוא 6

הנה מעם יהוה צבאות יגעו עמים בדי אש 7

ולאמים בדי ריק ייעפו 8

פשר הדבר על מטיף הכזב אשר התעה רבים 9

לבנות עיר שוו בדמים ולקים עדה בשקר 10

בעבור כבנדה לוגיע רבים בעבודת שוו ולהרותם 11

במ[ע]שי שקר להיות עמלם לריק בעבור יבואו 12

למשפטי אש אשר גדפו ויחרפו את בחירי אל 13

כיא תמלא הארץ לדעת את כבוד יהוה כמים 14

יכסו על הי[ם]   פשר הדבר [כיא] 15

בשובם [...]ל ... [מטיף] 16

Column XI

הכזב ואחר תגלה להם הדעת כמי 1

היים לרב הוי משקה רעיהו מספח 2

חמתו אף שכר למען הבט אל מועדיהם 3

פשרו על הכוהן הרשע אשר 4

רדף אחר מורה הצדק לבלעו בכעס 5

חמתו אבית גלותו ובקץ מועד מנוחת 6

7   יום הכפורים הופיע אליהם לבלעם

8   ולכשילם ביום צום שבת מנוחתם שבעתה

9   קלון מ(כ)בוד שתה גם אתה והרעל

10   תסוב עליכה כוס ימין יהוה וקיקלון

11   על כבודכה

12   פשרו על הכוהן אשר גבר קלונו מכבודו

13   כיא לוא מל את עורלת לבו וילך בדרכו

14   הרווה למען ספות הצמאה וכוס חמת

15   [א]ל תבלענו לוסיף [קלון וקיק]לון ומכאוב

16   [כיא חמס לבנון יכסך ושוד בהמות...]

Column XII

1   יחת(כ)ה מדמי אדם וחמס ארץ קריה וכול יושבי בה

2   פשר הדבר על הכוהן הרשע לשלם לו את

3   גמולו אשר גמל על אביונים כיא הלבנון הוא

4   עצת היחד והבהמות המה פתאי יהודה עושה

5   התורה אשר ישופטנו אל לכלה

6   כאשר זמם לכלות אביונים ואשר אמר מדמי

7   קריה וחמס ארץ פשרו הקריה היא ירושלים

8   אשר פעל בה הכוהן הרשע מעשי תועבות ויטמא את

9   מקדש אל וחמס ארץ המה ערי יהודה אשר

10   גזל הון אביונים מה הועיל פסל כיא פסל יצרו

11   מסיכה ומרי שקר כיא בטח יצר יצריו עליהו

12   לעשות אלילים אלמים פשר הדבר על כול

13   פסלי הגוים אשר יצרום לעובדם ולשתחות

14   להמה והמה לוא יצילום ביום המשפט

15   ה[וי אומר] לעץ הקיצה [עורי לאב]ן דומה

16   [הוא יורה הנה הוא תפוש זהב וכסף]

17   וכל רוח אין בקרבו ויהוה בהיכל קדשו]

Column XIII

1   הס מלפניו כול ה[א]רץ פשרו על כול הגוים

2   אשר עבדו את האבן ואת העץ וביום

3   המשפט יכלה אל את כול עובדי העצבים

4   ואת הרשעים מן הארץ

Glossary of Hebrew Terms

I have preferred simple Hebrew transliterations and, therefore, have abjured diacritical markings. Beginning *aleph*s also are not transliterated. In transliterating the Hebrew letter *tzadi*, I use "*z*", despite confusions in transliterating *zayin*, in order to conserve the common spelling of expressions like *Zaddik*, Zadok, Nazoraean, etc. (there are several *tzadis*, but few *zayins*). I preferred the double "*s*" in *Hassidim*.

abeit-galuto, a defective expression in 1QpHab, xi.6 connected with the arrest/ destruction of the Righteous Teacher. While obscure and usually translated "House of his Exile", it most likely has a different meaning altogether relating to the Wicked Priest's *judicial conspiracy* to destroy the Righteous Teacher, i.e., "he pursued (after) the Righteous Teacher to destroy *him* in *his* hot anger in *his Beit-Galut*"—meaning, "*his Beit-din*"/"*Beit-Mishpat*"/"*his* Guilty Trial". In fact, as we show, it probably relates to "the High Priest's House" where the Sanhedrin was "exiled" from the Temple Mount in the days preceding the Uprising against Rome.

Aharonim/Dor ha-Aharon, the Last/Last Generation; the opposite of *ha-Rishonim*, the First. Just as the First Covenant was associated with "the *Rishonim*", the New Covenant was associated with "the *Aharonim*" of the Last Times; note how Paul refers to himself as "last" in 1 Co 15:8, a nuance not lost in New Testament parodies of the expression, cf. also *ha-Kez ha-Aharon* (the Last Era or Last End) and *Aharit ha-Yamim* (the Last Days).

'Am/'Amim, "People"/"Peoples". In the Habakkuk *Pesher* and Damascus Document referring to people—primarily Gentiles—"led astray" by a guilty Establishment and its "ways" (cf. CD, viii.8, 16, and 47 and 1QpHab, viii.5, 11, and ix.5). Particularly the plural has the sense of "Herodians", i.e., "the Kings of the Peoples" (CD, viii.10); cf. also "*Yeter ha-'Amim*"— "the Additional Ones of the Gentiles" for Romans below.

'amal, "works", *'amalam*, "their works"; equivalent to "suffering works" or "works with soteriological force" as per the usage in Is 53:11f.—where it

occurs in conjunction with other familiar Qumranisms, such as *"Da'at"*, *"Rabbim"*, *"nephesh"*, *"Zaddik"*, etc.). In 1QpHab, viii.2 and x.12, used in relation to both "Jamesian" works and "Pauline" works, the former (with *"amanatam"* below) in the context of eschatological exegesis of Hab 2:4; the latter, the "empty works" of "the Liar"/"Empty Man".

Amanatam, "their Faith". A pregnant expression in 1QpHab, viii.2 found together with *"'amalam"* in the exegesis of Hab 2:4's "the Righteous shall live by his Faith" and interpreted to mean, their Faith in the Righteous Teacher; in ii.2 and ii.4 the usage *he'eminu* ("believed"/"did not believe") is an ironic reference to the central focus of the teaching of the "Man of Lying"/"Scoffing".

'amod/'omdim, "stand up"/"standing"; usually translated in Qumran texts as "come"/"coming", but evoking Ezek 37:10's "they stood up" and carrying something of the connotation of "be resurrected"; cf. precisely this use in Dan 12:13 and its reflection in *Lam. R*, ii.3.6. Found in the Damascus Document both in the context of eschatological exegesis of the Zadokite Covenant and allusion to the Messianic return; for the latter, see also *Lam. R*, intro, xxiv, applying this usage to the "return of Moses and the Patriarchs". There is also a direct relationship with "the Standing One" in Jewish Christian/Elkasaite/Ebionite ideology directly related too to the idea of "the Primal Adam" in these traditions.

'Ani (pl. *'Aniyyim*), also *'Anayyei-Arez*, "the Meek" or "Downtrodden"; one of the sect's several interchangeable forms of self-designation. The equivalent of similar New Testament allusions; used synonymously with *"Ebionim"*/ "the Poor", and *"Dallim"*.

'Anshei-(H)amas, "Men of Violence"; a synonym of *'Arizim/'Arizei-Go'im* below and most likely "the Men of War" in CD, viii.37—"who walked with the Man of Lying". In 1QpHab, viii.11 the allusion is to the guilty "Riches", which the Wicked Priest "collects" through them.

Anshei-Hesed, the Men of Piety or Pious Ones equivalent to the *"Hassidim"*; mistranslated as "Famous Men" in Ecclesiasticus.

Anshei Kodesh-Tamim, "the Men of Perfect Holiness"; equivalent to such other Qumran usages characterizing communal membership as "the Men of Perfect Holiness" or the "Perfection of Holiness" (*Anshei-Tamim ha-Kodesh*), "the Perfect of the Way" (*Tamimei-Derech*), and "the Poor Ones of Piety" (*Ebionei-Hesed*); cf. Paul on "Perfection of Holiness" in 2 Co 7:1. Probably meant to imply *Perfect* Naziritism.

'Arizim, "the Violent Ones"; connected in 1QpHab, ii.6 and 10f. with "the Man of Lying", and "Covenant-Breakers"; cf. the parallel New Testament expression "Men of Violence" and the *"Anshei-(H)amas"*/" *'Amim"* above.

'Arizei-Go'im, "the Violent Ones of the Gentiles"; in 4QpPs 37, ii.20 and iv.10 they play an analogous role to Josephus' "Idumaeans" and "pay back" the Wicked Priest for his destruction of the Righteous Teacher.

'Avlah, Unrighteousness, Evil or Sinning; sometimes translated as "Lying" as in

"the township on Lying" erected by the Liar in 1QpHab, x.6 or the imagery of 1QS, iv.9–17.

'avodah, work in the sense of "service" or "mission". To be distinguished from the more soteriological " *'amal*" above and "*ma'aseh*"/"*ma'asim*" below. Often used when discussing the "mission" or "service" of the Liar (cf. *'avodat-shavo*—worthless work; 1QpHab, x.11 and *'avodat-tum'ah*—work of pollution; 1QS iv.10) and those breaking off association with him in CD, viii.30, 1QS, viii.22, and ix.8; see also *le'ovdam*, serving them (i.e., serving idols) in 1QpHab, xii.14.

balla'/Bela', as used in the Temple Scroll, varying the language of Num 4:20 and Job 20:15 and playing on all the "swallowing" language at Qumran from Belial to *leval'o*/*leval'am*/*teval'enu*; possibly important for linking the notice in 11QT, xlvi.10 to the Temple Wall Affair directed against Agrippa II. Cf. "Bela' ", an Edomite King in Ge 14:2ff. .and 36:32f. and its variations "Belial" (CD, iv.14f. and 1QH, iv.10) and "Balaam" (Rev 2:14ff., 2 Pe 2:15, and Jude—the first three all making allusion to "nets" and "snares"; the last, "food sacrificed to idols"). One should also compare this to the claim Acts makes on behalf of Paul and his possible "Benjaminite" ancestry.

Beit ha-Mishpat, "House of Judgement"; in 1QpHab, viii.2 used in conjunction with " *'amalam*", "*Amanatam*", "doing *Torah*", and "being saved" in the "eschatological exegesis of Hab 2:4., x.3 concretizes it as the actual decision or decree of eschatological Judgement of "Fire and brimstone" which God delivers through His Elect "in the midst of many Nations" on all Gentiles and Jewish backsliders; cf. "*Mishpatei-Esh*" in x.13, 2 Pe 2:9, Jude 15, Rev 20:4ff., etc., and "*Mishpat*", "*Yom ha-Mishpat*" below.

Beit-Yehudah, the House of Judah or simply *Jews*; as used in 1QpHab, viii.2 to be distinguished from the Ephraim usage in 4QpNah, i.e., Jews as opposed to Gentile "*Nilvim*" misled by a Lying Teacher. Together with " *'Osei-Torah*", it restricts the soteriological efficacy of the exegesis of Hab 2:4 in a twofold manner, that is, only to Jews, and of these, only to *Torah*-Doers; cf. too its use in the eschatological exegesis of Ezek 44:15 in CD, iv.11.

be'orot, "in skins"; as used in 11QT, xlvii.13ff., always connected to "things" or "food sacrificed to idols", a key element in James' directives to overseas communities as conserved in Acts 15:29 and 21:25 (in Acts 15:20, "the pollutions of the idols") and reflected in 1 Co 8:1ff., 10:19ff., 2 Co 6:16 (note the specific reference to "Belial" and "Light" and "Dark" imagery), and Rev 2:14ff. (note the attribution of the license to consume such "food" to "Balaam" and the allusions accompanying it to "snare" and "fornication" as in CD, iv.13ff. In regard to this last, one should note the possible play on "Be'or", the father at once of both "Bela' " and "Balaam". This kind of word-play is known in *b. San* 105a in the *Talmud*).

beza', profiteered, as in 1QpHab, ix.5 on how "the Last Priests of Jerusalem profiteered from the spoils—or looting—of the Peoples" (" *'Amim*", i.e.,

Herodians and "Violent Gentiles" generally); cf. the same usage in CD, viii.7.

Bnei-Zadok, the "Sons of Zadok"; usually considered to imply genealogical descent, however as used at Qumran—particularly in the Damascus Document—incorporating a play on the meaning of the root *Z-D-K* and carrying thereby a figurative sense; equivalent to many parallel usages like "Sons of Light", "Sons of Truth", "Sons of Righteousness", etc.; when used eschatologically, also equivalent to New Testament expressions like "Sons of Resurrection" (even "Sons of God").

Bogdim, "Traitors", an important expression in the *Pesharim* and the Damascus Document, denoting those within the Community who "turned aside from the Way" no longer following the Law (CD, i.12f.). In 1QpHab, ii.1ff. referred to with "the Man of Lying" as "Covenant-Breakers" and synonymous with "the House of Absalom and those of their persuasion" in v.8ff. These did not "believe" what they heard "in the End of Days" from the Righteous Teacher. That these include "Violent Gentiles" is made clear from the "*'Arizei-Go'im*" usage and a comparison of CD, viii.4f. with viii.16; cf. New Testament inversions/parodies.

Chohanei-Yerushalaim ha-Aharonim, in 1QpHab, ix.4f. "the Last Priests of Jerusalem" who "profiteered from the spoil of the Peoples" and whose wealth would be given over in the Last Days to the Army of the *Kittim*; probably reflective of first-century euphemisms like "High Priests"/"Chief Priests".

Da'at, Knowledge, a basic concept at Qumran very much connected with the terminology of Is 53:11 and the process of Justification generally; in some vocabularies, "*Gnosis*".

Dal (pl. *Dallim*), "the Poor" or "the Meek", related to "*'Ani*" above and "*Ebion*" below.

Derech, "the Way", related to 1QS, viii–ix's exegesis of Is 40:3, the Noachic "Perfection" notation, "Straightening", and New Testament "Way" allusions; often inverted when "the Way of the People(s)", the Way "of the Kings of the Peoples", and "the Ways of the Traitors", "Abominations", "Uncleanness", "fornication", etc. are at issue.

Ebion (pl. *Ebionim*), "the Poor"; in 1QpHab, xii.3ff. related to the predatory activities of the Wicked Priest and his destruction of the Community's Leadership. Another of the sect's interchangeable forms of self-designation, as well as the name applied by the early Church to "Jewish Christians".

Ebionei-Hesed, "the Poor Ones of Piety" (1QH, v.23); another of the sect's interchangeable forms of self-designation combining, like such parallel usages as "*Tamimei-Derech*", "*Nimharei-Zedek*", "*Anshei Kodesh-Tamim*", etc., two fundamental notations.

Emet, "Truth", a basic concept at Qumran; together with *Hesed, Zedek,* and *Da'at* perhaps the most basic; often used in conjunction with *Derech*, Foundation and Cornerstone imagery, and *Da'at*. An expression like "Sons of Your

Truth" parallels formulations like "Sons of Light", "Sons of Zadok", "Sons of *Hesed*", and corresponding New Testament allusions.

'Ezah/'Azat ha-Yahad, "Council" or "Community Council", with interesting resonances with "the Jerusalem Council"; also having the possible connotation of "their approach" or "their persuasion" as in " *'azatam*" in 1QpHab, v.10.

ger-nilveh, resident alien. An important allusion playing on the sense of "joining" or "being attached to" of "*nilveh*". Its use in 4QpNah, ii.9 prepares the way for a clearer understanding of the exegesis of "the Zadokite Statement" in CD, iv and elucidation of "the *Peta'ei*-Ephraim" in 4QpNah, iii.5f.; see *nilvul/Nilvim* below.

geviyyah/geviyyat, sometimes translated "body", but actually "corpse"; a pivotal usage for correctly identifying the Wicked Priest in 1QpHab, ix.1f.'s "they inflicted the Judgements of Evil by committing on him the outrages of Evil pollutions in taking vengeance on *the flesh of his corpse*".

hamato, "his wrath"; in 1QpHab, xi.5f., the "angry wrath" with which "the Wicked Priest pursued the Righteous Teacher". Though thought in xi.14f. to relate to his "drunkenness", the allusion, which plays on and inverts xi.6's imagery of "anger" and "consuming", is to that Divine "Cup of Wrath" which would be "poured out" upon the Wicked Priest. Cf. Rev 14:9f. in precisely this vein: "He shall drink the Wine of God's Wrath poured unmixed into the Cup of His Anger, and he shall be tormented in Fire and brimstone ..." For the latter image see 1QpHab, x.5 (also relating to the Wicked Priest): "He will judge him with Fire and brimstone."

Hassidim, literally "the Pious Ones"; the original behind the expression Hassidaeans and probably the basis of the Greek transliteration "Essenes"; cf. "*Anshei-Hesed*" and the "*Ebionei-Hesed*" above.

Hesed, "Piety"; the first part of the "*Hesed*" and "*Zedek*" dichotomy, descriptive of man's relationship to the Deity, i.e., "thou shalt love the Lord thy God". Taken with the second, "loving one's neighbor" or "Righteousness towards one's fellow man", the two comprise the sum total of "the commands of all Righteousness" and epitomize the "Opposition" ideological orientation; the root of the terminology "*Hassidim*".

hittif, "pouring out"/"spouting"; as in CD, viii.13's "of Lying". For CD, 1.14f. "the Man of Scoffing" (or "the Comedian") "poured out on Israel the waters of Lying leading them astray in a trackless void without a Way", which combines "Lying", "Jesting", "Spouting", and "leading astray" imageries with inverted allusion to "wilderness" and "Way" terminologies; see "*Mattif*"/"*Mattif ha-Chazav*".

hok, "statute" or "Law"; at the heart of 1QS, viii–ix's exposition of Is 40:3's "Way in the wilderness", "the Way" being "the study of the Law". The phrase, "zealous for the Law", specifically occurs in ix.23 accompanied by reference to "the Day of Vengeance"; cf. "*kin'at Mishpetei-Zedek*" in iv.4. Note CD, i.20's "*yapheiru hok*" to describe the "pursuit after" the *Zaddik*—

the synonym of 1QpHab, ii.6's *Mephirei ha-Brit* echoed too in 1QpHab, viii.17.

Hon, "Riches"; one of CD, iv.17ff.'s "Three Nets of Belial"; in CD, vi.14ff. and viii.4ff. (including "fornication" imagery), directed against the Establishment—probably Herodian; in 1QpHab, viii.10ff. and ix.4ff. related to the "gathering"/"robbing the Poor"/"profiteering from the Gentiles" activities of "the Last Priests/Wicked Priest".

lechalah/lechalot, the language of "destruction", applied in 1QpHab, xii.5f. to the conspiracy to destroy the Righteous Teacher and the Poor, i.e., "as he plotted to destroy the Poor", so too would "God condemn him to destruction"—in this context synonymous with "*leval'o*" "swallow him"/"*leval'am*" "swallow them".

leva l'o/leval'am/teval'enu, the language of "swallowing"/"destruction"; applied in 1QpHab, xi.5ff. to the confrontation between "the Righteous Teacher" and "the Wicked Priest" and the "destruction" of both. Its resonances with the "Bela'"/"Belial" equivalence are purposeful, not to mention the "*hayil bala'*" of 11QT, xlvi.10/Job 20:15 (i.e., "swallowing wealth"). Cf. also "Balaam" as "Swallower of the People" in *b. Sanh* 105a. In this sense, all aspects of the *B-L-'* usage were considered illustrative of the activity most characterizing the Herodian Establishment, i.e., "swallowing".

losif, the language of "gathering", applied in 1QpHab, viii.12 to the Wicked Priest's/Last High Priests' "gathering Riches" and "profiteering from the spoils of the Peoples" and a consonant harvest of blame.

ma'as, "reject"/"deny"/"speak derogatorily about"; a catchword for the legal posture of "the Lying Spouter" and those of his "Assembly" or "persuasion"; in 1QpHab, v.11f. the former "rejected" the *Torah* in the midst of their whole Assembly" or "Church". Cf. the parallel, more general, use in i.10, 1QS, iii.5f., and CD, vii.9, viii.18f., and 31f.

ma'asim/ma'aseihem, "works"/"their works"; generally "works of the Law," paralleling the usage in the Letter of James and the use of "*'amal*" in 1QpHab and Is 53:11. Also used with inverted sense as in 1QpHab, x.11f.'s the Liar's "instructing them in Lying works" (*ma'asei-Sheker*) and 1QS, iv.23's "*ma'asei-Remiyyah*", "Works of Deceit"; also see "*ma'asei-To'evot*" in 1QpHab, xii.8.

Ma'oz, "Protection" or "Shield"; in 1QH, vii.8ff. and 23ff. related to "Fortress", "strengthening", "building", "Wall", "Foundations", "Stone", and "Cornerstone" imagery; it parallels the "*Oblias*"/"Protection"/"Bulwark" allusion applied to James in early Church testimony and related to "Stone" and "Pillar" imagery in the New Testament generally.

Mattif/Mattif ha-Chazav, "the Spouter"/"Pourer Out of Lying"; a variation of the "*Ish ha-Chazav*" (the Man of Lying) and the "*Ish ha-Lazon*" (the Man of Jesting/Scoffing/Comedian) imagery at Qumran, incorporating plays on what appear to have been his characteristic activities, "pouring out" words or waters—even perhaps speaking with his "Tongue" or "in tongues"— and "Lying".

Mephirei ha-Brit, "Covenant-Breakers"; synonymous with "the *Bogdim*"/"House of Absalom" in 1QpHab, ii.1ff. and v.8ff., and related to the "breaking" charge in Ezek 44:7ff. and Ja 2:10ff. The opposite of 1QS, v.2ff's "Sons of Zadok" as "Covenant-Keepers".

Migdal, "Tower"/"Fortress"/"Bulwark"; in 1QH, vii.8ff. applied together with the language of "Strength", "Stone", "Wall", "Cornerstone", "building" and "Foundations" imagery to the person of the Righteous Teacher.

Mishpat, "Judgement"; used in 1QpHab, v.4ff. in conjunction with "*Beit ha-Mishpat*" above; expressive of that Judgement God would make by "the hand of His Elect" (i.e., "the Bnei-Zadok" in CD, iv.3f.) on all Gentiles and backsliding Jews; cf. "*Beit ha-Mishpat*" above, "*Yom ha-Mishpat*" below, and 1QS, iv.4's "*kin'at Mishpetei-Zedek*" ("zeal for the Judgements of Righteousness"—the opposite of 1QpHab, ix.1's "*Mishpetei-Rish'ah*").

Moreh-Zedek/Moreh ha-Zedek, the "Righteous Teacher" or "the Teacher of Righteousness".

nephesh-Zaddik (see also *nephesh-Ebion* and *nephesh-'Ani*), "the soul of the *Zaddik*"; terminology remounting to Is 53:11f. paralleling "heart" and "body" imagery generally at Qumran and in Ezek 44:7ff., etc. Cf. CD, i.20 where "*nephesh-Zaddik*" is used synonymously with "*Moreh ha-Zedek*" and "*nephesh-Ebion*" and "*nephesh-'Ani*" in 1QH, ii.32, iii.25, v.6, etc.

niddah/niddat, "unclean"/"uncleanness"; often used at Qumran in conjunction with the imagery of "*tum'ah*" (pollution), as for instance in 1QpHab, viii.13, CD, xii.1f., 1QS, iv.10 ("*Darchei-Niddah*", replete with "Lying" and "fornication" imagery), and the Temple Scroll generally.

nilvu/Nilvim, "joined"/"Joiners"; evoked in 4QpNah, iii.5 in relation to the "*Peta'ei*-Ephraim" and in eschatological exegesis of Ezek 44:15 in CD, iv.3 (also echoed in 4QpNah, ii.9's "*ger-nilveh*"). Es 9:27 concretizes it as connotative of Gentiles "attaching themselves" to the Jewish Community, which in turn helps elucidate the "Ephraim"/"City of Ephraim"/"Simple Ones of Ephraim" usages. Probably synonymous in other vocabularies with the terminology "God-Fearers".

Nozrei ha-Brit/Nozrei Brito, "the Keepers of His Covenant"; cf. Ps 25:8ff., and Ps 119, where the expression is used synonymously with "*Shomrei ha-Brit*"—the qualitatively precise definition of "the Sons of Zadok" in 1QS, v.2ff.; also "*britcha yinzor*" in Deut 33:9 and 4QTest. The allusions "*Nozrim*"—Hebrew terminology denoting "Christians"—and "Zadokites" can be viewed, therefore, as variations on a theme.

'oseh ha-Torah/'Osei ha-Torah, "doing *Torah*"/"the Doers of the *Torah*"; the expression "*'Osei ha-Torah*" limits the soteriological scope of the exegeses of Hab 2:3 and 2:4 in 1QpHab, vii.11ff. to "*Torah*-Doers in the House of Judah". "Doers"/"doing"/"Breakers"/"keeping" usages are also reflected in the language of Ja 1:22ff. "*'Oseh ha-Torah*" defines xii.4f.'s "*Peta'ei-Yehudah*", distinguishing it from 4QpNah, iii's "*Peta'ei*-Ephraim" and tying it to the "Keepers of the Covenant" terminology. The root of "*ma'aseh*"/ "*ma'asim*".

Peta'ei-Yehudah/*Peta'ei*-Ephraim, "the Simple Ones of Judah"/"Simple Ones of Ephraim"; in 1QpHab, xii.4f. the former are the "*Torah*-doing" Community rank and file. In 4QpNa, iii.5f. the latter must be associated with Gentile "*Nilvim*", who, it is hoped, "will once again join themselves to Israel" (cf. "*ger-nilveh*" in ii.9). In 8f. they are associated with being led astray by "Deceivers . . . teaching their Lies, a Tongue of their Lies, Deceitful lips, and misleading the Many". Cf. also the use of "Little Ones" and "Samaritans" in New Testament usage.

Rabbim, "the Many", used at Qumran to designate the rank and file of the Community, who were presumably the beneficiaries of the justifying activities (whether via "suffering works" or imparted "Knowledge") of the Righteous Teacher/Community Council; the usage goes back to the vocabulary of Is 53:11f.—cf. also its use in the Dan 12 passage noted above. Its sense is reversed in 1QpHab, x.11's "wearing out Many with worthless work" and 4QpNah, ii.8's "leading Many astray" both relating to activities of "the Man of Lying".

Rasha'/*Resha'im*, "Evil"/"Evil Ones"; usually connected in the *Pesharim* to "the Wicked Priest", but sometimes, as in 1QpHab, v.9f., to the "Man of Lying".

Remiyyah, "Deceit"; in 1QS, viii.22 and ix.8 tied to covert infractions of the Law and in 1QS, viii.22ff., ix.8ff. (reflected in CD, viii.30) to consonant bans on work, table-fellowship, or common purse; cf. "Deceit"/"Deceitful works" in 1QS, iv.9 and 23 and "Deceitful lips" in 4QpNah, ii.8.

Rishonim, "the First"; to be viewed in conjunction with allusions to "the Last" and resonating with New Testament parodies of both; in CD, i.4ff. and iv.9, specifically denoting the *Zaddikim* of old (or "the Forefathers") with whom God made "the First Covenant".

Ruah-Emet, in 1QS, iv.21 (amid allusion to baptism, etc.), "Spirit of Truth"; a variation of the language of the "Holy Spirit". In viii.12 this relationship to "the Holy Spirit" is made explicit. Also to be viewed in the context of several contraries more or less typifying "the Spirit" of "the Lying Scoffer", i.e., "Lying", "fornication", "insults", "Evil", "Darkness", etc. in 1QS, iv.9ff.

shavo, "worthless"; in 1QpHab, x.10f. used to characterize the Community's perception of the Liar's activities, i.e., "the Worthless City" and the "worthless service with which he tires out Many" (cf. Ja 1:26 on his "worthless Religion", "heart of Deceit", and "Tongue").

Sheker/*ma'asei-Sheker*, "Lying"/"works of Lying"; the terminology is part and parcel of the "Lying"/"Spouting"/"boasting" imagery at Qumran. Often accompanied by allusion to "the Tongue" or "lips" and used in conjunction with reference to "works", baptismal imagery, or "leading astray".

Shomrei ha-Brit, "Keepers of the Covenant", 1QS, iv.2ff.'s qualitatively precise definition of "the Sons of Zadok", harking back to allusions in Ezek 44:6ff, and Psalms; note the parallel represented by "*Nozrei-Brito*" and the contrast represented by "*Mephirei ha-Brit*"/"Covenant Breakers".

Tamim/Tamimim, "the Perfect"; also sometimes, "Perfection"—a fundamental notion at Qumran based on references to Noah in Ge 6:9 as "Righteous and Perfect in his Generation"; the relationship to the parallel New Testament notation (cf. Mt 5:48, 19:21, Ja 1:4,, 17, 25, 2:22, etc.) is intrinsic.

To'evot, "Abominations"—*Darchei-To'evot*, "Ways of Abominations" in 1QpHab, viii.12f. Here and in xii.8, those of the Wicked Priest, particularly his "pollution of the Temple"/"Temple treasure" through violent tax-collecting and "robbing the Poor". Part and parcel of the language of "polluting the Temple"/"breaking the Covenant" in Ezek 44:6ff.; in the Temple Scroll, related to forbidden foods (xlviii.6), marriage with nieces (lxvi.11f.; also referred to as *"niddah"*), and Gentiles (lx.17ff. and lxii.16).

Tom, "Perfect"/"Perfection"; *Tom-Derech/Tamimei-Derech*, "Perfection of the Way"/"the Perfect of the Way"; also linked to expressions based on Is 40:3 like *"Yisharei-Derech"*, "the Straight" or "Upright of the Way".

tum'ah/teme' ha-Mikdash/yitame' et Mikdash-El, "pollution"/"pollution of the Temple of God", generally tied to a demand for "separation" (cf. 11QT, xlvi.9ff. and CD, iv.17ff.); with *"To'evot"* part and parcel of the charges relating to the admission of foreigners into the Temple in Ezek 44:7, as well as in consonant "Zadokite"/"Zealot" ideologies. As used in 1QpHab, xii.8f., directed against the Wicked Priest who did not "circumcize the foreskin of his heart" (Ezek 44:9), and in viii.13, 1QS, v.19f., and CD, xii.1f. linked to *"niddah"*.

yazdik-Zaddik (yazdiku-Zaddikim), the "Justification" ideology at Qumran based on the terminology of Is 53:11 (and to a lesser extent, Is 5:23); cf. also its use in Dan 12:3 above and see *"Zaddik"* and *"Zedakah"* below.

yazzilem/yazzilum, "save them"/"be saved"; the language of "Salvation", associated with the language of the "House of Judgement"/"Day of Judgement". The first in 1QpHab, viii.1f.'s exegesis of Hab 2:4 refers to the "Salvation of the Righteous"; the second in xii.14ff., the condemnation of "the Servants of Idols (Gentile Idolators) and Evil Ones" (here backsliding Jews; cf. 2 Pe 2:9 and 3:7).

yehalluhu, "pollute it". This plural usage is attached to the singular allusion to *"balla' "/"Bela' "* in 11QT, xlvi.11 and forms the background to "the Zadokite Statement" in Ezek 44:6ff., where the ban on "bringing strangers uncircumcized in heart and flesh into My Temple to pollute it" is enunciated.

Yeter ha-'Amim, "the Remnant" or "Additional Ones of the Gentiles"; in 1QpHab, ix.7 specifically identified with "the Army of the *Kittim* ", i.e., the Romans; see *'Amim*.

yikboz, "gathering"; in 1QpHab, viii.11 and ix.5 having to do with the *Darchei To'evot* or "gathering" activities of the Wicked Priest/Last Priests via the instrument of Unruly Gentiles; in this context "gathering" wealth—see also *Iosif*.

Yom ha-Mishpat, "Day of Judgement", linking up with the usages *"Mishpat"/*

"*Beit ha-Mishpat*" and "*yazzilem*"/"*yazzilum*" and used eschatologically in 1QpHab, xii.14 and xiii.2f., i.e., "on the Day of Judgement God would destroy all the Idolators and Evil Ones from the Earth".

Zaddik/Zaddikim, "the Righteous"/"the Righteous One(s)"; the terminology is highly developed in Jewish *Kabbalah* and Jewish Resurrection theory. Via the Is 53:11 "*yazdik-Zaddik*" conceptuality, the basis of "Justification" theorizing, Qumran's esoteric exegesis of Ezek 44:15, and the "purist Sadducee" Movement.

zamam/zammu, "conspired"; in 1QpHab, xii.6 relating to the Wicked Priest's *judicial* conspiracy "to destroy the Righteous Teacher"/"Poor"/"Simple of Judah doing *Torah*". In 1QH, iv.7ff. The usage applies to both "the Sons of Belial" (Herodians) and their "nets", not to mention all "Scoffers of Deceit"/"Scoffers of Lying" (*Malizei-Chazav*) who lead the people astray "with Smooth Things", "give vinegar to the thirsty", and whose "works are boasting".

zanut, "fornication", one of "the Three Nets of Belial"; in CD, iv.17ff. marrying nieces and divorce; in viii.5 tied to Riches and incest. Part and parcel of James' directives to overseas communities (cf. too Ja 1:14f., 4:1ff., and Rev 2:14), the imagery of which pervades Qumran; e.g., 1QS, iv.10's "zeal for lustfulness, *ma'asei-To'evot* in a spirit of *zanut*, and *darchei-niddah* in the service of pollution" and *par contra* 1QpHab, v.4ff.'s Elect of God "not lusting after their eyes" (cf. 2 Pe 2:13f.).

Zedek, "Righteousness"; with *Hesed*, the fundamental notation at Qumran. Taken together these two represent the basic ideological orientation of all "Opposition" groups in the Second Temple Period; the second of the two "all Righteousness" Commandments, i.e., "loving one's neighbor as oneself" or "Righteousness towards one's fellow man", which moves easily into a consonant demand for economic equality and an insistence on poverty.

Zedakah, also translated as "Righteousness", but having the form of a verbal noun implying something of the sense of "Justification", i.e., in place of sacrifice, one "was justified" by charity.

Note on Translation and Transcriptions

In my early work, most translations followed the work of Solomon Schechter, R.H. Charles, Chaim Rabin, Philip Davies, A. Dupont-Sommer, G. Vermes, T.H. Gaster, M. Burrows, and John Allegro. Later, after I found it necessary to do translations myself, I followed my own.

For the transcriptions of the Community Rule and Habakkuk *Pesher*, I also consulted the work of M. Burrows, John Trever, W.H. Brownlee, A.M. Habermann, and E. Lohse. Where reconstructions went, sometimes I was guided by these; sometimes, my own; and sometimes, declined to reconstruct at all. This depended upon what made sense in translation.

INDEX